What better way to introduce today's students and tomorrow's criminal justice practitioners to the world of criminal justice administration than through a set of well-constructed ethnographic reports detailing the lived experiences of the participants in the process? This is a welcome addition to the field.

—**Malcom M. Feeley**, *Professor of Jurisprudence and Sociology, University of California at Berkeley*

Voices represents a robust effort to understand the lived experience of criminal justice system participants. The ethnographic selections are engaging, readable, and expose students to the broad array of players. The book's unique insider/outsider perspective provides probing and incisive accounts of key issues facing the field today.

—**Bruce Jacobs**, *Professor of Criminology, University of Texas, Dallas*

The book brings various practitioners in the criminal justice system to life through ethnographic research. The collection puts a human face on the system and will draw students to the subject. It will also remind academics why they entered the field.

—**Ralph Weisheit**, *Distinguished Professor of Criminology, Illinois State University*

D0218857

Criminology and Justice Studies
Series Editors: Britt Chester
Shaun L. Gabbidon

Criminology and Justice Studies seeks to publish brief and lengthier manuscripts that make both intellectual and stylistic innovations. Our goal is to publish works that model the best scholarship and thinking in the field today, but in a style that connects that scholarship to a wider audience, including advanced undergraduates, graduate students, and the general public. We envision these works filling the gap between academic monographs and encyclopedic textbooks by making innovative scholarship accessible to a large audience without the superficiality of many texts. Series topics will include the causes and consequences of crime, the globalization of crime, crime control policy (domestic and international), crime prevention, organizational approaches to the study of the criminal justice system, decision-making in the criminal justice system, terrorism and homeland security, and immigration and crime.

voices from criminal justice

Voices from Criminal Justice, Second Edition, gives students rich insight into the criminal justice system from the point of view of practitioners, as well as outsiders—citizens, clients, jurors, probationers, or inmates. These qualitative and teachable articles cover all three components of the criminal justice system, ensuring students will be better informed about the daily realities of criminal justice professionals in law enforcement, courts, and corrections. At the same time, the juxtaposition of insider and outsider views allows students to look beyond the actual content of the articles and develop their own views about the functions and flaws of the criminal justice system on a societal level.

This innovative reader, now with seven new articles designed to stimulate discussions and promote critical thought, is perfect for undergraduate criminal justice courses in the United States, and has proven to be an effective companion or alternative to traditional introductory textbooks. *Voices from Criminal Justice*, Second Edition, also offers a framework for more advanced students in special issues or capstone courses to synthesize information from earlier courses and develop their own views of American justice.

Heith Copes is a Professor in the Department of Justice Sciences at the University of Alabama at Birmingham. His primary research combines symbolic interactionism and rational choice theory to better understand the criminal decision-making process. His recent publications appear in *British Journal of Criminology, Crime and Justice: A Review of Research, Criminology, Justice Quarterly* and *Social Problems* and he has received funding from the National Institute of Justice.

Mark R. Pogrebin is a Professor of Criminal Justice in the School of Public Affairs at the University of Colorado, Denver. He has authored and co-authored six books, the most recent, *Guns, Violence and Criminal Behavior*. He has published over 50 journal articles and chapters published in anthologies. He is a field researcher whose past studies have all used qualitative methods.

voices from criminal justice

insider perspectives, outsider experiences

second edition

edited by

heith copes

and

mark r. pogrebin

NEW YORK AND LONDON

First published 2011
by Routledge

Second edition 2017
by Routledge
711 Third Avenue, New York, NY 10017

and by Routledge
2 Park Square, Milton Park, Abingdon, Oxon, OX14 4RN

Routledge is an imprint of the Taylor & Francis Group, an informa business

© 2017 Taylor & Francis

Library of Congress Cataloging in Publication Data
A catalog record for this book has been requested

ISBN: 978-1-138-19344-4 (hbk)
ISBN: 978-1-138-19347-5 (pbk)
ISBN: 978-1-315-63934-5 (ebk)

Typeset in Minion
by RefineCatch Limited, Bungay, Suffolk

Heith Copes To Purvis and Otha Lee Copes, my grandparents, who helped to keep me grounded.

Mark R. Pogrebin To my lovely grandchildren Elyza, Mila and Ian. You brighten my life.

Contents

Kurtz, Linnemann, and Williams examine the historical role of the police
matron and how the legacy continues to define women's status in the
current police and correctional workforce.

Dabney and his co-authors conducted an ethnographic study of homicide
investigations in a large urban police department and focused on those
occupational factors that cause job related stress.

Vera Sanchez and Rosenbaum examine how police officers socially
construct race within Latino and African American neighborhoods.

Pogrebin and Poole explore the consequences of working undercover for police officers. They show that working undercover has a significant impact on how police interact with informants, criminals, other officers, and their families.

Pogrebin, Chatman, and Dodge analyze the social-organizational relationships and interactions that relegate African-American police women as outsiders within their own police department.

Gau and Brunson explore the tension between procedural justice and order maintenance policing as it affects the self-reported experiences with police by young inner-city minority youth.

Durán concentrates on the relationship between police and gangs in two cities where suspected gang members perceive being stopped by police as racial and ethnic profiling.

Stretesky, Shelley, Hogan, and Unnithan examine the perceptions of the families of cold-case homicide victims to determine their interactions and relationship with law enforcement detectives assigned to their case.

Table of Contents

DioGuardi examines experienced capital judicial participants' (defense
lawyers, prosecutors, and judges) thoughts concerning the existence and use
of the death penalty.

Rosecrance argues that probation pre-sentence reports emphasize some
offender characteristics more than others. He explains how a stereotyping
process is used by officers who write these reports and how current offense and
prior criminal history determine a pre-scripted sentencing recommendation.

Konradi focuses on how victims of sexual assault prepare themselves for court
appearances. She also discusses survivors' views of the criminal justice process.

Goodrum explores, through an interactionist perspective, the families of
homicide victims' experiences with prosecutors and the criminal court system.

Fischer, Geiger, and Hughes study female drug-court program participants'
perceptions and evaluations of their current and past experiences while in
the program.

Hans and Sweigart focus on the decision-making process of jurors serving
on civil court trials and their opinions of trial lawyers' courtroom behavior
and communication skills.

Preface

This book came about when the two of us were discussing the value of ethnographic research for conveying the lived experiences of people. We recognized that many criminal justice students have never worked in the field and may have misguided notions of what it is like being a police officer, attorney, or correctional officer. The nature of most college courses dictates that students would not have the opportunity to learn what the day to day routines are really like. This book fills this gap in the education of criminal justice students by presenting the perspectives of those who work within the criminal justice system (i.e., practitioners) and from those who experience it as outsiders (i.e., citizens, clients, jurors, probationers, or inmates).

In deciding which articles to include in the book, we evaluated them on their methodological rigor, ability to artfully portray the perspective of those being studied, and their readability for students. By providing firsthand experiences of those who work in or are affected by the criminal justice system, these articles will inform readers about what they should expect when selecting a career in criminal justice. In addition, these articles are precisely the types of scholarly work that students enjoy reading. It has been our experience that students are much more receptive and willing to consume research that provides firsthand accounts of those being studied than they are to general textbooks or research involving complex statistical models that can be detached from personal experiences. Thus, those who adopt the book can expect and assume that students will read the assigned text.

We also believe that these articles will allow professors to better develop students' abilities to think critically about criminal justice issues. To foster such critical thinking, we have included questions after each article. These questions are designed to stimulate course discussion and to encourage students to make connections among the other articles and their own experiences. We recognize that sometimes it is necessary to test students to ensure that they have read the articles. Thus, we have also developed "fact based" questions to supplement the book. For those interested in copies of these questions please contact [please fill in publisher information].

Acknowledgments

We appreciate very much the support of Routledge in providing us with the opportunity to have a second edition of this book. In particular, we thank Pamela Chester, our managing editor, for her patience, insights, and enthusiasm for the book. We also thank our research assistants (Whitney Marsh at the University of Alabama at Birmingham and Myrna Chavez Heredia, Jessica Rosenthal and Porscha Carrol at University of Colorado, Denver) for putting up with a number of tedious, cryptic, and perhaps unreasonable requests. They have been patient, good natured, and diligent in their aid to us and we dare say that this book would have a publication date far in the future were it not for their efforts.

Introduction: Thinking and Reflecting on Criminal Justice Issues

Heith Copes and Mark R. Pogrebin

In the past several decades the size of the criminal justice system and the number of people interested in pursuing criminal justice careers has grown tremendously. Each year more and more students are majoring in criminal justice or enrolling in criminal justice classes. Introductory courses, once small and filled typically with majors, now seat large numbers of students from a variety of disciplines. In addition, the number of universities in the United States with doctoral programs in criminal justice and criminology has grown from 20 to 38 in the past 20 years. More people are graduating with doctorates in criminal justice/criminology than any time in history. Correspondingly, the amount of research on criminal justice related topics has increased dramatically. We now know more about the function of criminal justice bureaucracies and those who work in them than ever before.

While this rise in attention to criminal justice has brought about many positive changes, there is still a downside. With more majors and more information to cover in criminal justice courses, the amount of in-depth, critical examinations of the system, which is vital for effective teaching, has been hampered. Those who teach introductory courses in criminal justice typically rely on large textbooks that cover a wide range of topics, but with little depth (Withrow, Weible, and Bonnett 2004). Such textbooks eschew in-depth understanding of criminal justice occupations and issues and critical thinking for summary overviews. This trend is neither desired nor necessary.

In response to the changing nature of criminal justice courses we have put together this reader with two goals in mind. The first goal is to provide students with a richer, more realistic understanding of the lived experiences of those who work in the criminal justice system and those who find themselves in the system as outsiders (i.e., citizens, victims, or offenders). We think it is important that students of criminal justice know what it is really like to work in one of the three core components of the criminal justice system (policing, courts, and corrections). Traditional textbooks rarely provide insights into the day-to-day experiences of the people who make up the criminal justice system (as employees or outsiders). The articles we have selected buck this trend by using ethnographic methods to understand the system from those within it.

The second goal is to encourage more critical thinking about criminal justice issues. Traditional textbooks are geared primarily to provide summary overviews of knowledge in a given field. Textbook writers are forced to forgo depth of coverage so that they can include the large amount of material for a subject. Such styles of textbooks lend themselves to multiple choice, true false, and short answer questions. Thus, the ability to think critically and move beyond rote memorization is devalued. To overcome this limitation of most textbooks we place a stronger emphasis on making connections among the readings and on thinking about the root causes and unintended consequences of criminal justice issues and policies.

In selecting articles for this reader we sought to find those that could best help us reach our goals. With little doubt there are a number of methodologies that can offer insights into what it is like for police officers to arrest suspects, attorneys to defend clients they know are guilty, and for families of inmates to try to make sense of the confinement of their loved ones. We think, however, that the best suited methodology involves allowing study participants the opportunity to express their ideas, concerns, and thoughts in their own words. Instead of asking them to fill in boxes to predetermined categories on pen and paper questionnaires, we see greater value in letting individuals tell their stories of their own volition. Thus, the articles we selected all focus on ethnographies.

Providing Lived Experiences

Students majoring in criminal justice or criminology do so primarily to obtain an edge in landing a job as police officers, correctional officers, attorneys, probation officers, or some other criminal justice position. Except for those few who worked as interns during their college career most are unfamiliar with the day-to-day aspects of the job. Most educators would agree that it is important for students to understand what to expect when choosing or starting a new career. This compilation of articles includes information about what the day-to-day aspects of the job are like and how they are viewed by those outside their profession. While college textbooks provide some insights into what the job may be like, they seldom provide an insider's perspective. When they do it usually appears in small boxes separated from the text. Thus, professors are assigned the task of conveying what these jobs entail: a task that often proves difficult, given that many professors have not worked as a criminal justice professional in the field.

One of the primary goals of this reader is to fill this gap in the education of criminal justice students. Specifically, we have selected articles that provide insights into the three major aspects of criminal justice (policing, courts, and corrections) by presenting the perspectives of those who work within the system (i.e., practitioners) and from those who experience it as outsiders (i.e., citizens, clients, jurors, probationers, or inmates). All of the included articles use ethnographic and/or fieldwork methodologies because such methods are ideally suited to articulate how actors (in this case criminal justice practitioners and outsiders) make sense and understand their worlds (Spradley 1979, 1980). That is, each article provides the words and lived experiences of those who work in or who are affected by the criminal justice system. We have selected each article for their methodological rigor, ability to artfully portray the perspective of those being studied, and readability for students.

By providing empirical research from the perspective of those who experience the three components of the criminal justice system students (and possibly professors) will be better informed about the realities of the day-to-day job of criminal justice professionals. This includes discussing what it is "really" like to work as a police officer after going through formal training, how detectives handle the emotions of dealing with death, how probation officers determine if their clients are telling the truth, how prosecutors discredit witnesses to win decisions, and how women who work in jail deal with the stresses and strains of doing so. In addition, these readings will provide insights into what it is "really" like for young minorities to interact with police, how victims of domestic violence interpret the actions and demeanor of responding officers, how jurors view various types of attorneys and how this influences their decisions, how women experience incarceration, how juveniles experience probation, and what sex offenders think about their sentencing.

Too often when studying the various components of the criminal justice system people focus solely on the experiences of those who work in such positions. While much can be gained from their perspective, it does not provide a full picture of what happens in each stage of the criminal justice system. As such, if we are to understand the role of police, courts, and corrections in society it is important to understand how practitioners in each are viewed by those they come in contact with. One may ask: Why should we care what the public, especially the offending public, thinks about police, courts or corrections? The answer is simple. It is important to understand how those people view the agents of social control. By allowing these types of people to present their perspectives, police, judges, attorneys, and correctional officers (and others) can better evaluate the impact and efficacy of their policies and perspectives, a goal to which all criminal justice organizations should aspire. In addition, understanding the perspectives of others will offer those working in the criminal justice system insights into how their actions will affect the people over whom they have power. Knowing how bureaucratic policies are experienced by outsiders will likely go a long way in maintaining, or establishing, the legitimacy of the criminal justice system.

Critical Thinking

A second, but equally important, part of the readings requests that the students look beyond the actual content of the articles and use a "critical thinking" perspective to develop their own thoughts about the functions of the criminal justice system on a broader societal level. Critical thinking is not an easily defined concept. We all "know" what it means, but we have a hard time describing it when asked directly. To achieve some clarity on the issue, we use the American Philosophical Association's (Facione 1990) conceptualization, which states:

> We understand critical thinking to be purposeful, self-regulatory judgment which results in inter-pretation, analysis, evaluation, and inference, as well as explanation of the evidential, conceptual, methodological, criteriological, or contextual considerations upon which that judgment is based. CT [Critical Thinking] is essential as a tool of inquiry. As such, CT is a liberating force in education and a powerful resource in one's personal and civic life. While not synonymous with good thinking, CT is a pervasive and self-rectifying human phenomenon.

In short, "The successful application of these core CT skills requires that one take into reasoned consideration the evidence, methods, contexts, theories, and criteria which, in effect, define specific disciplines, fields, and areas of human concern" (Facione 2000: 65). Few of us have inherently developed these characteristics. Instead, they are learned and cultivated. This implies that anyone, and everyone, has the potential to think critically if encouraged and reinforced to do so.

One of our goals when constructing this reader is to encourage readers to develop and hone their critical thinking skills, especially when thinking about the criminal justice system. We think it is important for readers to analyze how all of the components of the criminal justice system affect the larger society in which they operate. Thus, we encourage readers to think bigger and more abstractly about the readings. While much can be gained simply from reading each article on its own, we think greater pedagogical benefits come when people seek to make connections among the various articles and other issues raised in class.

Consider the following example. Two articles in the policing section, by Durán, and Sanchez and Rosenbaum, both discuss policing in minority communities, but from two different perspectives. Durán concluded that Latino gang members were of the opinion that police profile racial minorities. On the other hand, Sanchez and Rosenbaum found that police socially construct a particular view of Latinos and African Americans in the neighborhoods they patrol and act upon their often negative definitions. Both of these studies point to the various ways in which communities formulate their attitudes toward one another. With the racial turmoil we have witnessed in the recent past between African Americans and police, the articles in this book should be analyzed so that new, improved public policies may be developed and incorporated to greatly advance minority–police relations. Critical thinking and informed discussion are the most positive processes to arrive at workable solutions for the existing problems that are currently causing a high degree of mistrust between police organizations and ethnic and racial minorities.

To encourage critical thinking, we offer critical thinking questions after each article that will introduce readers to issues to think about and reflect upon when using a critical eye. We do not mean for these passages to be exhaustive in their questioning. Instead, they are designed to whet the appetite for thinking critically and to stimulate discussion in class.

Consistent with the dictates of critical thinking we expect that students and professors are bringing their own experiences and interpretations to the readings and, thus, will be able to provide their own unique insights and connections as they read the articles.

Using This Anthology

The size of introductory criminal justice classes should not prevent professors from incorporating a book of readings that will enhance the descriptive information found in the majority of introductory texts. The purpose of this anthology and the advantages for exposing students to the in-depth content of each component of the criminal justice system has been discussed in the preceding pages. However, before being found guilty of redundancy, we turn to recent thoughts on teaching lower-level criminal justice classes by Garcia (2011: 23), who discusses her insightful goals for students:

> Textbooks are adequate for a number of lower division courses, but they allow students to be lazy because they do much of what students should do for themselves—consume a wide variety of topics and synthesize the information in a meaningful way.

In short, Garcia desires her students to be critical thinkers, as most professors wish their students to become.

The issue of how to accomplish this lofty goal when using a text and a reader for a large introductory criminal justice class is often perplexing. We offer a brief explanation for accomplishing this task in order for lower division students to become familiar with the realities of the justice system.

We have found it best to use a condensed version of the criminal justice text assigned to the class. Doing so allows for students to gain a comprehensive overview of the three components of the system without the large number of pages. In addition, and perhaps most importantly for students, it will also keep book costs down. After covering a particular subject section, we introduce the students to five readings about practitioners and five articles about those who experience the actions of the practitioners. This allows students to "experience" what it is like for practitioners and those with whom they interact when carrying out their duties.

To ensure that students read the articles, we either ask for volunteers or assign readings to students to present in class. In larger classes we often assign two students per article. We allot a certain amount of time to each presenter and ask them to highlight their article and be prepared to ask the class three in-depth questions or to raise three major issues. This usually gets the rest of the class involved in the conversation. Of course, instructors have to put time limits on each presentation and class discussion based on what they see as most appropriate for their classes. Based on our experiences using this pedagogical technique, students' responses have indicated a much higher degree of class involvement and more inclusive participation for the class as a whole. We replicate this procedure for each section of the criminal justice system covered in the course. Inevitably, our student class evaluations favor the anthology's real-life subject analysis over our lecture format when covering the text material.

A great advantage we have found when using our anthology in this way is that it has allowed us to become observers of student input and it places them in the new position of facilitator, at least during the article discussion time. They often find this empowering. Further, exams have reflected an increased understanding of the complexities that exist within criminal justice agencies and external policies that are formulated by various governmental bodies that directly affect the operation of the three components of the criminal justice system. In sum, we have observed a raised awareness of the functions and dysfunctions of the system by our students, and an increased expectation for their commentary and analysis of the existing problems that our society faces in crime control. We believe these improvements in student understanding and engagement are due to the use of articles that present the "lived experiences" of those who work in the criminal justice system and those who go through it more than our inherent teaching ability. It is our hope that others who use this book will have similar success.

References

Facione, Peter. 1990. *Critical Thinking: A Statement of Expert Consensus for Purposes of Educational Assessment and Instruction*. Millbrae, CA: California Academic Press.

Facione, Peter. 2000. "The Disposition Toward Critical Thinking: Its Character, Measurement, and Relationship to Critical Thinking Skill." *Informal Logic* 20: 61–84.

Garcia, C.A. 2011. "Teaching Tip: Found! Teaching Treasure in ASC Meeting Registration Bags." *The Criminologist* 36(3, May/June): 22–24.

Spradley, James. 1979. *The Ethnographic Interview*. New York: Holt, Rinehart, & Winston.

Spradley, James. 1980. *Participant Observation*. New York: Holt, Rinehart, & Winston.

Withrow, Brian, Kerry Weible, and Jennifer Bonnett. 2004. "Aren't They All the Same? A Comparative Analysis of Introductory Criminal Justice Textbooks." *Journal of Criminal Justice Education* 15: 1–18.

1 Police

The articles in this section are representative of qualitative studies that have been conducted on law enforcement officers and those they police. Because police are the most visible criminal justice agency, they are frequently in the public eye. Interest in their role within society has long been popularized by movies and television shows, which have enjoyed wide audiences on a national level. The popularity of police issues holds true for the news media, both print and television, and is reflective of the public's fascination with this occupation. We believe that much of the curiosity about the world of law enforcement has also had an effect on social science research. We would venture to speculate that there has been more research and published journal articles, academic books, and journalistic accounts about the police profession than any other component of the criminal justice system.

The five articles that constitute the police practitioners section of this anthology offer insights into an array of subjects within the police occupation. The topics which these articles address include gender and the division of labor in policing, the stress that homicide investigators experience, gender and racial discrimination in policing by black female officers, life as an undercover officer and the job's effects on them, and the influence of race on the day-to-day working interactions of officers. While there are certainly numerous other topics that could have been addressed, we believe these topics exhibit the variation in how officers think about their roles as police and how they go about their day-to-day jobs. It should become clear that each of the issues raised in the articles are all important aspects of policing. What is often less clear are the various unintended consequences of the actual behaviors and thoughts of police. As you read the articles you should think about these issues, even if not discussed directly in the article. Doing so will not only challenge prevailing notions of proper policing but may also allow you to seek solutions to emerging problems.

We also provide five articles that offer a glimpse into how citizens perceive police. These articles reflect the views of a range of individuals who have come into contact with police, including those who sought help from police and those who were sought out by police for perceived wrongdoings. Recent events relating to race and policing illustrate that interactions with police have a strong effect on perceptions about the quality of service provided by police. Young males who see their interactions with police as oppressive and instigated by others, clergy members who are interested in helping but still skeptical of police, secondary victims of homicide and their desire to get more from detectives, and domestic violence offenders who are being confronted (and arrested) all evaluate and understand police differently. By hearing the voices of citizens (innocents, victims, and offenders alike) police officers can gain insights into how they are perceived by the public and, ideally, how they can be more effective at their jobs.

A Practitioners

1

Reinventing the Matron: The Continued Importance of Gendered Images and Division of Labor in Modern Policing

Don L. Kurtz, Travis Linnemann, and L. Susan Williams

Abstract: *The current research examines the workplace images and responsibilities of female police officers in three departments. Ethnographic interviews with 28 officers in three Midwestern communities indicate that women in law enforcement are still viewed through a gendered lens, which shapes relations with fellow officers and the community. Images of female officers correspond to their early role in law enforcement as matrons charged with the care of female offenders and juvenile delinquents. Results indicate that female officers are expected to care for children, delinquents, and female victims regardless of personal preference or individual skills, and institutional practices tend to maintain women officers in the devalued position historically held by police matrons. Subtle interactions between officers and the belief in so-called natural feminine instincts are utilized to maintain patrol work as a masculine enterprise.*

Introduction

The American criminal justice system has a tradition of gender differentiation in both criminal offense patterns (J. Miller 1998) and the employment of those charged with the detection, prosecution, and management of criminal offenders (Britton 2003; Schulz 1995; Segrave 1995). Historically speaking, policing is one of the most gender-segregated occupations in American history, and it remains resistant to placing women in patrol positions because of perceptions of danger in these work environments. The first women employed in policing and corrections entered in the decidedly gendered position of matron. This limited role for women in the early criminal justice system focused on gender-essentialist traits as custodians of minor children. The prevailing thought of the time was that men lacked the innate nurturing skills needed to care for children, juvenile delinquents, and women offenders and victims (Wadman and Allison 2004). In addition, early women officers lacked powers of arrest and more closely resembled social workers than modern police officers (Schulz 1995; Wadman and Allison 2004). The use of matrons by police departments was a concession to middle-class reformers associated with the Progressive Movement and accompanying beliefs in the intrinsic abilities of women. This social movement involved a call to public service for early feminists that pushed many

White middle-class women into the public sector in schools, settlement houses, and police stations (Schulz 1995), and as early as 1845, New York City appointed part-time matrons. In 1878, Portland, Maine appointed the first full-time paid matron, and New York City, Denver, and Cleveland followed suit within six years (Wadman and Allison 2004).

The legacy of the matron continues to shape law enforcement and prison organizations to this day. Using aspects of gendered organization theory (Acker 1990; Britton 2003; Kanter 1977), the current study augments and extends prior research by examining officers' perceptions and beliefs about informal attempts to gender-segregate specific assignments, determining whether the matron concept still shapes beliefs about women officers and examining types of informal organization behavior used to maintain gender arrangements in police organizations.

Literature Review

Much research has focused on the gendered nature of the American workforce across multiple disciplines, exploring gendered behavior in medicine (Baxter, Cohen, and McLeod 1996; Field and Lennox 1996; Lambert and Holmboe 2005), law (Kay and Hagan 1998; Pierce 1995), the military (L.L. Miller 1997; Snyder 2003), and the criminal justice system (Britton 2003; Brown 1998; Kurtz 2008; Martin and Jurik 1996). In particular, the criminal justice system serves as fertile ground for examining gendered labor practices because of strong notions of gender among people in American society, criminal offenders, and those employed within the criminal justice system.

Acker (1990) provided an important theoretical contribution to this research; she argued that the gendering of organizations occurs along five interactive processes. The first is a division of labor, or gender-appropriate behaviors. The second is the creation of images—or an imagined social organization based on gender traditions—that account for, oppose, or reinforce the created divisions. The third involves the actual gendered interactions among people and is closely associated with the doing gender thesis—a perspective asserting that gender is actively constructed and maintained by gendered actors on a daily basis. The fourth component that produces gendered organizations is individual identity. Finally, gender as a social concept helps frame social and organizational structure and is a vital aspect of how individuals understand the practices and perceptions that dominate organizational culture (Acker 1990). For the purposes of the present research, three areas of gendered organizations—the division of labor, gendered images, and gendered interactions—provide a theoretical focus.

Few occupations in America have a pronounced history of gendering quite like police departments. Law enforcement established a gendered division of labor from its conception, and policing is still largely regarded as men's work today. During the first 100 years of law enforcement in the United States, women were formally excluded from employment in law enforcement (Wadman and Allison 2004), and women were not appointed as sworn officers until the early 20th century. Although there are conflicting accounts of who can be classified as the first female officer, most trace the early involvement of women in law enforcement to matrons (Britton 2003; Schulz 1995; Segrave 1995; Wadman and Allison 2004). The matron focused on caretaker duties such as ensuring that offenders had adequate clothing, food, and shelter; gender essentialism of the time assumed that male officers were ill-equipped to provide for the specific needs of women and children (Schulz 1995; Wadman and Allison 2004). These early foundations provided a context that shaped gendered behavior in policing even as women transitioned into patrol positions in the 1970s.

In 1972, Congress enacted Title VII of the Civil Rights Act, which prohibited discrimination based on sex, color, race, religion, or national origin and expanded coverage to public employment sectors (Schulz 1995). This effectively ended the legal exclusion of women from patrol functions and other criminal justice settings such as prisons (Britton 2003); however, the increase in women in patrol remained limited despite changes in the law. In 1971, fewer than 12 women were utilized as patrol officers. By 1974, this number had increased to more than 1,000, and by 1981 women represented more than 5 percent of sworn patrol officers (Schulz 1995). Currently women constitute approximately 13 percent of sworn officers in the United States (National Center for Women and Policing 2001), but some evidence indicates difficulty with recruiting and retaining women officers (National Center for Women and Policing 2000).

As women assumed patrol positions in the 1970s and 1980s, much of the division of labor from the early 20th century remained intact (Martin 1980), with women frequently pigeonholed into certain tasks associated with so-called feminine qualities (Moore 1999). Gender-segregated labor still encourages women to handle juvenile delinquents and female criminals, successfully pushing women into the same positions held by matrons (Brown 1998; Martin 1994; Westmarland 2001). Women are also overrepresented in domestic abuse departments, and the involvement of women in these units, initially heralded as positive movement by police agencies, is an example of how women officers get compressed into gender-specific tasks (Westmarland 2001). Furthermore, women are frequently pulled from patrol duties and forced to deal with incidents involving women or children (Brown 1998), and women rarely make it into the upper ranks of police departments because of discriminatory practices in regard to promotion (House 1993).

Despite the fact that women are more represented in modern policing than they were in the past, the lingering gendered division of labor, lack of advancement, and the underrepresentation of women result in a perception of tokenism in law enforcement (Archbold and Schulz 2008; Kanter 1977; Stichman, Hassell, and Archbold 2010). Kanter (1977) originally conceived of a token as an identifiable subgroup of people in an organization that represent less than 15 percent of total organizational demographics; she applied this concept to her study of gendered behavior in corporate America. She determined that tokens generally shared one of three experiences: assimilation, contrast, or visibility (Archbold and Schulz 2008; Kanter 1977; Stichman et al. 2010). A key concern for the application of tokenism to policing is the use of images of women officers in a manner consistent with Kanter's theory, in particular the contrast and visibility of female officers within police organizations.

Images of Women Officers

A recurring image of women officers is that they are weak and unable to fulfill job requirements (Britton 2003; Brown 1998; Segrave 1995; Wadman and Allison 2004). Images
of male officers generally focus on their physical prowess, whereas female officers are
viewed as a physical liability (Britton 2003; Brown 1998; Martin 1996; Schulz 1995). This
is the most consistent image of female officers, and it builds on a cultural tradition
that defines women as physically inferior. In modern policing physical altercations
are infrequent; however, the concern that physical requirements for officers have been
diluted to accommodate women remains salient. Many researchers have identified fears
by men that question the physical capabilities of women in violent criminal justice
settings. The concern that women are too weak to function properly in law enforcement
work shapes images of women officers and is used to reinforce the gendered division
of labor. These images construct powerful social forces that underline the status quo
in law enforcement and aid in the construction of police organizations, whether
deliberately or inadvertently; such practices buttress the gendered division of labor in
policing.

Some research has directly explored the influence of gender on the street-level behavior
of officers, with varied results (DeJong 2004; Lundman 2009; Paoline and Terrill 2004;
Rabe-Hemp 2008). Paoline and Terrill (2004) argued that gendered perceptions of women
officers frequently portray them as unwilling to appropriately utilize coercive authority.
However, their extensive research study of officer behavior in Indianapolis, Indiana
and St. Petersburg, Florida found little difference in the use of force between men
and women officers. Furthermore, Lundman (2009) found little difference in traffic
ticket decisions between men and women officers and concluded that the behavior was
"indistinguishable" based on gender. DeJong (2004) studied officers' attitudes in relation
to providing comfort to citizens and found that gender was not a significant factor in
officer behaviors or attitudes in consoling citizens, and that officers provide such comfort
in situations when citizens most require it. DeJong concluded that the findings indicated
"no evidence from the analysis that women are better or worse than men at the job of
enforcing the law" (p. 29).

These findings aside, some research indicates a robust and complicated relationship
between gender and the on-the-job behavior of officers. For example, Rabe-Hemp (2008)
found that gender influenced some officers' behavior but not others. In her research she
found that women officers were less likely to use "extreme controlling" techniques such as
threats, physical control, and actual arrest than their male counterparts. However, the
findings did not support the belief that women were more likely to use supportive techniques during citizen interactions. Still other research indicates that female officers are less
likely to use violence as part of their job. For example, Lonsway (2001) reported that
women use appropriate force in necessary situations; however, they are less likely to use
excessive force. Prussel and Lonsway (2001) also showed that women were less likely to use
excessive or deadly force.

Gendered Interactions

Acker (1990) argued that the third major gendered social structure involves interactions between individuals in an organization. Acker was concerned with how interactive processes produce gendered organizations. The dynamics of interactions in police organizations is an important aspect of the gendering process. Susan Martin's (1994) comprehensive research on five police agencies found that race, class, and gender guided organizational behavior, interpersonal interactions, and officer conduct. The interactions between men and women, among women, and between Black and White officers aligned with the historical context of policing as White and male. Male officers frequently discriminated against women officers, belittling their abilities or refusing to partner with them.

Interactions between men in law enforcement provide an additional social context for understanding gendered interactions in police agencies. Findings indicate that male officers reinforce the gender dynamics of their work environment in both formal and informal settings (Franklin 2005). Franklin (2005) used a male peer support model in her research, focusing on underlying social structures in the police subculture, including misogyny, hypermasculinity, and lack of deterrence, as factors contributing to the continued negative treatment of women officers. These groups offer significant support networks for male officers, and it appears that women officers do not have a similar support system. In these settings, men are free to discuss subjects that could result in negative sanctions in other settings (Martin 1996; Westmarland 2001). This cop culture develops as a shared response to organizational rules. Cop culture may be described as macho in orientation, sexist, crude, and sophomoric (Martin 1996); others have referred to this group behavior as the "John Wayne syndrome" (Kop and Euwema 2001). In regard to gender, cop culture is a subcultural understanding of how to interact in mixed company in order to remain in compliance with the official rules of law enforcement organizations but retain the masculine aura of policing.

The cop culture may, in fact, filter elements of the informal culture through aspects of formal officer training by highlighting gender differences in officer interactions during training. Haarr (2005) found gender discrimination and harassment to be a primary factor in the self-initiated dropout of female police recruits, and Prokos and Padavic (2002) found a strong hidden curriculum in the training of police recruits designed to encourage women officers' dropout or to exaggerate gender differences between officers. Prior research has also revealed that recruitment strategies that target women rely overly on traditional male-oriented recruiting methods and behavior expectations (National Center for Women and Policing 2000).

Another pattern of gendered interactions frequently identified in the literature is the domination of women through sexual harassment. All but two women in Martin's (1996) sample experienced sexual harassment on the job. In Brown's (1998) research, 70 percent of the female officers experienced some type of direct sexual harassment, and nearly half reported this as a frequent problem. Westmarland (2001) stated that "women officers are still being subjected to discrimination and harassment, partly due to traditional 'male' police culture which is very difficult to change" (p. 89). Police culture is male dominated and highly masculine, and the treatment of female officers provides sufficient evidence that it remains a noteworthy and ongoing problem.

The expansion of women into law enforcement created situations that challenge established gendered dichotomies and required adjustments to the division of labor, images, interactions, and the identity of police officers. The gendering of police organizations remains a salient, although often ignored, concern in law enforcement. Using qualitative interviews, the current research examines how gender images, interactions, and the division of labor influence the perceptions and job assignments of women police officers.

The current study augments and extends prior research by examining the following research areas. First, this research explores officer perceptions of existing informal attempts to gender-segregate women in specific assignments based on essentialist assumptions about women's abilities regardless of their actual interests or interpersonal skill sets. Second, we explore whether the matron concept continues to dominate beliefs about women officers, even in the 21st century. Third, we are interested in how informal organization behavior maintains gender arrangements in police organizations and how officers themselves influence this social structure. Finally, we explore points of change related to gender and areas of future transformation in organizational behavior.

Methods

This research involves semi-structured qualitative interviews with police officers from three mid-western agencies representing organizations of various sizes. In order to maintain confidentiality, we have altered the names of these departments and individual officers, and use pseudonyms throughout this article. The police organizations included in this research reflect their respective mid-western communities, and each embodies certain characteristics that potentially shape interactions and ideas about gender among officers. The samples of officers drawn from these three organizations approximated as much as possible the gender, race, and ethnic composition of each department. A purposive sampling technique was used in order to seek out officers representing particular characteristics. We also specifically targeted women officers and those in certain positions within each department, such as investigations. Each department offered unique challenges for accessing officers and had slightly different procedures for accessing officers. In all, more than 50 officers phoned or emailed responses, and formal face-to-face interviews occurred with 28 officers. Interviews lasted for an average of 50 minutes, with several lasting in excess of an hour and a half. The final sample included seven women and 21 men. Only three of the participants were racial or ethnic minorities. Multiple individuals chose not to participate in the research for various reasons, and time restrictions and scheduling difficulties also reduced the sample size. Although we could not ensure a representative sample, we took care to include both women and men in key positions and across a diversity of positions and experience.

Kiowa Police Department (KPD)

KPD is by far the largest and most bureaucratic agency included in this research, but it is still modest in size compared to departments located in considerable urban centers. The gender composition of KPD is quite reflective of traditional gender roles in policing, with few women holding higher ranks in the KPD bureaucracy. At the time of the interviews, the department employed 201 women; however, 114 of them worked in non-sworn positions. Among sworn officers, approximately 50 were female patrol officers, 10 were female detectives, and six women officers held the rank of sergeant or higher. The highest ranking woman officer was in the position of deputy chief.

Gaining access to interviewees in the Kiowa department required several steps and the assistance of the female deputy chief. Two of the authors met with the deputy chief on multiple occasions, discussed the purpose of this research, and provided information on the questions and informed consent approved by the university institutional review board. After receiving approval and feedback from the deputy chief, she then provided copies to the department's chief and other administrative officials, who then requested a direct meeting with the researchers. The principal researcher met with the KPD executive police board and further explained the purpose of the research. Although the chief admitted some apprehension about allowing this research, we received final authorization to interview officers.

KPD agreed to provide the research team with a random sample of 30 officers drawn from multiple shifts and divisions. The administrative office emailed the principal researcher a list with both email addresses and contact numbers for officers included in this sample. KPD required that the interviews occur away from the department, and we conducted interviews at a local university library on four separate days over a three-week period. The interview site was several hours' drive, and interview days, coupled with the restricted availability of some officers, limited the number of completed interviews. The final Kiowa sample included four women and seven men; however, three male officers directly refused to take part in the interview process. This portion of the sample included six patrol officers, three detectives, a community resource officer, and one captain. Again, the sampling produced limitations regarding generalizing to the entire KPD population, but the in-depth interviews provided significant details of individual officers' perceptions about their police work environment.

Queens Police Department (QPD)

The Queens community offers several unique factors that could influence police culture and organizational structures. Queens fits the classification of an isolated urban cluster and is located in a highly rural state. The culture encompasses both elements of the surrounding rural community as well as influences related to urban culture. In particular, a major university and a significant military installation encompass the community. In addition to performing normal law enforcement duties, QPD maintains the county jail, housed in the central law enforcement center. QPD patrols large geographic zones; however, the department is modest in size, with approximately 160 individuals and more than 90 sworn officers. At the time of the interviews, 115 of the 160 employees were male, and the vast majority of women were employed in non-sworn support functions. The organization employed six women in sworn patrol or investigative positions, but no women held positions higher than sergeant. Like many departments, QPD had a quasi-military structure, with four divisions: patrol, investigations, support, and the jail.

Interviewing officers in the Queens department was also a multiple-step process. The department was clearly concerned with the purpose of this research; nevertheless, the administration was mindful of the importance of university research because of its frequent interaction with the local college. Gaining permission to interview officers took more than two months from initially contacting QPD's administrators. The final approval required a face-to-face meeting with the director and several other ranking officers.

As with KPD, the Queens department provided a sample of officers drawn randomly from the department's three shifts and investigations. At our request, the department provided contact information on all women sworn officers, and we specifically attempted to interview these officers. In all, 12 interviews were completed with QPD officers, and the sample included seven patrol officers, two detectives, one sergeant, one lieutenant, and one captain. As with each of the other departments, few minority officers were included in the sample (only one QPD officer was a racial minority). One female officer and one male officer directly refused to take part in the interview process but did not provide direct reasons for their refusal. Two officers failed to complete interviews because of scheduling or other conflicts, and interview efforts were terminated after multiple attempts. It is unclear whether the scheduling failures were passive attempts to avoid the interview process or simply the by-product of difficult schedules.

Monterrey Police Department (MPD)

The city of Monterrey is the third community of interest in this research and is located in the Midwest on a major interstate highway. At the time of the interviews, the city had a population of roughly 7,000, and according to U.S. Census data the population was 97 percent White. Reflecting the city's population, MPD employed few officers; however, MPD fits with the majority model of policing because nearly 60 percent of all police departments in the United States have fewer than 10 officers (Weisheit, Falcone, and Wells 1999). MPD maintained a paramilitary organizational structure, albeit with a flatter hierarchy and less distance between line officers and supervisors. The sworn officers included a chief of police, one sergeant, three corporals, and seven patrol officers. The department also employed six communications officers, four of which were full-time employees. Although the city and corresponding patrol areas are not particularly high risk, the intersection of two major highways provides some potential for dangerous police operations.

The MPD law enforcement center houses both the city police and the sheriff's office. The portion of the sample drawn from MPD included five White males; the department employed no women in sworn positions.

The flat hierarchy and rural nature of MPD reduced some of the complications in the approval process encountered in the other agencies. The principal researcher contacted the MPD chief and received permission to conduct the interviews within a day. The chief of police agreed to the interview, as did the second-in-command, the day shift sergeant. The remaining three officers interviewed in Monterrey served primarily patrol functions in the community, but owing to the size restrictions of the department these officers had varied experiences in other functions, including investigations and animal control. The interviews were conducted in a meeting room located in the city's main street that the police department had purchased for training and other functions. Interviews covered officers from the first and second shifts and were completed in the course of one 12-hour visit to the department. All on-duty officers agreed to the interview process, but this procedure excluded those currently working the midnight shift. Officers in the department beyond the chief frequently rotated shifts, so the officers interviewed had experienced working the midnight shift at various times in their employment.

Interviews, Coding, and Limitations

The qualitative research design involved semi-structured interviews with individual officers from each department. The questionnaire used for these interviews is included in the Appendix. This instrument was part of a broader study of gender and stress among police officers and explored respondents' perceptions of their work environment, including questions on gender interactions, burnout, organizational stress, work-related stress, psychological health, physical health, negative behavioral patterns, suicide, and excessive force. The interviews utilized a flexible format style. This type of interviewing technique allows respondents to speak freely and lets the interviewee set some of the terms of the interview (Lofland and Lofland 1984).

The analysis of these interviews included a combination of coding specific themes identified by prior research and allowing additional themes to emerge from the interview process. All interviews were recorded and later transcribed for accuracy; quotes represent the direct words of those interviewed during the process. The design of the interview schedule allowed for open-ended responses to questions, with flexibility for follow-up questions related to officer responses.

As with all research, the current study has several limitations. The inductive and theory-driven process of qualitative research creates the potential for misinterpretation of the data owing to provincialism, emotional reactions, hasty conclusions, and suppressed evidence (Rubin and Babbie 1993). Within the current research, we attempted to avoid these pitfalls by evaluating all available evidence and ensuring that the data fitted with the balance of this evidence. This process also included thoroughly reviewing any information not included in the analysis, and the conclusions of this paper and data collected during emotional situations were further reviewed to ensure the theoretical focus of the conclusions. In addition, descriptions of observed emotion are included in the analysis at times. The direct or indirect refusal to interview may also have resulted in some level of selection bias within the sample, and in two departments the administration generated the contact list of potential interviewees. Although we have no reason to suspect selection or exclusion of specific officers by these departments, we cannot ensure that the provided lists were random.

This research has additional limitations and concerns specific to interviewing police officers. Peer bonds within policing can lead to intense secrecy and solidarity among officers, limiting their willingness to disclose observed gendered (and other) behavior. In fact, officers who report problems presented by their peers might fear retaliation from others within the department (Cancino and Enriquez 2004). The lead author, who has considerable experience working with police officers in a professional setting, conducted the interviews and took measures to build rapport. It appears that the officers in this sample were forthright and provided exceptionally candid responses, but there is no way to ensure the complete candor of respondents. In addition, immersion within the work culture may actually change the perception of the officer. Furthermore, the lead author's position as a researcher may have influenced responses by study participants. Nevertheless, the additional depth of knowledge gained by conducting these observations outweighs these limitations.

Findings

Findings indicate that officers observe strong informal attempts to gender-segregate women in specific assignments based on essentialist assumptions about women's abilities that directly correspond to traditional views of the matron. Interviews with officers indicate that images of policewomen generally follow one of three viewpoints, all of which appear to influence social interaction and, eventually, assignments within departments. First, many officers believe that women are naturally drawn toward cases involving women or children. Beliefs that women are inherently maternalistic, in part, justify gender-based assignments. Second, officers, including many women, believe that women in law enforcement are naturally more empathic and sensitive to the needs of victims, particularly if those victims are children or women who have been sexually assaulted. Part of this assumption is that officers tend to believe that women have better communication skills, which makes them more appropriate for dealing with highly emotional situations. Third, lack of physical strength remains a dominant representation of women officers that operates to restrict some of their field responsibilities.

Representations of women as naturally maternal are the strongest and most consistent images of women officers among interviewees. Examples of maternalistic women officers generally focus on interactions with children—specifically the idea that women naturally protect and comfort children. Larry, a patrol officer in Monterrey, provides a perfect example of such beliefs in the following statement:

> In fact one of the wrecks I worked. [Pause] I mean I have children and I am pretty good with children but in my mind when it was going on I was concerned with dealing with everything else. The female officer was dealing with the little kid. That was just her instinct. I don't know, he was a 3-year-old or something like that and she just calmed him down. The rest of us just got more into dealing with the hurt people. I can see an advantage with that and calming people down. I think they would have an advantage with that. Guys tend to once they get worked up, they stay worked up.

The text of Larry's statement evokes essentialist beliefs about women and provides a superlative example of how gendered images reinforce behavior in law enforcement settings. Terms like *instinct* intimate biological differences between men and women that guide behavior. Larry believes that in critical events, women are naturally inclined to deal with children while the men handle everything else.

Officers draw upon general social conceptions about women when marshalling stereotypical images of women's strengths in law enforcement situations, and these images persist even in departments with no women officers. Travis, a newly hired Monterrey officer at the time of his interview, provides just such a case. Monterrey historically has employed only two patrol women, and none in recent years, and Travis's interaction with women in law enforcement is limited to infrequent interagency collaboration with a female sheriff's deputy. Despite limited contact with women patrol officers, Travis has formulated strong beliefs about their contributions to policing.

> Women are probably better dealing with children. Although it may also bother them more when children are hurt in accidents or abused or stuff like that. I think that it may have been useful when we had a female officer on abuse calls, like child abuse or even conflicts in families.

Travis's statement suggests powerful stereotypical images of women officers that persist in policing even with limited contact between policemen and policewomen, particularly in situations that men equate as feminine. Although we cannot know for sure, these gendered images of women officers may not always correspond to actual observations of officers in field situations and could reflect broader cultural stereotypes. As noted earlier, research has not consistently shown that women officers provide different levels of comfort or emotional care (DeJong 2004; Lundman 2009; Rabe-Hemp 2008). This dynamic suggests that changing the images of women in law enforcement could prove arduous because most people—and perhaps police officers to an even greater degree—draw upon strongly entrenched stereotypes of women in American culture to support beliefs about the power of essentialist behavior in some patrol situations.

Images of women officers as emotionally sensitive and effective communicators harken to general views of women in society, and interviewees frequently draw upon this image when accessing the skills and behaviors of women officers. Such images imply that women are naturally more effective in dealing with human emotions. Ross, a Monterrey officer, vocalizes this viewpoint when asked about a most appropriate situation for a female officer:

"Probably instances when there needs to be a little more emotional tactfulness, like working with a child or somebody who is suicidal. They [women] might have an advantage."

It should not be surprising that the women in the sample also share many essentialist views about particular skills that women bring to law enforcement. This phenomenon showcases the power of gender dynamics in society and requisite effects on both men and women. Women, like men, frequently accept social arrangements as biological imperatives. Observe the following comments by Sherry, a Queens detective who works primarily with child abuse and sexual assault cases. "Oh absolutely! I think women, as the general rule, are more compassionate, more understanding, and more articulate. Not all, but as a general rule you can listen to people. We try to fix everything." Answering the same questions about women officers, Tamara offers a similar response: "[W]hat I see with the female officers, for the most part, they become more personable, I guess maybe they aren't trying to maintain an image . . . their people skills are better and they relate better for the most part." Both Sherry and Tamara have specific assignments in law enforcement that require excellent communication skills. Sherry investigates child abuse cases, and Tamara works as a community resource officer. These women also believe that they possess skills, based on their gender, that assist in these highly public appointments within their respective departments. This does not imply that these women are undeserving of their positions, but merely that their accounts of women officers fit better with specific assignments focused on communication skills than on traditional patrol behaviors. Furthermore, expectations of women officers develop because of either contrast effects or the visibility of their behaviors (Kanter 1977; Stichman et al. 2010). Specifically, the behavior of women in comforting situations may be more visible or may be used to contrast the behavior of men.

A final emerging theme related to images of women among interview subjects centers on the lack of an imposing physical stature, indicating that women are too small for certain law enforcement tasks. Interviewees frame concerns about the physical strength of women officers in two interrelated fashions. First, they focus on a lack of physical size as a disadvantage and an additional stressor for women officers. Second, respondents frequently identify physical stature as an advantage for men in law enforcement. Regardless of how officers frame this issue, it generates images of women as inferior and a potential liability in patrol situations and men as an asset to police organizations.

Images of women officers continue to concentrate on physical strength and body size, resulting in negative images of women officers. Consider, for example, a simple statement by a Kiowa patrol officer regarding difference between men and women in law enforcement: "Physical strength or if you had to control a subject. As far as decision making or ability to do the job, I don't think there is difference." Similar comments were provided by officers in Queens and Monterrey. For example, Joe states, "I think in terms of strength. I am going to put you [woman's name] there fighting a 300-pound gorilla down in [bar district]." Such thinking ignores the wide variation among individual officers of both genders and results in a general belief that women cannot function in certain tasks, further influencing the gendered division of labor.

Division of Labor

Interviews indicate that the gendered division of labor persists, particularly with certain tasks that remain highly masculinized or feminized, but that changes are based largely on informal action as opposed to formal exclusion via agency policy. The most notable informal practice among interviewees was the deliberate exclusion of women from certain highly masculine police functions. Serving on warrant squads and arrest teams appears to be one area of policing that maintains a masculine stronghold. Several of the women officers indicate that they are specifically excluded from these tasks, despite requests for such assignments, and they believe that administrators and supervisors marshal images of women in law enforcement that justify these practices. During an interview, Sara, a patrol officer in Queens, states,

> Yes, they very rarely take a female on a search warrant; they will take a man in case something goes wrong. I have repeatedly asked Lieutenant [Name] if I could go assist on a search warrant and he always picks a guy, even when I go to him and specifically request that I want to go help.

Exclusion from certain patrol assignments considered too rough for women is another example of the gendered division of labor. Queens officers, both men and women, reference walking patrols in the college bar district as an example of a beat that historically excluded women. Sherry specifically addresses this beat during her interview: "In the old days, I can remember you would volunteer to go the [bar district] and they would never pick the females to go because they always wanted to pick the tough-looking guys to do that stuff." Joe, who patrolled the bar district with a woman officer, was also aware of these exclusions:

> I had a partner that walked with me in [bar district]. She was the first female cop ever. Yet, I know for a long time that there was a lot of resistance from a lot of people because is she going to be able to fight off the 250-pound drunk that gets into a fight?

These comments vividly illustrate the gendered division of labor that remains in policing, but the inclusion and success of women in this walking patrol speak to some level of change. Note, however, that despite indication of change the officer's statement reflects gender-based concerns even while supporting his patrol partner.

Gendered images sometimes generate and appear to take on a life of their own in a process quite similar to the construction of urban legends. Many interviewees reference concerns that some citizens easily dismiss female officers. It is interesting that this belief seems more reflective of pre-existing images of female officers than actual events. Many men present the general concern that citizens, particularly men, will not follow the orders of women officers. The idea that citizens disrespect women officers, as with general images of women, may not entirely build on directly observed events and mirrors deep-seated beliefs about women. A Kiowa patrol officer provides such an example: "A suspect is going to look at them and say well she is just a little female you know and I am not really worried about them, something like that." When pressed to describe a specific example, this officer stated, "I can't think of one offhand, but I've heard of it happening." A patrol officer whose beat covered a rural section of Queens that is traditionally reserved for only male officers proffers another example of this phenomenon: "Yes, this is strange. I mean the size of some officers will turn a perpetrator a little more mellow or whatever than a female officer arriving at headquarters." Again, when this officer was pressed for more details he could not offer a specific situation when this behavior was directly observed. In fact, none of the officers in the sample provided specific situations when a female officer failed to control a male subject, yet interviewees frequently referenced judgments about their physical abilities.

Interactions

Gendered interactions described by most officers in this research appear to be the by-product of both gendered images and the existing division of labor. Gendered interactions occur in three general ways and have a profound influence on informal police culture. First, typical interactions occur between officers as routine aspects of their job during work hours. These interactions include any aspect of behavior taking place while officers are acting in an official capacity and include direct face-to-face contact, shift briefings, and memos or electronic communication. Second, interactions include off-duty relations between department members. Finally, gendered interactions occur between the public and law enforcement officers when gender becomes the focal point of exchanges.

Both men and women officers acknowledge that law enforcement workplaces are highly masculine. In fact, many officers use the words *guys* or *men* when talking about their employment atmosphere, seemingly ignoring the fact that women are in their occupational environment (except for in Monterrey). As one male officer states, "I mean it's just guys hanging out." Although the term *guys* is popular slang for large social groupings, the tone of the discussions, description of gender-segregated behavior, and acknowledgment of the masculine nature of interviewees' police work environments seem to indicate that the selected terminology actually reflects understandings about the limited social acceptance of female peers.

Respondents describe the police work environment as highly informal. Field officers in these three departments patrol alone, and work interaction occurs only prior to shifts, during joint calls, and when officers are working on cases at the station. Detectives and administrators interact in an office setting similar to most management-type positions, and they have significant face-to-face interaction with their peers. Regardless of their position, the officers' descriptions provide considerable insight into gendered interactions in law enforcement.

"I work with a bunch of men. I am the only female . . . my daily work environment right now is very gritty; it's not very politically correct." Chloe provides the previous statement to a simple question: "Describe your daily work environment for me." Although she carefully avoids words like *harassment* or *oppressive*, words like *gritty* and *politically incorrect* bring to mind negative gender-based behavior. A Queens officer reports that police interactions include "a lot of shit talking" and that officers "badger the hell" out of each other. These behaviors are not viewed as problematic; he believes they build cama- raderie between officers, describing this phenomenon as a "locker room mentality"— inferring images of men sitting around interacting. Although these interactions may appear harmless on one level, they also indicate the type of peer support among male officers that reinforces masculine behavior in police settings (Franklin 2005).

Contact among officers in non-work environments represents the strongest form of informal gendered interactions in the current research. As with any work setting, personal relationships develop and extend into the private lives of employees. During non-work hours, officers interact freely, apart from the formal organizational policies that restrict certain conduct and foster safe havens for macho culture.

Women are effectively excluded from non-work peer interactions by the purposeful action of men and the selection of activities designed to "naturally" eliminate women officers. Both men and women officers present strong beliefs about behavior that occurs off-duty, which fortifies gendered behavior at work. Take, for example, the highly gendered statement of a Monterrey patrol officer: "From what I can tell they are at least invited. You know, well, I'm sure they say [men officers] if you're going to a titty bar you may not invite them." This officer's statement speaks volumes about gendered interactions in policing. He believes that women are included during most leisure activities but also directly speaks to situations when masculine culture dictates the segregation of women. When male officers behave as "real men" supposedly do, they easily manage to exclude women.

Male officers do sometimes invite women officers to non-work activities that focus on drinking and social interaction. Although women officers are included in these social gatherings, the described behavior frequently remains masculine in nature. Joe provides an example of this behavior among officers in Queens:

> We will invite you . . . So when I say yes, they are included, it's because they are invited [women] and if they don't show up, that's on them. Yeah they are just as apt to get picked on and made fun of just like everybody else.

According to Joe, women are invited to these activities, but the men feel no obligation to adjust their behavior. So women can attend these events, subjecting themselves to teasing and derogatory treatment as one of the guys, or they can opt not to attend. Women must adapt to the masculine behavior or stay away; regardless, the masculine nature of these events is unchanged. Women are left with the double-bind of appearing aloof or modifying their behavior to match that of men.

Men frequently exclude women from non-work events that do not fit with feminine images. Interviewees regularly describe non-work interactions in terms of masculinized activities that women would not want to attend. Nate, for example, describes off-duty interactions in the following statement: "A bunch of guys get together to play video games, football, and stuff like that. Play cards maybe. Pretty active stuff, I think." Another officer, Ross, directly references gender segregation in non-work events in his statement: "In the past it has been more so, on the guys side of it, campouts or gatherings at someone's house. It often involves alcohol." Both of these men describe events that exclude women and involve interaction that centers on reinforcing masculinity by focusing on behaviors officers believe do not interest women or invoke the questioning of their gender identity.

Women officers in this sample are generally aware that their male peers do not invite them to certain activities. Sherry is cognizant of direct practices that exclude women officers from male-dominated off-duty interactions.

> A lot of the guys go and play poker together and the females aren't invited. In investigations our captain has poker night regularly and we aren't invited and that hurts our feelings. I would never go, but we aren't included in that; we're not part of that. I still think it's just because they are crude or disgusting but they are like that in the office anyway.

Women, like Sherry, know that they are not invited to events like poker night because the men choose to act in a "macho man" way and do not want to manage perceived negative reactions from women. During these events men reinforce their behavior and develop informal networks that allow policing to remain a mostly masculine enterprise. It is ironic that the behaviors these men are protecting women from are frequently displayed in the very workplace they both inhabit; masculinized behavior developed in non-work settings often spills into their work environments.

Despite the regularization of women in law enforcement, many men maintain beliefs that women are ill-equipped for policing, and this attitude is reflected in their treatment of women. Sherry, a female detective, describes this belief among her male peers.

> I was the only one here for a while and you take the brunt of everything because there are a lot of officers here who are still here who think women still don't belong in law enforcement . . . [Pause] Don't have a place in law enforcement or should only be certain things.

Beliefs about women in law enforcement extend beyond concerns over their ability to use physical force; women are assumed to be less effective as officers than their male counterparts. This standard relates to doing gender processes that see women as effective only in certain feminine employment sectors and assume them to be less worthy as officers because policing aligns with masculine ideals.

Interviews with officers in this sample describe aspects of gendered images, a gender-oriented division of labor, and gendered interactions that remain strongly entrenched in modern policing. Consistent with Acker's (1990) theory, police organizations remain highly masculine, and nearly every aspect of law enforcement preserves this social arrangement. This may, in part, explain the stagnated growth of women in policing, as they currently constitute approximately 13 percent of sworn officers in the United States.

Discussion

Interviews in the current study provide indications that social structure and individual actions in police organizations remain shaped by conceptions of gender, further building upon existing research. Given more than 30 years of successful mass employment of women in patrol functions, we would expect the matron image to fade. Yet, in the current sample officers describe images of female officers that correspond to law enforcement tasks managed by matrons, even if their daily work functions are inconsistent with these images. Apparently some aspects of the matron image are continually reinvented in modern policing.

Formal organizational restrictions limiting women to certain police posts have disappeared, but informal behavior based on gendered images seems to have assumed this function. Modern law enforcement equipment and training minimizes concerns that women cannot handle violent situations, yet these images remain prevalent today. One male officer recounted the success of a woman officer in a traditionally male patrol setting, specifically the Queens bar district, without truly challenging the image of women as physical liabilities. Envisioning women officers as inferior in certain tasks represents a subtle manifestation of masculine power. Compared to adjustments in formal policy, these informal behaviors, attitudes, and assumptions may prove especially resilient to change.

In order to protect masculine power in law enforcement and informal gender segregation, men need women to fail in certain masculinized aspects of the job. In this research gendered images of women work insidiously, even in imagined situations. Men frequently generate images of women officers that draw upon stereotypes of their physical abilities and emotional propensities. Fears that women could falter in physical fights abound among male officers in this sample, despite the fact that no officer could provide specific examples of women failing to arrest a violent suspect or placing other officers in harm's way. In some cases, officers make strong gender-specific assumptions about women officers despite having only peripheral contact with female officers. Ultimately the gendered image of women as liabilities protects the masculine image of men and provides an informal culture that allows these sexist assumptions to continue. The current research cannot determine whether these imagined failures of women are deliberately or unconsciously created, but they clearly demonstrate the amazing resiliency of patriarchy in American society.

The research findings also reveal the staying power of the matron image of women officers and ideas that women have a proclivity toward emotional labor. This dynamic becomes a self-generating and powerful force in policing that continues the status quo by encouraging administrators to believe that women are more effective in certain tasks. Consequently, certain matronly tasks remain mostly the domain of women officers.

Some respondents seem to indicate that segregating women from certain assignments, like walking patrols in violent settings, is a natural result of gender differences in size and strength and is designed to protect women from potential danger. This finding conforms to much prior research on women officers that focuses on their physical prowess and on beliefs about women being a physical liability (Brown 1998; Martin 1996; Schulz 1995).

The safety of women officers—in both practice and imagery—reinforces the masculine aura of law enforcement by protecting established images of men and women. The protection of women officers from potential violence is not truly about women; it is about preserving the power of men. Participation in warrant and SWAT teams lingers as a masculine endeavor that separates ordinary officers from the truly fearless tough guys of policing. This behavior safeguards masculinity in police work environments by preserving certain positions. The other side of this relationship is that masculine power also protects men from carrying out matronly tasks within the organization.

If policing is to reach gender equality, police departments and criminal justice educators must actively aid in changing these outdated matronly images of women officers. The changes must continue to focus on both powerful stereotypes of women officers and specific beliefs about their skill sets in policing.

Community-oriented policing may offer some aspects of change from traditional masculine police behavior expectations for both men and women officers. Community-oriented policing arose from a desire to increase police–community partnerships, foster public relations and community satisfaction, and improve the effectiveness of crime control measures (Scheider, Chapman, and Schapiro 2009). The acceptance of women could increase as police agencies continue to move toward a new breed of police officers that focus on community policing behaviors and communication skills (Rabe-Hemp 2008), not because of essentialist beliefs, but because it is reflective of emerging views of law enforcement skills. For example, a lack of observed gender differences in the use of coercion in Paoline and Terrill's (2004) research was partly attributed to the community policing practices within the departments studied. In the current research some of the positive stereotypes of women as emotionally supportive and excellent communicators correspond well to aspects of community policing. However, community policing alone may not alleviate gender-based attitudes and behaviors, as some research shows variability in applications of practices like community policing by gender (Eterno 2006). Furthermore, the power of status and decision-makers often remains outside the venue of community policing so the programs are not always fully integrated into police service delivery.

Formal organizational behavior still plays a rather significant role in continuing change in police behaviors. In particular, organizational training practices and job assignments could significantly influence the tenor of police culture and job expectations. Furthermore, prior research has found an informal curriculum in the training of police recruits designed to encourage women officers' dropout or to exaggerate gender difference between officers (Prokos and Padavic 2002). Recruitment education, shift meetings, field training, and other organizational instruction should shift attention away from the importance of physical size and brute force by focusing on offender de-escalation techniques, communication skills, intelligence, and cognitive decision-making as earmarks of affective policing (Stichman et al. 2010). This could also include the selection of case examples, training stories, and practices that focus less on contrasting or exceptional behavior linked to gender stereotypes (Stichman et al. 2010). Some research indicates that police organizational behaviors in Norway that are less focused on macho practices and more accepting of women officers produce fewer gender differences in work outcomes, social support, and other attitudes and behaviors (Burke, Richardsen, and Martinussen 2006).

Official job assignments also offer a potential area for change. Although women enjoy full participation in patrol duties, findings indicate both informal and formal attempts to gender-segregate women in specific assignments based on essentialist assumptions about women's abilities. However, officers also indicate some degree of change and hope for the future. The recent addition of women to walking patrols in Queens offers an excellent example of change despite remaining stereotypes. Forced gender integration and cross-gender partnering in traditional gender-segregated units may foster additional change (Stichman et al. 2010). What is indisputable is that any policy that includes a gender quota system would meet, at a minimum, with informal resistance despite the fact that gender-specific job assignments already exist. Changes on such a scale could also reduce some elements of the tokenism currently observed because of the limited presence of women in these units. Finally, it is important that women continue to advance to higher ranks within departments (Archbold and Schulz 2008).

The informal police culture remains a powerful roadblock to major behavioral change (Cancino and Enriquez 2004). The normative standard in policing pushes officers toward risk-seeking behavior. Officers who attempt to avoid perilous situations can be stigmatized as cowards and treated accordingly (Hickman et al. 2001). The police subculture values the most masculine behavior. Violence and risk-taking are encouraged, cautious and analytical policing dejected, and violations of secrecy punished. This social context restricts rapid change in law enforcement agencies. Police organizations should specifically target the informal subculture and encourage officers, staff, and administrators to assume a funda-mental role in changing informal behavior. In particular, officers must be clear that seemingly harmless masculinized behavior plays a role in continued ideology and essentialist beliefs (Franklin 2005). Having a full understanding of the negative impact of this subculture could aid the change process. In addition, officers should encourage some non-masculine off-duty activities that involve both men and women. The pervasive police culture and the strangle-hold of masculine power question the effectiveness of any formal organizational policy to address informal practices; however, organizations should expand their efforts in this area.

An interesting emphasis in future research could focus on the increased generation of imagined failures of women in law enforcement tasks. Given the urban legend quality of stories about women's patrol shortcomings, such imagery could expand as a protective mechanism for more masculine positions. Recall that these images of women persist with no equivalent example for men, despite countless instances of women succeeding in diffi-cult situations.

Finally, the findings provide implications for the recruitment and retention of women officers. Prior research indicates that many police organizations have failed to develop appropriate recruiting strategies to target women officers and rely overly on traditional male-oriented recruiting methods (National Center for Women and Policing 2000). Departments primarily attempt to develop gender-neutral language, policies, and promo-tional practices in order to reduce discrimination concerns among officers. However, such policies ignore the evidence that women may face unique work behavior, such as sexual harassment (Brown 1998; Martin 1996; Westmarland 2001) and tokenism (Morash, Kwak, and Haarr 2006). Proactive policies such as those described here will improve police work environments for women and positively affect recruitment and retention.

Appendix

Interview Schedule

1. Please tell me a little about your background in law enforcement.
2. Describe your daily work environment for me.
3. How would you describe what is most stressful about working in law enforcement?
4. Is stress in law enforcement different for male and female officers?
5. Have you ever experienced physical or psychological problems that you believe are related to job stress?
6. Describe for me the characteristics of a good police officer.
7. What do you consider to be professional burnout?
8. In your opinion, what does the public expect of a police officer in your community?
9. Do you hear other officers talking about emotional or psychological distress attributed to their employment in law enforcement?
10. Have you ever thought that your employment in law enforcement has caused emotional or psychological distress in your own life?
11. Do you know of any officers who have seriously thought about taking their own life?
12. Have you ever seriously thought about taking your own life?
13. Have you known or suspected that fellow officers may have been overlooked for certain assignments because of race, gender, sexual orientation, or physical characteristics?
14. Do you ever feel that you are less likely to get chosen for certain assignments because of who you are?
15. Do you feel that your administration supports officers who are in trouble? Please explain.
16. Are you able to talk about stressful events or personal burnout with your peers?
17. Do you know or suspect that an officer has become violent while on the job? Off the job? If so, what do you suspect is the cause or triggering factor?
18. Have you ever observed open hostility between officers? In your opinion what precipitated the problem?
19. Have you ever observed an officer become violent at work? How did you handle this situation?
20. Is there an expectation that officers handle these situations informally? Is there an expectation of loyalty or secrecy?

21. What would happen to an officer in your department if they reported a peer for using excessive force?
22. What steps has your department taken to reduce officer burnout?
23. How do officers interact with each other when they are not on the job?
24. Are female officers equally included in non-work peer interactions?
25. Do officers talk with each other about stressful events?
26. Can you think of instances in which a male officer has an advantage over a female officer? Can you think of instances in which a female officer has been treated differently in your department because of her gender?
27. Can you think of instances in which a female officer has an advantage over a male officer? Can you think of instances in which a male officer has been treated differently in your department because of his gender?

Critical Thinking

There is an enduring perception within law enforcement that females lack the physical strength necessary to be effective officers, but possess superior interpersonal skills necessary to deal with children and victims of abuse. These ideas form the basis for gender-based segregation, particularly among special units (warrant serving team). How has the female officer matron image changed over the past 30 years and how can community-oriented policing change the rampant gender inequality present within law enforcement? What other policies could address this issue?

References

Acker, Joan. 1990. "Hierarchies, Jobs, Bobies: A Theory of Gendered Organizations." *Gender and Society* 4: 139–158.

Archbold, Carol A. and Dorothy Moses Schulz. 2008. "Making Rank: The Lingering Effects of Tokenism on Female Police Officers' Promotion Aspirations." *Police Quarterly* 11: 50–73.

Baxter, Nancy, Robert Cohen, and Robin McLeod. 1996. "The Impact of Gender on the Choice of Surgery as a Career." *The American Journal of Surgery* 172: 373–376.

Britton, Dana M. 2003. *At Work in the Iron Cage: The Prison as Gendered Organization*. New York: New York University Press.

Brown, Jennifer. 1998. "Aspects of Discriminatory Treatment of Women Police Officers Serving in England and Wales." *British Journal of Criminology* 38: 265–282.

Burke, Ronald J., Astrid M. Richardsen, and Monica Martinussen. 2006. "Gender Differences in Policing: Reasons for Optimism." *Policing* 29: 513–523.

Cancino, Jeffrey M. and Roger Enriquez. 2004. "A Qualitative Analysis of Officer Peer Retaliation." *Policing* 27: 320–340.

DeJong, Christina. 2004. "Gender Differences in Officer Attitude and Behavior: Providing Comfort to Citizens." *Women & Criminal Justice* 15: 1–32.

Eterno, John A. 2006. "Gender and Policing: Do Women Accept Legal Restrictions More Than Their Male Counterparts?" *Women & Criminal Justice* 18: 49–78.

Field, David and Angela Lennox. 1996. "Gender in Medicine: The Views of First and Fifth Year Medical Students." *Medical Education* 30: 246–252.

Franklin, Cortney A. 2005. "Male Peer Support and the Police Culture: Understanding the Resistance and Opposition of Women in Policing." *Women & Criminal Justice* 16: 1–25.

Haarr, Robin. 2005. "Factors Affecting the Decision of Police Recruits to 'Drop Out' of Police Work." *Police Quarterly* 8: 431–453.

Hickman, Matthew J., Alex R. Piquero, Brian A. Lawton, and Jack R. Greene. 2001. "Applying Tittle's Control Balance Theory to Police Deviance." *Policing* 24: 497–519.

House, Cathryn H. 1993. "The Changing Role of Women in Law Enforcement." *The Police Chief* 60: 139–145.

Kanter, Rosabeth M. 1977. *Men and Women of the Corporation*. New York: Basic Books.

Kay, Fiona M. and John Hagan. 1998. "Raising the Bar: The Gender Stratification of Law-Firm Capital." *American Sociological Review* 63: 728–743.

Kop, Nicolien and Martin C. Euwema. 2001. "Occupational Stress and Use of Force by Dutch Police Officers." *Criminal Justice and Behavior* 28: 631–652.

Kurtz, Don L. 2008. "Controlled Burn: The Gendering of Stress and Burnout in Modern Policing." *Feminist Criminology* 3: 216–238.

Lambert, Emily M. and Eric S. Holmboe. 2005. "The Relationship Between Specialty Choice and Gender of U.S. Medical Students, 1990–2003." *Academic Medicine* 80: 797–802. .

Lofland, John and Lyn H. Lofland. 1984. *Analyzing Social Settings*. Belmont, CA: Wadsworth.

Lonsway, Kim. 2001. "Police Women and the Use of Force." *Law and Order* 49(7): 109–114.

Lundman, Richard J. 2009. "Officer Gender and Traffic Ticket Decisions: Police Blue or Women Too?" *Journal of Criminal Justice* 37: 342–352.

Martin, Carol. 1996. "The Impact of Equal Opportunities Policies on the Day-to-Day Experiences of Women Police Constables." *British Journal of Criminology* 36(4): 510–529.

Martin, Susan E. 1980. *Breaking and Entering*. Berkeley: University of California Press.

Martin, Susan E. 1994. "Outsider Within the Station House: The Impact of Race and Gender on Black Women Police." *Social Problems* 41: 383–401.

Martin, Susan E. and Nancy Jurik. 1996. *Doing Justice, Doing Gender: Women in Law and Criminal Justice Occupations*. Thousand Oaks, CA: Sage.

Miller, Jody. 1998. "Up It Up: Gender and the Accomplishment of Street Robbery." *Criminology* 36: 37–66.

Miller, Laura L. 1997. "Not Just Weapons of the Weak: Gender Harassment as a Form of Protest for Army Men." *Social Psychology Quarterly* 60: 32–51.

Moore, Dahlia. 1999. "Gender Traits and Identities in a Masculine Organization: The Israeli Police Force." *Journal of Social Psychology* 139: 49–68.

Morash, Merry, Dae Hoon Kwak, and Robin Haarr. 2006. "Gender Differences in the Predictors of Police Stress." *Policing* 29: 541–563.

National Center for Women and Policing. 2000. *Recruiting and Retaining Women: A Self-assessment Guide for Law Enforcement*. Washington, DC: Author.

National Center for Women and Policing. 2001. *Equality Denied: The Status of Women in Policing 2000*. Los Angeles, CA: Author.

Paoline, Eugene A. and William Terrill. 2004. "Women Police Officers and the Use of Coercion." *Women & Criminal Justice* 15: 97–119.

Pierce, Jennifer L. 1995. *Gender Trials: Emotional Lives in Contemporary Law Firms*. Berkeley: University of California Press.

Prokos, Anastasia H. and Irene Padavic. 2002. "There Oughtta Be a Law Against Bitches: Masculinity Lessons in Police Academy Training." *Gender, Work and Organization* 9: 439–459.

Prussel, Deborah and Kim Lonsway. 2001. "Recruiting Women Police Officers." *Law and Order* 49(7): 91–96.

Rabe-Hemp, Cara E. 2008. "Female Officers and the Ethic of Care: Does Officer Gender Impact Police Behaviors?" *Journal of Criminal Justice* 36: 426–434.

Rubin, Allen and Earl Babbie. 1993. *Research Methods for Social Work*. Pacific Grove, CA: Brooks/Cole.

Scheider, Matthew C., Robert Chapman, and Amy Schapiro. 2009. "Toward the Unification of Policing Innovations Under Community Policing." *Policing* 12: 694–718.

Schulz, Dorothy Moses. 1995. *From Social Worker to Crimefighter: Women in United States Municipal Policing*. Westport, CT: Praeger.

Segrave, Kerry. 1995. *Policewomen: A History*. Jefferson, NC: McFarland.

Snyder, Claire R. 2003. "The Citizen-Soldier Tradition and Gender Integration of the U.S. Military." *Armed Forces and Society* 29: 185–204.

Stichman, Amy J., Kimberly D. Hassell, and Carol A. Archbold. 2010. "Strength in Numbers? A Test of Kanter's Theory of Tokenism." *Journal of Criminal Justice* 38: 633–639.

Wadman, Robert C. and William Thomas Allison. 2004. *To Protect and Serve: A History of Police in America*. Upper Saddle River, NJ: Pearson.

Weisheit, Ralph A., David N. Falcone, and Edward L. Wells. 1999. *Crime and Policing in Rural and Small-Town America*. Prospect Heights, IL: Waveland Press.

Westmarland, Louise. 2001. *Gender and Policing: Sex, Power and Police Culture*. Portland, OR: Willan.

2

A Qualitative Assessment of Stress Perceptions Among Members of a Homicide Unit

Dean A. Dabney, Heith Copes, Richard Tewksbury, and Shila R. Hawk-Tourtelot

Abstract: *Existing research on stress among police assumes the presence of uniform stressors across job roles and borrows from generic stress instruments to tap stress types and levels. The present study draws upon interviews with 26 members of a metropolitan homicide unit to provide an inductive vantage point on stress perceptions within a specialized area of policing. We provide evidence that the occupational and organizational forms of stress detailed by these officers are shaped largely by the unique nature of homicide work. The unique task-related stressors observed include the complexities of homicide crime scenes, time pressures, case assignment factors, paperwork demands, and long-term ownership over individual case files. A series of structural issues from both within and outside the police agency are identified as organizational stressors unique to homicide work. We conclude with a proposed theory of homicide investigator stress and implications for future research.*

Over the past several decades scholars from various disciplines have produced an abundance of literature on how "first responders" experience and respond to stress (Malasch, 1982; Patterson, 1992). Prominently featured in this literature is research that focuses on stress and coping among law enforcement personnel. Scholars generally agree that members of the policing profession are subject to a multitude of stressors, that these stressors are correlated with negative events on and off the job, and that individuals employ a host of coping strategies to mitigate these negative conditions and outcomes (Abdollahi, 2002; Stevens, 2008; Terry, 1981; Waters and Ussery, 2007). Reviews of the police stress literature suggest that the scholarship is replete with multiple avenues of measurement, data collection, and empirical interpretation, which makes it difficult for researchers and practitioners alike to flesh out the complex nature and dynamics of stress in policing. As such, there exists considerable disagreement as to the dimensions of stress experienced by police officers, how to most effectively measure said dimensions, and how the kinds and levels of stressors vary across demographics and by department size and location (Lord, Gray, and Pond, 1991; Malloy and Mays, 1984; Terry, 1981; Waters and Ussery, 2007).

We contend that much of the disagreement and confusion can be traced to the fact that scholars have rarely imposed an inductive frame on the topic. In a rush to yield generalizable and theoretically informed findings, researchers have borrowed or extended conceptual frameworks and/or stress-related indices from other social science disciplines and applied them to large samples using a deductive approach. This approach rests on the assumption that stress can be operationalized generically across one or more police departments and that there exists a one-size-fits-all conceptual model that can account for the nature and dynamics of stress within law enforcement. A more reasonable approach assumes that the source and form of the stressors are influenced significantly by the nature of the police work in question and the organizational context within which the work occurs.

The present study uses inductive ethnographic methods to shed light on manifestations of stress among officers tasked with the investigation of homicide.[1] We chose this group for several reasons. First, there are unique characteristics associated with the occupational context of doing homicide work. The caseload in homicide is generally lighter than other units but investigators work in an "on-call" status and may thus be called to a crime scene without warning. In addition, for homicide investigators acute stress levels are high, as "mundane" calls do not exist; someone will always have just had their life cut short and the resultant crime scene is likely to be populated with emotional onlookers (e.g., distraught friends and family of the victim) and scrutinizing members of the media. Furthermore, homicide work is mentally demanding, as investigators have to endure long hours, reconstruct events in chaotic crime scenes, comprehend a breadth of forensic science, and work with uncooperative witnesses and suspects. Sustained focus and coordination are also critical for homicide investigators. Unlike cases in other units, the lead detective usually maintains primary responsibility for the case file from response to the crime scene through final disposition, regardless of how long it takes or how involved the tasks become. Scholars suggest that these forms of chronic stress may have more deleterious effects on officers than the acute stress experienced while fielding calls (Hickman, Fricas, Strom, and Pope, 2011).

A second reason we focus on homicide investigators regards unique aspects related to the organizational context of homicide work. Homicides are relatively rare events, even for a metropolitan police force. Yet, homicides are designated as the highest priority crimes and investigators are expected to bring them to a prompt and just resolution. Unit and departmental command staff routinely inquire about specific cases and expect immediate results. Moreover, homicide cases are subject to heightened scrutiny by outsiders, including the media, prosecutors, elected officials, and the public. While other areas of police work yield external scrutiny, homicide is generally considered to be well above average in this regard (Innes, 2003).

Collectively, these organizational and occupational characteristics produce qualitatively, and perhaps quantitatively, different stress manifestations for homicide investigators relative to other police personnel. These factors make understanding stress related to homicide investigators particularly important. By examining how stressors emanate from the way that the work is organized and operationalized, we hope to better inform the ongoing conceptual and methodological discussion of stress within law enforcement.

Stress and Policing

Studies from a variety of disciplines have sought to document the nature, extent, and consequences of stress among police officers. This literature is often contradictory and inconclusive, a likely by-product of the interdisciplinary nature of the research (Abdollahi, 2002). What most do agree on is that there are numerous sources of stress for police officers and this stress has psychological and physical consequences.

It is generally agreed that the sources of stress stem from two broad areas. The first involves occupational stressors, which emerge from the tasks and inherent dangers of police work roles. For example, police typically rank being in shoot-outs and high-speed chases as the most stressful aspects of their jobs. Although contentions about the dangers of police work may be exaggerated (Zhao, He, and Lovrich, 2002), there is always the potential for an officer to either use or become the victim of lethal force, and this often leads to them rating such situations as highly stressful (Patterson, 1992; Violanti and Aron, 1994, 1995).

The second broad category of stress includes organizational stressors. Day-to-day aspects of the job structure, such as strict hierarchies and chains of command, size of the department, overbearing rules and regulations, rotating shift work, and institutional pressures to reduce crime, have all been shown to be major sources of stress (Brooks and Piquero, 1998; Brown and Campbell, 1990; Violanti and Aron, 1994, 1995). It is important to note that organizational stressors may emanate both from structural issues within the law enforcement agency and other agencies with which law enforcement works closely, including the courts and other public officials (Ayres and Flanagan, 1994; Kroes, 1985). Such organizational issues are usually seen to be more influential and important for law enforcement officers' experiences than are occupational or task-based stressors (Gershon, Barocas, Canton, Li, and Vlahov, 2009; Kop, Euwema, and Schaufeli, 1999; Lord, 1996; Shane, 2010; Storch and Panzarella, 1996). For example, Amaranto, Steinberg, Castellano, and Mitchell (2003) found that organizational stressors were over six times more influential on officers' experiences than were task-based stressors. Scholars have also sought to discern individual variations in the sources and consequences of stress for police officers. Race shows a strong association with stress levels; non-white officers tend to report higher levels of stress than white officers (Dowler, 2005; Garcia, Nesbary, and Gu, 2004; Morash and Haarr, 1995). For women, the issue of a perceived "token status" appears to be related to increased stress (He, Zhao, and Ren, 2005; Morash, Haarr, and Kwak, 2006). It is further observed that organizational sources of stress may have differential impacts on male and female police officers, especially as stressors impact officers emotionally and in their performance of personal/family obligations (He, Zhao, and Archbold, 2002). In addition, factors related to an officer's career trajectory appear to be related to the experience of stress among police officers. It is during the middle part of officers' careers that stress levels are most acute (Violanti and Aron, 1995). In a similar vein, research shows that one's position in the agency's hierarchy is related to experienced levels of stress. Specifically, lower ranking officers, such as patrol officers and sergeants (as front-line supervisors), report higher levels of stress than others (Brown and Campbell, 1990; Violanti and Aron, 1995).

Interestingly, though, what remain largely missing in the literature on police stress are assessments of experiences by officers of various specialty units and functions. In addition to neglecting the experiences of officers carrying out specialized law enforcement tasks, there are two other primary limitations in the previous research. First, previous studies tend to over-rely on quantitative measures of stress, coping, and consequences (for notable exceptions see Kroes, Margolis, and Hurrell, 1974; Toch, 2002). The majority of research that investigates stress among police relies on general stress scales (e.g., Deschamps, Paganon-Badinier, Marchand, and Merle, 2003; Lord et al., 1991; McCarty, Zhao, and Garland, 2007; Van Patten and Burke, 2001). At times these scales are adapted for policing, but not always. The use of in-depth interviews and inductive data analyses stand to provide greater insight into the nature of police stress than general stress surveys. The subjective nature of stress suggests that it is necessary to assess how people recognize, interpret, and make sense of potential stressors. By using an inductive approach, it is possible to develop scales and diagnostics that are more refined and specific to the population being studied.

A second limitation of the existing literature is that the majority of police stress research relies on sampling that aggregates officers at the departmental level (Hickman et al., 2011). Doing so assumes that the variety of factors that have stress-producing effects on both task-oriented and organizational pressures operate uniformly for most officers. This is clearly not the case. Officers in other units are not only exposed to different types of stressors but the routinization and bureaucratization of their jobs leads to particular interpretations and experiences of the stressors (Kroes, 1985). While homicide detectives experience many of the same stressors faced by other law enforcement officers, the actual tasks and expectations associated with homicide investigations likely yield unique stressors. In spite of this, the current research detailing the sources of stress for homicide detectives and the consequences of stress is sparse and underdeveloped.

Stress and Homicide Work

The limited research on stress among homicide investigators focuses either on highly specific types of homicide investigations (e.g., child homicide) or on providing a general overview of job-related stressors (Sewell, 1994; Van Patten and Burke, 2001). For example, Van Patten and Burke (2001) demonstrate that detectives who are involved in investigating child homicides have especially high levels of stress. The emotional difficulty of investigating offenses against children is well known, and it is not surprising that detectives in such cases experience high levels of stress (see also Krause, 2009). Alternatively, Sewell (1994) provides a conceptual framework for understanding the sources of stress that are unique to homicide investigators as a class. Drawing explicitly upon his own experiences and anecdotes from other investigators, Sewell outlines a variety of potential stressors for homicide investigators. The stressors he identifies may be grouped into three general categories: pressures to do their work effectively and efficiently, encountered barriers to success generated by structural issues both within and outside the police agency, and investigators' personal reactions and experienced consequences of attempting to achieve but not succeeding fully in their goals.

Within the category of pressures to do the work effectively and efficiently is recognition that homicide investigators carry the "awesome burden" of being responsible for investigating and solving the most important crime (Sewell, 1994, p. 566). This burden can weigh heavily on investigators, as they place great demands on themselves to manage and solve the case. When coupled with time pressures (e.g., a large caseload and the call for a prompt resolution of each), many investigators become consumed with the task or occupational aspects of their investigations.

Sewell (1994) identifies a perceived lack of support from the judicial system, recognition of the failure of social support services in the community that could both assist those affected by homicide and prevent homicides, and interagency rivalries, competition, and lack of cooperation in investigations as examples of structural issues that yield stress among homicide investigators. He describes the necessity to deal with the significant others of homicide victims as another specific organizational pressure facing homicide detectives. When investigating an offense, detectives have to deal with highly emotional, demanding, distraught, and disoriented friends and family members. These emotions are often heightened when one or more friend or family member becomes a suspect in the investigation.

Finally, Sewell (1994) contends that there exist reciprocating forms of frustration, anger, and fatigue that manifest themselves as personal forms of stressors with which homicide investigators must contend. These largely psychological and emotional reactions evolve out of constant exposure to violence and its consequences, and may lead investigators to "feelings that society is lawless beyond control, communities are too insensitive to sights of violence, and little effective rehabilitation or punishment exists" (Sewell, 1994, p. 571). While not fitting neatly under either the organizational or occupational rubric of stressors, this third category of stressors may be especially important in that "the very emotion resulting from stress can simmer and cause further stress," which in turn "often materializes in anger and hostility directed against superiors, suspects, the system, and even the uninvolved" (Sewell, 1994, p. 572). This leads to the suggestion that individual-level perceptions shape how investigators experience and respond to job stress.

While Sewell's framework for the stress experiences of homicide investigators is clear and logical, it is nonetheless anecdotal. Referring to the paucity of research on homicide stress, Henry (1995, p. 95) noted, "To date, no attempt has been made to explore systematically the impact of exposure to death upon police officers or their subculture." Unfortunately, this claim remains true today. The present study seeks to fill this gap through an investigation of the experiences of members of one large metropolitan police department homicide unit. Specifically, we rely on semi-structured interviews coupled with extensive fieldwork to inductively identify the aspects of their jobs that homicide investigators find the most stressful. Doing so will provide an empirical validity check of Sewell's proposed framework. More importantly, systematic observations about the nature and dynamics of stress within specialty units, such as homicide, will serve as a viable point from which to develop a middle-range theory of police stress. Such a theory will incorporate inductive observations relevant to specialty units, and deductive points of logic that have been shown to apply to policing in general. Armed with such a conceptual tool, scholars can then begin to propose and pursue future research directions that operationalize and test the tenets of a middle-range theory. Presumably, more effective interventions and policy initiatives could then follow.

Methods

This study relies on ethnographic data collected from homicide investigators employed by a single metropolitan police department. The department in question has an authorized force of just under 2,000 officers, who are responsible for a jurisdiction of just under 150 square miles.[2] This jurisdiction faces considerable levels of property and violent crime. The homicide unit is a centralized entity that is tasked exclusively with investigating homicides, kidnappings, officer involved shootings, and all suspicious non-vehicular deaths. At the time of the study, the unit comprised 26 sworn officers and a handful of support staff who handled an annual caseload of approximately 100 homicides. Late in 2008, the lead author was granted access to all members of the homicide unit, including officers and administrators. The unit commander introduced the researcher at a unit-staff meeting, and the researcher briefed all sworn officers in the unit about the purpose and scope of the project. The researcher was assigned a ride-along time with interested participants. Before the ride-along sessions, the detailed study aims and procedures were provided to prospective participants with an informed consent document. All 26 sworn members of the unit consented to participate.

Approximately 300 hours of fieldwork were conducted over the course of a nine-month data collection effort (2009–2010). These activities included ride-along sessions with 19 investigators, five line supervisors holding the rank of sergeant, and two lieutenants with unit command responsibilities. Each ride-along lasted for at least the duration of an eight-hour shift with additional time spent in the squad room and in social settings interacting with unit members in a collective format. Significant rapport was developed with the investigators during this time. During moments of down time and immediately after leaving the research setting, the lead author used a digital recording device to take notes of key observations. These recordings were later transcribed verbatim.

In addition to this fieldwork, face-to-face, semi-structured interviews were conducted with all 26 sworn members of the unit. A major advantage of the semi-structured interview is that it allows respondents to answer questions in their own words with minimal direction from the interviewer, with the flow of the discussion determined in part by the officer. This leads to a more natural description of events by the respondent. The main disadvantage of this approach is that the responses can sometimes be wide-ranging and not every respondent may cover all issues. The interviews lasted between 90 and 150 minutes and were designed to take on a conversational format driven by an interview guide. The goal was to stimulate discussion around a predetermined set of topics. An interview guide built around a dozen core topics was designed to prompt discussion about one's work history, perceptions of the homicide investigator's role, and to probe the perceived nature of various forms of occupational, organizational, and personal stressors potentially affecting homicide work. While there was no expectation that the topics would be covered in order or during one sitting, the research plan called for each officer to be engaged on all the topics during the course of the interview. Interviews were audio-recorded and transcribed verbatim. The data were subject to thematic content analysis using the NVivo software program and the following series of theoretical observations were generated inductively.

Event or Occupational Stressors

The nature of homicide work produces a number of unique circumstances that act as potential stressors on homicide investigation unit members. These circumstances appear to be relatively routinized within investigators' daily work experiences and generally mirror those detailed in Sewell's (1994) conceptual framework. More precisely, these task-related issues include that the nature of homicide work involves repeated exposure to homicide crime scenes, time pressures, staffing rotations that dictate when officers are assigned lead investigator roles, paperwork demands, and long-term ownership over individual case files (i.e., from crime scene to final verdict). Our interview data reveal that each of these occupational or event characteristics yield perceived stress in unit members.

Working Crime Scenes

Crime scenes present a host of potential stressors for members of a homicide unit. Many of these factors are simply unwavering realities of the job (i.e., location or condition of the dead bodies), while others are the deliberate outcome of human action or error. Interviews revealed that homicide officers downplay the significance of the former and highlight the latter.

In the eyes of a homicide investigator, dead bodies are part of the job. They learn to dehumanize them and treat them as evidence rather than as someone's sons or daughters. Thus, investigators claimed that the presence of dead bodies did not cause them undue stress. When asked directly if gruesome crime scenes are stressful, a veteran sergeant in the unit replied:

> I have seen it [the gore] a million times, from maggots coming out of the body to decapitation. You become desensitized to it. . . . You don't look at it like, "poor guy;" you look at it like evidence. Let's get to work, you know? I mean I have sat next to a guy that has been in the woods with maggots

crawling out of his eye sockets and ate a double stack from Wendy's. This intern she was like, "How in the world can you eat with that smell?" And I am like, "What smell?"

Referring to the repeated exposure to death and gore, an investigator with almost two years on the unit said:

> It's part of a job and I'm not trying to take any dignity or humanity away from someone, but you know I have to do this every day. . . . You have to learn how to control your emotions and not let your emotions control you. And I control mine, you know? I don't allow it to bother me. I don't think about it . . . I've been on some stinky crime scenes and you just go, "Well, whatever." You know, it's just part of the job and I think that's part of what it is; we accept that this is our job, so we have to do this.

Perhaps because death is such a routine part of the job the investigators did not perceive this aspect of the crime scene as being too stressful. Alternatively, failing to "get it right" at the crime scene was consistently mentioned as a major source of acute stress for these investigators. As one investigator said bluntly, "if someone is still alive and they're in pain there's things that I can do to help them. The only thing that I can do to help this dead person is make sure I get this right." Regardless of the complexity of the task before them, the wealth or dearth of physical evidence, and the skills or lack thereof of other law enforcement representatives, the homicide team cannot return to a crime scene the following day to gather new evidence.[3] As one five-year veteran investigator in the unit said:

> If an interview doesn't go right or if a statement doesn't go right, you can call that person back in, you can re-interview them. . . . You only got one shot at a crime scene. So, if that's screwed up or evidence is contaminated or lost or whatever, that's the only chance you ever get at that. So, I mean that's the beginning of the investigation and often times the most crucial.

Echoing this sentiment about the crime scene, an investigator who had been on the unit for about two years said, "You don't want to miss it because you will never have that scene again and to me that's the stressful part. I got to make sure I get enough right there that's gonna assist me in my investigation and then the prosecution will put this guy away. If I don't get it, I blew, I blew it." Time and again, officers noted how the pressure of gathering the right information weighed heavily on the members of the homicide unit.

Per standard operating procedure in the department under study, the lead homicide investigator has primary authority over the crime scene and all agency staff who are present. This means that they must make sure all support staff are going about their designated tasks, that uniformed officers have cordoned off an appropriate-sized area and made a crime scene log of all persons present, and that other homicide unit members are securing witnesses, taking measurements of the crime scene, drafting a crime scene sketch, and canvassing the area. This can be an enormous endeavor, yielding significant occupational stress for the lead investigator. This is reflected in the following account from a three-year veteran of the unit:

I had a case at that nightclub. . . . When I got on the scene, there were still probably 150 people there. My crime scene log was five pages long. You gotta kind of sift through the people, get the information, pull out the key people that you're gonna interview that night. You know, try to determine who didn't see shit and was just in the other side of the building and get them out, but still record their information. . . . It's crazy and chaotic even when you get there 20, 30, 45 minutes later, it's still crazy and chaotic. Then you have family coming up and you're trying to secure witnesses and you don't have enough people on the scene. Your crime scene's not big enough. . . . It's just everything.

Lead detectives consistently maintained that they do not stress much about what goes on outside of the crime scene tape, as that is the responsibility of uniformed officers. Conversely, interactions with persons present inside the crime scene tape were repeatedly noted as a potential or likely source of stress. Uniform personnel often engage in behavior that compromises the integrity of the investigation. Given that these are sworn law enforcement officers who "should know better," their transgressions are described as stress inducing. As one veteran investigator said:

[Uniformed officers] don't want to go the extra mile. They want to cop attitudes, cut corners. We have a lot of problems with them responding to scenes and taking information from a witness and letting the witness go and then it takes that much more time to go find the witness or just basic commonsense things.

Another commented, "I'd say the biggest thing that's stressful about a crime scene is getting there and officers aren't doing what they're supposed to do, they've messed things up. . . . That's like the number one rule, don't contaminate the crime scene."

Homicide investigators also frequently cited crime scene unit personnel as a major source of stress on the murder scene. In the department in question, these are civilian personnel trained and tasked with visually documenting the crime scene and collecting physical evidence. In more egregious cases, investigators noted that the actions of the crime scene technician can compromise the integrity of the entire case due to errors or oversights. This was seen as particularly stressful to the homicide investigator who knows that he or she is the individual who holds primary responsibility for the overall investigation and will likely be expected to testify in court about any errors or issues attributed to poor follow-through on the crime scene. This is evident in the following quote from an investigator with four years in the unit:

Our crime scene unit is stressful to me, because they're missing a lot and it's not anything you could do. You're just not getting it done from them and you can't go back out [to the crime scene]. I always get the feeling like they don't want to be there . . . I've never gotten the feeling like they're actually trying to help you. They're just trying to get through it.

The interviews uniformly demonstrate that homicide investigators go about their work in a very methodical, non-emotional manner. The routine exposure to dead bodies is mitigated by a sterile approach to blood, human loss, and the like, as such conditions are deemed beyond their control. Conversely, trying to direct, supervise, and manage crime scene personnel and rely upon these people to competently preserve and gather all relevant evidence is a clear source of acute stress. Summarizing the occupational stressors emanating from crime scenes, one investigator said,

> I've got the family to worry about, I've got the victim, I got the ME's [Medical Examiner's] Office, I got witnesses, I've got a whole big crime scene, I got to worry about patrol, I've got to worry about my crime scene tech missing something or I got to worry about my Crime Scene Tech not doing a walk through.

Noticeably absent from this list is the presence of dead bodies.

Time Pressures

In most homicide units, case assignments are made on a rotational basis; lead investigators or investigation teams are placed in an order so that members know who will receive lead responsibility on the next case. The rotation order is often depicted on a white board so that all unit members or teams are aware of the number of murders that must occur before they assume primary responsibility for a case. Investigators use the term "being up" to refer to their time at or near the top of the rotation. They are in an on-call status when they are "up"; when the next "body drops," regardless of whether they are on duty or not, they must report immediately to the crime scene. This places serious stress on investigators, as they cannot plan personal and family functions, and must limit the location of social events. The indecision and stress is illustrated well in the following quote from a three-year veteran of the unit:

> Well the first thing, at least with me, is like, "Fuck, I'm almost up again." Especially when you get to like two or three [on the list]... "Is it gonna be on my off days? Is it gonna be in the middle of the night?" ... It's always a guessing game; you just don't know where it's gonna fall. I guess the not knowing is the biggest thing. "Do I have another beer? Do I plan something with my family or whatever?" So you'll start thinking about it. But what if you're that number one person for five, six, seven weeks? Now you start guessing on where's this thing's gonna fall. It's just a guessing game. You feel that relief once I get the call the first question I ask is, "Are they dead yet? Just tell me they're dead." Because the worst thing is getting called in on somebody that may or may not die.... And then you could be out of the rotation for a couple of days and then you could be back up. It's a roller-coaster.

Echoing this sentiment an investigator with just over one year in the unit said:

> You know you're gonna get that call. You could be in the middle of celebrating someone's birthday or your daughter's dance recital or a nice dinner out with your girl or wife or whoever and you gonna have to put that down and come in to do your job and they might not see you for 12, 16, 24, 48 hours.... You got to call home; you have childcare issues, so that is immediately stressful.

Homicide investigators are subject to a new set of time pressures once called to a crime scene. While the homicide team tries to be deliberate and methodical in its crime scene work, there is a palpable sense that they need to make progress on the investigation. Unit members press to reconstruct the events leading up to the murder, interview key individuals, identify a solid suspect, and notify family members of the loss (all while also being in command of the crime scene and other personnel present). In the hours immediately following the death, these tasks are accomplished in a team format, with multiple members of the homicide unit descending on the crime scene along with medical examiners, crime scene technicians, and uniform officers. As time passes, those with long-term responsibility over the case must forge ahead. Investigators go from being overwhelmed by a mass of support staff to trying to achieve significant results on their own or in a small group. Investigators routinely spend long hours on the crime scene, only to follow these up immediately with a barrage of interviews with potential suspects and witnesses, track down family members, contact credit card or cell phone providers for pertinent records, and/or pull criminal records and assemble photo line-ups, making fatigue an important occupational stressor. As a nine-year veteran investigator noted, "It's like a dog, you're gonna hunt. And if you have to take a nap, take a nap, because nobody's gonna work it as hard as you. This last homicide I had, I was so tired, I needed two hours so badly it ain't funny." Another commented, "There's some cases that you know you need to put in the time. You need to put in the time. You need to manage your time. Sometimes you have to do that 48 hours straight. You don't want to do it, you got to do it."

Having multiple open cases at once poses another time-related occupational stressor. Time-sensitive leads often present themselves simultaneously for multiple cases. The investigator must prioritize this work and find ways to progress his or her entire caseload in an effective and efficient manner. As one 14-year veteran investigator noted, "When you're bombarded with a lot of cases, you prioritize and you move the cases you can solve quicker. And then sometimes you continuously get bombarded with one case after the other and then years go by before you could ever go back to something." Having unsolved cases that one believes can be advanced was repeatedly cited as a point of tension for investigators. As a 10-year veteran detective noted, "You always have those open cases that you go back and ask, 'Did I do everything?' And they bother you."

Once a case is cleared by arrest, a new set of time demands are encountered. Courts will set "non-negotiable" hearing dates. The prosecutor will often call the investigator to testify or follow up on evidentiary issues according to his or her own scheduling constraints with little concern for the investigator's time. To this point, a veteran sergeant explained:

> Court is a bear.... Probably the second biggest frustration is the courthouse.... We're on call for cases for a month at a time. You know, they can call you at any time to go. You sit down there for eight, nine hours and they don't get called on the stand.

As one investigator put it, "Oh, they don't give a shit if it's your off day, or you work morning watch. That is a huge pain in the ass. 'Cos they'll say, 'Oh no, you gotta come in.'"

Paperwork Demands

The typical robbery or burglary case file is relatively thin, including a small stack of reports and evidentiary documents assembled by the lead investigator and support personnel. To a large degree, the robbery or burglary investigator assembles his or her own case file and passes it along to prosecutors. However, with a homicide case file there are routinely several inches of materials, including a host of evidentiary documents and supplemental reports provided by every individual who was party to the investigation. This includes the first officer on the scene, the medical examiner's office, crime lab personnel, crime scene technicians who processed evidence, and the numerous members of the homicide unit who assisted in the investigation by interviewing witnesses, canvassing the community, drawing crime scene diagrams, and the like. All witness and suspect interviews must be included in written or video form. In short, the files can be quite large, complex, and unwieldy. This is a critical part of the work role and the investigators know it; as the unit commander said bluntly, "Your files are looked at. I mean your files have to be in order. You have to be able to do paperwork. This job just requires you to put a good file together." Not surprisingly, then, investigators almost always reported that collecting and compiling case file materials is a significant source of stress, one that is unique in scope and complexity to the homicide investigator. Referring to the factors that shape how to best construct a case file, an investigator who was a four-year veteran of the unit commented:

> Write a story. Document everything. Everything! Because you know when it goes to trial, everything hinges on you. . . . A lot of guys are fearful of the documentation because you know when it goes to trial everything hinges on you. The spotlight is on you. And then you know that defense attorney has a year or two years to look over through your file and figure out what I need to do to make him look incompetent. And that's one of the most stressful things when you come in you know you got one person gonna make you look good. You got that one person try his best to destroy your credibility.

Adjudication Demands

Once the case file is assembled and a copy is passed along to the prosecutor, the homicide investigator will most likely be subject to a spate of court hearings to justify the legitimacy of his or her decisions and conclusions. This process is far more intense and prolonged for the homicide investigator than it is for other detectives. If all goes well, the case proceeds to trial. If it does not and the case is dismissed on a legal "technicality," the homicide investigator experiences frustration watching his or her hard work disintegrate. In the metropolitan jurisdiction under study, a full year will usually pass between the arrest and the scheduled trial dates. During this time, the investigator will likely be responsible for an additional five to ten cases, each with its own unique circumstances and problems. Once the trial date arrives, the lead investigator and all members of the homicide unit who played a role in evidence collection can expect to be called to the witness stand. This necessitates one becoming reacquainted with the case, and disentangling its details from all the other cases that he or she has been a part of in the interim. This process was consistently described as stress inducing. As one investigator reflected, "Did I put the best file together? Am I gonna get hammered in court? Am I gonna look like a fucking idiot when I get up on the stand? . . . You don't want to look like an idiot when you go to court." Another detective, this one a nine-year veteran on the unit, spoke of the gamesmanship of court testimony and how it is stressful:

> They'll keep me up there for three or four hours and then me and him [defense attorney] will go at it. This is my chance to shine. This is your all-star game.... There's loopholes in everything and those little fucking rat finks [defense attorneys] over there they know the loopholes and they try to get everything out of you they can.

Organizational Stressors

A significant amount of the interview content sought to explore the form and content of organizational stressors experienced by homicide investigators. It was found that structural issues from both within and outside the police agency generate stress for the investigator. Perceived internal sources include managing the pressures that come from the high-priority status of homicide cases, navigating the bureaucratic processes associated with case assignment and case processing, and wrestling with the tight-knit nature of the homicide unit culture. Organizational stressors that originate from outside the police department include pressures from the media, actors within the adjudication process, community stakeholders, and members of the public.

Administrative Pressure

Within the department under study, it was standard practice for at least one homicide sergeant and the lieutenant (unit commander) to be present at every crime scene. Usually joining these unit-level superiors were the major who oversees the Major Crimes Section and at least one patrol lieutenant or major. If the crime is high profile, one could expect the presence of an upper-level superior, perhaps even the Chief of Police, and one or more members of the district attorney's (DA) office. Beyond the justice system personnel present, a homicide crime scene is sure to attract multiple-media outlets, onlookers, and frequently key stakeholders from the community (politicians, neighborhood activists, or faith leaders). Homicide investigators cannot help but be aware of these various spectators of their work. As one sergeant who had worked in homicide for nearly 10 years said:

> Some of these [young investigators] get overwhelmed with the pressure of the media. I mean if there's a bigger media story this year I don't know what it is. The media, the supervisors, the fact that he's still catching [additional homicide] cases. This isn't just the one case that he's working on [as lead detective]. He's working this and he's working other things and I think that we do a huge disservice to some of the young detectives that come over here that we just don't give them the training on how to juggle pressures, cases, and prioritize what you have and what you need. You know, it's like I guess a MASH Unit.

Once the crime scene is cleared and the homicide investigator embarks on the investigation, he or she can expect follow-up inquiries from police superiors both within and outside the homicide unit. Within the unit, sergeants and lieutenants will query progress, inject theories about case details, and/or possible directions to explore. This comes in addition to the formal case reviews noted previously and often engenders resentment and stress due to the lack of investigative experience of most supervisors. As one seasoned investigator noted, "I don't think if you took anybody from our command staff and said, 'show me how to work a murder,' I don't think they would have the foggiest clue." Referring more pragmatically to the unit commander, an investigator with three years in the unit noted, "He [the lieutenant] wants them [offenders] locked up as fast as freaking possible. So, he was riding my ass about locking up the guys."

Beyond the unit, the investigator can expect a homicide case to remain on the radar of upper administrators. Not only are the majors and chiefs keenly aware of year-to-date clearance rates, they routinely expect briefings on individual cases. Speaking about the heightened attention to homicide cases, one investigator noted, "The whole chain of command staff is a little more involved, from the lieutenant on up. And passing the information becomes a number one priority. I got to explain to the uppers why this [arrest] hasn't happened yet. I think their pressure becomes my pressure." The department under study functioned using a Compstat model. This accountability-driven management system calls for weekly crime analysis briefings in which a room full of 50 to 100 mid- and upper-level administrators consider crime events and crime patterns from the previous week and expect commanding officers to detail plans to address the workload before them. In this regard, the centrality of open homicide cases and corresponding patterns was described by many as further adding to the stress on the unit.

Unit Culture

There are unique characteristics about the organizational culture of a homicide unit that produce pressures for homicide investigators as they go about their work. For one, all unit members tend to work in contiguous space and spend significant time together. They eat meals together, discuss case details with one another, and often socialize outside of work. Everyone knows everyone else's personal and professional business, which frequently produces stressful interactions. It is not that these cultural pressures do not exist in other units, but rather that they are more intense and palpable in a homicide unit. This is reflected well in the following quote:

> [There's] definitely a lot of inter-shift competition. . . . Every once in a while you hear a guy say, "Oh, you got a bone [easy case]. You can finally close one, huh?" So yeah, there's some of that. . . . I don't want to hear it because it's already on my mind and it bothers me.

There are other structural aspects of a homicide unit that add to the organizational stress. For one, there is a decidedly social nature to the workload and productivity. Front and center in every homicide unit is a "homicide board" that details all the case assignments for each investigator and documents for all to see his or her open and closed cases for the current and previous year. This generates competition, ridicule, and bravado from unit members. Referring to the homicide board, one fledgling investigator said:

> A lot of people could tell you probably better about my cases than I could. . . . You really don't want to leave a board full of open cases. It's just not cool. It's not good for business. It's not good for the public. You just, if you're leaving them open every year it's no coincidence, there's something wrong with you. . . . I think everybody knows when you got to get it done. If you are not going to get it done, they will find somebody else who will. We are known to be the best of the best here. We work the hardest cases here. If you can't handle it they will find somebody that can.

At every turn, from the constant ribbing that senior members dispense to fellow investigators, to the prominently featured homicide board to the localized rituals,[4] the organizational culture of the homicide unit serves to push unit members to achieve the highest standards. While at times a source of reinforcement for the successful unit members, these traditions also serve as stressors when expectations are not met.

External Demands

Members of a homicide unit face additional structural pressures originating from entities outside of the police organization. These include demands imposed by other justice system officials, the media, and public stakeholders that resonate in the minds of homicide unit members. Chief among the stress-inducing interactions are those with members of the judiciary and the DA's office. As an investigation unfolds, detectives must abide by due process afforded to all criminal suspects. In the days and weeks following an arrest, investigators are mandated to secure search-and-arrest warrants and appear before a judge for requisite hearings (e.g., first appearance, evidentiary hearings, and arraignment). However, judges are not always accessible at the odd hours of a homicide investigation and do not consult homicide detectives when setting court hearings. These obstacles weigh upon homicide investigators as they seek to preserve evidence, advance investigations, and go about their multitude of time-sensitive work responsibilities. While all police officers must respect and work within the same due process stipulations, the fact that a homicide investigator assumes sole responsibility for a case file from crime scene to verdict means that they encounter these organizational prerogatives more frequently and more intensely than their fellow officers. Moreover, they are well aware that the consequences of losing a homicide case on a technicality are far more troubling than losing a property crime case on similar grounds.

As the homicide investigator draws in on his or her prime suspect, he or she is inclined to consult with members of the DA's office to seek advice about whether probable cause exists to make an arrest. If the DA's office is not invested in a case, the arrest charges are likely to be dismissed. There exists a subtle but important disconnect between the goals of the homicide investigator and those of the prosecutor. The former is focused on meeting evidentiary standards to effect a lawful arrest and get a killer off the street. The latter shares these concerns but also factors in the likelihood of securing a conviction based on the facts of the case. This perceived disconnect often yields tension between the two justice entities. A 10-year veteran investigator captured this point well:

> You got some DAs that are not too helpful on the investigative side of it. They want all these elements in the case and it's like we're not gonna get that. This is the best we're gonna do. So they don't want to try the case. Then you got some of the younger DAs that want the case handed to them with a bow and a nice little string to it. Then sometimes they don't make a big enough argument. They'll dead docket a case or have a case dismissed because they feel as though that person goes out and kills somebody and the first thing they say is, "The police didn't do this or the police didn't do that."

Once all the pre-trial hearings have been resolved and a murder case is set for trial, the homicide investigator returns to his/her caseload to advance open investigations and await the next one in the rotation. To the detective, he or she no longer has primary responsibility for the case; the prosecutor's office takes over in this regard. That said, organizational stressors remain. As the trial date approaches, investigators are often subject to demands from the DA's office to further develop case materials. Court appearances are often not well coordinated by the DA's office and homicide investigators are made to "waste" a day sitting in the courthouse for their turn on the witness stand. Similarly, prosecutors often cut plea agreements or dismiss a case without fully articulating their logic or satisfying the investigator of the veracity of their decision. This produces additional strains on the homicide investigator that are seemingly more significant than those faced by other police officers. For one, the homicide investigator invests far more time in the average case. Second, and more importantly, the suspect is an alleged murderer and the public safety threats associated with setting the accused free are more severe. As one investigator with five years on the unit noted:

> Our agenda a lot of times is different than their agenda. Our agenda is to identify and build up enough PC [probable cause] to arrest the person and their agenda is to convict this case. "We aren't gonna try it if we don't think we can get a conviction." And that leads to a lot of frustration to the [homicide] guys, because there is enough to go to trial.

Members of the media exert additional demands on homicide unit personnel. This begins at the crime scene where multiple media outlets routinely scramble to get a sound bite from someone in the unit about what happened and where the initial investigation stands. Few other forms of crime scene produce this level of media attention. As a homicide investigation progresses, especially if it takes on a high-profile status, members of the media inquire further into the details of the case. At times, their reporting efforts are seen by investigators as compromising the integrity of the case. In the department under study, the unit or section commander handles crime scene media inquiries but investigators are afforded no protection from the follow-up reporting of the media. Here, the big concern is the control of information so as to not compromise the case outcome. As one rookie investigator noted,

> The media can go against you when they put too much information out there for you. It may be some information that we could have used later. So that's gonna hurt you if they put it out there. So sometimes they help you and sometimes they hurt you. I just don't think you need give them too much. Let them [superiors] just give them [the media] enough to keep the interest going.

Stakeholders within the community pose yet another source of organizational stress upon members of a homicide unit. These include grief-stricken families and friends of the victim, faith leaders, politicians, community activists, and even curious or persistent residents (Stretesky, Shelley, Hogan, and Unnithan, 2010). While their level of intervention varies widely across murder investigations, members of the homicide unit frequently encounter demands for more information or added investigative efforts. Regardless, due to the enormity of the crime, outside forces tend to expect immediate positive results. Speaking about the perspective of a victim's family, a rookie investigator noted:

> They don't care about the other cases. You know, you might be having your twelfth homicide of the year. You might have had two in a month and then you get this one. But no one wants to hear [excuses]. They want to know how come six months in and my baby's case is still open. You know they are wearing your phone out [calling constantly]. You got some family that will flat just wear you out, and that's stressful. I know it's got to be stressful to them because it, sometimes it is to me.

For the homicide investigator, these demands come without the context of external entities knowing the full details or directions of the investigation and/or without sensitivity for the rest of the investigator's caseload. In short, politicians and other community entities want answers irrespective of whether these added insights will help or hinder the work of the detective.

Discussion

The ethnographic data from this study suggest that homicide investigators experience high and unique sources of job-related stress, including pressures to succeed effectively and efficiently, barriers to success arising from both internal and external to the agency structural issues, and personal reactions and experiential consequences of not fully succeeding in their efforts. The present study provides important, initial evidence and documentation of the stressors experienced by police officers involved in investigations of homicides. In particular, interview and observational data identify various occupational and organizational factors that generate stress among members of the homicide unit.

Compared to other police detectives or patrol officers, what may be unique about the stress experiences of homicide investigators identified herein is the intensity of the stress and the specific sources from which these identified stressors arise. For police performing general investigation and/or patrol duties, performance pressures, structural barriers to success, and personal reactions to crime scenes, suspects, witnesses, victims' loved ones, and other agency personnel may be significantly less frequent than those experienced by homicide investigators. While there is a need for additional research to solidify this assertion, it raises the possibility that homicide investigators should be expected to experience greater levels and more intense stress than others within the department.

The event characteristics that give rise to stress for homicide investigators may be unique to their specific niche in law enforcement. However, in contrast, many of the occupational stressors are similar to those reported by patrol officers (the typically studied members of law enforcement). Indeed, bureaucratic elements of law enforcement may have important, negative impacts upon police performance (Dowler, 2005; Morash et al., 2006; Zhao et al., 2002). Sewell (1994) notes astutely that homicide investigators are not immune to these standard bureaucratic pressures. As such, homicide investigators experience the "regular" acute stresses of policing in addition to the chronic stressors that are often highly emotional, time-pressured, and necessitate well-documented tasks specifically associated with homicide investigations.

We found that many of the characteristics of the job that one would expect to be very stressful (i.e., death and gruesome crime scenes) are in fact viewed as manageable. Repeated exposure to dead bodies was described as a necessary condition of the job. Organizational and occupational stressors are not. Thus, it was common for investigators to lay blame for stress onto outsiders. Homicide investigators appear to be more troubled with the factors that they deem to be controllable. Incompetent and/or apathetic crime scene investigators, micro-managing superior officers, meddling media, frustrated families, and judicial practitioners driven by goals that conflict with those of the homicide investigator were the primary sources of stress. It is likely that this ability to externalize the sources of stress is what makes homicide investigators resilient. If they were to internalize the many problems that can and do go wrong with investigations, detectives would likely be overwhelmed by pressure and self-doubt. Blaming others may free them up to focus on the important and necessary demands of the job and overlook the frequent brushes with the worst of humanity.

Developing Middle-range Theory on Police Stress

The previous findings suggest the utility of a broader theory of stress for homicide investigators, perhaps even police in general. By moving up a level of analysis, we can look for more general stressors than the nuanced ones presented above. Doing so allows for more generalizable data and broader understanding of the causes of stress. A closer examination of the results suggests that the "awesome burden of homicide" brings with it unique stressors. Sewell (1994, p. 566) observes that "citizens and detectives alike have ranked murder as the most important crime." In answering this point, a detective from Simon's (1991) ethnographically inspired investigation of the Baltimore homicide unit said, "Homicide is the major leagues, the center ring, the show. It always has been" (p. 17). This burden of being tasked with the highest-priority job in the department is at the root of the general and chronic stressors common to homicide investigators. While outsiders may think that working with dead bodies, grieving families, and outraged, frightened, or otherwise impaired communities are major sources of acute stress, we did not find this to be the case. Instead, the stressors may be grouped into three categories: (1) responsibility for high-priority cases; (2) uncertainty throughout cases; and (3) potential scrutiny from others.

For obvious reasons, solving homicide cases takes high priority within police departments. With high priorities comes a heightened sense of responsibility. In most police departments, those assigned to a particular homicide case are given full responsibility for handling it from outset to conclusion. This involves collecting relevant information at the crime scene, following leads, interviewing witnesses and suspects, keeping up with paperwork, and eventually presenting enough information to prosecutors to clear the case. Being responsible means that investigators have little leeway for error or uncertainty. They must be comprehensive, in command, and without error. They must also take responsibility for crime scene operations, be in command of staff who may be uninterested or untrained, and supervise the scene and others' activities. As lead detective, they must deal with inquiries, uncertainties, and requests from victims' families, uniformed officers, superiors, media, community members, and all who enter the crime scene. On top of all of these responsibilities, the homicide investigator must respond to and manage time demands. They know that the chances of solving the case decrease as time passes and they know the community and agency superiors are impatient about homicide case outcomes. There exist high-profile responsibilities within all police assignments and it stands to reason that the unique aspects of homicide work will be stress-inducing for unit members.

Stress that comes from job aspects not directly emerging from activities at crime scenes includes uncertainty. Uncertainty for homicide investigators arises from not knowing when they will catch a case, whether they are effectively managing follow-up investigations, when they will be called to court, and if their case files are sufficiently thorough. They must cope with ambiguities in information and processes, insecurities about how each case is progressing, and the reactions of other constituencies. These pressures begin before a case is even assigned to an investigator, through its final disposition by the criminal justice system. As with task prioritization, uncertainty is a core part of all police work and should be expected to be stress-inducing.

The high priority of the job also means that homicide investigators are under constant scrutiny from inside and outside the department. Scrutiny is assumed for homicide detectives, and is likely to come from both within the law enforcement agency, and from interested and invested constituencies in the community. This scrutiny begins when they first appear at the crime scene. Inevitably, the crime scene is populated by onlookers who are watchful and critical of any potential missteps the investigators make. Much of this scrutiny is driven by assumptions and misunderstandings about what investigators can and should do to work a crime scene. The scrutiny continues throughout the course of the case, and may be intensified when their case files are examined by prosecutors and others in the judicial system. Prosecutors need proper documentation to either convince the defense to accept a plea or win the trial. The defense team is looking for mistakes to weaken the prosecution's case. In short, both sides are examining the files and procedures with a careful eye. Any mistakes fall on the shoulders of the lead homicide investigator. Given the top-down bureaucratic structure of police organizations, stress researchers should more carefully consider these conditions as they manifest themselves in the police samples under study.

Stress is an inevitable component of all occupations, especially policing. In developing this broader theory of homicide investigator stress, we do not mean to imply that police departments should seek ways to eliminate the occupational and organizational demands that contribute to stress; rather we are suggesting that they should be aware that various stress manifestations exist. For instance, investigators acknowledged that pressure from above and within the unit to solve cases weighed heavy on them. The homicide board, with its graphic depiction of solved and unsolved cases, was a frequently cited source of stress. However, decades of stress research suggest that not all stress is negative. In fact, some stress, commonly referred to as eustress, can lead to enhanced performance. It is possible that being responsible for cases and being scrutinized pushed them to be better investigators. Thus, before administrators rush to remove such visible components of homicide investigator culture, more needs to be known about how stress affects investigators.

The practical implications of these results are clear in that homicide investigators in urban police departments have significant demands on their time, energies, emotions, and managerial skills. Homicide investigation is a job that is distinctly different from other law enforcement roles in structure, process, and experiences of stress. Therefore, it should be recognized and treated as such. Support services for homicide investigation unit members need to address the unique task-oriented stresses that are common for such officers, as well as the organizational stressors that are similar to those experienced by all officers.

Study Limitations

This study, while providing data-based documentation of the unique task and occupational stressors experienced by police homicide investigators, is not without limitations. First, the sample is drawn from a single municipal police department, one with a fairly heavy overall caseload. The fact that the officers interviewed in this research work in such an environment may well be important in the construction of their identification and experience of job-related stressors. Second, while documenting the presence and experiential consequences of these stressors, we are unable to identify specific and precise ways in which these stressors are experienced by officers of differing demographics, professional experience, and personalities, all of which likely affect experiences of stress. Such tasks remain to be addressed, and future researchers are urged to engage such questions. A third limitation is that stressors arising from organizational or occupational sources may well vary across agencies of differing cultures, degree of urbanization in communities being policed, and bureaucratic idiosyncrasies of specific agencies. The present study is based on data from a single metropolitan police department with a unique organizational culture; this may significantly limit generalizability.

Future Research Directions

While the present study provides significant advances in understanding and theorizing stress experienced by homicide investigators, it also points to the need for continued research on the issue. In concluding his overview, Sewell (1994, p. 580) acknowledges the need to evaluate his model and suggests that "the first item in a research agenda would be to assess quantitatively the impact of stress-causing and stress-reducing practices." While such an approach is most certainly of value, we argue that it is more important to first document the presence of these stressors by drawing on systematically collected data, which was the goal of the present study. Now is the time that it is appropriate to employ a quantitative methodology to examining the severity, impacts, and responses to such stressors, knowing that they in fact are present. Such a study may now be more clearly outlined, drawing upon the findings of the present analysis. Moreover, such studies would allow scholars to test and refine the broader theory of police stress we proposed. Specifically, large samples of police officers could be used to determine the effects of responsibility, scrutiny, and uncertainty on police officers of all types, especially homicide investigators.

It is also important to continue a qualitative line of inquiry focusing on how the findings of this study may generalize to other jurisdictions, and to other specialized dimensions of law enforcement work. Based on the findings of the present study, it may now be feasible to develop practical methods and instruments for both assessing and monitoring stress experiences of homicide investigators. Such an endeavor is critical for maintaining high-quality investigations—if investigators are identified as experiencing high levels of stress they may be less likely to function effectively and efficiently (Vuorensyrja and Malkia, 2011). Such a situation would not only inhibit effective investigations in the short term, but would likely also contribute to ongoing stress and increases in frustration and physical, psychological, and emotional consequences (including burnout) for investigators. Therefore, the development of easily implementable instruments for monitoring the key components and contributors of homicide investigator stress may directly contribute to more effective (and efficient) investigations. Such instrument construction should draw upon inductive efforts, such as this one, but must be expanded to include additional qualitative inquiries that seek to identify and theorize contextually specific stressors in policing. Armed with these results, instrument development and validation may then be undertaken that combines the inductive observations from studies such as this one with the deductive materials present in existing measurement protocols. It is only then that we will begin to gain an informed and effective means of measuring and then combating stress within policing.

In the end, this study makes clear that members of police homicide investigation units experience significant degrees of job stress. The occupational and organizational stressors they experience appear to be bound to the nature of the work assignment. Conceptually, the stresses experienced by homicide investigators can be reduced to the issues of responsibility, uncertainty, and scrutiny. While many of the specific stress-inducing aspects of their jobs that give rise to heightened responsibilities, uncertainties, and scrutiny are similar to those also experienced by their police peers not engaged in homicide investigations, for homicide investigators more frequent and intense stress experiences emanate from the unique aspects of taking on the "awesome burden" of homicide investigation.

Critical Thinking

Due to the homicide unit's particular mix of intense occupational experiences and organizational demands, a complex and individualized amount of stress results for those investigators. How are these stressors experienced differently by homicide investigators than from other law enforcement officials? Are homicide investigators more troubled by the conditions of the job or organizational and occupational stressors? Why?

Notes

1. In the present study, we focus solely on manifestations of stress. Issues pertaining to negative psychological or physiological outcomes of stress or the manner in which officers manage or cope with stress are beyond the scope of this inquiry.
2. The descriptions of the agency under study are intentionally vague in an effort to respect confidentiality assurances that were extended at the outset of the research project.
3. Such a course of action raises contamination and legitimacy issues that can undercut the case in court.
4. After clearing their first case, members of the unit are ceremoniously given a Fedora-style hat, which he or she then wears while on the job.

References

Abdollahi, M.K. 2002. Understanding police stress research. *Journal of Forensic Psychology Practice*, 2: 1–24.

Amaranto, E., Steinberg, J., Castellano, C., and Mitchell, R. 2003. Police stress interventions. *Brief Treatment and Crisis Intervention*, 3: 47–53.

Ayres, R. and Flanagan, G. 1994. *Preventing law enforcement stress: The organization's role*, Washington, DC: U.S. Department of Justice.

Brooks, L. and Piquero, N. 1998. Police stress: Does department size matter? *Policing: An International Journal of Police Strategies and Management*, 21: 600–617.

Brown, J.M. and Campbell, E.A. 1990. Sources of occupational stress in the police. *Work and Stress*, 4: 305–318.

Deschamps, F., Paganon-Badinier, I., Marchand, A., and Merle, C. 2003. Sources and assessment of occupational stress in police. *Journal of Occupational Health*, 45: 358–364.

Dowler, K. 2005. Job satisfaction, burnout, and perception of unfair treatment: The relationship between race and police work. *Police Quarterly*, 8: 476–489.

Garcia, L., Nesbary, D.K. and Gu, J. 2004. Perceptual variation of stressors among police officers during an era of decreasing crime. *Journal of Contemporary Criminal Justice*, 20: 33–50.

Gershon, R.M., Barocas, B., Canton, A.N., Li, X., and Vlahov, D. 2009. Mental, physical, and behavioral outcomes associated with perceived work stress in police officers. *Criminal Justice and Behavior*, 36: 275–289.

He, N., Zhao, J., and Archbold, C. 2002. Gender and police stress: The convergent and divergent impact of work environment, work–family conflict and stress coping mechanisms of female and male police officers. *Policing: An International Journal of Police Strategies and Management*, 25: 687–708.

He, N., Zhao, J., and Ren, L. 2005. Do race and gender matter in police stress? A preliminary assessment of the interactive effects. *Journal of Criminal Justice*, 33: 535–547.

Henry, V.E. 1995. The police officer as survivor: Death confrontations and the police subculture. *Behavioral Science and the Law*, 13: 93–112.

Hickman, M.J., Fricas, J., Strom, K.J., and Pope, M.W. 2011. Mapping police stress. *Police Quarterly*, 14: 227–250.

Innes, M. 2003. *Investigating murder: Detective work and the police response to criminal homicide*, Oxford: Oxford University Press.

Kop, N., Euwema, M., and Schaufeli, W. 1999. Burnout, job stress and violent behavior among Dutch police. *Work and Stress*, 13: 326–340.

Krause, M. 2009. Identifying and managing stress in child pornography and child exploitation investigators. *Journal of Police and Criminal Psychology*, 24: 22–29.

Kroes, W.H. 1985. *Society's victim: The police officer*, Springfield, IL: Charles C. Thomas.

Kroes, W.H., Margolis, B.I., and Hurrell, J.J. 1974. Job stress in policemen. *Journal of Police Science and Administration*, 2: 145–155.

Lord, V. 1996. An impact of community policing: Reported stressors, social support and strain among police officers in a changing policing department. *Journal of Criminal Justice*, 24: 503–522.

Lord, V.B., Gray, D.O., and Pond, S.B. 1991. The police stress inventory: Does it measure stress? *Journal of Criminal Justice*, 19: 139–149.

Malasch, C. 1982. *Burnout: The cost of caring*, New York: Prentice-Hall.

Malloy, T.Y. and Mays, G.L. 1984. The police stress hypothesis: A critical evaluation. *Criminal Justice and Behavior*, 11: 197–224.

McCarty, W.P., Zhao, J., and Garland, B.E. 2007. Occupational stress and burnout between male and female police officers: Are there gender differences? *Policing: An International Journal of Police Strategies and Management*, 30: 672–691.

Morash, M. and Haarr, R. 1995. Gender, workplace problems, and stress in policing. *Justice Quarterly*, 12: 113–140.

Morash, M., Haarr, R., and Kwak, D. 2006. Multilevel influences on police stress. *Journal of Contemporary Criminal Justice*, 22: 26–43.

Patterson, B.L. 1992. Job experience and perceived job stress among police, correctional, and probation/parole officers. *Criminal Justice and Behavior*, 19: 260–285.

Sewell, J.D. 1994. The stress of homicide investigations. *Death Studies*, 18: 565–582.

Shane, J.M. 2010. Organizational stressors and police performance. *Journal of Criminal Justice*, 38: 807–818.

Simon, D. 1991. *Homicide: A year on the killing streets*, New York: Owl Books.

Stevens, D.J. 2008. *Police officer stress: Sources and solutions*, Upper Saddle River, NJ: Prentice-Hall.

Storch, J.E. and Panzarella, R. 1996. Police stress: State-trait anxiety in relation to occupational and personal stressors. *Journal of Criminal Justice*, 24: 99–107.

Stretesky, P.B., Shelley, T., Hogan, M.J., and Unnithan, N.P. 2010. Sense-making and secondary victimization among unsolved homicide co-victims. *Journal of Criminal Justice*, 38: 880–888.

Terry, W.C. 1981. Police stress: The empirical evidence. *Journal of Police Science and Administration*, 9: 61–75.

Toch, H. 2002. *Stress in policing*, Washington, DC: American Psychological Association.

Van Patten, I.T. and Burke, T.W. 2001. Critical incident stress and the child homicide investigator. *Homicide Studies*, 5: 131–152.

Violanti, J.M. and Aron, F. 1994. Ranking police stressors. *Psychological Reports*, 75: 824–826.

Violanti, J.M. and Aron, F. 1995. Police stressors: Variations in perceptions among police personnel. *Journal of Criminal Justice*, 23: 287–294.

Vuorensyrja, M. and Malkia, M. 2011. Nonlinearity of the effects of police stressors on police burnout. *Policing*, 34: 382–402.

Waters, J. and Ussery, W. 2007. Police stress: History, contributing factors, symptoms, and interventions. *Policing: An International Journal of Police Strategies and Management*, 30: 169–188.

Zhao, J., He, N., and Lovrich, N. 2002. Predicting five dimensions of police officer stress: Looking more deeply into organizational settings for sources of police stress. *Police Quarterly*, 5: 43–62.

3

Racialized Policing: Officers' Voices on Policing Latino and African American Neighborhoods

Claudio G. Vera Sanchez and Dennis P. Rosenbaum

Abstract: *Vera Sanchez and Rosenbaum argue that knowing how police perceive those whom they patrol is vital for understanding the complicated relationship between police and citizens. Thus, they interview patrol officers to learn how they socially construct race within African American or Latino neighborhoods. They show that police often spoke of African American communities as being morally deficient, while defining residents of Latino neighborhoods as being hard-working, good people. These perceptions of communities then affected the way in which police dealt with citizens residing in the communities.*

Since the 1960s, conflict between urban police forces and minority communities has been a staple topic for the media and researchers in the United States. The police have been accused of racially biased decision-making that contributes to racial profiling, disrespectful encounters, excessive force, and, ultimately, disproportionate minority confinement. Unfortunately, much of what is known about the police is disseminated through media images and newspapers, often showcasing sensationalized cases of police use of excessive force; the experience of policing minority communities—from the viewpoint of police themselves—remains elusive. Researchers who study biased policing (Barlow and Hickman Barlow, 2000; Cohen, 1996; Platt, Frappier, Ray, Schauffler, Trujillo, and Cooper, 1982) have introduced pioneering theoretical frameworks to the scientific community, yet fewer works incorporate a police perspective (Barlow and Hickman Barlow, 2002; Dowler, 2005; Ioimo, Tears, Meadows, Becton, and Charles, 2007; Moskos, 2008b). Because police officers are the primary gatekeepers to the criminal legal system and their power to arrest has considerable consequences for minority youth and adults, understanding their perspective about the communities they serve is of the utmost importance. The objective of this study, therefore, is to explore the experiences of urban municipal officers who police predominately low-income, minority communities, and how they perceive, or perhaps even racialize, Latinos and African Americans within those neighborhoods.

Focusing on populations of power, as a unit analysis, is long overdue because the trend in criminological and social research is to study downward, minorities, or disadvantaged groups, with the objective of interpreting their experiences. In contrast, a careful study of police experiences may offer insight regarding the exercise of power and legal authority in our society. The police have been issued with legitimate authority to initiate street and vehicular stops, make arrests, and employ deadly force (Fyfe, 1988). Their behavior, then, may improve or worsen the plight of those with whom they interact. Exploring the attitudes, perspectives, and experiences of police officers vis-à-vis the minority communities they serve should help advance our understanding and interpretation of police behavior in the field and ultimately provide guidance to improve police–minority relations. Issues about race and class biases in policing may be more fully understood and contextualized by hearing the voices of police officers who work in low-income minority neighborhoods.

Public Perceptions of The Police

Police–minority interactions and perceptions of each other are complex and multifaceted. Much of what we know about this relationship stems from research on public attitudes toward the police, where minorities have expressed the most distrust and negative sentiment. African Americans, overall, report the most pessimistic attitudes toward the police followed by Latinos and then Whites (Schafer, Huebner, and Bynum, 2003; Skogan and Hartnett, 1997; Weitzer and Tuch, 2004). Further, attitudes vary by contextual and socioeconomic variables. Weitzer (2000) finds that middle-class African Americans in Washington, DC voice more positive views of the police than their low-income counterparts, although their attitudes remain less positive than those of Whites. Brown and Benedict's (2002) review of the literature concludes that higher status Whites report greater appreciation for, and confidence in, the police than higher status African Americans. In contrast, studies centered on low-income immigrant Latino communities, while few, highlight intense fear and apprehension toward the police by community residents (Carter, 1985; Skogan, 2006), fears occasionally attenuated through intensive community policing efforts (Torres and Vogel, 2001). All in all, minorities, both Latinos and African Americans, have consistently expressed more negative views of the police than Whites, and contextual and socioeconomic factors contribute to skew these perceptions (Cao, Frank, and Cullen, 1996).

Attitudes toward the police may also vary by the type of contact minorities experience—either voluntary citizen-initiated (e.g., calling the police for assistance) or involuntary police-initiated (e.g., being stopped; Langan, Greenfield, Smith, Durose, and Levin, 2001). African Americans experience more involuntary encounters with the police in comparison to Whites (Lundman and Kaufman, 2003). Rusinko, Johnson, and Hornung (1978) indicate that voluntary police contact is a precursor to positive attitudes toward the police as opposed to involuntary contact. Although positive contact mitigates negative attitudes for African Americans, overall they continue to report more negative views of the police than Whites. Even though direct contact has been linked with negative attitudes toward the police (Jesilow, Meyer, and Namazzi, 1995; Scaglion and Condon, 1980), contact is not a prerequisite for negative perceptions (Hurst, Frank, and Browning, 2000). Rosenbaum, Schuck, Costello, Hawkins, and Ring (2005), for example, find that one recent contact alone is insufficient to fuel negative attitudes toward the police, and instead, vicarious experience (e.g., knowing someone with a negative experience) and possessing preconceived negative views about the police will accentuate negative perceptions of a recent encounter. Finally, in Skogan's (2006) review of the literature, what he describes as an "asymmetry" in police–citizen encounters reveals that negative contact overshadows positive experiences by 4 to 14 percentage points. That is, negative experience has a larger impact than positive experience on views of the police ("Bad news travels faster than good news"). Involuntary contacts, however, are not devoid of social context. Generally, low-income, high-crime contexts, due to high crime volumes and unique organization of the neighborhood, are susceptible to a style of policing that structures involuntary stops. If low-income, high-crime neighborhoods place minorities at risk for involuntary stops and searches, then displeasure with the police among minority residents is predictable.

Overall, past research indicates that minorities report more negative attitudes toward the police than Whites; unfortunately, the majority of studies reviewed rarely incorporate a police perspective or the effects of neighborhood context on police work. Serious attention to low-income and high-crime neighborhoods may also provide insight about police–community dynamics, police–minority conflicts, and the unique challenges which police officers face. Neighborhood conditions, such as poverty and violent crime, may intensify aggressive policing and conflicts between the police and community residents (Kane, 2002, 2003). Hearing the voices of police officers who work in low-income minority neighborhoods, therefore, may improve our understanding of police–citizen encounters.

The extant literature reveals that Latinos and African Americans share negative images of the police and social scripts of what police do, but how do officers experience low-income minority neighborhoods and their residents? Aside from police surveys and official data, which capture general attitudes toward the community and community policing functions (see Lurigio and Rosenbaum, 1994; Skogan, 2005), researchers have given less attention to police officers' own perceptions of community residents in minority neighborhoods. There are frequent discussions of "police culture" in the policing literature, as well as early fieldwork on the subject (National Research Council, 2004), but race and ethnicity are not the central focus. Concepts such as danger, suspicion, group loyalty ("us vs. them"), and cynicism are commonplace in previous analyses (Skolnick, 1966). Race may be the "elephant in the room," but it is rarely examined in detail.

Policing and Neighborhood Context

A body of research suggests that racial disparities in policing are ubiquitous, and attitudinal measures of minorities and official records corroborate with these data, yet an examination of neighborhood context can improve our understanding of the relationship between the police and the public (Schuck, Rosenbaum, and Hawkins, 2008). Few works have focused on how police officers negotiate or experience low-income minority neighborhoods. In addition to race, which is considered a possible source of biased policing, neighborhood context may be equally important in examining police harassment, profiling, and other types of police behavior.

Research shows that policing styles, including but not limited to harassment and excessive force, vary by neighborhood conditions (Klinger, 1997; Rosenbaum, 2007). Kane (2002) concludes that minorities residing in disadvantaged neighborhoods are recipients of over-policing (Kane, 2002). Terrill and Reisig (2003) find that the police exercise excessive force in neighborhoods where serious offending (e.g., homicide rates) and concentrated disadvantage (e.g., percent of poverty, level of unemployment, and number of female-headed households) are endemic. The authors conclude, however, that race is a proxy for neighborhood disadvantage, because minorities are often segregated to high-crime and low-income areas. Terrill and Matrofski (2002) find that police officers are more likely to apply excessive force toward males, minorities, youth, and those living in disadvantaged environments. However, Terrill (2005) shows that police officers often exercise less force than is legally permitted despite extreme situational exigencies; alternatively, when young minority males reside in high-crime communities, the continuum of force escalates even when suspects are not resistant. These results suggest that neighborhood context helps explain aggressive policing. Whether race plays a role during police–suspect encounters is difficult to determine without exploring police officers' experiences in minority neighborhoods.

Although excessive police force varies by neighborhood and suspect characteristics, other scholars contend that officer behaviors, although often read as mistreatment, may reflect not biased but proactive policing in low-income contexts. McCluskey and Terrill (2005) indicate that "Officers who receive repeated complaints may not actually be so-called problem officers, but rather proactive officers." (p. 143). The authors suggest that "problem officers" score higher at proactive stops and interrogations in the field but score no differently in terms of physical force or discourtesy. Complaints against an officer, then, or being labeled as a problem officer may be interpreted by some as evidence of actually doing good police work. Quilian and Pager (2001) argue that the symbolic face of criminality in the public perception—the African American or minority male—has been shaped by neighborhood context; neighborhoods facing severe crime problems experience high volumes of calls for service that require an immediate police response. If the public routinely demands police presence in some neighborhoods, coupled with intense lobbying for arrest (Black and Reiss, 1970), then the public and the police may play a role in contributing to what appears to be biased policing. In addition, the emergence of data-driven "hot-spots policing" demands that greater police attention be given to high-crime minority neighborhoods (Rosenbaum, 2006). Past research reveals that police behavior is shaped by both suspect characteristics (e.g., race) and neighborhood context (e.g., calls for service and crime incidents); what remains unclear is how the police officer's mindset and interpretation of race and neighborhood context contribute to the outcome.

Overall, research indicates that police behavior and style vary by neighborhood conditions, yet few studies have explored how the police experience and perceive minority communities. What characteristics of low-income minority neighborhoods are salient to police officers? How do police officers describe low-income communities? A better understanding of how police perceive neighborhood conditions and local residents may shed light on their behavioral responses and the mediating processes involved.

Research Questions

The following research questions guided this qualitative inquiry:

1. Are police officers attuned to public dissatisfaction from residents in minority communities and how do they interpret or respond to it?
2. How do police officers perceive race, racialize, or socially construct race?
3. What aspects of Latinos and African Americans do police officers focus on when expressing their views about these groups?
4. What language do police officers use to describe low-income minority neighborhoods?

Methods

The data for this study were collected as part of a larger project on minority trust and confidence in the police consisting of self-reports from police officers, community adults, and community youth collected via focus groups, in-person interviews, and/or telephone interviews (Rosenbaum et al., 2005). This study is a qualitative inquiry that draws on the in-person interviews with police officers.

Interviews

Ten interviews were conducted with police officers in each of four racially distinct neighborhoods (i.e., Latino or African American) in a large Midwestern city, for a total of $N = 40$ interviews. The interviews were conducted at police precincts, generally in vacant offices or roll-call rooms. The watch commanders selected the police officers but participation was voluntary and informed consent procedures followed the institutional review board approved protocol. The interviews ranged from 30 minutes to one hour in length. Field notes were jotted down in notebooks and interviewers recorded the data into an electronic document shortly thereafter.

Once the actual interviews commenced, some of the officers appeared reluctant at times to discuss what they perceived as sensitive police practices. Secrecy within the police culture has been documented previously (Manning, 1977; Westley, 1970). Occasional single-word answers and repetitive assurances were meant to suggest that "everything was perfect" in the communities that they policed. For example, many officers denied that racial profiling occurred in their beat, although many admitted that such practices were common in other parts of the city. Other police officers, however, were more candid about their feelings. They did not appear concerned with being politically correct and offered in-depth information to the interviewers.

Communities

The communities were selected based on their ethnic composition and quality of police–community relations. Data from telephone surveys were used to identify neighborhoods where police–community tensions were moderately strong. Census 2000 data were used to identify neighborhoods that were predominately African American, Latino, or White. Field observations from the research team were used to identify neighborhoods that were comparable on visible factors such as residential-commercial mix, housing quality, and levels of disorder. Approximately 10 communities were purposively selected and a narrowing process occurred through a combination of input from the research team, field notes about the various communities, and neighborhood profiles.

Researchers drove around and documented detailed neighborhood descriptions, including the physical structures, businesses, and the people, as well as an overall subjective feeling of the context. The researchers noted in a high-crime, low-income minority neighborhood

> Currency exchange, liquor stores, mechanic shop, empty lots, empty and boarded up rentals, church, abandoned industrial building . . . lots of people on the streets, lots of cars and foot traffic. Guys hanging out on the corner, all African American. A group of kids shouted at us.

From this process, four communities in the city were selected for this study (two African American, two Latino). Police beats within the boundaries of the four communities were included in the study and used as the basis for selecting police officers.

See Table 1 for a description of the demographics of the neighborhoods studied in this large Midwestern city, based on Census 2000 information. The percentage of households living below the poverty line for each of the neighborhoods exceeds the average for the city. The neighborhoods are also racially homogeneous, have lower median incomes, and have fewer homeowners than the typical neighborhood in the city. These communities may be considered low income and high crime, based on Census 2000 data, field accounts, and crime data.

Table 1 Neighborhood Demographics

Neighborhood	Percent below Poverty	Percent of One Race	Median Income	Home Ownership	Percent below 9th Grade	Homicide per 100,000
African American A	27.1	97.04	33,081	45.78	5.2	33
African American B	24.1	89.70	33,663	39.54	9.6	29
Latino C	26.5	83.0	32,320	36.0	39.9	24
Latino D	31.1	43.4	36,667	33.6	23.3	22

Note: This table shows the demographic characteristics of the neighborhoods studied, such as percentage of individuals living below the poverty line, percentage of racial group of interest (Latino or African American), median income, percentage of residents who own their home, percentage of individuals over 25 years of age with education levels below the ninth grade, and homicide in the neighborhood per 100,000.

Results

Six distinct themes emerged from the voices of the police officers. Each is described in the following with corresponding documentation.

Theme 1: Police Officers Feel Misunderstood and Unwelcome in Minority Neighborhoods

Researchers have reported accounts of hostile and aggressive police personalities (Chambliss, 1994; Skolnick, 1966), but in the current study, the police describe themselves as the victims of community abuse—they report feeling frustrated and angry that they are unappreciated and even resented in minority neighborhoods. Police officers were keen to offer verbal and behavioral indicators of community dissatisfaction with their presence.

> Everybody friendly downtown—they say hi. We don't get that here. We hear "F*** the police" and other stupid comments.
>
> (Police Officer, African American neighborhood A, White, Male)

> They see you as the enemy. The only time people deal with you is when they are in some kind of trouble or going through a crisis—a robbery or burglary for example. They don't stop police to say "Hi, how are you doing?" . . . not everybody is a bad person but when you go to somebody's house it's because there is something wrong. And when there is a potential to get hurt the first thing you will protect is yourself because you know you will get hurt from the people you are supposed to be serving. Then they become your enemy.
>
> (Police Officer, Latino neighborhood D, Latino, Male)

The behavioral displays such as "staring and spitting on the floor" or verbal statements such as "F*** the police" suggest to the police that they are unwelcome in the neighborhood.

Officers are very aware of the tension between them and minority residents. According to the respondents, statements such as being "at war" with segments of the community or being perceived as "the enemy" highlight the conflict police officers negotiate on a daily basis with the public. When officers feel unappreciated and unwelcome, they find it more difficult to be good public servants to victims and others who need their assistance. As one officer noted, "Most feel it is hard to help people in the community."

Theme 2: The Police Contend That Their Views of the Community Are Shaped Largely by the Community's Attitudes and Actions Toward Them

Often in a defensive tone, officers talked about citizens' complaints of unjustified police harassment, intergenerational transmission of antipolice values, and police interference with people's illegal activities.

We Harass Them for No Good Reason

According to police officers, minorities assume that they are being hassled unjustifiably. Officers indicate that these reactions occur in the course of routine police work—for instance, attending to traffic violations, clearing corners, and making arrests when crimes are committed.

> "Those bastards." [community people say] . . . they call us and don't like us when we get there. We're all racist and lock up their sons and daughters for no good reason.
>
> (Latino neighborhood C, Police Officer, White, Female)

> Community has this perception/thoughts that we are going to stop them, ask for the driving license, the insurance. They are not aware of the laws like drinking in public areas—they don't know the laws are to protect them. People drinking in the park cause problems but they think that we are harassing or bothering them.
>
> (Latino neighborhood C, Police Officer, Little Village, Latino, Male)

Intergenerational Transmission of Disrespect and Attitudes About the Police

Officers also reported that family upbringing encourages negative sentiments toward the police. The comments of police officers suggest that some individuals are socialized to respect the police and others have been raised to disrespect the police. According to some police officers, parents actively discourage their children from showing any positive regard toward the officers. Several officers described how family socialization contributes to dissatisfaction with the police.

> They pass this hatred down to their children. If little kids try to wave to us they tell them, "don't say hi to the police".
>
> (Latino neighborhood C, Police Officer, White, Male)

> They [community residents] try to provoke the police and start fights. They're brought up thinking that the police are bad. I've seen little kids point their guns at the police. It's night and day when you look at how they respect the police.
>
> (Latino neighborhood C, Police Officer, Latino, Male)

They Are Doing Bad Things—Drug Dealers and Gangs—and Do Not Want Us To Interfere

Officers indicated that public disrespect for the police is due, in part, to police interrupting law-breaking behavior. The police reported stopping people drinking in the park or putting drug dealers out of business as reasons why police are resented. But some officers expressed a more conditional, nuanced understanding of public sentiment that varies by type of citizen.

> If they're drug dealers, they're going to be mad. We're putting them out of business. The majority of people are glad we're out there.
>
> (African American neighborhood A, Police Officer, White, Male)

> No one is afraid of the police unless they are doing wrong . . . most officers feel the people in the area are decent and realize a small segment causes most problems. Tensions do exist but the source can be narrowed down considerably (e.g., Most tensions are with families at a specific address who have members that are in trouble with the police).
>
> (Latino neighborhood D, Police Officer, White, Male)

In sum, officers' views of the community are shaped by their assessment of the community's negative assessment of police activity. Officers believe that in minority communities young people are taught by older generations to distrust the police, good abiding citizens perceive routine police work as harassment, and serious offenders do not appreciate police interference with their illegal activities.

Theme 3: A Person's Age Is a Stronger Determinant of Judgment by the Police
Than a Person's Race or Ethnicity

Police officers report a consistent apprehension toward young people in all communities. Not a single neighborhood was found, regardless of racial or ethnic composition, where the police failed to report tension with youth and alternatively felt more appreciated by older segments of the community. If the police were only racially motivated, one would not expect officers to consistently report positive images about older minority adults in these racially homogeneous minority neighborhoods. In contrast to the belief that police officers would express negative stereotypes across an entire neighborhood, they tended to emphasize their satisfaction with many law-abiding and "good" residents in high-crime, economically disadvantaged, Latino and African American communities. Many statements made by police officers indicate that they felt appreciated by older residents and were occasionally flattered by young children who expressed positive regard.

> Older people love us. Others hanging on the corners will spit and eyeball you. Little kids will wave.
> (African American neighborhood A, Police Officer, White, Male)

> The male Black between 16 to 25 hate us and they are not going to like the police. Older Blacks are better . . . age plays a big role in attitudes about us.
> (African American neighborhood A, Police Officer, White, Male)

Police officers believe that older people's positive opinions of them stem from living in fear of offenders and youth gangs and that the police serve an important public safety function. Police officers indicate that older residents are occasionally too demanding of police services, but overall they are grateful for their service.

> Older people are glad when they see the police in the area, they feel safer. Younger people are disrespectful and don't care. If we try to get them off the corner they would either still stand there or just come back later.
> (African American neighborhood B, Police Officer, Latino, Male).

> Older adults are more comfortable but are upset that we can't do more. They have to set up "Gang Hot Spots" to stop loitering of juveniles. Older adults want police to do more.
>
> (African American neighborhood B, Police Officer, Latino, Male)

All in all, police officers report dissatisfaction with youth in every neighborhood. Police officers believe that young people make disrespectful comments while older people support police efforts to enhance public safety by removing youth from corners and cease their illegal activities. Police officers rarely spoke about race explicitly, in contrast to their many comments about "rowdy" or intractable youth. When profiling occurred, age was the dominant theme rather than race or ethnicity.

Theme 4: Police Officers Were More Likely to Moralize, Rather Than, Racialize Homogenous African American Communities. But They Blamed Both Individuals and Society for the Observed Failures

To define morality, officers made references to the goodness or badness of an individual's character rather than the racial makeup of the person. The comments made by officers suggest that they frown upon what they believe is a faulty socialization of children, disapprove of a perceived questionable work ethic, and are critical about what they understand to be a failure of neighborhood residents to perform informal social control and proactive community activities (e.g., keep the streets clean). In many cases, police officers view African American neighborhoods as "war-zones," individuals "without hope," where "no one seems to be working." In addition, it was uncommon for police officers to overtly use the words Black or African American when describing the negative attributes of African Americans and their neighborhoods. The extent to which race is interwoven into the subtext of these narratives is difficult to unveil given that many police officers today are sensitive to the importance of making politically correct statements in public. In any event, the words tend to focus on the moral character of the neighborhood as a whole.

> Neighborhood looks like a nuclear war zone-blighted, sad but true . . . high domestic abuse, high birth rate, high incidence of violent crime against persons.
>
> (African American neighborhood A, Police Officer, White, Male)

> I wouldn't know how to begin. It's filthy over here. All the structures are in disarray. From the look of the inside of their houses, they don't care how they live. Fences are in disrepair, garages falling apart, and there's garbage everywhere . . . they have no respect for anybody. They don't respect their moms, nobody.
>
> (African American neighborhood A, Police Officer, Latino, Female)

Other officers made moral statements yet were also empathetic to the issues faced by these communities, making external attributions, such as Section 8 housing and lack of opportunities, to explain the plight in these neighborhoods. Officers reported dissatisfaction with the social issues and conditions of the neighborhood but expressed a deeper appreciation and understanding of the individuals residing in these urban contexts.

There's lots of garbage. The buildings are falling apart . . . the houses are pretty dirty. There's tons of narcotics. There's quite a bit of violence to solve, lots of problems. It's a population that needs help, and they're not able to solve their problems with words. Among this urban disaster, many people are just trying to live their lives. They go to work to make money.

(African American neighborhood A, Police Officer, White, Male)

It's drug infested and the worst beat in the district . . . people from the projects are moving into the neighborhood . . . they're bringing the same problems and lifestyle into an otherwise good neighborhood.

(African American neighborhood B, Police Officer, African American, Male)

The comments by police officers suggest that they focused on the moral aspects of African American neighborhoods. The social organization of the neighborhoods—what they believed was a poor work ethic, questionable transmission of prosocial values to children, and disinterest in improving the neighborhood—were often mentioned. Other officers also highlighted the preceding neighborhood conditions but also expressed a deeper understanding of people's plight within these environments.

Theme 5: The Concept of Racial Profiling Is Illogical or Nonsensical to Police Officers Working in Racially Homogeneous Environments

Racial profiling is typically defined as police decisions that are influenced by the race of the citizens they encounter. From a police perspective, this concept is not meaningful when police officers are working in predominantly Latino or African American neighborhoods.

The beat is all Black and so it would only be profiling if I stopped every White person on the block. So if a White person is stopped then one could say it is profiling but if a Black person is stopped it's hard to see how that could be profiling.

(African American neighborhood A, Police officer, White, Male)

Not in the minority neighborhood. There is no way you could be racial profiling in a minority neighborhood where there are only Hispanics and Blacks. Community don't really understand what racial profiling means. Mexicans say, "you stopped me because I am Mexican," when the neighborhood is Mexican.

(Latino neighborhood C, Police Officer, Latino, Male)

Police officers also indicated that the race of the officer makes it difficult to participate in racial profiling. Minority officers, they argued, cannot be accused of profiling. Furthermore, they argued that working with minority officers makes racial bias by White officers unlikely. Hence, police officers used their own or their partner's race to rationalize the improbable nature of racial profiling.

Personally, they think that I don't like them because I'm White. My partner is Hispanic and they think that he's sold out.

(Latino neighborhood C, Police Officer, Little Village, White, Female)

Yes, if they see Hispanic or White officers stopping people they think they are messing with them. They don't have the same feelings if it is a Black officer stopping them.

(African American neighborhood B, Police Officer, African American, Female)

But given that racial profiling is politically and organizationally disapproved of, few individuals will admit to racial bias or profiling. Nevertheless, officers were perplexed about the possibility of biased law enforcement within largely African American or Latino communities and urged the research community to develop alternative conceptualizations of racial profiling for these communities.

Theme 6: Police Officers Racialized African Americans in the Lowest Crime Latino Neighborhood

The Mexican neighborhood that had the lowest crime rate and lowest proportion of African Americans of the four neighborhoods studied is the only setting where police racialized or overtly expressed negative racial comments about African Americans and positive statements about Mexicans. Not even in the Puerto Rican community, where half of the population consists of African Americans, did the police officers report a negative image of race. Police officers described the north side (i.e., the African American section) in negative terms and the south side (i.e., Mexican section) in positive terms. Some officers even characterized the Latino gang members as polite and friendly. Mexicans were racialized favorably. Although drug markets and gangs were mentioned, Mexicans were commended for their work ethic and internal social organization within the community, and immigrants were characterized as coming to the United States to improve their life chances.

Latinos Positively Racialized

They care about their neighborhood, go to [police-community] meetings. The Hispanic section, and the Italian section . . . they are more cooperative.

(Latino neighborhood C, Police Officer, White, Female)

It's primarily Hispanic . . . working-class people. There are gangs here. It is evident that they're here. Being on the beat, you see them. And when people get arrested you know who they are. My beat is very congested . . . there are some apartments where we go into basements and they are converted into six different units with one communal restroom and no kitchen. I mean they're like the size of this (gestures around the cubicle we are talking in).

(Latino neighborhood C, Police Officer, Latino, Male)

Difference Between Latinos and African Americans

The neighborhood is half Mexican and half Black and the two halves are night and day. The Black side is depressing. There's a lot of ignorance there. People get used to it, we get used to it. We get cynical. Most of the people on the Mexican side work and go through life to the best of their ability.

(Latino neighborhood C, Police Officer, White, Female)

You have to change your personality when you go to the north end [African American section]. You can't be cordial or polite. I know this from my experiences. All of the officers know this. The south end [Mexican side], there's no tension. There is a little gang trouble. But, the north end there's more violence and more tension. The housing is bad and people just stand on the street corner drinking.

(Latino neighborhood C, Police Officer, Latino, Male)

The officers described Mexicans and African Americans and their racial characteristics differently in the predominately Mexican community. Some officers stated that the differences were like "night and day." Community tensions, disrespect for the police, street drinking, and violence were some key differences noticed by police officers between the Latino and African American areas of the same neighborhood. The problems in the neighborhood, at least for the officers interviewed, originated from the different characteristics of racial and ethnic groups (Mexicans vs. African Americans) and police officers' interpretation of their law-abiding behavior.

Discussion and Conclusion

Police conceptions of minority communities are heavily influenced by the perceived quality of their encounters with the public and whether the officers feel respected by community residents. Consistent with prior research that identifies the "us versus them" mindset in the police culture (Chambliss, 1994), the narratives of police officers in our sample underscore the extent to which they feel misunderstood, disliked (even hated), and abused in minority communities. Officers feel that most of the negative sentiment originates from African American instead of Latino residents, and particularly from young people. Whether older residents really have a more positive regard for the police or have simply learned to suppress their feelings and interact with the police in less threatening ways is uncertain. In any event, these perceived responses from the community, in turn, seem to play some role in shaping officers' judgments and feelings about the communities they serve. Police officers do not hold undifferentiated views of minority communities. Rather, they seem to distinguish easily between Anderson's (1999) "decent families" and "street families." Officers feel appreciated by the former and disrespected by the latter.

Police appear less able to make refined distinctions in their perceptions of neighborhood youth. Police have particularly harsh feelings about youth in minority neighborhoods, describing them with a wide range of negative attributes. No particular subset of youth is immune from this criticism. In a nutshell, officers feel that youth and young adults have no respect for them and, therefore, the feelings and behaviors can be reciprocated. They cite a number of possible reasons for minority youth disliking them, particularly the dynamics of family and peers. Two "lay theories" are posited by the police regarding the intergenerational transmission of negative attitudes about the police: On the street, young adults (often gang members in their twenties) teach the younger teenagers to hate the police. In the family, the parents teach the pre-teen children to hate the police.

Intergenerational transmission of information about the police is a vicarious process (Rosenbaum et al., 2005) and such explanations by the police of negative community sentiment do not include direct experience as a factor in shaping the judgments of younger adults toward the police. Perhaps youths have their own experiences with the police to draw upon as well. From the police narratives in the current study, only occasionally do the officers recognize their own role in these long-standing conflictual relationships with young minorities. The reality of urban policing is that young people are the primary targets of aggressive policing designed to control crime and disorder (Brunson and Weitzer, 2009; Jones-Brown, 2007). National and local data indicate that young minority males are stopped and searched at much higher rates than other segments of the population (Skogan and Steiner, 2004). Furthermore, in some cities the new focus on hot-spots policing results in substantially more police officers deployed to high-crime minority neighborhoods, primarily to make contact with young residents on the streets (Rosenbaum, 2006). Granted, many of these younger adults are not entirely innocent and no one knows that better than the officers on the street. Often they belong to gangs, deal drugs, use guns to resolve conflict, and exhibit considerable disrespect for the police and other authority figures. Research indicates that young adults also use their street authority to intimidate older members of the community (Wilkinson, 2007). Nevertheless, one theme from interviews with adults and youth in these same communities is that youth are "picked on" by the police and that police are unable to distinguish between the "good" and "bad" kids (Rosenbaum et al., 2005). Training, workshops, and supervision to address these concerns could go a long way toward improving the situation,

Although community policing efforts have successfully motivated older adults within minority neighborhoods to attend police–citizen meetings (Skogan and Steiner, 2004), an alternative vision is for the police to actively build relationships with young people. Perhaps community policing programs could give more thoughtful attention to strengthening police–youth relations and address the unique obstacles to achieving this goal (e.g., being considered a "snitch," differential power inherent in police–youth dynamics, and developmental factors such as a contempt for authority). In addition, police officers who engage in foot or bicycle patrol (vs. motorized patrol) are more likely to get to know local youth and be able to distinguish between those who are "troublemakers" (e.g., gang members) and those who are not.

Police officers may not racialize but rather moralize African American neighborhoods. Manning (1977) suggests that police rhetoric emphasizes their crime control capabilities, but more often they serve moral objectives—removing alcoholics, prostitutes, and noisy youth from the streets. Some police officers in our sample, consistent with the findings of Moskos (2008a), viewed African American communities as morally deficient. Officers reported a feeling that many community residents "did not care about anything." Although police officers acknowledged their distaste for crime, they also stressed family dysfunction, negative socialization of children, a faulty work ethic, and physically chaotic environments as salient descriptors, especially within African American neighborhoods. Broken windows theory suggests that police work is more about order maintenance than law enforcement (Kelling and Coles, 1996; Sousa and Kelling, 2006; Wilson and Kelling, 1982), and this may include the expectation that the police will maintain the moral order (e.g., by removing rowdy youth and prostitutes, extinguishing drug markets, and arresting gang members). Although policing disorder is often popular with local residents and is arguably responsive to community concerns, these activities are also controversial because of the political and cultural issues around defining disorder. In any event, the difference between racialization and moralization is theoretically precarious. Our definition of racialization, one of many, is "to impose racial character on or to perceive or experience in racial terms." The findings here suggest that officers infrequently imposed racial ascriptions through their words to residents in homogeneously African American neighborhoods.

Furthermore, officers often made reference to the "good" people in the neighborhood, empathizing with their plight of coping with a troubled environment. Hence, their moral sentiments were not directed at everyone in the community but, rather, at individuals believed to possess characteristics that were precursors to crime and delinquency—being unemployed, having anti-police values, not caring about the community, and so forth. Muir (1977) found that the officers he interviewed had a strong sense of morality and immorality, and they equated deviance with immorality. Similarly, officers in our sample reported a clear and strict notion of morality and were unwilling to tolerate segments of the community they believed were responsible for creating community violence via maintaining drug markets, gang affiliation, and participation in other illicit activities—behaviors diametrically opposed to the mission of the police department.

The findings of this study, across four communities, suggest that urban police officers do not racialize or make racial characterizations of entire communities, except in situations where different racial and ethnic groups border each other in the same district and appear to have different levels of disadvantage. One community in our study, where African American and Latino neighborhoods were adjacent and shared the same police officers, provided a unique opportunity to examine racializations and social constructions of race. This setting seemed to encourage invidious comparisons between the groups, with Latinos being positively racialized and African Americans being negatively racialized by the police.

The mechanisms underlying this racialization process are unclear, but several sources of variation deserve mentioning. These two minority neighborhoods within the same police district were described by the police as different in several ways. The African American neighborhood, in comparison to the Latino community, was characterized as having (1) more serious street-level problems with violence, gangs, and drug markets; (2) more serious physical and social disorder problems such as drinking in public (although this is debatable); and (3) more non-criminal behavior in the community that is negatively valued by the police. Two types of non-criminal behavior are noted: a more negative demeanor toward the police and a poor work ethic. Certainly, these variables may interact in complex ways. For example, the police are forced to intervene more often when violence and disorder problems occur and, in turn, these encounters are often negative, thus introducing potentially more problems with civilian (and police) demeanor. In any event, this study suggests that when police officers are given the opportunity to make comparisons between racial and ethnic groups within their beats, racialization is more likely to occur and the comparisons are more likely to favor Latinos than African Americans for a host of reasons. And these comparisons are not always based in fact. For example, officers implied that Latinos were more inclined to attend local community meetings, but these types of statements are inconsistent with the facts (Skogan, 2002).

The police acknowledge that racial profiling is a popular concern, but they are totally befuddled by the concept and feel it does not apply in police beats that are racially homogeneous. How can a police officer profile someone when everyone in the neighborhood is African American or Latino? While this argument is logical, in these narratives we also find subtle indications that racial homogeneity gives police officers license to stop anyone, anywhere, for anything, without concern about racial bias. Furthermore, officers felt that if they, themselves, were a minority or if they had a minority partner, they were completely protected from complaints about racial profiling.

The primary purpose of this article was to understand how the police experience minority communities and, specifically, whether race plays a role in how officers perceive and interpret events and people in African American and Latino neighborhoods. The findings suggest that police are attuned to race in heterogeneous neighborhoods where different racial and ethnic groups live side by side. But for homogeneous minority neighborhoods, a new conceptualization of racialization or biased policing may be needed to understand police interpretations of the environment. For example, officers claim that racial profiling is not possible where working in all-minority neighborhoods. Organizational (rather than individual) decisions may explain why some neighborhoods receive more aggressive policing than others. Police organizations that measure performance by the statistics (e.g., arrests, gun seizures, drugs, money) and that deploy large numbers of police officers to minority communities to combat "hot spots" of crime could be accused of "racially profiling communities" (rather than individuals) and contributing to disproportionate minority mistreatment, arrests, and confinement (Rosenbaum, 2006).

Finally, we need to acknowledge that the absence of police talk about race does not imply that race is not an underlying driver of judgments, especially given cultural sensitivities about racism. More subtle methods of inquiry may be required in future research on this topic.

Critical Thinking

The authors show that race affects the way in which officers perceive and interpret events and people in African American and Latino neighborhoods. How much do you think that these labels affect the way that police use discretion in these neighborhoods? Do you think that the unequal use of discretion plays a role in how African American and Latino citizens respond to police? Could this be at least a partial explanation for varying crime rates in the neighborhoods?

References

Anderson, E. (1999). *Code of the streets.* New York: Norton.

Barlow, D.E. and Hickman Barlow, M. (2000). *Police in a multicultural society: An American story.* Prospect Heights, IL: Waveland Press.

Barlow, D.E. and Hickman Barlow, M. (2002). Racial profiling: A survey of African American police officers. *Police Quarterly, 5,* 334–358.

Black, D.J. and Reiss, A.J. (1970). Police control of juveniles. *American Sociological Review, 35*(1), 63–77.

Brown, B. and Benedict, W. (2002). Perceptions of the police: Past findings, methodological issues, conceptual issues and policy implications. *Policing: An International Journal of Police Strategies & Management, 25,* 543–580.

Brunson, R.K. and Weitzer, R. (2009). Police relations with White and Black youths in different urban neighborhoods. *Urban Affairs Review, 44,* 858–885.

Cao, L., Frank, J. and Cullen, F.T. (1996). Race, community context, and confidence in the police. *American Journal of Police, 25*(1), 3–22.

Carter, D.L. (1985). Hispanic perceptions of police performance: An empirical assessment. *Journal of Criminal Justice, 13,* 487–500.

Chambliss, W.J. (1994). Policing the ghetto underclass: The politics of law and enforcement. *Social Problems, 41*(2), 177–194.

Cohen, D.S. (1996). Official oppression: A historical analysis of low-level police abuse and modern attempt at reform. *Columbia Human Rights Law Review, 165*(28), 165–199.

Dowler, K. (2005). Jobs satisfaction, burnout, and perception of unfair treatment: The relationship between race and police work. *Police Quarterly, 8,* 476–489.

Fyfe, J.J. (1988). Police use of deadly force: Research and reform. *Justice Quarterly, 5,* 165–205.

Hurst, Y.G., Frank, J. and Browning, S.L. (2000). The attitudes of juveniles toward the police: A comparison of black and white youth. *Policing: An International Journal of Police Strategies & Management, 23*(1), 37–53.

Ioimo, R., Tears, R.S., Meadows, L.A., Becton, B.J. and Charles, M.T. (2007). The police view of bias-based policing. *Police Quarterly, 10,* 270–287.

Jesilow, P., Meyer, J.O. and Namazzi, N. (1995). Public attitudes toward the police. *American Journal of Police, 14*(2), 67–88.

Jones-Brown, D.D. (2007). Forever the symbolic assailant: The more things change, the more they stay the same. *Criminology & Public Policy, 6*(1), 103–122.

Kane, R.J. (2002). The social ecology of police misconduct. *Criminology, 40,* 867–896.

Kane, R.J. (2003). Social control in the metropolis: A community-level examination of the minority group-threat hypothesis. *Justice Quarterly, 20,* 265–295.

Kelling, G.L. and Coles, C.M. (1996). *Fixing broken windows: Restoring order and reducing crime in our communities.* New York,: Martin Kessler Books.

Klinger, D.A. (1997). Negotiating order in patrol work: An ecological theory of police response to deviance. *Criminology, 35,* 277–306.

Langan, P., Greenfield, L., Smith, S., Durose, M., and Levin, D. (2001). *Contacts between police and the public: Findings from the 1999 national survey.* Washington, DC: Bureau of Justice Statistics, U.S. Department of Justice.

Lundman, R.J. and Kaufman, R.L. (2003). Driving while black: Effects of race, ethnicity, and gender on citizen self-reports of traffic stops and police actions. *Criminology*, *41*, 195–201.

Lurigio, A.J. and Rosenbaum, D.P. (1994). The impact of community policing on police personnel: A review of the literature. In D.P. Rosenbaum (ed.), *The challenge of community policing* (pp. 147–166). Thousand Oaks, CA: Sage.

Manning, P.K. (1977). *Police work: The social organization of policing*. Cambridge, MA: The Massachusetts Institute of Technology.

McCluskey, J.D. and Terrill, W. (2005). Departmental and citizen complaints as predictors of police coercion. *Policing: An International Journal of Police Strategies & Management*, *28*, 513–529.

Moskos, P. (2008a). Two shades of blue: Black and white in the blue brotherhood. *Law Enforcement Executive Forum*, *8*(5), 57–86.

Moskos, P. (2008b). *Cop in the hood: My year policing Baltimore's eastern district*. Princeton, NJ: Princeton University Press.

Muir, W.K. (1977). *Police: Streetcorner politicians*. Chicago, IL: University of Chicago Press.

National Research Council. (2004). *Fairness and effectiveness in policing: The evidence*. Washington, DC: National Academies Press.

Platt, T., Frappier, J., Ray, G., Schauffler, R., Trujillo, L., and Cooper, L. (1982). *The iron fist and the velvet glove: An analysis of the U.S. police* (3rd edn). San Francisco, CA: Synthex Press.

Quilian, L. and Pager, D. (2001). Black neighbors, high crime? The role of racial stereotypes in evaluations of neighborhood crime. *The American Journal of Sociology*, *3*, 717–767.

Rosenbaum, D.P. (2006). The limits of hot spots policing. In D. Weisburd and A.A. Braga (eds), *Police innovation: Contrasting perspectives* (pp. 245–266). New York: Cambridge University Press.

Rosenbaum, D.P. (2007). Police innovation post 1980: Assessing effectiveness and equity concerns in the information technology era. *Institute for the Prevention of Crime Review*, *1*, 11–44.

Rosenbaum, D.P., Schuck, A.M., Costello, S.K., Hawkins, D.F., and Ring, M.K. (2005). Attitudes toward the police: The effects of direct and vicarious experience. *Police Quarterly*, *8*, 343–365.

Rusinko, W.T., Johnson, K.W., and Hornung, C.A. (1978). The importance of police contact in the formulation of youths' attitudes toward police. *Journal of Criminal Justice*, *6*, 53–67.

Scaglion, R. and Condon, R.G. (1980). Determinants of attitudes toward city police. *Criminology*, *17*, 485–494.

Schafer, J.A., Huebner, B.M., and Bynum, T.S. (2003). Citizen perceptions of police services: Race, neighborhood context and community policing. *Police Quarterly*, *6*, 440–468.

Schuck, A., Rosenbaum, D., and Hawkins, D. (2008). Influence of race/ethnicity, social class, and neighborhood context on residents' attitudes toward the police. *Police Quarterly*, *11*, 496–520.

Skogan, W.G. (2002). *Community policing and "the new immigrant": Latinos in Chicago*. Washington, DC: U.S. Department of Justice.

Skogan, W.G. (2005). Citizen satisfaction with police encounters. *Police Quarterly*, *8*, 298–321.

Skogan, W.G. (2006). Asymmetry in the impact of encounters with police. *Policing & Society*, *16*(2), 99–126.

Skogan, W.G. and Hartnett, S.M. (1997). *Community policing, Chicago style*. New York: Oxford University Press.

Skogan, W.G. and Steiner, L. (2004). *Community policing in Chicago, year ten: An evaluation of Chicago's alternative policing strategy*. Chicago, IL: Illinois Criminal Justice Information Authority.

Skolnick, J.H. (1966). *Justice without trial: Law enforcement in a democratic society*. New York: Wiley.

Sousa, W.H. and Kelling, G.L. (2006). Of "broken windows", criminology, and criminal justice. In D. Weisburd and A.A. Braga (eds), *Police innovation: Contrasting perspectives* (pp. 77–97). New York: Cambridge University Press.

Terrill, W. (2005). Police use of force: A transactional approach. *Justice Quarterly*, *22*, 107–138.

Terrill, W. and Matrofski, S.D. (2002). Situational and officer-based determinants of police coercion. *Justice Quarterly*, *19*, 215–248.

Terrill, W. and Reisig, M. (2003). Neighborhood context and police use of force. *Journal of Research in Crime and Delinquency*, *40*, 291–321.

Torres, S. and Vogel, R. (2001). Pre and post-test differences between Vietnamese and Latino residents involved in a community policing experiment: Reducing fear of crime and improving attitudes towards the police. *Policing: An International Journal of Police Strategies & Management*, *24*, 40–55.

U.S. Census. (2000). *State and county housing unit estimates*. Retrieved from http://www.census.gov/.

Weitzer, R. (2000). Racialized policing: Residents' perceptions in three neighborhoods. *Law and Society Review*, *34*(1), 129–155.

Weitzer, R. and Tuch, S.A. (2004). Race and perceptions of police misconduct. *Social Problems*, *51*, 305–325.

Westley, W.A. (1970). *Violence and the police: A sociological study of law, custom, and morality*. Cambridge, MA: The Massachusetts Institute of Technology.

Wilkinson, D.L. (2007). Local social ties and willingness to intervene: Textured views among violent urban youth of neighborhood social control dynamics and situations. *Justice Quarterly, 24*, 185–220.

Wilson, J.Q. and Kelling, G.L. (1982). The police and neighborhood safety. *Atlantic Monthly, 249*(3), 29–38.

4

Vice Isn't Nice: A Look at the Effects of Working Undercover

Mark R. Pogrebin and Eric D. Poole

Abstract: *Undercover work is important for proactive policing, but it can create a number of negative consequences for those who work undercover. Using interviews with undercover officers from federal and municipal agencies, Pogrebin and Poole examine the consequences for working undercover for police officers. Specifically, they discuss the impact of working undercover upon officers' interactions with informants, suspects, interpersonal relationships with family, and readjustment to routine police duties.*

Undercover police operations have increased greatly since the 1970s (Marx, 1988). An extensive body of work has addressed a variety of issues involving covert police activities, such as deceptive tactics (Skolnick, 1982), criminal inducements and entrapment (Marx, 1988; Stitt and James, 1985), corruption (Pogrebin and Atkins, 1979), and moral dilemmas and ethical decision-making (Schoeman, 1986). These studies have generally dealt with criminal justice policy implications of undercover operations; little attention has focused on the effects of undercover work on the officers themselves (Girodo, 1984, 1985).

In this study, undercover work was defined as assignments of police officers to investigative roles in which they adopt fictitious civilian identities for a sustained period of time in order to discover criminal activities that are not usually reported to police or to infiltrate criminal groups that are normally difficult to access (see Miller, 1992). This study examined the consequences of working undercover for police officers. Focusing on role dynamics and situated identity in undercover assignments, it explored the impact of work experiences on officers with respect to their interaction with informants and suspects, interpersonal relations with family and friends, and readjustment to routine police activities.

The Nature of Undercover Work

Assignments to undercover units are avidly sought and highly valued. The selection process typically is intense and very competitive. Most undercover police units require interested officers to make application in the form of a request to transfer, which is followed by a series of rigorous interviews and assessments to screen out all but the best qualified for the specialized unit. Since an elite few are actually selected for undercover assignments, these officers enjoy a professional mystique associated with the unique nature of their work.

Undercover assignments allow officers wide discretionary and procedural latitude in their covert roles. This latitude, coupled with minimal departmental supervision, allows the undercover agent to operate with fewer constraints, exercise more personal initiative, and enjoy greater professional autonomy than regular patrol officers. Manning (1980) cautioned that such conditions may lessen officer accountability, lower adherence to procedural due process, and undermine normative subscription to the rule of law.

Marx (1988) further argued that police subcultural norms of suspicion and solidarity may take a conspiratorial turn as undercover agents adopt a protective code of silence not unlike that characteristic of organized crime. Covert intelligence-gathering procedures and processes become highly insular, almost peripheral to routine police operations. There develops a need-to-know doctrine in which information is strictly guarded and selectively shared. The secrecy required for clandestine police work offers rich opportunities for self-aggrandizement, with many agents developing an exaggerated sense of power. As Marx (1988: 161) concluded, "the work has an addictive quality as [officers] come to enjoy the power, intrigue, excitement and their protected contact with illegality."

The undercover agent typically must operate alone; moreover, the deeper the level of cover required in the investigation, the more isolated the officer becomes (Williams and Guess, 1981). Direct and sustained management of covert activities is practically impossible because of the solitary nature of the work. When supervision is lax or nonexistent, undercover officers are prone to cut corners, which may lead to an end-justifies-the-means type of attitude (Manning, 1980). In addition to the inadequate supervision, often there are no written departmental policy guidelines covering undercover operations for officers to rely on in lieu of direct supervisory control. Even when policies are explicated in departmental operations manuals, typically they are neither known nor followed by officers (Farkas, 1986).

Lack of supervision and effective policy guidelines diminish operational accountability and responsibility at the department level, leaving officers in the field to fend for themselves. Consequently, undercover agents often devise their own operational procedures in order to accomplish unit objectives. These officers develop individualized styles of working, relying on personal expertise and judgment (Marx, 1985, 1988).

Methods

Three federal law enforcement agencies and eight municipal police departments located in the greater Denver metropolitan area participated in the present study. The researchers approached each agency with a request to obtain the names of officers who were currently or formerly assigned to undercover operations and who would be available for personal interviews with the researchers. Utilizing the lists of study volunteers provided by the respective agencies, the researchers contacted each officer initially to determine his or her length of undercover experience and present assignment. The officers were then stratified according to these two variables so that a wide range of work experiences, from entry to termination of undercover work, would be tapped. Next, 20 officers who were currently working undercover were selected—ten having less than three years and ten having three or more years of undercover experience, and 20 officers who were not currently assigned to undercover operations were also selected—ten having fewer than three years and ten having three or more years of prior undercover experience. The sample of 40 officers comprised 35 men and five women. Their ages ranged from 28 to 45 (mean = 37), and their undercover experience ranged from one to seven years (mean = 4).

All interviews were conducted at the respective agencies in either subject offices, private conference rooms, or interrogation rooms. Each interview lasted for approximately two hours and was tape-recorded with the subject's consent. An unstructured in-depth interview format was used, which relied on sequential probes to pursue leads provided by subjects.

The Impact of Undercover Work

Informant Relations

Since officers must learn to operate on their own much of the time and since undercover work is proactive, one of the most critical requirements is the ability to cultivate informants for information on illegal activities and for contacts with active criminals. The relationship between an officer and an informant is to a great extent symbiotic, since they come to rely on one another for services they can obtain only from each other. The cooperation of informants in supplying information is fundamental in most police intelligence-gathering operations. Deals and bargains must be struck and honored for cases to be made. Informant relations are really exchange relations. For example, Skolnick (1975) noted that at each link in the chain of a narcotics investigation, officers must make arrangements with suspects in order to move to the next higher level in the criminal organization responsible for the purchase, manufacture, and distribution of the narcotics. According to one federal agent,

> An informant is the easiest, quickest way to do police work. . . . [He] can walk you in the front door and take you directly to the crook and introduce you face-to-face.

Officers must develop and maintain stable relations with informants who can provide reliable information over time. The incentives that officers can offer informants to secure their cooperation or compliance often involve a carrot-and-stick approach. One officer provided several examples of the tactics he has used with his informants:

> Getting cases dropped . . . or dealing with probation officers for not going hard on them. Lobbying district attorneys or city attorneys about the cases, or getting bonds reduced so that they can bond

> out of jail. . . . Getting their cars released from the pound so they can get their wheels back. I have
> even loaned them money out of my own pocket.

Left to their own personal devices in working with informants, however, some officers
may resort to questionable practices:

> We would have the person arrested by other officers, not knowing why they were involved. They
> usually were arrested for misdemeanor warrants. We would then get them out of jail in return for
> information. It would appear to the informant that we were doing him a favor.

A related problem involves officers' discretion to overlook illegal activities of informants in order to preserve access to information. This practice may cause agents to lose
their sense of perspective regarding the relative importance of their operations in crime
control; that is, these officers may come to believe that the types of crimes they are fighting
pose a greater public safety concern than the offenses committed by their informants. The
immediate justice meted out through arrests of informants for their crimes seems to be far
outweighed by the long-term crime control benefits that may be realized only through the
use of information these individuals provide. This utilitarian view may be advanced even
by police administrators, who emphasize the larger public safety view of crime control;
that is, these administrators convey the view that the activities of street criminals may be
ignored for the purpose of getting at the "heavy hitters" who run criminal organizations.
As one officer observed,

> You see captains and lieutenants using people and not putting them in jail for certain warrants so
> that they can get more information. . . . You see there is no problem doing it even though it was a
> violation of the operations manual. We feel if the captain can do it, and do it in front of us like that,
> then we can do it.

This reliance on active criminals for information about other active and ostensibly
more serious criminals creates a variety of challenges to the integrity of police work. For
example, informants are not bound by procedural due process constraints. Moreover, the
tolerance of informant lawlessness by law enforcement officials in the interest of securing
information may blur the line between legal and illegal police practices.

> [Informants] . . . are going to screw up, so you've got to cover their ass. I've had to do things on
> several occasions, like setting up some guy, just to clear an informant. . . . You just know that when
> they screw up . . . they're always able to turn around and offer something that makes up for that.

On the other hand, many officers are sensitive to the risks involved in depending on
informants for information to do their jobs. Informant information may be faulty and, if
acted upon, could jeopardize, compromise, or embarrass the officer. One federal agent
illustrated the problem:

> The main basis for our intelligence and what we go by in initiating investigations usually is a confi-
> dential informant, who are criminals themselves, which makes their motives suspect. I have seen

cases where we were sure as we could be about a suspect, and we have been wrong. Our information came from an informant who had been corroborated in the past and had been pretty trustworthy, and you still get burned.

The officer–informant relationship is driven by reciprocity but grounded in deceit. Both the agent and the informant must create illusions in the dual roles they play—both pretend to be people they are not. Credibility and reliability are tenuous commodities where misrepresentation of self is the key to continued relations.

Informants, as active participants in illicit enterprises, are part of the cover that affords police access to criminals (Manning, 1980); however, the illegal activities informants engage in while working for the police pose a problem of control. Police undercover operations must not disrupt routine criminal processes, which include illegal behavior by informants. Thus, it is not uncommon for informants to take advantage of their protected status by pursuing more criminal opportunities. For police, it is imperative that informants' motivations for cooperation be judged and their roles in undercover operations monitored. Assessing informant motivation and directing informant participation are critical in managing undercover operations. The observations of officers typify this perspective:

> A guy that is motivated by money is pretty easy to control. The ones that are into revenge are also easy to control, because if they think they are getting back at someone, or as long as you keep them thinking that you are doing this to get back at so-and-so, they are okay. . . . The hard ones to control are the ones who are doing it because it's fun or a game to them. They think they are smarter than you. . . . You control snitches by strength of personality—letting them know your rules and . . . knowing their motivation.

> You never take anything they [informants] do for granted. I put myself in their position and ask, "What's in it for me?" You then get a feeling for what they're doing and why. What you don't want is surprises.

As Levine (1990: 45) noted, " 'Never trust a snitch' . . . is one of the most important proverbs in the unwritten bible of a narc." Many undercover officers have echoed this sentiment, often adding that informants do not deserve to be treated well. After all, informants typically commit a range of criminal acts, and they may be perceived as no different than the offenders who are being targeted. Two agents sized up their informants as follows:

> [Y]ou can't turn your back on them for a second or they will bite you. They lie to you all the time. They are untrustworthy. They have the morals of an alley cat.

> [I]nformants are some of the sorriest excuses for human beings imaginable—like sociopaths, no conscience. They're just looking out for themselves. . . . I have dealt with some real scum bags, and you can feel awfully dirty later on.

From such sentiments arise purely utilitarian justifications for the manipulation of informants and their treatment as disposable by-products of undercover operations.

For example, several officers noted that it would be counterproductive to become too concerned about the personal well-being of an informant simply because informants are expendable; that is, once a police operation concludes, an informant may be cut off from the department or, in some cases, arrested and prosecuted. For many veteran officers informants become almost invisible, blending into the background of the criminal environment. There is no affect associated with their dealings with informants; personal relations are feigned for instrumental purposes. One officer summed up this approach:

> Informants can appear to be our friends and we can appear to be theirs; however, they are a necessary tool of our trade and must be treated that way.

In contrast, some officers experience genuine feelings of concern for informants as individuals. They point out that they frequently must establish and nurture relationships with key informants over extended periods of time. Such relations inevitably lead to a mutual exchange of personal information. It is not surprising that these relationships may foster conflicting emotions among officers:

> I have sympathy for some of my informants. . . . You spend a great deal of time working with them and listening to their problems. Basically, you are their keeper while they are working for you. You start to feel responsible for what they do. You wonder why their life is such a mess. I try to keep that separate, but you really can't.

While relations with informants pose significant problems for officers, close association with targeted criminals heightens the challenges of the undercover role considerably. As the next section shows, the stakes are higher and the costs of deception greater.

Identification with Criminals

As noted previously in this article, undercover infiltration into criminal networks requires the use of techniques that include presenting a false identity in interaction with offenders in their environment. However, the agent is not feigning his or her entire presentation of self. Much of his or her genuine self is actually incorporated into the false identity created. After all, he or she is playing a role, and, like a method actor, the officer actually strives to identify personally with the part:

> You have to learn to be an actor because you're pretending to be somebody you're not. . . . [Y]ou're pretending to be a crook, and the crook thinks you're a crook, so you must rely on personal experience.

The officer's job is actually made easier through incorporating much of him- or herself into the performance. As one undercover agent observed:

It's best to tell as few lies as possible. The fewer lies you tell, the easier the lies are to remember and keep straight. And your lies should be related to your personal life experiences. This makes recall easier.... You should not attempt to change your life history ... because you are likely to confuse what you said to each crook.

In a Federal Bureau of Investigation study of its special agents who were involved in deep undercover operations, many operatives were found to experience profound changes in their value systems, often resulting in overidentification with criminals and a questioning of certain criminal statutes they were sworn to enforce (U.S. Department of Justice, Federal Bureau of Investigation, 1978). Two federal agents in the present study reported these types of problems in their long-term undercover assignments:

I identified very strongly with the bad guys.... Even though these people were breaking the law, they had some fairly good reasons for doing it.... I realized everything wasn't black and white. Everything became kind of gray.

It didn't take me long to get into the way of thinking like the crooks I was running with. I started identifying with these people very quickly.... [P]art of it was identifying with them and part of it was trying to fit in with them.

The deep undercover operative who lives under false pretenses for months or years necessarily forms close relationships with those under investigation, as well as with their associates, friends, or families. There are subtle assimilation processes involved in undercover work, since officers must adjust and adapt to an unfamiliar criminal subculture; consequently, officers may take on, in greater or lesser degree, the folkways, mores, and customs of that criminal subculture. For some, the net result is having their conventional outlook undermined and conventional bonds of social control weakened. Such processes free up the officer to engage in non-conventional activities characteristic of the criminal primary group with which he or she affiliates, as illustrated in the following report:

You get into a case where you are undercover for a very long period of time, where you are acting like a puke-ball for a year or more in order to make a huge case. I mean, you start hanging around these guys and start picking up their bad habits ... doing things that are not really related to the case and hanging out with people you shouldn't be with.

Undercover operatives come to share many experiences with those under investigation in order to be perceived as authentic. While this sharing heightens officer credibility, it also promotes bonding, which in turn fosters understanding of and sympathy for the targeted individuals:

You are only human and you get to know and like a lot of people. When you're a year with these people, they become your friends. You share your problems with them ... [and] they make sacrifices for you.

Prolonged and intense interaction within a criminal network leads to emotional conflicts. Since deception requires a dual self-identity for the agent, there is constant tension between loyalty and betrayal in performing an undercover role and an uneasy moral ambiguity, as revealed in the following remarks of a narcotics officer:

> There are cases that you don't want to see come to an end because you don't want to arrest them. You like the people. You hate to see their lives ruined. You hate to think about what they are going to think about you. . . . You would like to just slide out of the picture and never be seen again.

The observations of the next two officers indicate that they felt morally tainted by the undercover experience.

> It is something that you have to live with that just doesn't go away. It nags and eats at you. You feel really bad about it—all the people that got caught up . . . [in the operation], and their lives were ruined and their kids' lives.

> Knowing what I know now, I don't think I could ever work narcotics again. . . . I know I've changed. Certainly more cynical about what we're doing. . . . And for what? To dirty ourselves like the crooks?

The work orientations and habits developed by undercover officers often have spillover effects on their interpersonal relations with family and friends. These problems are described in the next section.

Relations with Family and Friends

Undercover assignments may disrupt or interfere with an officer's family relationships and activities. As Marx (1988: 166–167) observed, undercover work exerts pressure on interpersonal relations because of "the odd hours, days, weeks away from home, unpredictability of work schedules, concern over safety, late night temptations and partying that the role may bring, and personality and life style changes that the agent may undergo."

Some undercover officers have difficulty separating the traits and attributes associated with their deceptive criminal roles from their normal demeanor in conventional social roles. They experience role strain in shifting between the criminal identity at work and the conventional identity at home:

> Trying to be what the crooks were caused me some real problems with my wife right off the bat. We would go to a social gathering and I would end up off in some corner staring into the back yard and probably drinking too much, because I didn't like the pressure. People would come up and ask me what I did for a living and I had some cockamamie story I would give . . . it was always some lie.

For some officers, adopting a deceptive criminal identity for an undercover assignment essentially precludes their assuming their conventional identity while off-duty. As a veteran agent observed,

> There are a lot of guys who I don't think have been able to put their undercover role aside when they go home. When they work undercover, they are always undercover.

In Farkas' (1986) study of former and current undercover police officers in Honolulu, 41 percent reported adverse changes in interpersonal relations with family and friends, 37 percent experienced stress in associating with family and friends in public, and 33 percent expressed anxiety over not being able to discuss their assignments with family and friends. In the following observations, officers in the present study have provided firsthand accounts of the types of problems revealed in the research by Farkas (1986). First, an officer described some of the disruptive effects of his work on family relationships:

> [A] lot of times I was involved in undercover operations where I would spend so much time away from home. . . . Then you go home grumpy. You don't feel like doing anything with the family. They want to go out for a burger. I just got through eating fifty burgers in the last two weeks. . . . The last thing I want to do is go out and get in the car. So, undercover work messes up your family life a lot.

Second, being in an active undercover role will often cause officers to worry about the safety of their families when they are with them in public; there is concern about the possibility of chance encounters with suspects or criminal associates who know the officers by undercover identities:

> [W]e may have gone to a shopping mall or somewhere with my family and see somebody who may be involved in a case or may know who you are, so you wouldn't want your family to be part of it. So, I found myself limiting my activities . . . to pretty much just staying at home with the family. Or when I did go out, not taking them with me. This isolation was definitely stressful for all of us.

Third, the need to maintain secrecy in covert operations restricts communication with family and friends, heightening feelings of uncertainty and danger associated with the work:

> I was totally isolated from my family and friends. I couldn't tell them where I was . . . how [I was] doing or what [I was] working on. . . . [It] was extremely painful and upsetting [and frightening] to them. . . . My whole family really took a beating over that period of time.

Law enforcement organizations rarely prepare officers or their families for the kinds of interpersonal problems they are likely to face as a result of an undercover assignment. Two former narcotics officers in the present study lamented the negative effects in hindsight:

> I would give anything if prior to working undercover I would have known some of the pitfalls and some of the pressures that were going to be put on my family situation.

> Things got kind of crazy . . . out of control, really. I lost perspective on a lot of things, including my wife and kids, and she ended up divorcing me. . . . I should have seen it coming, but I was so into my work that it didn't matter at the time. Nothing mattered at the time.

A common theme of undercover work that runs through the dramatic lifestyle changes revealed above is a "separation of self." Undercover work typically requires officers to adopt a criminal persona, distancing themselves from a conventional lifestyle. This transformation involves isolation from police peers, family members, and friends, as well as from conventional places where activities with these individuals normally occur. These people and places provide the emotional, psychological, social, and moral bearings for conventional living. To a great extent, these bearings reflect and reinforce one's personality, a part of the self; thus, the separation of that part of the self is akin to a loss of identity. Officers working undercover are expected to seem to be people they are not through role-playing; however, their isolation in those roles may actually foster real changes in attitudes, values, beliefs, manner, habits, demeanor, character, and identity. Operatives may begin to think and feel like the criminals they are impersonating. Who they are, or are becoming, may be confusing to family, friends, and colleagues. These individuals are perceived as different. The relational landscapes are altered, and the situations are disorienting.

Return to Routine Police Work

Ending an undercover assignment and returning to patrol duty can be awkward for many officers. These former operatives often experience difficulty in adjusting to the everyday routine of traditional police work. Farkas (1986) reported that former undercover agents frequently suffer from such emotional problems as anxiety, loneliness, and suspiciousness; moreover, they experience disruptions in marital relations. Similarly, Girodo (1984) noted that the return to regular police duties after a lengthy assignment as an undercover operative is analogous to coming down from an emotional high. Officers in this situation often report feeling lethargic and depressed as well as experiencing self-estrangement in their new assignments. After six years in an undercover unit, this former narcotics agent described his adjustment problems:

> I was well trained for something else. What am I doing here? At times it hits you hard. For three months on graves I didn't want to hear about vice and narcotics. I didn't want to see them, hear about them, or know anything about them. I just didn't want any contact because it was painful. . . . I don't blame anybody. I knew I was going to be rotated out . . . but yet I feel cheated somehow.

Two former undercover officers commented on the psychological impact of being transferred back to patrol:

> I was really pissed off. I had a short fuse and would go off for no reason at all. I guess I was even trying to provoke some sort of response.

> I was bored and restless and resented what I was doing. I just didn't feel good about myself and was mad at everybody. I didn't feel anybody understood what I was going through because they hadn't done the things I had.

Many of the problems associated with reassignment to patrol duties may be attributed to decreased autonomy and diminished personal initiative in job performance. For example, working a certain geographic area of the community, responding primarily to radio-dispatched calls for service, handling non-criminal cases, and being subject to closer supervisory monitoring of activities all make for less exciting work experiences than those enjoyed in undercover assignments (Marx, 1988). A veteran officer reflected upon what he missed the most following his transfer to patrol after five years in an undercover unit:

> The excitement in undercover work is, to me, the ultimate. An officer is actually doing something and creating things that are happening. He comes back on the street and back to a daily routine.... I still miss the close-knit unit and having the kind of freedom and control we did.

Former undercover agents generally see themselves as having developed and honed special skills as a result of their undercover experiences; consequently, they feel that their talents and abilities are wasted in routine assignments. As the following comments show, officers view their return to patrol as the functional equivalent of a demotion:

> It's like stepping backwards. I mean, you have accomplished a lot of things ... [in] seven years in undercover. You get better and better over time and suddenly you're sent back to where you were seven years ago—right back at the bottom.

> Narcotics is not a glamorous job. You got to be tough mentally. You get that only from experience.... Narcotics officers should be assigned on a permanent basis and not rotated out after a set number of years.... I'll never be able to adjust to patrol; my career is ruined.

For several former narcotics officers the return to routine police duties was even more devastating; they expressed deeply held personal beliefs and commitment concerning the societal importance of their undercover work. As undercover narcotics agents, they saw themselves not just on the "front lines" fighting the war on drugs; they also felt they had assumed even greater risks by going undercover "behind enemy lines" to infiltrate and destroy criminal networks. Their experiences were intense, inherently dangerous, and exciting. Some of these officers actually perceived themselves as engaged in a perverse form of trench warfare, as soldiers whose mission was to win the war on drugs one dealer at a time. The following comment is representative of this sentiment:

> Highly committed members of an elite narcotics unit want no part of ordinary police duties ... handling DUIs, domestics, and noise complaints.... Drugs are our number one problem, and I got tremendous satisfaction getting drug traffickers off the street.... There is a drug war going on out there, and it bothers me a lot I'm no longer ... doing my part.

Finally, Girodo (1985) noted that some attributes thought to be beneficial in an undercover assignment (e.g., deceptive, manipulative, inclined toward risk-taking) may have adverse consequences in routine police work. For example, ex-undercover officers tend to adopt a more proactive approach to policing, with an emphasis on the "strategic management" of suspects. As one former undercover investigator explained:

> I talk to arrestees differently. I am always looking for what information they can give me as opposed
> to throwing them in jail and forgetting about them like I did before I was in undercover. Now all I
> think about is, "Can I get something out of them?"

Undercover officers are likely to have developed a different working style and
demeanor—often characterized by heightened suspicion, cynicism, and caution—that
may escalate conflict in interaction with suspects or undermine citizen satisfaction and
confidence in service calls. Such consequences have led several officers to stress the need
for a decompression period; that is, former operatives need time off for gradual reentry
into their new assignments:

> I think it's extremely dangerous to go back on the street in uniform and deal with citizen complaints
> just off a long undercover assignment. You're just not ready to handle those types of problems. . . .
> I mean, you're not comfortable or as confident as you should be. And I guess you try to make up for
> that with a lot of bravado. . . . You really need some time away to get things straight again.

For many officers, an understanding of the dramatic changes they have undergone as a
result of their undercover experiences arises only in retrospect, after they have had time to
appreciate the stark contrast between the demands of their former and current work
assignments fully.

Conclusions

Unlike police officers with conventional assignments, undercover agents tend to operate
primarily within criminal networks. The agent's ability to blend in—to resemble and be
accepted by criminals—is critical for any undercover operation. Deception is continuous
and must be adhered to consistently for the illusion to be maintained; that is, the officer's
appearance and demeanor must seem natural and genuine.

An operative is required to adopt an alternate identity. The undercover officer must be
a good improviser in order to perform convincingly in accordance with the role demands
of a false identity. When a person's identity is changed, even for the temporary purpose of
acting a part, the individual comes to view him- or herself differently; he or she is not the
same person as before. This identity transformation helps the officer fit in with those of
the criminal world in which he or she now operates. It is not unexpected, then, that
prolonged participation in a criminal subculture may create role conflicts for the officer.

In addition, the officer must manage a split between conventional and non-conventional
identities. Typically, undercover work requires the officer to obtain new identification
documents, to change appearance (e.g., clothes, hairstyle, beard, makeup, etc.), and to
alter demeanor, speech, and lifestyle in order to fit in with suspects. Over an extended
period of time, undercover pursuits tend to isolate the officer from contact with friends
and relatives, thus limiting or precluding participation in conventional activities. The
undercover officer is often far removed, both physically and emotionally, from support

systems and institutional symbols that serve to define his or her conventional self. Without such relational ties to reinforce his or her normal identity, sustained interaction with law violators threatens to undermine the maintenance of a conventional self-concept. The line separating the self-concept associated with the role of an undercover cop and the self-concept tied to the responses of deviant others who reinforce the role performances becomes increasingly blurred. The norms of police ethics may thus be turned upside-down in undercover work.

Critical Thinking

One of the major findings from this study is that working undercover can exact a heavy toll on detectives. Consider the article by Stenross and Kleinman about emotional labor. How do you think working undercover affects the emotional labor of being a detective? In what ways do you think working undercover exacerbates the difficulties detectives experience when interacting with innocents, victims, offenders, and their families?

References

Farkas, G. (1986). Stress in undercover policing. In *Psychological services for law enforcement*, ed. J.T. Reese and H.A. Goldstein. Washington, DC: U.S. Government Printing Office.

Girodo, M. (1984). Entry and re-entry strain in undercover agents. In *Role transitions: Explorations and explanations*, ed. V.L. Allen and E. van de Vliert. New York: Plenum Press.

Girodo, M. (1985). Health and legal issues in narcotics investigations: Misrepresented evidence. *Behavioral Sciences & the Law* 3: 299–308.

Levine, M. (1990). *Deep cover*. New York: Delacorte Press.

Manning, P.K. (1980). *The narc's game: Organizational and informational limits on drug enforcement*. Cambridge, MA: MIT Press.

Marx, G.T. (1985). Who gets stung? Some issues raised by the new police undercover work. In *Moral issues in police work*, ed. F.A. Elliston and M. Feldberg. Totowa, NJ: Rowman and Allanheld.

Marx, G.T. (1988). *Undercover: Police surveillance in America*. Berkeley, CA: University of California Press.

Miller, G.I. (1992). Observations on police undercover work. In *Order under law* (4th edn), ed. R.G. Culbertson and R. Weisheit. Prospect Heights, IL: Waveland Press.

Pogrebin, M.R. and Atkins, B. (1979). Some perspectives on police corruption. In *Legality, morality and ethics in criminal justice*, ed. N.N. Kittrie and J. Susman. New York: Praeger Publishers.

Schoeman, F. (1986). Undercover operations: Some moral questions about S. 804. *Criminal Justice Ethics* 5: 16–22.

Skolnick, J.H. (1975). *Justice without trial: Law enforcement in democratic society* (2nd edn). New York: John Wiley & Sons.

Skolnick, J.H. (1982). Deception by police. *Criminal Justice Ethics* 1: 40–54.

Stitt, B.G. and James, G. (1985). Entrapment: An ethical analysis. In *Moral issues in police work*, ed. F.A. Elliston and M. Feldberg. Totowa, NJ: Rowman and Allanheld.

U.S. Department of Justice, Federal Bureau of Investigation (1978). *The special agent in undercover investigations*. Washington, DC: U.S. Department of Justice.

Williams, J. and Guess, L. (1981). The informant: A narcotics enforcement dilemma. *Journal of Psychoactive Research* 13: 235–245.

5

Reflections of African American Women on Their Careers in Urban Policing: Their Experiences of Racial and Sexual Discrimination

Mark Pogrebin, Mary Dodge, and Harold Chatman

Abstract: *Pogrebin, Dodge, and Chatman examine the social organizational relationships and interactions that position African American policewomen as outsiders within their own department. Their exclusion arises not only from dominant white males but also from subordinate groups, such as white female and black male officers. They find that persistent and pervasive patterns of perceived sexual and racial discrimination permeate the work environment for African American policewomen. Black women often experience gender discrimination related to professional abilities, job performance, and supervisory responsibilities. They also experience racism in the form of derogatory remarks, and in the areas of hiring and promotion. Their marginal status based on gender and race is also readily apparent in their relationships with other officers.*

Introduction

The experience of African American women in a largely white male-dominated occupation is almost entirely lacking from the research literature. Overall, research on the experiences of minority women has been limited in number and restricted in scope (Gilkes 1981). Studies of black women have been regarded as deviant cases or incorporated into studies of women in general with the primary focus on white women's universal experiences (Collins 1986; Gilkes 1981). Few systematic studies have focused on discrimination against minority women (Nkomo 1988; Schroedal 1985). This research explores gender and race discrimination as experienced by black female police officers.

Historically, occupational norms have been linked to work segregation by sex (Coser and Rockoff 1971; Jacobs 1989; Laws 1979; Stockard and Johnson 1980). Sex typing by specific jobs, though arbitrary, follows one basic rule: men and women are different and should be doing different things. Such stereotypical thinking has long sustained the stigmatization of those who violate norms of occupational segregation, thus reinforcing sex-role typing in the workplace. Sex-role stereotypes function to keep women in ancillary and supportive roles, rather than in positions of independence, authority, and leadership (Safilos-Rothschild 1979).

Early studies and contemporary literature reveal that women who have entered a variety of traditional male occupations have faced discriminatory hiring assignments and practices, opposition from co-workers, and inadequate on-the-job training (Gray 1984; Gruber and Bjorn 1982; Kanter 1977; Meyer and Lee 1978; O'Farrell and Harlan 1982; Swerdlow 1989; Walshok 1981). Policewomen remain a marginalized, unaccepted minority, not only in the United States but also in other countries, despite a long history of involvement in policing (Brown 1997, 2000; Dene 1992; Heidensohn 1992; Reiner 1992). Women officers may be labeled by their male counterparts as interlopers, who have invaded male territory. By entering an occupation that is perceived as masculine in nature, women may be seen as intruders into the male police officers' self-defined role of brave, strong, and courageous protectors of the community (Yoder 1991). Women who enter the profession and hold their own as good police officers often present a threat to the masculine self-perception and image that male police wish to maintain. The cop culture, described by Reiner (1992: 124), is one of "old-fashioned machismo" (for a discussion of this problem in the UK see Brown 2000).

The marginalization of policewomen is well documented, but generally ignored within law enforcement agencies. The informal "canteen" cop culture is entrenched in offensive humor, sexual stereotypes, and harassment (Balkin 1988; Brown 1997; Fielding 1994; Heidensohn 1992; Hunt 1990; Martin 1990; Reiner 1992; Young 1991). Reiner (1992) suggests that internal solidarity among police officers coupled with social isolation masks conflicts within the organization. Consequently, the divisions between male and female officers are rarely addressed by administrators and are exacerbated by informal rules embedded in the masculine subculture. The "cult of masculinity" continues to denigrate, condescend, and deny full access to women who seek policing careers (Young 1991).

The problems of acceptance for African Americans in police work appear to be particularly acute. Alex (1969) argued that African American males often experience "double marginality" as a result of the expectations held by the dominant majority for their dual roles as minority group members and as police officers. Belknap and Shelley (1992) concluded from their study of policewomen that race played a role in how minority females were perceived within their departments. Further, they suggest that black policewomen were less likely than white policewomen to believe that male police recognized them for good police work. Belknap and Shelley also found that black female police officers experience double marginality as a result of being a woman and a member of a racial minority. Black female police officers, who face the additional obstacles associated with gender discrimination, seem to suffer from marginality to a much greater degree than their male minority counterparts.

Black women's occupational experiences in the police world point to the existence of racism and sexism which Collins (1990) believes are an integral part of male domination over women in occupations that are defined as male-oriented. When sexism and racism are two dominating factors that are prevalent in an organization, it remains unclear which attribute, race or gender, is the principal cause of the differential treatment (Martin 1994; West and Fenstermaker 1995; Yoder and Aniakudo 1997). Lewis (1977), however, noted that many black women perceive race as a more important factor for their subordinate positions than gender. For black policewomen it may be unclear whether discriminatory behavior toward them is the result of gender or of racial bias. Martin (1994) concluded from her study that 77 percent of white policewomen reported facing sex discrimination from male officers while 61 percent of black females reported racial discrimination and 55 percent reported sex discrimination as the more frequent experience. Clearly, there is evidence to suggest that both sexual and racial discriminatory practices may be widespread throughout police departments in the United States.

Minority police and women are also subject to special stressors such as exclusion from the informal channels of support and information, as well as ostracism and overt racial or sexist comments by white officers (Ellison and Genz 1983; Morash and Haarr 1995). Martin (1994), who studied the social and work relations of black policewomen, found that the forms of exclusion black females experienced were poor instruction communication; peer hostility and ostracism through the silent treatment; over-supervision; exposure to dangerous situations; and inadequate back-up by male officers. Strained relationships among officers cause additional stress for many female policewomen (Pogrebin and Poole 1998; Yoder, Adams, and Prince 1983). In addition, black women often experience degrading stereotyping (Dill 1979). According to Docner (1995) in a study of police officer retention patterns, black females leave the job at a much higher rate compared to all other police—on average during their fourth year. One important reason for early termination may be the direct result of exclusionary practices that black women experience in a white male environment.

Methods

This research focused on African American policewomen who work in an urban police department. The department has approximately 1,400 sworn law enforcement officers of which only 21 are black females—all of whom served as respondents in this study. The median age of the women was 37 years old (range = 21–51). Their police employment ranged from one to 22 years. Their educational background varied from high school to postgraduate degrees, with more than half having attended or graduated from college.

Interviews were conducted at the respondents' homes, in restaurants, on ride-alongs, and at off-duty jobs. Each interview lasted for approximately 90 minutes and was tape-recorded with the subject's consent. A semi-structured interview format was used, which relied on sequential probes to pursue leads provided by the women, allowing the officers to identify and elaborate on important domains they perceived to characterize their experiences in police work. The interview tapes were transcribed for qualitative data analysis, employing grounded theory techniques advanced by Glaser and Strauss (1967).

Findings

Gender Discrimination

The majority of officers in this study experienced a wide variety of discrimination. The respondents indicated mixed feelings concerning which discriminatory practice—gender or race—was most prevalent. Sexual and racial discrimination can be subtle. Often the recipient is unaware of the discrimination, as demonstrated by one respondent who stated: "I think a lot of times we don't realize we are just being discriminated against, and we put it off on something else. So sometimes it's hard to identify." In contrast, another officer described being a black woman in a predominantly white male organization as "just being a double minority, black female, you are going to have it, you know, three times as hard." Rhode (1989) differentiates between sexual and racial discrimination—the latter is often motivated by the intent to degrade and disempower, while the former is motivated by paternalism. The results show that gender appears to take precedence over race in terms of sexist behavior in three areas: professional abilities, job performance, and supervisory duties.

Discrimination based on gender was seen as a common problem among the women interviewed. One woman stated: "I find it more directed at the fact that I'm a woman as opposed to I'm black. If there is any kind of negative feelings ever, it's always the woman thing." When reflecting upon what she would tell her daughter about being a minority policewoman, this officer related the following thoughts concerning race and gender:

> Hopefully by the time she [is] old enough, some things [will] have changed. But I would have to tell her that there is prejudice among the police in the department, not only because she's black, but because she is a woman. In my personal experience, I've faced a lot more prejudice or negative remarks because I was a woman, more so than because I was black.

Another respondent described her view of the discrimination she experienced during her struggle to enter the Homicide Bureau: "I had more trouble getting there because of being a woman than I did because I was black." Similarly, one officer claimed that gender discrimination is more relevant to the status of minority women in the department than race. She explained that white males are less likely to perceive black women as a threat compared to black males. Consequently, she believes that "black females tend to suffer more from gender-related issues than racial issues."

In instances where sexism is overt and rather easy to identify, we found that black women experience similar treatment from both black and white males. Male officers of both races share some of the same gender attitudes when judging female police. In an incident at the training academy, a young black recruit commented: "Why's those bitches here? You guys, you should be cooking, fixing dinner for your husband."

In another example, a lesbian policewoman related her treatment by white male peers in the gang unit:

> The guys really resented the fact that I don't sleep around with anybody. They put things on my locker, nasty notes, anti-gay material, anti-woman material, pornographic pictures. The toilet I would go in on the weekends, and I'd be the only female there, would be overflowing with excretion. It was just unbelievable.

The issue of potentially threatening situations and the male officer's desire for masculine back-up by fellow officers may make gender a more important factor than race to male officers in certain circumstances. This is expressed pointedly by a female minority officer. Here, gender rather than race, appears to be the important variable:

> They [white males] don't know if in a fight they can count on you. I think that this is their main concern. Will you be there in the end? Will you be there side-by-side fighting with me? I think that's more of a concern for them. They know a black guy's going to fight and be there for them. You know what I'm saying? A white male police officer doesn't, in my opinion, have to worry in his mind whether or not the black male is going to be there as his partner fighting and protecting him or what needs to be done. However, the white male is definitely wondering about what a female is going to do, not what this black female is going to do, but what is this female going to do?

Police Subculture Exclusion

Male police officers in the Vice Squad displayed a paternalistic attitude toward one of the interviewees when she was temporarily assigned to the unit. The minority female officer was required to visit a topless bar with some of her male peers. The males working with her felt she shouldn't be exposed to this environment. The respondent expressed her views on this behavior:

> Then the night guys, they were like embarrassed. They were embarrassed to take me to a topless bar where women were dancing. We were supposed to be there, I mean this is our job. I mean they can go out there and watch women shake their pussy in their face and everything, but if they go with a female officer, then they are embarrassed that I'm there.

A few women described blatant incidents when they were excluded from mainstream communication. One respondent, for example, received the clear message that she was not a valued member of the team and that she would never be accepted as part of the unit no matter what she did in the way of accomplishments on the job. She noted:

> I was being left out of the information loop; therefore, I didn't have the information when I'd go on calls. I was being completely left out. If I did not come in and research an incident on my own, I would not know. The guys in my unit would get together and have coffee and lunch. They would make sure they'd get on the air and call out that they were going to coffee. They would specifically name names, this is who is invited to coffee, and I would be the only one on the east side left out. It got really bad. I knew that this was becoming a real bad situation when I had three armed suspects at the shopping center at gunpoint, and I'm calling for help. All the people in my unit were sitting at Denny's, and they never gave me back-up.

Failing to provide back-up when a peer is calling for help on the radio is probably the most flagrant act of malfeasance for police officers. Yet, according to this respondent, she often encountered this type of behavior. Few examples of exclusion can be more unambiguous than your peers knowing you are in a dangerous situation and ignoring your calls for assistance.

Specialized assignments in various areas of police departments are looked upon as earned rewards for good police work. Women have a difficult time obtaining these assignments and often higher ranking police, who select officers for these positions, feel that women are incapable of performing adequately. In one instance, a black woman discussed her struggle to get into the elite Homicide Bureau:

> I knew from past experience with the captain there that he didn't think that Homicide was an appropriate job for a woman. Then because of a female captain, I got the job in Homicide. You never know what new battle you've got to fight. You don't know if it will be a battle because of sexism or it will be because of racism.

Paternalistic behavior toward female officers may be problematic in the areas of supervision and evaluation. A female line patrol officer found herself in a frustrating situation that she believed resulted from stereotypical attributes ascribed to women. This woman explained how her sergeant's patronizing attitudes toward women resulted in an unfair evaluation. According to the interviewee, the sergeant said: "I don't think you're going to make a very good officer. You're too nice. You actually talk to people."

The acceptance of women in police work remains problematic for many male officers, and supervision by a woman is even more difficult to accept. Perhaps men view women who have more experience, expertise, and knowledge as threatening. One officer described the difficulty with men who refused to accept her knowledge of various aspects of police work:

> No, they don't look at me as a senior officer because I am female and don't any male officer want a female to teach them anything or think they can be taught anything by a female officer who happens to be black.

Women at the supervisory rank experience difficulties with male police officers working under their direction. Even in these instances, where the authority comes with the rank, male police often are uncooperative. A black female sergeant explained her problems with men whose attitudes about working for a woman caused real problems in her unit:

> You have got to be prepared to face a lot of discrimination because there are a lot of men that point blank refuse to work for you, not only because you're a female, but because you are a person of color and they will not hide that. They do not care what kind of alleged discipline might happen to them because of it.

Racial Discrimination

The officers interviewed were exposed to racist as well as sexist attitudes within the organization. For these respondents race also cast them as outsiders. This point was made in a somewhat different way by one woman, who said: "believe it or not, I think that racism is more open. Sexism is more subtle." The racism experienced by participants was most apparent in the derogatory racial remarks made by fellow officers in their presence. Racism was also a predominant theme in hiring and promotion.

In their study of minority policewomen on the Los Angeles Police Department, Felknes and Schroedal (1993) found that minority female officers reported receiving racial slurs from their supervisors and peers. Approximately 40 percent of black women officers and 36 percent of Hispanic women police claimed that they had experienced such verbal abuse. They also report that non-white females in the department are the recipients of a greater degree of discrimination than their white female peers or male minority police. This research indicates that derogatory racial remarks were common for women in this study. The following sums up a respondent's feelings about white officers who made derogatory racial remarks in front of her:

> Young white cops discriminate against minorities openly. The thing that scares me is that the older officers maybe know how to hide it better, but the newer officers, it's real blatant. You can go to a call with them, they will call someone a nigger in front of you and not think twice.

When racial remarks are made openly by police officers, one would expect that their superiors would take action against such utterances and that punitive sanctions would be forthcoming. Unfortunately, superiors often ignore such remarks. One of the most disturbing aspects of their Los Angeles study, noted Felknes and Schroedal (1993), was management's obvious tolerance of racial remarks. When complaints were made to the organization about particular racist and sexist groups, complainants were told that the remarks and discriminatory behavior were only jokes and pranks. Those interviewed experienced similar reactions by their superiors:

> If you make those command officers or anybody else of rank above you accountable for the actions of the people who work for them and follow the police manual, then maybe we could get some people for discrimination. The diversity training we went through is just documented bullshit; there is no one to enforce it.

Police officers often know that racial remarks are overlooked by their department. The lack of punishment for those police who continually disparage minorities may encourage openly racial remarks. Overt sexist remarks, however, are taboo because police managers appear to be more willing to enforce sex discrimination policies. One woman explained that blatantly sexist acts were prohibited, but "it's okay to make racist comments openly because nobody is beating anyone across the head and getting disciplined for that." One officer explained: "it's serious when your administrators are not aware of certain words and terms that are sensitive to black people. Because they are not aware of it they perpetuate the problem."

The fact that both black male and female police officers are such a small percentage of the overall organization may explain why some white policemen feel free to openly verbalize racial slurs about minority citizens without fear of reprisals. Obviously, such derogatory statements do little to help improve relations between black and white police officers. One woman stated:

> You hear it all the time in the way they describe suspects. For people that are supposed to be trained, intelligent people, who feel that blacks can't do the job and aren't educated enough, they themselves are

blatantly ignorant when they try to describe different ethnic groups or when they use a lot of ethnic slang when they are on the radio or off the radio or just out on a call out of the earshot of the commanders. They figure, what the hell, what are they going to do? Fire me? They really don't give a shit.

Black police officers may discover that being culturally different is seldom tolerated within the organization. Griffin (1997) notes that black police officers are segregated by culture in their own organizations. According to the black policewomen we interviewed, the non-acceptance of black culture by the majority of white police tends to isolate minority officers. One respondent questioned how black individuals can be expected to leave their race behind when it is repeatedly thrown back in their face: "I don't make an issue of my race, it's just who I am. I walk in, I'm black. That's just the way it is. I have heard them call me 'bitch', 'fucking bitch', and 'black bitch'."

Yamoto (1995) argues that racial prejudice shapes minority self-perception. According to Yamoto, racism results in the acceptance of mistreatment by some people by leading them to believe that being treated with little or no respect is to be expected because of their race. Others may respond differently, choosing to fight racial disrespect whenever they encounter it, as one respondent suggested:

> When we hear someone calling someone a "spic", we can't just sit there and say, "O.K., dang, I'm glad he didn't call me a 'nigger'." We have to react to that, too. It's not just on us, it's not just a black thing. Prejudice is prejudice. You have to react to it. You have to take a stand and let them know that it's not going to be tolerated whether they're calling someone "nigger" or "spic" or whatever.

Hiring and Promotion Issues

Some white officers may believe that police departments hire blacks because of their minority status. A simultaneous perception by dominant white males is that minorities who are hired under affirmative action guidelines are unqualified for the positions they attain. The following excerpt exemplifies a respondent's perception that white officers believe that people of color who are on the police force were hired as a result of rigged selection schemes:

> You come on the department, and you're told you're only hired because you're black. They had a hiring quota. They had a different list for blacks and a different list for whites. We are told that the tests are fixed for you to pass and all this other garbage.

The black policewomen in this study were commonly told that they were unqualified or that they would be unable to measure up adequately once they began street patrol. The following response indicates that, from the interviewee's perspective, white male officers perceive minorities as a threat to the status quo: "I mean there is still racism and prejudice, and they still think black people don't belong on this job anyway."

The attitude on the part of many white officers toward black women, as expressed by the women, leads one to conclude that white males see black females as unqualified to be police officers. One respondent stated: "The whites' attitude was that they lowered standards for us to get in, which is a lie. Then they would say that it doesn't mean just because they hired you that we're going to keep you."

Once on the job for a period of time, some black women actually attained advancement in the department. White males reacted negatively in those rare instances when this occurred. One black woman made detective after only three-and-a-half years on the force. She commented on the "heartaches" and "jealousy" that accompanied her promotion. She explained that fellow officers believed that her accomplishments were because "she's a black female." The same officer was told the following concerning her promotion to the Detective Bureau: "I heard a detective say, 'It's strange to me that they would promote you at this time. They only did it because you are black.'"

White male police seem to have a difficult time distinguishing between merit and preferential treatment for minorities when they are promoted. Such a pervasive attitude on the part of white male police was expressed by another woman, who stated: "Since I've been here, all I have seen is gripes, and I hear complaints about blacks who only get promoted 'cos they are black." She explained, "If a white person winds up lower on the list than a black person, and that black person gets promoted, it's only because he's black." Clearly, the women perceive that their white male peers believe that both black women and men receive preferential treatment as a result of race. In reality, few blacks have been promoted above the rank of sergeant in this department. A reaction to these allegations concerning the promotion of minorities being based on race is exemplified by the following statement of one respondent:

> I can't explain it, except that it makes no sense to me that every time a person of color, or a black person is up for promotion, it always seems like, they can't quietly get promoted and go on with their lives. There's always gotta be some issue surrounding either who they are or how they got to where they were. It's not like that with white officers. White officers make rank every day, and you never hear all of the other issues like you do with black officers.

One participant explained that many black officers feel that not standing out improves their chances for advancement:

> I think with black officers it plays a part in how they make decisions. That's why I always think for blacks in order to get where you want to, you have to try to be as neutral as possible without compromising yourself or without demeaning yourself. You have to be as neutral as possible in their world because it makes them [white police] feel uncomfortable.

Remaining neutral and not making waves, while simultaneously not demeaning oneself, places a minority police officer in a compromised position. To gain a promotion requires the presentation of a non-controversial and conforming image to white police supervisors. Paradoxically, members of a minority who need to stand up against racism must submerge their self-image to exhibit the characteristics required for promotion.

One woman provided an additional reason for the problematic nature of minority promotion. She raised the issue of the comfort level which whites require: "I think they are afraid to put black people in charge. It doesn't have anything to do with our qualifications, it has to do with if we make them comfortable." According to the majority of respondents, conditions for black officers are unlikely to improve. One woman, for example, stated: "They are never going to allow blacks on this job to constitute more than the quota for the population. And now that mandatory hiring for minorities no longer exists, I think I see it going backwards." In the areas of hiring and promotion of minority police, the majority of black women officers believe conditions are not improving fast enough in the department to make notable differences during their working lives.

A Shared Pride

Black policewomen appear to be excluded from the police subculture both internally and externally. Martin (1994) claims that black women have limited expectations of climbing onto the pedestal as many white women do or of becoming one of the boys. Black women, Martin notes, have been able to distance themselves from the police culture and to adopt a more critical view of it as well as find a place in which they feel comfortable. This may be one reason black women avoid off-duty social contact with both white and black male officers. A respondent explained:

> So as a rule, I would say black women don't have time to socialize with other cops. The black women that I know already feel under siege for being black, for being female, so I don't have time to be playing hanky-panky with anybody.

Black female respondents said that often they view their white female peers as needing protection from male officers when involved in threatening street encounters. The women we interviewed prided themselves in not having to be as dependent on male officers to rescue them in similar situations. A shared pride in their ability to handle tough circumstances as a result of their lifelong experiences exists among these officers and is exemplified by the following remark: "It's like black women since they have been on the bottom for so long, are a lot stronger than white women. Just internally stronger." The respondents also felt that white women were overly concerned with being accepted by higher status white males, often at the expense of other women, as noted by the following statement: "I've seen some women really go at it. I mean not physically, but I'm talking about back stabbing, the rumors, the cut throatness."

The perception of support by black male officers for black female officers varied widely by respondent. Some of the women officers believe that their presence on the police department actually improved black males' status position among the white male officers of the department. From the perspective of some black policewomen, many black male officers are deliberately not supportive of black women as a result of their own minority status in the department. One woman explained her viewpoint of the situation: "The black men, even on this job, are just a little bitty cut of society, and they don't support black women." Another woman offered a functional explanation for the lack of support black females receive from their black male counterparts. She said: "I found them non-supportive, self-interested. I don't know if they were conscious about it, they had gone into a protective stance, and that's where they stayed. So it was to protect themselves and you had to deal with looking after yourself." Protecting one's self-interest may be linked to conscious perceptions black male police have concerning their desire for inclusion within the police organization. In short, being overtly and enthusiastically supportive of black women police may not be beneficial to a minority male's occupational status due to prejudices on the part of many white males who control the politics of the department.

Black female officers in this study also experienced alienation from white male officers. A woman commented that "the majority of white officers are kind of afraid of black women. They don't know what to do with us. How to categorize us. Where to put us. They don't understand us." Many of the women seemed to feel that white policemen stereotype women to keep them subordinate. A respondent discussed one stereotype that she believed was prevalent: "Unless you are a little blonde-headed, beautiful looking floozy with a nice ass and good boobs; you know they don't want anything to do with you for showing that you are a Tarzan and you can pick up a stolen car or shoot 20 rounds." Overall, the women indicated that they perceive white officers with skepticism and usually appear to distrust their intentions. Being accepted into the police subculture is difficult for black women who are cognizant of the separation that color makes within the department. One respondent stated: "On this job, they really want you to believe we're all one. But once you take your uniform off and you're driving home, boom! You're black again. You're not blue."

Conclusions

The experiences of African American police officers in this research show a pervasive pattern of racial and sexual discrimination. It appears that black policewomen suffer from a threefold dilemma occupationally. They are female members of a minority group in a white male-dominated organization. Formal and informal organizational norms contribute to the continuing marginalization of minorities and women. Research on the social organization of policing shows that officers adjust their working relationships and interactions with their own perceptions of the social and political departmental environment as well as their own interests and experiences in the organization (Fielding 1988; Haarr 1997). Tolerance of sexist and racial behavior, along with discriminatory hiring and promotional practices, perpetuates discrimination, exclusive subcultures, and stereotyping among police officers.

Although many of the policewomen were able to contextualize and separate problems related to either sexist or racist behaviors, they also acknowledge the combined effect of being a woman and a minority as a unique problem. Historically, the treatment of race and gender as mutually exclusive categories has resulted in isolating black women from feminist theory and anti-racist policy discourse based on a discrete set of experiences that ignores multi-dimensionality (Crenshaw 1991). Denial of the intersection of race and gender forces women to devalue the part of the self that does not fit or is not accepted with a particular category (Williams 1991). The problem is exacerbated for African American policewomen because of their dual marginality in a predominately male organization.

Occupational obstacles that African American policewomen face may diminish as an increasing number of women enter the workforce, though support of their peers both off and on the job is a crucial element for reducing discrimination. Few people, however, are willing to align themselves with those at the bottom. Martin (1994) asserts that white and minority women see acceptance by male officers of the same race as more important than the support of other women, for both work-related and social reasons. The respondents focused overwhelmingly on the need for racial solidarity. One woman believed, for example, that "there is an understanding that we need to look out for each other; that we need to take care of each other." The women we interviewed understand the importance of a cohesive and supportive group, but many feel that they are unable to come together to discuss their problems. The women also recognize that this lack of unification perpetuates their problematic experiences. Some officers, however, noted positive change and increased support among minority members of the department.

Despite affirmative action mandates and research which shows that women make satisfactory police officers (Martin 1992), females comprise only 10 percent of all municipal police officers in America (Polisar and Milgram 1998; Reaves 1989). Female police often experience hostility and resentment from their male peers (Balkin 1988; Belknap and Shelley 1992; Brown 1997; Herrington 1993; Townsey 1982). Discrimination against women officers is prevalent and continuous (Coffey, Brown, and Savage 1992; Erez and Tontodonato 1992). This negative treatment is thought to be an important stress factor for women officers (Anderson, Brown, and Campbell 1993; Balkin 1988; Poole and Pogrebin 1988; Wexler and Logan 1983). It is unlikely that the opportunities for black female officers will improve unless police departments hire more black women. The organizational subculture must change from within before minority groups will gain acceptance, fair treatment, and job satisfaction. Women will continue to be viewed as outsiders as long as sexist and racist behaviors are tolerated.

Critical Thinking

The authors find that discrimination in the workplace has had a lengthy history for racial minorities and women. Although there have been gains made in hiring and promotion, these groups are still under-represented in police departments today despite equal opportunity laws passed some years ago. Why do you think this is? Are women and minorities not attracted to such positions or are they blocked from gaining entry into them? How do you think community perceptions of police affect the decisions of women and minorities to choose policing as an occupation?

References

Alex, H. (1969) *Black and Blue*. New York: Appleton, Century, Crofts.

Anderson, R., Brown, J., and Campbell, E. (1993) *Aspects of Sex Discrimination Within the Police Service in England and Wales*. London: Home Office Police Research Group.

Balkin, J. (1988) Why policemen don't like policewomen. *Journal of Police Science and Administration* **16**, 24–38.

Belknap, J. and Shelley, J. (1992) The new lone ranger: Policewomen on patrol. *American Journal of Police* **12**, 47–75.

Brown, J. (1997) European policewomen: A comparative research perspective. *International Journal of the Sociology of Law* **25**, 1–19.

Brown, J. (2000) Discriminatory experiences of women police. A comparison of officers serving in England and Wales, Scotland, Northern Ireland and the Republic of Ireland. *International Journal of the Sociology of Law* **28**, 91–111, doi:10.1006/ijsl.2000.0119.

Coffey, S., Brown, J., and Savage, S. (1992) Policewomen's career aspirations: Some reflections on the role and capabilities of women in policing in Britain. *Police Studies* **15**, 13–19.

Collins, P. (1986) Learning from the outsider within: The sociological significance of black feminist thought. *Social Problems* **33**, 14–30.

Collins, P. (1990) *Black Feminist Thought: Knowledge, Consciousness, and the Politics of Empowerment*. New York: Routledge.

Coser, R. and Rockoff, G. (1971) Women in the occupational world: Social disruption and conflict. *Social Problems* **18**, 535–554.

Crenshaw, K. (1991) Demarginalizing the intersection of race and sex: A Black feminist critique of antidiscrimination doctrine, feminist theory, and antiracist politics. In *Feminist Legal Theory*, ed. K.T. Bartlett and R. Kennedy. Boulder, CO: Westview Press, pp. 57–80.

Dene, E. (1992) A comparison of the history of entry of women into policing in France and England and Wales. *Police Journal* **65**, 236–242.

Dill, B. (1979) The dialectics of Black womanhood. *Signs* **4**, 543–555.

Docner, W. (1995) Officer retention patterns: An affirmative action concern for police agencies. *American Journal of Police* **14**, 197–210.

Ellison, K. and Genz, J. (1983) *Stress and the Police Officer*. Springfield, IL: Charles Thomas.

Erez, E. and Tontodonato, P. (1992) Sexual harassment in the criminal justice system. In *The Changing Roles of Women in the Criminal Justice System*, ed. I, Moyer. Prospect Heights, IL: Waveland, pp. 227–252.

Felknes, G. and Schroedal, J. (1993) A case study of minority women in policing. *Women and Criminal Justice* **4**, 65–89.

Fielding, N. (1988) *Joining Forces: Police Training, Socialization, and Occupational Competence*. New York: Routledge.

Fielding, N. (1994) Cop canteen culture. In *Just Boys Doing the Business: Men, Masculinity and Crime*, ed. T. Newburn and E. Stanko. London: Routledge, pp. 46–63.

Gilkes, C. (1981) From slavery to social welfare: Racism and the control of Black women. In *Class, Race and Sex*, ed. A. Swerdlow and H. Lessing. Boston, MA: G.K. Hall, pp. 288–300.

Glaser, B. and Strauss, A. (1967) *The Discovery of Grounded Theory: Strategies for Qualitative Research*. Chicago, IL: Aldine.

Gray, S. (1984) Sharing the shop floor: Women and men on the assembly line. *Radical America* **18**, 69–88.

Griffin, J. (1997) African Americans in policing. In *Policing America: Methods, Issues, Challenges*, ed. K. Peak. Uppersaddle River, NJ: Prentice-Hall, p. 357.

Gruber, J. and Bjorn, L. (1982) Blue-collar blues: The sexual harassment of women auto-workers. *Work and Occupation* **4**, 271–198.

Haarr, R. (1997) Patterns of interaction in a police patrol bureau: Race and gender barriers to integration. *Justice Quarterly* **14**, 53–85.

Heidensohn, F. (1992) *Women in Control? The Role of Women in Law Enforcement*. Oxford: Clarendon Press.

Herrington, N. (1993) Female cops. In *Critical Issues in Policing*, ed. R. Dunhamand G. Aldert. Prospect Heights, IL: Waveland, pp. 361–366.

Hunt, J. (1990) The logic of sexism among police. *Women and Criminal Justice* **2**, 3–30.

Jacobs, J. (1989) *Revolving Doors: Sex Segregation and Women's Careers*. Stanford, CA: Stanford University Press.

Kanter, R. (1977) *Men and Women of the Corporation*. New York: Basic Books.

Laws, J. (1979) *The Second X: Sex Role and Social Role*. New York: Elsevier.

Lewis, D. (1977) A response to inequality: Black women, racism and sexism. *Signs* **3**, 339–361.

Martin, S. (1990) *On the Move: The Status of Women in Policing*. Washington, DC: Police Foundation.

Martin, S. (1992) The interactive effects of race and sex on women police officers. *The Justice Professional* **6**, 155–172.

Martin, S. (1994) Outsider within the station house: The impact of race and gender on Black women police. *Social Problems* **41**, 383–400.

Meyer, H. and Lee, M. (1978) *Women in Traditionally Male Jobs: The Experiences of Ten Public Utility Companies.* U.S. Department of Labor, Employment, and Training Administration. Washington, DC: U.S. Government Printing Office.

Morash, M. and Haarr, R. (1995) Gender, workplace problems and stress in policing. *Justice Quarterly* **12**, 113–135.

Nkomo, S. (1988) Race and sex: The forgotten case of the Black female manager. In *Women's Careers: Pathways and Pitfalls*, ed. S. Rose and L. Larwood. New York: Praeger, pp. 133–150.

O'Farrell, B. and Harlan, S. (1982) Craftworkers and clerks: The effect of male coworker hostility on women's satisfaction with nontraditional jobs. *Social Problems* **29**, 252–265.

Pogrebin, M. and Poole, E. (1998) Sex, gender, and work: The case of women jail officers. In *The Sociology of Crime, Law, and Deviance*, ed. J. Ulmer. Greenwich, CT: JAI Press, pp. 105–124.

Polisar, J. and Milgram, D. (1998) Strategies that work. *Police Chief*, October, **42**.

Poole, E. and Pogrebin, M. (1988) Factors affecting the decision to remain in policing: A study of women officers. *Journal of Police Science and Administration* **16**, 49–55.

Reaves, B. (1989) *Police Departments in Large Cities, 1987.* Washington, DC: U.S. Department of Justice, Bureau of Justice Statistics.

Reiner, R. (1992) *The Politics of the Police* (2nd edn). Toronto: University of Toronto Press.

Rhode, D. (1989) *Justice and Gender: Sex Discrimination and the Law.* Cambridge, MA: Harvard University Press.

Safilos-Rothschild, C. (1979) *Sex Role Stereotypes and Sex Discrimination: A Synthesis and Critique of the Literature.* U.S. Department of Health, Education, and Welfare, National Institute of Education. Washington, DC: U.S. Government Printing Office.

Schroedal, J. (1985) *Alone in a Crowd: Women in the Trades Tell Their Stories.* Philadelphia, PA: Temple University Press.

Stockard, J. and Johnson, M. (1980) *Sex Roles.* Englewood Cliffs, NJ: Prentice-Hall.

Swerdlow, M. (1989) Men's accommodations to women entering a nontraditional occupation: A case of rapid transit operatives. *Gender and Society* **3**, 373–387.

Townsey, R. (1982) Black women in American policing: An advancement display. *Journal of Criminal Justice* **10**, 455–468.

Walshok, M. (1981) *Blue-collar Women: Pioneers on the Male Frontier.* New York: Anchor Press.

West, C. and Fenstermaker, S. (1995) Doing difference. *Gender and Society* **5**, 178–192.

Wexler, J. and Logan, D. (1983) Sources of stress among women police officers. *Journal of Police Science and Administration* **11**, 46–53.

Williams, P.J. (1991) On being the object of property. In *Feminist Legal Theory*, ed. K.T. Bartlett and R. Kennedy. Boulder, CO: Westview Press, pp. 165–180.

Yamoto, G. (1995) Race and racism. In *Race, Class, and Gender*, ed. M. Anderson and P. Collins. Belmont, CA: Wadsworth Publishing, pp. 71–75.

Yoder, J. (1991) Rethinking tokenism: Looking beyond numbers. *Gender and Society* **55**, 178–192.

Yoder, J. and Aniakudo, P. (1997) Outsiders within the firehouse: Subordination and difference in the social interactions of African American women firefighters. *Gender and Society* **11**, 324–341.

Yoder, J., Adams, J., and Prince, H. (1983) The price of a token. *Journal of Political and Military Sociology* **11**, 327–337.

Young, M. (1991) *An Inside Job.* Oxford: Clarendon Press.

B Outsiders

6

Procedural Justice and Order Maintenance Policing: A Study of Inner-city Young Men's Perceptions of Police Legitimacy

Jacinta M. Gau and Rod K. Brunson

Abstract: *Jacinta Gau and Rod Brunson examine young men's self-described experiences with order maintenance policing. They interviewed 45 male adolescents who resided in disadvantaged neighborhoods in St. Louis, Missouri about their experiences with involuntary interactions with police. They find that young men perceive much bias in interactions with police. For them, police stops are simply harassment for being young and black. The authors conclude that order maintenance policing strategies have negative implications for police legitimacy and crime control efforts via their potential to damage citizens' views of procedural justice.*

Police and citizens often hold vastly different views of law enforcement practices. Where order maintenance policing efforts are concerned, this discrepancy may be especially pronounced. Many police administrators and politicians assert that aggressive enforcement of low-level criminal activity sends a strong message to potential offenders that officers will not tolerate even the slightest transgressions. By altering the social meaning of disorder, zero tolerance initiatives are intended to create an environment of perceived constant surveillance (Bratton and Knobler, 1998; Kelling and Coles, 1996; Wilson and Kelling, 1982; see also Greene, 1999).

Citizens' perceptions of such tactics, however, may be quite different from those of police and city leaders. Proactive policing initiatives directed at minor offenses exemplify the state's exertion of a level of power disproportionate to the severity of the crimes being committed (Harcourt, 2001); that is, the state brings its law enforcement power down forcefully against offenses that some might consider non-serious or even downright trivial. There is no consensus as to whether the state is justified in employing such extraordinary measures. In addition, evidence suggests that some order maintenance strategies may disparately affect disenfranchised persons such as minorities and the poor (Roberts, 1999; see also Duneier, 1999), as these efforts are not always distributed evenly throughout social strata.

Standing in juxtaposition to the concept of order maintenance policing are the notions of procedural justice and police legitimacy. Procedural justice is the process-based criterion by which individuals evaluate whether they were treated fairly (Tyler and Wakslak, 2004) and it can mean the difference between satisfied and disaffected citizens. The policing literature contains ample evidence attesting to the importance of procedural justice in police–citizen encounters (e.g., Tyler, 1990; Tyler and Folger, 1980), even when such interactions result in arrest (Bouffard and Piquero, in press; Paternoster, Brame, Bachman, and Sherman, 1997; see also Sherman, 1993).

Uniting the concepts of order maintenance policing and procedural justice makes clear the potential for conflict. On the one hand, order maintenance supporters tout the strategy as an indispensable crime-fighting tool (e.g., Dilulio, 1995; Kelling and Bratton, 1998; Kelling and Coles, 1996). On the other hand, aggressive policing can leave citizens feeling humiliated, violated, or even victimized (e.g., Brunson, 2007; Duneier, 1999; see also Sherman, 1993). The popularity of aggressive order maintenance policing among police executives and politicians has, unfortunately, outpaced academic research regarding the strategy's capacity to reduce crime (Worrall, 2006) and scholars' efforts to better understand its impact on police–community relations (see Roberts, 1999). The need for more research concerning the effects—both direct and collateral—of aggressive order maintenance policing is clear.

Some researchers have examined the effects of order maintenance policing on crime and/or fear. Most have relied on survey research or official crime data and have typically focused on adult citizens' general perceptions of disorder, crime, and fear (Bennett, 1991; Braga et al., 1999; Hawdon, Ryan, and Griffin, 2003; Katz, Webb, and Schaefer, 2001; Novak, Harman, Holsinger, and Turner, 1999; Sampson and Cohen, 1988). Quantitative data derived from adult samples, however, capture only a thin cross-section of society and overlook those who may be the very ones who have the most to say about the effectiveness and collateral consequences of order maintenance policing.

In-depth interviews offer a unique opportunity to focus on the experiences of people who have been subjects of involuntary police contacts. Order maintenance policing strategies are supposed to send a particular message to active and potential law-breakers, but it is not at all clear whether or how that message is being received by its intended recipients. Some researchers have undertaken qualitative examinations of these issues in order to gain more in-depth, nuanced understandings of individuals' experiences (Carr, Napolitano, and Keating, 2007; Carvalho and Lewis, 2003; Chesluk, 2004; Duneier, 1999; Golub, Johnson, and Taylor, 2003) and some have interviewed offenders to investigate their perceptions about crime, disorder (St. Jean, 2007), and aggressive policing (Golub et al., 2003). Again, these studies have revolved primarily around adults' accounts, with little attention paid to juveniles' experiences (for an exception, see Carr et al., 2007). This is an unfortunate oversight, since youth are disproportionately involved in violent crime, both as perpetrators and victims (Blumstein, 2000), a fact that supports in-depth examination of their views on order maintenance policing.

The present study contributes to the literature on aggressive policing initiatives in two ways. First, we examine the experiences and perceptions of those who often bear the brunt of proactive policing efforts: urban, adolescent males. This group is disproportionately targeted for street stops, pat-downs, and arrests (Fagan and Davies, 2000; Hemmens and Levin, 2000; Spitzer, 1999). By considering young men's accounts, we have the potential to better understand whether order maintenance policing accomplishes its goal or if the consequences outweigh any possible benefits. Second, we are able to compare the involuntary police experiences of law-abiding young men with those of active offenders. This allows us to examine whether perceptions of and experiences with mistreatment by police are unique to those youth who are involved in serious delinquency, or if, conversely, these negative experiences transcend delinquency status.

Procedural Justice, Police Legitimacy, and Aggressive Order Maintenance

While movies, news reports, and other media sources affect people's perceptions of the police, personal experience with officers also ranks high on the list of influential factors (Cheurprakobkit, 2000; Skogan, 2005; Weitzer and Tuch, 2002). Citizens value police professionalism (Cheurprakobkit and Bartsch, 2001), and tend to feel better about brushes with the criminal justice system, in general, when they believe that they were treated fairly (Thibaut and Walker, 1978; see also Casper, Tyler, and Fisher, 1988; McEwen and Maiman, 1984; Tyler, 1984). It is, therefore, not enough for police to plow headlong into their law enforcement mission—they must also consider the evenhandedness with which they execute their duties (Skogan and Frydl, 2004; Tyler and Folger, 1980). Failure to do so has the potential to reduce their legitimacy and ultimately undermine their capacity to influence citizens' behavior and effectively control crime.

Procedural justice fosters a belief in the legitimacy of police (Sunshine and Tyler, 2003) and inspires greater compliance with the law (Lind and Tyler, 1988; McCluskey, Mastrofski, and Parks, 1999). Put simply, believing in the legitimacy of the police and of the criminal law leads people to internalize a moral obligation to obey the law. This framework stands in opposition to a purely instrumental, deterrence-based system of compulsory compliance predicated upon the threat of punishment for misconduct (Tyler, 1990). Compliance with the law is greater when people follow it because they believe in it rather than because they are afraid of being caught and punished. It is, therefore, not just *what* police do that is important but, also, *how* they do it. Failure to adhere to principles of procedural justice can reduce public support for police and, in the long run, may even increase crime (Bouffard and Piquero, in press; Paternoster et al., 1997; Sherman, 1993; see also Braithwaite, 1989; Hay, 2001).

The legitimacy that procedural justice engenders is a necessary component of any policing paradigm, including order maintenance. Aggressive policing tactics carry the potential to undermine police legitimacy for at least two reasons. First, the focus of order maintenance policing—so-called "disorderly" behavior—etudes precise articulation of the specific behaviors that should be considered unacceptable and of the reasons why these behaviors are deleterious to community well-being. Disorder-related infractions generally do not have obvious victims but are, rather, violations of general public order and standards of conduct (see, e.g., Wilson and Kelling, 1982). The idea of "public (dis) order" is far more definitionally fluid than are criminal codes delineating particular prohibited behaviors. Symptomatic of this underlying conceptual ambiguity is a lack of clarity in disorder-related laws and codes, which allows for subjective and potentially arbitrary law enforcement (Roberts, 1999).

Vague or overly broad statutes provide little guidance to individual officers working the streets (Hemmens and Levin, 2000; Roberts, 1999; see also *Chicago v. Morales,* 1998). Officers face many situations wherein there is no apparent "right" way to proceed. Under these circumstances, police may turn to suspect characteristics or the sociostructural environment for help in deciding on the best course of action. The likelihood of these extralegal factors seeping into criminal justice agents' decision-making is greatest when legal factors (e.g., offense seriousness, evidence of criminal activity) are murkiest (Kalven and Zeisel, 1966; Reskin and Visher, 1986; Spohn and Cederblom, 1991). An abundant body of knowledge has established that police decisions can be affected by a suspect's race and/or social standing (Alpert, Dunham, and MacDonald, 2004; Mastrofski, Reisig, and McCluskey, 2002; Skogan, 2005), gender (Brunson and Miller, 2006a), demeanor (Engel, Sobol, and Worden, 2000; Klinger, 1996; Lundman, 1996; Worden and Shepard, 1996), and the environment wherein a given police–citizen encounter transpires (Fagan and Davies, 2000; Klinger, 1997; Meehan and Ponder, 2002; Terrill and Reisig, 2003). This gives rise to decision-making that citizens may perceive as arbitrary even when officers have no intention to discriminate and are unaware that they are conveying such an impression.

Seemingly capricious decisions can undermine the public's trust in police because fairness is one of the attributes that individuals desire most from officers (Skogan and Frydl, 2004). When citizens trust the police to exercise their powers fairly and to distribute justice equitably, they are more supportive of officers having a wide range of discretion (Sunshine and Tyler, 2003). Even citizens who have involuntary police contacts express greater satisfaction afterwards if they believe the officer treated them fairly (Tyler and Folger, 1980). Conversely, people who believe that the police engage in unfair practices, such as racially discriminatory policing, express much lower support for and trust in the police (Tyler and Wakslak, 2004).

The second reason that aggressive order maintenance policing may run counter to procedural justice and police legitimacy is that the linchpin of some order maintenance policing strategies—stops-and-frisks—can harm police–citizen relations. Stops-and-frisks are commonly used by police departments that seek to reduce social disorder. Officers may be directed to watch for disorderly behaviors in progress, such as loitering or aggressive panhandling, or for behaviors that are about to take place, such as youths preparing to paint graffiti. Stops can be of pedestrians or vehicles, though in the present study most respondents experienced the former. Stops are not confined to order maintenance activities and also take place when officers suspect persons of being about to commit serious crimes, so any police department using stops-and-frisks for order maintenance purposes will see stops for serious crimes mixed in.

In theory, order maintenance policing efforts—even those with a stop-and-frisk emphasis—do not have to conflict with procedural justice or police legitimacy. The desire for police protection and effective law enforcement transcends racial and economic lines, and even groups who have historically suffered injustices at the hands of police want something done about local crime and disorder (Brooks, 2000; see also Bobo and Johnson, 2004). The concern, though, is not what order maintenance looks like in theory but, rather, how it plays out in practice. Even Wilson and Kelling (1982), the original architects of broken windows and order maintenance policing, recognized the potential for this strategy to go sour. The fact that order maintenance deals in relatively low-level, non-serious offenses means that there is a lot of room for police discretion, and this discretion, in turn, means there is considerable latitude for order maintenance tactics to be applied in a discriminatory fashion. In the present study, the focus is on the practical aspects of order maintenance policing.

A heavy reliance on stops-and-frisks can reduce individuals' respect for and desire to comply with police because those on the receiving end may view these tactics as unfair and/or heavy-handed. Aggressive stops-and-frisks are a staple of many order maintenance policing efforts (see Braga et al., 1999; Fagan and Davies, 2000; Spitzer, 1999). Vehicle and pedestrian stops require only reasonable suspicion that "criminal activity may be afoot" (*Terry v. Ohio*, 1968, p. 30), as opposed to the higher standard of probable cause necessary to make an arrest. Investigatory stops are, therefore, key to allowing police to legally interfere with the voluntary movement of "suspicious persons" even when police do not have legal standing to arrest these individuals.

Stops-and-frisks are an important tool for police to have at their disposal, but they do carry risks for both actual and perceived misuse. Proactive policing strategies that revolve around widespread use of field interrogations can lead to the frequent stopping of "troublemakers" even when these people are not committing crimes or behaving suspiciously (Brunson and Miller, 2006b). Instances of frequent, unwelcome police contact have the potential to lead certain segments of the population to believe that police openly dislike them (Brunson, 2007).

It has also been documented that police often conduct stops-and-frisks illegally. Determining how often unlawful searches and seizures take place is difficult because officers will likely avoid documenting activities they know to be prohibited (Skogan and Frydl, 2004). Evidence from field observations suggests that a substantial portion of stops and pat-downs would not pass constitutional muster should they be challenged in court. Most people who are subjected to unconstitutional searches, however, are not formally arrested and therefore have no opportunity to vindicate the violation of their rights (Gould and Mastrofski, 2004). Any system of law or government that wishes to be seen by its masses as legitimate must obey its own laws (Lind and Tyler, 1988), and the police, therefore, must adhere to the law if they expect citizens to do likewise. Unfortunately, studies of officer compliance with search and seizure laws paint a disturbing picture. Although most police follow constitutional guidelines much of the time, a substantial minority of stops-and-frisks are conducted unlawfully (Skogan and Frydl, 2004; Skogan and Meares, 2004).

There are other problems associated with the widespread use of stops-and-frisks that threaten citizens' sense of fairness and procedural justice. Evidence suggests that police stop different racial groups at disparate rates. In particular, African Americans are subjected to pedestrian and vehicle stops at rates disproportionate to their representation in the population, a phenomenon that stems more from area rates of poverty (Fagan and Davies, 2000) and racial composition (Meehan and Ponder, 2002; Spitzer, 1999) than from differential offending patterns across race. Blacks, moreover, may be stopped without cause more often than whites are, as evidenced by whites' greater likelihood of being arrested after a stop-and-frisk (Spitzer, 1999).

Individuals' perceptions of racially biased policing have important implications for procedural justice and police legitimacy (Wilson, Dunham, and Alpert, 2004). Specifically, research concerning citizens' attitudes toward police has consistently found that black adults and adolescents report more dissatisfaction and distrust than their counterparts from other racial groups (Hurst and Frank, 2000; Hurst, Frank, and Browning, 2000; Leiber, Nalla, and Farnworth, 1998; Taylor, Turner, Finn-Aage, and Winfree, 2001). In addition, police can unwittingly contribute to impressions that they harbor personal animosity toward certain groups (Brunson, 2007).

In sum, an over-reliance on stops-and-frisks to carry out order maintenance policing can have implications for police legitimacy because it can damage citizens' perceptions of the fairness with which police utilize their law enforcement authority. The current study pits the procedural justice and police legitimacy framework against aggressive order maintenance policing to examine the interactions of these perspectives in practice.

Methodology and Study Setting

Data for this study come from a larger study investigating the lived experiences of black and white male adolescents residing in disadvantaged St. Louis neighborhoods. The present investigation is based on information obtained from surveys and in-depth interviews with 45 male adolescents who were interviewed between the fall of 2005 and the spring of 2006. The data collection focused exclusively on young males because research has identified them as a group for whom unwelcome police attention is commonplace in the U.S.A. (Hurst et al., 2000). Only a handful of studies, however, have offered an in-depth investigation of young men's perceptions of and experiences with the police.

Respondents ranged in age from 13 to 19, with a mean age of 16. Participation in the study was voluntary and respondents were assured confidentiality. They were paid $25 for participating. Sampling was purposive in nature. Respondents were recruited with the assistance of community-based organizations working with at-risk adolescents. Staff members were asked to identify and approach young men who were known to live in distressed neighborhoods in the city, interviews lasted approximately one hour, and all except one were conducted in private offices at each location.

The goal was to interview young males who were either currently involved in or at risk for involvement in delinquent activities, as these youths would likely have more involuntary contacts with police. In other words, purposive sampling was designed to compile a sample of young men who likely had experiences with police and whose experiences may have been unfavorable. We did not, however, seek out persons known to have had negative encounters or who had overtly expressed hostility toward the police. The sampling was not intended to be representative of all young people living in distressed St. Louis neighborhoods. The interview team consisted of four graduate students. Two were African American and two were white; each student primarily interviewed same-race respondents. The black interviewers and one of the white researchers were from the same communities as many of the research participants.

Data collection began with the administration of a survey and followed with a taped interview. The survey supplied baseline information about young men's perceptions of police in their neighborhoods. Respondents were asked how often they believed the police: do a good job enforcing laws; respond quickly to calls; work hard to solve crimes in the neighborhood; are easy to talk to; are polite to people in the neighborhood; do a good job preventing crime; and harass or mistreat people in the neighborhood. Youths were then asked whether they had been personally mistreated by the police and whether they knew someone who had been mistreated. These surveys functioned as the basis for some quantitative analyses to complement the qualitative findings. The qualitative data were gathered using a series of open-ended questions that explored youths' experiences with and observations of the police, including detailed renderings of their encounters. Reliability was strengthened by cross-checking participants' responses to the survey and in-depth interview questions, and by probing for detailed accounts during the interviews.

The data are restricted to young men's accounts and perceptions of their encounters with St. Louis police officers. In the following discussion of respondents' experiences with officers, we do not take for granted that the youths' descriptions of incidents are necessarily correct or that they have provided full accounts in all instances. We are mindful that citizens may misinterpret police officers' behaviors and motives. Nonetheless, what matters for the present study is precisely how youths described their experiences, observations, and attitudes toward the police. The interviewers attempted to enhance the validity and reliability of the data by asking youths about their experiences at multiple points across the two interviews, by inquiring about their observations of police actions as well as personal experiences, and by probing for detailed, concrete descriptions of events.

Study Findings

Several respondents reported having had both personal and vicarious experiences with police harassment. Nearly half reported having experienced direct harassment and six out of ten claimed that someone they knew had been harassed or otherwise treated poorly by the police. The qualitative data revealed that respondents were especially resentful of aggressive police tactics when they were in what they considered law-abiding contexts. Further, they believed that "doing nothing wrong" should have been enough to insulate them from involuntary stops and physically intrusive searches.

Respondents' unfavorable views on police courtesy stemmed in part from their perceptions of widespread police harassment in their neighborhoods. Study participants' detailed accounts of what they viewed as heavy-handed policing tactics seemingly undermined police legitimacy by weakening officers' moral authority in the eyes of community residents.

Aggressive Order Maintenance Policing: Widespread use of Stops-and-Frisks

Respondents felt that their neighborhoods had been besieged by police and they reported that law enforcement efforts on their streets consisted primarily of widespread stops-and-frisks. Many study participants came to view this style of policing as overly aggressive and they characterized their involuntary contacts with the police as demeaning and of inordinate frequency.

Nearly 78 percent reported having been stopped by police at least once in their lives and the number of times they reported having been stopped ranged from one to 100 times (mean = 15.84). It is clear from this that the youths in this sample had extensive personal experience with police in stop-based situations. Over 45 percent of respondents also said that they had been arrested at least once in their lifetime, and 22 percent reported having been arrested in the past six months. Again, this demonstrates that many of these youths were no strangers to direct experiences with police.

Young men reported that police frequently stopped and questioned them for "no reason." Study participants believed that the poor treatment they received from the police was multi-faceted and was intimately tied to their status as poor, urban males. For example, Maurice said, "[The police] assume you run the streets, steal cars or smoke weed because you dress a certain way, like baggy pants or a long T-shirt and Nike brand shoes. They consider you as a gang member just because of what you were wearing or how you talk." In agreement, Nate explained, "It's the way we dress and talk. [Police] pretty much stereotype people.... They think if kids do saggin' pants and grills, gold [teeth] in they mouth, [that] we punks or we ain't no good." Likewise, Kyle commented, "We look thuggish, so [the police] treat us like thugs. ... But if you grew up in a perfect neighborhood, the [police] treat you like you're a human being."

There was a slight racial difference among respondents in terms of their likelihood of receiving such treatment. White study participants had less troubled relationships with and more positive views of the police than did black respondents. Whereas black and white youths alike reported experiencing unwelcome police encounters, the frequency was less for whites, who primarily risked being stopped in a more narrow set of situations.

Study participants also specifically mentioned the aggressiveness of officers' actions. For instance, James noted, "[Police officers] ride around and see what's going on, but some be harassing. They just jump out on you, tell you to put your hands up." Similarly, Derek observed, "[The police always] harass us, constantly think we stealing and robbing." And David reported, "Me and my friends was walkin' and I guess [the police] thought we was hangin' on the corner. [The police] rode up and pulled us over. First thing they said was,

'Get on the hood [of the patrol car].' . . . They told us to spread our arms and legs and then searched us." These types of police behaviors directly contravene the concept of procedural justice. For people to believe that the police are fair and that the force they wield is legitimate, they must see officers' actions as reasonable and equitable (see Sunshine and Tyler, 2003; Tyler and Wakslak, 2004). Officers who appear to act on caprice or malice can threaten citizens' notions of justice.

Young men regarded officers' proactive policing practices as insidious and believed that officers attempted to restrict their movement within the neighborhood by threatening to arrest them for minor ordinance violations (i.e., demonstrating, loitering, trespassing, and peace disturbance). Many respondents attributed officers' poor treatment of them to the types of neighborhoods they lived in. For example, Darius observed, "[The police] will lock you up for anything." Further, several young men said that friends and relatives were reluctant to visit because of the pervasiveness of aggressive policing in their communities. Mike explained, "[My neighborhood] is hot, real hot. [The police] lockin' you up for anything, just for trespassin'. . . . You gotta meet people down the street, or out on the corner to get picked up." A handful of young men also expressed concern about visitors' well-being. For instance, Raynard noted, "I was talking to [some] of my friends, and they was just getting ready to leave my house and had started walking down the street. The police pulled up and started patting them down for no reason." Respondents' determinations that officers' actions were guided, in part, by the characteristics of the neighborhood offers further confirmation of previous researchers' findings that neighborhood context can shape police behavior (Fagan and Davies, 2000; Klinger, 1997; Meehan and Ponder, 2002; Terrill and Reisig, 2003).

Respondents appeared to understand the need for crime-control efforts in their neighborhoods. They also acknowledged that as part of the law enforcement mission it was sometimes necessary for officers to detain and question "suspicious-looking people." The majority of our study participants could not understand, however, why police would target them when they were engaged in clearly lawful activities. For instance, Todd and his friends were detained by officers as they walked home from school: "The police got out of the car and were like, 'What ya'll doing?' I said, 'We're coming home from school.' [The officer] was like, 'What's in the book bags?' He came over and started checking but couldn't find nothing but books." Similarly, Martez described how he and his friends were subjected to a series of physically intrusive searches while in what they considered to be an unquestionably law-abiding context:

> We was playin' basketball and [my friend] put a wristband in his gym bag. . . . The police thought it was some crack so they stopped him and was harassing him, like, "where it's at?" He was like, "I ain't got nothin'." After they checked him, they checked all of us. Only thing they found was wristbands, white wristbands. . . . [The police officers] took all six of us in [to the station] and was checkin' our mouth[s] and [other body parts] . . . to see if we have drugs and they found out [that] we didn't.

As Martez's account points out, police interactions with respondents and their associates were not just experienced as invasive, but were also physically intrusive. Further, young men seldom considered avoidance of arrest following involuntary police contact to be appropriate conciliation. For example, Jamal described an encounter with police. He noted, "The [police] stopped me and they ran my name and said I needed an [identification card] 'cos I wasn't in the system. [The officer] was like, 'I'm not arresting you [but] can I put you in handcuffs though and run your name?'" Jamal's, Martez's, and Todd's accounts illustrate what many young men considered the arbitrariness of officers' decisions to stop, question, and search them. Further, even though Jamal realized that he was not under arrest, he took exception to the public humiliation of being placed in handcuffs like "a common criminal" while the officer called in his personal information.

Some respondents spoke directly to the effects that these seemingly groundless police actions had on the respondents' ensuing behavior toward the police. Respondents who believed they had done nothing wrong were more likely to defy police commands and were more likely to adopt an outwardly hostile demeanor toward the officers. Maurice recounted a time when officers suddenly surrounded him as he sat on the front porch of his home. Maurice recalled,

> This one policeman said, "[Do] you live here?" I said, "Yeah." He said, "Come down here." I said, "No." He said "Why you refuse to come down here?" I said 'Cos this my front [and] I can sit on it. Why you messin' wit me?" He said "Well, you shouldn't be on the front porch. Come down here, sir." I walked into the house.

Young men's accounts thus provide strong support for prior researchers' notions of procedural justice and the consequences of police actions that run afoul of fairness (e.g., Mastrofski et al., 2002; Tyler, 1990). We next analyze what happens when stops-and-frisks (justified or not) turn ugly. We investigate in detail study participants' encounters with discourteous officers and how their perceptions of these situations helped undermine police legitimacy.

Officer Discourtesy: Eroding Police Legitimacy

It was not simply that study participants took issue with being stopped, questioned, and searched on a frequent basis—most young men were especially troubled by the way officers spoke to them during these unwelcome interactions (see also Mastrofski et al., 2002; Tyler and Wakslak, 2004). Specifically, they reported that officers were routinely discourteous and that they used inflammatory language, racial slurs, and name-calling. For example, Kyle said, "[The] police will drive by and yell, 'You get off the corner or we're gonna . . . whoop your asses.'" Similarly, Antwan noted that the police shouted at him and his friends to "get ya'll asses off this corner. What the fuck are ya'll big, stupid motherfuckers doing?" And Lorenz said:

> We was [sitting] in the car; we was just sittin' in there. [Police] got us out the car, check[ed] us and said he found some drugs in the car. And [the officers] said, "One of ya'll goin' with us." [To decide]

they said, "Eeny, meeny, miny, moe, catch a nigga by his throat," and locked up my friend because he was the oldest.

While most of our respondents said that police occasionally spoke harshly to them, they reported that officers were more apt to direct demeaning and offensive language toward blacks. For example, black study participants said that officers frequently used racial slurs. Bob explained, "[Police] like to curse at people for no apparent reason. They shout bitches, hoes, niggers." Other young men linked officers' crude language to racist attitudes. For example, Martez offered, "I think cops [are] racists. That's what I think because they call us niggas." In addition to undermining police legitimacy, discourteous language was viewed by several respondents as dehumanizing. For instance, Antwan complained, "I'm a citizen and a human being just like [the police]. I deserve respect." There was no apparent relationship between officer race and the use of derogatory language toward respondents; in fact, most respondents did not mention the race of the police officers at all and, when asked, said they believed that officers' race is not a factor in the way they treat citizens. One exception to this trend was black study participants who reported that African American officers were more likely to show concern for their well-being.

Prior research has shown that citizens' demeanor is often influenced by police officers' behavior toward them (Wiley and Hudik, 1974); thus, aggressive or demoralizing police actions have the potential to inflame a situation and expose citizens to more serious kinds of malfeasance. For example, Tommie noted, "There was a fight in the neighborhood and a bunch of people was standing around. [The police] was like, 'Ya'll gotta go home,' and somebody said, 'We ain't gotta go nowhere.' They thought it was me and the officer said, 'I'll have you missing [cause your disappearance].'" Officers also took exception to being questioned about the appropriateness of their conduct. For instance, Jamal observed, "I guess [the police] thought we were fina run. He was like, 'Why you guys walkin' away?' My friend kept asking, 'What did we do?' The police was like, 'I should punch you in the mouth.'" Respondents argued that officers routinely provoked youths in order to have a reason to physically assault them. James explained:

It was the Fourth of July, and the police thought I had been shooting off fireworks. When they jumped out I didn't have no fireworks, but I did have a lighter. [One of the officers] was like, "We should beat your ass [just] for having this." I just looked at him. . . . I wasn't gonna respond to him like, "Yeah right," [because] he would have just hit me.

Young men's accounts provide evidence of the potential for serious ramifications when those charged with enforcing the law do so in a manner that is unjust or even illegal.

The Experiences of Law-abiding vs. Law-violating Young Men

In all, more than one-third of the young men reported participating in serious delin-quency within the last six months. On the other hand, almost all of the youths reported having engaged in minor forms of delinquency or status offenses, including: skipping classes; being loud or rowdy in public; avoiding paying for things; drinking beer or liquor; stealing $5 or less; lying about their age to get into someplace or buy something; or running away. Thus, our sample captured variations in delinquent involvement. It is, of course, worthy of note that all 45 of the teens interviewed did come from disadvantaged areas and were considered to be at risk for delinquency even if they had never actually committed any criminal acts. A sample of low-risk youths from a wealthier area of the city might have produced different findings. We see this not as a validity issue but as an indication that care should be taken when generalizing these results to youths of other backgrounds.

While one might expect that individuals involved in crime or serious forms of delinquency would report having more negative police contacts relative to law-abiding respondents, young men's accounts revealed few systematic differences in the nature and extent of their experiences with aggressive policing. Specifically, both serious delinquents and non-delinquents complained of what they considered to be frequent, routine harassment by police. Our research suggests that young men came to understand that no matter how hard they tried, they were not able to convincingly present themselves to officers as law-abiding, even when they were just that.

Discussion

This study was an effort to better understand the intersection of procedural justice and aggressive order maintenance policing. Interview data from 45 young men in a socioeconomically disadvantaged urban area revealed that these citizens harbored ambivalent feelings about the police. While study participants recognized that the police had a difficult job to do, they questioned the wisdom and utility of relying heavily on stops, frisks, and field interviews. In particular, respondents resented what they considered to be unfair, aggressive targeting by police. They believed their socioeconomic status and/or race made them *de facto* "suspicious persons" in the eyes of officers and that, as a result, they were subjected to heightened and unwarranted levels of police scrutiny. Study participants perceived officers' widespread use of stops-and-frisks for suspected disorderly behavior as a form of harassment because they sometimes felt that they had done nothing to merit such treatment. Several respondents expressed the view that police judged them based on their clothing, accessories, friends, and/or the neighborhoods in which they resided. They felt that police would use the inferences they drew from these surface characteristics as justification for stopping, questioning, and/or frisking them even when they were not engaging in crime. Overall, young men reported feeling that they were perpetually under officers' gaze.

Several respondents believed that police treated citizens differently depending on where they encountered them. These findings are especially troublesome. In particular, using neighborhood-level characteristics as heuristic devices for decisions regarding how to treat residents could further exacerbate one's perception that the police act unfairly toward them. Citizens of disadvantaged neighborhoods run the risk of feeling that they are being judged on the basis of the neighborhoods in which they live (Jones-Brown, 2007). Such a perception could strain the already tense relationship between police and poor, minority citizens.

Another theme that emerged from the analyses was respondents' feeling that officers were frequently discourteous and even verbally abusive. In addition to the potentially deleterious effects that such disrespectful treatment of citizens may have on police legitimacy, this kind of behavior also increases the likelihood that police–citizen encounters will be rife with animosity emanating from both parties. Prior research shows that citizen demeanor can influence police actions and, therefore, help determine whether an encounter is civil or confrontational (Engel et al., 2000; Klinger, 1996; Lundman, 1996; Worden and Shepard, 1996). This finding indicates that people, such as the young men under study here, who are subjected to routine maltreatment at the hands of police may begin approaching police encounters with an uncooperative demeanor. Outward displays of hostility toward police could put police on edge in anticipation of possible verbal or physical attack. Whether or not the encounter turns violent, the mutual suspicion and distrust exuded by police and citizens could leave both with negative feelings about one another.

The broad conclusion is that aggressive order maintenance manifesting in the form of widespread stops-and-frisks can compromise procedural justice and, therefore, undermine police legitimacy. This has a wide range of implications for police policy, both at the level of the patrol officer who interacts with the public daily and at the administrative level where departmental missions and philosophies are forged. Prior research has documented that tattered faith in officers' ability to carry out their duties fairly and equitably can spark a decline in public support for police organizations (Sunshine and Tyler, 2003; Tyler and Wakslak, 2004) and in the public's compliance with the criminal law in general (Bouffard and Piquero, in press; Lind and Tyler, 1988; Paternoster et al., 1997; Sherman, 1993; Tyler, 1990). Police agencies that embrace order maintenance therefore need to be aware of the possible ramifications of this strategy; specifically, they need to cast a keen eye toward the collateral consequences of waging a battle against social disorder. Police–community relations are already strained in many cities and neighborhoods, especially those that are socially and economically distressed (Renauer, 2007; see also Klinger, 1997; Sampson and Bartusch, 1998), and aggressive order maintenance could hit these shaky alliances particularly hard.

Study participants' accounts underscore the need for police agencies to ensure that officers engaging in order maintenance and other aggressive policing activities carry out their duties fairly and equitably and that they adhere to strict standards of professionalism. The fact that many of the youths' experiences analyzed in the present study involved stops, frisks, and other activities that fell short of formal arrest is no reason to take these young men's accounts less seriously. Stops-and-frisks that do not result in arrest may seem harmless because the citizen is not subjected to formal sanctions. Formal sanctions, however, are but one potential consequence of stops-and-frisks—there also are a host of informal outcomes such as shame, embarrassment, anger, and feelings that one's personal integrity has been violated. For these reasons, stop-and-frisk policies should not be taken lightly and police departments should be cognizant of the profound effects that even these relatively informal police procedures can have for police–citizen relations.

As described earlier, order maintenance policing entails a large amount of officer discretion, and abuse of this decision-making power can discredit police in the eyes of community members. The establishment of boundaries for the exercise of discretion could help ensure that officers are allowed enough discretion to do their jobs but are not granted unbridled decision-making authority. Clear guidelines should be in place so that officers know when it is (and is not) appropriate to stop citizens and how intrusive frisks may (or may not) be under different circumstances. Academy and in-service trainings should educate officers on the laws of search and seizure and on the importance of upholding citizens' rights for both the legal purpose of evidence suppression and for social reasons, such as the need to promote healthy relationships with the community. Police administrators and supervisors should promote a culture of respect within the department and make it clear that mistreatment of citizens will not be tolerated within the organization.

Public awareness campaigns and the solicitation of feedback from citizens could help police ensure that the crime-reduction strategy they have chosen has not compromised perceptions of fairness and justice. One vital component of a strategy such as order maintenance is notifying the community of the types of behaviors police will be cracking down on so that citizens know in advance what actions are likely to draw the attention of police. A notification policy such as this could also serve as a check on police behavior, as a public statement declaring that police will be watching for certain activities obligates officers to limit their enforcement efforts to only those persons whose behavior clearly falls within the prohibited realm. As demonstrated in the current study, a constant source of frustration among the vast majority of respondents was that the police routinely stopped them for what they perceived to be no valid reason.

Efforts are also necessary to force into the open a dialogue about sensitive issues such as the long-standing tension between police and some of society's traditionally marginalized groups. Officers may believe in good faith that what they are doing is a legitimate and effective effort at crime control, and that their actions (e.g., stops, frisks, and/or field investigations) are justifiable even when premised more on gut-level suspicion than on observations of unlawful activity. It is important for officers to understand the damage that such factually groundless stops-and-frisks can do over time. A two-way exchange of information between police and the local community could elucidate to each group the other's reasons for responding the way they do sometimes. Police departments have a tendency to shy away from candid discussions with the public concerning uncomfortable or potentially volatile topics such as citizens' perceptions of racial discrimination. Many departments that have confronted these issues head-on have improved police–community relationships (Harris, 2007), an example that should help dispel the lingering fear that continues to hold other departments back.

In a similar vein, allowing community members to express their opinions about local problems and police performance can help assure citizens that the police department is attentive and genuinely concerned about working with the community. Feeling that one's voice has been heard and taken seriously is, as discussed earlier, integral to procedural justice and police legitimacy (Paternoster et al., 1997; see also Thibaut and Walker, 1978). Respectfulness, moreover, is very important to citizens and something that many residents of poor, urban areas feel they do not typically receive (Stoutland, 2001). Police executives and supervisors can make it clear to patrol officers and others who deal with the public regularly that professionalism and respectful treatment toward all citizens is non-negotiable. Internal guidelines that require officers to be courteous and professional in all their dealings with the public can reduce citizen complaints against officers without hindering officers' law enforcement capabilities (Davis, Mateu-Gelabert, and Miller, 2005; Greene, 1999). After all, fairness and effectiveness are complementary—not competing—principles of policing (Skogan and Frydl, 2004).

Critical Thinking

The words of these young males suggest that they and the police have differing perceptions of what constitutes disorder, which clearly leads to conflict between the two groups. Why would most assume that the perspective of disorder presented by police is in fact accurate? Should police and policy-makers take the perception of those they police (including those who may violate the law) into account when developing and instituting policy? Is it possible that police can enforce the law and protect citizens while also maintaining respect with youth in these areas?

References

Alpert, G.P., Dunham, R.G., and MacDonald, J.M. (2004). Interactive police–citizen encounters that result in force. *Police Quarterly, 7*, 475–488.

Bennett, T. (1991). The effectiveness of a police-initiated fear-reducing strategy. *British Journal of Criminology, 31*(1), 1–14.

Blumstein, A. (2000). Disaggregating the violence trends. In A. Blumstein and J. Wallman (eds), *The crime drop in America*, pp. 13–44. Cambridge: Cambridge University Press.

Bobo, L.D. and Johnson, D. (2004). A taste for punishment: Black and white Americans' views on the death penalty and the War on Drugs. *Du Bois Review, 1*, 151–180.

Bouffard, L.A. and Piquero, N.L. (in press). Defiance theory and life course explanations of persistent offending. *Crime & Delinquency*. DOI: 10.1177/0011128707311642.

Braga, A.A., Weisburd, D.L., Waring, E.J., Mazerolle, L.G., Spelman, W., and Gajewski, F. (1999). Problem-oriented policing in violent crime places: A randomized controlled experiment. *Criminology, 37*(3), 541–580.

Braithwaite, J. (1989). *Crime, shame, and reintegration*. Cambridge: Cambridge University Press.

Bratton, W.J. and Knobler, P. (1998). *Turnaround: How America's top cop reversed the crime epidemic*. New York: Random House.

Brooks, R.R.W. (2000). Fear and fairness in the city: Criminal enforcement and perceptions of fairness in minority communities. *Southern California Law Review, 73*, 1219–1270.

Brunson, R.K. (2007). "Police don't like black people:" African-American young men's accumulated police experiences. *Criminology & Public Policy, 6*(1), 71–102.

Brunson, R.K. and Miller, J. (2006a). Gender, race, and urban policing: The experience of African American youths. *Gender & Society, 20*, 531–552.

Brunson, R.K. and Miller, J. (2006b). Young black men and urban policing in the United States. *British Journal of Criminology, 46*, 613–640.

Carr, P.J., Napolitano, L., and Keating, J. (2007). We never call the cops and here is why: A qualitative examination of legal cynicism in three Philadelphia neighborhoods. *Criminology, 45*, 445–480.

Carvalho, I. and Lewis, D.A. (2003). Beyond community: Reactions to crime and disorder among inner-city residents. *Criminology, 41*(3), 779–811.

Casper, J.D., Tyler, T., and Fisher, B. (1988). Procedural justice in felony cases. *Law & Society Review, 22*(3), 483–508.

Chesluk, B. (2004). "Visible signs of a community out of control:" Community policing in New York City. *Cultural Anthropology, 19*(2), 250–275.

Cheurprakobkit, S. (2000). Police–citizen contact and police performance: Attitudinal differences between Hispanics and non-Hispanics. *Journal of Criminal Justice, 28*, 325–336.

Cheurprakobkit, S. and Bartsch, R.A. (2001). Police performance: A model for assessing citizens' satisfaction and the importance of police attributes. *Police Quarterly, 4*(4), 449–468.

Chicago v. Morales, 527 U.S. 41 (1998).

Davis, R.C., Mateu-Gelabert, P., and Miller, J. (2005). Can effective policing also be respectful? Two examples in the South Bronx. *Police Quarterly, 8*(2), 229–247.

Dilulio, J., Jr. (1995). Arresting ideas [electronic version]. *Policy Review, 74*, 12–17.

Duneier, M. (1999). *Sidewalk*. New York: Farrar, Straus & Giroux.

Engel, R.S., Sobol, J.J., and Worden, R.E. (2000). Further exploration of the demeanor hypothesis: The interaction effects of suspects' characteristics and demeanor on police behavior. *Justice Quarterly, 17*, 235–258.

Fagan, J. and Davies, G. (2000). Street cops and broken windows: Terry, race, and disorder in New York City. *Fordham Urban Law Journal, 28*, 457–504.

Golub, A., Johnson, B.D., and Taylor, A. (2003). Quality-of-life policing: Do offenders get the message? *Policing: An International Journal of Police Strategies and Management, 26*(4), 690–707.

Gould, J.B. and Mastrofski, S.D. (2004). Suspect searches: Assessing police behavior under the U.S. constitution. *Criminology & Public Policy, 3*, 315–361.

Greene, J.A. (1999). Zero tolerance: A case study of police policies and practices in New York City. *Crime & Delinquency, 45*(2), 171–187.

Harcourt, B.E. (2001). *Illusion of order: The false promise of broken windows policing*. Cambridge, MA: Harvard University Press.

Harris, D.A. (2007). The importance of research on race and policing: Making race salient to individuals and institutions within criminal justice. *Criminology & Public Policy, 6*, 5–24.

Hawdon, J.E., Ryan, J., and Griffin, S.P. (2003). Policing tactics and perceptions of police legitimacy. *Police Quarterly, 6*(4), 469–491.

Hay, C. (2001). An exploratory test of Braithwaite's reintegrative shaming theory. *Journal of Research in Crime and Delinquency, 38*(2), 132–153.

Hemmens, C. and Levin, D. (2000). Resistance is futile: The right to resist unlawful arrest in an era of aggressive policing. *Crime & Delinquency, 46*(4), 472–496.

Hurst, Y.G. and Frank, J. (2000). How kids view cops: The nature of juvenile attitudes toward police. *Journal of Criminal Justice, 28*, 189–202.

Hurst, Y.G., Frank, J., and Browning, S.L. (2000). The attitudes of juveniles toward the police: A comparison of black and white youth. *Policing, 23*, 37–53.

Jones-Brown, D. (2007). Forever the symbolic assailant: The more things change, the more they remain the same. *Criminology & Public Policy, 6*, 103–122.

Kalven, H. and Zeisel, H. (1966). *The American jury*. Boston, MA: Little, Brown.

Katz, C.M., Webb, V.J., and Schaefer, D.R. (2001). An assessment of the impact of quality-of-life policing on crime and disorder. *Justice Quarterly, 18*(4), 825–876.

Kelling, G.L. and Bratton, W.J. (1998). Declining crime rates: Insiders' views of the New York City story. *Journal of Criminal Law & Criminology, 88*(4), 1217–1231.

Kelling, G.L. and Coles, C.M. (1996). *Fixing broken windows*. New York: Simon & Schuster.

Klinger, D.A. (1996). More on demeanor and arrest in Dade County. *Criminology, 34*, 61–79.

Klinger, D.A. (1997). Negotiating order in patrol work: An ecological theory of police response to deviance. *Criminology, 35*, 277–306.

Leiber, M.J., Nalla, M.K., and Farnworth, M. (1998). Explaining juveniles' attitudes toward the police. *Justice Quarterly, 15*, 151–174.

Lind, E.A. and Tyler, T.R. (1988). *The social psychology of procedural justice*. New York: Plenum Press.

Lundman, R.J. (1996). Demeanor and arrest: Additional evidence from previously unpublished data. *Journal of Research in Crime and Delinquency, 33*, 306–323.

Mastrofski, S.D., Reisig, M.D., and McCluskey, J.D. (2002). Police disrespect toward the public: An encounter-based analysis. *Criminology, 40*, 515–551.

McCluskey, J.D., Mastrofski, S.D., and Parks, R.B. (1999). To acquiesce or rebel: Predicting citizen compliance with police requests. *Police Quarterly, 2*, 389–416.

McEwen, C.A. and Maiman, R.J. (1984). Mediation in small claims court: Achieving compliance through consent. *Law & Society Review, 18*(1), 11–49.

Meehan, A.J. and Ponder, M.C. (2002). Race and place: The ecology of racial profiling African American motorists. *Justice Quarterly, 19*(3), 399–430.

Novak, K.J., Harman, J.L., Holsinger, A.M., and Turner, M.G. (1999). The effects of aggressive policing of disorder on serious crime. *Policing: An International Journal of Police Strategies & Management, 22*(2), 171–190.

Paternoster, R., Brame, R., Bachman, R., and Sherman, L.W. (1997). Do fair procedures matter? The effect of procedural justice on spouse assault. *Law & Society Review, 31*(1), 163–204.

Renauer, B.C. (2007). Is neighborhood policing related to informal social control? *Policing: An International Journal of Police Strategies & Management, 30*(1), 61–81.

Reskin, B.F. and Visher, C.A. (1986). The impacts of evidence and extralegal factors in jurors' decisions. *Law & Society Review, 20*(3), 423–438.

Roberts, D.E. (1999). Race, vagueness, and the social meaning of order-maintenance policing. *Journal of Criminal Law & Criminology, 89*(3), 775–836.

Sampson, R.J. and Bartusch, D.J. (1998). Legal cynicism and (subcultural?) tolerance of deviance: The neighborhood context of racial differences. *Law & Society Review, 32*(4), 777–804.

Sampson, R.J. and Cohen, J. (1988). Deterrent effects of the police on crime: A replication and theoretical extension. *Law & Society Review, 22*(1), 163–189.

Sherman, L.W. (1993). Defiance, deterrence, and irrelevance: A theory of the criminal sanction. *Journal of Research in Crime and Delinquency, 30*(4), 445–473.

Skogan, W.G. (2005). Citizen satisfaction with police encounters. *Police Quarterly, 8*(3), 298–321.

Skogan, W.G. and Frydl, K. (2004). *Fairness and effectiveness in policing: The evidence*. Washington, DC: The National Academies Press.

Skogan, W.G. and Meares, T.L. (2004). Lawful policing. *Annals of the American Academy of Political and Social Science, 593*, 66–83.

Spitzer, E. (1999). *The New York City police department's "stop & frisk" practices: A report to the people of the State of New York from the Office of the Attorney General*. New York: Office of the Attorney General of the State of New York.

Spohn, C. and Cederblom, J. (1991). Race and disparities in sentencing: A test of the liberation hypothesis. *Justice Quarterly, 8*, 305–327.

St. Jean, P.K.B. (2007). *Pockets of crime*. Chicago, IL: The University of Chicago Press.

Stoutland, S. (2001). The multiple dimensions of trust in resident/police relations in Boston. *Journal of Research in Crime and Delinquency, 38*, 226–256.

Sunshine, J. and Tyler, T.R. (2003). The role of procedural justice and legitimacy in shaping public support for policing. *Law & Society Review, 37*(3), 513–547.

Taylor, T.J., Turner, K.B., Finn-Aage, E., and Winfree, L.T., Jr. (2001). Coppin' an attitude: Attitudinal differences among juveniles toward the police. *Journal of Criminal Justice, 29*, 295–305.

Terrill, W. and Reisig, M.D. (2003). Neighborhood context and police use of force. *Journal of Research in Crime and Delinquency, 40*, 291–321.

Terry v. Ohio, 392 U.S. 1 (1968).

Thibaut, J. and Walker, L. (1978). A theory of procedure. *California Law Review, 66*, 541–566.

Tyler, T.R. (1984). The role of perceived injustice in defendants' evaluations of their courtroom experience. *Law & Society Review, 18*(1), 51–74.

Tyler, T.R. (1990). *Why people obey the law*. New Haven, CT: Yale University Press.

Tyler, T.R. and Folger, R. (1980). Distributional and procedural aspects of satisfaction with citizen–police encounters. *Basic and Applied Social Psychology, 1*(4), 281–292.

Tyler, T.R. and Wakslak, C.J. (2004). Profiling and police legitimacy: Procedural justice, attributions of motive, and acceptance of police authority. *Criminology, 42*(2), 253–281.

Weitzer, R. and Tuch, S.A. (2002). Perceptions of racial profiling: Race, class, and personal experience. *Criminology, 40*(2), 435–456.

Wiley, M. and Hudik, T. (1974). Police–citizen encounters: A field test of exchange theory. *Social Problems, 22*, 119–127.

Wilson, G., Dunham, R., and Alpert, G. (2004). Prejudice in police profiling: Assessing an overlooked aspect in prior research. *American Behavioral Scientist, 47*, 896–909.

Wilson, J.Q. and Kelling, G.L. (1982). The police and neighborhood safety: Broken windows. *Atlantic Monthly*, March, 29–38.

Worden, R.E. and Shepard, R.L. (1996). Demeanor, crime, and police behavior: A reexamination of the police services study data. *Criminology, 34*, 83–105.

Worrall, J.L. (2006). Does targeting minor offenses reduce serious crime? A provisional, affirmative answer based on an analysis of county-level data. *Police Quarterly, 9*(1), 47–72.

7

Urban Youth Encounters with Legitimately Oppressive Gang Enforcement

Robert Durán

<u>Abstract</u>: *Robert Durán explores how police assigned to suppress gangs interact with inner-city Mexican Americans. Using ethnographic measures and insights from prior membership in a gang, the author suggests that stereotyping Mexican American communities as gang "infested" and equating gangs as synonymous with crime allows for differential policing that no longer emphasizes criminal acts, but rather perpetually criminal people. He concludes by arguing that gang enforcement is over-inclusive and embedded with practices that create opportunities for the abuse of authority.*

Policing of urban youth of color has changed greatly since the 1980s when the concept of gangs began to legitimize and open the door to more aggressive forms of law enforcement. Violating an individual's civil rights became less of a concern as barrios and ghettos began to be equated with breeding grounds for gangs and criminality: the terms being used interchangeably. Gang members have been primarily characterized in large cities as male (97 percent), poor (85 percent), and of the following racial and ethnic groups: Latino (47 percent), black (38 percent) and very rarely as white (8 percent) (National Youth Gang Survey, 2009). Both Latinos and blacks are three times overrepresented on gang lists compared to their proportion of the population in the United States, whereas whites are 12 times underrepresented. In addition, involvement in gangs has been found to increase self-reported involvement in delinquency and crime than non-gang members (Battin, Karl, Abott, Catalano, and Hawkins, 1998; Bjerregaard and Smith, 1993; Curry, Ball, and Decker, 1996; Esbensen and Huizinga, 1993; Miller, 1992; Thornberry, 1998). Thus, two profiles merge into a social created reality: (1) gang members are primarily black and Latino; and (2) gang members self-report more criminal activity than non-gang members.

In response to this image of a new "urban predator" a large number of cities since the mid-1980s have created specialized gang units to support a "war on gangs" that will eliminate this alleged threat. As a society we are bombarded with a "law and order" view of gangs and their communities. The History Channel's "Gangland" has commercialized this criminal image with the help of law enforcement and gang member bravado. Police officers routinely recognize how such a war on gangs is hindered by traditional constitutional protections, but have developed support to create methods and tactics to sidestep disapproval; in essence gang suppression/oppression has become legitimated.

Police officers and those involved in gangs often occupy different social worlds. Nationwide, law enforcement continues to be white (80 percent) and male (90 percent) (Reaves and Hickman, 2004). Differences in age, class, race and ethnicity, and living location do not support an equal relationship between those who enforce the law and the individuals considered outlaws (i.e., gang members). Officer behavior and the reasons for the stop will shape urban youth demeanor, as will the historical relationship between police and minority communities. The key strategy for urban youth is to decrease interactions with law enforcement. Avoidance is important because both legal (majority of the time) and illegal behavior can result in a stop. In this article, I will provide an "urban youth of color" point of view when describing interactions between police and individuals considered gang members. I will explore how these interactions are oppressively unequal, yet legitimized and encouraged by dominant society.

Gangs and Their Policing

Gangs have achieved an almost mythical status through news media, movies, music, and portrayals from law enforcement. Yet, empirical evidence suggests that much of these portrayals may amount to nothing more than a moral panic. Klein (2004, 2007), who has studied gangs for over 40 years, found that most gang crime is minor; most gang activity is noncriminal; street gangs are social groups; street life becomes a part of gang culture; and the community context in which gangs arise is often ignored. He argued that most gang activity is mundane, and far from the excitement described by gang members or law enforcement (Klein, 1995). Vigil (2002, 2007) reported that most youth, even in the poorest neighborhoods, do not join gangs. Estimates are that approximately 4 to 14 percent of all urban youth join a gang and the duration of membership is often short. Moore (1978, 1991), who has conducted the longest ongoing field research with gangs (more than 15 years), described how barrio youth are cut off from the American dream, including equality, justice, and economic betterment. Most Americans will never experience this minority experience of failure with public institutions, and thus gangs, drugs, and prison have become normal in these segregated settings. Under 20 percent of her interviewees reported coming from "gang families" despite these gangs existing for more than 45 years at the time of the study. Moreover, the main activities of these gangs included hanging around and partying rather than chronic offending and violence. Sánchez-Jankowski's (1991, 2008) ten years of ethnographic research of gangs in three cities found that gangs do not represent a menace, but rather serve as a legitimate means to maximize security in poor neighborhoods. Brotherton and Barrios (2004) argue that urban youth struggle to create their own communities in a society that shows little inclination to meaningfully include them and instead the dominant framework focuses upon repressive techniques.

Contrary to ethnographic research data finding normal behavior for gang members and less prevalent involvement in criminal activity, the increased involvement of law enforcement in urban barrios and ghettos highlights a post-civil rights form of racism where myths are more important than reality. Justification of gang enforcement simply calls for a "kernel of truth" that some violent incident occurred and now *all* gang members are the problem. Such panics have occurred, to some degree, in daycare centers (de Young, 1998), with the legislation of drugs (Reinarman, 2003), and with marginalized groups in society (Cohen, 1980; McCorkle and Miethe, 2002; Zatz, 1987). Mainstream, white society offers support by encouraging more aggressive tactics disregarding how the segregated communities of color will be targeted. These repressive and oppressive strategies have been found by gang researchers to enhance the marginalization of poor minority communities. Werthman and Piliavin (1967, p. 57) described this as "ecological contamination." These researchers found that gang members and police occupy separate cultural and structural conditions. A mere perception of a gang neighborhood could infect many suspicious persons who lived there and subject these residents to police officers' discretion and to their power to investigate, which creates problems of law.

Researchers have tracked the growth of gang enforcement and specialized units targeting gangs (Huff and McBride, 1993; Katz, 2003; Katz and Webb, 2006; Klein, 1995, 2004; Needle and Stapleton, 1983; Spergel, 1995). Through a survey of 261 police departments, Klein (1995) found that intelligence gathering, crime investigation, and suppression were the most common police actions against gangs, and that many states had instituted increased consequences for gang-related crimes. Spergel (1995) agreed that a vigorous "lock-em-up" approach remained the key action of police departments, particularly in large cities with acknowledged gang problems. Since the 1980s, more than 360 gang units began operating nationwide to respond to the perceived and actual threat caused by gangs (Katz, 2001). Katz and Webb (2006), who studied gang units in four cities (Albuquerque, Inglewood, Las Vegas, and Phoenix) by interviewing police officers and participating in ride-alongs, found many units lacking in governing policies, procedures, rules, and training. The gang units' insufficient knowledge of gangs often led to officers engaging in prohibited street enforcement tactics and falsifying official reports. Most gang unit problems originated from a decoupled organizational style, where they operated separately from the police department. Operating autonomously from the police department is thought to have played a role in facilitating the illegal activities of the Los Angeles CRASH unit and Chicago gang unit. The two researchers encouraged efforts to control gangs but advised that such efforts would require adjusting current forms of gang enforcement to be more effective.

Analyzing the impact of policing and communities of color by using gang labels is enhanced by the incorporation of the work of Erving Goffman and Elijah Anderson. Goffman (1959, 1963, 1982) analyzed interactions as a type of performance. He described how first impressions shape subsequent treatment. Maintaining face is deemed highly important for each actor and thus the best way to prevent role threats is to avoid contact. Impression management can provide structure to social encounters. There are individuals who are treated as stigmatized in society due to their race and/or behavior. This differential impact on an identity can reduce the life chances of stigmatized groups and such negative labeling can be concentrated within certain neighborhoods. Anderson (1990) reported how black men in public are perceived and treated as predators. Individuals within the community are unable to determine law-abiding black males and others. Race becomes a master status where in a context of racism is labeled deviant in public places (Hughes, 1945). According to Anderson, urban youth use images of dangerousness to prevent others from threatening their safety. This aggressive presentation of self receives peer approval and reduces victimization. Goffman provides a guide for analyzing interactions and Anderson offers a framework for exploring these interactions with urban youth of color.

My study of urban youth interactions with police due to gang enforcement is developed from two different cities: Ogden, Utah, and Denver, Colorado. Both cities have similar levels of poverty and economic, ethnic, and racial segregation. The urban sections of the city, barrios and ghettos, have higher levels of socioeconomic inequality and higher concentrations of blacks and Latinos. In this chapter I examine how young people in Latino neighborhoods perceive the legitimacy of police. In doing so, I discuss how the use of violence by police maintains a hostile relationship between communities of color and law enforcement, and compare the control of space (i.e., urban barrios and ghettos) and racial and ethnic groups to previous historical attempts to eliminate marginalized groups.

Methods

The research reported in this article is based on my life experiences with gangs as both a member and ex-gang member (1992–2010), my research of gangs in Ogden, Utah (1997–2006) and Denver, Colorado (2000–2006). Ethnographic methods allowed me the opportunity to associate with gang members, associates, and urban youth in the community and directly observe police stops. I used ethnographic research methods such as direct observation, casual interaction, semi-structured interviews, introspection, photography, and videotaping to collect these data.

I observed over 200 police stops (47 of these stops included Gang Units) in all areas of these two cities for three years. Most of my time involved patrolling nightlife areas such as cruising boulevards and minority communities because this is where most police activity was concentrated. The use of police scanners helped me travel to the segregated white suburbs when an infrequent stop was made. Observation of stops along cruising boulevards allowed me to witness a wide variety of racial and ethnic group encounters with the police. Overwhelmingly, these areas were adjacent to communities of color which aided my ability to patrol both areas. All of the observed gang unit stops included Latinos, followed by blacks and Asians. I used this information to compare urban youth experiences with police officers and the media. Observing the inequality of policing was enhanced by my ethnographic walks and study of the five highest concentrated black, Latino, and white census tracts.

My participant observation was supplemented with 123 interviews: 64 gang members, 12 ex-gang members, 38 gang associates, and nine youth who had no affiliation with gangs. My interviewees included 102 males and 21 females who were primarily Latino (78 percent) or black (11 percent). Ninety-seven percent of my interviews were with members of racial and ethnic minority groups. These interviews reflect associations with 20 different gangs in two different cities. All of these individuals have at one time or another lived or continued to live in the barrio or ghetto areas of these cities. Ogden is a small city of 77,226 residents located within a mid-sized metropolitan area of slightly more than a million people. Denver is a mid-sized city of 554,636 residents located within a large-sized metropolitan area of more than two million people. Twenty-nine to 34 percent of residents are Latino.

Targeting Minority Neighborhoods with the Gang Label

Regular patrol officers often did not know how to distinguish gang members from non-gang members and thus primarily considered the entire urban youth of color population as possible suspects for membership. Gang Units utilized the "duck" profile for determining gang membership: "If it looks like a duck, quacks like a duck, then it's probably a duck." This unsophisticated form of profiling differentiated urban youth based on appearances, but because many youth dressed in a similar way it made it difficult to separate members from non-members. Discerning gang membership is not always easy for urban youth either. Individuals appearing (i.e., clothing, tattoos, vehicles) to belong to a rival gang, along with their family members and friends, can often enhance perceptions of danger. Many urban youth appear to enjoy this dangerous image until confronted by a rival gang, when quickly denying membership can hopefully de-escalate a potential violent encounter.

Before joining a gang, I associated with a total of four gangs, of which three groups were allies and one was a rival. One evening, I was hanging out with two individuals who were associates of the rival gang. As I drove my car into a fast-food parking lot, my friends and I were quickly approached by 11 young men excited to physically attack us. Quickly and pleadingly we announced that we were not gang members and after several minutes of questioning one of the individuals who confronted us was about to verify the accuracy of these claims. Thus rival gangs often mirror the police in providing a blanket level of suspicion toward the entire group of individuals until information is obtained proving or disproving membership. There is however a difference for members who belong to a particular gang, and then it is clearly known who has been jumped in and who still maintains an associate or outside role to the gang. Associates are potential candidates for inclusion into the gang but for various reasons have not been formally initiated.

Gang members and urban youth often shared a similar background and living situation, while on the contrary the police and urban youth are often direct opposites. Structural issues of race and ethnicity were more than likely replicated in such unequal interactions.

In Ogden, Utah, the entire police department of 140 sworn officers is almost all white, whereas two-thirds of the listed gang members are Latino. In Denver, Colorado, one-third of the 1,550 sworn personnel but more than 90 percent of the listed gang members are considered non-white. Such differential numbers in regard to racial and ethnic diversity have played a role in enhancing divisions between the police and minority communities. In addition, as reported in Denver, several police officers of color are often accused of being more racist and violent than their white counterparts by many community members. Thus, reducing the historical division will more than likely also require structural changes that go beyond diversity initiatives. Not all police officers were the same in attitude, demeanor, or use of discretion. The variable types of officers was clearly reported during interviews and while observing police interactions with urban youth. Some officers were considered friendly, professional, and attempting to do a good job of enforcing the law. Indeed, several interviewees considered police important in the community to stop criminal activity. On the other hand, participants saw another segment of the policing population as perceiving themselves as superior to urban youth of color and did everything possible to reinforce this dominate and controlling personality. These officers were despised and hated.

Interacting with Suspected Gang Members

Urban youth claimed that if you are black or brown you will always be treated as a crime suspect or gang member. Some behaviors can enhance this profiling such as style of dress and associating with more than one individual in public. Denying gang membership often carried little support when an officer's "duck" profile was met. This made interactions between police and urban minority youth tense because the origin for the stop was often vague and the type of officer confronted unknown. Urban youth believed that the police will often attempt to incite or provoke an incident in order to justify increased harassment, searches, and arrests. The overall goal for urban youth is to avoid the police. When this is not possible they try to be respectful and to remain silent.

Intelligence gathering was a key component of police suppression tactics. Donner (1980) reported that surveillance conducted with people and groups was justified on preventive grounds against violence. However, police intelligence gathering has allowed the labeling of entire racial and ethnic groups, especially men, as gang members (Durán, 2009a, 2009b; Johnson, 1993; Lopez, 1993). Once people land on such lists, it becomes more likely that their future acts will be discovered, prosecuted, and dealt with punitively (Anderson, 1990). Gang lists in Denver and Ogden do not require criminal activity for admission and they remain in the file for at least five years. For police officers to create these lists, urban youth were repeatedly asked to what gang they belonged. According to the police department gang protocol, people who admitted gang membership satisfied the first and primary requirement for being placed on a gang list, yet most people denied membership. The police used different tactics to discover gang involvement, ranging from talking nonchalantly to coercion. Most respondents interviewed who were not involved with gangs believed that officers suspected them of lying in denying membership. Officers would search for clues by asking individuals to pull up their shirts, looking for tattoos, or asking what high school they attended, to denote possible gang membership. Tone, a 28-year-old "convict" who chose to stay away from a gang lifestyle, said:

> They [police] would throw a couple different gang names at me and ask me which one I belonged to and I would say none. But they would always look like they didn't believe me if you didn't tell them what they wanted to hear.

Anne, a 24-year-old gang associate from Ogden, said:

> I was pregnant and me and my friend were cruising and we were just sitting there parked and the cops came over and a couple other people were parked there and they were in a gang but they said we couldn't be loitering around there. And right away they were yelling at us what gang were we in. I said, "I'm not in a gang," and he said, "Don't lie," like yelling at me, "don't lie." I was like, "I'm not in a gang." And then he asked, "Why you around all of these gang members if you're not in a gang?" I was pregnant and a girl hanging out with another girl and so it made me pretty mad. And frustrated too because I kept telling him but he wouldn't let it go. He kept saying, "You're in a gang! Tell me!"

Although Anne was associating with gang members, she was not a member. A large number of people in the barrio know someone in a gang, but this does not make them a member. Individual gang membership created a stereotype that spread to everyone living in the barrio of this particular racial or ethnic background. Police officers could then use the gang label to legitimate all interactions with the urban minority community. These labels were then maintained by the presumption of clear and precise policies and guidelines that countered all forms of legal challenges and the negation of complaints, yet no one outside the gang unit had access to the police files to verify its accuracy.

Others whose family members were involved in gangs were often treated as members of the gang. Monique, a 22-year-old from Ogden who had two brothers involved in gangs, mentioned how the police automatically assumed she was a member and treated her poorly. Lucita, a 25-year-old associate with a traditional gang who had two brothers who were previously involved in gangs, concurred with this negative treatment when she said:

> For a while there I was getting pulled over a lot. They assumed I was affiliated with so and so, they see you one time with this one person, therefore you have information that you are withholding from them or they think you know the whereabouts of an individual. Stuff like that. You get harassed and you get them on your back you can't get them off. They are on you constantly and they will pull you over for anything. I think they put the word out, look for this vehicle with this person driving.

Lucita in fact wished the police were friendlier with her and the Latino community. A higher level of trust and mutual support could provide the ideal that the police were actually here to protect and serve.

Frequent disrespect from the police was unanimously reported by more than 97 percent of the urban youth interviewed, and they took little time to recall instances of verbal and body language abuse. Although Mastrofski, Resig, and McCluskey (2002) reported that police disrespect was very rare (4 percent of all police stops) almost half of these incidents were unprovoked. The police attempted to dominate these interactions with the power of the law, authority, and entrusted discretion. Mack-one, a 24-year-old ex-gang associate from Denver, said:

> They treated me bad. They thought I was a gang member. They didn't really do any physical harm to me but, verbally they definitely thought of me as a lower human being.

Although acting civil and cordial may not be a requirement for policing, these stops produced feelings of anger, distrust, and hopelessness, particularly when police could do whatever they wished and get away with it. Everyone interviewed could cite examples of being treated disrespectfully and then simply told to go on their way once officers found no reason to take the stop further (the majority of the time). Police officers' "fishing expeditions" would not always pay off. Anne, the 24-year-old gang associate from Ogden, said:

> They're dicks; they don't care, and they don't care if you're a girl. I had one of the gang cops search me, and I know that is against the law. Not search me but pat me down, like really pat me down! I know they are not supposed to do that, and I told him, "You can't pat me down." I'm like, "You're supposed to have a female officer." He was all, "You don't tell me what to do." You know, just their little attitude, they'll put you down to your face. You're nothing, you're a piece of shit. They totally don't have any respect for anybody who is a gang member or who they think is a gang member. I don't know how they choose the gang task force but they don't seem to understand anything about gangs. All they focus on is getting them off the street and into jail. It's awful.

Smiley, a 23-year-old ex-gang associate, said:

> They treat you like you are lower than everybody you know, like you are a bad person, like you are always committing felonies or that you are involved in crime. They just treat you with no respect. They just treat you like you are scum or something, like you are a bad person.

These two interactions between Mexican American community members and the police highlight the perception that the police are attempting to gather intelligence to bring individuals down and disrespect them during the process. Police officials applied the gang label primarily to Latinos and blacks, thus increasing the likelihood that the only people who could be perceived as non-gang members were whites. Gang intelligence gathering was blatantly discriminatory when Gang Unit officers would stop countless Latinos and blacks and leave groups of whites alone. Conducting sweeps on groups of white youth and justifying it with gang reasoning had the potential to put Gang Unit funding and continued operations in jeopardy. Police officers' repeated profiling based on stereotypical perceptions and coercive intelligence on urban youth justified increased funding, increased gang legislation, and the movement to relocate greater numbers of this population to the penitentiary.

Interacting with Confirmed Gang Members

Gang-labeled urban youth, those who were on the gang list or completely meeting the duck profile, were approached differently because they were seen and treated as constant criminals even when abiding by the law. Police perceptions shaped gang membership as a "master status" that combines ascribed and achieved statuses with the belief of lifelong gang involvement (Hughes, 1945). Changing this image was very difficult for gang members, particularly those attempting to leave the gang lifestyle. D-loc thought gang members were treated three times worse than non-gang members by the police. Based on my research and experiences, D-loc's claim was supported by my observations of gang members encountering a greater frequency of stops and increased levels of scrutiny. Many police stops of gang members would begin with ordering these urban youth out of their vehicle and telling them to put their hands up in the air or lie face down on the ground. The officers drew their guns more frequently on gang-confirmed individuals than others and attempted to investigate assumed gang involvement and planned activities. Law enforcement stops of gang members held a greater potential for abusive conduct because they often took the continuum of force to occasionally require fighting violence with violence. To reduce the potential danger to officers, a gang stop was more than likely to proceed in the following order: (1) Stop. (2) Order suspect out of the vehicle at gunpoint. Tell suspect to raise both hands in the air and walk backwards. (3) Frisk upper and lower body: this can be done with the suspect standing up or being told to kneel or lie face down on the ground. Possibly place in handcuffs and have sit on the curb. This will often be done for each individual in the car. (4) Question each suspect about guilt and participation in gang and crime. (5) Run background check for warrants on each individual. Take photographs of tattoos and ask suspects to take pictures throwing gang signs. These types of stops are frustrating and annoying to encounter. For gang members, it becomes part of life and you simply "suck-it-up," but let some middle- or upper-class youth go through this routine and they will quickly counter with formal complaints that get acknowledged. In the barrios and ghettos, such complaints are ignored.

Cyclone, a 25-year-old ex-gang member and ex-prison inmate, said:

> I got labeled as a known violent gang member and never been caught of a gang crime with anybody and it's odd because they label you as that and it's not a good label because it sticks with you for life. When I get pulled over it doesn't matter who I am with they pull me out of the car and pat me down. Every time. I mean they run my name, the NCI report comes up that says I am a violent person and they wait for three or four more cops to show up and then they get me out of the car just to check me. While I am with my family, my kids, I am getting discriminated. They've embarrass me in huge way with the people I'm with. They will tell the people I'm with I'm a bad influence or I'm trouble.

Cyclone was adamant that the police have consistently tried to hurt him and also have not provided personal protection to prevent his victimization from rival gangs. Raul, an 18-year-old ex-gang member from Denver, said:

They [police] mess with you all of the time. Like if you are a gang member they be stopping you all of the time. Checking to see if you have any weapons, some of these police officers are racist, they think we are all violent and do bad crimes but I think we are different. One time they stopped us and they were taking off our shirts and checking if we had any gang tattoos. Writing things on their computer, about when they stopped you, what gang tattoos you have. They even took pictures of me one time, and I don't know why.

Raul adamantly denied the police viewpoint when describing his friends and how it differed greatly from the violent and criminal projection given by law enforcement.

Respondents interviewed claimed that both Denver's and Ogden's police departments often used excessive physical force. Although researchers for the Bureau of Justice Statistics (Greenfeld, Langan, and Smith, 1999) reported that the use of force occurred in under 1 percent of all encounters with citizens during the year of their survey, at least 34 percent of my respondents had experienced physical abuse one or more times. Sixty-five percent of this misconduct occurred during an arrest and in an isolated area during evening hours. Individuals were more likely to be victimized by police in impoverished black and Latino neighborhoods. The full level of abuse and misconduct in these cities has not been exposed in the same way as the infamous Rampart CRASH division case with detailed investigations and hearings. Nevertheless, several of my respondents were adamant that officers similar to the character played by Denzel Washington in the movie *Training Day* exist in the Denver and Ogden police departments.

Problematic urban conditions and minority presence have resulted in police violence being used proactively rather than simply reacting to a criminal threat (Jacobs and O'Brien, 1998; Terrill and Resig, 2003). The Latino and black communities recognized that a simple stop or interaction with the police had a variety of outcomes that were seen as legally permissible, but that law enforcement officers were not going to treat whites living in their racially segregated suburbs with the same type of aggression. Holmes (2000) reported that there are reliable data to conclude that southwestern Latinos are targets of police brutality based on his study of civil rights complaints filed with the U.S. Department of Justice. Furthermore, Kane (2002) reported that a growth in the percentage of the Latino population increased police misconduct.

The captain of the Denver Gang Unit assured me that many policies and protections were instituted to prevent misconduct from happening within his city. Nevertheless, two Denver gang officers were charged for not logging at least 80 pieces of drug evidence into the police department property bureau after making numerous arrests and issuing tickets for marijuana possession and paraphernalia (Vaughan, 2000). One of these officers was accused of harassing and brutalizing gang members within the Denver area, and this may be the reason he was shot by a suspected gang member during a questionable traffic stop (Ritter, 2003, Decision Letter; 2004 Interviews). The alleged gang member was also shot and killed during this incident. Denver had a high rate of police shootings; from 1980 to 2008 231 people were shot and 103 people killed by the Denver Police Department.

In another Denver case, an off-duty gang officer was driving home late at night after getting off work and became involved in an incident in which he fired six shots at a Salvadorian immigrant, who died at the scene. Forensic evidence contradicted the officer's testimony about whether the immigrant was holding a gun (Lowe, 2001). An ex-military and highly decorated African American man filed a racial profiling complaint against the Gang Unit. He described how several gang officers stopped him without cause, crashed into his wife's car, and held him down at gunpoint while directing lewd remarks at his wife (Lindsay, 2004). Nevertheless, the Gang Unit claimed they had few complaints. Rodney, an African American and Latino resident who was a gang associate from Denver, told me:

> I wish every gang member would actually report the abuse that they would go through by the Denver Police Department. Then we would have a better picture of what the role is that unit plays. But the gang members don't feel like they have a right to report when they have been beat up. If they actually took the time to document this stuff we would actually see the Denver Police is putting in more work than anybody. They function as a gang. [They said they had low amounts of complaints that come from that unit?] They said they have a low amount of complaints; yeah they do, because the people they are attacking are scared to complain. A lot of times, I don't even want to say scared, they don't feel empowered to complain. They feel like they are a gang member so they just have to deal with what they got.

The Ogden Gang Unit was the least prepared for dealing with "harassment" practices by their officers because their white officers were rarely formally challenged or questioned about how they operated. Therefore, the Ogden Gang Unit practiced a higher number of profile stops than Denver. Jay, a 27-year-old ex-Ogden gang member, said:

> I think that some of their methods and tactics are a little on the borderline of police brutality, or excessive force. One of my friends who works at the police department is in close contact with the Gang Unit, told me that this one officer hates little gang members. He is one of the head guys and has been in there for like 27 years or so, and he specifically hates little gang bangers you know. He calls them on whether it be a fist fight, a weapons fight, whatever. He will physically challenge them, you know, you bring your stick and I'll bring mine. I guess they figure they got to do what they got to do.

Jay saw the need in the community for better policing. This drove him to continue pursuing the possibility of one day becoming a police officer himself.

Several community members challenged Ogden Gang Unit officers for their role in inciting a riot with about 75 urban youth of color at a hip-hop concert. The officers had received a call that alcohol was present and, when they attempted to enter the building, security officials denied them entrance. As a result, several people were beaten with police batons and charged with felony rioting (Gurrister, 2003). After this case was turned over to the FBI for investigation, one of the key officers suspected of brutality began to target the individual who filed the complaint (Gurrister, 2004a). Several individuals in Ogden have attempted to take their complaints against the Ogden Police Department to court. Such actions, they believe, have resulted in retaliation. In 2010, the city of Ogden passed the first gang injunction in the state of Utah against 485 individuals listed as a member of one gang. The injunction makes it a class B misdemeanor to associate with members listed as part of the gang, sets a curfew of 11 p.m., and denies possession of alcohol or guns. The injunction was not set to a particular neighborhood as were other injunctions but rather the entire 27 square miles of the city. These increased law enforcement powers have only further encouraged police officers to continue their level of racial profiling and harassment. The American Civil Liberties Union has been attempting to legally challenge these actions in Utah's Supreme Court.

Human Rights Watch (1998, p. 2) argued that

> race continues to play a central role in police brutality in the United States. Indeed, despite gains in many areas since the civil rights movement of the 1950s and 1960s, one area that has been stubbornly resistant to change has been the treatment afforded racial minorities by the police.

Their research involving 14 cities reported that habitually brutal officers, usually a small percentage on the force, might receive repeated complaints but were usually protected by other officers and poor internal police investigations. These data mirrored the city of Denver, where it was discovered that a small number of officers accounted for the largest proportion of shootings. Cyclone, the 25-year-old ex-gang member and ex-prison inmate, said:

> I've been beaten by cops before. I was running from the police and I was drunk. I wrecked a car and I got out and started to run and I noticed there were five different counties of cops. There were cops from every district surrounding me. I laid down on the ground and the cop that jumped on me started punching me in back of the head. I went into County [Jail] and let them know that I was having serious migraines and I showed them the bumps on my head. They took a report and that's all that was ever said. They didn't do anything to the officer that whupped my ass. I got charged with resisting arrest and was tied to the bumper of a car. [How many times do you think he hit you in the back of the head?] Probably about four of five. [What were you doing?] I was in handcuffs on my stomach while his knee was in my back, and the other cops were watching. They know something happened. If I wasn't in cuffs when he was hitting me I would have defended myself. They have the reports on the bumps on my head, severe handcuff marks on my arms; I couldn't feel my left hand for nearly an hour after they took the cuffs off.

Cyclone did his best to stay employed and help raise his children in a setting where he believed the police preferred that he was dead or incarcerated.

Several of the interviewees also believed that undocumented immigrants were treated worse by police. Mirandé (1987) suggested that immigrants were especially vulnerable because they lacked resources and familiarity with the justice system. Immigrants also reported fewer instances of abuse because they feared deportation. Nite Owl, an undocumented 17-year-old gang member, said:

> One time I was walking, and they [police] told me stop, and I stopped, and they didn't tell me to turn around or anything they just came up and tackled me. They hit me two times with their stick and put the cuffs on my hands. Maybe they could say I'm sorry we messed up or something, but they didn't say nothing like that. They just sorry, it wasn't you. I said it wasn't me and they said shut up, so I didn't say anything.

Nite Owl viewed his situation as being in the wrong place at the wrong time, but there was nothing he could have done to prevent his receiving a severe beating. Nationwide, and in both Denver and Ogden, U.S. Immigration and Customs Enforcement have worked with Gang Units to launch raids against undocumented immigrants who are allegedly involved with gangs. As of September 7, 2010, Immigration and Customs Enforcement claims to have removed 176,736 "criminal aliens" from the United States with this program, which began in 2006 (http://www.ice.gov/pi/nr/1009/100928denver.htm). Despite the reason for the raid being for criminality and gang membership, never was a separate court hearing instituted to determine the accuracy of either claim.

Conclusion

In an ideal world, gangs are the bad guys and the cops are the good guys. But in this social world of urban neighborhoods of color, the roles are often reversed. Gangs often serve as the social and protective group in the neighborhood whereas the police are seen as acting as a gang. Such contradictory roles do not lend themselves to better community and police relationships. My previous publications have focused on how this labeling occurs (Durán, 2009a) and how the community responds to these abuses (Durán, 2009b). This article has concentrated on the interactions between police and gangs. I did not find that Gang Unit officers or law enforcement officials were incorrect in all criminal stops, but rather the majority of gang enforcement stops were predicated on non-criminal activity and included more non-gang members. The barrio residents were not anti-police. They *were* against the profiling and demeaning treatment. The end result of aggressive differential policing was greater division between the barrio and law enforcement.

Bonilla-Silva (2003) and Feagin (2010) have argued that whites have developed powerful explanations to justify racial and ethnic inequality. One of these explanations involves the ability to use agency (choice) to supersede the power of structure. Many individuals may argue that these urban youth get what they deserve for "choosing" to dress like, associate, or belong to gangs. Although this article did not focus on the activities of gangs or the structural reasons that have shaped their creation, such viewpoints are the dominant propaganda disseminated and accepted for mainstream suburban residents who live outside of the barrio and ghetto. Yes, some individual gang members commit atrocious acts and deserve to be held accountable, as do rogue officers who remain protected by departments operating under a code of silence. The explanation of choices, however, does not get to the root of this inequality and the repeated patterns of friction that maintain forms of polarization.

Other individuals may argue that the individuals interviewed in my study are lying; that upstanding police officers do not harass or mistreat youth, and that responses of law enforcement are controlled by legal guidelines of reasonable suspicion and probable cause. Urban youth are more than likely acting suspiciously to bring such legal oversight in their direction. These mainstream arguments have in fact encouraged such targeted law enforcement practices to continue unabated. "Truth" from members of minority groups is regularly dismissed in police departments where claims of misconduct are rarely substantiated.

As long as an officer can demonstrate five gang members stopped out of 50 in this population, then it is good police work to prevent future criminality. It does not really matter if standards of reasonable suspicion or probable cause become stretched to include legal behavior. Most of these urban youth will never file a complaint or plead not guilty. Most will take a plea bargain or simply accept their treatment as routine. Those lowest in social power rarely possess the legal recourse or the professional networks to stop such treatment. I was continually amazed from my interviews and observations of police how legitimized such aggressive law enforcement has become. I have wondered where the lawyers or advocacy groups were to change this structural inequality.

Despite mainstream white racial frames of "choice" and "untruthfulness," there were a significant number of observed patterns of unequal treatment from police toward racial and ethnic minority group members living in segregated urban environments. The most powerful and relevant critique I have seen on ghetto neighborhoods and oppressive treatment was not explored in the United States but rather in Germany where ghettos were created to segregate Jews from the rest of the population. In the long run these ghettos were replaced with concentration camps. In the United States, prisons are the result of segregated neighborhoods, and the aggressive law enforcement and under-protection from victimization makes this a reality. There is no doubt that issues of context play a significant role in Denver and Ogden. Urban barrios and ghettos across the United States most likely exist on a continuum of worst to slightly worse than average. The community in southern New Mexico, where I live now, has negative conflicts with the police but at a much lower rate than Denver and Ogden. Durkheim described the coming together of individuals as *sui generis:* a creation unique unto its own. There is no doubt that a structural conflict exists between police and urban youth of color. As long as these structural inequalities exist in society, racial and ethnic minorities will continue to experience differential treatment from law enforcement and their voices of opposition will be ignored. And the gang label will continue to serve its purpose.

Critical Thinking

Without a doubt Durán's study and his interpretation of what his participants revealed is affected by his race and his former participation as a gang member; however, we should not take this to mean that his findings are wrong. When reading this article, think about how the level of rapport and understanding with gang members allowed Durán to get them to open up to him. How do you think the social and cultural distance between police and citizens contributes to problems? Do you think it would help if police departments made concerted efforts to hire police from the communities they patrol? In short, is diversity among police a good thing for improving community relations?

References

Anderson, E. (1990). *Streetwise: Race, class, and change in an urban community*. Chicago, IL: University of Chicago Press.

Battin, S.R., Karl, G.H., Abott, R.D., Catalano, R.C., and Hawkins, D.J. (1988). The contribution of gang membership to delinquency beyond delinquent friends. *Criminology*, 36, 93–115.

Bjerregaard, B. and Smith, C. (1993). Gender differences in gang participation, delinquency, and substance use. *Journal of Quantitative Criminology*, 9, 329–355.

Bonilla-Silva, E. (2001). *White-supremacy and racism in the post-civil rights era*. Boulder, CO: Lynn Rienner.

Brotherton, D.C. and Barrios, L. (2004). *The Almighty Latin King and Queen nation: Street politics and the transformation of a New York City gang*. New York: Columbia University Press.

Cohen, S. (1980). *Folk devils and moral panics: The creation of the mods and rockers*. New York: St. Martin's Press.

Curry, G.D., Ball, R.A., and Decker, S.H. (1996). *Estimating the national scope of gang crime from law enforcement data*. Research in Brief. Washington, DC: U.S. Department of Justice, Office of Justice Programs, National Institute of Justice. NCJ 161477.

de Young, M. (1998). Another look at moral panics: The case of satanic day care centers. *Deviant Behavior*, 19, 257–278.

Donner, F.J. (1980). *The age of surveillance: The aims and methods of America's political intelligence system*. New York: Alfred A. Knopf.

Durán, R.J. (2009a). Legitimated oppression: Inner-city Mexican American experiences with police gang enforcement. *Journal of Contemporary Ethnography*, 38, 143–168.

Durán, R.J. (2009b). Over-inclusive gang enforcement and urban resistance: A comparison between two cities. *Social Justice: A Journal of Crime, Conflict and World Order*, 36, 82–101.

Esbensen, F. and Huizinga, D. (1993). Gangs, drugs, and delinquency in a survey of urban youth. *Criminology*, 31, 565–589.

Feagin, J.R. (2010). *The white racial frame: Centuries of racial framing and counter-framing*. New York: Routledge.

Goffman, E. (1959). *The presentation of self in everyday life*. Garden City, NY: Anchor.

Goffman, E. (1963). *Stigma: Notes on the management of spoiled identity*. New York: Simon & Schuster.

Goffman, E. (1982). *Interaction ritual: Essays on face-to-face behavior*. New York: Pantheon.

Greenfeld, L.A., Langan, P.A., and Smith, S.K. (1999). *Police use of force: Collection of national data*. Washington, DC: U.S. Department of Justice, Bureau of Justice Statistics and National Institute of Justice. NCJ 165040.

Gurrister, T. (2003). Police tactics queried: Union station case builds. *Standard Examiner*, October 23.

Gurrister, T. (2004a). FBI probing Ogden incident. *Standard Examiner*, February 22.

Gurrister, T. (2004b). Officer accused of payback arrest. *Standard Examiner*, April 1.

Holmes, M.D. (2000). Minority threat and police brutality: Determinants of civil rights criminal complaints in U.S. municipalities. *Criminology*, 38, 343–367.

Huff, C.R. and McBride, W. (1993). Gangs and the police. In A.P. Goldstein and C.R. Huff (eds), *Gang intervention handbook* (pp. 401–415). Champaign, IL: Research Press.

Hughes, E.C. (1945). Dilemmas and contradictions of status. *American Journal of Sociology*, 50, 353–359.

Human Rights Watch. (1998). *Shielded from justice: Police brutality and accountability in the United States*. New York: Human Rights Watch.

Jacobs, D. and O'Brien, R.M. (1998). The determinants of deadly force: A structural analysis of police violence. *American Journal of Sociology*, 103, 837–862.

Johnson, D. (1993). 2 out of 3 young black men in Denver are on gang suspect list. *New York Times*, December 11.

Kane, R.J. (2002). The social ecology of police misconduct. *Criminology*, 40, 867–896.

Katz, C.M. (2001). The establishment of a police gang unit: Organizational and environmental factors. *Criminology*, 39, 37–73.

Katz, C.M. (2003). Issues in the production and dissemination of gang statistics: An ethnographic study of a large midwestern police gang unit. *Crime and Delinquency*, 49, 485–516.

Katz, C.M. and Webb, V.J. (2006). *Policing gangs in America*. New York: Cambridge University Press.

Klein, M.W. (1995). *The American street gang: Its nature, prevalence, and control*. New York: Oxford University Press.

Klein, M.W. (2004). *Gang cop: The words and ways of officer Paco Domingo*. Walnut Creek, CA: AltaMira.

Klein, M.W. (2007). *Chasing after street gangs: A forty-year journey*. Upper Saddle River, NJ: Pearson Prentice Hall.

Lindsay, S. (2004). Police acted "inappropriately." *Rocky Mountain News*, April 21.

Lopez, C. (1993). List brands 2 of 3 young black men. *Denver Post*, December 5.

Lowe, P. (2001). Panel, police see different theories in glass shards: Glass, gun and blood focus forensic battle. *Rocky Mountain News*, November 24.

Mastrofski, S.D., Resig, M.D., and McCluskey, J.D. (2002). Police disrespect toward the public: An encounter-based analysis. *Criminology*, 40, 515–551.

McCorkle, R.C. and Miethe, T.D. (2002). *Panic: The social construction of the street gang problem.* Upper Saddle River, NJ: Prentice Hall.

Miller, W.B. (1992). Revised from 1982. *Crime by youth gangs and groups in the United States.* Washington, DC: U.S. Department of Justice, Office of Justice Programs, Office of Juvenile Justice and Delinquency Prevention. NCJ 156221.

Mirandé, A. (1987). *Gringo justice.* Notre Dame, IN: University of Notre Dame Press.

Moore, J.W. (1978). *Homeboys: Gangs, drugs, and prison in the barrios of Los Angeles.* Philadelphia, PA: Temple University Press.

Moore, J.W. (1991). *Going down to the barrio: Homeboys and homegirls in change.* Philadelphia, PA: Temple University Press.

National Youth Gang Survey. (2009). National Youth Gang Survey Analysis. Retrieved [September 30, 2010] from http://www.nationalgangcenter.gov/Survey-Analysis.

Needle, J.A. and Stapleton, W.V. (1983). *Police handling of youth gangs.* Reports of the National Juvenile Justice Assessment Centers. U.S. Department of Justice.

Reaves, B.A. and Hickman, M.J. (2004). *Law Enforcement Management and Administrative Statistics, 2000: Data for individual state and local agencies with 100 or more officers.* Bureau of Justice Statistics.

Reinarman, C. (2003). The social construction of drug scares. In P.A. Adler and P. Adler, *Constructions of deviance: Social power, context, and interaction* (pp. 137–148). Belmont, CA: Wadsworth/Thomson Learning.

Ritter, B. (2003). Investigation of the shooting death of Anthony Ray Jefferson, March 7. Available at: http://www.denverda.org/Decision_Letters/02Jefferson.htm.

Sánchez-Jankowski, M. (1991). *Islands in the street: Gangs and American urban society.* Berkeley, CA: University of California Press.

Sánchez-Jankowski, M. (2008). *Cracks in the pavement: Social change and resilience in poor neighborhoods.* Berkeley, CA: University of California Press.

Spergel, I.A. (1995). *The youth gang problem: A community approach.* New York: Oxford University Press.

Terrill, W. and Resig, M.D. (2003). Neighborhood context and police use of force. *Journal of Research in Crime and Delinquency*, 40, 291–321.

Thornberry, T.P. (1998). Membership in youth gangs and involvement in serious and violent offending. In R. Loeber and D.P. Farrington (eds), *Serious and Violent Offenders: Risk Factors and Successful Interventions.* Thousand Oaks, CA: Sage Publications.

Vaughan, K. (2000). Charges filed against two cops veteran gang officers accused of destroying evidence in "at least" 80 criminal cases. *Rocky Mountain News*, Section Local, 20, July 20.

Vigil, J.D. (2002). *A rainbow of gangs: Street cultures in the mega-city.* Austin, TX: University of Texas Press.

Vigil, J.D. (2007). *The projects: Gang and non-gang families in East Los Angeles.* Austin, TX: University of Texas Press.

Werthman, C. and Piliavin, I. (1967). Gang members and the police. In *The police: Six sociological essays.* ed. D. Bordua. New York: John Wiley & Sons.

Zatz, M.S. (1987). Chicano youth gangs and crime: The creation of a moral panic. *Contemporary Crisis*, 11, 129–158.

8

The Role of Law Enforcement in Making Sense of the Unimaginable

Paul B. Stretesky, Tara O'Connor Shelley, Michael J. Hogan, and N. Prabha Unnithan

<u>Abstract</u>: *Paul Stretesky and colleagues sought to understand how the families of murder victims whose case has turned cold make sense of the crime and view the detectives assigned to the case. Using interviews with family members of murder victims (e.g., parents, siblings, spouses, children, aunts, uncles, grandparents, and friends of the victims) the authors discover that family members consider frequent and productive communication with law enforcement personnel to be important in their quest to make sense of the events, but such communication seldom occurs. The majority of participants think that communication is sporadic, information is inadequate or erroneous, and that police have given up on the investigation. Participants interpret the decrease in communication as a symbol for the way police trivialize the murder and the well-being of family members. Many participants assume that police think that the case does not warrant a proper investigation because of officers' prejudices against characteristics of the victims. These participants claim that because of the victim's race, religion, sexual orientation, profession, prior behavior, affiliations, or habits, officers are unwilling to launch an adequate investigation.*

Every day I do hurt. I hurt every day. Every day I do. My whole life has changed. I'm just existing. I am not living. I think once they find out who hurt my son, maybe I can start living again. I just get up and I just go. I'm not living right now. I'm just goin' through the motions, really, to be honest with you. You know, once they find who hurt my son, maybe I can start living again.

(Mother of an unsolved murder victim)

Colorado law enforcement recorded 151 murders in 2008. National data suggest that approximately one-third of these homicides will remain unsolved or unresolved for more than a year. According to the Families of Homicide Victims and Missing Persons Inc., there are more than 1,500 "cold-case" murders in Colorado that date back to 1970. Our research draws upon the perceptions of the families and friends of cold-case homicide victims to determine how they see their interactions with law enforcement to better understand how those interactions may assist or hinder bereavement. Throughout this research we define the family and friends of unresolved and unsolved homicides as "co-victims" (Hertz et al., 2005).

While grieving is always a difficult process, homicide co-victims often suffer from what mental health specialists refer to as complicated grief—grief made even more difficult by the traumatic nature of the loss. The ability of co-victims to make sense of what has happened to their loved one can determine how they grieve, how they see themselves, and how they see others in a post-loss world. We argue that the grieving process can be compromised in cases where murders go unsolved for an extended period. This is true because unsolved murder cases are characterized by ongoing uncertainty, fear, and intense anger, leaving co-victims with little information and, eventually, little hope of ever making sense of the murder. This study examines the role law enforcement plays in that process by drawing upon interviews with 37 family members and friends of unsolved murder victims to better understand if and how communications with the criminal justice system affected their ability to make sense of their loss. The co-victims we interviewed held mostly negative views of police and prosecutors because those criminal justice officials failed to locate information about the murder. These negative feelings toward law enforcement intensified over time. In some cases, co-victims viewed the failure of the criminal justice system to resolve the murder to be based on discrimination against the victim or the victim's behavior. We conclude with some modest suggestions to law enforcement about what they can do to attenuate the problem of secondary victimization and promote bereavement.

Sense-making

An extensive amount of research has focused on the concept of sense-making, or the notion that victims create a subjective understanding of their loss (Currier et al., 2006, 2008a; Frankl, 1963; Pakenham, 2008; Updegraff et al., 2008). For the purposes of this research we define sense-making as a form of meaning-making that focuses on understanding the murder, and thus contributes to post-loss identity reconstruction. The ability to make sense of a loss is thought to play a central role in bereavement therapy because it aids in the re-creation of the self post-loss (Armour, 2006). Thus, sense-making may alleviate some of the anguish associated with the death of a loved one (Park and Folkman, 1997). People suffering from the loss of a significant other find themselves asking questions about the circumstances surrounding their loss as well as questions about who they are in a post-loss world. While the process of sense-making is thought to be restorative, the most difficult losses fail to make sense. While studies of sense-making have expanded to include many types of trauma (cancer, suicide, accidents, homicide), the concept has not been studied in the context of unsolved homicide co-victims. Sense-making among these particular co-victims seems particularly relevant because it is likely to be extremely difficult to construct any type of post-loss meaning when the circumstances surrounding a murder are unknown, uncertain, and ongoing (Armour, 2006; Bucholz, 2002). Uncertainty surrounding murders creates significant fear of the unknown that may extend to fear of living without a loved one to fear that the killer will return.

Grief

The idea that grief progresses through normal stages is widely accepted in the bereavement literature, and recent empirical evidence suggests a sequence through the following stages: disbelief, separation distress, depression-mourning, and recovery (Maciejewski et al., 2007). However, grief stage theory largely focuses on depressive symptoms, and therefore does not account for more complicated patterns of grief that may often be attributed to traumatic loss (Maciejewski et al., 2007). Traumatic loss is typically defined in terms of a sudden violent death characterized by a fatal accident, suicide, or homicide (Norris, 1990). Malone (2007: 384) also notes that when a loved one is murdered, the emotional and psychological processes of grieving may not follow the traditional stages of grief. In addition, Weiner (2007: 2962) has recently argued that it may be counterproductive and dangerous to apply normal patterns of grief to traumatic loss (see also Silver and Wortman, 2007).

As a result, researchers have developed the notion of complicated grief (or "traumatic grief": see Prigerson et al., 1999) to better characterize the typical bereavement associated with horrific events such as murder (Armour, 2006; Bucholz, 2002). Complicated grief is thought to be a reaction to stress response syndrome and is associated with long-lasting painful emotions that are severe (Prigerson et al., 1995). Individuals suffering from complicated grief have trouble accepting death and resuming life. Prigerson et al. (1995: 22), for example, report that symptoms of traumatic grief include "searching, yearning, preoccupation with thoughts of the deceased, crying, disbelief regarding the death, feeling stunned by the death, and lack of acceptance of the death." In addition to complicated grief, homicide co-victims may also suffer from post-traumatic stress disorder (PTSD). Amick-McMullan et al. (1991: 545) discovered that 23.3 percent of homicide co-victims developed PTSD. The American Psychiatric Association (2000) also reports that homicide co-victims exhibit clinical symptoms that include PTSD and acute post-traumatic stress. PTSD is thought to be associated with feelings of "disbelief, anger, shock, avoidance, numbness, a sense of futility about the future, a fragmented sense of security, trust, and control" (Prigerson et al., 1999: 67). Stress among homicide co-victims may also be related to physical illness (see Baliko and Tuck, 2008). In short, individual grief as a response to stress is often complicated and can vary tremendously in "duration, intensity, and complexity" (Malone, 2007: 384).

The Criminal Justice System and Bereavement

Unsolved homicide co-victims often turn to the criminal justice system for answers to aid their bereavement (Bucholz, 2002); however, research suggests that interactions with the criminal justice system can also intensify victimization (see Bucholz (2002) for homicide co-victims; see Karmen (2007) for review). Unfortunately, individuals who report a violent loss such as a murder are also likely to be the least successful at making sense of that loss

(Armour, 2006). Recently, Updegraff et al. (2008) have suggested that in the case of severe trauma people are less likely to find meaning but also more likely to search for meaning. The study of the role that others, such as criminal justice actors, can have in the process of sense-making among unsolved homicide co-victims is largely neglected. By showing disapproval and distancing themselves from victims and co-victims, criminal justice personnel can cause additional harm (Ryan, 1971). This occurs because interactions (or a lack of interactions) between police, prosecutors, and co-victims can themselves be traumatic and therefore complicate grief by causing additional stress among co-victims (Bucholz, 2002). This phenomenon, known as secondary victimization, is often reported by homicide co-victims (Rock, 1998). Unfortunately, few studies have linked sense-making to secondary victimization by examining co-victims' perceptions of their interactions with law enforcement.

Co-victims report facing many challenges with respect to the criminal justice system and often describe their interactions with the system as extremely frustrating (Bucholz, 2002; Baliko and Tuck, 2008). Bucholz (2002) argues that for these co-victims, justice may be perceived as being "minimized, delayed, or denied," leading to feelings of outrage and powerlessness. Rock (1998: 76) argues that a co-victim's alienation from the justice process "constitutes one of the most potent symbolic assaults suffered by families in the wake of murder."

Recently, Baliko and Tuck (2008) reported that homicide co-victims reported feelings of anger and dissatisfaction due to the criminal justice process. These feelings may impede sense-making by co-victims, especially unsolved homicide co-victims. Updegraff et al. (2008: 710) suggest that "in the context of negative events, having an explanation [of the event] should lessen the emotional impact and facilitate long-term adaptation." In the case of unsolved homicides, then, there is considerable reason to suspect that sense-making is especially difficult because many aspects of the crime are not known and because the offender is still at large. Thus, interactions with criminal justice officials about the murder and possible events leading up to the crime may be critical to the sense-making process because these agencies have access to information and are responsible for gaining information about their loved one's murder. It is for this reason that we examine unsolved homicide co-victims' experiences with the criminal justice system as it relates to their perceptions of sense-making.

Methods

Thirty-seven co-victims were interviewed for this study and represent 29 separate cold-case murders that occurred in ten law enforcement jurisdictions throughout Colorado, including rural, urban, and suburban jurisdictions. Sixty percent of the co-victims in this study were white, and 76 percent were female. The mean age of co-victims interviewed was 57. The cold-case murders covered in this research occurred, on average, 15 years prior to the study. The oldest murder took place 40 years prior to the interview and the most recent murder occurred one year prior to the interview. Twenty co-victims were the parents and nine co-victims were the siblings of the murder victim. The remaining co-victims represent spouses, children, aunts, uncles, grandparents, and friends of murder victims. Interview questions were designed to focus on the level, quality, and intensity of the co-victims' communications and interactions with the criminal justice system, rather than on the features of the unsolved case. The interviews lasted from one to four hours and were conducted in the co-victim's home, office, or other private place. Interview responses were coded to identify general themes and statements about relationships among categories of observations. The ensuing analysis revealed sense-making as a major issue, and thus the observations and perceptions of co-victims' experiences with the criminal justice system as impacting sense-making directed the empirical generalizations and themes described below.

Findings

Findings are organized according to four major themes that emerged from our interviews and relate to sense-making. These themes focused on: (1) perceptions about the lack of communication in the investigation; (2) perceptions about law enforcement's reaction to the victim's status; (3) perceptions about prosecutors' unwillingness to charge strongly suspected murderers with a crime, and (4) co-victims' responses to perceptions of police inactivity. The first three themes demonstrate how law enforcement inhibits sense-making among unsolved homicide co-victims and the fourth theme addresses the victim's response to this perceived inactivity. Names of co-victims used in this article are pseudonyms.

Lack of Communication

The nature and frequency of communication with co-victims was important to sense-making among co-victims. All but one of the co-victims reported that they were dissatisfied with the current level of communication with law enforcement. Thirty-four of those co-victims believed that the police were no longer actively investigating their unsolved homicide. Over time all co-victims reported a decrease in communication. This decrease is symbolic to co-victims and suggests that their loved ones' murders, and their lives by extension, are not important. Thus, co-victims' negative perceptions about police communication and competence increase over time. Once communication with law enforcement stopped, most co-victims lost hope in the criminal justice system, which impacted sense-making by (1) complicating their post-loss understanding of justice, and (2) limiting information about the case. This lack of communication, then, appears to prevent sense-making and may lead to secondary victimization through the promotion of complicated grief.

Hallie, whose son was murdered approximately one year prior to the interview, emphasizes the importance of police communication with her family. She believes that the police were taking the murder seriously because they kept in constant contact and had a favorable impression of the detective assigned to her son's case.

HALLIE:	*He was a very good investigator. He kept in communication very well. [Detective] would return my phone call, if not the same day, the next day or so.*
INTERVIEWER:	*So when you called, he called back and gave you an update?*
HALLIE:	*Yeah, I think he did a good job, actually, knowing and finding out things. I have no problem with [Detective]. He's really good. He communicated with me and he's working hard.*

Hallie underscores the importance between communication and information. She held out hope that her son's murder could be solved because the detective was still responsive to her requests for information. She also emphasized that finding out what happened and who killed her son will help with post-loss resolution:

Every day I do hurt. I hurt every day. Every day I do. My whole life has changed. I'm just existing. I am not living. I think once they find out who hurt my son, maybe I can start living again. I just get up and I just go. I'm not living right now. I'm just goin' through the motions, really, to be honest with you. You know, once they find who hurt my son, maybe I can start living again.

For Hallie, and for many other co-victims, catching the killer may aid in sense-making because it implies that justice does exist and that information about the case will help with resolution. Unlike nearly all other homicide co-victims, however, Hallie felt that the detective was forthcoming about the murder and potential killer. Thus, the attention to communication by law enforcement appears to send a critical and symbolic signal so that she may eventually be able to live again because the murder is important and information is forthcoming.

Mark and Molly's comments are more reflective of co-victims whose cases remain unsolved. Their teenage daughter was murdered nearly 20 years prior to the interview and, like Hallie, they agree the police did a good job communicating during the initial investigative stages. Mark and Molly both felt that subsequent communication with the police dropped off significantly. Thus, they suggest they will never make sense of the murder or receive justice. They suggest that the police no longer communicate or worry about solving their daughter's murder:

It just started to get cold, so they didn't—they used to call us up, but now, they don't seem to have anything new. . . . There's no updates. It's kind of like the same thing over and over: no money, no time.

These feelings of despair about the lack of information led Mark and Molly to the police department to examine their daughter's case file. Both Mark and Molly indicated that it was important for them to look at the file, but without any additional information their ability to discover why this happened is clearly diminished. The couple continue to ask the same questions they did immediately after the murder.

Now, after all these years, I've mellowed out a lot and I don't feel that much hate. It's still there. I don't think I'll ever lose it. . . . I don't know, it's like that until you find the person who did it. Maybe

> you'll have some closure after that, but until then, everybody you look at, the same thing crosses your mind. Is that the person? . . . Who would want her dead?

Thus, for Mark, the uncertainty about the murder was clearly associated with a lack of information about who may be responsible. It could be anybody. Mark and Molly also believe that law enforcement has given up on the case and views the family's inquiries concerning the status of the murder investigation as bothersome. This perception of law enforcement has intensified Mark's sense of injustice and his feelings of hate and fear.

Co-victims report that the lack of communication by the police department was especially apparent and harmful when detective reassignments occurred without notification. Seventeen co-victims told the interviewer that a change in the primary detective assigned to their murder case signaled that the case was no longer a police priority. Thus, reassignments were painful because they signaled that law enforcement had given up the quest for justice. These co-victims believed they would never have the important details they needed to understand the world post-loss. Seventeen homicide co-victims reported that they had endured several of these "reassignments." Most co-victims could not identify the detective currently assigned to their cold case. Such admissions to the interviewer were emotionally distressful to the co-victim and signaled potential secondary victimization. This was clearly the case with Quinton, who was a teenager at the time his father was murdered.

> The families are not notified when the detective changes. I mean, I even asked [the Department], "Is he [the detective who initially investigated my father's murder] still here?" "Yeah, he still works here." So that part I think is more hurtful than anything else, to feel like, OK, this person has literally taken control of a murder investigation that has impacted our family in more ways than most people can ever comprehend, and then for us to just kind of become a project that goes by the wayside.

The fact that the detective was reassigned led Quinton to question the veracity of the detective's commitment. For Quinton, the detectives assigned to the case played a central role in helping the family make sense of the crime. In short, most co-victims believed that a change in the primary detective assigned to the case signaled a decrease in departmental commitment to their investigation because, they argued, the detectives probably believed that the cases were not solvable. This left co-victims with a feeling of hopelessness that they would never discover what had actually happened.

While perceptions about changes in detectives were common, they were not universal. Two co-victims noted that the initial interactions with the primary detectives in charge of their cases were so negative and the detectives so unresponsive that they welcomed the change. In both cases the new detectives assigned to the case appeared more willing to share more information, which appeared to be associated with sense-making and notions of justice. Gwen, whose son was murdered 12 years prior to the study interview, notes that information increased with the reassignment of the first lead detective:

> About three years after my son was murdered [detective] started workin' on the case. And he gave me more information than I've ever had in the years that it happened. He brought other people in and started interviewing them again. He talked to both my twin boys and myself, and he was trying

to get in touch with the girl that he was livin' with at the time, but she would never go down there. And the person that was with him when he got shot, he would never go. It's just like, I think they know who did it, but they won't tell who did it, it's a situation like that. All the years that this case has been here, [detective] was the one that gave me more information than anybody.

Notions of a post-loss sense of justice also emerged alongside the lack of information. For example, 11 co-victims believed that the police perceived their calls as bothersome and problematic. In these 11 instances, co-victims reported that the police were trying to cover up the fact that they had no leads or did not (at the time) believe the case was a murder. For example, Winnie's daughter was murdered nearly 15 years ago and she still calls the police department every year for an update. Winnie reports that the police are not willing to talk to her because they believe the case is unsolvable. Winnie notes that she may never get resolution and justice:

INTERVIEWER: *So you've had no update over the past few years?*
WINNIE: *None. Because whenever you call, you get the same thing. "We just had a forest fire or whatever, don't you know? And you're worried about your dead daughter? We've got a forest fire." So unless I have the mental fortitude to deal with it, it just backlashes too much into my current existence now, just tryin' to meet everyday needs and stuff like that. So I try not to deal with that too much for right now.*

Winnie was able to get some information about her daughter's murder from another source and noted the importance of that information to the interviewer. She clearly believes that God played a role in bringing her the information about her daughter so that she could make sense of life post-loss and become a better Christian.

The feeling that co-victims were bothering law enforcement when they asked for information to help make sense of the unsolved crime, then, is not uncommon. Many co-victims called the police to find out that even the detective assigned to their unsolved homicide reported that they had very little (if any) knowledge about the circumstances of the murder. These feelings about law enforcement leave co-victims angry and pessimistic about coming to resolution about the case. Most co-victims reported that these experiences left them feeling like they had been victimized a second time and they reported that this intensified their struggle to make sense of justice and the police role in that process during pre- and post-loss while at the same time dealing with the stress of their traumatic and ongoing loss (e.g., the unsolved murder of their loved one).

The Role of Race, Ethnicity, and Gender

Sixteen co-victims reported that they thought the murder of their loved one was not being adequately investigated because the police believed the case was less worthy of investigative resources since the victim was somehow "unconventional" (i.e., the victim was black, Hispanic, poor, and/or was involved in drugs or prostitution). A total of four homicide co-victims in this sample perceived that their family member's case was not adequately investigated because of their race. These co-victims appear to have made sense of the fact that the case was unsolved by drawing upon larger prejudices in society to help explain the perceived police response. Several co-victims even argued that the case was solvable and information about the murderer and murder exists.

Unlike black co-victims, Hispanic co-victims argued that factors such as drug use, domestic violence, or gang membership also affected the investigation into their family member's murder because it is the perception of most police that Hispanics engage in these illegal activities. Orlando emphasizes that his murdered brother was not in a gang, but that the police treated the case as a gangland murder and thus did not investigate the case vigorously. Orlando and his mother Olivia report that the police told them that the victim's gang activity and membership caused his death. They became extremely angry at the police because they were presented with an account of the murder that was not compatible with their sense-making.

> There's nobody working on the case right now. We know they're very, very busy. It's not like my brother is the only murder case. There are a lot of other cases. It's not like somebody else's case is more important or my brother's case is more important than somebody else's. It doesn't matter who the person is or what they've done, they've still been murdered. It's not like, 'This person's a very bad guy so we're just gonna push his case over here.' That should be a priority, but not put anybody's case to the side just because they feel that it's gang-related or this person's a drug dealer or anything like that. Anybody should have the right for their case to be solved and worked on.

Victor also talked about the importance of race in his daughter's three-year-old murder investigation. He argued that race is the reason his daughter's murderer was still at large. He expressed anguish that the murder would never be solved and that he had no information about the case, and also reported feeling both helpless and depressed. Victor's lack of agency caused him to view the police as an obstacle to catching his daughter's killer(s).

> Here's a black child . . . probably used drugs. You know she did some prostitution. And that's just the way it is. I don't think that's gonna change for a while. I do not believe the police department's gonna change. Why won't the police department change? Because the power that be is not gonna do anything to institute change within the police department. They will always be able to tell me, "Well, we just don't know," and there won't be a thing that I can do about it. I really can't put pressure on these people.

Thus, Victor believes that the police will not give him information to help him make sense of the case because his daughter is black. Moreover, Victor has given up hope that the police will find the killer and has come to the conclusion that the case is unsolved because of his daughter's race. Police and prosecutors may unintentionally send signals to co-victims that their deceased loved one was at least partially responsible for being murdered and may suggest to co-victims that some cases may be more deserving of investigation than others (Karmen, 2007). It is not possible to know what signals law enforcement sent Victor in this case, but it is clear he believes that racism has played a direct role in the way his case was handled by law enforcement, and that has prevented him from ever seeing the killer brought to justice or gaining some insight into the mysterious circumstances surrounding the murder of his daughter.

Past deviant or illegal behavior on the part of the murder victim can also impact a co-victim's ability to make sense of the murder and cause them to question the effort police put into an investigation. Sometimes this feeling is perpetuated by the media, who spread what co-victims consider to be lies about the murder victim (Armour, 2006), and that further prevents sense-making and complicates grief. Thus, at the same time that co-victims seek to convey a conventional image of the murder victim to the public, and to stop any negative public judgments, they also worry about the impact such perceptions may have on the murder investigation and their notion of what happened in the case.

Karla, for instance, believed that her husband's murder was not being investigated because his bad reputation was emphasized in local newspapers when describing his death. As Karla was fighting the newspaper, law enforcement began asking questions about her husband's untoward past. Even though the information about Karla's husband later turned out to be false, and the newspaper retracted the story, she continues to believe that the police are still influenced by those reports and her husband's delinquent past. Thus, even when she was in the initial stages of making some sense of the unsolved murder she perceived the police were undermining her belief in her husband as a good person:

> I believe that they aren't doing anything. I feel that my husband had a lot of run-ins as a juvenile, as a young adult, with law enforcement, a lot of city police knew him and his brother by name. And I believe that it's felt there's one less troublemaker on the streets. If I looked at his past, he was still human. He still deserves the same effort that they would put into anyone else's murder. He's got family. He had two kids. They ask me all the time, "How come So-and-so's in jail for this murder, but nobody's in jail for killing my dad?" He's human. He does have family regardless of what kind of past he had. No one deserves to be shot and killed.

Paula's perceptions are similar to Karla's. While Paula explains that her brother was an alcoholic and needed help, she also argues that he often went out drinking late at night and was known to carry around a large sum of money. She believes that the police did not take her brother's case seriously because of his risky behavior. She could not make sense of her brother's murder with the accounts that the police had given and was still trying to identify the killer, get justice, and come to some resolution about the murder. The inability of the police to accept or even acknowledge her account of her brother's murder caused Paula great anger and distress:

> In fact, when my son and sister-in-law and I went and kind of walked that whole area after [my brother's] death, I found some items that might have been kicked out of a car that was parked there, and that's where those people said that car was parked. I picked those items up, and I've still got them. It's like, packets of crackers and stuff like that. But the [department] didn't want to hear anything like that. It was like, No, this was a drunk [that] got hit, and that's the end of the story.

Moreover, Paula, like other co-victims in this study, is upset that the police refuse to take seriously the evidence she has collected. Such reports appear to be consistent with yet an additional secondary victimization on the part of unsolved homicide co-victims who reported high levels of stress over their perceptions of what evidence may be important to the case.

Self-investigation

An inability to make sense of the murder and to bring the killer to justice appears to complicate co-victims' grief. Most families longed for communication from law enforcement which indicated that the case was still active and that new information about the case would be forthcoming as their questions about the case developed through the process of trying to make sense of the murder. Co-victims' perceptions that the police were not investigating the case and providing appropriate levels of information, however, delayed the restorative process. This lack of information pushed many co-victims into action. Sixteen co-victims indicated some sort of self-initiated effort in trying to solve their loved one's murder. Thus, they tried to make sense of the case by solving it themselves. Molly explained that she often wanted to investigate her own case given the response she sometimes gets from law enforcement when she asks if they have any leads on her daughter's killer.

> That's another thing I pick up on when we go over there, they say, "Do you have anything new for us?" It's like, are we doing the investigating now? I know some people do if they have something like this in their family. They go out and investigate. But that's a special kind of person, I think. Not everybody can do that. You have to give up your life. Follow all the leads you can, whatever. Not everybody can do that. But I kind of feel like they throw it back on us, like they feel like we're accusing them of not doing anything. "Do you have anything for us?"

This reported reaction is similar to Goffman's (1952) notion of betrayal in "cooling out the mark" where co-victims report that they have come to realize that the police, who are supposed to be on their side throughout the process, have really been trying to distance themselves from the murder case because (co-victims believe) it cannot be solved. Co-victims report that these feelings challenged their sense of justice and caused them considerable additional anger and stress—feelings that are counterproductive to the notion of sense-making and represent yet another victimization by the criminal justice system.

In other instances, co-victims actually conducted their own investigations to make sense of the case. Debra, for example, reports that she consulted with her detective prior to conducting an interview for fear of jeopardizing her daughter's case. However, she wanted to know why and how her daughter was murdered. She believed that she could gain information about the reason for her daughter's murder and that would ultimately help the prosecutors gain a conviction:

> Let me tell you right now, I went out on my own and interviewed people I thought I wanted to talk to. I always told [detective] "I'm going to do this." And he would say, "Back off," or like he did with [witness] he'd say, "Wait till after the trial because I don't think he should talk to you before the trial."

Several co-victims in this sample were working vigorously to solve their loved one's murders. However, these co-victims perceived that the detectives working their cases thought that this investigation was unnecessary and potentially harmful. Self-initiated detective work caused a number of hardships for co-victims, ranging from financial strain to mental instability to threats of harm and violence. However, co-victims persisted in these investigative efforts in order to gain information that would help them identify the murderer and make sense of the murder. For example, Xandria, who believed she had identified her daughter's killer, reports that the police initially did not take her investigation seriously. She was convinced, despite all the resistance from the police, that her daughter's boyfriend had killed her. In the end, and only after the suspect was convicted of another murder, Xandria reports that the police did use the evidence she collected to build a case against her daughter's murderer. Xandria's investigation consisted of videotapes obtained from the convenience store where her daughter was last seen and interviews of potential witnesses and informants. She spent a large portion of her time searching for her daughter's body and looking for physical evidence. She believed that she had made sense of the case through her investigation of events. In a matter of a few years, her intense investigation into her daughter's case interfered with nearly every aspect of her life, caused her to lose her business, and she nearly died from poor health exacerbated by extreme stress.

> If you look in the police evidence box, 98 percent of the evidence is from [me]. And they are lucky they even have a case. And you know, people just—I still have family members that I—it's very strained because they say, "You should let the police do their job." And [my ex-husband] and I say, you know, we hope they never know. We hope they never have our experience—they never need to know, if you don't do it, nothing happens.

In the end, Xandria's ability to make sense of the case helped her to find resolution despite the fact that the killer had not yet been brought to justice. The fact that the murderer was still free did present Xandria with some anxiety, but she was again healthy, working, and going about her life.

Caroline also spent years collecting evidence resulting in extreme financial hardship and periods of homelessness. She invested considerable time reconstructing her mother's murder and interviewing people involved in the case and its investigation in order to make sense of her mother's murder and see resolution in her case. Caroline invested an immense amount of time and money in her investigation:

> I had to pay. I've got thousands of dollars, which is horrible, because I don't make thousands of dollars, in paperwork. But I had to have it in order to first understand and second of all, to make anybody else listen. I had to bring their own paper to them and prove it. . . . I went and I read page for page for page. And then I broke it down into investigators, witnesses, and I got online and I started finding people and people would give me numbers to people and I would contact them and—it wasn't like it was an all-day, every-day thing, but it was consuming, and I wanted to know what happened. And the more questions I had, the more I would get a run-around or the more answers I got, it would lead me to different branches. Some people would open the door and welcome me, and some people [told me to leave].

After years of investigation Caroline was able to make sense of the murder, and her mother's killer was eventually convicted of the crime. Caroline reported that her investigation provided her with a sense of what happened to her mother and the prosecution provided her with affirmation of that sense-making in a public forum. Importantly, she notes that when she talked with the judge she received affirmation:

> He [the judge] apologized to me because he was on bench when it originally happened. He said, We let you down, we let your mother down, we let your folks down, and I feel terrible about that. I am very proud of you for all that you've accomplished. It is what it is. I went for the truth and not out here for brownie buttons or anything other than to keep it out there, to get the law enacted, and to hopefully prevent somebody else. I don't think it would prevent somebody else from doing it, although it makes people aware of who he is, he can't fly through life any more.

Thus, Caroline was able to make sense of her mother's murder and have that resolution affirmed in a public forum. While she reports that she is still suffering because of her mother's murder, she is in the unique position of finding resolution in her case.

Unfortunately, most family members did not get as much information about their case as Caroline and Xandria. While most unsolved homicide co-victims worked their loved ones' cases with determination, they often report having little understanding of investigative techniques and lacked adequate resources, protection, and support. Paula worked on her brother's unsolved murder case for several years before coming to the conclusion that it would remain unsolved.

PAULA: *Like I said, after working so hard all those years, I just decided, okay, patience. Let [my brother's case] cool down. Let it take its own course and maybe something will come out of it.*

INTERVIEWER: *That must have been hard, to just let it die down. It sounds like those first two years you were working and trying to work on your brother's case. I assume when you say kids . . .*

PAULA: *I have one, but I had just hurt myself, and I was working in pain every day and trying to work on my brother's case, and everything, and I wasn't getting much rest and everything between the nightmares and pain and everything else, just after a few years, I couldn't do it anymore. So I thought, OK, this is it. I'm not getting anywhere. I'm just going around in circles and pounding my head against the wall. Let it cool down and have patience. Get back into it later.*

Paula was unable to make sense of her brother's murder and, after years of investigation, had to step back because of the toll it was taking on her family and her health. She was forced to choose between trying to make sense of her traumatic loss and losing her husband, job, and health.

In the end, the fact that many co-victims could not get information about their unsolved murder led them to see the criminal justice system as an under-resourced bureaucratic organization incapable of solving many crimes. As noted previously, this realization intensified co-victims' feelings of despair and suspicion.

Implications for Bereavement and Criminal Justice

The Federal Bureau of Investigation (FBI, 2008) reports that 38.8 percent (or 6,568) of the 16,929 murders and non-negligent manslaughters that occur in the United States will not be immediately solved. Hawkins (2008) recently noted that the clearance rate for homicides dropped from 91 percent in 1963 to 61 percent in 2007. These data suggest that many co-victims are faced with conditions that may lead them to complicated and prolonged forms of grief, and that the circumstances of their interactions with law enforcement may cause them to be especially prone to forms of secondary victimization at the hands of the criminal justice system. Co-victims of unsolved homicides report that they are in a position where they are unable to find meaning or to make sense of the murder because of the enormous amount of uncertainty that surrounds the unsolved homicide combined with the fact that their notions of justice are undermined in their interactions with law enforcement. In short, without resolution to a case, sense-making on the part of co-victims is difficult at best. It is clear that co-victims believe that the criminal justice system is often at odds with their capacity to develop a sense of understanding about their loss. Without critical information about the case, many co-victims are never able to construct such an understanding.

With respect to a lack of information, crime victims often turn to the criminal justice system to get information about the murder (Bucholz, 2002). In that respect, cold-case co-victims are no different than most crime victims in wanting information about the crime. Specifically, co-victims clearly asserted that they wanted more information about the murder to help them understand what had happened. This notion is compatible with the process of sense-making and suggests that it may be hard to construct post-loss meaning when circumstances surrounding the death are unknown and uncertain. Consistent with the notion of sense-making, co-victims reported that information about the case would help them formulate some type of resolution. Thus, many co-victims became extremely frustrated when the system served to limit or even intentionally block their access to information. Co-victims reported that this lack of information extended their bereavement and many were still grieving, despite the passage of time.

The co-victims interviewed for this study were nearly universal in their belief that the police stopped actively investigating their case when it turned cold (i.e., after one year). These perceptions are based on co-victims' observations that law enforcement failed to provide regular case updates, return phone calls, or notify co-victims of personnel changes. Co-victims believed that better communication by law enforcement would lead to additional information to help them understand what happened and give them hope that the case was still being investigated. Instead, they lived with large amounts of uncertainty about the facts of the case and what, if anything, the police were doing to catch the killer. The lack of information implied to co-victims that the criminal justice system did not take the murder seriously.

We also discovered that several co-victims believed that the lack of contact that signaled the end of the investigation was the result of race, ethnicity, economic status, or deviant behavior. In short, the co-victims interviewed for this study indicate that the lack of communication made grieving more difficult because it increased uncertainty about what was being done in the case and because it signaled that victim characteristics might prevent the case from being solved.

A post-loss understanding of criminal justice may also be problematic because several co-victims could not understand why their case was not prosecuted when the system could identify the murderer. As noted before, co-victims reported that law enforcement told them they know who did it, "but could not prove it." It is clear that these co-victims have little faith in notions of justice and fairness. Again, these co-victims report that they are frustrated by the system and believe that criminals have more rights than the victims. The sense-making literature indicates that it is difficult to construct a post-loss identity under such conditions (Armour, 2006). Frustration with the criminal justice system and a need to find the murderer led several co-victims to actively investigate their own cases. These investigations were usually not successful and sometimes dangerous.

Co-victims continually report that above all, and as one would expect, they would like their cases resolved. For example, a co-victim in Baliko and Tuck's (2008: 31) study of the interaction between co-victims and homicide offenders points out, "I don't hold it as a grudge . . . no need to live bitter . . . as long as you got him in custody, and he's going to be somewhere."

While solving cases is clearly the priority, there are policies that police and prosecutors can adopt to reduce uncertainty and facilitate notions of justice. These policies should aid in the promotion of sense-making among co-victims. First, this research suggests that police departments should adopt a policy to contact co-victims when the detectives investigating the cold case change. Only one Colorado jurisdiction claimed to have such a policy in place at the time of our interviews. Thus, two co-victims in this study reported that the police did contact them when there was a change in the lead detective. We believe a department policy to notify co-victims of detective changes could be easily implemented within jurisdictions. Ideally, detectives handling the cases would make contact with the co-victims.

An alternative would be to amend a state's victims' rights act to include such contact as mandatory. As with other mandatory victims' rights notifications, co-victims who wished to be notified could simply ask the department to alert them of a change. For example, in some states victims can provide a written request under the state's victims' rights acts if they would like to be notified of cold-case updates.

Co-victims suggest that updates about who is working on the case would signal that the case is active and important. The policy of notifying cold-case co-victims of detective changes may also reduce the belief by many co-victims that cases are not pursued because of victim characteristics (i.e., race, ethnicity, or deviance). This is because co-victims appear to be likely to draw upon notions of race, ethnicity, and victim status when there is a lack of communication between co-victims and law enforcement. As noted earlier, many cold-case co-victims did not know who was working the case and, by extension, believed that nothing was being done because the victim was black, Hispanic, or lived an unconventional lifestyle.

Second, this research suggests that departments should adopt a policy of allowing co-victims to examine their cold-case files when possible. Dannemiller (2002: 7) suggests that "deaths are upsetting in proportion to uncertainty that surrounds them." Thus, law enforcement agencies can also adopt policies that reduce case uncertainty by promoting better communication about the investigation. This is because co-victims of unsolved homicides report that they are unable to find meaning or make sense of the murder because of the enormous amount of uncertainty that surrounds the unsolved homicide. Co-victims in this study suggested that sharing information, and when possible case files, is helpful. If co-victims' perceptions about communication with law enforcement were more positive than negative (see, for example, follow-up with bereaved next-of-kin of critical care patients in Cuthbertson et al. (2000)), this may help attenuate this potential form of secondary victimization by removing impediments to sense-making. Despite law enforcement arguments to the contrary, the few co-victims interviewed in this research who were allowed to look over police and prosecutor case files report that the information they gained from the process was helpful in bereavement. Thus, this strategy should become standard, when feasible, among law enforcement agencies when charges cannot be filed, as it may provide a sense of understanding about what information the police and prosecutors have regarding the murder.

This proposed policy is likely to be controversial because law enforcement culture is not one where information is readily shared with outsiders and because sharing some types of information may jeopardize a case. However, it is important to note here that several co-victims did believe that looking over evidence might also benefit the case because it may help co-victims provide information that is useful to law enforcement. Thus, some co-victims asserted that if they were more involved in the investigation, for example, it might improve the likelihood that a case would be solved. Such a policy of sharing information might also reduce the motivation for some co-victims to engage in their own murder investigations due to a perception that nothing was being done by police.

Third, states should consider revising victims' rights acts to *retroactively* provide for various types of victims' support services to unsolved homicide co-victims. Because the bereavement process is delayed, there may be many co-victims who were not eligible or who did not receive information about victims' assistance when their loved ones were murdered.

Fourth, law enforcement personnel who interact with unsolved homicide co-victims should be trained in complicated grief. While we have found that some departments have pursued such training, it is not likely to occur in rural areas where agencies operate on limited budgets. Agencies must have a policy to engage in regular, empathic communication with families and loved ones of unsolved homicides, including contacting the families and loved ones when law enforcement personnel assigned to the case are changed. We believe that families and loved ones of murder victims, when possible, should be able to review case files and discuss possible theories with law enforcement personnel and prosecutors.

In the end, we hope that the information obtained from this study is also useful because it encourages future research on sense-making among cold-case co-victims. Especially important in terms of future research are issues of race, ethnicity, and class as indicators of secondary victimization among cold-case co-victims. Our finding that the status of the victim may inhibit sense-making has important consequences for social inequality. Thus, any additional research in this area should focus some attention on what may be done to better promote sense-making among traditionally disadvantaged and marginalized populations.

Critical Thinking

The results of the present study bring to mind several larger issues. At what point should detectives give up on a case that has gone cold? Is it possible that characteristics of the victim do affect the way in which police pursue the case? One would hope that race, gender, and class would not influence how police handle a murder investigation, so we must ask ourselves: are the perceptions of these family members accurate or is their grief clouding their perceptions?

References

American Psychiatric Association. 2000. *Diagnostic and Statistical Manual of Mental Disorders* (4th edn). Washington, DC: APA.

Amick-McMullan, A., D. Kilpatrick, and H. Resnick. 1991. Homicide as a risk factor for PTSD among surviving family members. *Behavior Modification* 15: 545–559.

Armour, M. 2006. Meaning making for survivors of violent death. In *Violent Death*, edited by Edward Rynearson (pp. 101–121). New York: Routledge.

Baliko, B. and I. Tuck. 2008. Perceptions of survivors of loss by homicide: Opportunities for nursing practice. *Journal of Psychosocial Nursing and Mental Health Services* 46: 26–34.

Bucholz, J.A. 2002. *Homicide Survivors: Misunderstood Grievers*. Amityville, NY: Baywood Publishing.

Currier, J.M., J.M. Holland, and R.A. Neimeyer. 2006. Sense-making, grief, and the experience of violent loss: Toward a mediated model. *Death Studies* 30: 403–428.

Currier, J.M., J.M, Holland, and R.A. Neimeyer. 2008a. Making sense of loss: A content analysis of end-of-life practitioners' therapeutic approaches. *OMEGA–Journal of Death and Dying* 57: 121–141.

Cuthbertson, S.J., M.A. Margetts, and S.J. Street. 2000. Bereavement follow-up after critical illness. *Critical Care Medicine* 28: 1196–1201.

Dannemiller, C.H. 2002. The parents' response to a child's murder. *OMEGA—Journal of Death and Dying* 45: 1–21.

Federal Bureau of Investigation. 2008. *Crime in the United States, 2007*. Washington, DC: U.S. Department of Justice, Federal Bureau of Investigation. Retrieved May 28, 2009 (http://www.fbi.gov/ucr/ucr.htm).

Frankl, V. 1963. *Man's Search for Meaning*. New York: Washington Square Press.

Goffman, E. 1952. On cooling the mark out: Some aspects of adaptation to failure. *Psychiatry* 15: 451–463.

Hawkins, K. 2008. More people are getting away with murder in the U.S. *Associated Press*. Released Monday, December 8, at 4.06 p.m. EST.

Hertz, M.F., Prothrow-Stith, D., and Chery, C. 2005. Homicide survivors: Research and practice implications. *American Journal of Preventive Medicine*, 29: 288–295.

Karmen, A. 2007. *Crime Victims: An Introduction to Victimology*. Belmont, CA: Wadsworth.

Maciejewski, P.K., H.Z. Baohui, S.D. Block, and H.G. Prigerson. 2007. An empirical examination of the stage theory of grief. *JAMA—Journal of the American Medical Association* 297: 716–723.

Malone, L. 2007. In the aftermath: Listening to people bereaved by homicide. *Probation Journal* 54: 383–393.

Norris, F. 1990. Screening for traumatic stress: A scale for use in the general population. *Journal of Applied Social Psychology* 20: 1704–1718.

Pakenham, K. 2008. Making sense of caregiving for persons with multiple sclerosis: The dimensional structure of sense making and relations with positive and negative adjustment. *International Journal of Behavioral Medicine* 15: 241–252.

Park, C. and S. Folkman. 1997. Meaning in the context of stress and coping. *Review of General Psychology* 1: 115–144.

Prigerson, H.G., E. Frank, S.V. Kasl, C.F. Reynolds 3rd, B. Anderson, G S. Zubenko, P.R. Houck, C.J. George, and D.J. Kupfer. 1995. Complicated grief and bereavement-related depression as distinct disorders: Preliminary empirical validation in elderly bereaved spouses. *American Journal of Psychiatry* 152: 22.

Prigerson, H.G., M.K. Shear, S.C. Jacobs, C.F. Reynolds 3rd, P.K. Maciejewski, J.R. Davidson, R. Rosenheck, P.A. Pilkonis, C.B. Wortman, and J.B. Williams. 1999. Consensus criteria for traumatic grief. A preliminary empirical test. *The British Journal of Psychiatry* 174: 67–73.

Rock, P. 1998. *After Homicide: Practical and Political Responses to Bereavement.* Oxford: Oxford University Press.

Ryan, W. 1971. *Blaming the Victim.* New York: Vintage.

Silver, R.C. and C.B. Wortman. 2007. The stage theory of grief. *JAMA—Journal of the American Medical Association* 297: 2692.

Updegraff, J.A., R.C. Silver, and A. Holman. 2008. Searching for and finding meaning in collective trauma: Results from a national longitudinal study of 9/11 terrorist attacks. *Journal of Personality and Social Psychology* 95: 709–722.

Weiner, J.S. 2007. The stage theory of grief. *JAMA—Journal of the American Medical Association* 297: 2692–2693.

9

Victims' Voices: Domestic Assault Victims' Perceptions of Police Demeanor

B. Joyce Stephens and Peter G. Sinden

Abstract: *Joyce Stephens and Peter Sinden interviewed domestic violence victims whose assailants had been arrested under mandatory arrest policies to determine how these victims perceived police. Interestingly, but perhaps not surprisingly, the number of interactions for domestic violence had a strong impact upon how victims perceived the responding officers. One-time victims thought that police understood what they were experiencing and genuinely cared about their well-being. Whereas first time victims saw police as caring and warm, it appears that successive encounters led to increasing dissatisfaction with the way police handled the situation. These victims began to interpret police responses to them as antagonistic, unsympathetic, and unconcerned. This is in stark contrast to those who had fewer interactions with police.*

More than a decade has passed since the findings of the Minneapolis Experiment were reported. The Minneapolis Police Department was the testing site for an investigation of the deterrent effect of three different law enforcement responses to domestic violence situations. Of the three responses—arrest of perpetrator, separation of the parties for a cooling off period, and counseling/referral to social services—the arrest option was associated with the lowest rate of recidivism after a six-month follow-up. Widely disseminated by researchers and policy-makers and given maximum exposure by the media, this study was a major catalyst for changes in how the justice system responds to the problem of intimate violence. Quickly following the release of this report, police departments nationwide began to institute reforms; chief among them was the adoption of pro-arrest policies with regard to perpetrators of domestic violence. In some states legislatures passed mandatory arrest statutes, sparking a contentious policy debate that continues to divide groups concerned with the formulation of domestic violence policies.

Various interest groups, including victims' rights advocates, feminists, academics, and criminal justice officials, have contributed to the ongoing dialogue about mandatory arrest laws for domestic assault. Mandatory arrest continues to receive strong endorsement from legislators and criminal justice spokespersons, although confidence in the strongly deterrent consequences of pro-arrest laws was dealt a severe blow when replication studies failed to confirm the Minneapolis results. Supporters argue that not only will such reforms lower victim risk, but in addition they will result in improved police response and an increase in victims' confidence in the criminal justice system. Underrepresented in this policy debate have been the perspectives and experiences of the victims themselves.

Arguably, it is the victims who have the most to gain (or lose) from the current trend toward a more aggressive law enforcement treatment of family violence, but we know little about victims' experiences with the new laws and their interactions with law enforcement officers. Their voices are needed to inform and guide efforts to evaluate the changes in law enforcement practices.

Review of the Literature

Legislative reforms and changes in law enforcement practices reflect an increased societal intolerance of violent crimes committed against family members. Victims of violent acts by intimate partners have been the object of much concern, but the subjects of only limited research that explores their perceptions and experiences with police interventions. This paucity stands in contrast with the relatively large number of published studies of police attitudes and responses to domestic violence.

Existing research on victims' points of view may be categorized into two periods, corresponding approximately to the time before and the time after the widespread enactment of laws that authorized or mandated warrantless, probable cause arrests for misdemeanor assault. In the early 1980s, two studies addressed issues relevant to victims' perceptions of police officers' victim-related attitudes.

In a self-administered questionnaire, Pagelow (1981) asked a sample of 143 domestic violence victims to respond to the item, "What was the attitude and the behavior of the police toward you?" Of the participants, 53 reported favorable attitudes, 78 reported unfavorable attitudes, and 12 reported neutral attitudes. Bowker's (1982) survey of victims found that they had a number of concerns, including the demeanor displayed by the police. Reluctance to arrest, failure to listen or provide encouragement, reassurance, or material aid were mentioned as examples of police insensitivity to the needs of victims. More recent research in Canada (Radford, 1987) and Holland (Zoomer, 1989) reported similar patterns of police insensitivities.

Victim-centered research during the second period remains sparse. Kennedy and Homant (1984) and Brown (1984) recorded favorable evaluations of police conduct in their surveys of victims. In Kennedy and Homant's sample of residents of shelters for battered women, 63 percent characterized the police as very or a little helpful. Brown also found a favorable evaluation of the police in his survey of victims; 71 percent thought that the police were concerned and helpful, whereas only 21 percent thought the police were rude, angry, or blaming.

Buzawa, Austin, Bannon, and Jackson (1992) and Buzawa and Austin (1993) concluded that victims' approval ratings of the police increased when victim preferences with regard to arrest were followed and when victims perceived that they were not trivialized or belittled by the police. Muraoka's (1996) survey of 61 residents of a shelter in Omaha had the respondents rate their experiences with the police. Respondents rated recent experiences as slightly more satisfactory than past experiences, and a majority cited interpersonal reasons for their approval. Prominent among the reasons they gave were that police treated them with respect, police listened and understood, and police did not blame victims.

It is probably not surprising that much of the current research is system oriented in that it involves issues of concern to law enforcement and the criminal justice system generally. Deterrence and recidivism are priority matters for those formulating system responses to domestic violence; however, as the policy debate about appropriate institutional responses moves forward, it is critical to understand the dynamic between police and victims. It is essential to explore the perspectives and experiences of victims in detail and in depth, including those who have encountered intervention by officers acting under the requirements of a mandatory arrest law. As of now, such a study has not been done.

Method

In January 1996, the State of New York began implementation of the mandatory arrest provision of the Family Protection and Domestic Violence Intervention Act (*Criminal Procedure Law of the State of New York*, 1996/1967). This legislation requires police to make arrests when a family offense misdemeanor has been committed against a member of the same family or household. To study victims' experiences and perspectives, we conducted interviews with 25 victims whose assailants had been arrested under the provisions of the new law.

The participants were referred to the researchers by the director of a victim witness assistance program located in a semi-rural county in western New York State. Taped interviews that averaged 1.5 to 2 hours provided the data for our study.

Of the interviewees, 24 were female and one was male. The youngest was aged 21 and the oldest was aged 51, with a median age of 33 years. All but one were Caucasian (one participant was Native American). The ethnic and racial homogeneity of the sample was reflective of the small town and village populations in the rural county in which they lived. A majority ($n = 13$) were divorced from their assailants at the time of the study, three had divorces pending, seven were single, and only two remained married. They had an average of two children. Eleven participants had completed high school, 12 had some college, one had a bachelor's degree, and one had completed some graduate-level courses. Most of the interviewees were employed ($n = 19$) and two were students. Incomes ranged from less than \$10,000 ($n = 5$) to \$42,000 ($n = 1$). Most of the interviewees ($n = 21$) reported annual incomes of less than \$20,000.

Findings and Discussion

We were especially interested in two aspects of the participants' experiences: their perceptions of police demeanor toward them and their assessment of the officers' handling of the arrest event. This article is a report on our findings with regard to the first issue. By *demeanor* we are referring to the participants' perceptions of the attitudes of the police as expressed in their behavior toward the victims and assailants. Thus, from the point of view of the victims, the manner in which the officers conducted themselves was reflective of the officers' beliefs and assumptions about the victim, the perpetrator, the nature of their relationship, and the type of relationship the officer should establish with the participants. As perceived by the victim, an officer's actions (or inactions) could convey a wide spectrum of attitudes—concern, sympathy, seriousness, boredom, frustration, anger, contempt, indifference, and so forth. A hostile officer who makes it clear by his demeanor that domestic disputes are not his idea of real police work confirms a victim's feelings of worthlessness and fears that nothing will be done to change her situation. That she deserves a nonviolent life and will be safe can be affirmed by the presence of an officer whose manner expresses concern and seriousness of purpose.

Participants with a Single Police Encounter

Nearly three-quarters ($n = 18$) of the participants had had multiple encounters with the police prior to the arrest event. Of the seven whose single experience with law enforcement culminated in their assailant's arrest, three described the officers' demeanors in positive terms. Their comments depicted the officers as "great," "genuinely concerned," "very attentive," and "very caring." For these victims, the actions of officers were not simply objective events but reflected officers' assessments of the moral worth of the victims. Verbal reassurances that the victim had done the right thing by notifying the police, listening to the victim's account without showing impatience or trying to rush it, offering to transport her to the hospital and other forms of assistance had conveyed the message that the victim's situation was being taken seriously and merited police intervention.

One participant was surprised at the police response, stating that she had not thought they would pay that much attention or care that much about what happened to her. Another individual, who had gone to the police department after being assaulted by her ex-husband, described her interaction with a lieutenant in glowing terms. As important to her as explaining her rights and showing her how to apply for an order of protection was his willingness to spend a considerable amount of time with her, allowing her to "work up" to telling the humiliating details of the assault. Furthermore, the officer gave her his office phone number, advising her to call him directly if she had further questions. The most unexceptional acts—making the person feel comfortable, asking about her children, offering her coffee or a tissue—took on a weightier meaning in that, for the victims, these acts signified that they deserved to be treated well.

Of the victims who described a negative encounter with the police, I reported that she "got the third degree" from state troopers who gave every indication of discrediting her account. From their first remark, "So what did you do?," these officers made it clear that they were neither interested nor concerned about the victim and her children. When the victim asked to be allowed to leave (her hand was bleeding), the trooper insisted that she wait with her children in a truck and then left, returning half an hour later to grill her about the situation. The victim was especially upset that they did not offer her the use of their first-aid kit to treat her injured hand. The troopers continued to express doubt as to her credibility by suggesting that she "must have done something," although eventually they did arrest her assailant. Another dissenter expressed strong dissatisfaction with the deputies who did not "give a crap" about which one they arrested and whose "attitude" made things worse for her and her children.

Participants with Multiple Encounters with Police

For the majority of participants with previous and multiple encounters with law enforcement, nearly all ($n = 16$) described negative and psychologically bruising experiences with the police that had occurred prior to the arrest event. We identified four common types of police demeanor that had been corrosive in their effects on victim confidence and satisfaction with law enforcement.

Minimizing the Situation

A common experience of the participants was to be confronted with officers whose demeanor conveyed the message that they doubted the seriousness of the victims' situation. The ways in which officers appeared to the victims to downplay the gravity of what had occurred were legion. In some cases, the discounting of the victim's appeal for help was pointed and explicit. When one victim showed the officer her finger which had been broken by her boyfriend, his reply was "that's no big thing." Another officer, presumably tired of dealing with the same violent husband, told his victim, "Hey, husbands kill wives all the time." A majority of the participants in this study had encountered law enforcement officials who "just brushed it off" or "treated it like a joke." In the words of these women, officers "acted like it was just a domestic, no big deal, just a part of life." Not atypical were the remarks made to one victim by a responding trooper that "Well, what do you want me to do about it? He'll just be back tomorrow."

Victims felt particularly humiliated when their violent relationships were a source of humor to officers. During the interviews, in their words and body language, the participants expressed bitterness toward officers who laughed and "giggled" at their predicament. Usually, such moments of levity occurred when the officer took the perpetrator aside to speak privately.

Victims drew their own conclusions when the events prompting them to notify the police were downplayed and treated as not serious. They drew conclusions about the unreliability of law enforcement and, by extension, the justice system. They also drew conclusions about the meaning of intimate violence to the police: It is not important and you are not important.

Disbelieving the Victim

Also undermining victim–police interactions were the participants' beliefs that officers did not believe their version of events. Disbelief was expressed in several ways: verbal challenges to the victim's explanations, accusations that both parties were culpable, statements that the victim had provoked (and thus was responsible) for the altercation, and so forth. Victims were less likely to be believed if they had been drinking and if they were not married to their abusers. Some victims were not believed when they asserted that they had restraining orders. In one case, the officer ignored the victim's document, insisting that it was irrelevant unless the police department also had a copy. Several hours later the department found its copy.

Discrediting the victim's accounts was also accomplished by threatening to arrest both parties and take the children into custody. The latter threat sent a chilling message to victims that their own physical safety might be gained at too high a price. Most of the participants doubted that the police were genuinely ignorant of what had happened; rather, they suspected that the officers were reluctant to credit their stories for other reasons. Such reasons included frustration with having to make repeated calls, disgust with emotional victims, and sympathy with the male ("The Brotherhood," as one participant put it) as a consequence of having been manipulated by the perpetrator.

We Don't Care

Destructive to victim–police interactions was a police manner that conveyed attitudes of unconcern and indifference. Even when they were believed, victims' trust in officers was undermined when they perceived the police as being unmoved by their situation. Participants felt belittled by a police style that focused solely on getting the facts. Participants were critical of officers who did not show concern for them, or compassion or sympathy. Although they appreciated efficiency (especially with regard to the time it took for police to arrive) and professionalism, they were alienated when confronted with police reserve and flat affect.

One participant, contrasting the demeanor of the two officers who arrived together, described one as "nonchalant, cold . . . he just didn't care," whereas the other "listened to me . . . was very, very sympathetic . . . made me feel good about myself . . . never made me feel small." All of the individuals we interviewed judged the police not only on their behavioral responsiveness (i.e., quick arrival, taking charge, ensuring the victim's safety) but also their emotional responsiveness (i.e., concern and compassion for the victim).

Macho Cop

According to the participants, they often encountered arrogant police officers whose rude and even contemptuous treatment of them was especially demoralizing. With considerable passion, they offered example after example of insolent police conduct toward them. Many of these victims were convinced that the police viewed them and their problems as undeserving of police time or effort. Such convictions had been reinforced over time and after repeated abrasive experiences with law enforcement officials.

When one victim, in tears, asked the responding sheriff's deputy, "What can I do?," his retort, "I have no idea and I wasn't the one who married him," conveyed a clear message of scornful dismissal. Another participant was stunned when an officer suggested that she must be "awfully good in bed" for her ex-husband to continue his stalking and harassment of her. One woman who, after waiting more than an hour for the police to arrive asked what had taken them so long, described the officers' response: "He was cocky, really kind of macho acting and said, 'Oh, you're going to complain about the service. I'll just turn around and leave.' I didn't dare say more because he got nasty."

Some of the participants wondered if the officers they had dealt with might be abusers themselves. An example of this was the woman who, before going to the emergency room, overheard her abusive boyfriend joking around with the state trooper, who said, "Oh boy, you must have really pissed her off. She'll be back, they never leave for long. You should keep your woman in line." The participants made it clear to the interviewer that experiences such as these engendered feelings of futility and shame, and reinforced their suspicions that the police viewed them with contempt.

Police Demeanor and the Arrest Event

Thus far, we have considered the victims' perceptions of police demeanor during previous situations that did not result in an arrest. Now we shall present findings that pertain to those victim–police encounters that culminated in their partner being arrested.

Police demeanor toward the assailants was also of interest to us, as presumably it implicitly carries meaning with regard to their attitudes toward the victims. However, we were unable to obtain these data for most of the cases, as only four of the participants were present at the assailants' arrests. Three described the police as allowing the assailants to verbally abuse them (the victims) before making the arrest. The lone male in our sample was convinced that the officers' reluctance to arrest his abusive spouse was due to their incredulity, indeed discomfort, when dealing with a male victim of abuse.

For the 21 participants not present at the actual arrest, we obtained data on their assessments of police demeanor toward them based on the interactions that led directly to the arrests. Of the participants, 15 (71%) depicted police attitudes and behaviors toward them in positive terms, free of demeaning or negative qualities. As these participants explained, the officers listened to them, believed them, showed concern, were sympathetic and helpful, explained their rights and available services, and treated them with respect.

Representative of this group was the woman who recounted with gratitude how the deputy "calmed me down and listened to my problems. He treated me really good, actually. The last thing he said, 'You don't have to be treated like this. Not even for him,' and he pointed at my kid, and I just remembered that." Another participant felt reassured by the thorough manner with which the officer addressed her complaint, attributing this to genuine concern on his part. "Detective [name] encouraged me to think about my options—arrest, an order of protection. He is excellent. I'm going to write a letter of recommendation for him because he is very, very, very good. He really cares."

Participants who described police demeanor in positive terms emphasized the following: listening to the victim (this is not merely getting the facts of the crime, but permitting the victim to talk about related problems in the relationship), believing the victim, taking the victim's situation seriously, informing the victim of options and services (explaining them and answering questions), reassuring the victim that he or she (and their children) will be protected, and showing understanding and concern for the victim.

This last aspect of police demeanor—empathy with the victim—was of paramount significance. Whatever else they did or failed to do, said, or did not say, the officers' willingness to show a human face overlay other considerations. From the victims' viewpoint, the nature of their relationship with the police was to a larger degree contingent upon whether the officers seemed to understand and were emotionally moved by their plight. Victim attribution of meaning to all components of the police presence (asserting authority, establishing order, implementing legal procedures, etc.) was filtered through this primary aspect of police demeanor.

Three of the participants' evaluations of police demeanor were conflicted. For two of these individuals, their experiences with several officers during events resulting in the arrest produced divergent impressions of police attitudes. An example of this is the woman who sat, weeping and ignored, for three hours in the troopers' barracks, during which time she overheard officers in an adjacent room laughing and talking about her. Then, "I just went to pieces. My God, I've been here three hours. Nobody has talked to me. What is wrong with these people?" Eventually, a "very, very nice, sympathetic sergeant" wrote up the report.

> I was just so thankful for him. He made me feel safe. He constantly asked did I need some water. He handed me tissues. Those other officers did absolutely nothing for me, nothing. But he was incredible. He listened to my problems. He really made me feel good.

One-third ($n = 7$) of the participants were very critical of the police officers' attitudes and conduct toward them. Chief among the sources of dissatisfaction were victims' beliefs that the officers had been dismissive of the gravity of their situation and their failure to show concern for victims. A repeating theme in this study, victim trust, is undermined in interactions with officers who, by their manner, seem indifferent to victims' suffering and dismissive of the seriousness of victims' concerns. The potential for victim alienation is magnified as officers, adhering to their own procedures, are perceived by victims as hiding behind protocol and dealing with victims only reluctantly and without any real interest in them.

The participants drew conclusions about the attitudes of the police based on virtually any and every aspect of the officers' behaviors. A brusque, no-nonsense style was likely to be experienced by victims as rudeness and arrogance. Officers who did not immediately stop the abusers' verbal attacks were assumed to be hostile to the victims. Similar to other crime victims, these individuals wanted the police to instantly accept their version of events, bitterly resenting any indication that the police doubted their story. Shared by many of the respondents, one type of explanation of police motives and attitudes alleges pervasive police skepticism and victim-blaming in domestic violence situations. As one participant stated,

> The police make you look like you're probably wanting the relationship and you're not telling all the truth. It's like, she's half nuts or something. They think, oh no, she's on an emotional run. And they discredit you. They think women are too emotional. They think he didn't mean to, we'll give him another chance.

In addition to lack of compassion, another recurring motif was the complaint that the police were unwilling to spend enough time listening to participants, but instead limited the interaction to a narrow focus on legal aspects of the participants' acts. To the participants, not listening to their problems clearly reflects an overall disinterest in their condition.

> They don't want to, really. They want facts and I understand. But, if you talk to someone long enough, you'll see the real person. You'll see the pain and hurt and [how] they're caught and don't know how to get out.

For victims, listening and talking constitutes a necessary first step to helping them; when the police are unwilling or unable to do this, it is easy for victims to attribute hostile attitudes to the police.

In five of the cases, trust in the police reached a nadir when they made specific threats to the victim—three victims were told they might be arrested, and two victims were told that their children could be taken from them. Whether intended by the police as a strategy to achieve a truce between fractious spouses or to reprove victims whose seemingly intractable problems engender frustration, even disgust, the victims imbued these threats with two meanings. First, police actually know who has broken the law, but, because of their denigration of victims of domestic crimes, want to dispense with them as quickly as possible. As one participant recounted her reaction to this threat, "It's got to be like common sense. The sheriff knew that he [ex-husband] was full of poo poo. I think he knew exactly what had happened. They said, 'well, that's what he says and we don't know what happened.'" The second meaning for victims is that these threats are real—if they are not careful, the police will arrest them and their children will be taken from them.

The legacy of distrust was especially marked for the five participants who had generalized their assessments of specific individuals to all law enforcement. These women viewed the police as a kind of male club, loyal to each other, sympathetic to male abusers, and either indifferent or actively hostile to women. Two alleged that their abusers had personal connections with the police that enabled them to act with impunity. In their words,

> There's a lot of men police officers like a club and everybody knows it. There's a brotherhood between policemen. I represented an ex-wife trying to screw over her husband. I represented what

can or maybe has happened to them. If I was a man, I'd'a been arrested and gone for life. But, "when you're dead, give us a call." They told me in different ways than words that he is going to do what he is going to do and, "oh yeah, we'll be investigating it."

The police are chauvinist. They aren't fair to women still. They aren't fair. I never got concern, I don't feel, as a woman. And that officer I dealt with previously, I believe he's an abuser himself. I tried to be calm. They don't like it when you're nerved up and talking a lot. And the police cover up for each other. And I'm tired of it. The state police lost everything I filled out. They said, "We're dismissing it." So, I thought the law isn't on my side. If the law isn't on your side, what are you going to do?

Conclusion

This study has focused on aspects of police demeanor that are of great concern to victims of intimate violence. We described the following four categories of police demeanor of which most victims were critical: (1) minimizing the situation, (2) disbelieving the victim, (3) we don't care, and (4) macho cop. From the victims' perspectives, listening and believing are the first steps that police must take to begin the process of helping them, but this is not enough to guarantee police credibility in the eyes of victims. Victims want the police to show empathy for them and their situation. Victims expect the police to act effectively on their behalf, but equally importantly they want the police to treat them as worthy of police concern and intervention.

A provocative finding was that, when compared with earlier (non-arrest) encounters with law enforcement, the tendency was for participants to have more positive assessments of police demeanor during the arrest event. Optimistically, it may be that police attitudes are changing as a consequence of new training and reforms in police policy. On the other hand, it is possible that by this point victims are so relieved at the arrest of their tormentors that they tend to remember only the positive aspects of their encounters with the police. It could even be that one consequence of involvement with a victim witness program is a more positive victim perception of criminal justice officials, including the police. However, existing research does not support this explanation.

Whatever the reasons for this change, it is clear that the experiences and preferences of victims must in some measure be represented in the criminal justice system's reform agenda. Feminist, academic, and advocacy groups have purported to speak for the victims of intimate violence. Legislators and police administrators have moved rapidly to criminalize acts that historically were of little interest to the state. The new harshness has been driven by system needs; in particular, concern over the public's lack of confidence in its justice institutions. The danger is that the most important group of all may be sidelined during the national debate about the future of our society's response to domestic violence. Lacking victim input, the formulation of policies may continue to be shaped by ideology and pragmatic politics. Yet, if these policies are to be credible and effective, they must be informed by the voices of victims.

Critical Thinking

These findings suggest that police change the way they interact with repeat victims and imply that police think that those who stay with abusers do not deserve continued respect and concern. If this is the case, how will such attitudes affect the reporting of domestic violence? At what point do victims think that the lack of concern, and possible ridicule, from police is not worth calling them? If women do stop calling police for help in these situations, are they truly getting equal protection under the law?

References

Bowker, L.H. (1982). Police services to battered women: Bad or not so bad? *Criminal Justice and Behavior, 9*, 475–496.

Brown, S.E. (1984). Police responses to wife beating: Neglect of a crime of violence. *Journal of Criminal Justice, 12*(3), 277–288.

Buzawa, E.S. and Austin, T. (1993). Determining police response to domestic violence victims. *American Behavioral Scientist, 36*, 610–623.

Buzawa, E.S., Austin, T.L., Bannon, J., and Jackson, J. (1992). Rule of victim preference in determining police response to victims of domestic violence. In E.S. Buzawa and C.G. Buzawa (eds), *Domestic violence: The changing criminal justice response* (pp. 256–269). Westwood, CT: Auburn House.

Criminal procedure law of the State of New York. (1996/1967). Section 140.10/4. Flushing, New York: Looseleaf Law Publication.

Kennedy, D.B., and Homant, R.J. (1984). Battered women's evaluation of police response. *Victimology: An International Journal, 9*, 174–179.

Muraoka, S.M. (1996). *Use of police services by victims of domestic violence.* Unpublished doctoral dissertation, University of Nebraska.

Pagelow, M.D. (1981). *Woman-battering: Victims and their experiences.* Beverly Hills, CA: Sage.

Radford, J. (1987). Policing male violence—policing women. In J. Hammer and M. Maynard (eds), *Women, violence and social control* (pp. 30–45). London: Macmillan.

Zoomer, O.J. (1989). Policing women battering in the Netherlands. In J. Hammer, J. Radford, and B. Stanko (eds), *Women, policing and male violence* (pp. 125–154). London: Routledge.

10

We Trust You, But Not *That* Much: Examining Police–Black Clergy Partnerships to Reduce Youth Violence

Rod K. Brunson, Anthony A. Braga, David M. Hureau, and Kashea Pegram

Abstract: *This article examines activist black clergy involvement in local youth violence reduction initiatives and efforts to improve police–minority community relations in Boston, Massachusetts. In-depth interviews were conducted with activist black clergy, community organizers, and Boston Police Department (BPD) managers. Study findings highlight how the work of a specific group of black ministers supports that of BPD and vice versa. The research suggests that police–black clergy partnerships can improve police legitimacy in minority communities and enhance informal social control elements of youth violence prevention strategies.*

Introduction

Police departments, unfortunately, often do not have strong relationships with community members in disadvantaged, minority neighborhoods where violent crime problems tend to concentrate. Scholars have long recognized the persistent problem of fragile police–minority community relations. In fact, prior research concerning citizens' attitudes toward police has consistently found that blacks report more dissatisfaction with and distrust of the police than their counterparts from other racial groups (see, e.g., Skogan and Frydl, 2004; Weitzer and Tuch, 2006). This is an important concern because neighborhood residents are more apt to assist police in the performance of their duties if they view the police favorably. There are many historical reasons for the poorer assessments of the police held by African Americans; these include the harms generated by over- and under-policing black neighborhoods, a lack of diversity in several police departments, the concentration of police misconduct in black neighborhoods, and other concerning issues disproportionately affecting African Americans (see, e.g., Brunson and Miller, 2006; Kane, 2002; Terrill and Reisig, 2003). Indeed, in recognizing these persistent problems, many contemporary community policing programs are focused on stimulating improved relationships with minority communities.

In many African American communities, the black church functions as a central social institution. Beyond serving the religious and spiritual needs of parishioners, several black churches are involved in community organizing, social service activities, and political action (see DuBois, 1903; Frazier, 1963). Whereas the historical significance of the black church is well documented, scholars have paid less attention to its role as a potent social institution in community crime control and prevention efforts. It stands to reason that numerous police–community initiatives would be connected to faith-based institutions given that "African American residents of urban disadvantage neighborhoods create their own civil institutions—the church being one—to deal with community-based problems" (Mears and Corkan, 2007, p. 1378). While there are some promising case studies (e.g., Mears, 2002; Winship and Berrien, 1999), the available research has not elicited the kind of information that would allow scholars, community leaders, and policy-makers to acquire deeper understandings of the nature and extent of these police–clergy partnerships.

The current study examines the relationships between activist black clergy and police managers involved in youth violence reduction initiatives and efforts to improve police–minority community relations in Boston, Massachusetts. We conducted in-depth interviews with three key constituencies: Boston Police Department (BPD) managers, Boston TenPoint Coalition (TPC) black ministers, and community organizers working in disadvantaged Boston neighborhoods. It is important to note from the outset that our study does not take a position on whether faith-based initiatives have the potential to reduce criminal behavior, whether spirituality is a key ingredient to increasing community cohesion, or any other issues in the broader debate on religion and crime. Our inquiry centers on understanding the advantages and challenges of police partnerships with leaders of a ubiquitous social institution in black neighborhoods—the black church.

This study highlights that the degree to which community policing efforts are successful hinges largely on a police department's ability to forge and maintain mutually beneficial relationships with organizations that can effectively broker trust between neighborhood residents and police. Further, our results suggest that police–clergy partnerships, in particular, have the potential to improve police–community relations and garner community support for crime control initiatives. The broader implications are that police administrators should work to identify key intermediaries to community-based organizations and local social institutions that could deliver critical social control elements to police crime prevention strategies. Finally, we recognize that not all black churches will "answer the call"; instead crime control efforts will likely be led by a small but active few that have a disposition and capacity for civic action, making the "identification" aspect all the more important.

Black Churches, Crime, and the Police

Scholars have long recognized the prominent role that black churches[1] have played in various facets of African Americans' lives (DuBois, 1903; Frazier, 1963). In fact, commentators have consistently identified black churches as important social institutions for its members—beginning with slavery, during emancipation, throughout the Civil Rights era, and in contemporary campaigns for social justice (Billingsley and Caldwell, 1991; Cavendish, 2000; Lincoln, 1974). Thus, black churches have shouldered the weighty responsibility for attending to the purposeful and systematic exclusion of African Americans from full participation in many segments of society (Cavendish, 2000; Lincoln, 1974; Pattillo-McCoy, 1998). Further, a number of historians have credited black churches for effective organizing, while simultaneously accepting responsibility for parishioners' well-being beyond the four walls of places of worship (Billingsley and Caldwell, 1991; Pattillo-McCoy, 1998). For example, Cavendish (2000) notes, "African Americans have historically looked to their churches as their chief source of culture, music, values, community cohesion, and political activism" (pp. 66–67).

The available research suggests that black churches can be important sources of social capital and could serve as important elements of "collective efficacy" in African American neighborhoods. Collective efficacy is generally defined as "social cohesion among neighbors combined with their willingness to intervene on behalf of the common good" (Sampson, Raudenbush, and Earls, 1997, p. 918) and has been revealed to be inversely related to high levels of violent crime in neighborhoods. In disadvantaged neighborhoods where social control mechanisms offered by the family, school, and other institutions may be weakened, the social policy implication is to facilitate black churches, either alone or in partnership with secular institutions, to exert informal social control or enhance shared expectations of residents in a way that controls and prevents serious violence.

Efforts to address delinquency have led to pioneering research concerning the role of the church as a protective factor that helps build and strengthen neighborhood social networks.[2] For example, in measuring concepts, such as one's religiosity and church involvement in relation to delinquency, scholars have found that youth who are more active in church are also less likely to engage in various forms of both serious and minor delinquency (Johnson, Jang, De Li, and Larson, 2000; Johnson, Larson, De Li, and Jang, 2000). Launched in 2000, the Amachi mentoring project in Philadelphia, a collaboration of inner-city congregations (mostly black churches), Big Brothers/Big Sisters, Prison Fellowship (a national prison ministry), Public/Private Ventures, and others, was designed to mentor the children of prisoners with the intent of breaking the cycle of imprisonment in disadvantaged neighborhoods (Johnson, 2011; Jucovy, 2003). By 2002, Amachi was operating through volunteers from 42 churches and some 517 children had been paired with mentors. According to Johnson (2011), 82 percent of the mentors were African American and 8 percent were Latino. Most striking was that 34 percent of the mentors were African American males—a critically important but difficult to recruit group of volunteers in inner-city communities.

Forming effective working partnerships with black churches seems to be a logical mechanism through which police executives can strive to build better relationships with the black community. Black communities have a much higher density of churches per 100,000 residents than white communities (Sampson, 2012).[3] In domestic and international polls, many measures suggest that African Americans are consistently among the most religious people in the world (Gallup and Castelli, 1989). In fact, relative to white

Americans, African Americans "attend church more frequently, participate in other church-related affairs more often, and belong to more church-affiliated organizations" (Ellison and Sherkat, 1995, p. 1415). Drawing on the civil rights literature, it would seem that black churches represent potentially powerful local social institutions to carry out community-based actions to address violent crime problems.

It is important to recognize that one area of concern among many black church leaders has been persistent, tenuous police–minority community relations (Billingsley and Caldwell, 1991). Graphic images of untoward police brutality from the Civil Rights era have for many Americans come to symbolize the long-standing, troubled relationship between police and black citizens (Bass, 2001; Websdale, 2001). Further, black church leaders routinely occupied the front lines of some of the most violent clashes between police and African American protesters, reflecting a regrettable but undeniable part of U.S. history. An abundant body of research has revealed that residents of disadvantaged urban areas routinely bear the brunt of frequent, unwelcome police contacts (e.g., arrests, pat-downs, and pedestrian stops) (Brunson and Miller, 2006; Weitzer and Brunson, 2009). Specifically, recurring, negative police experiences have dire consequences for the legitimacy of law enforcement officers and public confidence in the criminal justice system (Brunson, 2007; Brunson and Weitzer, 2009).

It stands to reason then that prolonged levels of heightened racial animus between neighborhood residents and local police also have dire implications for police–community relations and black citizens' perceptions of aggressive crime-control efforts. And while perhaps not rising to the same level in seriousness or egregiousness of previously documented incidents of police malfeasance, there is no shortage of contemporary, unsettling accounts of black persons' alleged mistreatment at the hands of police (Brunson, 2007; Stewart, Baumer, Brunson, and Simons, 2009). The widespread diffusion of these unsettling narratives increases the likelihood that neighborhood residents will come to view local policing initiatives as racially biased (Brunson, 2007; Stewart et al., 2009; Weitzer, 2002).

Damaged police–minority community relations have the potential to undermine police legitimacy and thwart their ability to implement effective crime control initiatives. For example, people who believe that officers routinely engage in discriminatory acts express less trust in the police (Tyler and Wakslak, 2004). Citizens are more willing to support officers' crime-fighting efforts, however, when they believe that police will dispense justice equitably (Sunshine and Tyler, 2003). Interestingly, the importance of procedural justice for increasing police legitimacy is also confirmed by individuals who report having unwelcome police interactions but express greater satisfaction following such encounters if they believe the officer treated them fairly (Tyler and Folger, 1980).

Crawford, Lister, Blackburn, and Burnett's (2005) research on plural policing in England and Wales is relevant to the current study (see also Crawford, 2008; Crawford, Blackburn, Lister, and Shepherd, 2004). Specifically, they note that "good community consultation at both strategic and operational levels was identified as important in establishing and maintaining community engagement and helping to build constructive and informed relationships" (2005, p.x). Thus, Crawford et al. (2005) observe that high levels of police–community engagement have the potential to increase residents' willingness to come forward with information on local crime.

While there is prima facie evidence that black churches could serve as important partners to the police in their pursuit of improved police–community relations and more effective crime-control strategies, there is little systematic research that specifically examines these partnerships. Research in Chicago, however, suggests there are perhaps two divergent narratives about the potential of black clergy in mobilizing communities to control crime. In an effort to reduce youth violence rates on Chicago's West Side and strengthen police–community relationships, the Chicago Police Department (CPD) and several hundred African American churches organized prayer vigils in May 1997 (Mears, 2002; Mears and Corkan, 2007). These prayer vigils were credited with establishing stronger working relationships between clergy and the police, enhancing police legitimacy in the black community, and improving police officer perceptions of West Side residents. The West Side prayer vigil was also credited with initiating a critical rethinking of the CPD's community policing strategy as the City of Chicago became more interested in supporting similar local grassroots events involving churches and faith-based institutions (Mears and Corkan, 2007). Collaborations between police and churches were argued to enhance the community efficacy of poor minority neighborhoods in Chicago. Similarly, Skogan (2006) reported that about one-third of all community policing beat meetings in 1998 were held in churches, especially in predominately African American communities where the link between the community policing program and churches was observed to be particularly strong.

Sampson (2012), however, suggests that black churches may deliver little in terms of collective community-based action. He specifically examined whether the density of churches and other community-based nonprofit organizations impacted the collective action underway in Chicago's predominately black communities. While the density of nonprofit organizations was positively related to collective efficacy, Sampson (2012) found "that the density of the churches is *negatively* related to collective efficacy and one of its core indicators—trust" (p. 205). In explaining this surprising result, Sampson (2012) suggests that the impact and legacy of concentrated disadvantage in black communities has made it difficult for churches alone to establish the trust among local residents needed to facilitate collective action. Moreover, he suggests that just because a church is located in a particular community does not mean that its interests coincide with that community or that its parishioners necessarily live in that community. Interestingly, Sampson (2012) also reported that religious leaders in Chicago had stronger inter-institutional connections to politicians when compared to connections with leaders in community, business, education, and law enforcement organizations.

McRoberts (2003) examined black churches in Boston's Four Corners neighborhood, one of the densest neighborhoods for churches in the city. He found that most African American churches in Four Corners were led and attended by "outsiders" with little investment in the surrounding neighborhood. Rather, these churches were located in Four Corners due to cheap rents. McRoberts (2003) further noted that most of the congregations were not actively engaged in neighborhood revitalization or improvement efforts. In fact, in terms of social and physical disorder, many of the structures remain shuttered during the week, looking uninviting and offering little in terms of additional eyes on the street and potential for improved community guardianship.

Boston's Police–Black Clergy Partnership

Boston received national acclaim for its innovative approach to preventing youth violence in the 1990s (Butterfield, 1996; Witkin, 1997). The well-known Operation Ceasefire initiative was an interagency violence intervention that focused enforcement and social service resources on a small number of gang-involved offenders at the heart of the city's youth violence problem (Kennedy, Piehl, and Braga, 1996). The Ceasefire "pulling levers" focused deterrence strategy was associated with a near two-thirds drop in youth homicide in the late 1990s (Braga, Kennedy, Waring, and Piehl, 2001). While the sudden decrease in youth homicide was surprising and certainly newsworthy, the Boston approach was also noted for its extraordinary police–community relationship spearheaded by a small network of activist black clergy (Berrien and Winship, 2002; Winship and Berrien, 1999). In his review of the so-called "Boston Miracle," Johnson (2011) further credits these black ministers with reducing complaints against police by 60 percent during the 1990s. Given the history of poor race relations in the City of Boston, it was remarkable that any group of black community members were able to forge such a highly productive partnership with the BPD.

The development and trajectory of Boston's unusual police–clergy partnership has been extensively documented elsewhere (Braga, Hureau, and Winship, 2008; Braga and Winship, 2006; Berman and Fox, 2010; Berrien and Winship, 2002; Winship, 2005; Winship and Berrien, 1999). However, a brief summary is necessary here. A series of well-publicized scandals emanating from highly aggressive and indiscriminate policing tactics, poor management practices, and corruption led to an extensive overhaul of the BPD's command staff personnel, organizational structure, mission, and tactics during the early 1990s. A community policing plan was implemented and the Youth Violence Strike Force (YVSF, initially known as the Anti-Gang Violence Unit) was created to disrupt ongoing gang conflicts and focus on more general youth violence prevention work. While these changes were important in creating an environment where the police could collaborate with the community, residents of Boston's poor minority neighborhoods remained wary of and dissatisfied with a police department that had a long history of abusive and unfair treatment.

In 1992, a loosely allied group of activist black clergy formed the TPC following a gang invasion of the Morningstar Baptist Church. During a memorial for a slain rival gang member, mourners were attacked with knives and guns (Berrien and Winship, 2002; Winship and Berrien, 1999). In the wake of that outrage, TPC ministers decided that they should attempt to prevent the youth in their community from joining gangs, and also that they needed to send an anti-violence message to all youth, whether gang-involved or not.

The TPC initially included some 40 Boston-area churches with Reverends Jeffrey Brown, Raymond Hammond, and Eugene Rivers as its key leaders.[4]

Initially, the ministers assumed an adversarial role to the BPD and were highly critical in the public media of police efforts to prevent youth violence (Braga and Winship, 2006; Winship and Berrien, 1999). However, as TPC ministers worked the streets, they started to form effective relationships with particular YVSF officers and to develop a shared understanding of the nature of youth violence in Boston: only a small number of youth in the neighborhoods were involved in violence; many of these gang-involved youth were better served by intervention and prevention strategies, and only a small number of these gang-involved youth needed to be removed from the streets through arrest and prosecution strategies.

While TPC ministers were not initially involved in the development of Operation Ceasefire, they soon played key roles in the implementation of the gang violence strategy and, more broadly, served as central brokers in the management of positive relationships between the BPD and Boston's minority community. Through their involvement in Ceasefire, TPC ministers became part of the process of determining which gang interventions would occur and when. In addition, they, along with others, gave gang members the message that they had a choice: stop the "gang banging" and they would be helped—with school, a job, family; continue, and the full weight of the law (and the community) would come down on them, with every possible lever being used to see that they were incarcerated. The transparency and involvement in the enforcement process built trust and further solidified a functional working relationship between the community and the BPD. In turn, by engaging a process through which they were meaningfully and appropriately accountable to the community, the BPD created the political support, or "umbrella of legitimacy," that it needed to pursue more focused and perhaps more aggressive intervention than would have been possible otherwise (Winship and Berrien, 1999).

TPC ministers also worked with the BPD to manage negative publicity by the local media after several potentially explosive events ranging from the beating of a black undercover officer by uniformed police to the accidental death of a 75-year-old retired minister who suffered a fatal heart attack after a botched drug raid (Braga and Winship, 2006). In these cases, TPC ministers took two positions. First, they demanded that the police department take responsibility for its actions—investigate incidents thoroughly and hold those involved accountable. Second, after it was clear that the BPD was accepting responsibility, the ministers communicated to the community that the police were in fact reacting appropriately. This, in turn, prevented these situations from becoming racially explosive and provided the police with the continued political support they needed in order to undertake policy innovations, such as Ceasefire. The ministers also performed this dual role with regard to fatal police shootings, eight of which occurred over a 22-month period between 2000 and 2002 (Winship, 2005).

The BPD–TPC partnership seems to offer a potentially powerful way for police departments to manage tenuous relationships with minority communities and, simultaneously, to enrich community-based responses to violent crime problems. While their operational capacity has waxed and waned over time (Braga et al., 2008), Boston TPC maintains its mission to end violence in Boston through the participation of faith-based institutions in citywide crime prevention efforts.[5] In addition to continuing its involvement in Operation Ceasefire, the TPC supports prisoner reentry initiatives, female delinquency prevention programs, and community crisis intervention teams.

It is important to note here that data used in previous narrative accounts of the BPD–TPC relationship were limited to small numbers of interviews with key clergy and police personnel, material from local and national media accounts, and a small number of ethnographic observations.[6] Research on Operation Ceasefire simply acknowledged TPC clergy as important partners in the interagency working group and provided a narrative account of their role in communications with gang-involved youth (see Kennedy et al., 1996; Braga et al., 2001). Based on these modest data-collection efforts, a number of important policy-relevant claims have been made about the BPD–TPC relationship. In this study, we closely examine *how* these partnerships: (1) improved police legitimacy in black communities, and (2) enhanced police crime prevention and control efforts. Finally, the existing literature on the BPD–TPC partnership does not examine the challenges involved in maintaining productive police–clergy working partnerships. Our research explicitly identifies some persistent issues that arise in the day-to-day work of these two very different groups.

Study Setting and Methodology

Our research was framed as a qualitative case study of the contemporary BPD–TPC partnership with a focus on the three specific issues identified above. Case studies generally represent empirical research inquiries that investigate phenomena within their real-life contexts (Yin, 2009). Case studies provide in-depth examinations of people, groups, and events that facilitate description, exploration, and explanation. As such, the case study approach drawing upon extensive qualitative interviews with clergy, police, and community organizers was an appropriate method to learn more about how these partnerships to improve police legitimacy, enhance community crime prevention efforts, and face the challenges that arise in managing these partnerships. However, given their tight focus on specific phenomena, case studies can have limited generalizability when extrapolating key findings to other people, places, and contexts. While our findings are limited to the study site and its current context, we believe that the careful documentation of the nature of police–black clergy partnerships in one setting can yield important insight on plausible steps that can be taken to address a persistent and ubiquitous problem present in most U.S. cities: poor relationships between the police and minority communities.

The current study enjoys a design advantage over prior examinations of the BPD–TPC partnership, and, in fact, most qualitative research of police–minority community relations. Specifically, data for this article are drawn from systematic face-to-face interviews with 70 very knowledgeable individuals: 30 inter-faith TPC clergy, 30 BPD managers of varying rank and experience, and 10 community organizers working in disadvantaged, high-violence Boston neighborhoods. The interviews were conducted between spring 2012 and fall 2012. All respondents were recruited with the assistance of community liaisons (for the clergy and community organizer interviews) and the BPD command staff (for police manager interviews). The research team also used snowball sampling procedures to enroll additional participants by obtaining the help of those previously interviewed to introduce other persons suitable for inclusion in the study. The interviews were voluntary, and civilian respondents were paid $25 (in the form of a retail gift card) for their participation and promised strict confidentiality.[7]

Sampling was purposive: key informants were asked to identify and approach individuals for participation in the research, namely persons who were known to work in the study neighborhoods. The goal was to interview activist clergy, police managers, and community organizers, the vast majority of whom had decades of experience working in disadvantaged Boston neighborhoods as these individuals would likely have extensive knowledge regarding current and previous efforts to combat youth crime. Thus, sampling was designed to include three specific groups of persons with considerable experiential knowledge and insight regarding the foundation and evolution of the BPD–TPC partnership.

BPD managers were selected based on a priori knowledge that they had worked an assignment that would have put them in the position to partner with TPC clergy to address violent crime problems. These assignments included working in the YVSF, in the BPD School Police Unit, as a Community Service Officer, as a member of the Safe Street Teams,[8] and as a Captain or Lieutenant Detective in a BPD district that provides police services in high violent crime areas.

Few studies have offered an in-depth examination of whether and, if so, how the work of the police supports the mission of black churches and vice versa. Specifically, we asked a series of questions about the nature of police–clergy relationships in Boston and probed respondents for guidance regarding how best to strengthen these relationships. Our study allowed for a detailed examination of these issues with three groups of constituents. The interview schedule was semi-structured, consisting of both closed- and open-ended questions that allow for considerable exploration.[9] We sought to improve reliability by cross-checking and probing study participants' responses to the interview questions. Interviews lasted for approximately one hour and were conducted in private spaces. Except when respondents refused, the interviews were digitally recorded (audio only, however), transcribed, and analyzed by the authors.

In the analysis, we selected statements that illustrated themes consistently found throughout the data. The quotes used were not atypical, with the exception of a few issues that we indicate were mentioned by a small number of respondents. We were also careful throughout the data analysis to ensure that the emerging themes correctly reflected respondents' descriptions. Thus, the research team utilized grounded theory methods to identify recurrent topics, in addition to less common but salient issues (Strauss, 1987).

Study Participants

Boston Police Department

Ninety percent of police respondents were male ($N = 27$) and slightly more than 73 percent were white ($N = 22$). The respondents ranged from 35 to 63 years old with a mean age of 43.8 years. A diversity of BPD management positions were represented among the subjects ranging from front-line supervisors (sergeants and lieutenants) to the upper echelons of the command staff structure (captains, deputy superintendents, and superintendents). At the time of the interviews, the most frequently held rank of the subjects was sergeant ($N = 9$, 30.0%) followed by deputy superintendent ($N = 7$, 23.3%). A majority of the BPD subjects were assigned to patrol forces (Bureau of Field Services, $N = 17$, 56.7%), followed by detective management positions (Bureau of Investigative Services, $N = 9$, 30%), and the Office of the Police Commissioner ($N = 4$, 13.3%). On average, the respondents had served as BPD officers for 23.8 years with a range of 14 to 33 years of police experience.

TenPoint Coalition Clergy

Eighty percent of the ministers were male ($N = 24$) and all but two were black ($N = 28$, 93.3%). These study participants were between the ages of 29 and 73 with a mean age of 49.4 years. Ministers reported having worked in disadvantaged Boston neighborhoods on average for 19.8 years. Our clergy sample comprised the following religious affiliations: African Methodist Episcopal ($N = 2$, 6.7%), Baptist ($N = 13$, 43.3%), Catholic ($N = 2$, 6.7%), Pentecostal ($N = 7$, 23.3%), and Presbyterian ($N = 1$, 3.3%). Finally, 16.7% ($N = 5$) of our clergy respondents were nondenominational.

Community Organizers

Eight of the ten community organizer respondents were male (80%), and two were female. Seven respondents were (70%) identified as black, one (10%) as Latino, one (10%) as white, and one (10%) as mixed race. The community organizers ranged in age from 26 to 62, with a mean age of 38 years. They further served an array of Boston's neighborhoods, particularly those that were majority nonwhite and disproportionately affected by violence. Although the primary neighborhoods served ranged from Dorchester ($N = 5$) to Mattapan ($N = 1$), the subsample had a wealth of work experience throughout the city. Aside from Dorchester, Roxbury, and Mattapan, several community organizers also mentioned experience working in South Boston, Jamaica Plain, and the South End. While only four respondents in the subsample (40%) currently serve as outreach workers to gang-involved individuals (tasked with reducing serious youth violence), a unique feature of this group is that 90 percent ($N = 9$) had served as gang outreach workers at some point in their careers, giving them a unique and longitudinal perspective regarding on-the-ground policing efforts of the BPD and the outreach and service work of the TPC.

Study Findings

Our main objective here is to provide a more nuanced understanding of two central claims offered in prior research on the TPC–BPD partnership (i.e., increased police legitimacy and enhanced community crime prevention) and to investigate one important but previously overlooked policy area. We begin by examining study participants' reports that the BPD gained increased legitimacy in the eyes of Boston's black community by establishing strong working relationships with the TPC. Next, we investigate respondents' views that TPC involvement in BPD crime prevention initiatives provided mechanisms for officers to improve rapport with high-risk youth and their families as well as convey their anti-violence message to gangs. Finally, we analyze each constituency's detailed accounts to highlight how particular individuals in particular organizations relied on their pre-existing relationships, and built on mutual trust and respect to successfully navigate the daily challenges of police and clergy working together. The current study supports, refines, and extends prior research on the topic, resulting in an improved and more holistic understanding of the TPC–BPD relationship.

Improved Legitimacy as an Important Outcome of Police–Clergy Partnerships

Study participants from the three constituencies almost uniformly identified improved police legitimacy with minority communities as the primary benefit of the BPD–TPC working partnership. Here, we adopt the definition of police legitimacy used by the National Research Council's Committee to Review Research on Police Policy and Practices: "the judgments that ordinary citizens make about the rightfulness of police conduct and the organizations that employ and supervise them" (Skogan and Frydl, 2004, p. 291; see also Tyler, 2004). As the Committee suggests, perceptions of legitimacy are, by definition, subjective, and legitimacy "lies in the hearts and minds" of the public. The police are more effective in achieving their goals when citizens trust the police and view them as legitimate authorities.

While everyone mentioned the importance of the TPC relationship to improved police–community relations, the majority of BPD managers ($N = 22$, 73.3%) explicitly recognized that the clergy provided them with an important mechanism to develop enhanced trust, transparency, and legitimacy with black communities. These officers explained that there was a long history of bad relations between the BPD and the black community that improved over the course of the 1990s. The development of strong working relationships with the TPC clergy helped address some long-standing grievances with the provision of policing services in black neighborhoods and maintain open lines of communication on ongoing issues when tensions arise. BPD Manager Delaney said:

> We are dealing with two different worlds. In the eighties and nineties, we didn't trust each other and we didn't understand each other at all. [The BPD] changed the way we did policing [by adopting community policing] and partner[ing] with anyone who wanted to work with us to make the streets safer. The ministers became, perhaps, our most important partner in changing community perceptions of our work. Things aren't perfect . . . there will always be problems that come up . . . but we communicate with each other now.

Seventeen officers (56.7%) described the value of clergy members in explaining police actions in tense situations to the community, such as police-involved shootings or apparent excessive uses of force in apprehending offenders. These BPD managers suggested that TPC clergy were able to provide the department with a "moment of pause" to explain incidents and deal with any bona fide police transgressions before community members protested in streets or, possibly, rioted. Commenting on a recent video recording of an arrest of a young black male that appeared, at first blush, to involve excessive use of force, BPD Manager Mallett reported:

> I can understand why the community may have gotten the wrong impression about that [incident]. However, [the forced used] wasn't excessive . . . the officer did what he was trained to do. While there were some initial protests, it was important that the clergy and other community leaders gave us a chance to explain the officers' actions. . . . The story in the [Boston] Globe turned out really good for us . . . the Reverends' comments in the paper [that the arrest did not involve excessive force] helped cool things down.

The same BPD managers also observed that relationships with the TPC clergy enhanced their ability to have open conversations about the nature of violence in black neighborhoods and how their gang enforcement strategies did not seek to target all young black males indiscriminately. For instance, BPD Manager Dawson observed:

> Many community meetings before the [TPC] partnerships weren't very productive. The residents often took a very defensive stance when talking about gangs and shootings. You would hear things like . . . "you only call them *gangs* because they are a bunch of young black guys hanging on the corner . . ." or "why don't you do something about the drugs that are coming into the neighborhood? Our kids aren't responsible for that and the drugs are causing most of the violence . . ." with one of the Reverends by your side, it is much easier to have an honest talk about what is going on. . . . [Members of the black community] are much more likely to trust your opinion and defer to your judgment on enforcement actions when a minister is on your team.

Ten officers (33.3%) recognized that it was particularly valuable to consult with clergy members on planned law enforcement operations before implementation.[10] The discussions were focused on the strategic elements of overall enforcement plans. BPD managers reported two related benefits. First, BPD managers received valuable feedback on how the community might perceive the enforcement strategy so they could consider tempering any actions that the community might find overly harsh or draconian. As BPD Manager

Mamalian suggested, "it is always a good idea to present your ideas to the ministers first and hear out any concerns they have before you act." Second, a priori conversations with TPC clergy helped BPD inform the community of the real goals of the law enforcement action and the careful consideration through which targets were selected. BPD Manager Bonner commented,

> We can't rely on the media to get it right for us . . . we need to make sure the community gets it right from the people it trusts. It is powerful when a minister says to residents that our enforcement actions were focused on reducing violence in the neighborhood rather than some misguided comments about the police wrongfully hassling young black men.

The vast majority of TPC clergy ($N = 23$, 76.6%) emphasized that their ability to forge an effective partnership with the BPD centered largely on their success at brokering trust from community members. Further, faith leaders also understood that if they were able to enhance neighborhood residents' trust of them, it might extend to BPD, resulting in increased police legitimacy. Specifically, as did BPD managers, our clergy respondents pointed to how the BPD often sought advice from TPC leadership about planned enforcement strategies because police believed that they were able to accurately communicate the minority communities' moral voice and conscience. Reverend Lindsey noted:

> I know from being on the inside that the [TPC] is consulted almost immediately by the police department when there is going to be a change of strategy [,] the first calls that are made are to the people who are a part of the [TPC]. [The black clergy] have been supportive of the police while at the same time maintaining their individual voice, which is important. And the community has to believe and know that the [TPC] has their interest at heart as paramount . . . that no one's cutting deals in order to give support to the police [arbitrarily] when it may go against the valid interest of the community.

As recognized by Winship and Berrien (1999), TenPoint provided the BPD with an "umbrella of legitimacy" and an opportunity to address seething community tensions in the aftermath of questionable police actions. Reverend Shegog remarked, "I think the police are glad that [TPC] is there because of course some of the incidences that the Coalition has dealt with and will deal with [the police] don't have to deal with. And it's kind of like a buffer for [the police] and they know that." Ten of our clergy (33.3%) mentioned the complexities inherent in simultaneously representing the communities' interests and preserving positive relationships with the BPD. For instance, Pastor Rooks said, "the majority of people come to the conclusion that if sometimes the police are mad with you, the Mayor is mad with you, and sometimes the community is mad with you, you're probably trying to be honest . . . I think the position TenPoint and other groups have tried to play is being honest brokers and honest partners in this process." Likewise, Pastor Rodgers commented,

> I think clergy took a pragmatic approach to police–community relations . . . [deciding] we're going to praise the cops that are doing the right thing and shine a light on the cops that aren't, but primarily we're going to focus on the cops who are doing the right thing. Build some goodwill with the department and begin to work from within. And address the concerns of the community that way.

Of the three interview sub-samples, the community organizer sub-sample was the least sanguine in its views regarding the TPC's role in promoting police legitimacy. Half of the community respondents ($N = 5$) believed that the TPC played a role in improving police–community relations in Boston. Tilly summarized the views of this subset of the community sample, stating:

> In the 1990s, [TenPoint] was a part of the puzzle. The fact that we could do saturation policing to cool off crime waves was great, and this was due in part to TenPoint. They don't do much directly with youth—they don't have a lot of capacity, and frankly their volunteers aren't very good and don't like the type of kids they are supposed to work with. Their main thing was political, not direct service.

Like Tilly, the majority of community organizers understood the TPC's role in both building police relations and preventing street violence as largely symbolic and political. Half of the sample ($N = 5$) praised the TPC for serving as a "voice" for the black community.

Enhancing Community Crime Prevention and Control Efforts

The BPD managers were well aware that, in general, police departments benefit from strong relationships with community members in their efforts to control and prevent serious violent crime problems in urban settings. It seemed to be common knowledge among the police respondents that community support and involvement in police programs can enrich their violence prevention effectiveness in many ways. While particular police respondents identified varying mechanisms, several common themes emerged. For the BPD's community and problem-oriented policing initiatives, TPC ministers relayed information from residents and encouraged community members to provide valuable insights on the underlying conditions and dynamics that caused violent crime problems to persist in specific neighborhoods and particular hot spots. TPC clergy were also recognized as important conduits to community groups and local social networks that could add important informal social control elements to police crime prevention plans. For enforcement-based initiatives, such as Operation Ceasefire, clergy provided complementary voices at offender call-ins and helped connect social services to gang youth and their families. Strong relationships with TPC clergy were credited with holding some potential in forwarding investigative efforts. The willingness of community members to step forward as witnesses was critical in BPD efforts to hold violent offenders accountable for their crimes.

Two-thirds of the BPD managers ($N = 20$) valued the enhanced "information sharing" that partnerships with TPC clergy offered. Through community meetings held at churches such as the Twelfth Baptist Church in Roxbury or at faith-based organizations such as the Ella J. Baker House in Dorchester, BPD managers reported learning about community concerns (such as problematic drug houses, certain groups of disorderly youth, and a lack of police presence in particular areas) and specific incidents that may not come to the attention of the police (such as simmering feuds among youth that could escalate to more serious violence). The officers also saw the strong benefits in providing the clergy with information to communicate to community members in violent areas. As BPD Manager Dobkin reported,

> residents seem more comfortable sharing information in meetings facilitated by their clergy . . . we can also use the meetings as opportunities to let residents know what we are doing about crime and whether they are actually at risk of being victims . . . it helps manage expectations and fear.

The majority of our clergy respondents ($N = 18$, 60%) consistently identified reciprocal and responsible information sharing between themselves and the police as an important by-product of the BPD–TPC relationship. In fact, the ability to share intelligence was fundamental to ministers' unwavering belief that the work of the TPC supported that of the BPD and vice versa. For example, Reverend Weems pronounced, "it's a partnership because [the police and clergy] connect and talk and [the BPD] even shares intelligence with clergy." Reverend Wooten noted, "It's a robust working relationship that helps the police do their job." And, Reverend Arnette explained,

> We walk a thin line and I don't mean it in a negative way with the Boston police. We have a good relationship and I don't think that we could do as good of a job without the support of the police. . . . part of their patrol awareness of the neighborhood is to know that we're out there. We're in those high crime areas so they drive by and see [us]. They're available to help us do our job.

In agreement, Reverend Shegog remarked, "The presence and the rapport that [Ten Point] have built up with the city, with the Mayor, with the police, that makes a difference." Finally, Reverend Ackles elaborated on what he considered to be mutual benefits to the police–clergy partnership:

> [We] have a police department that is committed to community policing, but community policing has to be more than holding a series of neighborhood meetings and having those usual suspects come out and talk. . . . What happens when you have faith community activists out there understanding the problem and the issue of violence and all its interactions, you have another group of people who can help build a community policing platform that leverages the best of both worlds. I think an ideal relationship does just that.

Ministers also reported relishing opportunities to share information with the police. At the same time, however, church leaders recognized their weighty responsibility as trusted confidants and were reportedly extremely careful regarding how they shared information obtained from neighborhood residents. For instance, Reverend Weems commented, "[We] have to be very mindful of the confidentiality piece and how it plays out in the lives of young people . . . they need to know that as clergy I'm not just throwin' all of their business out there." Church leaders also understood how they might be instrumental toward helping challenge anti-snitching campaigns often credited with stifling the flow of information from troubled inner-city communities to the police (see Rosenfeld, Jacobs, and Wright, 2003; Woldoff and Weiss, 2010).

Many BPD managers believed that it was strategic to include clergy in their violence prevention plans because ministers gave them a powerful way to interact with troubled youth and their families ($N = 18$, 60%), help connect these youth to services and job opportunities ($N = 15$, 50%), and send pro-social service and moral/spiritual messages ($N = 10$, 33.3%) to active street criminals and gang members. BPD Manager McNulty commented:

> We often do home visits with ministers to talk to parents about how their kids are involved in gangs and headed toward a bad life outcome.... We are just trying to make sure they are aware what their son is doing and that we can get them some help to get him headed down the right road. If it was the police alone at the front door, most parents in these neighborhoods would not let us in and not want to talk with us about their kid. Many of them don't trust us and worry that we are there to lock their kid up, ... The ministers reassure them that the visit isn't about making arrests and that the conversation might benefit the kid's future ... they give us a way in that front door that wouldn't be there if the ministers weren't our partners.

In discussing the role of TPC clergy in Operation Ceasefire gang call-ins, BPD Manager Dawson reported:

> It is powerful when a respected member of the community, who knows many of the gang kids in the room, stands up and says, "We're tired of losing our young men to gun violence. We're tired of losing our young men to the criminal justice system ... please put your guns down and end this senseless violence. Please take advantage of the services and opportunities presented to you here ... if you don't, we support law enforcement in doing what they need to do (intensive enforcement) to keep our community safe." A message like that gets [the gang members'] attention and shows that no one supports what they are doing out there.

Finally, while the BPD managers did not specifically use academic terms like "informal social control" or "collective efficacy" in their responses, nearly two-thirds ($N = 19$, 63.3%) mentioned that the ministers could deliver collective community action and work to improve cohesion among residents to protect against continued violence in particular neighborhoods.

Similar to the BPD managers, the majority of clergy respondents ($N = 20$, 66.6%) consistently touted community members' organized efforts as the linchpin of sustained crime reduction. For example, Reverend Stewart observed, "What made the police thing even possible is that the black community owned crime in their community. Nothing that the [BPD] attempted to do, Ceasefire, anything, had any possibility until there was a consensus in the black community led by the black clergy that black on black violence was going to be owned and not excused and justified." Likewise, Pastor Triplett explained, "our responsibility as a community is to raise our young people and to make sure that we're doing the best we can not just by our own households but also with our neighbors or by our neighbors because a good man takes care of his family but a great man takes care of his neighborhood and community."

More than half of our church leaders ($N = 17$, 56.6%) reported participating in a number of specific local crime control and prevention efforts. They consistently said that these initiatives afforded them unprecedented opportunities to establish greater rapport with neighborhood residents. For example, pastors and members of their congregation periodically marched through nearby high crime neighborhoods, singing, praying, and distributing leaflets about regular worship services (encouraging residents to attend). Activist clergy referred to this particular activity as "community walks" and touted their potential importance for ministering to and mobilizing the public around youth violence reduction strategies. For example, Reverend Ackles said, "[I want people to] sort of look at the faith group contribution like a streetwise Red Cross if you will. You got people who are out there to help you, not to hurt you. People welcome that kind of help." Similarly, Reverend Pettigrew explained, "walking the streets gives you the opportunity to be in that community before something really happens so when it does happen, people already know about you, you've been out there, they feel more comfortable with you, talking with you, maybe coming to your church." Likewise, Pastor Nero noted, "[community walks] are a step in the right direction because it's getting the church out of the four walls and into their community to meet and greet people . . . the community appreciates seeing people of faith walking, praying and being a part of their local neighborhood." As highlighted above, church leaders viewed community walks as a proactive approach toward reducing the negative consequences stemming from sporadic episodes of neighborhood violence by connecting with and building trust among neighborhood residents.

The Challenges of Partnerships

Among the varying concerns raised by BPD managers, the most consistent problem in partnering with clergy involved the difficulty they had navigating existing minister rivalries and managing the infighting among the clergy ($N = 18, 60\%$).[11] BPD Manager Majeski described how a BPD-supported "gang truce" was nearly derailed by two feuding TPC clergy who were supposed to serve as peace facilitators for gang members on opposing sides of the gang rivalry. He commented, "the gang kids seemed more willing to make peace with each other than the ministers were." In general, BPD managers were concerned that working with any particular minister might cause other ministers not to work with them. Similarly, they also worried about jeopardizing long-standing relationships with ministers if they launched new partnerships with other clergy on similar types of issues. As BPD Manager Ianello lamented, "my orientation is to work with anyone who can help me keep the community safe . . . unfortunately, this sometimes runs up against the complicated social world of the ministers. I need a scorecard to keep track of their problems with each other . . . and a metal detector to avoid any unseen landmines that might derail my [violence reduction] plans." Six out of ten (60%) community organizers also mentioned difficulties in partnering with TPC because of personal conflicts between the ministers. Organizer Bivins noted:

> One of the challenges [in working with the TPC] is you couldn't even bring [TPC] folks in the same room together! They were always trying to figure out—as the street guys say—who was going to [profit]. And some of them wanted to take the whole pie. There was a lot of backstabbing and selling

each other out for what amounted to crumbs at the table. It's just not uncommon for these guys to stab each other in the back. There were many times I'd ask myself, "Are these guys just talking, or are they about the work?"

BPD managers also observed that, beyond particular TPC ministers, there were not enough clergy doing work on the streets in the community ($N = 15$, 50%). Too many clergy seemed to prefer to stay in the church and service their congregation rather than engage the surrounding community. Reflecting on his experiences leading Safe Street Teams in different neighborhoods, BPD Manager Stone complained:

> When I was working in the Bowdoin and Geneva area, my team had a great relationship with [name and church removed]. We dropped by the church every weekday to help neighborhood kids with homework in their afterschool program, we walked the streets of the neighborhood together and talked to residents about problems and concerns, and we worked together on the gang violence problem ... when I took over the Heath Street team, I immediately visited all the local churches in my area. None of the clergy seemed too interested in actually doing something about crime in the neighborhood ... the only problem I've worked on with one of those local churches involved community concerns over parking during their services.

Similarly, in discussing his lack of partnerships with clergy from churches in his Safe Street Team area, BPD Manager Thornton observed:

> Most of the congregation members for the churches in my area don't live there. They commute in from the suburbs and other parts of the city ... many of the residents from Orchard Gardens [a housing project with high levels of violence] go to the bigger churches, like Jubilee and Morningstar Baptist, on Blue Hill Ave [located more than a mile away in another police district].

BPD managers suggested that there needed to be more consistency from the active TPC clergy in these partnerships ($N = 12$, 40%). Some complained that certain TPC clergy only showed up at big media events surrounding horrific incidents, such as the shooting of a child, but were not there for the day-to-day work, a view that was supported by the community organizers. BPD Manager Dobkin observed, "if there are cameras there, you can count on *all* the reverends being there." Others suggested that the TPC clergy who were willing to do the work were spread too thinly across multiple initiatives and this caused their inconsistency and unavailability for strategic prevention work. For instance, BPD Manager McNulty commented, "Reverend [name removed] is terrific. I wish I could clone him. The problem is that there are not enough ministers doing this work and everyone wants him on their projects. He sometimes misses meetings and can't help me with my stuff because he is way overcommitted."

Although the community organizers spoke of the TPC's lack of capacity largely in terms of their inability to deliver on expectations of direct services, similar to BPD complaints of TPC ministers being spread too thinly, 40 percent of the community sample ($N = 4$) mentioned that the TPC's power was concentrated too heavily in the hands of a small number of individuals. For the community organizers who mentioned this, this led to two key problems. First, the concentration led to personality-driven (rather than problem-/issue-driven) responses to youth violence. The dark side of institutional arrangements that function primarily through individual relationships is that they can be inefficient when a personal relationship is not in place to fit an organizational need. For example, community organizers cited examples of key TPC ministers only working with people and neighborhoods that they were comfortable with and trusted, and thus neglected other neighborhoods and their problems. Second, community organizers raised the long-run concern that the TPC's concentrated leadership failed to develop younger clergy leaders across the city and enroll them in the civic partnerships.

There was also a grouping of varied concerns held by BPD managers on the credibility of particular TPC clergy members. It is important to note here that these concerns were attributed to specific clergy members within the TPC and did not necessarily represent their general opinion of the organization. In summary, 22 (73.3%) BPD managers articulated that their trust in the clergy was highly personalized to particular ministers rather than to the entire TPC movement. One-third of BPD managers ($N = 10$) felt that certain clergy were not involved with the residents of disadvantaged black neighborhoods and that they did not actually represent the views of that community. As BPD Manager Velez commented, "some of them are nothing more than opinion-givers without a real constituency." Another ten BPD managers (33.3%) were concerned that particular ministers played "both sides of the fence" with police and community. The officers suggested that certain ministers would praise the police or express understanding to their faces and then made matters worse by harshly criticizing them to the community. They simply felt uncomfortable collaborating with certain TPC clergy members because they were too political (8, 26.7%) and self-aggrandizing (7, 23.3%). BPD Manager Majeski noted that "some of them are nothing more than politicians." BPD Manager Dawson noted, "I tend to avoid the ministers who show up at the press conferences in their $1000 suits and drive $80,000 Mercedes . . . those guys tend to care about themselves more than anything else." BPD respondents' abrasive comments regarding some clergy are not surprising given police cynicism. Further, it is worth noting that whereas our clergy generally agreed with certain BPD officers' remarks about some of their colleagues (e.g., clergy who routinely showed up at media events following tragedies but were seldom seen interacting with neighborhood residents in the streets), they were much more diplomatic in the way they articulated these points.

Interestingly, whereas our clergy respondents repeatedly mentioned the importance of trust regarding their work with citizens and the police, bouts of distrust seemingly jeopardized their relationships with both groups. For example, our clergy respondents said that some community members were quite suspicious of individual TPC ministers' own agendas. For instance, Pastor Rodgers explained, "the point is that everyone can't be a star, someone who has a magnetic personality . . . you need people in the trenches who have heart, passion . . . cos when the stars start to have friction . . . when they go off on speaking engagements, have a moral lapse . . . if things fall apart, you still need leaders." Pastor Nero commented on how clergy members' internal conflicts seemingly undermined citizen trust:

> One of the larger reasons why we haven't been able to overcome some of the issues that we've been fighting for 20 plus years is because the people in power are so distrustful of each other that they have the same gang warfare, turf beef that the kids have . . . you got the same beef that the kids have and you want them to stop and you holding on to grudges that you've had for ten plus years. It's crazy! It's crazy!

Further, respondents explained that some community members openly questioned the extent to which the TPC operated independently from the BPD. For instance, Reverend Wooten observed, "I would suspect that some folk would say that Ten Point and the police is too cozy." Likewise, Reverend Cokely noted, "some people distrust the fact that some clergy have close relationships with the police . . . some people would prefer that you didn't work with the police at all." Finally, Pastor Rodgers quipped, "to be totally frank, there have been times when people have said that the police *are* the clergy . . . that the clergy protect the police and make it seem that things aren't as bad as they really are."

Citizens' skepticism of the BPD–TPC relationship was seemingly a by-product of long-standing tensions between the BPD and the black community. For instance, Reverend Weems noted, "the police have to learn how to be honest, open, and transparent . . . one of the problems is that people don't trust the police because they do not approach them in an amicable way. They always are antagonistic and try to intimidate." Similarly, Reverend Glasgow noted, "it's the challenge of the community. . . . The mistrust, the distrust [of police]. . . . The track record of what we often see with police officers . . . whether it's a misuse of authority vs. seeing a family member hurt by an officer . . . it's just a tremendous sense of mistrust." Reverend Weems observed, "the police need to understand that how you engage with people, their communication, they need to improve in that area." Further, several clergy described the relationship between the police and Boston's minority youth as especially tumultuous. For example, Pastor Edwards explained:

> Most young folks don't view [the police favorably]. Most young folks dislike them. It's a lack of trust there . . . [youths] feel injustice. They feel like they're targets . . . they may not be doing anything, but they're getting stopped anyway . . . in [the black] community the young folk don't look at the police as protection as they do in white communities. They look at them as an adversary . . . the police department needs to do more within the community to establish a rapport with the young folks and speak to them and not just look at them suspicious[ly] like [they're] up to something, but create a dialog with them.

Finally, Reverend Shegog implored members of the BPD "to treat our young men and women like they were their [own] children."

The accounts noted above beg the question whether, and if so, how the TPC, and by extension the BPD, could reasonably forge relationships with individuals who were at times somewhat cynical of each partner's motives. Reverend Ackles, however, explained that improved police–minority community relations and any resulting crime control benefits required changes in the approaches of both groups. He noted:

> There is a negative history between the community and the police department and so there needs to be some effort on the part of the police department to approach things differently. And on the part

of the community, they also have to begin to approach things differently out of necessity. Out of expediency probably initially, but eventually those relationships have to be forged if we are going to be able in a combined way to most effectively address the violence in the community.

The majority of clergy ($N = 21$, 70%) mentioned that, while they may harbor residual skepticism of BPD as an organization, given its history, they had more confidence in individual officers with whom they had established strong, long-term relationships centered on mutual trust and respect. For example, Reverend Birdsong reported, "I grew up with a lot of the Boston police and a Superintendent. ... I have rapport with them. The Commissioner that we have now is much more on the scene [than his predecessor]. He goes to houses, [and meets with] families, which makes a difference. ... He's not a person that says you can't touch him. ... You can talk to him." Likewise, Reverend Arnette said, "our biggest supporter is the Police Commissioner." Pastor Rooks also noted:

> Back in the beginning [of the police–clergy partnership] I think the sense often was that there were local police and folks scattered within the department who got it ... now I'd say pretty reliably that the Commissioner and to some extent the command structure gets it ... you [also] have community service officers that get it, youth service officers who get it ... the remaining challenge is to continue to sell [community policing] to the patrol officer, to the detectives, to the gang unit officer that the [strategy] is the best approach over the long haul ... you still have a lot of [BPD officers] who think in terms of busts, arrests, and 911 calls answered ... you still got that ... it's like any other culture. It's a long, hard slog to turn it around.

It appears that both our BPD and TPC respondents perceived police–clergy relationships as occurring mostly between individual officers and pastors rather than permeating either institution.[12] For instance, Reverend Reed observed, "the [police officers] we *know*, that we built a relationship with, we trust. There are some we don't have a relationship with probably because they don't trust what we do and we don't trust them." Finally, Pastor Griggs remarked, "there are officers whose fathers that I know [and] worked with and the sons are now [police officers] doing gang work but those are based on real relationships that are trustworthy relationships." This same idea of person-to-person (rather than organization-to-organization) partnerships was echoed in community organizer descriptions of TPC–BPD collaborations. As community respondent Shawan put it, "As far as collaboration between agencies—officially—that just never works in Boston. I would just collab[orate] person to person. Using big entities to work together just never works."

The variability of views offered by our clergy respondents highlights the diversity in the black community regarding attitudes toward the police—an aspect missing from many prior studies. Specifically, our findings demonstrate that black citizens, even those residing in high crime neighborhoods, can be generally supportive of the police as agents of formal social control while simultaneously being critical of particular crime prevention strategies (e.g., stop, question, and frisk). In fact, even those individuals expressing the most trepidation about the overall fairness and effectiveness of the BPD recognized the importance of having a legitimate voice through the TPC. For example, Reverend Tucker remarked,

> I don't necessarily work *with* the police. I don't at all. I don't get in their way and I hope we have meetings where we are asking them not to get in ours. I would like to believe [that there's] a mutual respect. They've been hired by the society at large. It's what it is. So I have to navigate through that. Not around it, through it.

Discussion

This qualitative analysis of police–black clergy partnerships provides further evidence that such collaborations can be highly beneficial to urban police departments and the African American citizens they serve. It is also important to note, however, that this study does not claim that police–black clergy partnerships in Boston have directly resulted in improved relationships between the police and all black residents or produced noteworthy reductions in serious youth violence in black neighborhoods.[13] Further, while our results may not be widely generalizable, our methodological approach and data analysis raise important issues that may guide future research on this important topic. Specifically, more wide-reaching evaluation research is clearly needed to determine the independent effects of these types of partnerships on police–community relations and youth violence. Nevertheless, given the persistent problem of poor police legitimacy in black neighborhoods, we believe that urban police departments should be working to develop strong working relationships with black churches. This is particularly true in highly disadvantaged neighborhoods suffering from serious violence where the church may be the only functional social institution.

Our qualitative inquiry was designed to provide a deeper understanding than previous accounts of the role of police–black clergy partnerships in improving police legitimacy and enhancing community-based crime prevention efforts. These contemporary interviews strongly support and refine prior work on the emergence of this collaboration during the 1990s. Our constituent groups reported that the BPD gained increased legitimacy in the eyes of Boston's black community by forming strong working relationships with the TPC. BPD managers recognized that the BPD–TPC relationship facilitated an improved dialog between the police and black residents and generated opportunities for black citizens to convey long-standing and ongoing concerns about the nature of policing in their neighborhoods. BPD managers suggested that the involvement of TPC clergy in their crime control interventions provided an improved way to connect with high-risk youth and their families as well as strengthening their anti-violence communications with gangs. BPD managers also noted that they routinely called upon the TPC to represent the moral voice of the community and facilitate many important facets of informal social control. Further, BPD managers explained that the TPC was highly effective in explaining questionable police actions to an often anxious and skeptical black community, providing the BPD with "a moment of pause" during volatile situations. The BPD also routinely sought feedback from TPC leadership prior to launching potentially controversial crime control strategies in black communities.

Our clergy respondents valued highly their ability to garner citizen trust and judiciously extend it to the BPD. Pastors were acutely aware of the "fine line" they were required to walk, constantly considering community needs while working as earnest partners to the BPD. Black clergy respondents particularly appreciated the benefits of reciprocal and responsible information sharing. They were able to provide police with some insights on particular recurring violent crime problems and specific violent events. In turn, TPC clergy received new information on violent crimes and the general content of police response to those crimes that could be shared with concerned community members. TPC clergy also reported appreciating the opportunity to assist the BPD in shaping law enforcement responses to outbreaks of violence in ways that minimized unintentional harms to the black community. In these settings, they worked with BPD managers to ensure focused rather than indiscriminate enforcement responses that were blended with social service and opportunity provision elements. Community organizers generally recognized the value of the BPD–TPC partnerships for improving policing responses in black neighborhoods.

These partnerships aid urban police departments in strategic and programmatic ways. Both broad sets of action share the common theme of extending an "umbrella of legitimacy" to the police (Winship and Berrien, 1999) and enhancing their ability to work with residents of black neighborhoods. Black clergy can be very helpful to the police in managing citywide political discussions on appropriate policing strategies. The explicit involvement of black clergy in these discussions signals to the black community that the police department seeks their input on problems and proposed programs, values transparency in decision-making and the resolution of community concerns, and embraces accountability to community leaders. At a programmatic level, black clergy can help police by mobilizing local communities to act against violence, sharing information on the nature of violent crime problems in particular places, and appealing to troubled youth and their families to take advantage of services and opportunities rather than persisting in high-risk activities. It is worth noting here that most contemporary theoretical and policy discussion of improving police legitimacy focuses on improving police–citizen encounters through the application of procedural justice principles (see, e.g., Tyler, 2004). Police departments need to recognize that, in addition to procedurally just encounters, there are multiple pathways they can pursue to improve their legitimacy in the minds and hearts of the public they serve (see Skogan and Frydl (2004) for a discussion of varied approaches). As Crawford and colleagues (2005) recommend, community engagement and helping to build constructive and informed relationships certainly represent an important complementary pathway to changing citizen perceptions of police as legitimate authorities.

Previous research did not examine the ongoing challenges that arise from types of collaborations (Berrien and Winship, 2002; Winship and Berrien, 1999; but see Berman and Fox, 2010). In the absence of further evidence, policy-makers and practitioners are left with a sense that there are few, if any, problems and that these partnerships are rooted in deep trust that permeates a majority of the individuals who comprise these two very different institutions. In our study, participants across constituent groups reported challenges associated with the BPD–TPC partnership. BPD managers and community organizers alike often found it difficult to navigate the complex political terrain of clergy relationships and bemoaned what they perceived as a lack of involvement of far too many black church leaders. While a number of BPD managers and community organizers questioned the sincerity of specific TPC clergy, they did not disparage the entire organization. Further, those respondents appeared to reserve the harshest criticisms for black church leaders whom they considered to be detached and self-absorbed. Clergy respondents also mentioned problems stemming from their BPD partnership. For instance, TPC clergy at times wondered whether certain colleagues were more interested in capturing the media spotlight than working earnestly for the black community. Indeed, Berman and Fox (2010) observed that squabbling among partnering agencies, highlighted by internal and external TPC disputes over credit and grant funding, contributed to the eventual cessation of Operation Ceasefire in the early 2000s (see also Braga et al., 2008). TPC study participants also reported periodically drawing the ire of certain black citizens who took particular exception to their "cozy" relationship with the BPD. Interestingly, the majority of TPC clergy readily acknowledged having lingering misgivings about the BPD as an organization due to a long history of perceived racial discrimination at the hands of the Boston Police. A number of pastors and BPD managers reported, however, having established long-term relationships with individuals from the other organization. Both BPD managers and clergy were adamant that these relationships were founded on mutual trust and respect. Further, it is important to recognize that these were seemingly highly idiosyncratic associations, confined to a small number of people (a handful of true believers in the BPD and in the TPC), and operating within a modest number of neighborhoods.

As note above, the strongest and deepest relationships occurred between individuals, not institutions, and were developed over long periods of time. In fact, while acknowledging the value of the BPD–TPC partnership, both BPD managers and clergy expressed skepticism about individuals from the other organization whom they did not know and/ or trust. BPD managers and community organizers routinely expressed frustration over the uneven distribution of activist black clergy across Boston's neighborhoods. Certain black churches did not serve the immediate neighborhood in which they resided and some black clergy were simply not interested in getting directly involved in local violence prevention work. Similarly, clergy respondents noted that many BPD officers were not interested in engaging them as partners.

These observations suggest that effective, ongoing police–black clergy partnerships in Boston are uncommon and surprisingly fragile. Police departments and community leaders need to ensure that these relationships are not limited to partnerships among a small number of people who focus on a limited number of areas in cities. Moreover, police manager, clergy, and community organizer respondents alike expressed concern that the small number of pastors and officers who coordinated the bulk of their joint actions were nearing retirement and investments were not being made in the development of the next generation of TPC and BPD partners. Boston, and other municipalities seeking to promote these partnerships, face the common problem of bringing innovative and effective programs "up to scale" (see, e.g., Welsh, Sullivan, and Olds, 2010). The participants had a number of ideas on how these partnerships could be spread to a broader set of neighborhoods and individuals. These included TPC-led faith-based summits to stimulate interest among uninvolved clergy, the inclusion of TPC clergy as guest speakers in BPD Academy classes on community policing, the introduction of local clergy at roll call in BPD districts, the attendance of local officers at church services, and other suggestions. Given the promise of these partnerships, more work needs to be done to understand how these relationships can be stimulated and broadened to include a wider range of participants from both organizations.

Finally, it is important to note that black clergy do not necessarily represent the views of the entire black community. Not all residents go to church and church-going residents may have divergent views on particular issues. Equally importantly, some local clergy may not be well suited to deliver community involvement in crime prevention plans. Indeed, Sampson (2012) suggests that it is unreasonable to expect that churches alone can establish the trust among local residents needed to facilitate collective action. Police officers may be tempted to view clergy members as reliable "short cuts" to working with residents in black neighborhoods. While our research suggests that churches should be a focal institution for police partnerships, community policing programs need to be geared toward engaging a broader set of community members that best represent a particular neighborhood's concerns and capacities to respond to local problems.

Critical Thinking

The authors discuss the historical instances of abuse that have pitted law enforcement officials against people of color. What social factors put black clergy in a position to bridge this gap and partner with law enforcement to influence their community and impact crime control? Do you think that this partnership could lead to any negative outcomes? What other social institution within oppressed communities could be beneficial in establishing collective efficacy?

Notes

1. Although we make frequent reference to black churches, parishioners, and clergy, we are fully aware and appreciate the diversity that exists among them. Further, we attempted to capture such religious diversity within the black community in the study design.
2. A voluminous literature exists regarding the relationship between religion and individual offending (see, e.g., Freeman, 1986; Hirschi and Stark, 1969; Johnson, Jang, De Li, and Larson, 2000; Johnson, Larson, De Li, and Jang, 2000). As mentioned at the outset of this article, an analysis of this relationship is not the focal point of the current study. However, in a recent systemic review examining the relationship between religious involvement and delinquency, Johnson (2011) found that the vast majority of studies "report an inverse beneficial relationship between religion and some measure of crime and delinquency" and that hardly any studies linked religion with a "harmful outcome" (p. 78). Reflecting on this body of research, Cullen (2010) argues that the study of religion should be an integral part of the criminological enterprise and a vibrant subfield within the discipline.
3. Please note that we are not conflating density with religiosity. The density of black churches is in part—if not mostly explained—by low overhead costs and the presence of "storefront" churches. African American communities in many cities are overwhelmingly disadvantaged, with exceptionally low real estate costs.

4. We interviewed all three reverends and assigned them pseudonyms.

5. http://www.nationalgangcenter.gov/SPT/Programs/43.

6. In their popular article on TPC in *The Public Interest*, Winship and Berrien (1999) do not specify any data-collection methods or analytical techniques. Berrien and Winship (2002) mention observing police–clergy crime prevention meetings and conducting interviews with clergy, police officers, and others. However, they do not specify how many meetings were observed or how many individuals were interviewed. Newspaper articles are referenced throughout both papers. Personal communication with Christopher Winship (March 2012) suggests repeated interviews with three lead clergy (Hammond, Brown, and Rivers), routine presence at crime prevention meetings occurring at one faith-based organization (the Ella J. Baker House) during the mid- to late 1990s, occasional interviews with other clergy and support staff, and interviews with a small number of BPD managers.

7. We were prohibited from compensating BPD managers.

8. The BPD Safe Street Team program assigns teams of officers (one sergeant and six patrol officers) to persistent violent crime hot spots in Boston on a permanent basis. These officers are required to patrol on foot and/or bicycles in the hot-spot area, form partnerships with local residents and business owners, use problem-oriented policing to address crime problems, and arrest offenders (see, e.g., Braga, Hureau, and Papachristos, 2011).

9. The instruments were intended to tap into consistent themes but were revised slightly because some questions were not relevant to each of our three groups.

10. It is important to note here that sensitive tactical elements, such as investigations of particular individuals or the use of confidential informants and undercover officers in specific areas, were not discussed with ministers.

11. Similarly, in Chicago, relationships between many of the black churches were marred by cleavages resulting from religious ideologies and the demographics of each church's congregation (Mears and Corkan, 2007).

12. To illustrate the importance of trust, both clergy and BPD study participants pointed to Operation Homefront—an intervention and prevention initiative where YVSF officers and clergy visit the homes of at-risk students previously identified by school personnel. When necessary, the police–clergy teams make referrals to a number of local social service agencies who conduct follow-up visits with and provide resources to the families. Our respondents were adamant that due to its voluntary nature (i.e., parental consent), such a program would not have been possible without considerable community trust in the police–clergy relationship.

13. As described earlier, there is some indirect empirical evidence that BPD–TPC partnerships improved police relationships with the community by virtue of fewer complaints lodged against Boston police officers after the partnership was developed in the early to mid-1990s (see Johnson, 2011). There is also some indirect empirical evidence that police–black clergy partnerships can be very helpful in reducing youth violence. TPC clergy were the lead community partners in the Operation Ceasefire strategy that was associated with a large reduction in youth homicides in Boston during the 1990s (Braga et al., 2001).

References

Bass, S. (2001). Policing space, policing race: Social control imperatives and police discretionary decisions. *Social Justice, 28*, 156–176.

Berman, G. and Fox, A. (2010). *Trial & error in criminal justice reform: Learning from failure*. Washington, DC: The Urban Institute Press.

Berrien, J. and Winship, C. (2002). An umbrella of legitimacy: Boston's police department—Ten point coalition collaboration. In G. Katzmann (ed.), *Securing our children's future: New approaches to juvenile justice and youth violence* (pp. 200–228). Washington, DC: Brookings Institute Press.

Billingsley, A. and Caldwell, C.H. (1991). The church, the family, and the school in the African American community. *The Journal of Negro Education, 60*, 427–440.10.2307/2295494.

Braga, A.A. and Winship, C. (2006). Partnership, accountability, and innovation: Clarifying Boston's experience with pulling levers. In D. Weisburd and A. Braga (eds), *Police innovation: Contrasting perspectives* (pp. 171–187). New York: Cambridge University Press.

Braga, A.A., Hureau, D.M., and Papachristos, A.V. (2011). An ex-post-facto evaluation framework for place-based police interventions. *Evaluation Review, 35*, 592–626.

Braga, A.A., Hureau, D., and Winship, C. (2008). Losing faith? Police, black churches, and the resurgence of youth violence in Boston. *Ohio State Journal of Criminal Law, 6*, 141–172.

Braga, A.A., Kennedy, D.M., Waring, E.J., and Piehl, A.M. (2001). Problem-oriented policing, deterrence, and youth violence: An evaluation of Boston's operation ceasefire. *Journal of Research in Crime and Delinquency, 38,* 195–225. 10.1177/0022427801038003001.

Brunson, R.K. (2007). 'Police don't like black people': African American young men's accumulated police experiences. *Criminology & Public Policy, 6,* 71–102.

Brunson, R.K. and Miller, J. (2006). Young black men and urban policing in the United States. *British Journal of Criminology, 46,* 613–640.

Brunson, R. K. and Weitzer, R. (2009). Police relations with black and white youths in different urban neighborhoods. *Urban Affairs Review, 44,* 858–885.10.1177/1078087408326973.

Butterfield, F. (1996). In Boston, nothing is something. *New York Times,* November 21, p. A20.

Cavendish, J.C. (2000). Church-based community activism: A comparison of black and white Catholic congregations. *Journal for the Scientific Study of Religion, 39,* 64–77.

Crawford, A. (2008). Refiguring the community and professional in policing and criminal justice: Some questions of legitimacy. In J. Shapland (ed.), *Justice, community and civil society: A contested terrain* (pp. 125–156). Cullompton: Willan.

Crawford, A., Blackburn, S., Lister, S., and Shepherd, P. (2004). *Patrolling with a purpose: An evaluation of police community support officers in Leeds and Bradford city centres.* Leeds: Centre for Criminal Justice Studies, University of Leeds Press.

Crawford, A., Lister, S., Blackburn, S., and Burnett, J. (2005). *Plural policing: The mixed economy of visible patrols in England and Wales.* Bristol: The Policy Press.

Cullen, F.T. (2010). Toward a criminology of religion: Comment on Johnson and Jang. In R. Rosenfeld, K. Quinet, and C. Garcia (eds), *Contemporary issues in criminological theory and research* (pp. 151–162). Belmont, CA: Wadsworth.

DuBois, W.E.B. (ed.). (1903). *The Negro church.* Atlanta, GA: The Atlanta University Press.

Ellison, C.G. and Sherkat, D.E. (1995). The "Semi-involuntary Institution" Revisited: Regional Variations in Church Participation among Black Americans. *Social Forces, 73,* 1415–1437.

Frazier, E.F. (1963). *The Negro church in America.* New York: Schocken Books.

Freeman, R.B. (1986). Who escapes? The relation of churchgoing and other background factors to the socioeconomic performance of black male youths from inner-city poverty tracts. In R. Freeman and H. Holzer (eds), *The black youth employment crisis* (pp. 353–376). Chicago, IL: University of Chicago Press.10.7208/chicago/9780226261829.001.0001.

Gallup, G. and Castelli, J. (1989). *The people's religion: American faith in the 90's.* New York: Macmillan.

Hirschi, T. and Stark, R. (1969). Hellfire and delinquency. *Social Problems, 17,* 202–213.10.2307/799866 [CrossRef].

Johnson, B.R. (2011). *More God, less crime: Why faith matters and how it could matter more.* West Conshohocken, PA: Templeton Press.

Johnson, B.R., Jang, S.J., De Li, S., and Larson, D. (2000). The invisible institution and black youth crime: The church as an agency of local social control. *Journal of Youth and Adolescence, 29,* 479–498.10.1023/A:1005114610839.

Johnson, B.R., Larson, D.B., De Li, S., and Jang, S.J. (2000). Escaping from the crime of inner cities: Church attendance and religious salience among disadvantaged youth. *Justice Quarterly, 17,* 377–391.10.1080/07418820000096371.

Jucovy, L. (2003). *Amachi: Mentoring children of prisoners in Philadelphia.* Philadelphia, PA: Public/Private Ventures and the Center for Research on Religion and Urban Civil Society.

Kane, R.J. (2002). The social ecology of police misconduct. *Criminology, 40,* 867–896.10.1111/crim.2002.40.issue-4.

Kennedy, D.M., Piehl, A.M., and Braga, A.A. (1996). Youth violence in Boston Gun markets, serious youth offenders, and a use-reduction strategy. *Law and Contemporary Problems, 59,* 147–196.10.2307/1192213.

Lincoln, C.E. (1974). *The black church since Frazier.* London: Schocken Books.

McRoberts, O.M. (2003). *Streets of glory: Church and community in a black urban neighborhood.* Chicago, IL: University of Chicago Press.

Mears, T.L. (2002). Praying for community policing. *Yale Law School Legal Scholarship Repository, 90,* 1593–1634.

Mears, T.L. and Corkan, K.B. (2007). When 2 or 3 come together. *William and Mary Law Review, 48,* 1315–1387.

Pattillo-McCoy, M. (1998). Church culture as a strategy of action in the black community. *American Sociological Review, 63,* 767–784.10.2307/2657500.

Rosenfeld, R., Jacobs, B.A., and Wright, R. (2003). Snitching and the code of the street. *British Journal of Criminology, 43,* 291–309.10.1093/bjc/43.2.291.

Sampson, R.J. (2012). *Great American city: Chicago and the enduring neighborhood effect.* Chicago, IL: University of Chicago Press.10.7208/chicago/9780226733883.001.0001.

Sampson, R.J., Raudenbush, S.W., and Earls, F. (1997). Neighborhoods and violent crime: A multilevel study of collective efficacy. *Science, 277,* 918–924.10.1126/science.277.5328.918.

Skogan, W.G. (2006). *Police and community in Chicago: A tale of three cities.* New York: Oxford University Press.

Skogan, W. and Frydl, K. (eds). (2004). Fairness and effectiveness in policing: The evidence. *Committee to Review Research on Police Policy and Practices. Committee on Law and Justice, Division of Behavioral and Social Sciences and Education.* Washington, DC: The National Academies Press.

Stewart, E., Baumer, E.P., Brunson, R.K., and Simons, R.L. (2009). Neighborhood racial context and perceptions of police-based racial discrimination among black youth. *Criminology, 47*, 847–887.10.1111/crim.2009.47.issue-3.

Strauss, A. (1987). *Qualitative analysis for social scientists.* New York: Cambridge University Press.10.1017/CBO9780511557842.

Sunshine, J. and Tyler, T.R. (2003). The role of procedural justice and legitimacy in shaping public support for policing. *Law & Society Review, 37*, 513–547.

Terrill, W. and Reisig, M.D. (2003). Neighborhood context and police use of force. *Journal of Research in Crime and Delinquency, 40*, 291–321.10.1177/0022427803253800.

Tyler, T.R. (2004). Enhancing police legitimacy. *Annals of the American Academy of Political and Social Science, 593*, 84–99.10.1177/0002716203262627.

Tyler, T.R. and Folger, R. (1980). Distributional and procedural aspects of satisfaction with citizen–police encounters. *Basic and Applied Social Psychology, 1*, 281–292.10.1207/s15324834basp0104_1.

Tyler, T.R. and Wakslak, C.J. (2004). Profiling and police legitimacy: Procedural justice, attributions of motive, and acceptance of police authority. *Criminology, 42*, 253–282.10.1111/crim.2004.42.issue-2.

Websdale, N. (2001). *Policing the poor: From slave plantation to public housing.* Boston, MA: Northeastern University Press.

Weitzer, R. (2002). Incidents of police misconduct and public opinion. *Journal of Criminal Justice, 30*, 397–408.10.1016/S0047-2352(02)00150-2.

Weitzer, R. and Brunson, R.K. (2009). Strategic responses to the police among inner-city youth. *Sociological Quarterly, 50*, 235–256.10.1111/tsq.2009.50.issue-2.

Weitzer, R. and Tuch, S. (2006). *Race and policing in America: Conflict and reform.* New York: Cambridge University Press. 10.1017/CBO9780511617256.

Welsh, B.C., Sullivan, C.J., and Olds, D.L. (2010). When early crime prevention goes to scale: A new look at the evidence. *Prevention Science, 11*, 115–125.10.1007/s11121-009-0159-4.

Winship, C. (2005). End of the miracle? Crime, faith, and partnership in Boston in the 1990s. In R. Smith (ed.), *Long march ahead: African American churches and public policy in post Civil Rights America* (pp. 171–192). Durham, NC: Duke University Press.

Winship, C. and Berrien, J. (1999). Boston cops and black churches. *The Public Interest, 136*, 52–68.

Witkin, G. (1997). Sixteen silver bullets: Smart ideas to fix the world. *U.S. News and World Report*, December 29, p. 67.

Woldoff, R.A. and Weiss, K.G. (2010). Stop snitchin': Exploring definitions of the snitch and implications for urban black communities. *Journal of Criminal Justice and Popular Culture, 17*, 184–223.

Yin, R.K. (2009). *Case study research: Design and methods* (4th edn). Thousand Oaks, CA: Sage.

II Judicial

Whereas the police are highly visible in the community, the opposite is true for the criminal courts. The media image of actors in the judicial arena is one characterized by frequent criminal trials, with each side battling for truth within an adversarial environment. Although this image may be true on occasion, it is not how the adjudicative process operates in reality. Over 90 percent of criminal cases are officially disposed of by plea bargaining agreements that take place between the prosecutor's office and defense attorneys. Often these behind-the-scenes deliberations occur over a very short period, although not always, as one of the authors in this section points out.

Conducting qualitative research in courthouses, attorneys' offices, and judge's chambers is no easy task. But studies conducted through painstaking observation and interviewing have lifted the hidden operational processes of courtroom decision-making that have seldom been well understood, especially for outsiders and those going through the system. Ingratiating one's self with the courthouse work group and developing rapport for purposes of gaining entrée over a sustained time is an absolute necessity if one is to attain some degree of insider status. It is only by being there and witnessing firsthand how criminal cases are handled that researchers can formulate theoretical propositions to explain the informal judicial decision-making process that affects all cases.

The articles selected for the first part of this section represent qualitative approaches that analyze some of the most important issues facing the criminal courts today. Although they may overlap somewhat, these articles provide an opportunity for the reader to see and understand why the judicial system works the way it does. Topics include organization of the court and decision-making process, court workgroup members and their perspectives of the death penalty, views of a prosecuting attorney, criminal defense lawyers' occupational choices and their representing capital case clients, and reasons for probation officers sentencing recommendations are found in this section.

The articles included in the second part of this section analyze the perspective of those who are involved in the court system for short terms and are, for the most part, outsiders to the goings-on of the judicial bureaucracy. They do not make their living by being attorneys or judges. Instead, they were either brought to the court out of civic duty (e.g., as jurors or witnesses) or they are there because they were either the victim or culprit of a crime. Although not comprehensive, we have chosen research studies in both sections that cover most of the important issues addressing due process questions and the court systems' treatment of criminal defendants. It is through these field study efforts that we have come to better comprehend the practices of actors in our criminal courts.

A Practitioners

11

Representing the Underdog: The Righteous Development of Death Penalty Defense Attorneys

Sarah Goodrum, Mark Pogrebin, and Matthew W. Greife

Abstract: *Research on criminal defense attorneys offers conflicting views of their work, as the product of immoral double agents and also passionate cause lawyers, raising questions about our knowledge of their motivations and development. We know even less about the development of death penalty defense attorneys and what life experiences lead them to this work. The qualitative study uses symbolic interactionist theory to examine in-depth interviews with 15 death penalty defense attorneys practicing in a western state. The evidence reveals three key phases in their development: (1) a passion for civil rights issues starting in early childhood, (2) a disenchantment with law school, and (3) a pivotal internship experience with a public defender's office. The findings prove important for guiding the education and training of death penalty defense attorneys and for reconciling the disparate portrayals of these attorneys in the literature.*

For a death penalty eligible defendant in the United States, the criminal defense attorney acts as a confidant, advisor, and therapist. The experiences these defendants have with their lawyers determine whether they live or die.[1] The stakes could not be higher. Death penalty defendants are true underdogs, in every sense of the word. They typically represent the most economically destitute, socially isolated, and publicly disliked members of society; their personal histories and legal cases often sound like long uphill battles. The defense attorneys representing these defendants invest their heart and soul into their cases, and the work proves emotionally and personally exhausting.[2] In addition, research suggests that criminal defense law continues to be among the least well-compensated areas of legal practice,[3] and the public tends to view criminal defense attorneys in general and death penalty defense attorneys in particular with disdain.[4]

Given the social stigma, moderate compensation, and emotional investment associated with death penalty defense work, others find it hard to understand why these highly skilled attorneys want to represent death penalty defendants. The American legal system creates a challenging environment for defense attorneys and for opponents of the death penalty.[5] Practicing death penalty defense attorneys have asked themselves if they are "serving to legitimate the system by helping to provide sanitized executions, executions with the aura of legalism and therefore the appearance of fairness."[6] This study seeks to understand the development of death penalty defense attorneys by asking the attorneys themselves about the life experiences that led them to practice in a small, challenging, and moderately compensated area of law. Exploring their personal and professional development reveals the foundational life experiences that shaped their desire to work in death penalty defense. The findings inform law school educators, legal career counselors, and defense attorney training.

While we know little about the development of criminal defense attorneys and death penalty defense attorneys, several studies have examined the *work* of criminal defense attorneys. This research presents contradictory characterizations of criminal defense attorneys as selfish double agents[7] and selfless cause lawyers.[8] The portrayals of criminal defense attorneys as both immoral double agents and zealous advocates prove difficult to reconcile. Of course, *death penalty* defense attorneys may represent a uniquely driven group of cause lawyers.[9] This qualitative study of 15 defense attorneys specializing in death penalty cases in a western state helps clarify those conflicting portrayals and sheds light on their development.

The research proves important for several reasons. First, the defense attorney bar is a relatively small and young group. The National Association of Criminal Defense Lawyers was founded in 1958, and the American Bar Association first developed Criminal Justice Standards in 1968. Thus, studying the development of death penalty defense attorneys improves our understanding of the training and socialization of these lawyers in partic-ular and of this area of the American legal field in general. Second, death penalty defense attorneys work for the federal government, state government, and in private practice. However, most of these lawyers practice in federal or state government offices and repre-sent indigent defendants; their salaries are paid by the government. Yet, on a daily basis, they are appointed by the court and engage in legal battles against the other legal profes-sionals in the system—police officers, prosecutors, and judges. Thus, they represent a uniquely positioned group of lawyers—representing the underdog—and identifying problems with the state's evidence and prosecutor's case. As public defenders and what some call "cause lawyers," they are fighting the system while also acting as a representative advocating for the ideals of the system. Finally, previous research suggests that criminal defense lawyers and other "cause lawyers" are not well paid[10] and are disliked by the public.[11] What might lead someone to choose a specialty area that is both stigmatized and not well compensated? These ironies powerfully illustrate the conflict in American values at play in this profession. On the one hand, the government pays for the defense of indi-gent defendants—demonstrating a value for this work in theory. On the other hand, the stigmatization and moderate compensation associated with public defense work reflects the lower prestige of this legal profession in practice. Guided by the research on defense attorneys' work, the development of attorneys in other areas of specialty, and the symbolic interactionist framework for the career model, this study explores the following research question: What leads to a career in criminal defense work with a specialization in death penalty defense?

Literature Review

The Work of Defense Attorneys

Two areas of literature guide this study: the literature on criminal defense attorneys' work and the literature on the socialization of lawyers in other areas of specialty. The research on defense attorneys' work provides two rather conflicting viewpoints. In his landmark study on public defenders, sociologist David Sudnow observed the way public defenders managed cases and represented indigent clients.[12] Sudnow found that public defenders mediated between prosecutors and their defendant clients by trying to convince their clients to accept a plea deal. In addition, to streamline their heavy caseloads, defenders developed a "normal crime" classification scheme. The scheme allowed them to quickly identify the common features of any one type of offense (e.g., burglary, homicide, assault). Common features included the amount of damage done, the location of the crime, the seriousness of the injury to the victim, and the use of a weapon. When a client's offense was typical of other crimes in the category and fit the "normal crime" scheme for that offense, the defender pursued a plea agreement with greater confidence. Participant observations of criminal courts in California revealed that public defenders acted more like coaches than advocates for their clients, helping them prepare for court rather than helping them fight charges.[13] According to Sudnow's research, the public defender

> will not cause any serious trouble for the routine motion of the court conviction process. Laws will not be challenged, cases will not be tried to test the constitutionality of procedures and statutes, judges will not be personally degraded, police will be free from scrutiny to decide the legitimacy of their operations, and the community will not be condemned.[14]

While the same principles apply to public and private defense attorneys, the nature of the clientele is different, as is the nature of the client–attorney relationship. Research consistently finds that criminal defendants view their publicly appointed and government paid defense attorneys as less qualified and less invested in them than privately hired defense attorneys, making the client–attorney relationship a difficult one to manage for public defenders.[15] Skolnick found that defendants felt hostile toward and more critical of their court-appointed defense attorneys than privately hired defense attorneys.[16]

More recent research on defense attorneys' work offers a more positive outlook. For instance, relying on in-depth interview and participant observation data, Emmelman found that public defenders carefully evaluated the strength of the prosecution's case in plea bargains in three main stages, and the process they used to prepare for a plea bargain proved similar to that of preparing for trial.[17] Etienne offers compelling evidence to support the notion that "cause lawyering" represents a critical aspect of criminal defense work.[18] Cause lawyers "use their legal skills 'to pursue ends and ideals that transcend client service.'"[19] Etienne's finding that defense attorneys felt driven by deeply held moral beliefs,[20] and these personal motivations and previous research contradict the public perception that they are "amoral (if not immoral) 'hired guns' who, for the right price, would do anything to get their guilty clients off."[21]

Anecdotal accounts from practicing criminal defense attorneys suggest that beliefs in morality and social equality fuel interests in this area of law.[22] However, Margolin has warned, "[C]riminal defense is not a profession for the apathetic. It places enormous pressure on you and demands most of your time."[23] Death penalty defense work proves particularly demanding.[24] Mello felt called to fight the unfairness of the system's administration of the death penalty, force the government to address and answer these problems of inequality, and use strong advocacy to illustrate the arbitrariness and unfairness of capital punishment in the U.S.[25] He admitted that others often had a hard time understanding his motivations, asking, "Why do you represent people who are sentenced to death? Isn't it depressing?"

The Development of Lawyers

While we know little about the development of death penalty defense attorneys, we know a great deal about the development of attorneys in other specialty areas. Levin's study of the socialization of immigration lawyers described the backgrounds and legal practices of immigration lawyers working in private practice.[26] Levin found that personal family histories of immigration—from a parent or grandparent—often shaped their professional interest in immigration law, along with their desire to help people.[27] One participant explained, "[M]y father's family had a whole refugee history and my mother's family also and so that was like one aspect of it and then the other aspect of it was that I was interested in doing public service—public interest work . . . I felt [the work] was valuable."[28] Landon argues that the local community context (or the community of practice) in which lawyers work shapes their professional development more than their training in law school.[29] Etienne described African American and Latino/a defense attorneys as feeling driven to work in criminal defense to give back to their communities.[30] It remains unclear, however, what childhood, family, or community of practice experiences might fuel an interest in death penalty defense work.

Data Collection and Analysis

The data for the study come from a larger project on death penalty defense attorneys conducted in 2012 and 2013 in a mid-sized western state. To protect participants' confidentiality, the state's name is not revealed in this or other studies to come from the project. The state's Public Defenders' Office is nationally recognized for its high-quality training of criminal defense attorneys and death penalty defense attorneys. As a result, the state and these defenders provide an excellent opportunity for a study on the development of death penalty defense attorneys. These lawyers help train other defense attorneys around the country and they set the standard for death penalty defense work in the U.S. Thus, the "community of practice" for defense attorneys in the state is strong and close-knit.[31]

The study includes 15 participants, an admittedly small sample for a sociological study. It is important to note, however, that the population is extremely small. We estimate that fewer than 5 percent of practicing attorneys specialize in criminal defense law and fewer than 1 percent of practicing attorneys specialize in death penalty defense law in the U.S.

According to the state's defense attorney bar, we conducted in-depth interviews with all 15 of the death penalty defense attorneys practicing in the state (or 3 percent of the population of death penalty defense attorneys in the U.S.). Purposive sampling was used to identify and recruit 12 participants[32] and snowball sampling was used to recruit three participants.[33] To recruit participants, we sent letters to all 15 attorneys requesting their involvement in the project, but not one of them responded to the letter. To follow up, we contacted each participant via phone, and in several cases we called the participant multiple times before finally talking with them about an interview. Not one of the potential participants reached via phone declined to participate and these interviews continued until we exhausted the list of known death penalty defense attorneys in the state. Like other research suggests, public defenders have heavy caseloads, few case resources, and limited time.[34] In addition, more than 25 percent of participants worked as both a public defender with a heavy caseload and as an administrator in the state's public defender's office. It is understandable why several potential participants felt hesitant to do an interview simply because of the time commitment the meeting required. Once they agreed to an interview, all participants were talkative and candid about their backgrounds, law school training, and work experience.

The third author conducted all of the interviews and relied on an active and unstructured approach to the interviews.[35] Each interview took approximately one hour. Participants were asked four closed-ended questions about their careers (e.g., college, law school, internship, number of cases). They were also asked to describe their years of experience in criminal defense work. Participants were asked open-ended questions about their personal backgrounds (e.g., family, childhood), law school experiences, and death penalty defense work. These three categories of questions included: (1) I would like to start with your basic background information. Where did you grow up? What did your parents do for a living? Where did you go to college? What got you interested in law? Is there anything about your background that led you to criminal defense work? (2) Where did you go to law school? What did you think of law school? (3) What got you interested in criminal defense law? Can you tell me about your first job? Can you tell me about your first case or client? All interviews were tape-recorded and transcribed.

Sample Profile

Four of the 15 participants were female. All participants were white. Nine participants had worked in both private practice and in the public defender's office, and six participants had worked in the public defender's office only. Fourteen of the 15 participants had worked on death penalty trials; one of the participants worked specifically on death penalty appeals. None of the participants focused solely on habeas proceedings. Participants had between 18 and 41 years of experience in criminal defense work with an average of 29 years of experience. Fourteen of the 15 participants were currently practicing defense attorneys; one participant had recently retired as a defense attorney. Because we only interviewed death penalty defense attorneys from this mid-sized state, the findings may or may not represent what all death penalty defense attorneys would say about their development. The high quality of criminal defense attorney training in the state may make these respondents more passionate about and personally invested in defense work than defense attorneys from other states.

Findings

Mead says, the self "has development; it is not initially there, at birth but arises in the process of social experience and activity."[36] When study participants reflected upon the life experiences that led to their work in death penalty defense, we better understand the meaning of these experiences and their motivations. Goffman's career model celebrates the notion that social development occurs in phases, and at any given juncture in life, multiple paths can be taken.[37] As sociologists, we seek to identify the patterns that emerge in the development of people in a particular study population. The career model helps illustrate the individual's thought processes when consciously choosing the steps to a particular destination, as well as the fortuitous circumstances and "processing encounters" that helped shape their development.[38] These findings reveal the righteous development of death penalty defense attorneys.

Three major phases emerged in participants' responses to questions about what led them to work in death penalty defense law: (a) a passion for social and political issues starting in early childhood (the pre-lawyer phase), (b) a disenchantment with law school (the lawyer education phase), and (c) a pivotal internship experience with a defender's office during college or law school (the crystallizing experience phase). All three themes reflect participants' yearning to find social meaning in their life and work and to fight against injustice in society, and many participants described this searched-for meaning as culminating in a desire to help others, particularly disadvantaged others.

The Pre-entry Phase of the Death Penalty Defense Attorney Career

For most defense attorneys, the first phase in the development of their career arose in early childhood, or what Schein would call the pre-entry phase of the career.[39] Fourteen of the 15 participants recalled feeling a passion for social and political causes early in childhood, including the civil rights movement, the Vietnam War, and environmental protection.

In some cases, these passions emerged as the result of family socialization or religious educational experiences. In other cases, these passions emerged when participants witnessed a racial injustice (e.g., segregation, discrimination) or historical crisis (e.g., Kent State Massacre, Detroit Race Riots). For most participants, these pivotal experiences sensitized them to social problems, raised their consciousness about disadvantaged others, and predisposed them to an ethically oriented career.[40] Frank Stephens and Natalie Dresner, defense attorneys with 33 and 17 years of experience, respectively, in criminal defense work, said:

> [Mine] is a Jewish family and both of my parents considered themselves [to be] progressive-minded-liberals . . . [T]hey were involved in . . . the civil rights movement and supportive of the civil rights movement.
>
> (CDL#3, 33 Years of Experience, Private and Public Practice, Trials)

> My parents are both lawyers [and] my folks are activist-type people. There was a lot of civil rights activism in our household. My father eventually became a human rights lawyer.
>
> (CDL#14, 17 Years of Experience, Private and Public Practice, Appeals)

Frank and Natalie's parents' support for the civil rights movement provided a sensitizing socialization experience that predisposed them to an affinity for fighting for racial equality in society. Evan Leeman, a defense attorney with 18 years of experience, said:

> Intellectually, [my mother] agreed with civil rights, the ERA and the like, but [she] never actually [protested] out in the streets[s].
>
> (CDL#10, 18 Years of Experience, Public Practice, Trials)

Several participants indicated that it was the cultural and political timing of their upbringing, not their parents' beliefs that shaped their interest in justice for all. Together, Edward Zellner, Frank Stephens, and Steven Randolf had more than 100 years of experience in defense work, and all three believed that growing up during the 1960s set the stage for their careers in death penalty defense.

> I was a child of the Sixties . . . [So,] my radicalization basically came from being a child of the sixties, being in Ohio [learning about the Kent State University shootings], [and the] Vietnam War.
>
> (CDL#7, 40 Years of Experience, Private and Public Practice, Trials and Appeals)

> I went to high school in those formative years of the Sixties. [1] graduated in '71 from high school. I was . . . involved in anti-war protests even in high school, because of course, that was going on at the time.
>
> (CDL#3, 33 Years of Experience, Private and Public Practice, Trials)

> I grew up in Detroit, and I was 16 years old when the race riots happened in 1967. I took many pictures of the riots. I think seeing those events unfold opened me up to new experiences. [In looking back, I think] that's when I started to sympathize with the grievances that many minorities had.
>
> (CDL#11, 31 Years of Experience, Public Practice, Trials)

During the "pre-entry" stage of a career, the individual undergoes anticipatory socialization and begins to adopt the values, beliefs, and behaviors that align with the group she/he hopes to join.[41] In the case of death penalty defense work, participants did not necessarily begin "anticipatory" socialization with the hope of joining the death penalty defense attorney group. Most of them did not yet know that they wanted to be a defense attorney. Instead, they experienced what might be better called a sensitizing or consciousness-raising experience where they developed an awareness of social problems and political tensions and they started to sympathize with poorly treated groups. That sympathy and the sensitivity to injustice that came with it put them on a path toward a calling that allowed them to address injustice in their daily work. Of course, symbolic interactionists would note that not everyone incorporates these sensitizing socialization experiences into the "me" part of the self, where they adopt the values and beliefs as their own for the long term.[42]

While we might assume that these familial and cultural socialization experiences would move participants to participate in protests and marches, only a handful of participants actually became *active* participants in the civil rights movement and in the anti-war efforts of the 1960s and 1970s. Edward Zellner said,

> I fought in riots against the Vietnam War. I was a total [activist in college].
> (CDL#7, 40 Years of Experience, Public Practice, Trials)

However, he was in the minority. Most participants supported the sentiments behind civil rights and anti-war demonstrations, but their accounts indicate that they did not qualify as "high-commitment activists" where they marched, boycotted, and rallied for the cause.[43] Roger Garriott attributed his lack of involvement in demonstrations to timing.

> When I was in college, it was sort of post-Vietnam [and] the big time protests were gone. [Instead], I was involved in things in college and [in] law school [like] the American Civil Liberty Union and National Lawyers' Guild, but I was never on the front lines. I was never a big protester.
> (CLD#6, Public Practice, Trials)

Other participants explained that they felt an affinity for the values behind the movement but did not participate in the movement. Oscar Delaney explained:

> I was aware of the [civil rights movement and anti-war] protests, but I didn't actually march on Washington or anything.
> (CDL#13, Private and Public Practice, Trials)

Sherkat and Blocker's panel study of protesters and non-protesters suggests that "high-commitment" protesters tend to seek careers that reflect the values and beliefs championed by the cause.[44] The findings presented here, however, indicate that participants did not have to be "big protesters" of the 1960s and 1970s to feel an affinity for a legal career in public service. For the most part, death penalty defense attorneys were low-commitment activists or distant supporters of the social movements of the 1960s and 1970s. Yet, they still sought an educational and a professional path that allowed them to "sustain political orientations, promote interactions with networks of likeminded or receptive individuals, and obtain political power and influence," just as Sherkat and Blocker's "high-commitment activists" did.[45]

For one participant, religious upbringing served as the sensitizing socialization experience that shaped her career choice. Tina Carter, a defense attorney with 23 years of experience, described her Catholic school education and upbringing as an important influence in her decision to become a criminal defense attorney. She said:

> My parents sent all of their kids to a Catholic school . . . [It taught] me to be a good person and not judge people. So, all of the good things they taught me, I still to this day appreciate and believe that it formed who I am. And I probably would not have ended up being a public defender if I didn't have that education . . . [They taught me things] like don't judge other people, be kind to the poor, be kind to criminals, help people who are hungry, forgive seven times seventy, turn the other cheek, all those things . . . I think that's a great way to live.
>
>   (CDL#4, Public Practice, Trials)

Tina's Catholic education socialized her to a belief system that complemented the defense of indigent people accused of serious criminal acts, which Mead would describe as the "me" part of the self or the internationalization of others' beliefs and values.[46] She intentionally sought a career that supported that "orienting schema" and she found that the best way to live those ideals was through death penalty defense work.[47] Tina, however, was only one of two participants to reference religious upbringing as providing the sensitizing socialization experience that provided the foundation for a career in death penalty defense law. The other participant, Natalie Dresner, said her Jewish upbringing taught her to stand up for others and fight against injustices in the world (CDL#14, Private and Public Practice, Appeals).

Participants described themselves and their career interests as a product of these childhood experiences with their parents, civil unrest, and religious education, but symbolic interactionists would emphasize the role of the self in the formulation of these interests. Individuals do not passively internalize social or cultural messages, like parents' political beliefs, the civil rights movement, or the anti-war effort.[48] Instead, the individual actively considers the issues confronting him or her, reflects upon them, interprets the meaning of them, and after some consideration decides how to respond to them. Witnessing the civil rights movement or race riots does not *determine* one's career as a defense attorney; instead, individuals choose their own behavior and thus their own path within the surrounding social structural and cultural environment.[49] Social psychologists might argue that when these participants saw the negative effects of large social structures (e.g., socioeconomic class, government) on individual people, in the news and in everyday social encounters, they felt called to respond. "[I]n most societies these [large social structures] serve as social boundaries having important consequences for life chances."[50]

Other participants recalled a particular historical event or community experience as shaping their interest in fighting injustice through criminal defense work—such as the 1967 Detroit riots (discussed above) or the 1970 Kent State University shootings. Elliott Young, a trial veteran and head of the state public defender's office, recalled the racial tension in Kentucky between the student bodies at the predominantly white University of Kentucky and the predominantly black University of Louisville while he was in college. He recalled how in the 1960s and 1970s Kentucky never played Louisville in basketball, despite the strong in-state rivalry between the schools, because the "wealthy white school refus[ed] to play the inner-city black school" (CLD#2, Private and Public Practice, Trials). While he recalled those racial tensions and the busing policies in Louisville in the 1970s in vivid detail, he said they did not influence his decision to become a criminal defense attorney. He said the Kent State massacre, where officers with the Ohio National Guard fired shots on unarmed Kent State University students engaging in and observing a protest over the U.S.'s involvement in the Cambodian Campaign, led him to criminal defense work. The shootings left four students dead and one paralyzed. Elliott said:

> In 1970, Kent State happened [and I was 13 years old] . . . and I was going into my rebellious teenage years. I was astounded that the government of Ohio was allowed to call out the National Guard and kill college students, over [their] First Amendment rights . . . I still point to that day as sort of the defining moment that pushed me into doing Constitutional criminal defense work . . . No one was ever prosecuted for those shootings and I was just horrified.
>
> (CDL#2, 31 Years of Experience, Private and Public Practice, Trials)

Elliott's feelings of outrage over the shootings and sense of injustice that no one was ever prosecuted for them fueled his interest in the ideals and principles of criminal defense work. While a cursory reading of Elliott's comments might give the impression that he wanted to serve as a prosecutor, a closer review of his comments reveals that he wanted to serve in a role that allowed him to hold the government accountable. Indeed, Etienne said that the criminal defense attorney participants in her study wanted to fight the government and "described their work as upholding individual rights and liberties, or Constitutional rights."[51]

Other participants witnessed race riots in their high school or racial injustices in their communities. Eric Mason, a defense attorney with 33 years of experience, said:

> [My high school] was shut down for 6 weeks during my junior year in high school because of the race rioting. So, my junior year, as well as my senior year in high school [were] totally chaotic educationally because there were huge upheavals . . . afterwards, police officers were patrolling the hallways and it was a very violent background in high school. Fights all the time.
>
> (CDL#9, Private and Public Practice, Trials and Appeals)

Mary Vinson, one of the few female defense attorneys working in the state, witnessed outright racial discrimination against African American children when her family was stationed at a military base in Georgia in the 1960s. She said one incident in particular framed her interest in civil rights and race relations.

> I was raised in Georgia during the 1960s. What probably motivated me more than anything in my life [to become a death penalty defense attorney] was living in Georgia, while my father was stationed there. When we lived on the army base, we knew black people in town. [When] we lived off the base, [we learned that] white people did not associate with black people. [For example,] there was a community pool, and they bused black kids to our pool. None of my neighbors would swim in the pool any more. So, having that awakening about what was going on [between whites and blacks in the community] made me become interested in civil rights. I just think we need to be a better world.
>
> (CDL#1, 26 Years of Experience, Public Practice, Trials)

For Mary, these events profoundly shaped her view of the world and her role in it. In high school, she decided to become a lawyer, and in college, she majored in diversity studies. As Mead might say, she considered the event and organized for action—a career fighting for civil rights.[52] She said that "having that awakening" about race relations in Georgia influenced her desire to work on civil rights issues. Mary continued:

> I thought I was going in the direction of becoming a civil rights lawyer and then somewhere in my undergrad career, I realized the best place to do that was criminal law.
>
> (CDL#1, 26 Years of Experience, Public Practice, Trials)

Mary initially defined her career path as a civil rights lawyer, but like several other participants who started with an interest in civil rights or environmental law, Mary soon realized that criminal law was the best place to build "a better world" with her law degree. Goffman suggests that people try to present themselves as moral human beings.[53] For death penalty defense attorneys participating in this study, the pursuit of a "better world" and of "fighting for the underdog" represented important moral work. Mary said:

> I became really interested in criminal law because I . . . realized that's where the government has the potential to be more oppressive when it comes to issues of race and I think one of the driving factors always as a public defender [for me] has been just the impact the judicial system has had on minority communities . . . [W]e have an over-representation of minorities in the criminal justice system . . . So, it's a moral kind of thing.
>
> (CLD#1, Public Practice, Trials)

When asked why they chose to pursue death penalty defense work in particular, other participants discussed their desire to fight for the underdog and also fight against racism. Roger Garriott (quoted at the start of this article) and Sullivan Draper said:

> I've always liked working for the underdog [and] the criminal defendant certainly is an underdog in the system. I'm appalled at some of the racism and classism that continues to exist in America and this is one way to fight that sort of thing.
>
> (CDL#6, 33 Years of Experience, Public Practice, Trials)

> I always kind of liked the underdog. I liked the idea of arguing . . . I always sort of had an anti-authoritarian streak. Just sort of not liking authority, I mean it wasn't anything, the point of [out right rebellion], it was just sort of a mild undercurrent in my personality where I think that fit in well.
>
> (CDL#5, 25 Years of Experience, Private and Public Practice, Trials)

Participants' reflections help explain the experiences and events that provided the foundation for a career in criminal defense. While these accounts do not reflect a predetermined path to death penalty defense law, they do hint at a willingness to question the status quo and help disadvantaged others. The finding that most participants did not actively engage in protests or marches suggests that participants felt inclined to raise these questions and offer this help in the context of an established system, not by striking out against the system or by vehemently opposing it on their own.

In the first premise of symbolic interactionism, Blumer says, "Human beings act toward things on the basis of the meaning that the things have for them."[54] The theory argues that to indicate something is to extricate it from its setting, to hold it apart, and to give it meaning. These attorneys gave meaning to injustices in the world, and they actively sought an education and a career that allowed them to address and oppose those injustices—from *inside* the criminal justice system. Etienne explained that criminal defense lawyers are not really anti-government; they are "anti-government misconduct or abuse."[55]

The finding that participants felt personally called to represent the underdog, to champion racial equality, and to fight authority (even the government) reflects a very different characterization of defense attorneys than captured by Sudnow, Skolnick, and Blumberg.[56] Two possible reasons for the stark contrast in the findings presented here compared to previous research include: (1) the method of data collection, and (2) the focus on *death penalty* defense attorneys. First, Sudnow, Skolnick, and Blumberg relied primarily on participant observation data, which may not have captured all of the personal motivations for defenders' work.[57] This study and other recent research,[58] on the other hand, relies on in-depth interview data from the defense attorneys themselves, offering more insight into the presuppositions shaping their career decisions. Second, as a small subset of the defense attorney population, death penalty defense attorneys may prove more passionate and personally motivated than other defense attorneys.[59] Of course, the life experiences shaping the desire to work on death penalty defense did not come easily; law school, the next step in participants' careers, proved a difficult phase of the death penalty defense attorneys' professional development.

The Lawyer Education Phase in the Death Penalty Defense Attorney Career

In the second premise of symbolic interaction, Blumer argues that meaning arises from social interaction with others, and these social interactions can create changes in meaning.[60] Like with other things, the meaning of a law degree changes over time and over the course of the law school education.[61] These changes, however, do not always come easily, particularly for the social-cause-oriented first year law student. In these cases, the first year of law school can prove particularly intense.[62]

For the death penalty defense attorneys participating in this study, law school proved a difficult time. These participants disliked law school and one dropped out (but later returned). Two participants described their experiences with law school:

> Oh, I hated it. In fact after the first year, I quit. I said, "I want to be a criminal defense lawyer. I don't know why I gotta do all this other stuff." I didn't like the teaching method. I didn't like the subjects. I didn't much like my teachers. I didn't have a very good attitude. So, I quit for a year . . . [but] I went back and suffered through it and got my degree.
>
> (CDL#6, 33 Years of Experience, Public Practice, Trials)

> I did not like law school . . . I mean, I think as an institution and as an intellectual pursuit, it's a wonderful, nuanced, foundational thing. I think it's wonderful. But I wouldn't say that it was [wonderful] for me.
>
> (CDL#11, 31 Years of Experience, Public Practice, Trials)

Of course, it may be the case that many law students dislike law school, and of course, the current study does not include data from other lawyers to offer a comparison. These participants' comments indicate that these feelings of disenchantment led them to question but not abandon their interest in law.

The symbolic interactionist principle that meaning arises in social encounters (not in social isolation) helps explain these negative evaluations of law school. In the pre-lawyer phase of their careers (in childhood), participants perceived their law school education as a way to "do good" in society and improve the world. They sought a "moral kind" of education and career (CDL #1). They saw a law degree as a path to public service. Participants' *definition* of a law school education, however, was not always shared by their professors or classmates. Not only did others *not* share their definition, they also did not appear to value participants' definitions. Participants' expectation that a law degree would allow them to pursue public service law did not get validated in law school. These differences—and even conflicts—in the meaning of a law school education created frustration and disappointment among participants. For those who entered law school knowing that they wanted to make "a better world," many of the required courses in the law school curriculum (e.g., property, contracts) seemed unnecessarily difficult and even boring.

Other participants described their fellow classmates as a primary reason for their dislike of law school. Tina Carter said:

> I did not like law school, any of it, really. Most of the people I went to law school with were just very different from me . . . They were so intense about things that didn't seem all that important to me. The studying and the competition for grades, points of view, you know. I was there for a purpose, did it, and moved on . . . We [just] saw the world differently. We just did not have a lot in common.
> (CDL#4, 23 Years of Experience, Public Practice, Trials)

Death penalty defense attorneys' passion for moral and social issues may have alienated them from fellow law students with more conservative political views and more business-oriented legal interests. Erlanger and Klegon's panel study on changes in attitudes about public interest work among law students over time indicates that students' political attitudes changed very little over the course of the three-year education.[63] The values and beliefs that Tina and other participants held at the start of law school did not abate over time, despite the fact that their professors and classmates did not share the same values and beliefs. The finding that this isolation existed but did not derail participants from their public service calling reflects a slight departure from research on marginalization in other types of public service law.[64]

Interestingly, several participants described the type of people that work in criminal defense work as an important draw for them. Sullivan Draper said:

> I remember the public defender's conference is held every year in June [pseudo-month] and so I just took off from [law] school [and] went to that . . . I was walking along [the hotel corridor] and I look in this room and here's all these very sophisticated or well-dressed people that didn't look like what I expected and I figured out that [it] was an insurance sales thing. [But] I [kept] going down the hall

and then here's a much more ragtag group of folks and it was public defenders. And it's like, [I thought], "These are [the] folks I really enjoyed meeting." Once you see the whole system come together, you take all the classes, you see the sort of passion for representing the dispossessed. That [conference] was a fairly cementing event [for me].

(CDL#5, Years of Experience, Private and Public Practice, Trials)

Tina Carter admitted:

I like the kind of people who become public defenders. They seemed less stuffy, less arrogant, more real life: [they] cussed more, drank more, had really good parties, [and were] fun to hang out with.

(CDL#4, 23 Years of Experience, Public Practice, Trials)

While law school students' values and beliefs do not change radically over the course of the three-year degree, Erlanger and Klegon found that students' interest in pursuing a legal career with a public interest element, specifically a public defender or prosecutor, declined somewhat.[65] The findings presented here suggest that students' interest in criminal defense work may decline over the course of law school, in part because of the norms and values expressed within law school culture, as well as the small number of criminal law and constitutional law courses.

For the death penalty defense attorneys participating in this study, their law school experiences tested their definition of a law degree and their commitment to criminal defense work. When taken within the context of Erlanger and Klegon's earlier findings, these conflicts of meaning may discourage some students from pursuing public service law altogether.[66] Symbolic interactionists note how the meaning of things arises in and gets changed over the course of social encounters[67] but as participants' experiences in law school indicate, these changes can create distress and even dissatisfaction. Having one's definition of the situation challenged and even dismissed may lead some to feel negatively about the law school curriculum, teaching style, and student body. Participants felt disappointed. These death penalty defense attorneys said they "did it, and moved on," "suffered through it," and "could not wait to get out [of law school]." It was not until participants got to have their first internship experience with a public defender's office or legal aid clinic that they felt validated in their chosen legal specialty. The internship experience represents the third and final phase in the social development of the death penalty defense attorney, and it can be thought of as a crystallizing social experience when participants just "knew" they were meant to be criminal defense attorneys.

The Internship Phase in the Death Penalty Defense Attorney Career

The greatest influence shaping participants' decision to work in criminal defense law came from a pivotal internship experience in college or law school. For the law students disillusioned with the law school curriculum, the internship with a public defender's office or a legal aid clinic proved life-changing and life-affirming. They finally found their legal training exciting and fulfilling. Symbolic interactionists might say that participants found a place where their meaning of a career in law matched others' meaning, and this match proved to be a "godsend" and the "greatest experience." Sullivan Draper recalled:

> My second year of law school, I was really lucky that a new criminal-practice clinic was added. The [law school] got a new professor. They added a trial practice with the legal aid clinic. We actually had real clients. I signed up for that and it was a godsend . . . It was a one-semester program. I fell in love with it immediately.
>
> (CDL#5, 25 Years of Experience, Private and Public Practice, Trials)

Sullivan said he felt "lucky" and "fell in love" with it immediately. The language participants used to describe their internships reflect their deeply held desire to find purpose in their education and fulfillment in their work. They did not just want to *like* their work or their clients. They wanted to love it. Sullivan continued participating in the clinic, and then he landed a summer internship with the local public defender's office. He said:

> [Then] in my second year, I got an internship with the public defender's office. That summer was literally just the greatest experience of my life at that point. I was an intern for an attorney who was a long-time public defender, a really good trial lawyer. I was handed a stack of files that was a couple of feet high. These were cases that were mine to handle that summer. They were all misdemeanor cases, real clients . . . I was practicing under the Student Practice Act. At the end of the summer, they told me that they could not pay me anymore. I told them that I did not care; I just wanted to keep working there. I worked throughout my third year of law school.
>
> (CDL#5, 25 Years of Experience, Private and Public Practice, Trials)

Edward Zellner had a similar experience. He said:

> What happened is after my second year in law school, I got into the legal aid and defender program, which was great. So finally I could actually go to court and do stuff . . . After my second year in law school, I applied and got one of thirteen [legal aid association] grants for a summer internship with a public defender. I was sent to Camville [pseudonym]; so I went to Camville and they paid my summer being an intern down there, which was great. I got to do everything . . . Go to jail, talk to guys in jail; [I] helped out in a couple trials . . . [I] actually, got to strategize and those guys are still my friends.
>
> (CLD#7, 40 Years of Experience, Public Practice, Trials)

These internship experiences proved particularly important—for helping participants find their place in the legal field, renewing their interest in the law, and validating their desire to help others with their degree. The internship restored their enthusiasm for the law and confirmed their interest in criminal defense, which meant a great deal given their difficulties with classes and classmates in their first two years of law school. They had finally found a legal setting where their own definition of a legal career matched others' definition. They no longer felt "marginalized" where people didn't "quite know how to make sense of us," like the legal aid practitioners in Zaloznaya and Nielsen's study.[68]

Merolla and colleagues' study of undergraduates' participation in a science-training program, which they call a "proximate social structure" (e.g., family, social club, athletic team),[69] provides some insight into the significance of internship experiences in death penalty defense attorneys' identity. When students participated in a science-training program with other like-minded students, they increased their commitment to and identification with the scientist role. The authors recognize that large social structures (e.g., race, class, gender) and intermediate social structures (e.g., neighborhoods, schools, associations) create boundaries that either increase or decrease the likelihood of an individual's success in a particular endeavor (e.g., completing high school, attending college, graduating college, pursuing a science career). *Proximate* social structures, on the other hand, provide a stage where people can learn and practice the role.[70]

Symbolic interactionists would call a proximate social structure a micro-level or small group social interaction,[71] and they find these more intimate social interactions to be crucial to identity formation. Thus, an internship with a public defender's office or a legal aid clinic may act as a proximate social structure that enhances law students' commitment to and reaffirms their identification with a somewhat unpopular legal specialty. "[P]ersons will act in ways they perceive as consistent with the meanings they attach to particular role identities . . . [and within identity verification, people] seek to verify an identity standard, or a set of meanings about who one is, by aligning their own actions toward this standard and through attempts to manipulate the reflected appraisals of others."[72] Death penalty defense attorneys found a place for aligning their own identity standards in their internships, and their internship experience helped counteract their sense of dissatisfaction with law school and it reaffirmed their commitment to the defense attorney identity.

Discussion and Conclusion

The death penalty defense attorney quoted at the start of this article said that he liked the idea of representing "the underdog" and fighting "racism and classism" in his work, reflecting his heartfelt commitment to helping the disadvantaged and improving society. The findings presented here represent a major shift in the portrayal of criminal defense attorneys in the law and society literature, contradicting Blumberg's depiction of defense attorneys as self-interested double-agents[73] but supporting Etienne's depiction of criminal defense attorneys as passionate cause-lawyers.[74] While many participants knew early on that they wanted to pursue law and to help others, the notion that death penalty defense work was the best path to that end was not always obvious or even easy. In fact, most participants said they did not recall having an opinion about or engaging in debates about the death penalty in their formative years. Instead, their accounts reflect a slow, gradual movement toward a career first in criminal defense work and then in death penalty defense work. Drawing on Goffman's career model of development,[75] participants' accounts suggest three main phases leading to the death penalty defense attorney career: (1) a passion for social and political issues starting in early childhood (the pre-lawyer phase), (2) a disenchantment with and dislike for law school (the lawyer education phase), and (3) a pivotal internship experience with a defender's office during college or law school (the crystallizing experience phase).

In the first phase, participants discussed the impact that their awareness of racism, the civil rights movement, and the anti-war effort of the 1960s and 1970s had on them. Despite the fact that all participants were white, they described sympathizing with "the grievances minorities had" and felt a desire to make "a better world" at a very young age. In the second phase, the law school education phase, participants' altruistic interests got challenged. Participants hated law school, including the course topics, their fellow students, and professors' teaching styles. One participant even quit law school for a year. In the third and final phase, an internship with a public defender's office served as a major turning point in their career, validating them and their interests. One participant described the internship as a "blessing" and a "godsend." Mead might say that these law school students had finally found a legal community that supported their views and interests.[76] The validation that came with the internship proved critical to their development and to their completion of law school.

Using the symbolic interactionist perspective, we might argue that death penalty defense attorneys' ability to take the role of the other—disadvantaged others—shaped their career selection.[77] However, participants' accounts do not actually indicate that they put themselves in *individual others' shoes*, as symbolic interactionists might expect of sympathetic people. Taking-the-role-of-the-other allows people to imagine another person's viewpoint, and this role-taking is important in sympathy. Yet, we do not hear participants saying, "I knew my African American friend John must have felt discriminated against when all the whites left the city pool after he jumped into the water" or "I wondered what it felt like to lose a child in the Kent State Massacre and not have a trial." Instead, participants' accounts indicate that they considered and reflected upon the attitudes of *society as a whole* (not of individual people), which Mead calls the *generalized other*.[78] Symbolic interactionists argue that people in power define the generalized other.[79]

The findings indicate that participants consciously reflected upon the meaning of racial injustice and government oppression for American society, and little-by-little they came to find a career that allowed them to take action to benefit American society and to redefine the generalized other. The death penalty defense attorneys participating in this study recognized the prevalent (albeit shifting) social values of the time period, and they made a conscious decision not to internalize those traditional values. They sought out a career that allowed them to both resist the pull of traditional values reflected in the generalized other and champion a cause to change them—on behalf of their individual clients and for the benefit of larger society. One participant explained:

> I'm a big fan of the rule of law. I mean, it's fundamental to any advanced civilization and [a] criminal defense lawyer—by holding the government and the cops and the prosecutors to the rule of law—[I can] help ensure the rule of law. So, in some ways, [this job is] really a very conservative kind of job—maintaining the status quo. In other ways, it's a very radical kind of a job—because you're attacking the government and the powers that be in virtually every case.
>
> (CDL#6, 33 Years of Experience, Public Practice, Trials)

The notion that death penalty defense attorneys fight the system as a legal actor within the system places them in the ideal position to recognize societal values, acknowledge those values, and then fight against them in their daily work.

As Margolin has said: "[C]riminal defense is not a profession for the apathetic."[80] Symbolic interactionists would point out the challenge of having a foot in both worlds; one must see and understand current societal values, and one must identify the ways to up-end those values—in both individual cases and for the larger system. Edward Zellner, a death penalty defense attorney with 40 years of experience, used the analogy of a trampoline to explain this challenge. He said:

> You see, everybody [in the courtroom] is on a trampoline. The judge is bouncing and the DA is bouncing and they want me to bounce to the same tempo, right? Well, I've got to figure out a way to stop and pop ... Otherwise, [the judge and prosecutor are] gonna just bounce you right along to the ole' gas chamber. So, you don't become that guy. You don't become helpful [saying], "Judge, oh, I've got that for you." "Judge, can I help out?" "Oh, judge, I'll waive taking that record." You *can't* be that guy.
>
> (CDL#7, Public Practice, Trials)

Elliott continued by saying:

> [You see,] I'm the most dangerous person in the courtroom because I don't care ... It's a huge attitudinal change.

The attitudinal change reflects a deep understanding of the social values (i.e., the tempo) and a thoughtful resistance to the pull toward those values, also known as the generalized other. In her reflections on her own work as a defense attorney, Arguedas has explained, "First and foremost, it is *not* our responsibility to concern ourselves with what society, our friends, or our neighbors think or do when we defend our clients."[81] Elliott's above-quoted reflection that "I don't care" further supports this notion, and Mead's generalized other provides a way of framing this finding. As Etienne has suggested, defense attorneys are cause lawyers, working hard to help the underdog. These findings suggest that death penalty defense attorneys feel particularly called to their cause.[82] They felt honored to work for the cause. Considering himself fortunate, Edward Zellner said, "[H]ow [many] people ... get to be involved in a serious ... cause-oriented thing that [becomes] your life? ... Not many people do, you know?"

Over the course of their development, death penalty defense attorneys navigated several paradoxes, including (1) upholding sacred societal values (e.g., constitutional rights, equality, right to counsel) while representing people who have committed profane criminal acts, (2) hating law school for being a place that did not support their values, beliefs, or career interests—despite the fact that those beliefs, values, and interests are what make our country great, and (3) fighting the government while working for the government. Future research should consider the toll that these ironies take on death penalty defense attorneys' development, well-being, and career.

Critical Thinking

The defendants in death penalty cases provide attorneys with multiple challenges, one of which is that their clients have committed extremely heinous crimes which usually result in a great deal of media coverage to the detriment of the accused. In short, the public often comes to despise the accused. Why then do these lawyers not only take on the task of defending these defendants but do so rigorously and with much dedication in their role as a criminal lawyer?

Notes

1. Paul Kaplan, Forgetting the Future: Cause Lawyering and the Work of California Capital Trial Defenders. 14 Theoretical Criminology 211 (2010).
2. Suzanna Sheffer, Fighting for Their Lives: Inside the Experience of Capital Defense Attorneys (2013).
3. John P. Heinz et al., Urban Lawyers: The New Social Structure of the Bar (2005).
4. See Johnnie Cochran, How Can You Defend Those People?, 30 Loy. L.A. L. Rev. 39 (1996–1997): Abbe Smith and Monroe H. Freeman, How Can You Represent Those People? (2013).
5. Austin Sarat, The Killing State: Capital Punishment in Law, Politics, and Culture (1998).
6. Michael Mello, Another Attorney for Life, in Facing the Death Penalty: Essays on a Cruel and Unusual Punishment 87 (Michael L. Radelet ed., 1989).
7. See Abraham S. Blumberg, The Practice of Law as Confidence Game: Organizational Cooptation of a Profession, 1 Law & Soc'y Rev. 15 (1967).
8. Margareth Etienne, Criminal Law: The Ethics of Cause Lawyering: An Empirical Examination of Criminal Defense Lawyers as Cause Lawyers, 95 J. Crim. L. & Criminology 1195 (2005).
9. Sheffer, supra note 2.
10. Heinz et al., supra note 3.
11. See Cochran, supra note 4; Smith and Freeman, supra note 4.
12. David Sudnow, Normal Crimes: Sociological Features of the Penal Code in a Public Defender Office, 12 Soc. Probs. 255 (1965).
13. Jerome H. Skolnick, Social Control in the Adversary System, 11 J. Conflict Resol. 52 (1967).
14. Sudnow, supra note 12, at 273.
15. Roy B. Fleming, Client Games: Defense Attorney Perspectives on Their Relations with Criminal Clients, 2 Am. B. Found. Res. J. 253 (1986).
16. Skolnick, supra note 13.
17. Debra S. Emmelman, Gauging the Strength of Evidence Prior to Plea Bargaining: The Interpretive Procedures of Court-Appointed Defense Attorneys, 22 Law & Soc. Inquiry 927 (1998).
18. Etienne, supra note 8.
19. Etienne, supra note 8, at 1198.
20. Etienne, supra note 8, at 1196.
21. See Sudnow, supra note 12; Skolnick, supra note 13; Blumberg, supra note 7.
22. Gerald B. Lefcourt, Responsibilities of a Criminal Defense Attorney, 30 Loy. L.A. L. Rev. 59 (1996–1997).
23. Ephraim Margolin, Remaining Hopeful in a Hopeless System, 30 Loy. L.A. L. Rev. 88 (1996–1997).
24. Sheffer, supra note 2.
25. Mello, supra note 6.
26. Leslie Levin, Guardians at the Gate: The Backgrounds, Career Paths, and Professional Development of Private U.S. Immigration Lawyers, 34 Law & Soc. Inquiry 399 (2009).
27. Levin, supra note 26.
28. Levin, supra note 26, at 410.

29. Donald D. Landon, Clients, Colleagues, and Community: The Shaping of Zealous Advocacy in Country Law, 10 Am. B. Found. Res. J. 81 (1985).
30. Etienne, supra note 8.
31. Lynn Mather et al., Divorce Lawyers at Work: Varieties of Professionalism in Practice 6 (2001).
32. Earl Babbie, The Practice of Social Research (1995).
33. Bruce Berg, Qualitative Research Methods for the Social Sciences (2001); Patrick Biernacki and Dan Waldorf, Snowball Sampling, 10 Soc. Res. Methods 141 (1981).
34. Etienne, supra note 8; Sudnow, supra note 12.
35. See James Holstein and Jaber Gubrium, The Active Interview (1995).
36. George Herbert Mead. Mind, Self and Society (1989).
37. Erving Goffman, The Presentation of Self in Everyday Life (1960).
38. Goffman, supra note 37.
39. Edgar H. Schein, The Individual, the Organization, and the Career: A Conceptual Scheme, 7 J. Applied Behav. Sci. 401 (1971).
40. See also Etienne, supra note 8.
41. Schein, supra note 39.
42. Mead, supra note 36.
43. Darren E. Sherkat and T. Jean Blocker, Explaining the Political and Personal Consequences of Protest, 75 Soc. Forces 1049 (1997).
44. Sherkat & Blocker, supra note 43.
45. Sherkat & Blocker, supra note 43, at 1065.
46. Mead, supra note 36.
47. Sherkat & Blocker, supra note 43, at 1065.
48. Mead, supra note 36.
49. See Mead, supra note 36.
50. David Merolla et al., Structural Precursors to Identity Processes: The Role of Proximate Social Structures, 75 Soc. Psychol. Q. (2011).
51. Etienne, supra note 8, at 1211.
52. Mead, supra note 36.
53. Goffman, supra note 37.
54. Herbert Blumer, Symbolic Interactionism: Perspective and Method (1969).
55. Etienne, supra note 8, at 1213.
56. See Sudnow, supra note 12; Skolnick, supra note 13; Blumberg, supra note 7.
57. Sudnow, supra note 12.
58. Etienne, supra note 8; Emmelman, supra note 17.
59. Mello, supra note 6.
60. Blumer, supra note 54, at 4.
61. Howard S. Erlanger and Douglas A. Klegon, Socialization Effect of Professional School: The Law School Experience and Student Orientations to Public Interest Concerns, 13 Law & Soc'y Rev. 11 (1978).
62. Erlanger and Klegon, supra note 61.
63. Erlanger and Klegon, supra note 61.
64. Marina Zaloznaya and Laura Beth Nielsen, Mechanisms and Consequences of Professional Marginality: The Case of Poverty Lawyers Revisited, 36 Law & Soc. Inquiry 919 (2001).
65. Zaloznaya and Nielsen, supra note 64, at 30.
66. Zaloznaya and Nielsen, supra note 64, at 30.
67. Blumer, supra note 54; Mead, supra note 36.
68. Zaloznaya & Nielsen, supra note 64, at 930.
69. Merolla et al., supra note 50.
70. Merolla et al., supra note 50.
71. Mead, supra note 36.
72. Merolla et al., supra note 50, at 167.
73. Blumberg, supra note 7.
74. Etienne, supra note 8.
75. Goffman, supra note 37.

76. Mead, supra note 36.
77. Mead, supra note 36.
78. Mead, supra note 36.
79. Mead, supra note 36.
80. Margolin, supra note 23, at 99.
81. Christina C. Arguedas, Duties of a Criminal Defense Lawyer, 30 Loy. L.A. L. Rev. 7 (1996–1997).
82. Etienne, supra note 8.

12

How Can You Prosecute These People?

Paul Butler

Abstract: *The prosecution and defense attorneys are both moral actors who have a role to play in the judicial process. In this article, former federal prosecutor Paul Butler examines the role of defense counsel and compares it with the district attorney's responsibilities, and claims both sides play an important part in the justice regime. Much of Butler's viewpoints are discussed in the morality of trial work in both defense and prosecution. Other issues are included in his essay: helping victims, guilty pleas, racial justice, and innocence and guilt are important items discussed.*

Defense attorneys are frequently asked the "cocktail party" question: "how can you represent those people?" Prosecutors are rarely asked "how can you prosecute those people?" It's a good question—and maybe harder to answer, in many respects, than the defense attorney question. It is interesting that we do not demand the same moral accountability from prosecutors that we do from defense attorneys about the work they have chosen.

But people do ask prosecutors sometimes. When I was a prosecutor, the people who asked it were usually African Americans. I would not call it a cocktail party question because the people who asked generally weren't the cocktail party type. They were poor and working-class folks whose sons or grandbabies had gotten caught up in the criminal justice system. I'll call it the "courthouse hallway" question because that was the usual forum.

The courthouse hallway question was often an accusatory look rather than a form of words. It came from relatives of the person on trial, defense attorneys, and sometimes, if I hadn't done my voir dire right, jurors. It made me feel like I was the one on trial, like I had done something wrong.

The question also seemed like a kind of racial profiling; I thought I got the question more because I am African American, although perhaps that was just my guilty conscience. This is what the question seemed to signify: now was the first time that a professional black man had ever paid much attention to their kid and it was only because that professional black man—me—was trying to get the kid locked up.

Here I will provide a brief account of how I could have—and did—prosecute those people, and then compare the debate about the ethics of defense work to the new debate about the ethics of prosecution work. I will also examine some morally problematic aspects of the work of prosecutors and conclude with a brief comparison of the ethics of defense versus prosecution in an age of mass incarceration and extraordinary racial disparities in punishment.

How and Why I Prosecuted Those People

I became a prosecutor because of my experiences as a young African American man. The times I wasn't being harassed by police and security guards, I was being harassed by other young black men. Stopped and questioned by the former, robbed of my lunch money by the latter.

I wanted to use my law school education to address the two most vexing criminal justice issues for blacks—overenforcement of the law and underenforcement of the law—at the same time. So I joined the US Department of Justice as a trial attorney.

My plan was to go in as an undercover brother. It's the classic liberal response—to infiltrate the oppressor to try to create change from the inside. I thought nobody would be in a better position to make a difference than me.

Young black men are the most frequent victims of crime and the most likely to be charged with crimes. I could have responded the way that lots of my brothers do—by not trusting anybody. You walk through your hood and you glare at the dope boys on the corner, who make your community feel unsafe. Then, when the squad car slowly rolls by, and the cops take a good look at you, you glare at them too.

But I was an idealist. And being a prosecutor seemed to be the perfect solution to the long-standing concerns that African Americans had about both civil rights and public safety. In the segregated neighborhood in Chicago where I grew up, blacks made the same claims about law enforcement that they do now. The times that my neighbors were not complaining about how the police treated them, they were complaining that the police were never there when they needed them.

These claims seemed contradictory, but they were both accurate. And unfortunately things have not changed much now, when the United States has almost 1 million black people in prison.

The African American prosecutor lives at the intersection of crime control and racial disparities in criminal justice. Most fail, as I did, to make the difference they hope to make because their tool—locking people up—is too blunt an instrument. In the adversarial system of American criminal justice, prosecutors are forced to choose a side. So they end up enforcing selectively applied criminal laws, defending the police, and locking up a lot of black people.

Who gets prosecuted in the United States is politicized and racialized. The cities that have the highest number of incarcerated blacks are often the same as the ones with the most African American prosecutors.

But when African American prosecutors talk among themselves and say, "I wouldn't trust this guy in a dark alley," they could be talking about the police as easily as their most recent defendant. Black prosecutors are still black, which means they have their own stories about being racially profiled.

People ask if, when I was a prosecutor and I got stopped by the cops, I told them what I did for a living. Yes, but it didn't always make a difference. It didn't make a difference the time I told the cop that I was a prosecutor, and he smirked and said, "So you probably know this already"—and then he read me my *Miranda* rights.[1]

I became a prosecutor because I wanted to help victims, and not be one—of the police or of another black man. The police have a name for black-on-black crime: routine homicide. The closure rate on those cases is often less than 50 percent.

So there is a crying need for law enforcement interventions that actually work to keep communities of color both safe and free. I have explained elsewhere why my work as a prosecutor did not facilitate that effort.[2]

Here I want to examine why, given the vast inequities and draconian punishment that mark the American criminal justice regime, defenders—the people who resist this regime—are challenged more than prosecutors—the people who uphold it.

The Morality of Prosecution Work: A New Debate

The discussion about the ethics and morality of prosecution can be traced to Abbe Smith's seminal article "Can You Be a Good Person and a Good a Prosecutor?"[3] Professor Smith wrote: "We live in an extraordinarily harsh and punitive time, a time we will look back on in shame. The rate of incarceration in this country, the growing length of prison terms, the conditions of confinement, and the frequency with which we put people to death have created a moral crisis. Although, arguably, all those who work in the criminal justice system have something to do with its perpetuation and legitimacy, prosecutors are the chief legal enforcers of the current regime."[4]

In her book *Arbitrary Justice*, Angela Davis took prosecutors to task for practices that perpetuate racial disparities and recommended legal and policy interventions that might reduce those disparities.[5] In a chapter in my book *Let's Get Free: A Hip-Hop Theory of Justice*, I argued that "the adversarial nature of the justice system, the culture of the prosecutor's office, and the politics of crime pose insurmountable obstacles for prosecutors who are concerned with economic and racial justice."[6] That conclusion has been vigorously contested by many current and former prosecutors, some of whom have engaged me in public debates on the topic.

Legal scholars, and former defense attorneys James Forman and Jonathan Rapping, have also written critically about the morality of prosecution under the present conditions of American criminal justice.[7] In "Who's Guarding the Henhouse?," Professor Rapping castigates the prosecutor's office because it has become "more focused on conviction rates than the quality of the case resolution; has lost sight of the humanity of the people it prosecutes; and has minimized the import of the fundamental protections that are the foundation of our democracy." He states that "the ethical prosecutor should refuse to charge cases that the system is not funded to handle responsibly."[8]

So there is a growing critique of the morality of being a prosecutor in the United States in the twenty-first century. But that debate and the other debates about how defense attorneys can morally represent people accused of crimes are never recognized as related. In the next part, I want to flip the script by suggesting that some of the moral concerns expressed about defense attorneys are equally applicable to prosecutors.

Innocence and Guilt

The most serious moral concern many people have about defense attorneys is that they defend people who are guilty of the crime. Of course, the opposite is true of prosecutors: they sometimes prosecute, and even obtain convictions of, people who are innocent. While no well-meaning person desires this result, no one could deny that it occurs.[9]

The U.S. system of justice is based on the idea that we prefer the guilty to go free rather than the innocent to be convicted. This ideal is most famously expressed in the "Blackstone ratio" that it is "better that ten guilty persons escape, than that one innocent suffer." Thus when the defense attorney helps a "guilty" person go free, she is actually upholding an important principle of our democracy. The prosecutor who convicts an innocent person, on the other hand, subverts this ideal. It is strange, then, that "wrongful" acquittals seem to inspire more questioning about the role of the lawyer than wrongful convictions.

Perhaps the reason for the distinction goes to the intent or knowledge of each lawyer. Defense attorneys, the argument might be, sometimes know their client is guilty, whereas a prosecutor would not know that the defendant she is prosecuting is innocent.

I never prosecuted anyone who was innocent. I don't think. But of course I would say that, I was a prosecutor. Like most people drawn to this work, I possess a moral certainty about some things I cannot actually know.[10] In the cases I prosecuted I think the defendants were guilty based on the evidence (and because 90 percent of the time they pled guilty). The evidence is usually collected by the police, so my belief in the defendant's guilt also requires a certain amount of trust of the police. Yet the Supreme Court has described police officers as "engaged in the competitive enterprise of ferreting out crime," and for that reason they require judicial oversight when they seek search or arrest warrants.[11]

Prosecutors don't usually have time to second-guess the police or even to corroborate their work. An empirical study of prosecutor workloads found that in Houston, the average prosecutor handles 1,500 cases a year, in Las Vegas 800, and in Chicago between 800 and 1,000.[12] Professor Jonathan Rapping estimates that "with case-loads this high, the prosecutor who works fifty hours a week for fifty weeks per year will be able to devote between 1.66 and 3.125 hours to each case each year."[13] Thus the prosecutor's "knowledge" of guilt is mainly secondary and not well informed. It hardly seems the basis for the quality of information that any of us would desire in making a life-altering decision.

The risk of wrongful conviction is compounded by the bias that a defendant in a criminal case experiences from the moment he enters the courtroom. Moreover, prosecutors have more trials than almost any other litigator and they are often exceptionally able advocates. I believe, for example, that I have the skills that would allow me to get a conviction of an innocent person of a crime. Indeed, there is a saying that is a favorite of some prosecutors—one hopes it is said facetiously: "Convicting the guilty is easy. Convicting the innocent is the real challenge." In addition, defendants have little recourse once they are found guilty. Appeals are almost always focused on legal errors, not on innocence. Indeed, Supreme Court justice Antonin Scalia has stated, "This Court has *never* held that the Constitution forbids the execution of a convicted defendant who has had a full and fair trial but is later able to convince a habeas court that he is 'actually' innocent."[14]

In sum, prosecution incurs the risk of wrongful convictions, and this risk upsets democratic norms in a way that does not occur when a defense attorney wins an acquittal for someone who actually committed a crime. It is troubling, then, that the rhetoric about the morality of helping obtain inaccurate verdicts focuses on defense attorneys and not on prosecutors.

Helping Victims

The discourse about the ethics of criminal practice is sometimes framed by a good/evil dichotomy that is not particularly elucidating. Nowhere is this more evident than in the "prosecutor-as-protector-of-victim" trope. If prosecutors help victims, then what do defense attorneys do?

As a matter of trial practice, we know what defense attorneys do to victims. Defense attorneys interrogate victims, they cast doubt on their credibility, and they paint them as unobservant or malicious or complicit. In this narrative, the victim is presented as powerless, exploited, injured. Anybody who had a conscience would treat her with respect, and that is the opposite of how defense attorneys behave.

This narrative is incomplete, and to the extent it casts prosecutors as the victim's protector, it is misleading. As a prosecutor, I had several occasions to tell victims, "I don't represent you." The prosecutor's client is the government, not the victim. Victims are simply witnesses, with all the baggage that implies. Usually she is the star witness, so your most profound hope is that she doesn't mess up your case. In order to prevent that from happening, prosecutors "prepare" witnesses. This may involve coercion, for example, subpoenaing people to make them come to court even if they don't want to. It may involve harsh questioning or threats. The victim is supposed to tolerate it, based on the understanding that it's all in the service of punishing her victimizer.

Of course, people should be punished when they hurt others. The point is that in their zeal to prove that a crime occurred, prosecutors don't necessarily treat victims with dignity and kindness. For both sides, the victim is more or less a prop. This is disturbing to hear because we know that she is also a human being. But the trial lawyer's responsibility is to truss, manipulate, and fashion her into the teller of the story that the lawyer has created. People understand that this is what the defense attorney is doing, and that is a reason some people complain about defense attorneys. But prosecutors are also guilty of this sin.

In a more fundamental sense, defense attorneys are also helping victims—their clients. Virtually every person who commits a violent crime has been a victim at some point as well.[15] This is not to excuse the crime, but rather to place the act in a larger context, a context more like the real world, and less like the artificial constructs of "evidence" that the courtroom allows.

In the real world, the determination of "defendant," "victim," and "witness" is more random than it seems in the courtroom. "On any given Sunday," Lenese Herbert used to say when she was a prosecutor, "someone who is a victim today could have been a defendant yesterday and might be a witness tomorrow."[16] If it's the Sunday that she's the victim, she gets solicitude. If, on the other hand, it's the Sunday that she's the defendant, she is widely despised.

"Those People"

In the cocktail party question, "how can you represent those people?," "those people" are generally understood to be the guilty, as the preceding section discussed. But prosecutors also have clients. They represent "people" as well. Sometimes literally, as in New York and Illinois, which style their criminal cases "The People versus [the name of the defendant]." Otherwise, the prosecutor represents the people in the form of the state, like "California v. O. J. Simpson," or the "United States versus Bernie Madoff." What are the moral issues involved in representing "those people" in criminal prosecutions?

The Supreme Court, in some death penalty cases, has suggested that *the people* the prosecutor represents are emotional and vindictive. They need to be represented by a lawyer, the court says, because otherwise they might take matters in their own hands.[17] In their name, the prosecutor exacts a vengeance, thus circumventing the need for a lynching.

In drug cases, on the other hand, The People are situated differently than in violent crime cases. In drug cases The People are white, and middle class, and hypocrites, some of them. They tolerate a war on drugs selectively waged against low-income African Americans. Others use drugs just as much, or more, but they don't get prosecuted. The prosecutor is a key component of the machinery of this discrimination. How can she, knowing this, represent those people?

In *The Collapse of American Criminal Justice*, the late Harvard law professor William Stuntz described the American body politic as believing that "a healthy criminal justice system should punish all the criminals it can."[18] This perspective is the result of antiblack political appeals and sensational news broadcasts rather than a reasoned analysis of public safety. Of course, in a democracy, people have the right to make bad public policy. I simply want to point out that in the U.S. punishment regime, just as the defense attorney's client may not have clean hands, the prosecutor's client may at times have motives that are ill informed and even discriminatory.

Two Troubling Aspects of How Prosecutors Do Their Work

Thus far I have explained how three moral critiques of defense attorneys—that their work leads to inaccurate verdicts, that they treat victims unfairly, and that they represent people with antisocial interests—can also be applied to prosecutors. Now I will briefly identify some other qualities of prosecution that should give us pause about whether the work can be done ethically. This inquiry will also be in the service of elevating the *courtroom hallway question* to the central place that the *cocktail party question* presently enjoys in the discourse about the morality of criminal law practice.

Coercing Guilty Pleas

U.S. Supreme Court justice Anthony Kennedy has stated that "criminal justice today for the most part is a system of pleas, not a system of trials."[19] More than 90 percent of people who are charged with crimes end up pleading guilty. This is not because many of these defendants do not want to go to trial. Rather it is because prosecutors overcharge, in order to force the defendant to plead guilty to receive a lesser sentence.

In *Bordenkircher v. Hayes*, the Supreme Court blessed this practice.[20] Paul Hayes was charged with writing a bad check for $88.30. The prosecutor told him that he would recommend a sentence of five years if he pled guilty. If, on the other hand, he made the government go through the bother of a trial, the prosecution would seek life imprisonment.[21] Hayes went to trial, was convicted, sentenced to life, and the Supreme Court affirmed. The court recognized, however, that "the breadth of discretion that our country's legal system vests in prosecuting attorneys carries with it the potential for both individual and institutional abuse."[22]

Prosecutors have not taken the court's admonition about the potential for abuse to heart. Rather they have embraced the court's disinclination to regulate their discretion. Offering choices like those that Mr. Hayes was offered are routine practice for prosecutors, with horrific consequences. A reasonable innocent person, facing such a choice, might reasonably decide to plead guilty. Indeed, unless one's case would almost certainly lead to an acquittal, it might border on recklessness not to plead guilty. What prosecutors do, every day, is force people to give up one of their most precious constitutional rights, and one that is almost uniquely American: the right to trial by jury. This is not a necessary component of prosecutors' work; it simply makes their jobs easier. Comparing the moral critique of defense work, it is hard to find an analogue.

Dehumanization of Defendants

Some defense attorneys answer the cocktail party question by saying that it is not difficult to represent accused persons because defense attorneys get to know their clients as human beings. Remembering Sister Helen Prejean's admonition that "people are more than the worst thing that they have ever done in their lives," Rapping reminds us that criminal defendants are "sons and daughters, mothers and fathers, brothers and sisters. They may be cooks, sanitation workers, artists, or hairdressers. They are whole human beings with a lifetime of experiences that shape and define them."[23]

For prosecutors, on the other hand, defendants are the worst thing that they have ever done in their lives, or at least the most recent bad thing that landed them in criminal court. Few of us would want to be judged on this basis, but that is what prosecutors do. There is a certain level of hypocrisy; for example, prosecutors force defendants to suffer criminal consequences for some offenses, like drug crimes, and it is hard to believe that they would want the same for their family members or friends. The dehumanization of defendants by prosecutors is attributable in part to the adversarial system, which makes championing the defendant's cause the defense attorney's job. We can also blame the high caseload that most prosecutors carry; even if there was the inclination there, there is not the time to get to know the defendants as human beings. No matter that the prosecutor is the key player in a process that will fundamentally alter the life of the defendant.

What kind of expertise should be required when one human being wields so much power over another human being? How much knowledge should these persons be required to demonstrate about the role of poverty and race discrimination in causing people to make bad decisions? How much empirical data do they need on the most effective intervention of the state when someone has made a mistake? Exactly what bad acts by the defendant justify the unspeakable cruelties of the prisons to which prosecutors send people? And, in the absence of satisfactory answers to the questions, why are prosecutors called the "good guys?"

Racial Justice

Eric Holder, the first African American Attorney General, was also the first black chief prosecutor in the District of Columbia. He had a famous question that he asked prospective prosecutors in interviews: "How are you going to feel about sending so many young black men to jail?" Holder's question recognized that, for better or worse, this is the everyday work of many prosecutors.

I will conclude my chapter with a short meditation on the comparative racial equality components of prosecution and defense. If defense is racial justice work, then what is prosecution?[24]

Prosecutors assert a claim on this front as well as defense attorneys'. As I have already mentioned, one reason I became a prosecutor was to help remedy the problem of underenforcement of the law in the African American community. The prosecutor's racial justice intervention is to bring the equal protection of the law. This is a laudable goal, but it must be balanced against the reality that the criminal justice system is the primary legal manifestation of racial subordination in the United States.[25] The problem is that the prosecutor's instrument—prison—is too blunt. She needs a scalpel but she uses a sledge hammer.

Prosecutors labor in a system that produces extraordinary race disparities. The result of her work is a selective enforcement of certain criminal laws that has resulted in more African Americans under criminal justice supervision than there were slaves in 1850.[26] Even if prosecutors have been successful in helping minority communities receive the protection of the law—and I believe that they have—this does not ameliorate the substantial problems caused by overenforcement (especially of drug laws in the African American community, and the "crimigration" laws against Latinos).

For example, officers of the New York Police Department, in certain neighborhoods, stop black and Latino men for virtually any reason, and they rarely find anything incriminating. In one neighborhood, the cops made over 40,000 stops, and found just 25 guns—a hit rate of less than 0.1 percent.

Meanwhile, violent crime in that community is going up. The tragedy of racial profiling is not only that it's ineffective, but it's also that it makes many of its victims hate the profilers—whether they are police, security guards, or neighborhood watchpeople. And that causes a breakdown in trust that makes public safety even more problematic.

The main work of prosecutors in this regime is to defend the police and their tactics. If the police were actually making the community safer through their rough tactics, perhaps we could reluctantly tolerate it. But they are not. Can being complicit with a justice system this racially skewed, and this ineffective, ever be morally justified?

Conclusion

Perhaps the pat conclusion of this comparison of questions—the cocktail party defense question and the courthouse hallway prosecution question—should be that both sides have a role to play. Defense attorneys are moral actors and so are prosecutors. Both are important and necessary components in the American regime of crime and punishment.

But that conclusion is trite. It is not as nuanced as justice. It's not as complicated as equality. It's not as deep as truth.

A refrain frequently heard in prosecutor's closing statements is that people should be responsible for their choices. They should be held accountable. I want to say that this applies to the lawyers in the courtroom as well as defendants on trial. Defense attorneys and prosecutors have made choices motivated and constrained by ambition, personality, luck, and morality, among other things. They work in a system that some people have compared to slavery, to Jim Crow segregation, to an American gulag. They help implement, or fight against (or maybe defense attorneys do both[27]), the largest and most draconian punishment regime in the history of the world.

For people who are concerned about social justice or racial justice or economic justice, the answer to the question "how can you defend those people?" should be clear. This doesn't automatically lead to the conclusion that defense work is the best way to challenge the system, but there should be no doubt that individual human beings—"clients"—desperately need help. But for people concerned about civil liberties and equality under the law, "how can you prosecute those people?" is a more troublesome question. If the people you care most about are victims, and you have a relatively narrow view of what it means to be a victim, there is perhaps a coherent answer. But people with more expansive visions of social justice might require a more persuasive justification.

The "smart on crime" movement led by some progressive prosecutors, like Craig Watkins, District Attorney of Dallas, Texas; Kamala Harris, the Attorney General of California; and Cyrus Vance, Jr., District attorney of New York County, is limited reason for optimism. This movement focuses on reserving incarceration for violent crime, and repairing relationships between the police and disaffected communities. The U.S. Department of Justice, under Attorney General Eric Holder, has also promoted reconciliation between law enforcement and African Americans.

One day the answer to the question "how can you prosecute those people?" might be as persuasive as the answer to the question "how can you defend those people?" The reality that the first question isn't even asked much—outside the affected communities—demonstrates how far we are from that day.

Critical Thinking

Butler describes the "vexing" problem of law enforcement simultaneously over-enforcing and under-enforcing the law in black communities. In these communities, neighbors complain that the police mistreat them, yet also complain that the police are never there when they need them. What factors contribute to this emotional double-bind experienced by blacks? How does this perception manifest in community relations with the police? How can police improve these relationships to restore safe and free black communities?

Notes

1. Paul Butler, *Let's Get Free: A Hip-Hop Theory of Justice* (New York: The New Press, 2009), chap. 1.
2. Ibid., chap. 6.
3. Abbe Smith, "Can You Be a Good Person and a Good Prosecutor?," *Georgetown Journal of Legal Ethics* 14 (2001).
4. Ibid., 355.
5. Angela Davis, *Arbitrary Justice, The Power of the American Prosecutor* (New York: Oxford University Press, 2007).
6. Butler, *Let's Get Free*, 101–102.
7. Jonathan A. Rapping, "Who's Guarding the Henhouse? How the American Prosecutor Came to Devour Those He is Sworn to Protect," *Washburn Law Review* 51 (2012).

8. Ibid., 518.

9. For example, almost 300 people have been exonerated through postconviction DNA evidence since 1989. See "Facts on Post-Conviction DNA Exonerations," The Innocence Project, accessed September 28, 2012, http://www.innocencepro-ject.org/Content/Facts _on_PostConviction_DNA_Exonerations.php.

10. See Abbe Smith, "Are Prosecutors Born or Made?" *Georgetown Journal of Legal Ethics* 25 (2012).

11. Johnson v. U.S., 333 U.S. 10, 14 (1948).

12. Adam M. Gershowitz and Laura R. Killinger, "The State (Never) Rests: How Excessive Prosecutorial Caseloads Harm Criminal Defendants," *Northwestern University Law Review* 105 (2011).

13. Rapping, "Who's Guarding the Henhouse?", 539.

14. In Re Davis, 130 S. Ct. 1, 3 (2009) (emphasis in original).

15. This is sometimes referred to as the "cycle of violence." See Abigail A. Fagan, "Relationship between Adolescent Physical Abuse and Criminal Offending: Support for an Enduring and Generalized Cycle of Violence," *Journal of Family Violence* 20 (2005).

16. Butler, *Let's Get Free*, 111.

17. See Greg v. Georgia, 428 U.S. 153 ("In part, capital punishment is an expression of society's moral outrage at particularly offensive conduct. This function may be unappealing to many, but it is essential in an ordered society that asks its citizens to rely on legal processes rather than self-help to vindicate their wrongs.").

18. William J. Stuntz, *The Collapse of American Criminal Justice* (Cambridge, MA: Harvard University Press, 2011), 55.

19. Lafler v. Cooper, 132 S. Ct. 1376, 1388 (2012).

20. 434 U.S. 357 (1978).

21. Hayes was subject to a mandatory life sentence based on a "three strikes" law. Ibid., 359 n. 3.

22. Ibid., 365.

23. Rapping, "Who's Guarding the Henhouse?", 559–560.

24. A. Smith and M. H. Freedman (eds), *How Can You Represent These People?* (New York: Palgrave – Macmillan).

25. Michelle Alexander, *The New Jim Crow* (New York: The New Press, 2010).

26. Ibid., 175.

27. Monroe H. Freedman, An *Ethical Manifesto for Public Defenders*, 39 Valparaiso L. Rev. 911 (2006).

13

Calling Your Bluff: How Prosecutors and Defense Attorneys Adapt Plea Bargaining Strategies to Increased Formalization

Deirdre M. Bowen

Abstract: *Deidre Bowen examines the functioning of plea bargaining in an urban district attorney's office. Specifically, she focuses on the balance of power between the prosecutor and defense attorney and on how legal actors adapt to long-established institutional rules to attain efficiency and justice. She observed the process whereby defense lawyers find ways to equalize the balance of power when particular criminal cases do not fall under the "normal crimes" model. Her observations of the negotiation strategies between both sides of the plea bargaining process provide insight into whether prosecutors and defense lawyers behave differently under a rationalized system of plea negotiation as compared with a more traditional model that has historically been used.*

Introduction

Social scientists and legal scholars have long debated the suitability of plea bargaining as the dominant method for disposing of cases in the criminal justice system.

Bibas (2004c) suggests that the nature of plea bargaining reform should not focus on creating alternative systems, or eliminating plea bargaining, or reducing prosecutorial power in plea negotiations, but should instead create a balance of power by enhancing the power of other legal actors. Bibas (2004c) agrees with Uviller's (2000) suggestion that setting the criminal charges and negotiating pleas should be handled dispassionately and institutionally separately from the trying of cases. However, Bibas (2004c) also adds that limits should be placed on the types of plea offers made available.

In this ethnographic work, I concentrate on a rationalized approach to plea bargaining that the Superior Court in Seattle, Washington adopted, a system which happens to incorporate some of the ideas Bibas (2004c) and Uviller (2000) discuss. I examine the organizational structure and background of the Early Plea Unit (EPU) where non-drug felony plea negotiations take place, and explore the rules, the actors, and their perceptions of this model. I specifically focus on two questions: (1) whether and how attorneys create a balance of power in the pursuit of justice; and (2) whether attorneys behave differently under a new, highly rationalized model of plea bargaining compared to the models studied 30 years ago.

Literature Review

The legal and policy debate over plea bargaining has narrowed its focus to prosecutorial power within the criminal justice system. This shift in focus occurred both in the Supreme Court's observation in *Bordenkircher v. Hayes* (1978) as well as in the literature. The Court became increasingly concerned about the prosecutor's power to threaten more severe punishment or charges in retaliation for a defendant's rejection of a plea in favor of a trial. Specifically, as legislatures have responded to the public's call to get tough on crime measures by increasing prosecutorial powers, legal scholars have increased their criticisms over the use of these prosecutorial tools (Barkow, 2006; Bibas, 2004a; Stunts, 2004).

A division exists on how to respond to these plea bargaining criticisms. One camp advocates an outright ban on plea bargaining while the other suggests reform of a system that is here to stay. One such reform idea calls for a restructuring of the prosecutorial office from within. Uviller (2000) advocates a three-tiered prosecutorial approach to case disposition. This approach would address the concerns for achieving justice in an adversarial model of unbalanced power. He suggests that a case should be processed in a bifurcated manner. The investigation, where the appropriate charge is identified, and adjudication, where the appropriate punishment in exchange for a guilty plea is meted out, should occur in a neutral fashion with a dispassionate prosecutor who is not responsible for trying the case (Uviller, 2000, p. 1695). Only if and when the negotiations fall apart should a prosecutor take on a zealous advocacy role.

Wright and Miller (2002) propose a model akin to Uviller's (2000) approach, but place more emphasis on case screening resources as opposed to neutrality. The intended effect is to reduce the need for plea bargaining. Indeed, the results of their analysis demonstrated that plea bargains by charge or sentence reduction decreased substantially when prosecutors screened cases more effectively. Bibas (2004a) builds on these ideas by arguing that the best reforms will come from building a system of checks and balances that constrain prosecutorial power and have the effect of increasing defense attorneys' power (Bibas, 2004b). Prosecutors should focus on filing only the most serious and provable charges, stop charge bargaining, write down all plea offers, and obtain approval for them from a supervisor. More generally, Ma (2002) advocates that the United States follow a continental model of plea bargaining as found in France, Germany, and Italy. Again the emphasis is on restricting prosecutorial power by increasing control and supervision.

All of these writers stress that plea bargaining under an imbalanced system does not achieve justice, much less arrive at something akin to empirical or legal truth. While the criticisms and suggested reforms of plea bargaining have remained relatively consistent, the nature of the plea bargaining process in the current criminal justice system has not. Specifically, institutionalized plea bargaining embodies the criminal justice system's desire to create efficiency, calculability, predictability, and control in the processing of defendants (Ritzer, 1993).

Wright and Miller (2002) observe that empirical studies have ignored the inner workings of justice agencies and what values emerge in the production of justice. Yet, understanding the culture of these agencies within the context of these new approaches to plea bargaining is essential to developing policies around case processing reforms. As Mather (1979) observed almost 30 years ago, to understand the process of "sorting cases" that legal actors engage in, it is essential to describe the court behavior.

In this article, I examine an approach to plea bargaining that adopts some of the ideas suggested by Bibas (2004c) and Uviller (2000) at the King County Prosecutor's Office in Seattle, Washington. The King County Prosecutor's Office created the Early Plea Unit (EPU) originally in 1990 to increase efficiency in processing cases. The Prosecutor's Office revised the EPU again in 1999 to incorporate a highly rationalized process of negotiation that exists independently from the Trial Unit. This particular organizational approach happens to follow a lot of the recommendations of Uviller (2000) and Bibas (2004c): the charging and plea negotiating are handled institutionally separately from the trying of cases; the prosecutor charges conservatively, a supervising attorney reviews each action, and all plea agreements are written down.

While in King County all of the cases are being processed in the same institution, the charging attorney and plea negotiating attorney exist in independent units from the trial attorney and are not invested in trying the case. Therefore, according to Uviller (2000), these prosecutors are more likely to be dispassionate about the case. Only when it reaches the trial team should zealous advocacy appear. However, a key prosecutorial tool, the trial penalty, is available in King County, which tips the balance of power Bibas (2004c) and Uviller (2000) advocate. If the defendant declines to accept the offer given at the EPU, she or he not only faces the possibility of no plea negotiations with the trial prosecutor, or at least no better offer than the EPU offer; the defendant also faces the threat of additional charges, enhancements, or a recommendation of the high end of the sentencing range if convicted at trial.

Methods

This study came out of a larger research project examining new systems of plea bargaining and comparing them to the traditional model of plea negotiations at the King County Superior Courthouse in Seattle, Washington. I collected data from three sources in the King County Prosecutor's Office from February through December 2000. I chose this location for my research because it is one of only a handful of jurisdictions that is employing more rationalized and institutionalized systems of plea bargaining.

The population consisted of the prosecutors and their superiors who were part of the felony trial team, and the Early Plea Unit (EPU). In addition, private attorneys and the public defenders from the four corporations that are under contract with the Public Defender's Office were included in the study. Every attorney was Caucasian, almost evenly split between male and female, and in the 30 to 50 age range.

Three approaches were used to gather data for this research. First, direct observation was used to watch attorneys negotiate and process pleas of 42 cases in the Early Plea Unit.

Second, I interviewed a number of times, both formally and informally, over 25 attorneys involved in the plea system, and finally, I collected data on the characteristics and disposition of each case I observed from court documents, and created a database to both qualitatively and quantitatively analyze them. These observations occurred over a five-month period.

Results

Bureaucratic Organization of the King County Prosecutor's Office

The King County Prosecutor's Office ("KCPO") is located in the financial district of downtown Seattle. The Office occupies a number of floors in the King County Superior Court Building; it is the largest prosecutor's office in Washington State. Over 500 people are employed there, 240 of whom are prosecuting attorneys.

An executive group manages the four divisions that make up the Prosecutor's Office: Civil Division, Fraud Prevention, Family Support Division, and Criminal Division. The Criminal Division, the largest of the four divisions, has 156 attorneys. It comprises ten highly specialized units, one of which is the EPU.

After an arrest is made and the investigation is complete, the charge is filed by the King County (KC) Prosecutor's Office. The Prosecutor's Office has a specific set of internal guidelines on the rules used in filing charges and disposing of cases. These guidelines are used by the junior deputy prosecuting attorneys to assist them in filing the appropriate charges. In general, the guidelines advise that the defendant should be charged only for what can be reasonably proven and that the prosecutor should charge conservatively.

The KC Prosecutor's Office only files charges on the offenses that it is quite confident it can win at trial. It does not add additional charges just because the facts may allow for it, and it does not add enhancements. As part of its carrot-and-stick approach, the Prosecutor's Office encourages defendants to plead guilty early in the process of disposing of the case because it offers the best chance of receiving the lowest sentence for the fewest and least serious offenses. If the defendant decides not to plead guilty, and the case is assigned to trial, the KC Prosecutor's Office reserves the right to file additional charges and enhancements based on the facts of the case. Thus, the "stick" part of the process emerges as the trial penalty.

Under the conservative charging approach, the Prosecutor's Office asserts that the defense attorney knows exactly what to expect. If their client pleads guilty, then the low range of the appropriate sentence will be recommended. The defense attorney can advise their client as such, and the case can move forward without any continuances. Thus, defense attorneys are forced to accept the offer as-is unless they have truly identified legal challenges or evidentiary issues that require further attention. If the defendant chooses not to plead earlier on, the State will apply the "stick." Additional charges and enhancements are filed in preparation for trial, where both prosecutor and defense attorney have more time to investigate their legal worthiness.

After the arrest, the charges are set first by less experienced prosecutors in the Charging Unit. They investigate the case for the purpose of conservatively identifying only those charges that can be easily proven at trial. An experienced supervising prosecutor reviews each charge, and if the case is a non-drug, nonviolent class B or C felony, it is then transferred to the Early Plea Unit. The prosecutor's sole task in the EPU is to negotiate a plea for these cases. The pleas are written down and reviewed by a supervisor. If the case is not successfully negotiated at the EPU, the case is transferred to a third unit, the Trial Unit. There, it is assigned to the trial team to prepare for litigation, with clearly defined limitations on plea offers. Each stage is organizationally separate from the other.

Background and Purpose of the EPU

On its face, the charging guidelines as well as the purpose of the EPU seem to follow Uviller's (2000) proposal of dispassionate assessment of a case's worthiness for trial. According to the prosecutor, who negotiates within the EPU, it is to act as a checkpoint. Again, the language mirrors the goals articulated by both Bibas (2004c) and Uviller (2000): "To protect the process. The objective is to make sure we've got the right stuff for trial. If the case does not negotiate at EPU, then I give a heads up to the trial team about a potential issue" (EPU Prosecutor).

The defense community believes the real goal is efficiency. While their understanding is that the KCPO created the unit to increase efficiency in the processing of cases, one defense attorney observed: 'They could devote more resources if they really wanted to negotiate, but I think they are just as happy to go to trial" (Public Defender).

The Criminal Division Supervising Prosecutor stated in an interview that the KCPO established the EPU in 1990, indeed, as an efficiency measure. He observed that a review of cases showed that plenty of negotiations were occurring between prosecutors and defense attorneys, but the cases were staying in the system too long. The goal was to get cases processed in 30 to 45 days instead of eight to ten weeks. The KCPO developed internal standards to improve consistency, increase fair results, and to create greater access to the prosecutors for negotiations. The EPU, in its current form, emerged in 1999.

EPU Case Characteristics

In its present form, the EPU consists of one prosecutor who negotiates all non-drug, non-preassigned (to the trial team), nonviolent felony cases. These cases are known as mainstream cases. They largely consist of Class C and some Class B felonies. The supervising prosecutor of the EPU and the Trial Team makes decisions on an ad hoc basis as to whether a case should be preassigned to the Trial Team or sent to the EPU. The decision-making process seems to follow the supervisor's initial assessment as to whether they can be quickly negotiated based on the legal characteristics of the case, and the personal characteristics of the individuals involved in the case.

Institutional Rules, Process, and Norms of the EPU

The word "unit" is a bit of a misnomer as only one prosecutor negotiates with all the defense attorneys handling EPU cases. After the arraignment, in theory, the case is supposed to be plea bargained or set for trial at the case setting hearing within two weeks. This schedule is rarely followed. Defense attorneys as well as the EPU prosecutor requested an average of two continuances with each one lasting two weeks. Sixty percent of the cases seem to take a minimum of six weeks to process.

When the defense attorney is assigned the case, they go to the records department to request the case file for the EPU. In general, most defense attorneys don't go to EPU until a day or two before the case setting hearing. The defense attorney waits outside the EPU Prosecutor's office until she is available to discuss the case. Negotiations with the EPU Prosecutor can occur over several weeks. Continuances are used to allow time to examine any issues raised by the parties. The general issues raised tend to surround the offender score, whether the charge is supported by the facts, a clarification of the facts from witnesses or victims, consultation with the victim, or search and seizure issues.

The EPU process, as arranged by the institution in its present form, seems relatively straightforward to the newcomer. The organizational structure of the system, however, is teeming with frustrations for the defense community. It creates what Utz describes as "an atmosphere of cooperation under conditions of organizational conflict" (Utz, 1978, p. 4).

From the defense attorneys' perspectives, three factors prevent them from doing their job effectively. First, only one prosecutor is assigned to negotiate with approximately 50 attorneys who do business with the EPU on a regular basis. This increases the wait time significantly. In addition, when other defense attorneys are waiting outside the EPU office, the defense attorneys feel that the EPU prosecutor shortens their negotiation time and is quick to suggest a continuance for any issues raised. When defense attorneys are trying to assess whether a deal is likely, a continuance just creates a delay that must now be factored into the assessment of whether to pursue a plea. If a deal cannot be made, defense attorneys would like to quickly move on to the trial team. Continuances come at the expense of their clients, particularly those who are in pretrial detention. On occasion, the time taken to dispose of their case is longer than the sentence given. Finally, it is sometimes the case that no one is available to negotiate at all when the EPU Prosecutor is absent. Just as likely, the defense attorneys don't wish to negotiate with the substitute prosecutor because of the unpredictability it brings.

In an interview with a supervising prosecuting attorney, I raised these issues with him. He responded that the Prosecutor's Office has limited resources to work with and that the defense attorneys "all follow a cattle trail. They need to be more inventive about their practice. Change the way they spend their time." This interview offers the first hint of organizational tension that exists between defense attorneys and prosecutors.

Content and Sequence of Bargaining Discourse

Similar to Maynard's (1984) observations, the attorneys in this study engaged in a bargaining sequence that involved a "proposal" and "position report." In these negotiations, most defense attorneys enter the bargaining session silently waiting to see what the Prosecutor will propose. The offer will reveal some level of information about the Prosecutor's view of the case, or as Mather (1979) and Eisenstein and Jacob (1976) pointed out, the prosecutor's assessed "value" of the case. The defense attorney views it as an important strategy, similar to Maynard's (1984) "framing strategy," particularly in cases where they believe no factual or legal points exist to argue on behalf of the defendant. Furthermore, the reply techniques Maynard (1984) identified in his analysis are also used by these attorneys, specifically, the uses of utterances to delay a position report.

DEFENSE ATTORNEY:	*Last time we talked I think it was about scoring. [Defendant's offender score.]*
PROSECUTOR:	*Yes. We were looking at a 7 or an 8.*
DEFENSE ATTORNEY:	*Um.*
PROSECUTOR:	*"We need check on these felonies in California. . . . To see if the crimes are comparable felonies here.*
DEFENSE ATTORNEY:	*Huh?*
PROSECUTOR:	*We need to check the California code on the conspiracy to commit a crime.*
DEFENSE ATTORNEY:	*What crime?*
PROSECUTOR:	*Theft. I don't think the theft is comparable, but the conspiracy is.*
DEFENSE ATTORNEY:	*What happens when the DOC [Department of Corrections] doesn't agree with our scoring?*
PROSECUTOR:	*We would be willing to drop the theft, but not the conspiracy. Why don't we get a continuance and you bring me a copy of the California code next time you come in?*
DEFENSE ATTORNEY:	*If we go to trial, they'll split into two trials as one will be a misdemeanor.*
PROSECUTOR:	*If you set for trial, it will give us more time to figure out the circumstances of the California crimes and increase the offender score.*

In this exchange, the defense attorney uses a number of indirect utterances to get the Prosecutor to define her proposal without giving a clear position report until the end of the conversation. When the defense attorney does give a position report that threatens to reject the offer, the Prosecutor reminds him to whose advantage a trial would be. As Maynard (1984) observed, the attorneys will move to explicit bargaining and use formal justice if "convergence" does not occur between counsel. In addition, the defense attorney strategically uses the phrase "our scoring," suggesting the teamwork that should be involved in solving this issue.

Maynard (1984) also observed that facts and characteristics were not essential to case disposition, but rather charging and sentencing were the key to case disposition. Indeed, much of the content in the negotiations revolved around those ideas. However, both prosecutor and defense attorneys acknowledged that character could be an important part of the content. As Mather (1979) observed, defense attorneys use character to add "value" to a case when other factors cannot be argued. The defense attorneys and the prosecutor both agreed it could be used effectively, only if done strategically. In the following exchange, I asked the EPU prosecutor under what circumstances she would consider character.

PROSECUTOR: *Mental Health issues. Juveniles. Overall, I can't think about character because where is the dividing line? I let them say their piece, but I don't care, is that awful?*

INTERVIEWER: *Can they make their case in the sentencing hearing?*

PROSECUTOR: *Well, yes. Exactly. They can argue it there.*

From the defense attorneys' perspective, this was unfair. A key component in meting out justice was allowing for second chances. Character was a key determinant of that. According to defense counsel, the sentencing hearing seemed to be an ineffective, if not unpredictable, place to argue character because judges are so prone to follow the Prosecutor's sentencing recommendation. However, the defense attorneys did use character strategically in their negotiating and effectively added "value" to their case.

A significant theme observed in Maynard's (1984) discourse analysis, as well as in Feeley's (1979) and Mather's (1979) work, is that most of the negotiating involves implicit bargaining. The parties quickly come to an alignment of the shared value of the case. In the following exchange the attorneys view the offense as a "normal crime" and agree on the "going rate."

DEFENSE ATTORNEY: *Do you have an offer for me on this?*

PROSECUTOR: *A misdemeanor with restitution. Criminal Trespass?*

DEFENSE ATTORNEY: *This mother is driving me nuts. I'd never make it in Juvy [Juvenile Court] because of all the whiney mothers. I'd tell them it's their fault and get fired. So are we thinking along the same lines? Deferred Sentence? 12 month rec?*

PROSECUTOR: *Okay, but 20 days in custody and credit for time served. He'll be out at sentencing.*

DEFENSE ATTORNEY: *But you're not doing it out of the goodness of your heart. Hey, we're going to the game on Friday?*

PROSECUTOR: *Yeah, but he is still getting the benefit of it.*

There is no discussion about the facts of the case. Instead, the end result is agreed upon in the midst of non-legal discussion. What is also being communicated here is an acknowledgment by the Prosecutor that some incarceration period is included in the offer to justify the time the defendant has already spent in pretrial detention. When asked about this type of exchange the Prosecutor said, "A lot of times, when I know the attorney well, we just look at each other and agree on what needs to happen here. I feel like we work together on it. They know I'm reasonable and going for broke is not a good idea" (EPU Prosecutor).

This implicit bargaining was consistent with Feeley's (1979) and Mather's (1979) observations that in these less serious cases substantive justice was more appealing than formal justice. The challenge was balancing the costs of pretrial detention. On the one hand, the sentencing range is so small for less serious felonies that it would have been low risk to go to trial, or at least to investigate potential issues, but the time it would take to investigate and/or get to trial would mean the defendant often spent more time in detention waiting through continuances than serving his sentence. Therefore, pretrial detention became a strong motivator to plea bargain in less serious felony cases. In those cases where the defendant had spent more time in detention than the sentence agreed to in the plea bargain, the prosecutor made adjustments to the sentence offer, as noted in the previous negotiation exchange.

Cooperation Within the Workgroup

Despite the increasing tension around the organizational structure of the EPU, evidence of cooperation within the workgroup revealed itself in a number of ways. Overwhelmingly, attorneys took the view that they should work together to settle on the appropriate charge and punishment. When they did not agree, they respected each other's position to go to trial, but it often belied defense attorney resentment at "wasting time with the EPU." Overall, though, the attorneys' approaches in interacting with each other suggested a sense of familiarity and ease that comes from working together regularly over a long period of time.

Cooperation in the workgroup originates from an understanding of what the two parties are trying to achieve. Both sides know that the Court and Prosecutor's Office endorse plea negotiations to increase the efficiency of case processing. The defense attorneys acknowledged the seemingly objective approach taken by the EPU Prosecutor. If the case has problems, it should be investigated. The EPU Prosecutor explained her philosophy this way:

> It's a credibility issue. We tend to agree because I see my job as being objective. I advocate for the state, but I must make sure we can make our case. At the same time, I'm not going to tell them all the issues or hide them all either because that would mean ineffective assistance of counsel.

When defense attorneys questioned the facts, the charge, evidentiary, or scoring issues, the EPU Prosecutor always agreed to a continuance to investigate the case further. She willingly shared resources with the defense counsel and went so far as to point out potential issues that the defense counsel appeared to have not picked up on. In addition, when the defense attorney determined that trying the case was a better strategy, or that a request denied by the Prosecutor would be raised at the sentencing hearing, the EPU Prosecutor respected that position. The following example illustrates this behavior.

A defense attorney began negotiations on an assault case questioning whether the charge of assault in the third degree was appropriate given the facts of the case. The victim was the landlord who shared a house with the defendant. The victim confronted the defendant about not paying rent as well as his messy room. A fight ensued in which both parties were arrested, but only the defendant was charged. When the defense attorney did not elaborate on why assault in the fourth degree would have been more appropriate, the EPU Prosecutor handed him the charging standards to review. The defense attorney asked for help in looking them up. The Prosecutor read them aloud. Together, they listened to the 911 tape and examined the pictures of the injuries in light of the charging standards. The prosecutor then conceded:

PROSECUTOR: *It's an assault 4 (then jokes) with the stipulation that the defendant keep his room clean!*
DEFENSE ATTORNEY: *Agreed! I do have to check with my client though.*
PROSECUTOR: *If the defendant won't agree, just set it for trial.*

In this exchange, the parties clearly worked together in the dispassionate manner Uviller (2000) recommends to find the appropriate charge. The Prosecutor agrees to reduce the charge and wants a guilty plea in exchange for the low end of the sentence range recommendation. All of this is implicit bargaining. However, the defense attorney does not readily agree because there is an unspoken character issue of which both parties are aware. The defense attorney knows, however, that it would be bad strategy to articulate it explicitly. The victim is gay and the defendant is straight. The attorneys know socially sensitive characteristics can be problematic for a jury. The defense attorney is testing to see if there is an opportunity for further negotiation by leaving himself room to check with his client. The Prosecutor makes her position clear with the last statement. The tone of the exchange is pleasant and even includes a joke, but ultimately the prosecutor has made clear that she will not negotiate further.

Reasonableness seems to have its limits, and similar to Heumann's (1978) observations about "ungentlemanly" behavior, attorneys who raise frivolous legal issues that they cannot support are perceived as wasting the Prosecutor's time. In one case, the defense attorney came in for the initial negotiations and asked for a misdemeanor on an eluding police case. The defense attorney suggested that there was an identification issue, but did not elaborate. The Prosecutor disagreed and offered that perhaps there is a search issue instead. She advised the defense attorney to read the case law, and then they would ask for a continuance. The Prosecutor even read him the cite to the case. When he returns with the case law in hand, but does not actually argue the case, defense counsel's request for a misdemeanor is met with silence. The EPU Prosecutor explained her reaction: "I think we'll lose on the search issue, but it doesn't kill the case. Yeah, sure, I could have given him reckless endangerment, but I did not want to do it. Sometimes I'm surprised how unprepared they are. Why not argue why the case applies?".

On the other hand, some defense attorneys asserted that the Prosecutor was not always prepared either, but the defense attorneys claimed that this could be to their advantage. The defense attorneys entered these types of negotiations simply waiting for an offer, rather than arguing the case. On occasion, the Prosecutor would underestimate the value of the case, and the defense counsel perceived that the EPU Prosecutor gave a better offer than the "going rate." Defense counsel particularly relished these moments because they could go back to their clients and legitimately argue that the defendant got a discount off their "theoretical exposure." In other situations, when the offer was too good, defense counsel took it as a signal that something was wrong with the case and a better offer could be had if they waited and set it for trial.

Overall, defense attorneys felt that they operated in a subculture of cooperation, in which most cases were readily negotiated because of the shared knowledge and easy alignment in terms of "normal crimes" and "going rates." Most defense attorneys thought that the EPU had a place in the judicial system and that certain types of "no brainer" cases belonged there—victimless crimes in particular. The defense attorneys found they could work with the EPU Prosecutor in a cooperative manner, but certainly under tense circumstances. They believed that the lack of resources made available suggested that the Prosecutor's Office did not care about efficiency and fairness. Consistently, the defense attorneys voiced concern about the time it took to negotiate cases in the EPU because only one prosecutor was assigned to the Unit. Every request to investigate a case further meant a delay in resolving the case.

Decision-making and Adaptation to the Institutional Rules and Process

Despite the perceived impediments of the EPU's organizational system, the actors within the workgroup almost approached a sense of camaraderie as they completed their daily tasks. While the defense attorneys tolerated the structural arrangement of the EPU (less so as the study wore on), 80 percent expressed deep frustration about two institutional rules of the bargaining process. The first rule stated that once negotiations failed at the EPU, no negotiations *should* occur at the trial level, and if the case absolutely required them, the trial team could not offer a deal better than what was offered at the EPU. The second rule declared that negotiations were *not* available at all if a case bypassed EPU and was immediately set for trial. These rules were viewed as another form of a trial penalty.

   With regard to the first rule, every defense attorney had a story to tell about the deputy trial team offering a better deal than the EPU, only to have it withdrawn when the trial team discovered that the EPU had made a less attractive offer. One defense attorney explained it this way:

> There's almost an incentive not to submit the case to EPU and set it for trial. Because sometimes a deal is offered by the trial team and they can't make the offer because the EPU set a tougher deal, I had a defendant where three cases were involved. I said, "My guy will plead if two are dismissed." EPU said "one" and the trial deputy said "two" and then looked in the file and said, "I can't because of the policy on EPU offers. It's almost better not to open the can of worms [at EPU]."

The defense attorney's comment suggests that he is more confident in the second rule being broken: the trial team's willingness to negotiate even if the defense attorneys bypass the EPU because the trial prosecutor is facing the pressure of whether they can win at trial.

   The rule that the trial team cannot offer a deal better than the EPU causes additional angst, particularly when the defendant has been in pretrial detention. While the attorneys negotiate the case at the EPU, the defendant spends weeks or even months in jail only to have the process start all over again with the trial team. The additional time incarcerated may afford the defendant a better deal on paper only; overcoming the risks of trial and a more severe sentence could, in the end, lead to a better offer, but the amount of time he spends in jail waiting for two different prosecutors and his defense attorney to resolve the case may surpass his actual sentence.

   A defense attorney described the problem of the EPU in the following manner:

> The problem is that this is a traffic jam. You have to have continuances. I average three or four a case because you need the time to determine if there's a good defense. You're just shooting from the hip; both of us [prosecutor and defense attorney] need to get up to speed. Maybe one out of 30 to 40 cases do I get a deal on the first try.

Defense attorneys chose one of two ways to adapt to this situation. Typically, if the deputy trial attorney refused to negotiate or revised an offer to remain consistent with the EPU's offer, the defense attorneys approached the supervising trial attorneys.

The defense attorneys who tried this method were usually more senior than the deputy trial attorneys with whom they were negotiating. Public defenders, in particular, perceived that they had more success with the supervising prosecutors because of one key factor: history. According to one defense attorney:

> I go to the supervisor because I usually have a history with the supervisor. There is no substitute for history with a person. I'd love to work with someone I've bonded with in trial. We've bonded through the stress and we know how the disagreements will fall out.

The other adaptation employed by about 20 percent of the defense attorneys was to bypass the EPU and set the case for trial. Although the defense attorneys ran the risk of having the trial prosecutor enforce the second rule—no negotiating—they knew that if the case fell apart or the trial attorney had a full calendar, a deal could be made. The majority of defense attorneys informed me that they monitor the deputy trial attorneys' calendars. They deemed it good strategy to set the case for trial and have a "highly stressed prosecutor call for a deal."

Over 90 percent of the trial team prosecutors interviewed said that they would initially enforce the no-negotiation rule unless it was a private attorney unfamiliar with the process. However, every trial team prosecutor thought that each case should be negotiated if possible, but some noted that defense attorneys who bypassed the EPU should not receive as good a deal as those who followed the process. This prosecutor's opinion summarizes most of the trial team's view:

> Even if it's gone through EPU, I basically think the negotiating has to happen. Every case needs the opportunity to be resolved. I'm not trying to jumpstart a case, but every case can unravel, witnesses go missing or evidentiary issues come up. It's a mistake not to listen to the defense attorney. In my last eight or nine cases, I've given better deals in two or three cases [than the EPU].

The defense attorney is engaged in a two-part decision-making analysis, similar to the approach taken by the attorneys in Emmelman's (1996) work. First, the defense attorneys assess the value of the case based on the seriousness of the case, the strength of the evidence, and the background characteristics. The more serious the case, the more inclined defense counsel were to take it directly to the trial team and try negotiations there; particularly after engaging in part two of the analysis: the potential costs of delay by setting the case for trial after going to the EPU. The defense attorneys felt that the possibility of lost witnesses, better defense evidence emerging, and a clogged prosecutor calendar could all be used in their favor regardless of the risk of a trial penalty. In the end, the defense attorneys know that these rules are flexible. A plea bargain is possible with either the EPU or the trial team. Thus, the defense attorneys felt that they used this knowledge to create a balance of power.

Organizational Challenges of Having Separate Units Process the Same Case

Notwithstanding, the defense attorneys found the negotiating process challenging whether it was with the EPU Prosecutor or the trial team deputy prosecutors. They felt a truly effective negotiation could not occur if both parties were not approaching the bargaining with the same level of investment in the case. The defense attorneys thought that the EPU Prosecutor was too removed from the case because she would not actually be trying the case. She was not really eyeing the case for trial in the same way a defense attorney was because the EPU Prosecutor was not facing the same consequences of *trying* the case if the plea fell through. Consequently, she had less at stake than the trial attorney.

The following example illustrates this point. In two burglary cases, the defendants had substantial offender scores that significantly increased the lengths of their sentences. The EPU offers in both of these cases were at the higher end of the sentencing range because:

> There is nothing to lose by going to trial. I offered midrange because I was appalled by the offender scores. They're off the charts. Sure I could have gone lower, but I didn't want to. Let trial team deal with it, if they have to.

In this case there was a shared understanding as to the crime, but no convergence around the sentence length. The defense attorney was frustrated because he had to begin the negotiation process again with the trial team, under the guise that the trial team could not offer anything better; yet the EPU knew the defense counsel would try to get a better deal.

In fact, the trial prosecutor offered the minimum range in one of the cases, as he was unable to get any response from the victim. In the other case, the trial prosecutor kept the EPU offer open. The defense attorney advised her client to plead guilty. Ultimately, defense counsel obtained a significantly lower punishment at the sentencing hearing after describing in detail that the defendant had mental health issues for which he desperately wished to seek treatment. This shows how the defense attorney used the manipulation of his knowledge of the rules to his advantage at every stage. The trial attorney, having greater investment in the case, saw the need to plead out the cases. While discussing characteristics would not influence the EPU Prosecutor, or perhaps even the trial prosecutor, it did impact the judge's sentencing. Only if both the prosecutor and the defense attorney sign an "agreed" plea will the defense attorney not attempt to get a lower sentence at the sentencing hearing. Regardless, the defense attorney felt the case could have been processed more efficiently if the EPU Prosecutor actually had an investment in the case going to trial.

While Bibas (2004c) advocated greater supervision of plea agreements, defense attorneys thought there was too much supervision. Defense counsel felt that deputy trial prosecutors did not have adequate ownership over their cases. In comparing the organization of trial prosecutors in another county, one defense attorney observed: "In Thurston [county], the attorney has ownership over the case and they'll review it as if going to trial. They feel better about the job because they're independent thinkers. Deputy prosecutors here need approval for everything" (Private Defense Counsel).

In fact, the single biggest improvement that the defense attorneys wanted was for the deputy prosecutors to have more power over their cases. While the trial prosecutors examined the case as if going to trial, they did not have the ultimate say in whether a deal could be accepted. Again, the final decision went to a supervisor who would not be trying the case.

Furthermore, 75 percent of defense attorneys expressed bitter resentment toward the Prosecutor's Office in general. They could not understand why the institution was so unwilling to devote resources to increase the efficiency of both defense and prosecutorial tasks in the pursuit of justice. They felt that too much time was wasted on continuances because the EPU Prosecutor was overwhelmed with cases that needed further investigation. The defense attorneys in this study were continually under pressure to avoid delays not only for themselves, but also for their clients in pretrial detention. While the EPU Prosecutor certainly wanted to process cases, she was not facing a trial calendar pressure point like defense counsel. In that sense, for non-"no-brainer" cases, the defense attorneys felt that there was always an unequal balance of power at the EPU that could not be overcome without bypassing it, which came with risks.

At the end of the study, one defense attorney was so frustrated by this situation that he was conducting an experiment of his own. He was immediately setting all of his cases for trial to see whether he could obtain better outcomes faster than in the EPU alone or in an EPU/Trial Team combination because of his confidence in manipulating the rules to his advantage.

Discussion

This article has examined the internal machinations of a highly rationalized model of plea bargaining from the legal actors' perspectives. It has sought to answer three questions under this so-called reform model: (1) Do the behaviors, norms, and language of the attorneys differ from the more traditional models studied? (2) Does this institutionally separate model of case processing lead to the balance of power sought by Bibas (2004c) and Uviller (2000)? (3) If not, what adaptations, if any, are made by defense counsel to achieve some balance of power?

On one level, this model demonstrates an efficient and cooperative model of plea bargaining for those cases that fit Sudnow's (1965) "normal crimes" definition. While the structural organization and resource allocation of the EPU led to tension, the legal actors were able to come to an agreed-upon plea in over 70 percent of the cases that were processed through the EPU. Essentially, both defenders and prosecutors engage in routinization to efficiently process these cases. While cooperation abounds in the "no-brainer" cases, the adversarial nature of the trial emerges in the EPU when cases don't fit this model.

Norms, Language, and Behavior

The attorneys sort cases in the same way, relying on shared understandings of "normal crimes" and "going rates." While the name of the "normal" crimes has changed to "no-brainers," these attorneys work under a largely congenial workgroup setting, where a shared history appears to assist in the bargaining process. The bargaining sequence and content is remarkably similar to Maynard's (1984) descriptions. The attorneys engage in the same proposal and position report, with strategic uses of utterances and silences to delay responses. They use implicit bargaining for "no-brainer" cases and explicit bargaining for more complex cases. The attorneys also engaged in information control. They discuss mostly offender scores and sentencing more so than charging, but strategically mention character to add value to their cases when it is possible to do so. Finally, as Emmelman (1996) and others before her noted, case pressure does not appear to be a key motivator for defense attorneys in negotiating their pleas.

Balance of Power

While the norms, behavior, and discourse can appear to be significantly analogous, some key distinctions do emerge in this new setting and serve to decrease the balance of power in the prosecutor's favor. The EPU model appears to follow Bibas' (2004c) and Uviller's (2000) recommendations: separate charging, negotiating and trial units with differing levels of advocacy and investment in the case; high-level prosecutorial review of charges and pleas; charges conservatively filed and readily provable, with less charge bargaining; and all plea offers written down. However, this structural model does not create the general power balance Bibas (2004c) supports. Moreover, despite this structural organization, the EPU does not follow the ideological framework of neutrality as advocated by Uviller (2000). It engages in institutional retaliation through its threat of trial penalties, its no-trial team negotiation if the EPU is bypassed rule, and its no better offer than the EPU offer rule.

For the majority of cases, defined as no-brainer cases that can be easily aligned, this model seems to be highly effective, according to prosecutors and defense attorneys alike. For the remaining 30 percent of more complex cases, this model can be troubling. It appears to create even less efficiency, more strain, and less power for defense attorneys for a number of reasons.

First, the institutional rules around trial penalties and limited negotiation opportunities with the trial team are quite different from traditional models, and thus significantly impact prosecutorial power. The attorneys' behavior in this study more closely mirrored the attorneys' motivations in Feeley's (1979) work. The attorneys in this study felt compelled to plea bargain cases not because of resource conservation, but because of the threat of a trial penalty.

Second, while delay was a significant tactic employed by defense attorneys in earlier studies, it seemed to benefit the EPU in this study. The organizational structure and limited EPU resources in this study, however, meant that defense attorneys could not use delay as effectively. Because the EPU attorney was not taking the case to trial, she was not as concerned about a case going stale. Furthermore, the EPU Prosecutor knew that even if the case did get to trial and go stale, the trial prosecutor was under significant pressure to offer no better deal than what she had offered already.

The defense attorneys are put in a less powerful position when they have to consider the EPU Prosecutor's case pressure against their client's pretrial detention. Defense counsel worried about the ability to properly examine the legal issues in the case at the EPU, frustration from the EPU Prosecutor if she felt the continuances and investigation were unwarranted, and then further delays if they felt the case needed to be set for trial.

Third, differences in negotiation content also restrict defense counsel's bargaining power. Instead, more conversations were around sentencing or offender scores, which directly impact the sentencing range, rather than charges. In addition, character seemed to be used much more sparingly in this setting than in prior studies, where it was a key negotiating tactic. Under this organization structure, defense counsel experienced significant pressure to delay any character discussion until the sentencing hearing. However, defense attorneys often felt that arguing character at the sentencing hearing was futile because the judges deferred overwhelmingly to the prosecutors' recommendations. They asserted that the judge's deference to the prosecutors' recommendations meant that prosecutors held too much power in the system. Unlike in Mather's (1979) work, prosecutors in this study were not passive about sentencing.

Finally, an exchange relationship is essential to any negotiation. Both parties must feel that they are gaining from the bargain. However, in the EPU structural model, it did not feel as if an exchange was taking place. The defense attorneys could negotiate with only one EPU attorney who may have been too dispassionate in that she had little at stake if the deal fell through. Either way, the case would leave her desk without her taking it to trial. The defense attorneys had more at stake and more to gain from the deal.

Defense attorneys exhibited an undercurrent of distrust toward the EPU Prosecutor. When the prosecutor offered a deal lower than expected, the defense attorneys were just as likely to take the case to the trial team as when the deal offered was too high. They suspected that the prosecutor had reduced the case value because it was a weak case. Again, the perceived uneven investment in the case actually increased the adversarial tone at the EPU. The defense attorneys did not trust the EPU Prosecutor to act in a reasonable manner for non-"no-brainer" cases. Thus, by taking the case to the trial team, the defense attorneys were decreasing efficiency and increasing risks for their client.

Under the EPU model, the rules and penalties on plea bargaining attempted to remove the human element to increase predictability, efficiency, and fairness. Instead, they appeared to alienate the prosecutor and disempower the defense community. However, as will be seen in the next section, defense counsel used relationships and personalities to subvert these rules and achieve some modicum of justice.

Adaptations

Despite the frustrations articulated about the EPU, and in fact most attorneys lamented not being able to go straight to trial counsel in the non-"no-brainer" cases, the defense attorneys knew that the rules could be breached, meaning that some defense attorneys could equalize the power in the bargain. Specifically, the use of supervisors cut both ways for the attorneys. On the one hand, the supervisor may have appeared too dispassionate, even a hindrance, in disallowing the subordinate trial prosecutor's offer, while experienced defense attorneys used supervisors to their advantage. If they had a trial history with the supervisor, they could often get a better deal than what the less experienced trial prosecutor was offering them. Relationships, personality, and reputation were seen as key to their success in this maneuver.

The defense attorneys were also quite adept at acquiring bargaining power by side-stepping the EPU entirely. They were confident that in certain more serious, complex cases, the closer one got to trial, evidence and loss of witnesses could be turned to their advantage. In fact, defense counsel and prosecutors both agreed that they gave better "going rates" the closer the case came to trial in spite of rules to the contrary. In addition, defense counsel used trial prosecutors' case pressure to their benefit in exacting deals that were not available at the EPU or that were supposed to be available from the trial team. Ultimately, defense counsel also found highly effective ways to call the Prosecutor Office's bluff. However, much of this power was achieved because of the trial experience, history, and relationships that existed between defense counsel and trial prosecutors.

Conclusion

Despite the presence of structural changes advocated by Bibas (2004c), the neutrality Uviller (2000) suggests did not materialize in this reformed model of plea bargaining. Under the current organization of "reformed" plea bargaining in this study, efficiency was achieved at the EPU in 70 percent of the cases, but it is unclear whether justice was. The structure, resources, and rules lent considerably more power to the prosecutors than under the traditional model. While the attorneys in this study behaved remarkably similarly to the attorneys in traditional models when it came to processing "normal crimes," this imbalance in power led to tension and distrust in resolving more complex cases.

The defense attorneys were under significant pressure to screen cases in the midst of negotiating and minimizing continuances, particularly for clients in pretrial detention. In some cases this may have caused them to treat certain cases as "no-brainer" cases that may have deserved further legal attention. Under these circumstances, the defense attorneys tended toward substantive justice over formal justice. In addition, working under the threat of the trial penalty, no trial team negotiation rules, and further time delays, defense counsel experienced significant pressure to accept the EPU plea offers. This study suggests that recommendations are not enough, and that more should be done.

First, more resources should be allocated to Early Plea Units so that both prosecutor and defense counsel can carefully examine the case for triable issues without the burden of excessive time delays.

Second, neutrality is more likely to emerge if both parties have the same level of dispassion around the case. Defense counsel should be assigned to EPU cases in a similar model to the Prosecutor's Office. Certain defense counsels should work only on EPU cases. When both dispassionate parties agree that the case has a triable issue that cannot be pled out, then the case should be assigned to a new trial team, including a new trial defense counsel and a new trial prosecutor.

Third, the trial penalty should be removed. While there may be a sentence discount to provide an incentive in taking a plea, the state should act in good faith and charge only what it intends to prove at trial and remain consistent with that charge. If a triable issue emerges, defendants should not be punished for asserting their constitutional rights to trial.

The rules prohibiting plea bargaining between trial counsel should be eliminated. As has been shown, these rules can be subverted if a case starts to fall apart for either party. Furthermore, defense counsel will not bypass the EPU, nor have the incentive to do so, if they have confidence that counsel on both sides are dispassionately and efficiently reviewing the case.

Finally, the judges should play an active role in reviewing the sentence. If character is not an appropriate subject for the plea bargain, it is appropriate at the sentencing hearing. Judges should take careful note of the recommendation, but also review the presentence report and the evidence presented at the hearing to ensure the defendant is receiving a fair sentence given all aspects of the case. At this stage in the process, the judge is in the best position to ensure a balance of power in the disposition of the case.

At a minimum, the Prosecutor's Office should examine its screening procedures for the 30 percent of cases that do not get resolved in the EPU. Perhaps those types of cases should be immediately assigned to the trial team, where a more traditional model may be followed. As it stands now, this study suggests that we have not yet found a reform model of plea bargaining that addresses the concerns of legal scholars, social scientists, or practitioners.

Critical Thinking

The issues of case disposition and the court's demands for efficiency directly influence a defendant's actual sentence. Fairness needs to be taken into consideration when analyzing plea negotiations, as we have learned from Bowen's study. The balance of power lies with the prosecutor in the vast majority of criminal cases, which places defense attorneys at a real disadvantage in representing their clients' best interests. How does the uneven balance of power favoring prosecutors result in a defendant's opportunity to attain a just plea negotiation? What changes to the system do you think would lead to a more equal balance of power?

References

Barkow, R.E. (2006). Separation of powers and the criminal law. *Stanford Law Review, 58*, 989.

Bibas, S. (2004a). The Feeney amendment and the continuing rise of prosecutorial power to plea bargain. *Journal of Criminal Law & Criminology*, 94, 295–309.

Bibas, S. (2004b). The Feeney Amendment and the Continuing Rise of Prosecutorial Power to Plea Bargain. *Journal of Criminal Law and Criminology*, 94, 295-309

Bibas, S. (2004c). Plea bargaining outside the shadow of trial. *Harvard Law Review, 117*, 2463.

Eisenstein, J. and Jacob, J. (1976). *Felony justice: An organizational analysis of criminal courts*. Boston, MA: Little Brown.

Emmelman, D. (1996). Trial by plea bargain: Case settlement as a product of recursive decisionmaking. *Law and Society Review, 30*, 335–360.

Feeley, M. (1979). Perspectives on plea bargaining. *Law and Society Review, 13*, 199–249.

Heumann, M. (1978). *Plea bargaining: The experience of prosecutors, judges, and defense attorneys*. Chicago, IL: University of Chicago Press.

Ma, Y. (2002). Prosecutorial discretion and plea bargaining in the United States, France, Germany, and Italy: A comparative perspective. *International Criminal Justice Review, 12*, 22–52.

Mather, L. (1979). *Plea bargaining or trial? The process of criminal case disposition*. Lexington, MA: Lexington Books.

Maynard, D. (1984). *Inside plea bargaining: The language of negotiation*. New York: Plenum Press.

Ritzer, G. (1993). *The McDonaldization of society*. Newbury Park, CA: Pine Forge.

Stunts, W.J. (2004). Plea bargaining and criminal law's disappearing shadow. *Harvard Law Review, 117*, 2548.

Sudnow, D. (1965). Normal crimes: Sociological features of the penal code in the public defender's office. *Social Problems, 12*, 255–276.

Utz, P. (1978). *Settling the facts*. Lexington, MA: Lexington Books.

Uviller, R. (2000). The neutral prosecutor: The obligation of dispassion in a passion pursuit. *Fordham Law Review, 68*, 1695.

Wright, R. and Miller, M. (2002). The screening/bargaining tradeoff. *Stanford Law Review, 55*, 29.

Case Cited

Bordenkircher v. Hayes 434 US 357 (1978).

14

Examining the Death Penalty Insider Perspective: Capital Bench and Bar Interviews

Sherri DioGuardi

Abstract: *This study conducts semi-structured interviews with 27 death penalty insiders (nine judges, nine prosecutors, and nine defense attorneys) across three states. Prior research examined whether knowledge of capital punishment correlates with death penalty support (the Marshall Hypothesis). While prior research focused on opinions of laypeople, this study interviewed those with direct, hands-on experience to explore the knowledge-based, insider perspective. The majority (80%) of interviewee-respondents did not believe that the death penalty is necessary in light of life without the possibility of parole as an available sentencing option, and 62 percent did not support capital punishment. Qualitative data analysis reveals a wealth of insider information that advances death penalty knowledge and informs policy.*

It has been over 25 years since the first death row prisoner was released due to wrongful conviction. Since then, there have been 17 more DNA exonerations for death row prisoners; and, in terms of total criminal cases, 315 more exonerations (The Innocence Project, 2014). Despite wrongful convictions being publicized, the majority of the American public still supports the death penalty. Some scholars have attributed this persistence to Americans being ignorant of death penalty procedures or overinflating procedural safeguards (Acker, Bohm, and Lanier, 1998; Gross, 1998; Mello, 1996; Johnson, 1998). While death penalty insiders are fully informed and even contribute to procedural safeguards in capital cases, currently the "literature provides little scholarly assessment of the general subjective outlooks of any criminal court practitioner" (Weiss, 2003, p. 3)

Justice Thurgood Marshall wrote in *Furman v. Georgia* (1972) that the more informed people are about the death penalty, the more anti-death penalty they will be. A surfeit of public opinion research has been published on the death penalty (e.g., Durham, Elrod, and Kinkade, 1996; Zeisel and Gallup, 1989), and studies have been published that examine the issue from the perspective of capital juries (e.g., Bowers, 1995; Foglia, 2003, Geimer and Amsterdam, 1988), appellate capital defense counsel (Sheffer, 2013), and prison officials (Cabana, 1996; Lifton and Mitchell, 2000). Research has also been done with college students where their opinions on capital punishment were sought prior to learning about the death penalty and then were sought again after information acquisition to determine if support level changed. An *opinion hardening* phenomenon was also found where initial views on capital punishment were merely strengthened after death penalty knowledge was acquired (Lord, Ross, and Lepper, 1979). It may be that laypeople narrowly hone in on information that best supports a pre-established, emotion-based opinion (Bandes, 2008).

In comparison to the general public or college students, death penalty insiders are more fully informed, and their knowledge is firsthand because it is derived from direct, hands-on experience. Emotions should also play a lesser role in how capital case practitioners process and filter new knowledge because their training, experience, and practice (e.g., graduating from law school, passing a state bar exam, and participating in trials) require advanced reasoning skills and the ability to logically analyze information (DeGroff and McKee, 2006). The current study provided these death penalty insiders with the opportunity to voice their views on capital punishment.

Literature Review

There is a substantial body of literature on death penalty opinion. Findings confirm the complexity of this controversial issue because a multitude of variables, both individual and societal, correlate with death penalty support.

Research has looked at the relationship between death penalty knowledge and death penalty support (Bohm, 1989, 1991; Lambert and Clarke, 2001; Lambert, Camp, Clarke, and Jiang, 2011; Sarat and Vidmar, 1976; Vidmar and Dittenhoffer, 1981; Wright, Bohm, and Jamieson, 1995). The majority of that research was stimulated by Justice Marshall's *Furman* ruling (1972) in which he stated that people more informed about the death penalty would be less supportive of it, excepting those with an underlying belief in retribution. Studies were conducted with college students whose opinions on capital punishment were sought prior to being informed on the death penalty and who were then questioned again after information acquisition to determine if support level changed (e.g., Bohm, 1990, 2007; Lord et al., 1979). While some support was found for *Marshall's hypothesis* (Bohm, 1989; Bohm, Clark, and Aveni, 1991; Bohm and Vogel, 1991; Cochran, Sanders, and Chamlin, 2006; Patenaude, 2001; Sandys and McGarrell, 1995; Sarat and Vidmar, 1976; Vidmar and Dittenhoffer, 1981), studies also demonstrated that increased knowledge polarized opinions (Bohm, 1990; Lord et al., 1979). Students who declared themselves pro the death penalty at the onset ended up being even more supportive after receiving additional information, and the same was found for death penalty opponents. Researchers concluded that the opinion-strengthening effect of new knowledge resulted from people focusing only on those facts which reinforced their own pre-existing, emotion-based opinions (Bandes, 2008; Bohm, 2007; Bohm, Vogel, and Maisto, 1993; Lord et al., 1979). A rebound effect was also identified; the impact of new knowledge on death penalty support appeared to diminish over time (Bohm et al., 1993; Bohm and Vogel, 2004).

While all of these past studies greatly contributed to death penalty knowledge, the samples were comprised of people without direct knowledge of capital case proceedings.

If practitioners were sampled, the study tended to target one issue such as reactions to newly implemented law or perceptions of systematic error (McGarrell and Sandys, 1996; Ramsey and Frank, 2007a, 2007b). Much of what has been published on the capital practitioner experience was written from single-person perspectives (e.g., Kozinski, 2004; McCann, 1996; Salinas, 2006).

Multiple perspectives were somewhat explored when Whitehead, Blankenship, and Wright (1999) surveyed Tennessee legislators, chief prosecutors, and chief public defenders to determine differences in support levels. Whitehead et al. (1999) did not specify whether their sample had any capital case experience, but did find that chief public defenders were the only group not supportive of the death penalty. The other groups' death penalty support level decreased somewhat, however, when life without parole was offered as an alternative sentence option, and that finding is supported by extant literature (Bohm, 2007; Bowers, 1993; Durham et al., 1996; Jones, 2006). Both legislators and prosecutors revealed concerns about being politically harmed if they publicly opposed capital punishment, and their most frequent reason for favoring the death penalty was deterrence. Fairness was addressed; respondents were asked whether they agreed that Black-on-White murderers were most likely to be sentenced to death, and only 8 percent of prosecutors agreed with that statement, in comparison to 30 percent agreement by legislators and 90 percent by public defenders.

More recently, Sheffer (2013) interviewed 20 experienced post-conviction capital defenders in order to explore how death penalty appellate work impacted upon them emotionally. Her interviewees refer to themselves as adrenaline junkies who felt compelled to continue their work, despite the pressures and demands, due to the knowledge that they were vitally needed. They saw themselves as dedicated lawyers driven by a desire to represent the "underdog and to try to right wrongs" (p. 346).

Unlike the Sheffer (2013) study in which the objective was to specifically explore emotional experiences of post-conviction capital defense attorneys, the current study's goal was less restrictive by comparing and contrasting direct experience across all three capital roles (the judge, the prosecutor, and defense attorney). Interviews were with public, private, appointed, assigned, and retained defense attorneys whose experience ranged from lower level state trial courts to the highest level appellate courts in both the state and federal system. All 27 interviewees were given full opportunity to tell their own stories and present their own unique perspective.

Research Design

Because the goal of this study was to gain a deeper understanding of death penalty proceedings from the capital worker perspective, a qualitative research design was crucial.

A total of 27 capital case workers were interviewed from within the following three states: Ohio, Oregon, and South Carolina. These states were chosen because each had active death penalty statutes at the time of the study; they are geographically diverse (Northwest, Midwest, and Southeast United States); and, altogether, they represent the full range of Elazar's political culture typology (1972, 1984), which has been identified in the literature as a "powerful element" in explaining policy (Cook, 1979, p. 249), sentence severity, and criminal justice decision-making (Broach, Jackson, and Ascolillo, 1978; Eisenstein, Fleming, and Nardulli, 1988); and shown to be a determinant for death penalty implementation and frequency of use.

The two criteria used for selecting prospective interviewees are capital case experience and intrastate location. The semi-structured interview was the chosen format because it allows interviewees to tell their story in their own words, and it allows an interviewer to probe more deeply for details from each narrative (Charmaz, 2006).

Interviews averaged one hour in length and took place between May 31 and July 15, 2011. Interviewees were asked to generally describe their capital case experience, the magnitude of that experience, and whether or not they anticipated future involvement. All interviewees were queried about whether they had suggestions or recommendations for improving capital case proceedings. They were also asked whether they believed the death penalty was a necessary component in the current criminal justice system, and why or why not. That was followed up with the question: "Realizing that capital case litigation may be part of your professional job responsibilities, how do you personally feel about the death penalty?" Interviewees were urged to explain the basis for those beliefs. Lastly, they were explicitly given the opportunity to expand or elaborate. Sessions were tape-recorded and subsequently transcribed verbatim.

Findings

Range of Capital Experience

All interviewees had firsthand, direct experience with capital cases. That experience ranged from full participation in at least two bifurcated capital case trial proceedings (n=1) to direct involvement with over 50 capital cases (n=3). Some interviewees had multiple role involvement. Experience was grouped into three interval ranges. Slightly over 22 percent of interviewees had direct experience in 2 to 5 capital cases (n=6); 37 percent had direct death penalty experience in 6 to 19 cases (n=10); and 41 percent had direct participation in over 20 capital cases (n=11).

Thematic Findings

Economic Issues

"Super due process, to me, means you should have a Cadillac defense. Now what's being said is that a Kia is good enough," Anonymous Interviewee (AI) #6 stated. When wrongful convictions were revealed because of advances in DNA science, many states and counties jointly took action to provide more funding at lower court, post-conviction relief (PCR), and appellate levels. However, since that time, the economy has taken a steep downturn, which may be impacting upon capital funding.

> They have changed—you know—over my term of practice to being a little more penurious, a little more wary, and a little more savvy about—you know—the worst case scenario is they're giving you a half of a loaf, and they know it. They're giving you enough to insulate their record from a reversal, but they're not really giving you enough to do what you need to have done.
>
> (AI #13)

By restricting funding, defense attorneys feel forced to either go to the second-rate expert or settle for state-employed consultants. All interviewees conceded that currently their death penalty system is underfunded.

> The small counties can't afford a death penalty case; so—you know—if you did it in one county, you get a life sentence. If you did it in another county, you get the death penalty because of cost issues.
>
> (AI #13)

In certain impoverished counties, capital charges are not filed (or *noticed*, depending on the state) merely because those counties cannot afford the expense. Once the capital case quota in a county has been reached, the death penalty will be off the table or will remain merely as a bluff to secure a plea bargain.

Using the Death Penalty as Leverage

"Those who claim the death penalty is too costly never take into account the cases that are not litigated because of the death penalty existing as a leveraging tool" (AI #2).

One reason given for support is because without the death penalty as the high-level mark, aggravated murder cases will settle at a lower level. If life without the possibility of parole (LWOP) was, instead, the highest level of punishment, then the concern is that aggravated murders would end up eventually being released. "For any type of criminal case, the most severe penalty option moves the goal post where most cases will settle" (AI #1).

The Morality of the Death Penalty

> There have been times when I said that I'm going to have to answer to God for what I have done. And at times that has given me some angst, and then I thought: Well, did you do it responsibly? Did you do it for the right reasons? Did you do anything unethical? If you can answer those questions, then you can answer to God for it.
>
> (AI #20)

Many of the 27 interviews were intense, to the extent that the researcher-interviewer herself could not help feeling emotionally affected by the cracking voices, watering eyes, or shaking hands. Twice, interviewees broke down and cried. That provided insight as to how difficult it must sometimes be to maintain professional composure during death penalty proceedings.

> [I]n order to do this job, you have to pour your soul into it. If you do it [strictly] as a lawyer, this is pretty cool; you get out of it without getting hurt. It hurts a lot to do it right because you have to basically immerse yourself.
>
> (AI #6)

When interviewees were asked whether their death penalty opinions were based on moral or religious beliefs, 73 percent said they were morality-based (n=19). A little over 62 percent of judges felt that way (n=5); 67 percent of prosecutors (n=6); and 89 percent of defense attorneys (n=8). None of the interviewees believed that their opinions were founded on religious beliefs.

> I'm not a rabid "he's got to die" kind of guy. I mean it's just—I certainly believe in it. But, to me, if a jury decides to sentence him to life imprisonment, I don't go out and kick the dog or anything. It's like—you know—hey, that's their decision. And I don't—if they decide to sentence somebody to death, I don't pop the cork either.
>
> (AI #16)

Some prosecutors expressed distaste for the death penalty but were resigned to the fact that it was what the voters wanted. Others felt that in order not to be overwhelmed with personal angst, they had to believe in the morality of the death penalty. Some interviewees claimed that they hated the fact that the death penalty was necessary, but the presence of evil in the world made it so.

> Um, I hate that we have to have it. Okay? I do. I wish that people were not as evil as they are; that would be such a wonderful society to live in. All right? But we have mean and evil people that live amongst us, and I think they need to go, and so it's a hard decision.
>
> (AI #20)

Some judges expressed frustration with the system because of the requirements placed on them to regulate it and make it work perfectly when so many uncontrollable variables exist. More than a few judges confessed that the interview made it difficult for them because they were sworn to uphold the law (and the death penalty was the law in their state), and now they were being asked to look beyond the law and reveal personal feelings. For them, the law was often seen as a blinder, similar to what is placed on racehorses, so that they would not be distracted from the task in front of them. A few had experienced times during the course of a death penalty trial when they woke from a sound sleep besieged with doubts about the morality of it.

The Best of the Best

Neither capital prosecutors nor capital defenders make the kind of money that their level of education, skill, and trial experience would earn them in the private sector. The ones who stay in the field for any extended length of time tend to be strongly committed to their profession. "Most successful defense attorneys don't believe they're on a mission for God and separate themselves from their client. The ones that are the most obnoxious are the ones who take it all so very personally" (AI #7).

Those who specialize in capital litigation may find that their commitment over time becomes a crusade. Many capital defenders admit that unlike other major felony work where they strive to inject reasonable doubt and to hold the government accountable for proving guilt, in death penalty proceedings their goal is strictly to save the client's life. Prosecutors, on the other hand, feel a similarly strong responsibility to protect society. When prosecutors were asked about the necessity of the death penalty now that LWOP is available as a sentencing option and now that maximum security prisons have been built to resolve safety concerns, they expressed fears for the prison guards, the medical staff, and even other inmates.

The refrain heard over and over again from attorneys on both sides of the death penalty debate was, "I want to do right." Prosecutors and defense attorneys alike stated a prefer- ence for having their opponents be highly skilled capital litigators because that helped alleviate their fears about mistakes being made in the process:

> I would rather have a good lawyer on a case than a bad lawyer on a case. I don't worry about the— one, I know that the person on the other side from me is doing [the] job; so if something has happened wrong in the process, hopefully it will be found by the advocate on the other side.
>
> (AI #14)

Many defenders admitted to feeling like David to the government's Goliath and having had a lifelong desire to stick up for the underdog. A common sub-theme was found with the prosecutors being very service-oriented. As an example, most offered (without being asked) to help the researcher/interviewer navigate their cities by drawing maps or giving detailed directions. Many interviewees had been influenced by television shows they were exposed to in early childhood; others originally planned to go into corporate law or private defense law but were permanently sidetracked by taking on internships or first jobs at either a prosecutor's or public defender's office.

Respondents/interviewees revealed that it was not unusual for courtroom workers, whether prosecutor, defense attorney, or even judge, to get assigned to one death penalty case and then, no matter what the outcome, to declare "Never again!" This may be unfor- tunate because, according to interviewees, it takes multiple involvements before partici- pants will stop feeling as if they are walking on eggshells, and it is common for novices to second-guess everything. The possibility also exists that capital case workers will become so efficient that their focus on form will be at the expense of substance. Super due process requires capital defenders to leave "no stone unturned" in representing their clients, according to AI #6. Anonymous Interviewee #18 stated:

> I think ethically it's a real problem to be filing a motion that has no merit, but I'm doing it because it's a death penalty case; so I should just do everything. And I don't agree with that; so that's a problem. And, um, even though on one hand counsel are going through all these motions, a lot of

times to me what is stressful is it just looks like that's all they're doing—is going through motions as opposed to using a more case-specific, refined, focused effort in a case.

Interviewees told of times where written motions were filed that contained the wrong name of either the victim or defendant because filings were prepared hurriedly from templates. Due to the enormity of the task, there is a recognized risk that capital defenders will scramble to check off all their required to-do items and then not have any time or energy left over to put forth quality witness examinations, impassioned pleas, or creative arguments. This is what interviewees referred to as a *rote defense*, which may look marginally acceptable on the official transcript of proceedings (the appellate linchpin) but which falls far short of impressing the jury or of being effective.

The Worst of the Worst

We're not really charging the death penalty in the worst of the worst cases. So I would much rather see something—whether it's a grand jury review or whether it's a commission review, whatever it is—but to try to limit the number exposed to the death penalty to those really sociopathic, dangerous people who can't be held safely without an expense that's beyond what society can burden—or take on the burden, if that makes sense. It just seems like it's a very rare case where the state can't charge a death penalty case now.

(AI #4)

The majority of interviewees expressed concern that the death penalty in their states is not being reserved for the worst of the worst. Respondents related instances where the most vicious killers were allowed to plead to lesser sentences. One serial killer pled to LWOP in exchange for revealing where his victims' bodies were buried. Another multiple-victim killer fled the country, and the harboring country would not allow extradition until the state agreed not to seek the death penalty.

Super Due Process

"Presumption of innocence is an artificial bubble you place in one place and one place only: the courtroom" (AI #7). One judge admitted to being discouraged because many defense attorneys start out their case in the first phase by saying, "Okay. Let's talk about the death penalty." This gives everyone in the courtroom, including the jury, the impression that even the defendant's own attorney believes he's guilty.

And, of course, it is difficult to deal with the qualification of a jury without in some way mentioning the fact that—you know—we talk about the death penalty, but he hasn't even been found guilty yet, and so there's sort of like a seed being planted out there.

(AI #21)

Interviewees explained how hard it is to keep the high threshold of beyond a reasonable doubt from being lowered in capital case proceedings. Courthouse wisdom seems to be that the death penalty is only sought when the state's case is airtight. Also, everyone knows upfront—and even the *venire* learns on the first day—that the death penalty is the potential penalty, which may add a dire dimension to death penalty proceedings. This is in stark contrast to non-capital proceedings where merely mentioning a potential penalty can result in a mistrial.

When interviewees recounted their experiences, this refrain was often heard: "Guilt was not an issue in that case." When asked outright about the presumption of innocence during death penalty trials if guilt was never in doubt, one defense attorney expressed certainty that prosecutors would not risk going to trial on a capital case without insurmountable evidence of guilt.

> There's so much about capital law that is not only hollow and hypocritical but just flat-out topsy-turvy. You know, death is different; more process is due; all these pretended Pontius Pilate hand-washings repeatedly just to pretend that we are affording this person all the great protections twice, three times over.
>
> (AI #13)

Prosecutors were adamant that due process was present to an even greater extent than it was in noncapital cases. However, reservations were revealed. The biggest concern seemed to be the jurisdictional variation with capital charging and death penalty outcomes. Certain counties in all three states were known for aggressively seeking the death penalty and for having jury-eligible citizens who would always vote for death. Juries in one particular county were referred to as "the 12 Dobermans" (AI #25). Other counties never seek the death penalty regardless of the numbers of aggravated murders committed within their jurisdiction. Some counties consistently seek the death penalty but are known for having juries that always compromise with an LWOP verdict.

Another concern was the quality of the defense, which also appeared to be jurisdictionally related. In some areas there was the perception that aggressive defending was not tolerated; that appointments were given to a certain favored few who were more willing to compromise their client in order to maintain good relations with those having the most political power and/or controlling the purse strings. "I suppose it's like everywhere else in the country. There are certain house pets in the private bar that play the patron's game for appointments who keep getting them because they don't really put up a big fight" (AI #13).

Sometimes the client might be compromised inadvertently. This may occur merely as an unintended consequence of local courthouse culture.

> When we're here and we're trying cases in front of judges we see all the time—you know—sometimes there's a reluctance to try to cross that judge; so maybe death penalty counsel should be trained individuals in a central office and really not locally tied. Maybe you need some local counsel to assist in the jury selection or something to know more about the folks here, but if I'm beginning to try cases all the time in front of these judges, I may—whether I want to admit it or not, it may very well hamper me in really making a real—you know—really going to the mat when it's needed.
>
> (AI #19)

Concern about capital jurors' understanding of how to apply the law was also an issue. Anonymous Interviewee #12 opined that capital jurors probably used a preponderance of evidence standard (charges are more likely true than not) despite being instructed by the court to use the standard of beyond a reasonable doubt. In one state, new restrictions have recently been placed on *voir dire* examinations which prevent defense attorneys from effectively screening the *venire*. Also, instead of allowing individual *voir dire*, a new trend has been to question prospective jurors in small groups. Some jurisdictions have discontinued capital jury sequestration. While all of those interviewed supported America's jury system, many had reservations about capital juries being death-qualified.

The timing for appointment of defense counsel was identified as being problematic. Because the vast majority of defendants capitally charged are indigent, they are not appointed counsel until after the death penalty seek decision has already been made. Once elected, prosecutors announce publicly that they are going after the death penalty, it may be difficult for them to back down from that position even when new information later surfaces that might justify a softening stance. A privately retained attorney brought in early (at the suspect stage or even before) is in a much better position to advocate on the client's behalf and protect the defendant's rights. When the defense comes in later, important case decisions have already been made. Interviewees revealed that the state proceeds more cautiously and is more receptive to case disposition discussions when it knows the murder suspect has representation. On the other hand, problems can occur with privately retained counsel lacking sufficient trial skills and experience. One judge stated that the system works best when the capital defendant is either very wealthy or very poor (AI #10). Occasions were also recalled when prosecutors told defense attorneys upfront that even though the death penalty was being sought due to media scrutiny, the case would just get dragged along until public focus shifted, and then a deal would be offered.

Besides lower court-level variations, higher level court variances were identified. Certain federal circuit courts are known to the inner circle as being very liberal in their practice of reversing and remanding capital cases back for retrial on what might be considered as trite issues, whereas other federal circuit courts have the reputation for never ruling in favor of a capital defendant, no matter how valid the constitutional claim. It is similar with the three state supreme courts. In one state, it was identified as a running joke that its highest court will "stretch the taffy to affirm every capital conviction" (AI #13). Harmless error was seen by some as the catch-all phrase to keep capital convictions intact.

Measuring the Value of the Victim's Life

"A civilized society is not one that punishes less and less and less. It's one that is more discriminating about it" (AI #7). One aspect in particular was brought out by prosecutors which might explain, in part, some of the findings from past research regarding bias in death sentencing. The system itself forces its workers, as well as capital juries, to compare the value of a life by measuring one person's worth as compared to another.

You and I both know when we get to a jury that the jury is going to care a lot more about the armored car driver who was shot than about some damned crack-head who's out there selling poison to the kids. So which case are we going to get death on?

(AI #14)

Prosecutors, in screening out cases in which to seek the death penalty, evaluate the crime, the criminal, and even the victim. The latter assessment, rather than being racially motivated, is—as was explained—based on the prosecutor's perception of whether the victim is a true innocent, how much the impaneled jurors will care about that particular person's death, and whether their outrage will be sufficient to sustain a death penalty verdict. "We know in our experience that you're never going to get the death penalty unless you have a true innocent victim. It's just not going to happen" (AI #16).

The prosecutor is compelled to make these calculations because of the high costs attached to a death penalty pursuit. Experience has demonstrated to prosecutors that victims who have a shadier past—possibly as a consequence of low socio-economic status, chronic unemployment, substance use, or abuse—are viewed by sworn-in jurors as being less valuable to society; therefore, the price for murdering him or her will end up being discounted. As AI #14 explained it, the reality of the situation is that community members just "do not give a damn about the crack addict who is murdered."

A Sporting Event

"Death penalty has now become a giant game that only benefits the cottage industry" (AI #1). More than one interviewee used sports analogies to describe their experience with capital litigation, such as referring to it as being "the Super Bowl of criminal law" (AI #10) or the "Lawyers' World Series" (AI #5). Death penalty litigation is "addictive" (AI #13); and in comparison, other felony cases seem trivial. "The thing about death penalty work is it's so—you know—it's just so intense. You get so into it" (AI #23).

Also, most of these experienced capital attorneys went into law in the first place to litigate in front of juries. In civil law, litigation has decreased over the years; and, when it comes to the high-money cases, the established civil firms will usually not allow associates to try them. In criminal law, novice attorneys can try cases immediately at the misdemeanor level and get moved up the ladder to try felony cases fairly quickly. Now, in the modern era, with 95 percent of criminal cases being settled (Maguire, 2003), a considerable amount of capital cases can still be counted on to go to trial; and those trials are more grandiose than noncapital trials due to extended *voir dire*, the two-phase proceedings, and the risk of death being attached. Anonymous Interviewee #7 said that trying a capital one is "the most fun you can have with your clothes on." Others felt let down when a capital case was over, and they had to go back to more mundane criminal matters. Anonymous Interviewee #25 stated that it was like being forced to tail-gate after having recently been the star quarterback. Even capital judges may not be immune.

> There are a lot of judges who want to do death penalty cases. And I don't mean to sound disparaging of brothers and sisters on the bench, but some of them want to do it for the wrong reason. They want to do it because they're the big cases; they want to do it because they get a lot of attention.
>
> (AI #4)

In this study, however, the judicial interviewees were the least likely to appreciate the thrill aspect of these cases. Instead, they felt intense pressure to create a reverse-proof record.

> They are a pain in the butt both from the standpoint of the nature of what you are doing as well as the stringency of the rules, the requirements, the not screwing up, the not wanting to try it two, three, or four times. All of that comes into play.
>
> (AI #24)

Death Penalty Paradoxes

When asked, "Has being an active participant in the capital punishment system created any personal or professional concerns, conflicts, or stresses?" prosecutors explained how capital litigation was considerably less stressful for them than noncapital litigation. There are a variety of reasons: guilt or innocence is often not hotly contested; there is an established body of law regarding death penalty jurisprudence; more money is approved for hiring experts and/or consultants in capital cases; both capital prosecutors and capital defenders work in two-member teams; and there is always advance knowledge on exactly when the case will be tried.

> It isn't like a regular case where it's like a cattle call, and the docket tends to break out when cases plead out, and you scramble. For a capital case, you know it's coming. You have a specific date; you've got a job assigned to it; you've got a court reporter; you've got the lawyers lined up and all that. You have plenty of pretrial conferences to kind of get things on track if they start getting derailed, and so there is more certainty to it so you can—it's more organized than other types of criminal cases.
>
> (AI #26)

The interviews revealed another paradox with capital litigation. The better job that a defense attorney does, the less reversible error in the record; therefore, if a jury decides to bring in a death verdict—and, as was revealed over and over again, no matter how skilled you are in litigation, you can never be 100 percent certain what a jury is going to do—then that defense attorney has hurt, rather than helped, his client. For those capital defenders whose ultimate goal is to save their client's life, the temptation is great to deliberately insert error into the record. "It's an irony because the more fair to the defendant in some ways, the more we're making it so that there's no reversible error on the record. Know what I mean?" (AI #19)

Judges who may be personally anti-death penalty or merely ambivalent can be similarly conflicted. If they step in to protect the record when they feel a defense attorney is doing an improper job, then they are, in essence, paving the way for the death penalty to be affirmed upon review.

Summary of Interviews

Of the 27 interviews, 62 percent were non-supportive of the death penalty (n=16). One judge abstained from giving an opinion. All prosecutors, except for one in Ohio, were supportive. In contrast, all but one of the nine defense attorneys were non-supportive. Out of the eight judicial responses, 88 percent were anti-death penalty (n=7).

When interviewees were asked whether or not the death penalty was a necessary component in the criminal justice system, 80 percent of respondents (n=25) said that it was not necessary, and that included three of the nine prosecutors who agreed to answer that question. One prosecutor declined to respond because he or she felt that was a question best left for lawmakers to answer.

Interviewees were asked to make suggestions for improving the death penalty system in their state. One judge felt that was better left to the legislators. Six (one judge, one prosecutor, and four defense attorneys) felt the death penalty needed to be abolished. The issue of abolition was not addressed outright; the question asked whether they had suggestions for improving the death penalty in their state.

Seven interviewees suggested appellate reforms, and four of those suggestions were from prosecutors; one suggested eliminating the dual protection of Post-Conviction Relief (PCR) and habeas corpus because only one was sufficient to safeguard defendant rights; one prosecutor felt the process should be streamlined to eliminate delay between sentence and execution; another prosecutor felt that the issues preserved should be the same as for noncapital cases except to allow for any residual doubt issue to be reviewed. One judge also felt that the state post-conviction relief was redundant and was concerned with how expensive it had gotten in recent years. That dovetails with the comments of two prosecutors who suggested that better oversight was needed on appellate defense funding. One defense attorney suggested reform at two of the post-trial stages, that the habeas corpus needed to be a more meaningful review, and also that judges at the post-conviction relief hearings be required to draft their own orders instead of allowing the Attorney General's Office to do so (to ensure that the order is a more accurate and complete reflection of what actually occurred). A pernicious nationwide practice was described in PCR hearings where the winner has the power of the pen to subtly distort the facts in the court order, and those subtle distortions become presumptive truth in subsequent federal appeals.

Three suggestions were for bifurcated juries: one jury impaneled for the guilt/penalty phase, and a separate jury impaneled for the penalty phase. That suggestion was made by a judge as well as by two defense attorneys. Two judges and one defense attorney recommended that the decision to seek the death penalty in any case be taken out of a single prosecutor's discretion and either require a panel of statewide prosecutors or an appointed committee to make that decision.

Three defense attorneys recommended that defense funding be increased. One prosecutor suggested that death penalty prosecutions be state-funded. One prosecutor recommended better funding across the board.

Two prosecutors wanted to eliminate the requirement for unanimous verdicts in the sentencing phase and, instead, allow 11–1 or 10–2. Two defenders suggested that individual *voir dire* remain and that more meaningful jury–attorney exchanges be allowed. One interviewee suggested that standards for capital qualification be raised, and another defense attorney also expressed the need for better defendant representation. One interviewee was concerned about the jury sequestration rules being weakened and felt strongly that capital jury sequestration needed to remain regardless of the cost. Another recommended that the change of venue rule be relaxed, and one prosecutor recommended that jury charges be improved.

One Ohio respondent suggested an open file discovery more expansive than the one put in place earlier in the year. A South Carolina respondent recommended that statutory reform is needed to limit the amount of aggravated murders in which the death penalty could be sought. Another interviewee from South Carolina suggested that a capital defendant who wished to plead guilty be allowed to have a jury decide his penalty; at the present time the jury is required to be impaneled for both phases or for no phases; therefore, if a defendant pleads guilty, he must be sentenced by a judge. One Ohio interviewee asserted that fairer outcomes would be accomplished if indigent defense was brought into the case earlier, before the death penalty seek decision had already been made.

Discussion and Conclusions

This study examined death penalty opinions through the finely ground lens of knowledge and experience. To this researcher's knowledge, it is the first time that capital judges, capital prosecutors, and capital defense attorneys from three different states have been interviewed in depth about their views on the death penalty.

The majority (62%) of the interviewee-respondents in this study were not supportive of the death penalty. There were a number of reasons given for their non-support, such as the infallibility of the system; the moral opprobrium that killing is always wrong, even if done by the state; the idea that LWOP accomplishes the same objective; the high cost; the strain on the system; or the use of resources which would better serve society if applied elsewhere. However, the ones who did support it did so mainly for the reason stated by AI #7: "I have very little faith that true life will mean true life." This distrust in government aligns with Zimring's (2003) discursive analysis on cultural contradictions of American capital punishment because strong supporters of the death penalty "commonly express skepticism about alternative punishments such as life sentences without parole" (Messner, Baumer, and Rosenfeld, 2006, p. 583).

Qualitative analysis of the interviews revealed nine emergent themes: likening death penalty trials to sporting events; economic issues; plea bargaining as leverage; the best of

the best (quality representation); the worst of the worst (proportionality); measuring the value of a victim's life; super due process; morality issues; and death penalty paradoxes.

For capital attorneys, the two-stage death penalty proceeding has become their Super Bowl challenge. Capital judges did not appear to have that same appreciation for the sporting aspects of a death penalty trial, but the thrill aspects of capital work were previously noted by Sheffer (2013) during interviews with appellate defense attorneys.

Expense was a major theme, and the majority of all interviewees stated their belief that the death penalty is not needed because the LWOP sentence is a safer, more cost-effective alternative. Public opinion research has also shown that when the death penalty support question is extended to include harsh and meaningful sentencing alternatives such as "life imprisonment with absolutely no possibility of parole," overall death penalty support decreases (Jones, 2006, para. 5).

Unlike the Whitehead et al. (1999) study in which deterrence was a reason given for prosecutor death penalty support, no interviewee here identified deterrence as a basis for support. Instead, the main rationale for the death penalty being needed was its use as leverage to secure an LWOP plea. However, interviewees revealed that oftentimes capital defendants end up on death row because of their refusal to plead, even when doing so would be beneficial and life-saving. The concern is that too many death row inmates fit the description described by White (2006), who identified the typical capital defendant as being cognitively/emotionally deficient and averse to accepting favorable plea offers.

Suggestions were made to have some type of statewide oversight for capital charging decisions to eliminate geographic inequalities, promote proportionality, and ensure that the death penalty is being reserved for the worst of the worst. This type of regulation would also eliminate the ethically problematic victim–value calculus that may be occurring in death penalty charging decisions.

Prior research has suggested that most capital jurors decide punishment even before the innocence/guilt phase has been concluded (Bowers, 1995; Bowers and Foglia, 2002). This study found that defenders view their job as an uphill battle from the start. Except for three of them who had been extremely successful in bringing in not guilty verdicts for capital clients, defender-interviewees did not hold out hope for acquittals and were not optimistic about being able to keep clients from death row. If defense attorneys perceive their client's case as a lost cause from day one, then they may be conveying that lack of confidence to the sworn-in jury. Having a capital trial broken up into two parts makes it a challenge for defense to effectively mitigate in the second phase if they have already put forth an innocence claim in phase one (American Bar Association, 2003) because the jury will likely see that mitigation evidence as self-serving and manipulative (Sundby, 1998). A bifurcated jury may resolve this dilemma for defense.

Findings further suggest that death penalty insiders have reservations about super due process adherence. Expressed concerns were jurisdictional variance; quality of defense; integrity of prosecutor; death qualification of capital jury; not allowing individual *voir dire*; not sequestering the impaneled jury; and presumption of innocence. This study identified paradoxes and potential ethical dilemmas such as capital defenders on a life-saving mission who may feel forced to deliberately inject error into the record to provide appeal protection; and capital prosecutors who may be experiencing considerably less stress when involved with capital trials (as compared to noncapital murder trials) due to expanded resources, advanced scheduling, being relieved from regular caseload responsibility, and not being challenged on the issue of defendant's guilt. Findings were that capital judges felt conflict when compelled to intervene during a capital case in which they had concerns about a defendant's characteristics (e.g., low IQ, lack of social skills, legal system naiveté) or an attorney's performance.

Study Limitations and Suggestions

Given that this was a small sample size (n=27) and the research design was qualitative, the opinions expressed in this study may not be representative of other capital case practitioners, either in these states or in other states. It is suggested that studies in other states be conducted to determine whether the same (or similar) themes would emerge from interviewing death penalty insiders.

It is suggested that elected prosecutors be interviewed to find out how and why charging decisions are made and to determine their willingness to turn over death penalty-seeking discretion to a non-partisan decision-making panel. Also, expense vouchers could be analyzed to determine if expenses in death penalty proceedings have been increasing or decreasing over time. Capital cases settled with life pleas should be examined and compared to capital cases which went to trial in order to evaluate whether the death penalty is being reserved for the youngest, least educated, and most distrustful rather than for the worst of the worst.

Experienced capital case workers are a valuable, and largely untapped, resource for learning about the American death penalty. Society would be better served if policymakers put a system in place for periodically checking in with the front lines for feedback. Capital case practitioners are in position to pinpoint existing or emerging problems, and so it is imperative that their collective concerns be continuously heard and addressed.

Critical Thinking

Throughout the article, several capital litigation paradoxes were revealed. Explain these paradoxes. How do these apparent contradictions influence your own decision on the death penalty?

References

Acker, J. R., Bohm, R. M., and Lanier, C. S. eds. (1998). *America's experiment with capital punishment: Reflections on the past, present, and future of the ultimate penal sanction.* New York: Oxford University Press.

American Bar Association. (2003). Guidelines for the appointment and performance of defense counsel in death penalty cases. Retrieved from http://www.americanbar.org/content/dam/aba/migrated/legalservices/downloads/sclaid/death-penaltyguidelines2003.authcheckdam.pdf.

Bandes, S. A. (2008). The heart has its reasons: Examining the strange persistence of the American death penalty. In A. Sarat (ed.) *Studies in law, politics, and society special issue: Is the death penalty dying?* (pp. 21–52). San Diego, CA: JAI Press.

Bohm, R. M. (1989). The effects of classroom instruction and discussion on death penalty opinions: A teaching note. *Journal of Criminal Justice, 17*, 123–131.

Bohm, R. M. (1990). Death penalty opinions: Effects of a classroom experience and public commitment. *Sociological Inquiry, 60*, 285–297.

Bohm, R. M. (1991). American death penalty opinion 1936–1986: A critical examination of the Gallup polls. In R. Bohm (ed.) *The death penalty in America: Current research* (pp. 113–145). Cincinnati, OH: Anderson.

Bohm, R. M. (2007). *DeathQuest III: An introduction to the theory and practice of capital punishment in the United States*, 3rd edn. Cincinnati, OH: Anderson Publishing Co.

Bohm, R. M. and Vogel, R. E. (1991). Educational experiences and death penalty opinions: Stimuli that produces changes. *Journal of Criminal Justice Education, 2*, 69–80.

Bohm, R. M. and Vogel, R. E. (2004). More than ten years after: The long-term stability of informed death penalty opinions. *Journal of Criminal Justice, 32*, 307–327.

Bohm, R. M., Clark, L. J., and Aveni, A. F. (1991). Knowledge and death penalty opinion: A test of the Marshall Hypothesis. *Journal of Research in Crime and Delinquency, 28*, 360–687.

Bohm, R. M., Vogel, R. E., and Maisto, A. A. (1993). Knowledge and death penalty opinion: A panel study. *Journal of Criminal Justice, 21*, 29–45.

Bowers, W. J. (1993). Capital punishment and contemporary values: People's misgivings and the court's misperceptions. *Law and Society Review, 27*, 157–175.

Bowers, W. J. (1995). The capital jury project: Rationale, design, and preview of early findings. *Indiana Law Journal, 70*, 1043–1103.

Bowers, W. J. and Foglia, W. D. (2002). Still singularly agonizing: Law's failure to purge arbitrariness from capital sentencing. *Criminal Law Bulletin, 39*, 51–86.

Broach, G. T., Jackson, P. D., and Ascolillo, V. H. (1978). State political culture and sentence severity in federal district courts. *Social Science Quarterly, 86*, 683–703.

Cabana, D. A. (1996). *Death at midnight: The confessions of an executioner*. Boston, MA: Northeastern University Press.

Charmaz, K. (2006). *Constructing grounded theory: A practical guide through qualitative analysis*. Los Angeles, CA: Sage Publications.

Cochran, J., Sanders, B., and Chamlin, M. B. (2006). Profiles in change: An alternative look at the Marshall Hypothesis. *Journal of Criminal Justice Education, 17*, 205–226.

Cook, B. B. (1979). Sentencing problems and internal court reform. In P. F. Nardulli (ed.) *The study of criminal courts: Political perspectives* (pp. 131–169). Cambridge, MA: Ballinger.

DeGroff, E. A. and McKee, K. A. (2006). Learning like lawyers: Addressing the differences in law student learning styles. *Brigham Young University Education and Law Journal*, 499–550.

Durham, A., Elrod, P., and Kinkade, P. (1996). Public support for the death penalty: Beyond Gallup. *Justice Quarterly, 13*, 705–736.

Eisenstein, J., Fleming, R. B., and Nardulli, P. F. (1988). *The contours of justice: Communities and their courts*. Boston, MA: Little, Brown, and Company.

Elazar, D. J. (1972). Contemporary federalism in Germany and the future of federalism in America. *Publius, 2*, 1–3.

Elazar, D. J. (1984). *American Federalism: A view from the states* (3rd ed.). New York: Harper Collins.

Foglia, W. D. (2003). They know not what they do: Unguided and misguided discretion in Pennsylvania capital cases. *Justice Quarterly, 20*(1), 187–211.

Furman v. Georgia, 408 US 238 (1972).

Geimer, W. S. and Amsterdam, J. (1988). Why jurors vote life or death: Operative factors in ten Florida death penalty cases. *American Journal of Criminal Law, 15*(1), 1–54.

Gross, S. R. (1998). Update: American public opinion on the death penalty—It's getting personal. *Cornell Law Review, 83*, 1448–1475.

Johnson, R. (1998). *Death work: A study of the modern execution process* (2nd edn). Belmont, CA: Wadsworth Publishing Company.

Jones, J. M. (2006). *Two in three favor death penalty for convicted murderers*. The Gallup Organization. Retrieved from http://www.gallup.com/ poll/23167/two-three-favor-death-penalty-convicted-murderers.aspx.

Kozinski, A. (2004). Tinkering with death. In H. Bedau and P. Cassell (eds) *Debating the death penalty: Should America have capital punishment? The experts from both sides make their case* (pp. 1–14). New York: Oxford University Press.

Lambert, E. and Clarke, A. (2001). The impact of information on an individual's support of the death penalty: A partial test of the Marshall Hypothesis among college students. *Criminal Justice Policy Review, 12*, 215–234.

Lambert, E. G., Camp, S.D., Clarke, A., and Jiang, S. (2011). The impact of information on death penalty support, revisited. *Crime and Delinquency, 57*, 572–599.

Lifton, R. J. and Mitchell, G. (2000). *Who owns death? Capital punishment, the American conscience, and the end of executions.* New York: Harper Collins Publishers.

Lord, C. G., Ross, L., and Lepper, M.R. (1979). Biased assimilation and attitude polarization: The effects of prior theories on subsequently considered evidence. *Journal of Personality and Social Psychology, 37*, 2098–2109.

Maguire, K. (Ed.), (2003). *Sourcebook of Criminal Justice Statistics* University at Albany, Hindelang Criminal Justice Research Center. Table 5.46. Retrieved from http://www.albany.edu/sourcebook/pdf/t5.46.pdf.

McCann, E. M. (1996). Opposing capital punishment: A prosecutor's perspective. *Marquette Law Review, 79*, 649–706.

McGarrell, E. F. and Sandys, M. (1996). The misperception of public opinion toward capital punishment. *American Behavioral Scientist, 39*, 500–513.

Mello, M. (1996). *Against the death penalty: The relentless dissents of Justices Brennan and Marshall.* Boston, MA: Northeastern University Press.

Messner, S. F., Baumer, E. P., and Rosenfeld, R. (2006). Distrust of government, the vigilante tradition, and support for capital punishment. *Law & Society Review, 40*, 559–590.

Patenaude, A. L. (2001). May God have mercy on your soul! Exploring and teaching a course on the death penalty. *Journal of Criminal Justice Education, 12*, 405–425.

Ramsey, R. J. and Frank, J. (2007a). Wrongful conviction: Perceptions of criminal justice professionals regarding the frequency of wrongful conviction and the extent of system errors. *Crime & Delinquency, 53*, 436–470.

Ramsey, R. J. and Frank, J. (2007b). How to reduce the incidence of wrongful convictions: Current perspectives of criminal justice practitioners. *The Journal of the Institute of Justice & International Studies, 7*, 231–249.

Salinas, L. S. (2006). Is it time to kill the death penalty?: A view from the bench and the bar. *American Journal of Criminal Law, 34*, 39–108.

Sandys, M. and McGarrell, E. (1995). Attitudes toward capital punishment: Preference for the death penalty or mere acceptance. *Journal of Research in Crime and Delinquency, 32*, 191–213.

Sarat, A. and Vidmar, N. (1976). Public opinion, the death penalty, and the Eighth Amendment: Testing the Marshall Hypothesis. *Wisconsin Law Review, 17*, 171–206.

Sheffer, S. (2013). *Fighting for their lives: Inside the experience of capital defense attorney.* Nashville, TN: Vanderbilt University Press.

Sundby, S. E. (1998). The capital jury and absolution: The intersection of trial strategy, remorse, and the death penalty. *Cornell Law Review, 83*, 1557–1598.

The Innocence Project. (2014). DNA exonerations nationwide. http://www. innocenceproject.org/Content/DNA_Exonerations_Nationwide.php.

Vidmar, N. and Dittenhoffer, T. (1981). Informed public opinion and death penalty attitudes. *Canadian Journal of Criminology, 23*, 43–56.

Weiss, M. S. (2003). *Toward an understanding of public defender motivations.* Retrieved from ProQuest Digital Dissertations (3085122).

White, W. S. (2006). *Litigating in the shadow of death.* Ann Arbor, MI: University of Michigan Press.

Whitehead, J.T., Blankenship, M. B., and Wright, J. P. (1999). Elite versus citizen attitudes on capital punishment: Incongruity between the public and policymakers. *Journal of Criminal Justice, 27*, 249–258.

Wright, H. O., Jr., Bohm, R. M., and Jamieson, K. M. (1995). A comparison of uninformed and informed death penalty opinions: A replication and expansion. *American Journal of Criminal Justice, 20*, 57–87.

Zeisel, H. and Gallup, A. (1989). Death penalty sentiment in the United States. *Journal of Quantitative Criminology 5*, 285–296.

Zimring, F. E. (2003). *The cultural contradictions of American capital punishment.* New York: Oxford University Press.

15

Maintaining the Myth of Individualized Justice: Probation Presentence Reports

John Rosecrance

Abstract: *Probation presentence reports emphasize some offender characteristics more than others. John Rosecrance explains how a stereotyping process is used by probation officers who write these reports, and how their sentence recommendations to judges are determined on the use of a few relatively fixed factors (e.g., current offense and prior criminal history). Presentence reports are produced to provide the court with the illusion that each report is based on individual characteristics of the convicted person. However, Rosecrance questions whether probation agencies can really provide individualized justice as they claim to do.*

The Justice Department estimates that over one million probation presentence reports are submitted annually to criminal courts in the United States (Allen and Simonsen 1986: 111). The role of probation officers in the presentence process has traditionally been considered important. After examining criminal courts in the United States, a panel of investigators concluded: "Probation officers are attached to most modern felony courts; presentence reports containing their recommendations are commonly provided and these recommendations are usually followed" (Blumstein, Martin, and Holt 1983). Judges view presentence reports as an integral part of sentencing, calling them "the best guide to intelligent sentencing" (Murrah 1963: 67) and "one of the most important developments in criminal law during the 20th century" (Hogarth 1971: 246).

Researchers agree that a strong correlation exists between probation recommendations (contained in presentence reports) and judicial sentencing. In a seminal study of judicial decision-making, Carter and Wilkins (1967) found 95 percent agreement between probation recommendation and sentence disposition when the officer recommended probation and 88 percent agreement when the officer opposed probation. Hagan (1975), after controlling for related variables, reported a direct correlation of .72 between probation recommendation and sentencing. Walsh (1985) found a similar correlation of .807.

Although there is no controversy about the correlation between probation recommendation and judicial outcome, scholars disagree as to the actual influence of probation officers in the sentencing process. That is, there is no consensus regarding the importance of the presentence investigator in influencing sentencing outcomes. On the one hand, Myers (1979:

538) contends that the "important role played by probation officer recommendation argues for greater theoretical and empirical attention to these officers." Walsh (1985: 363) concludes that "judges lean heavily on the professional advice of probation." On the other hand, Kingsnorth and Rizzo (1979) report that probation recommendations have been supplanted by plea bargaining and that the probation officer is "largely superfluous." Hagan, Hewitt, and Alwin (1979), after reporting a direct correlation between recommendation and sentence, contend that the "influence of the probation officer in the presentence process is subordinate to that of the prosecutor" and that probation involvement is "often ceremonial."

My research builds on the latter perspective, and suggests that probation presentence reports do not influence judicial sentencing significantly but serve to maintain the myth that criminal courts dispense individualized justice. On the basis of an analysis of probation practices in California, I will demonstrate that the presentence report, long considered an instrument for the promotion of individualized sentencing by the court, actually de-emphasizes individual characteristics and affirms the primacy of instant offense and prior criminal record as sentencing determinants. The present study was concerned with probation in California; whether its findings can be applied to other jurisdictions is not known. California's probation system is the nation's largest, however (Petersilia, Turner, Kahan, and Peterson 1985), and the experiences of that system could prove instructive to other jurisdictions.

In many California counties (as in other jurisdictions throughout the United States) crowded court calendars, determinate sentencing guidelines, and increasingly conservative philosophies have made it difficult for judges to consider individual offenders' characteristics thoroughly. Thus judges, working in tandem with district attorneys, emphasize the legal variables of offense and criminal record at sentencing (see, e.g., Forer 1980; Lotz and Hewitt 1977; Tinker, Quiring, and Pimentel 1985). Probation officers function as employees of the court; generally they respond to judicial cues and emphasize similar variables in their presentence investigations. The probation officers' relationship to the court is ancillary; their status in relation to judges and other attorneys is subordinate. This does not mean that probation officers are completely passive; individual styles and personal philosophies influence their reports. Idiosyncratic approaches, however, are usually reserved for a few special cases. The vast majority of "normal" (Sudnow 1965) cases are handled in a manner that follows relatively uniform patterns.

Hughes' (1958) work provides a useful perspective for understanding the relationship between probation officers' status and their presentence duties. According to Hughes, occupational duties within institutions often serve to maintain symbiotic status relationships as those in higher status positions pass on lesser duties to subordinates. Other researchers (Blumberg 1967; Neubauer 1974; Rosecrance 1985) have demonstrated that although judges may pay lip-service to the significance of presentence investigations, they remain suspicious of the probation officers' lack of legal training and the hearsay nature of the reports. Walker (1985) maintains that in highly visible cases judges tend to disregard the probation reports entirely. Thus the judiciary, by delegating the collection of routine information to probation officers, reaffirms its authority and legitimacy. In this context, the responsibility for compiling presentence reports may be considered a "dirty work" assignment (Hagan 1975) that is devalued by the judiciary. Judges expect probation officers to submit noncontroversial reports that provide a facade of information, accompanied by bottom-line recommendations that do not deviate significantly from a consideration of offense and prior record. The research findings in this article will show how probation officers work to achieve this goal.

The research findings emphasize the importance of *typing* in the compilation of public documents (presentence reports). In this article, "typing" refers to "the process by which one person (the agent) arrives at a private definition of another (the target)" (Prus 1975: 81). A related activity, *designating*, occurs when "the typing agent reveals his attributions of the target to others" (Prus and Stratten 1976: 48). In the case of presentence investigations, private typings become designations when they are made part of an official court report. I will show that presentence recommendations are developed through a typing process in which individual offenders are subsumed into general dispositional categories. This process is influenced largely by probation officers' perceptions of factors that judicial figures consider appropriate; probation officers are aware that the ultimate purpose of their reports is to please the court. These perceptions are based on prior experience and are reinforced through judicial feedback.

Methods

The major sources of data used in this study were drawn from interviews with probation officers. Prior experience facilitated my ability to interpret the data. Interviews were conducted in two three-week periods during 1984 and 1985 in two medium-sized California counties. Both jurisdictions were governed by state-determinate sentencing policies; in each, the district attorney's office remained active during sentencing and generally offered specific recommendations. I did not conduct a random sample but tried instead to interview all those who compiled adult presentence reports. In the two counties in question, officers who compiled presentence reports did not supervise defendants.

Not all presentence writers agreed to talk with me; they cited busy schedules, lack of interest, or fear that I was a spy for the administration. Even so, I was able to interview 37 presentence investigators, approximately 75 percent of the total number of such employees in the two counties. The officers interviewed included eight women and 29 men with a median age of 38.5 years, whose probation experience ranged from one year to 27 years. Their educational background generally included a bachelor's degree in a liberal arts subject (four had degrees in criminal justice, one in social work). Typically the officers regarded probation work as a "job" rather than a profession. With only a few exceptions, they did not read professional journals or attend probation association conventions.

The respondents were generally supportive of my research, and frequently commented that probation work had never been described adequately. My status as a former probation officer enhanced the interview process greatly. Because I could identify with their experiences, officers were candid, and I was able to collect qualitative data that reflected accurately the participants' perspectives. During the interviews I attempted to discover how probation officers conducted their presentence investigations. I wanted to know when a sentencing recommendation was decided, to ascertain which variables influenced a sentencing recommendation decision, and to learn how probation officers defined their role in the sentencing process.

Although the interviews were informal, I asked each of the probation officers the following questions:

1. What steps do you take in compiling a presentence report?
2. What is the first thing you do upon receiving a referral?
3. What do you learn from interviews with the defendant?
4. Which part of the process (in your opinion) is the most important?
5. Who reads your reports?
6. Which part of the report do the judges feel is most important?
7. How do your reports influence the judge?
8. What feedback do you get from the judge, the district attorney, the defense attorney, the defendant, your supervisor?

In addition to interviewing probation officers, I questioned six probation supervisors and seven judges on their views about how presentence reports were conducted.

Findings

In the great majority of presentence investigations, the variables of present offense and prior criminal record determine the probation officer's final sentencing recommendation. The influence of these variables is so dominant that other considerations have minimal influence on probation recommendations. The chief rationale for this approach is "That's the way the judges want it." There are other styles of investigation; some officers attempt to consider factors in the defendant's social history, to reserve sentencing judgment until their investigation is complete, or to interject personal opinions. Elsewhere (Rosecrance 1987), I have developed a typology of presentence investigators which describes individual styles; these types include self-explanatory categories such as hardliners, bleeding-heart liberals, and team players as well as mossbacks (those who are merely putting in their time) and mavericks (those who strive continually for independence).

All types of probation officers, however, seek to develop credibility with the court. Such reputation building is similar to that reported by McCleary (1978) in his study of parole officers. In order to develop rapport with the court, probation officers must submit reports that facilitate a smooth work flow. Probation officers assume that in the great majority of cases they can accomplish this goal by emphasizing offense and criminal record. Once the officers have established reputations as "producers," they have "earned" the right to some degree of discretion in their reporting. One investigation officer described this process succinctly: "When you've paid your dues, you're allowed some slack." Such discretion, however, is limited to a minority of cases, and in these "deviant" cases probation officers frequently allow social variables to influence their recommendation. In one report an experienced officer recommended probation for a convicted felon with a long prior record because the defendant's father agreed to pay for an intensive drug treatment program. In another case a probation officer decided that a first-time shoplifter had a "very bad attitude" and therefore recommended a stiff jail sentence rather than probation. Although these variations from normal procedure are interesting and important, they should not detract from our examination of an investigation process that is used in most cases.

On the basis of the research data, I found that the following patterns occur with sufficient regularity to be considered "typical." After considering offense and criminal record, probation officers place defendants into categories that represent the eventual court recommendation. This typing process occurs early in the course of presentence inquiry; the balance of the investigation is used to reaffirm the private typings that will later become official designations. In order to clarify the decision-making processes used by probation officers I will delineate the three stages in a presentence investigation: (1) typing the defendant, (2) gathering further information, and (3) filing the report.

Typing the Defendant

A presentence investigation is initiated when the court orders the probation department to prepare a report on a criminal defendant. Usually the initial court referral contains such information as police reports, charges against the defendant, court proceedings, plea bargaining agreements (if any), offenses in which the defendant has pleaded or has been found guilty, and the defendant's prior criminal record. Probation officers regard such information as relatively unambiguous and as part of the "official" record. This comment by a presentence investigator reflects the probation officer's perspective on the court referral:

> I consider the information in the court referral hard data. It tells me what I need to know about a case, without a lot of bullshit. I mean the guy has pled guilty to a certain offense—he can't get out of that. He has such and such a prior record—there's no changing that. So much of the stuff we put in these reports is subjective and open to interpretation. It's good to have some solid information.

Armed with information in the court referral, probation officers begin to type the defendants assigned for presentence investigation. Defendants are classified into general types based on possible sentence recommendations; a probation officer's statement indicates that this process begins early in a presentence investigation.

> Bottom line; it's the sentence recommendation that's important. That's what the judges and everybody wants to see. I start thinking about the recommendation as soon as I pick up the court referral. Why wait? The basic facts aren't going to change. Oh, I know some POs will tell you they weigh all the facts before coming up with a recommendation. But that's propaganda—we all start thinking recommendation right from the get-go.

At this stage in the investigation the factors known to probation officers are mainly legally relevant variables. The defendant's unique characteristics and special circumstances are generally unknown at this time. Although probation officers may know the offender's age, sex, and race, the relationship of these variables to the case is not yet apparent.

These initial typings are private definitions (Prus 1975) based on the officer's experience and knowledge of the court system. On occasion, officers discuss the case informally with their colleagues or supervisors when they are not sure of a particular typing. Until the report is complete, their typing remains a private designation. In most cases the probation officers type defendants by considering the known and relatively irrefutable variables of offense and prior record. Probation officers are convinced that judges and district attorneys are most concerned with that part of their reports. I heard the following comment (or versions thereof) on many occasions: "Judges read the offense section, glance at the prior record, and then flip to the back and see what we recommend." Officers indicated that during informal discussions with judges it was made clear that offense and prior record are the determinants of sentencing in most cases. In some instances judges consider extralegal variables, but the officers indicated that this occurs only in "unusual" cases with "special" circumstances. One such case involved a probation grant for a woman who killed her husband after she had been a victim of spouse battering.

Probation investigators are in regular contact with district attorneys, and frequently discuss their investigations with them. In addition, district attorneys seem to have no compunction about calling the probation administration to complain about what they consider an inappropriate recommendation. Investigators agreed unanimously that district attorneys typically dismiss a defendant's social history as "immaterial" and want probation officers to stick to the legal facts.

Using offense and prior record as criteria, probation officers place defendants into dispositional (based on recommendation) types. In describing these types I have retained the terms used by probation officers themselves in the typing process. The following typology is community (rather than researcher) designated (Emerson 1981; Spradley 1970): (1) deal case, (2) diversion case, (3) joint case, (4) probation case with some jail time, (5) straight probation case. Within each of these dispositional types, probation officers designate the severity of punishment by labeling the case either lightweight or heavy-duty.

A designation of "lightweight" means that the defendant will be accorded some measure of leniency because the offense was minor, because the offender had no prior criminal record, or because the criminal activity (regardless of the penal code violation) was relatively innocuous. Heavy-duty cases receive more severe penalties because the offense, the offender, or the circumstances of the offense are deemed particularly serious. Diversion and straight probation types are generally considered lightweight, while the majority of joint cases are considered heavy-duty. Cases involving personal violence are invariably designated as heavy-duty. Most misdemeanor cases in which the defendant has no prior criminal record or a relatively minor record are termed lightweight. If the defendant has an extensive criminal record, however, even misdemeanor cases can call for stiff penalties; therefore such cases are considered heavy-duty. Certain felony cases may be regarded as lightweight if there was no violence, if the victim's loss was minimal, or if the defendant had no prior convictions. On occasion, even an offense like armed robbery may be considered lightweight. The following example (taken from an actual report) is one such instance: a first-time offender with a simulated gun held up a Seven-Eleven store and then returned to the scene, gave back the money, and asked the store employees to call the police.

The typings are general recommendations; specifics such as terms and conditions of probation or diversion and length of incarceration are worked out later in the investigation. The following discussion will clarify some of the criteria for arriving at a typing.

Deal cases involve situations in which a plea bargain exists. In California, many plea bargains specify specific sentencing stipulations; probation officers rarely recommend dispositions contrary to those stipulated in plea bargaining agreements. Although probation officers allegedly are free to recommend a sentence different from that contained in the plea bargain, they have learned that such an action is unrealistic (and often counterproductive to their own interests) because judges inevitably uphold the primacy of sentence agreements. The following observation represents the probation officers' view of plea bargaining deals:

> It's stupid to try and bust a deal. What's the percentage? Who needs the hassle? The judge always honors the deal—after all, he was part of it. Everyone, including the defendant, has already agreed. It's all nice and neat, all wrapped up. We are supposed to rubber-stamp the package—and we do. Everyone is better off that way.

Diversion cases typically involve relatively minor offenses committed by those with no prior record, and are considered "a snap" by probation officers. In most cases, those referred for diversion have been screened already by the district attorney's office; the probation investigator merely agrees that they are eligible and therefore should be granted diversionary relief (and eventual dismissal of charges). In rare instances when there has been an oversight and the defendant is ineligible (because of prior criminal convictions), the probation officer informs the court, and criminal proceedings are resumed. Either situation involves minimal decision-making by probation officers about what disposition to recommend. Presentence investigators approach diversion cases in a perfunctory, almost mechanical manner.

The last three typings generally refer to cases in which the sentencing recommendations are ambiguous and some decision-making is required of probation officers. These types represent the major consequences of criminal sentencing; incarceration, and/ or probation. Those categorized as joint (prison) cases are denied probation; instead the investigator recommends an appropriate prison sentence. In certain instances the nature of the offense (e.g., rape, murder, or arson) renders defendants legally ineligible for probation. In other situations, the defendant's prior record (especially felony convictions) makes it impossible to grant probation (see, e.g., Neubauer 1974: 240). In many cases the length of prison sentences has been set by legal statute and can be increased or decreased only marginally (depending on the aggravating or mitigating circumstances of the case).

In California, the majority of defendants sentenced to prison receive a middle term (between minimum and maximum); the length of time varies with the offense. Those cases that fall outside the middle term usually do so for reasons related to the offense (e.g., using a weapon) or to the criminal record (prior felony convictions or, conversely, no prior criminal record). Those typed originally as joint cases are treated differently from other probation applicants: concerns with rehabilitation or with the defendant's life situation are no longer relevant, and proper punishment becomes the focal point of inquiry. This perspective was described as follows by a probation officer respondent: "Once I know so-and-so is a heavy-duty joint case I don't think in terms of rehabilitation or social planning. It becomes a matter of how long to salt the sucker away, and that's covered by the code."

For those who are typed as probation cases, the issue for the investigator becomes whether to recommend some time in jail as a condition of probation. This decision is made with reference to whether the case is lightweight or heavy-duty. Straight probation is usually reserved for those convicted of relatively innocuous offenses or for those without a prior criminal record (first-timers). Some probation officers admitted candidly that all things being equal, middle-class defendants are more likely than other social classes to receive straight probation. The split sentence (probation and jail time) has become popular and is a consideration in most misdemeanor and felony cases, especially when the defendant has a prior criminal record. In addition, there is a feeling that drug offenders should receive a jail sentence as part of probation to deter them from future drug use.

Once a probation officer has decided that "some jail time is in order," the ultimate recommendation includes that condition. Although the actual amount of time is frequently determined late in the case, the probation officer's opinion that a jail sentence should be imposed remains constant. The following comment typifies the sentiments of probation officers whom I have observed and also illustrates the imprecision of recommending a period of time in custody:

> It's not hard to figure out who needs some jail. The referral sheet can tell you that. What's hard to know is exactly how much time. Ninety days or six months—who knows what's fair? We put down some number but it is usually an arbitrary figure. No one has come up with a chart that correlates rehabilitation with jail time.

Compiling Further Information

Once an initial typing has been completed, the next investigative stage involves collecting further information about the defendant. During this stage most of the data to be collected consist of extralegal considerations. The defendant is interviewed and his or her social history is delineated. Probation officers frequently contact collateral sources such as school officials, victims, doctors, counselors, and relatives to learn more about the defendant's individual circumstances. This aspect of the presentence investigation involves considerable time and effort on the part of probation officers. Such information is gathered primarily to legitimate earlier probation officer typings or to satisfy judicial requirements; recommendations are seldom changed during this stage. A similar pattern was described by a presentence investigator:

> Interviewing these defendants and working up a social history takes time. In most cases it's really unnecessary since I've already decided what I am going to do. We all know that a recommendation

is governed by the offense and prior record. All the rest is just stuffing to fill out the court report, to make the judge look like he's got all the facts.

Presentence interviews with defendants (a required part of the investigation) are frequently routine interactions that were described by a probation officer as "anticlimactic." These interviews are invariably conducted in settings familiar to probation officers, such as jail interviewing rooms or probation department offices. Because the participants lack trust in each other, discussions are rarely candid and open. Probation officers are afraid of being conned or manipulated because they assume that defendants "will say anything to save themselves." Defendants are trying to present themselves in a favorable light and are wary of divulging any information that may be used against them.

It is assumed implicitly in the interview process that probation officers act as interrogators and defendants as respondents. Because presentence investigators select the questions, they control the course of the interview and elicit the kinds of responses that serve to substantiate their original defendant typings. A probationer described his presentence interview to me as follows:

> I knew what the P.O. wanted me to say. She had me pegged as a nice middle-class kid who had fallen in with a bad crowd. So that's how I came off. I was contrite, a real boy scout who had learned his lesson. What an acting job! I figured if I didn't act up I'd get probation.

On occasion, prospective probationers refuse to go along with structured presentence interviews. Some offenders either attempt to control the interview or are openly hostile to probation officers. Defendants who try to dominate interviews can often be dissuaded by reminders such as "I don't think you really appreciate the seriousness of your situation" or "I'm the one who asks the questions here." Some defendants, however, show blatant disrespect for the court process by flaunting a disregard for possible sanctions.

Most probation officers have interviewed some defendants who simply don't seem to care what happens to them. A defendant once informed an investigation officer: "I don't give a fuck what you motherfuckers try and do to me. I'm going to do what I fuckin' well please. Take your probation and stick it." Another defendant told her probation officer: "I'm going to shoot up every chance I get. I need my fix more than I need probation." Probation officers categorize belligerent defendants and those unwilling to "play the probation game" as dangerous or irrational (see, e.g., McCleary 1978). Frequently in these situations the investigator's initial typing is no longer valid, and probation will either be denied or structured stringently. Most interviews, however, proceed in a predictable manner as probation officers collect information that will be included in the section of the report termed "defendant's statement."

Although some defendants submit written comments, most of their statements are actually formulated by the probation officer. In a sociological sense, the defendant's statement may be considered an "account" (Scott and Lyman 1968). While conducting presentence interviews, probation officers typically attempt to shape the defendant's account to fit their own preconceived typing. Many probation officers believe that the defendant's attitude toward the offense and toward the future prospects for leading a law-abiding life are the most important parts of the statement. In most presentence investigations the probation investigator identifies and interprets the defendant's subjective attitudes and then incorporates them into the report. Using this procedure, probation officers look for and report attitudes that "logically fit" with their final sentencing recommendation (see, e.g., Davis 1983).

Defendants who have been typed as prison cases are typically portrayed as holding socially unacceptable attitudes about their criminal actions and unrealistic or negative attitudes about future prospects for living an upright life. Conversely, those who have been typed as probation material are described as having acceptable attitudes, such as contriteness about the present offense and optimism about their ability to lead a crime-free life. The structuring of accounts about defendant attitudes was described by a presentence investigator in the following manner:

> When P.O.s talk about the defendant's attitude we really mean how that attitude relates to the case. Naturally I'm not going to write about what a wonderful attitude the guy has—how sincere he seems—and then recommend sending him to the joint. That wouldn't make sense. The judges want consistency. If a guy has a shitty attitude but is going to get probation anyway, there's no percentage in playing up his attitude problem.

In most cases the presentence interview is the only contact between the investigating officer and the defendant. The brevity of this contact and the lack of post-report interaction foster a legalistic perspective. Investigators are concerned mainly with "getting the case through court" rather than with special problems related to supervising probationers on a long-term basis. One-time-only interviews rarely allow probation officers to become emotionally involved with their cases; the personal and individual aspects of the defendant's personality are generally not manifested during a half-hour presentence interview. For many probation officers the emotional distance from offenders is one of the benefits of working in presentence units. Such an opinion was expressed by an investigation officer: "I really like the one-shot-only part of this job. I don't have time to get caught up with the clients. I can deal with facts and not worry about individual personalities."

The probation officer has wide discretion in the type of collateral information that is collected from sources other than the defendant or the official record. Although a defendant's social history must be outlined in the presentence report, the supplementation of that history is left to individual investigators. There are few established guidelines for the investigating officer to follow, except that the psychiatric or psychological reports should be submitted when there is compelling evidence that the offender is mentally disturbed. Informal guidelines, however, specify that in misdemeanor cases reports should be shorter and more concise than in felony cases. The officers indicated that reports for municipal court (all misdemeanor cases) should range from four to six pages in length, while superior court reports (felony cases) were expected to be six to nine pages long. In controversial cases (to which only the most experienced officers are assigned) presentence reports are expected to be longer and to include considerable social data. Reports in these cases have been as long as 30 pages.

Although probation officers learn what general types of information to include through experience and feedback from judges and supervisors, they are allowed considerable leeway in deciding exactly what to put in their reports (outside of the offense and prior record sections). Because investigators decide what collateral sources are germane to the case, they tend to include information that will reflect favorably on their sentencing recommendation. In this context the observation of one probation officer is understandable: "I pick from the mass of possible sources just which ones to put in the report. Do you think I'm going to pick people who make my recommendation look weak? No way!"

Filing the Report

The final stage in the investigation includes dictating the report, having it approved by a probation supervisor, and appearing in court. All three of these activities serve to reinforce the importance of prior record and offense in sentencing recommendations. At the time of dictation, probation officers determine what to include in the report and how to phrase their remarks. For the first time in the investigation, they receive formal feedback from official sources. Presentence reports are read by three groups important to the probation officers: probation supervisors, district attorneys, and judges. Probation officers recognize that for varying reasons, all these groups emphasize the legally relevant variables of offense and prior criminal record when considering an appropriate sentencing recommendation. Such considerations reaffirm the probation officer's initial private typing.

A probation investigator described this process:

> After I've talked to the defendants I think maybe some of them deserve to get special consideration. But when I remember who's going to look at the reports. My supervisor, the DA, the judge; they don't care about all the personal details. When all is said and done, what's really important to them is the offense and the defendant's prior record. I know that stuff from the start. It makes me wonder why we have to jack ourselves around to do long reports.

Probation officers assume that their credibility as presentence investigators will be enhanced if their sentencing recommendations meet with the approval of probation supervisors, district attorneys, and judges. On the other hand, officers whose recommendations are consistently "out of line" are subject to censure or transfer, or they find themselves engaged in "running battles" (Shover 1974: 357) with court officials. During the last stage of the investigation probation officers must consider how to ensure that their reports will go through court without "undue personal hassle." Most investigation officers have learned that presentence recommendations based on a consideration of prior record and offense can achieve that goal.

Although occupational self-interest is an important component in deciding how to conduct a presentence investigation, other factors are also involved. Many probation officers agree with the idea of using legally relevant variables as determinants of recommendations. These officers embrace the retributive value of this concept and see it as an equitable method for framing their investigation. Other officers reported that probation officers' discretion had been "short-circuited" by determinate sentencing guidelines and that they were reduced to "merely going through the motions" in conducting their investigations. Still other officers view the use of legal variables to structure recommendations as an acceptable bureaucratic short cut to compensate partially for large case assignments. One probation officer stated, "If the department wants us to keep pumping out presentence reports we can't consider social factors—we just don't have time." Although probation officers are influenced by various dynamics, there seems little doubt that in California the social history which was once considered the "heart and soul" of presentence probation reports (Reckless 1967: 673) has been largely devalued.

Summary and Conclusions

In this study I provide a description and analysis of the processes used by probation investigators in preparing presentence reports. The research findings based on interview data indicate that probation officers tend to de-emphasize individual defendants' characteristics and that their probation recommendations are not influenced directly by factors such as sex, age, race, socioeconomic status, or work record. Instead, probation officers emphasize the variables of instant offense and prior criminal record. The finding that offense and prior record are the main considerations of probation officers with regard to sentence recommendations agrees with a substantial body of research (Bankston 1983; Carter and Wilkins 1967; Dawson 1969; Lotz and Hewitt 1977; Robinson, Carter, and Wahl 1969; Wallace 1974; Walsh 1985).

My particular contribution has been to supply the ethnographic observations and the data that explain this phenomenon. I have identified the process whereby offense and prior record come to occupy the central role in decision-making by probation officers. This identification underscores the significance of private typings in determining official designations. An analysis of probation practices suggests that the function of the presentence investigation is more ceremonial then instrumental (Hagan 1985).

I show that early in the investigation probation officers, using offense and prior record as guidelines, classify defendants into types; when the typing process is complete, probation officers have essentially decided on the sentence recommendation that will be recorded later in their official designation. The subsequent course of investigations is determined largely by this initial private typing. Further data collection is influenced by a sentence recommendation that has already been firmly established. This finding answers affirmatively the research question posed by Carter (1967: 211):

> Do probation officers, after "deciding" on a recommendation early in the presentence investigation, seek further information which justifies the decision, rather than information which might lead to modification or rejection of that recommendation?

The type of information and observation contained in the final presentence report is generated to support the original recommendation decision. Probation officers do not regard defendant typings as tentative hypotheses to be disproved through inquiry but rather as firm conclusions to be justified in the body of the report.

Although the presentence interview has been considered an important part of the investigation (Spencer 1983), I demonstrate that it does not significantly alter probation officers' perceptions. In most cases probation officers dominate presentence interviews; interaction between the participants is guarded. The nature of interviews between defendants and probation officers is important in itself; further research is needed to identify the dynamics that prevail in these interactions.

Attitudes attributed to defendants are often structured by probation officers to reaffirm the recommendation already formulated. The defendant's social history, long considered an integral part of the presentence report, in reality has little bearing on sentencing considerations. In most cases the presentence is no longer a vehicle for social inquiry but rather a typing process which considers mainly the defendant's prior criminal record and the seriousness of the criminal offense. Private attorneys in growing numbers have become disenchanted with the quality of probation investigations and have commissioned presentence probation reports privately (Rodgers, Gitchoff, and Paur 1984). At present, however, such a practice is generally available only for wealthy defendants.

The presentence process that I have described is used in the great majority of cases; it is the "normal" procedure. Even so, probation officers are not entirely passive actors in this process. On occasion they will give serious consideration to social variables in arriving at a sentencing recommendation. In special circumstances officers will allow individual defendants' characteristics to influence their report. In addition, probation officers who have developed credibility with the court are allowed some discretion in compiling presentence reports. This discretion is not unlimited, however; it is based on a prior record of producing reports that meet the court's approval, and is contingent on continuing to do so. A presentence writer said, "You can only afford to go to bat for defendants in a few select cases; if you try to do it too much, you get a reputation as being 'out of step.'"

This research raises the issue of probation officers' autonomy. Although I depict presentence investigators as having limited autonomy, other researchers (Hagan 1975; Myers 1979; Walsh 1985) contend that probation officers have considerable leeway in recommendation. This contradictory evidence may be explained in large part by the type of sentencing structure, the professionalism of probation workers, and the role of the district attorney at sentencing. Walsh's study (1985), for example, which views probation officers as important actors in the presentence process, was conducted in a jurisdiction with indeterminate sentencing, where the probation officers demonstrated a high degree of professionalism and the prosecutors "rarely made sentencing recommendations." A very different situation existed in the California counties that I studied: determinate sentencing was enforced, probation officers were not organized professionally, and the district attorneys routinely made specific court recommendations. It seems apparent that probation officers' autonomy must be considered with reference to judicial jurisdiction.

In view of the primacy of offense and prior record in sentencing considerations, the efficacy of current presentence investigation practices is doubtful. It seems ineffective and wasteful to continue to collect a mass of social data of uncertain relevance. Yet an analysis of courtroom culture suggests that the presentence investigation helps maintain judicial mythology as well as probation officer legitimacy. Although judges generally do not have the time or the inclination to consider individual variables thoroughly, the performance of a presentence investigation perpetuates the myth of individualized sentences. Including a presentence report in the court file gives the appearance of individualization without influencing sentencing practices significantly.

Even in a state like California, where determinate sentencing has allegedly replaced individualized justice, the judicial system feels obligated to maintain the appearance of individualization. After observing the court system in California for several years, I am convinced that a major reason for maintaining such a practice is to make it easier for criminal defendants to accept their sentences. The presentence report allows defendants to feel that their case has at least received a considered decision. One judge admitted candidly that the "real purpose" of the presentence investigation was to convince defendants that they were not getting "the fast shuffle." He observed further that if defendants were sentenced without such investigations, many would complain and would file "endless appeals" over what seems to them a hasty sentencing decision. Even though judges typically consider only offense and prior record in a sentencing decision, they want defendants to believe that their cases are being judged individually. The presentence investigation allows this assumption to be maintained. In addition, some judges use the probation officer's report as an excuse for a particular type of sentence. In some instances they deny responsibility for the sentence, implying that their "hands were tied" by the recommendation. Thus judges are taken "off the hook" for meting out an unpopular sentence. Further research is needed to substantiate the significance of these latent functions of the presentence investigation.

The presentence report is a major component in the legitimacy of the probation movement; several factors support the probation officers' stake in maintaining their role in these investigations. Historically, probation has been wedded to the concept of individualized treatment. In theory, the presentence report is suited ideally to reporting on defendants' individual circumstances. From a historical perspective (Rothman 1980), this ideal has always been more symbolic than substantive, but if the legitimacy of the presentence report is questioned, so then is the entire purpose of probation.

Regardless of its usefulness (or lack of usefulness), it is doubtful that probation officials would consider the diminution or abolition of presentence reports. The number of probation workers assigned to presentence investigations is substantial, and their numbers represent an obvious source of bureaucratic power. Conducting presentence investigations allows probation officers to remain visible with the court and the public. The media often report on controversial probation cases, and presentence writers generally have more contact and more association with judges than do others in the probation department.

As ancillary court workers, probation officers are assigned the dirty work of collecting largely irrelevant data on offenders (Hagan 1975; Hughes 1958). Investigation officers have learned that emphasizing offense and prior record in their reports will enhance relationships with judges and district attorneys, as well as improve their occupational standing within probation departments. Thus the presentence investigation serves to maintain the court's claim of individualized concern while preserving the probation officer's role, although a subordinate role, in the court system.

The myth of individualization serves various functions, but it also raises serious questions. In an era of severe budget restrictions (Schumacher 1985), should scarce resources be allocated to compiling predictable presentence reports of dubious value? If social variables are considered in only a few cases, should courts continue routinely to require presentence reports in all felony matters (as is the practice in California)? In summary, we should address the issue of whether the criminal justice system can afford the ceremony of a probation presentence investigation.

Critical Thinking

The stereotyping of convicted offenders is in direct contrast to our judicial system's claim that each person found guilty of a criminal offense has individual characteristics taken into consideration during the sentencing process. In reality, however, the vast majority of presentence investigative reports for sentencing recommendations only perpetuate this illusion when the presentence investigation is actually more ceremonial than instrumental. This raises the question: should justice be more individualized? Regardless of your answer to this first question, why do you think this "myth" of individualized justice is maintained?

References

Allen, Harry E. and Clifford E. Simonsen (1986) *Corrections in America*. New York: Macmillan.

Bankston, William B. (1983) "Legal and Extralegal Offender Traits and Decision-making in the Criminal Justice System." *Sociological Spectrum* 3: 1–18.

Blumberg, Abraham (1967) *Criminal Justice*. Chicago, IL: Quadrangle.

Blumstein, Alfred J., S. Martin, and N. Holt (1983) *Research on Sentencing: The Search for Reform*. Washington, DC: National Academy Press.

Carter, Robert M. (1967) "The Presentence Report and The Decision-making Process." *Journal of Research in Crime and Delinquency* 4: 203–211.

Carter, Robert M. and Leslie T. Wilkins (1967) "Some Factors in Sentencing Policy." *Journal of Criminal Law, Criminology, and Police Science* 58: 503–514.

Davis, James R. (1983) "Academic and Practical Aspects of Probation: A Comparison." *Federal Probation* 47: 7–10.

Dawson, Robert (1969) *Sentencing*. Boston, MA: Little, Brown.

Emerson, Robert M. (1981) "Ethnography and Understanding Members' Worlds." In Robert M. Emerson (ed.), *Contemporary Field Research*. Boston, MA: Little, Brown, pp. 19–35.

Forer, Lois G. (1980) *Criminals and Victims*. New York: Norton.

Hagan, John (1975) "The Social and Legal Construction of Criminal Justice: A Study of the Presentence Process." *Social Problems* 22: 620–637.

Hagan, John (1977) "Criminal Justice in Rural and Urban Communities: A Study of the Bureaucratization of Justice." *Social Forces* 55: 597–612.

Hagan, John (1985) *Modern Criminology: Crime, Criminal Behavior, and Its Control.* New York: McGraw-Hill.

Hagan, John, John Hewitt, and Duane Alwin (1979) "Ceremonial Justice: Crime and Punishment in a Loosely Coupled System." *Social Forces* 58: 506–525.

Hogarth, John (1971) *Sentencing As a Human Process.* Toronto: University of Toronto Press.

Hughes, Everett C. (1958) *Men and Their Work.* New York: Free Press.

Kingsnorth, Rodney and Louis Rizzo (1979) "Decision-making in the Criminal Courts: Continuities and Discontinuities." *Criminology* 17: 3–14.

Lotz, Ray and John Hewitt (1977) "The Influence of Legally Irrelevant Factors on Felony Sentencing." *Sociological Inquiry* 47: 39–48.

McCleary, Richard (1978) *Dangerous Men.* Beverly Hills, CA: Sage.

Murrah, A. (1963) "Prison or Probation?" In B. Kay and C. Vedder (eds), *Probation and Parole.* Springfield, IL: Charles C. Thomas, pp. 63–78.

Myers, Martha A. (1979) "Offended Parties and Official Reactions: Victims and the Sentencing of Criminal Defendants." *Sociological Quarterly* 20: 529–546.

Neubauer, David (1974) *Criminal Justice in Middle America.* Morristown, NJ: General Learning.

Petersilia, Joan, Susan Turner, James Kahan, and Joyce Peterson (1985) "Executive Summary of Rand's Study, Granting Felons Probation." *Crime and Delinquency* 31: 379–392.

Prus, Robert (1975) "Labeling Theory: A Statement on Typing." *Sociological Focus* 8: 79–96.

Prus, Robert and John Stratten (1976) "Factors in the Decision-making of North Carolina Probation Officers." *Federal Probation* 40: 48–53.

Reckless, Walter C. (1967) *The Crime Problem.* New York: Appleton.

Robinson, James, Robert Carter, and A. Wahl (1969) *The San Francisco Project.* Berkeley: University of California School of Criminology.

Rodgers, T.A., G.T. Gitchoff, and I. Paur (1984) "The Privately Commissioned Presentence Report." In Robert M. Carter, Daniel Glaser, and Leslie T. Wilkins (eds), *Probation, Parole, and Community Corrections.* New York: Wiley, pp. 21–30.

Rosecrance, John (1985) "The Probation Officers' Search for Credibility: Ball Park Recommendations." *Crime and Delinquency* 31: 539–554.

Rosecrance, John (1987) "A Typology of Presentence Probation Investigators." *International Journal of Offender Therapy and Comparative Criminology* 31: 163–177.

Rothman, David (1980) *Conscience and Convenience: The Asylum and Its Alternatives in Progressive America.* Boston, MA: Little, Brown.

Schumacher, Michael A. (1985) "Implementation of a Client Classification and Case Management System: A Practitioner's View." *Crime and Delinquency* 31: 445–455.

Scott, Marvin and Stanford Lyman (1968) "Accounts." *American Sociological Review* 33: 46–62.

Shover, Neal (1974) "Experts and Diagnosis in Correctional Agencies." *Crime and Delinquency* 20: 347–358.

Spencer, Jack W. (1983) "Accounts, Attitudes and Solutions: Probation Officer–Defendant Negotiations of Subjective Orientations." *Social Problems* 30: 570–581.

Spradley, Joseph P. (1970) *You Owe Yourself a Drunk: An Ethnography of Urban Nomads.* Boston, MA: Little, Brown.

Sudnow, David (1965) "Normal Crimes: Sociological Features of the Penal Code." *Social Problems* 12: 255–276.

Tinker, John N., John Quiring, and Yvonne Pimentel (1985) "Ethnic Bias in California Courts: A Case Study of Chicano and Anglo Felony Defendants." *Sociological Inquiry* 55: 83–96.

Walker, Samuel (1985) *Sense and Nonsense About Crime.* Monterey, CA: Brooks/Cole.

Wallace, John (1974) "Probation Administration." In Daniel Glaser (ed.), *Handbook of Criminology.* Chicago, IL: Rand-McNally, pp. 940–970.

Walsh, Anthony (1985) "The Role of the Probation Officer in the Sentencing Process." *Criminal Justice and Behavior* 12: 289–303.

B Outsiders

16

Preparing to Testify: Rape Survivors Negotiating the Criminal Justice Process

Amanda Konradi

Abstract: *Amanda Konradi explores the strategies that rape survivors undertake in prepara-tion for court appearances and testimonies. She suggests that survivors' perceptions and expectations about various facets of the criminal justice process affect how victims prepare for the courtroom. Rape survivors typically employ one of six techniques when preparing for the courtroom. These techniques include adjusting their appearance to present an image of a respectable or moral woman, rehearsing testimonies in an attempt to sway judges, recruiting individuals to serve as credible witnesses or to provide emotional support, and educating themselves about their legal situation to strengthen their case. Overall, Konradi's findings indicate that many rape survivors become actively involved in the legal processes surrounding their cases.*

In trials and a variety of pretrial court events, including bond hearings, preliminary hear-ings, and motions, rape survivors come into the presence of their assailants and respond to direct and cross-examination about the details of the assaults perpetrated against them. With few exceptions, the prosecution of rape would not be possible without the participa-tion of survivors who are willing to attend court to testify. In spite of research which indi-cates that women are not passive in the face of rape attempts (Bart and O'Brien 1985; Caignon and Groves 1987; Kleck and Sayles 1990) and selectively bring assaults to the attention of the legal system (Greenberg and Ruback 1992; Williams 1984), rape survivors' active involvement in the process of prosecuting their assailants has not been extensively examined.

This article explores what rape survivors report they have done to prepare themselves for upcoming court appearances. It is explicitly an effort to analytically separate the victimization of rape (the act of sexual assault) from women's responses to it. I examine how rape survivors approach the legal process as an instrument, as a means to accomplish justice, and how they take on and shape the organizational role of victim-witness available to them. This article considers the following questions: How do survivors' knowledge and beliefs about the law and the legal process shape the strategies they use to prepare for court appearances? How do the cultural representations of rape with which survivors are familiar shape their self-preparation? How do survivors, as socially situated persons with ethnicity, age, class background, education level, friends, and families, draw on their various resources to negotiate the legal process? What other factors, including preparation received from prosecutors, shape survivors' preparation efforts?

I have chosen to focus on preparation because it falls between studies on reporting and those on courtroom appearances. It is also behavior that takes place out of the physical space controlled by legal personnel. In addition, examining survivors' self-preparation allows me to examine their orientations to preliminary hearings, in which they are far more likely to participate than trials. Survivors' preliminary hearing performances figure importantly in district attorneys' decisions to pursue pleas or go to trial.

Rape Prosecution Research

Researchers concerned with the prosecution of rape have primarily focused on the *behavior* of legal actors. Existing studies provide compelling evidence that legal actors underenforce, rather than overenforce, rape statutes (Polk 1985). They show that, under pressure to conserve institutional resources, legal personnel rely on stereotypes in making decisions to prosecute rape and that a persistent bias remains against women whose rape experiences do not conform to the classic stranger stereotype (Martin and Powell 1994). LaFree (1989) and Kerstetter (1990) report that police officers make decisions about doing the work to bring rape cases to the attention of prosecutors based on the personal attributes of survivors and their relationships with their assailants. Similarly, studies have found that prosecutors refuse to file felony charges or pursue cases through to trial when victims know their assailants, the use or threat of force is unclear, or victims report assaults in questionable parts of town (Frohmann 1991; Stanko 1981). Furthermore, judges are found to minimize sentences when victims do not fit stereotypes (Schafran 1993).

With respect to the prosecution of rape, researchers have primarily focused on how the demands of the trial process affect rape survivors. Their research has focused primarily on the emotional and psychological impact of the common practices of legal personnel. The frequently cited chapter in Holmstrom and Burgess's (1983) book, "The Rape Victim's Reaction to Court," explicitly identifies this analytic perspective. Examining the prosecution of rape from this perspective, a number of researchers have documented that survivors are frustrated and distressed when their claims are not taken seriously by police or prosecutors as well as when they are grilled during cross-examination sequences of trials (Holmstrom and Burgess 1983; Madigan and Gambel 1989). The result of this direction in research is that rape survivors' legal experiences are represented as what happens *to* them. We know quite a lot about how legal personnel structure the survivors' legal "career," particularly the early stages, but we know little about how survivors understand the legal process and respond to its constraints.

It is no accident, I believe, that the authors investigating legal personnel and raped women's reactions to institutional treatment primarily use the term *victim* to conceptualize the women they discuss. It is a powerful term that places the responsibility for sexual assault/rape on the perpetrator and highlights the very real psychological and physical trauma that may result from a violent attack. Used with reference to the criminal justice process, *victim* can also imply an objective lack of decision-making power. Many researchers investigating women's experiences with the criminal justice process in the 1970s and early 1980s intended for their research to contribute to the reform of abusive investigative and prosecution policies and rape statutes that made prosecution difficult and painful for the women involved. Their use of *victim* was thus politically strategic. Current researchers appear to have adopted the term whether or not they share the feminist reform agenda, because its usage has become somewhat conventional. However, conceptualizing raped women as victims appears to have had a constraining effect on the scope of investigation of how rape is processed through the criminal justice system. Having assumed victimization, many researchers have apparently assumed passivity on the part of raped women.

The nature of research into the processing of rape also reflects the difficulty of obtaining relevant data about survivors. To examine rape survivors' participation in prosecution, researchers must either follow them through the justice process and contend with the lengthy time frame of cases (months or years) or find a substantial number of women (or men) who are, or have been, involved in prosecuting their assailants and are willing to talk about the matter. With the absence of a public directory of rape survivors and the confidentiality mandated of most counseling and legal agencies, it is difficult to reach potential research participants. The access Holmstrom and Burgess (1983) gained in 1972, to the Boston hospital in which they began their study of the institutional processing of rape victims, could be very difficult to obtain in the present! In addition, given the low percentage of cases that get processed through to trial, it is also difficult to find rape survivors with courtroom experience. Polk (1985) estimated that fewer than 15 percent of cases ever reach the court phase. Researching the processing of rape from the standpoint of rape survivors can be very time-consuming. By comparison, the schedules of police and prosecutors are much more predictable, and their offices produce mountains of paperwork that may be used for triangulation.

Methods

Data for this study were collected through intensive *life history* interviews with 32 women who survived rape and participated in the prosecution of their assailants to the point of testifying in court. Given the lack of a directory of rape survivors and the restrictions on institutional access coupled with my concerns over potentially producing a homogeneous sample by recruiting through therapists or advertising alone, I elected to recruit participants in a variety of ways.

Getting information about the study to women was one part of the recruitment problem. The other challenge was to encourage women with a range of experiences to feel that they could speak to me about a stigmatizing experience. One of my early methodological decisions was to use my own experience with prosecuting my rapists as the basis of recruitment (Konradi 1993).

I conducted face-to-face and telephone interviews with survivors. Survivors who were currently involved in the prosecution of their assailants were interviewed several times. The interviews feature survivors' recollections of their interactions and behavior; thus, save for my observations, I do not have an "objective" record of interaction between survivors and legal actors. However, I gathered information that is not accessible through direct observation—reports of survivors' telephone conversations, reports of their behavior out of court, and reports of their thoughts off and on the witness stand. I also observed 12 court events and interviewed district attorneys and ancillary personnel to provide a context for my analysis.

The methods of recruitment I used were intended to produce a diversity of women in the study rather than to obtain a sample that would reflect the distribution of attributes that might be found among rape survivors involved in prosecuting their assailants in the general population. I was not successful in obtaining a racially diverse sample: 90 percent of the sample was white. Thus, the findings discussed below may omit culturally specific modes of preparation. I was more successful in obtaining socio-economic diversity: 37 percent were employed in blue- or pink-collar work, 27 percent were professionals, and three participants were unemployed high school students. A total of 63 percent had more than a high school education, and 23 percent of those had completed college. The participants ranged in age from 16 to older than 50. This is consistent with the fact that women of all ages participate in prosecution. Of the survivors, 59 percent did not know their assailants, 16 percent were raped by past or present intimates, and 25 percent were raped by other nonintimates whom they knew. Of the rapes, 59 percent were intraracial; 41 percent were interracial. In comparison to what is known about the characteristics of rapes that occur, this sample has an overrepresentation of interracial rapes and stranger rapes. In comparison to the characteristics of cases that get prosecuted, the study percentages are more consistent and possibly overrepresent nonstranger rapes. According to the sampling frame, all of the 32 women in the study were English speakers and were raped vaginally and/or orally and/or rectally. I have used pseudonyms throughout this article to guarantee the confidentiality promised the participants.

Findings

In the interviews, I noted six kinds of purposeful activities that the survivors engaged in to prepare for their time on the witness stand: appearance work, rehearsal, emotion work, team building, role research, and case enhancement. In the remainder of this article, I will describe these modes of preparation and discuss why and how survivors believed that such activities would help them meet the demands of the courtroom.

Appearance Work

While all survivors must dress in the morning before they go to hearings for probable cause and trials, slightly more than half of the survivors in this sample described purposefully creating an image through their clothing and makeup. Survivors sought to dress in ways that demonstrated respect for the court and in ways that conformed with visual standards separating real victims from women "who asked for it." Survivors' criteria were consistent with classic cultural stereotypes of rape. I use the term *appearance work* (Goffman 1959) to refer to survivors' intentional efforts to meet the stereotypic expectations they perceived jurors and judges to have.

It is easy to presume that this type of preparation is always carried out. However, the comments made by Cindy, a white 37-year-old pink-collar worker, about knowing what to wear and her serious concern about the apparel of the "co-victim" in her case underscore the fact that not all survivors engage in appearance work:

> No, she [the district attorney] didn't tell me what to wear, at all. You know, I mean, I knew. I knew that. I wish she had said something to the other victim. . . . They kept my case together with the attempted rape when he was caught. I wish the DA [district attorney] had said something to her and her family about how to dress in court, you know. I dressed conservatively, you know. Now she was coming in in tight pants, her brothers were there, and her brothers have long hair. Now I don't have anything against long hair, you know, but I mean, they looked like rock star wannabees, and then they got these girlfriends who look like, you know, rock star wannabees. These girlfriends that are in court with them, have like tight, short, skirts on [and] these little things that are exposing their midriffs, you know what I mean? So the jury is looking at this shit and thinking [about it] you know [laughs]. I mean, you know, that really affected things. I know it did, you know, it certainly affected the outcome [the jury was unable to reach a verdict].

While Cindy was intent on being perceived as a viable victim, the other victim-witness and her family did not seem to be concerned about the appearance-based attributions others might make.

The typical personas that survivors sought to project through appearance work were consistently conservative, businesslike, and nonsexual. Some survivors went to extra efforts to choose clothes that hid their bodies and to keep their makeup toned down. By the time Megan, an African American college student, finished dressing, only her head and hands were visible. She described her court attire as follows:

> A long, black floral dress, buttons down the front, about down to here [indicating her calf], and I wore boots. You couldn't see any of my body! [laughs] And not really, I don't usually wear makeup anyways, I just wear like a little lipstick, put my hair half up, I looked normal [laughing]

Connie and Theresa both viewed the court as business and dressed as they would for work. Theresa, a white 48-year-old woman, explained that a person who did not present herself in court in a businesslike way may not be believable:

> Well, I kind of had thought of what I wanted to wear, you know, something that was . . . something that I would normally just wear to work, you know, because I dress businesslike when I go to work

and so I thought you know, that that's the way it should be. I mean, you know, you're not gonna go to court in a miniskirt and be believable.

However, as Connie and Theresa drew upon their respective wardrobes for executive and clerical work, they appeared for their assailant's preliminary hearing in quite different attire. Connie wore a business suit, while Theresa came to court in more casual attire: a light-pink short-sleeved blouse, a pair of black crop pants sprinkled with pink flowers, and flat shoes. Thus, while these two white women of comparable age have similar perceptions of what the court requires, the way they implement their understanding reflects their class position.

As these two women's use of their work wardrobes indicate, survivors often based their court personas on an existing role and aspect of their self-conception. However, survivors chose with care the aspects of their personalities that they would reveal in court. Connie recalled consciously avoiding being the aspect of herself that she associated with backpacking, which is a dimension of her persona that would, perhaps, appear to be too self-reliant. On the other hand, Arlene, also a white middle-class woman, created a court persona that bore little resemblance to who she believed she was because she thought that court personnel might question her character. She became in appearance and manner what she hoped was the cultural embodiment of a "real rape victim":

> I dressed in a . . . in a very uncharacteristic way for me. I wore, you know, a skirt and a blouse and a jacket and hose and heels and all that stuff, I mean I looked the part that I wanted the court to think I was. . . . I have always been the kind of person that runs around in jeans and T-shirts as much as I can, and that's essentially what I was dressed in when I was raped, and I was very clear that I wanted there to be no question on the part of the court about my character, that I was going to play every game that I thought that they expected me to play, and I'm very good at that, I had been an actress for a while, and I had a good idea of how to create a . . . that kind of space for myself. . . . I did very consciously create a persona, it was not about who I was or who he was or what could have happened, it was about my objective that this fucker was going to jail, that's what was on my mind.

Most survivors' attention to their appearance involved selecting clothes from their closets that conformed with their images of victim-witnesses. However, several spent their own money and extra time to create their court image. Julianne, a white college student, described shopping for an "appropriate outfit":

> I remember when I was home I went shopping to make sure I had an appropriate outfit for court. . . . Something, um, conservative, something, um, something very presentable, um, nice, a dress, a skirt, a blazer. . . . I remember even shopping and thinking . . . I have to get clothes just to present myself, you know, um. . . . [On the day of court I] definitely wore waterproof mascara, that was like necessity item, and I had two different outfits and put them both on to see which one my parents thought was better.

Spending money to appear appropriately dressed cut across class lines. Thus, some poor and working-class women may take on a proportionally greater burden in preparing for trial than their middle- and upper-class peers.

Even in the absence of direct instruction from prosecutors, many survivors visually became "model victims" to make their cases stronger. Insofar as their actions were oriented to comply with cultural ideals of rape victims, they worked to support the prosecution effort. Other survivors reported that prosecutors led them to engage in appearance work because they told them how to dress for court. These women indicated that even when the attire requested was unpalatable to them, they followed the instructions they received. For example, 16-year-old Monica purchased a "silly dress" that the prosecutor requested she wear for her trial appearance after he decided that the dress shirt, blazer, and slacks she wore for the preliminary hearing made her look too old. Here, we see that Monica's perception of the businesslike nature of court is in contradiction with the district attorney's construction of her as the "victim" in the case.

In addition to appearing the part for others, appearance work may also make taking on the role of witness an easier task. Businesslike and modest clothing tends to restrict the wearer to businesslike and modest posture; thus, dress can be a small reminder to act the victim-witness part appropriately. Likewise, knowing that one is presenting oneself as a credible victim-witness can make it easier to put aside any doubts that one is not and to concentrate on the business of testifying.

Rehearsal

To convey their rape experiences convincingly to judges and juries, most survivors felt that they needed to give detailed accounts of their assaults. This was problematic for two reasons. For 29 percent of the survivors, the prospect of providing an adequately detailed account raised concerns about recall. They were unsure that they would be able to remember the specific details of the assault event, which usually transpired months or even years before. This made cross-examination, during which they expected to be held accountable for explaining their own as well as the assailant's actions, particularly worrisome. Other survivors were primarily concerned with adequately controlling their emotions during their potentially painful testimony. They knew that giving a detailed account would require them to get close to the experience of the rape. Many of the survivors thought such renewed closeness might bring forth strong feelings. They were anxious about the prospect of being overwhelmed with tears on the witness stand and being unable to complete their testimony. These two kinds of concerns prompted the preparation strategy of rehearsal.

Of the survivors, 25 percent reported rehearsing all or parts of their expected testimony to ensure an accurate portrayal of the assault event and to keep their emotions under control. Some survivors, like Natalie, a 26-year-old white Louisianan, prepared themselves by telling their stories to supportive friends and relatives. Unwilling to forget to include any details of her assailant's behavior, Natalie enlisted her husband to be an audience for her testimony the night before she was due in court. She explained,

> [W]hen I came home, you know, I knew that the next day that it was . . . it was my turn, it was my time, I would read over my [police] statement, and I would read over it and . . . I just wanted to know

from my own self that I was ready. Everybody kept on tellin' me that I was ready, that I was gonna be such a good witness. . . . I have to know that I'm ready and that's how I was feelin'. I had to be certain that I could get up there and say everything that happened to me and I didn't want to forget anything, um, all these little details or whatever. [The DA] said, you know, it's okay if you forget this or that or whatever, but I didn't want to, I wanted to say everything that he [her assailant] . . . that he had did to me. 'Cos I wanted to make sure that I was ready . . . I said, "Sam," my husband, "I know this is hard, but what I really need instead of just readin' my statement is to say it, to say what happened, and for you [to listen]." And he did, and um, and Sam bein' the supportive husband that he was, he did. I could tell that he didn't like it, he didn't wanna really listen to this again, um, 'cos he had just gotten finished readin' over this statement and everything after a year, when he had gone with me to [the DA's] office. And just rehashing everything over again for him was painful, but um, but he did it, he sat there and he listened to me and I got through it all and I didn't forget anything and I felt better.

Natalie learned that she could rely on her memory and describe explicitly what transpired between her assailant and herself; thus, she resolved her questions about her ability to recall:

When I went in to the courthouse Thursday, I mean I went up to [the DA], and I said, "NOW I'm ready," 'cause the day before I had told him, I'm not ready and I was scared and fallin' apart, but I told him that I was ready, I want to do it [testify] right now.

Other survivors rehearsed for their court appearances alone. One survivor who was troubled about conveying the sexual nature of her violation to a public court audience reported preparing statements. Prior to the court date, she selected the words to most comfortably describe how her assailant threatened and coerced her to orally copulate him. Alternatively, Arlene considered the account of the assault she had given police from the perspective of the defense attorney. She composed answers to the hardest questions that she could imagine him asking her, and then she practiced reciting them. On the day she went to court, she said that she knew that she would not fall apart on the stand. She recalled,

Well that thing about falling apart on the stand was [a problem]. I was very worried about it beforehand, but in the actual experience I had no question that I would do that. I had rehearsed it, I knew what I was going to say, and I had rehearsed the hard questions and how to say them. And [I] practiced it, and I knew that I wouldn't.

The last solo rehearsal effort involved visualization. To overcome her intense feelings and the tendency she had to cry when discussing the rape, one survivor explained that she would imagine herself successfully carrying out the role of witness, sitting on the witness stand testifying steadily with conviction.

Survivors who rehearsed their testimony in some fashion gained confidence that they could successfully talk about their assaults. They also entered court with a more complete sense of what they wanted to say, not just a general expectation that they would talk about the assault event. With the exception of a prosecutor's ability to object and temporarily stop interaction, survivors are alone in navigating cross-examination. One would expect that those survivors who are knowledgeable about their recall, who have identified language with which they are comfortable, and who have a clear sense of purpose would fare better in that interaction.

Emotion Work

I use the term *emotion work* to designate the efforts survivors made to produce feelings and emotional displays that they deemed appropriate to the courtroom before they entered it (Hochschild 1979, 1983). Of the survivors in this study, 29 percent recalled seeking actively to prepare themselves to achieve a courtroom demeanor that was consistent with idealized images of witnesses or victims. The feeling rules that accompanied the two ideal images and guided survivors' preparations were somewhat contradictory. The ideal witness was polite and composed, indicating honesty and an appropriate deference to the court's authority. Alternatively, the ideal victim was a woman overcome by tears brought on by recollection of the assault. Thus, while some survivors sought to repress displays of obvious anger or pain which would result in loss of emotional control or make their truthfulness suspect, others prepared themselves to lose emotional control and to cry on the stand.

In the following series of comments, Donna, a white working-class woman who went to trial twice, explains how she went about achieving different emotional states as her analysis of what was required to convince a jury changed. Prior to the first trial, Donna sought to achieve an inner calm and to preclude any show of emotion.

> DONNA: *So I had gone to one of the elders in my church and I said I want a blessing before I go to court. . . . So, um, they got all together and they gave me a blessing, and it was like the day before, and I was totally calm when I went through that first trial.*
>
> AUTHOR: *Because you thought you'd done what you could?*
>
> DONNA: *Yeah, I felt that I had done everything that I was supposed to do and I was determined I was not gonna cry.*

After the first jury was unable to reach a verdict, Donna decided to become a "real" rape victim. She chose not to receive religious solace and turned away emotional support. It had the desired effect; she fell apart on the witness stand. Her reconstruction of her thinking before the second trial follows:

> I had gone over the testimony that I knew I was gonna give, and I figured that I was . . . there was a part I was just gonna have to lose it on. And, I figured that was gonna be it and that's about the part that I did start to cry, and they called a recess and handed me some water and calmed me down, and then went on from there. But I figured that I was gonna have to, 'cos otherwise they weren't gonna believe anything. . . . Uh, CASA [a rape support service] offered to come and go with us to trial, but I said no, I didn't need anybody. I'd already made up my mind I was not gonna get a blessing this time, 'cos I was not gonna be calm, cool, and collected. If they [the jury] wanted somebody hysterical on the stand, they were gonna get one. And all I had to do was wait for [the DA] to push the right buttons 'cos I was sure he was gonna do that.

Other survivors' concerns about losing emotional control, which they believed would hamper their ability to complete their testimony in a rational, dispassionate way, led them to make pre-emptive emotive efforts. That is, they tried to work their feelings out before the court event. For example, Julianne tried to let herself cry freely as she went about her morning routine so that she might use up her tears before the preliminary hearing. In spite of her efforts to be calm, she cried through much of her testimony. However, as Hochschild (1979) has theorized emotion work, it is the effort to achieve feelings or displays of feeling that are consistent with some social ideal that is important. In making an attempt to produce a tearless calm to comply with her belief that the courtroom called for such affect from witnesses, Julianne did emotion work.

Successful emotion work prior to court can assist the survivor in achieving a courtroom demeanor that is consistent with her appearance and her story. Likewise, it can help her keep her mind on her testimony. In both of these ways, the survivor's emotion manage-ment efforts can assist a prosecutor's efforts. However, when a survivor feels that she must focus her energy on formulating and delivering her testimony, achieving a particular emotional display can be difficult. Constructing a particular courtroom demeanor is thus not a strategy that can be used by all survivors. For example, although 16-year-old Monica was told by the prosecuting attorney that a display of tears would be good during trial, she did not attempt to direct herself to achieve this emotional state. She explained to me that such an effort would have been wasted, because once she faced her assailant, she knew that she could not sustain a demeanor that was contrary to the way she really felt.

Team Building

The preparatory activity that survivors in the study most frequently reported (69 percent) was team building, recruiting specific people to attend court events with them. My use of the term *team* follows Goffman (1959), who identified persons who participated in maintaining an individual's performance as team members. Survivors described carefully selecting from among those individuals who were available to enhance their ability to achieve credible performances as victim-witnesses. They sought both emotional and instrumental support from other persons. Some survivors had teams of one; others orga-nized teams larger than six.

One of the more carefully considered support plans I encountered was described by the white clerical worker, Theresa. Sometime before the scheduled preliminary hearing, she evaluated her emotional and physical needs and asked two women to fill specific roles that she considered necessary to sustain a successful performance. One would sit by her on the stand and aid her ability to speak; the other would provide an audience for her testimony. She also recruited a third team member to ensure that her friend, who had been subpoe-naed, would have company and support as well.

Many survivors felt that they needed others to emotionally support them on the days they were called to testify, to endure the seemingly endless waiting in hallways and usually windowless victim-witness rooms with them and to provide a friendly face in the court-room during their testimony. While many persons may have been available to go to court with survivors, not all were chosen. Survivors constructed their emotional supports by weighing the investments of others against their own needs. They excluded from team membership those whose attention might be elsewhere, those who could not fully back them up, and those whose feelings might be hurt by hearing their testimony. The result was that persons who were close to the survivor, and who may have been involved in reporting decisions, were occasionally ruled out as team members. For example, a 20-year-old white college student, Joanna, asked her parents not to attend the preliminary hearing because they had not demonstrated unqualified support for her when she informed them that she had been raped. She felt that it would be easier to describe the assault event in the courtroom without having to worry about what they were thinking and feeling:

> So right before trial time, we had . . . we kind of had it out. I said, well, I said, "I don't want you there. I don't want you there at all." In fact, I said, "I feel like I need to be strong on that day, and I don't need to feel like I'm hurting your feelings by anything I might be saying on the stand."

Arlene, a white 34-year-old, also cautiously constructed her team from among those who were available. She asked only her sister and a male friend who was "sympathetic" to go to the preliminary hearing with her. She chose not to involve several sympathetic women friends who she believed were triggered by her assault and another man whose inability to control his anger made her uncomfortable. A third woman, Candace, a 34-year-old white immigrant, recruited her 20-something daughter to be her main support through the preliminary hearing and the trial that followed. However, she did not tell her adult son the details of her assault or when the preliminary hearing would be held, fearing the pain and anger that hearing her describe the attack would produce in him. She explained,

> He'll get angry and angry and angry and angry, you know, because the way he was brought [up]. He doesn't believe in these kind of things [rape], and I don't want him to see how people could hurt me, you know, [how] somebody we don't know could hurt me. Because he might keep that as a grudge or something, you know, to himself, you know. And I don't want him to feel that way, you know?

Staff members from rape crisis centers and victim-witness advocacy programs were sometimes sought for emotional support, specifically because survivors did not have to worry about their feelings and knew that they would provide unconditional sympathy. Of the 31 survivors in this sample, 10 reported requesting rape crisis or victim-witness personnel to attend court events with them. Anna, an African American working-class woman in her twenties, chose a victim-witness advocate to be in court with her to protect her mother and her boyfriend from details of the assault that would be revealed through her testimony. If an advocate was not available, she had planned to go through the preliminary hearing alone. Candace explained that she recruited a victim-witness advocate to join her daughter and herself for the preliminary hearing and trial, because she felt that she could not risk involving her friends in the proceedings. She was unsure of her friends' beliefs about rape and feared that they might reject her after learning the extent of her degradation or possibly hold her accountable for being assaulted. She assumed that the advocate understood the nature of rape:

> I like [the victim-witness advocate] to be there because [she] understood, I think. You know, even though they are your friend, maybe they don't understand the whole thing. You know, maybe they might hear something or whatever, then maybe change their mind [about you] or whatever. But [the victim-witness advocate], she understands. Maybe my friend[s] understand too, but I, I don't know. It's hard for me to bring them there to see, to know that private part of me, you know? They know what happened really, sort of. But I don't want them to hear the whole thing.

Candace's concern about maintaining privacy in the midst of the public court performance was echoed by other survivors. Several gave would-be supporters limited roles that balanced their need for encouragement with their desire to protect their privacy. Megan, an African American college student, for example, took a number of people with her to the courthouse for moral support, but she asked them to leave before she testified. She explained that only people immediately connected with the prosecution needed to know the details of the assault.

When several survivors found that would-be supporters were unwilling to respect their standards for team membership, they experienced a difficult situation. At the least, they felt annoyed. Sandra, a white college student, fled the courthouse when her boyfriend, whom she had requested not come, appeared anyway:

> I was in a big fight with Peter, and I told him that he couldn't go, and he didn't understand why. I said, "Well, you're not going, I don't want you there." And I remember the [courthouse] elevator opening, and it was Peter, and he was standing there and I freaked. And I went into this, like, . . . I'm leaving [mode]. I actually got into the elevator and went down, and I was, like, leaving the courthouse because Peter was there.

Members of the support system that Sandra had assembled went after her and brought her back. Her boyfriend realized that he was jeopardizing her participation in the case and left the courthouse.

Survivors also sought out team members who could increase their ability to affect the legal process. Some persons were selected for the knowledge they could impart to survivors. Others were included because they could be where the survivor could not. Survivors also recruited particular people in an effort to influence jurors.

Rape crisis counselors and victim-witness advocates were contacted for their knowledge of the legal process, as were friends who had prior experience with court events. In the absence of prosecutor contact, survivors believed that these team members could provide them with some idea of what to expect in the courtroom and the possible outcomes of the legal event. For example, Bernice asked an attorney friend who had previously worked for the district attorney's office to accompany her to court. Janice, who had no contact with the prosecuting attorney prior to the scheduled preliminary hearing, asked a co-worker who had recently been involved in a criminal proceeding to attend the preliminary hearing with her. Janice explained,

> She had been through, um, not this type of court hearing, her son had died in a motorcycle accident about a year before. When I started working there she was going back and forth to court. Um, basically she told me what was gonna happen, how long it was gonna take, because she'd been through

it before. Um, so, she offered to give me a ride [to court, and] I asked her if she would be there with me. And she said, fine, no problem. I asked her because she knew ... she had been through this before, and she kinda knew what was coming.

Survivors indicated that crisis workers, who were trained primarily to help a person work through her or his immediate response to rape, made good moral supports but often had a minimal grasp of the legal process and criminal procedure. Those who relied on victim-witness advocates generally found them to be well informed. However, several survivors reported that victim-witness advocates were sometimes close with information. It is probable that they were cautious about saying things that could undermine the prosecutor, because victim-witness programs are often associated with the district attorney's office in some way.

Team members also sat in the courtroom and observed for several survivors who were legally excluded from the courtroom. These "eyes and ears" then reported back to the survivor, keeping her abreast of the proceedings. Survivors recalled that receiving reports on the progress of the prosecution and defense helped them feel connected to the proceedings. In addition, they recognized that the information that team members relayed provided a context for them to construct testimony, if they were called back to the stand to testify.

Finally, several survivors reported that one of the reasons they encouraged other people to be present in the courtroom was to influence the jury. They indicated that they encouraged family members and friends to be present as a show of force—a visible representation that they were believed by a large number of people. Cindy's team-building effort was the most precisely focused toward influencing a jury. She reported that she sought out African American friends to be in the courtroom during the trial because they contradicted the race-bias argument she expected the defense attorney to make. It was her intent that the friends, along with the book by an African American woman author that she openly carried about, would dispel any perception that she was a white bigot with a vendetta against African American men. She explained her strategy:

The [trial was on the] Tuesday after the Saturday after the gubernatorial elections, so I ... needless to say, things are a little strange between blacks and whites at this point because David Duke [former Grand Wizard of the Ku Klux Klan] is running [for governor], you know. I mean that whole thing was the topic of conversation in Louisiana for the previous month. And you know, it just ... like I said, it made things very strange between black people and white people. Um, and I, ... you know, he [the Defense Attorney] was smart enough to kind of take advantage of all that. I think, he really set it up. So I found myself really consciously trying to, um, dispel that, you know. I had black friends in the courtroom with me, I was reading a book by J. California Cooper, who is a black woman writer, and I made sure that I was seen reading that book, you know what I mean? Um, you know, I did everything I could to try and dispel the whole kind of racial thing by manner and stuff.

Survivors' team building brings people into the legal process who can supply the survivor with orienting information in the absence of preparation from the prosecutorial staff. Team-building efforts also ensure that there will be people whom survivors trust and by whom they feel believed in the courtroom. Thus, survivors produce a sympathetic audience to whom they can direct their testimony. Finally, survivors may contribute to the prosecution effort by bringing into the courtroom people who symbolically underscore the validity of their claims to have been raped. Invested members of the court audience are an unexamined courtroom phenomenon worthy of additional investigation.

Role Research

Another way that survivors made an effort to manage the victim-witness role was to educate themselves about the parameters of the legal situation they would be entering. In the absence of precourt preparation from legal personnel, six survivors in this sample sought the guidance of persons with legal knowledge and/or engaged in library research to better understand rape law, the legal process, and the possible interactions they might have when appearing in court. By obtaining such information, they hoped they would become better witnesses and be better able to convey their testimony. Unlike the activities of appearance work, emotion work, or case enhancement (described below), such role research was not directed toward meeting cultural expectations about rape victims. It was focused on obtaining the knowledge or skills that survivors perceived to be necessary to participate effectively in a foreign "legal" space and to produce legally appropriate responses to questions. Many survivors mentioned reading books about coping with the trauma of rape that included chapters on criminal prosecution, which suggests a possible continuum of research activity. However, the efforts I have identified as role research stand out because the survivors were clearly intent on improving their grasp of the criminal justice process.

For example, Sandra and Joanna, both white and college students at the time that they were raped, described trying to find relevant information in their university libraries. They looked up legal terms and legal codes that defined rape as well as general court process information. Sandra recalled that although she put a lot of work into finding out information, she was not successful in obtaining all that she felt she needed:

> I was on this rampage of having this information, you know. [Sighs.] So I got a lot of information just from reading. I went to the library and found out about laws, um, the laws and what the defense attorneys could do, I mean, I read it in the [California Penal Code]. . . . I went to the library. It's like I felt I couldn't get any information [from court personnel]. Like, I had to go and read about it myself, and so that's what I did. I tried to read a lot about it, although it didn't [give me all I needed], you know, it's really not the same thing [as being talked to].

Joanna was more satisfied with the research effort she conducted and indicated that what she discovered guided her word choice while testifying. Specifically, Joanna reported that she learned that the State of Virginia differentiated between forced vaginal intercourse (rape) and sexual assault (forced sexual contact short of penetration) and that she needed to say the word *rape* while testifying rather than *sexual assault*, the term she used when reporting the incident to police. Megan, another college student, went to the university counsel's office for information. The four other survivors who researched their roles outside the college setting called therapists and lawyers for information about the law and legal procedure when it was not forthcoming from prosecutors and their assistants. The fact that all the college students undertook role research suggests that their presence in institutions for research and education shaped their response to the criminal justice system.

Role research helps a survivor gain information that she feels is necessary to successfully perform her role, and it is a productive way to become more involved in the legal process. The information obtained may ease her worry, thus boosting her confidence, and help her formulate her testimony in ways that support the prosecution effort. Furthermore, survivors who know more about the legal process and the way their testimony fits into a case constructed by the prosecutor may be better able to comprehend the logic of requests made by her or him. On the other hand, role research can be a frustrating experience for the survivor who comes to realize that her ability to obtain knowledge falls short of gaining a complete picture of the witness role. This can undermine confidence, as it did for Sandra.

Case Enhancement

The final group of preparatory activities, carried out by survivors, was directed to enhance the strength of "their" case. Of their own volition, nine survivors brought documents that corroborated their version of the assault event to the attention of legal personnel or to court with them. Their behavior reflected an understanding that the courtroom is a place where proof is required and that their testimony alone was not, on its own, sufficient evidence that a rape took place. This type of preparation cut across class lines. The two working-class survivors quoted below brought corroborative documents with them to hearings for probable cause. Theresa supplied a telephone bill which supported her claim that she called a particular friend immediately after the defendant left her home. This provided evidence of a *fresh complaint*, although she did not report the assault to the police until several weeks later. Recognizing the telephone bill as important evidence, the prosecuting attorney asked Theresa to provide a copy when the hearing was over. This is how Theresa accounted for bringing the bill with her:

> I hadn't even thought about the phone bill, until the day of the pretrial. I keep my phone bills, and I dug it out, and there it was, 1:03 on that night, I was on the phone with her for over 20 minutes.... You know, it's like, anything I can do to prove my case. I know that any documentation is that much better for me. And just like telling them [the DA and the detective], I talked with the people at rape crisis and stuff, there's documentation there, too, you know, they have logs. So yeah, I just feel that anything I can do to make my case more sound makes it that much better for me. And like the footwork with getting the people for my support group for that day, um, I've been able to do what I consider footwork to get some of the things done that I need done that will help my case. At least I think [they] will help my case, or help me get through it.

Rachel, a white 26-year-old, brought her daily diary to the attention of the prosecuting attorney several weeks before the scheduled hearing for probable cause because she thought it might help the prosecutor understand the history of her relationship with her assailant, her ex-husband. At the hearing, Rachel used the materials for reference. She explained to me,

> Well, I thought that anybody who knew our relationship . . . all our friends know what our relationship was like, they know that he manipulated me. Even friends that were his best friend are no longer friends with him because they don't like the way he treated me, or the kids. I just felt it was important that she [the DA] kinda knew a little bit of the history. So, I gave her that and that was a big chunk of our history, that one diary, the black book that they kept referring to [during the preliminary]. That was a big chunk of our history.

Katherine, a white medical assistant, brought a similar document to court with her, a date book that documented an escalating pattern of abuse by her domestic partner that went back months from the day of the rape. She explained to me that her previous experience with family court demonstrated the need for such specific information. During the hearing, she limited her answers to the contents of the date book.

While physical evidence of rape is collected by hospital personnel and police investigators, information regarding a survivor's mental state that may account for her behavior during or after a sexual assault is not. The materials supplied by the survivors quoted above provided support for their claims that they did not consent to intercourse in spite of their decisions to be in the presence of their assailants. Their case-enhancement efforts, like appearance work and emotion work, indicate that they were aware of and were trying to accommodate cultural stereotypes of "real rape."

When prosecutors made defense strategies known to survivors, a few reported producing evidence to counter them. For example, Natalie, a white legal secretary, brought eight years of employment evaluations to the prosecuting attorney after learning that the defense was planning to argue that she had precipitated the assault during a drug deal. She recalled,

> I knew that they didn't have anything to . . . to go on, they was gonna try to use drugs. His story was that he was my drug supplier and that, um, I had gotten upset because oh, he was gonna cut me off and I got mad and went crazy in the house, and that's how I got beaten up or whatever.

Natalie's provision of exculpatory evidence is particularly interesting because her case was one of the strongest I came across. Most of its attributes were consistent with classic rape stereotypes. She had been severely beaten about the head, such that she was taken to hospital in an ambulance and required stitches, and she contacted the police immediately. She also gave police an exceptionally detailed description of the defendant's tattoo. Despite all this, Natalie felt compelled to counter an argument that she recognized to be outrageous. Like the other women who provided evidence, she took personal responsibility for the successful outcome of prosecution.

The woman who took the greatest responsibility for the outcome of her case actually prepared it for prosecution. After the defendant was brought to trial once and the jury failed to reach a verdict, Donna and her husband gathered evidence, drew maps, photographed the area, insisted the prosecutor contact character witnesses for Donna, and constructed an argument for the prosecutor to use in a retrial.

In the cases I have discussed thus far, survivors provided concrete pieces of evidence to back up their claims, and they found that their efforts were accepted and incorporated by the prosecuting attorneys. However, other survivors' efforts to shape prosecution strategy with their ideas were not as well received. Julianne's experience provides a straightforward example of this point. She learned specifics of the defense attorney's strategy from a mutual friend to whom her assailant had spoken several weeks before the scheduled preliminary hearing and communicated the information to the prosecutor, hoping that a rebuttal would be planned. Instead, he brushed her concerns off without addressing the validity of her information. Unfortunately, Julianne's information was accurate. The defense attorney asked her about previous occasions when she had initially resisted sexual intercourse and then acquiesced, and he introduced some Polaroid photographs that depicted her in provocative poses. The judge called the preliminary hearing to a halt and recommended an immediate resolution. A plea agreement to significantly lesser charges was quickly arranged.

Prosecutors' acceptance of evidence and their rejection of ideas speaks to a boundary issue. Provision of tangible corroborative evidence falls within the bounds of appropriate witness behavior from the standpoint of prosecution. Providing strategy appears to tread on prosecuting attorneys' toes, as it challenges their right to determine whether and how prosecution will proceed. I suspect that Donna's efforts would have been dismissed as overly intrusive if the prosecutor had not failed to convict the defendant on his first attempt.

Case-enhancement efforts that bring to light documents that corroborate survivors' stories generally support prosecutors' efforts. Potentially, the information supplied by survivors can influence the way the prosecutor builds her or his case as well. If a survivor feels that her credibility is questionable, having something on paper to which she can refer during a hearing can build her confidence. In addition, when a survivor brings documents to court, she can limit her testimony to their content. This, in turn, can support prosecutors' efforts to keep the scope of survivors' testimony within narrow bounds.

Discussion

The findings in this study indicate that it would be unwise to assume that all rape survivors are passive bystanders in the legal process, just as it would be unwise to assume that they are passive in the face of rape. Faced with a new witness role and a responsibility to testify in the public courtroom forum, many survivors in this study actively prepared themselves for scheduled court events.

Incentives to Prepare

Study participants' preparation efforts were inspired by three interrelated concerns: conforming to cultural stereotypes of rape victims, managing themselves in a situation that they explicitly recognized as legal, and dealing with the potential emotional impact of participating in the court events. Some of the survivors in the study had contact with prosecutors prior to their initial court event and received directions as well as information from them. These directions—to obtain specific attire, to sustain a particular demeanor in court, to read through police reports, to stay away from the courtroom—were usually followed, but survivors often went beyond what was asked of them. For example, the majority of survivors in the study built courtroom teams, but none was instructed to do so by a prosecutor. The survivors who had no contact with the prosecutor until 30 or 45 minutes before preliminary hearings conceived of and carried out their preparation activities independently. Thus, rape survivors' preparation for court events cannot be conceptualized as solely determined by legal personnel (Konradi 1996).

Study participants' awareness of classic rape stereotypes encouraged their appearance work, emotion work, case enhancement, and instrumental team building. Through these preparation activities, they sought to present themselves as credible victims to judges and juries. Few of the survivors in the study knew what was legally required to establish rape, and many did not know the specific charges filed against their assailants before appearing to give their testimony at a hearing for probable cause. They did not know, for example, that to encourage a plea their assailants had initially been charged with attempted rape, and only if their testimony included a clear description of vaginal, oral, or rectal penetration would the charges be upgraded to rape. Thus, when they provided evidence, these women were not attempting to systematically establish penetration, specific force, or threat of force, some of the legal components of rape.

Some of the survivors in the study accepted the cultural stereotypes of rape as valid. Other study participants did not accept the cultural notions of rape as true but acknowledged that jury members and judges might well believe them. However, the strategies which believers and nonbelievers used to prepare themselves were similar, because members of both groups were intent on proving during their courtroom appearances that they were legitimate victims. Thus, appearance work, emotion work, case enhancement, and team building did not contest common cultural categories for understanding rape. As a result, even survivors who identified as feminist and were ideologically oriented to resist being dominated in court were engaged in affirming the belief systems that oppressed them. This paradox was occasionally painfully acknowledged when survivors reflected back on their experiences.

Social Aspects of Preparation

The findings of this study suggest that how participants took on the victim-witness role was very much determined by their membership in particular social worlds. Other persons provided audiences for participants' rehearsal efforts, and they were consulted when participants conducted research and composed their courtroom personas. How survivors in the study managed interaction and the particular ways they sought to meet cultural expectations, therefore, emerged from their daily experiences and intimate contacts. Teams, which many participants constructed to provide themselves with emotional support and encouragement, were also largely drawn from their close contacts. Although some survivors in the study reported making efforts to exclude people who might be pained by their testimony, this was not universally attempted or universally successful. Consequently, at least three women felt compelled to construct their testimony so as not to harm or offend their supportive listeners. The preparatory activity of team building also laid the groundwork for an additional layer of interaction in the courtroom between the survivor and nonlegal personnel. Ultimately, it does not serve legal personnel well to approach the victim-witness role as an individual role and themselves, despite their special relationship with rape survivors, as the sole shapers of survivors' actions in court.

The small number of women of color in the sample made group comparisons between white women and women of color difficult. However, racial/ethnic background does not appear to limit the kind of preparation in which survivors engaged. In the study, women of color and white women carried out each of the six preparation strategies. Among the rape survivors quoted above, Janice, Megan, and Anna were women of color, and the remainder were white. Exploring whether women of color, as a group, embark on additional unique preparation strategies, prepare more or less than white women, or use particular strategies of preparation more frequently than white women must be the focus of additional investigation.

Understanding the role that race plays in survivors' involvement in the prosecution of rape is not, however, simply a matter of asking if white women and women of color do the same things. It also involves exploring how survivors' understanding of cultural stereotypes about rapists and their victims and race relations shapes their behavior. This is particularly important in the case of interracial rapes. Some of the white women in this study who were raped by black men described their awareness of stereotypes of the "black rapist" at the time they entered the criminal justice system, and some expressed their belief that their assailants' race could make the prosecution's case more convincing to a jury. It is possible that such beliefs could translate into lack of self-preparation, although this was not explicitly stated by the survivors. However, such a supposition must not be casually generalized. Cindy's comments about building a courtroom team including black friends, because she expected a predominately black jury and was aware of heightened racial tension in her city, indicate that survivors of rape may respond to the race relations in their immediate geographic context. When rape survivors are knowledgeable that jury pools are drawn from specific geographic jurisdictions, this would seem likely.

Information provided by police or prosecutors can also make survivors attentive to their assailants' race or the expected race of jurors and shape their self-preparation. For example, Monica and Janice reported that prior to trial prosecutors informed them that race would play a role in their case. The prosecutor told Monica that she should not appear to be vindictive when she testified because the defendant claimed she "cried rape" out of fear that she would have a black baby. Janice was told that she would need to explain that she had previously frequented the predominately black club where she met her rapist and address the fact that her children were biracial (Asian black) to dispel jurors' concerns about racism. Interview questions focusing on this aspect of race would be a positive addition to future research about survivors' involvement in rape processing.

A greater variation in socioeconomic status and educational background existed in the study sample. The class differences among the women, as measured by these two indicators, also did not account for any substantial variation in preparatory behavior. Women who were highly educated and worked in professional capacities as well as women who were clerical workers with a high school education engaged in the full range of preparatory activities. Class status, however, did appear to contribute to the specific nature of team building and role research. Although women of all class backgrounds used rape crisis hot lines and drew victim-witness advocates onto their teams, it was several older, middle-class professional women who had lawyers as personal friends whom they could ask to accompany them to court. Young women attending college had access to extensive libraries and to the university counsel. Other role researchers relied on consulting experts by telephone. As with race, additional attention to the role of class in shaping survivors' preparation strategies would be worthwhile.

Like the civil plaintiffs studied by Merry (1990) and Conley and O'Barr (1990), many rape survivors in this study strategized and pursued their own agendas relative to their perceptions of courtrooms and the legal process more generally. To a great extent, their preparations supported the interests of the prosecution. However, some of the activities study participants carried out might not have the same effect. For example, women's efforts to prepare statements to defend their post-rape actions might work against a prosecutor's plan that revolved around presenting the survivor as a dupe of the assailant. In addition, team members who provided information about courtroom activity to excluded survivors gave them information which the prosecuting attorney did not know they had.

Critical Thinking

It is clear from Konradi's findings that the courtroom is a tremendous source of stress for victims of rape. In fact, the anxiety associated with the courtroom appearance is an explanation for why rape has a relatively low rate of reporting. How do you think anxiety and stress affect courtroom members' perceptions of the reliability or believability of rape victims' accounts and testimonies? Considering the article by Frohman, how do you think defense attorneys exploit this feature of rape trials to help their clients? If you were a defense attorney, would you exploit this feature in an attempt to get your client a favorable decision?

References

Bart, Pauline, and Patricia O'Brien. 1985. *Stopping rape: Successful survival strategies*. New York: Pergamon.

Caignon, Denise, and Gail Groves, eds. 1987. *Her wits about her: Self-defense success stories by women*. New York: Harper & Row.

Conley, John, and William O'Barr. 1990. *Rules versus relationships: The ethnography of legal discourse.* Chicago, IL: University of Chicago Press.

Frohmann, Lisa. 1991. Discrediting victims' allegations of sexual assault: Prosecutorial accounts of case rejections. *Social Problems* 38: 213–226.

Goffman, E. 1959. *The presentation of self in everyday life.* Garden City, NY: Doubleday.

Greenberg, Martin S., and R. Barry Ruback. 1992. *After the crime: Victim decision making.* New York: Plenum.

Hochschild, Arlie. 1979. Emotion work, feeling rules, and social structure. *American Journal of Sociology* 85: 551–575.

Hochschild, Arlie. 1983. *The managed heart: Commercialization of human feeling.* Berkeley: University of California Press.

Holmstrom, Lynda Lytle, and Ann Wolbert Burgess. 1983. *The victim of rape: Institutional reactions.* New Brunswick, NJ: Transaction.

Kerstetter, Wayne A. 1990. Gateway to justice: Police and prosecutorial response to sexual assaults against women. *Journal of Criminal Law and Criminology* 81: 267–313.

Kleck, G., and S. Sayles. 1990. Rape and resistance. *Social Problems* 37: 149–162.

Konradi, A. 1993. Discovering role modeling: An activist approach to the recruitment of rape survivors. Paper presented at the American Anthropology Meetings, November 17, Washington, DC.

Konradi, A. 1996. Understanding rape survivors' preparations for court: Accounting for the influence of legal knowledge, cultural stereotypes, personal efficacy and prosecutor contact. *Violence Against Women* 2: 25–62.

LaFree, Gary. 1989. *Rape and criminal justice: The social construction of sexual assault.* Belmont, CA: Wadsworth.

Madigan, Lee, and Nancy Gambel. 1989. *The second rape: Society's continued betrayal of the victim.* New York: Lexington.

Martin, Patricia, and R. Powell. 1994. Accounting for the "second assault": Legal organizations' framing of rape victims. *Law and Social Inquiry* 19: 853–890.

Merry, Sally Engle. 1990. *Getting justice and getting even: Legal consciousness among working-class Americans.* Chicago, IL: University of Chicago Press.

Polk, Kenneth. 1985. Rape reform and criminal justice processing. *Crime and Delinquency* 31: 191–205.

Schafran, Lynn Hecht. 1993. Maiming the soul: Judges, sentencing and the myth of the nonviolent rapist. *Fordham Urban Law Journal* 20: 439–453.

Stanko, Elizabeth. 1981. The impact of victim assessment on prosecutor's screening decisions: The case of the New York district attorney's office. *Law and Society Review* 16: 225–239.

Williams, L. 1984. The classic rape: When do victims report? *Social Problems* 31: 459–467.

17

Expecting an Ally and Getting a Prosecutor

Sarah Goodrum

Abstract: *Goodrum examines the experiences of the family members of murder victims, focusing in particular on interactions with prosecutors. The author describes two primary roles of prosecutors that are expected by grieving family members: the "key informant" and the "sympathetic warrior." Participants expected prosecutors and other court personnel to act as key informants in that family members demanded detailed information regarding all aspects of their loved one's cases, including minute details of the investigation, prosecution, and the probable outcome of the case. The prosecutors' role as sympathetic warrior was prompted by the participants' desires for court personnel to display empathy and compassion in dealing with the murder victims' cases and the participants' expectation that the prosecutor and other personnel understand and share the families' grief and anger.*

Me and the DA got into it a few times, because I didn't like what she was telling me [about her plan to seek a 15-year sentence for the defendant]. . . . That ain't your husband! . . . The DA needs to understand that when a life is taken, no matter what the circumstances may be, death is death. . . . [T]hey need to work a little bit more closely [with the family]

(Deidra Fiero, wife of 24-year-old man killed during a drug deal).

Since the 1970s, crime victims' rights advocates have fought to give victims a larger role in the criminal justice system in the belief that increased involvement would improve victims' satisfaction with the system and their recovery from the crime (see Kelly 1990; Kilpatrick and Otto 1987; Wiebe 1996). By 1995, all states in the U.S.A. had passed a victims' bill of rights, and in many states the prosecution-related rights proved most substantive (e.g., right to be informed of all court dates in the case, right to give a victim impact statement). Empirical evidence indicates, however, that these rights have brought little to no improvement in victims' satisfaction and recovery (Davis and Smith 1994; Elias 1984; Erez 1994, 2000; Erez, Roeger, and Morgan 1997; Kenney 1995), raising questions about what victims need from the criminal justice system. Recent survey research suggests that prosecutors may play a pivotal role in influencing victims' overall feelings about the criminal justice system (Carr, Logio, and Maier 2003), but few researchers have asked victims themselves what they want from prosecutors (for exceptions see Erez and Belknap 1998; Hare 2006; Konradi 1996, 1997).

Understanding victims' expectations of prosecutors may help explain the reasons for the lack of improvement in the overall victim–criminal justice system relationship in the post-victims' rights era. Admittedly, victims' views of prosecutors may be unrealistic or incorrect. However, symbolic interactionists—who emphasize the significance of meaning in everyday social encounters—would point out that these views prove important in informing victims' expectations and shaping their experiences (see Blumer 1969). Blumer (1969: 2) explains that people "act toward things [e.g., people, objects, or situations] on the basis of the meaning that things have for them." Thus, the meaning that victims attach to the prosecutor role (even if incorrect) guides their feelings about and behavior toward prosecutors, as well as their overall satisfaction with the criminal justice system and their recovery from the crime.

This study uses the symbolic interactionist perspective to examine victims' experiences with prosecutors and the criminal court system with a focus on people who have lost a loved one to murder ("bereaved victims"). The data come from in-depth interviews with 32 bereaved victims from Union County (pseudonym), nine criminal court workers (e.g., prosecutors, judges, and counselors) from Union County, and three crime victims' advocates based in Union County. Loss to murder proves a helpful focus for research on victims' experiences with prosecutors for three main reasons. First, a victimization to murder represents one of the most horrific types of criminal victimization, leaving victims with post-traumatic stress, anxiety, and depression (see Amick-McMullan, Kilpatrick, and Resnick 1991; Amick-McMullan, Kilpatrick, Veronen, and Smith 1989). The severity of the trauma exposes victims' and prosecutors' hidden assumptions about the prosecutor role and the victim–prosecutor relationship. Second, because of the seriousness of the crime, prosecutors tend to respond to murder cases with more intensity than to other types of criminal cases. Thus, if bereaved victims are displeased with prosecutors' responses to their loved one's murder case, other victims are likely to be displeased with prosecutors' responses. Finally, the stark contrast between prosecutors' stoic demeanor and bereaved victims' emotional devastation accentuates the two groups' different investments in the case. For bereaved victims, the case represents a profoundly personal pursuit; for prosecutors, the case represents a professional responsibility. These different viewpoints can make for awkward encounters in victim–prosecutor interactions, and this awkwardness may help explain the lack of improvement in victims' experiences. This study examines the ways victims define the prosecutor role with the idea that this definition influences victims' experiences with and perceptions of prosecutors and the criminal justice system; the study compares victims' definitions to prosecutors', counselors', and others' definitions—to consider whether conflicts of meaning create conflicts in victims' experiences with the criminal justice system. The research has implications for research on victims, victims' rights, the criminal justice system, and symbolic interactionist theory. The research also offers insight into the effectiveness of rights-oriented legislation in bringing positive change.

Literature Review

Empirical research repeatedly suggests that victims want more information about their cases and more involvement in criminal justice proceedings (Carr, Logio, and Maier 2003;

Erez 2000; Kenney 1995). Victims' rights legislation in the U.S.A. and elsewhere has tried to address these needs by guaranteeing victims the right to information on all of the court dates in their case and the right to make a victim impact statement to the court during the sentencing phase of the trial (Kelly 1990). The literature, however, offers mixed results on the ability of rights to improve victims' experiences with the criminal justice system. For example, in a study of the Australian criminal justice system, Erez et al. (1997) found that participation in a victim impact statement did not boost victims' satisfaction with the system, leading the authors to conclude that victim impact statements may not give victims the type of participation they want. Other research suggests that victims would rather have information about the case and interaction with criminal justice professionals than the opportunity to give a victim impact statement (Carr et al. 2003). Indeed, Riches and Dawson (1998) describe access to information as critical to bereaved victims' satisfaction with the criminal justice system.

For various reasons, however, access to information does not always help victims in the ways advocates and researchers expect. First, criminal justice workers often find that victims have difficulty understanding the legalities of the criminal justice system (Goodrum and Stafford 2003; Konradi 1997). Prosecutors working with rape survivors believed "it [did] not pay to put effort into explaining procedures thoroughly if the [survivor/witness did] not grasp the information" (Konradi 1997: 38). Second, the current literature does not reveal what specific types of information victims want from prosecutors or other criminal justice workers, leaving the request to give victims information open to faulty interpretation.

Some research suggests that victims may want regular interaction with prosecutors, not just information from them. Carr et al.'s (2003) survey of Philadelphia victims revealed that positive interaction with the prosecutor significantly related to overall satisfaction with the criminal justice system, feeling knowledgeable about the status of the case, *and* feeling connected to the prosecution of the case. The literature does not yet indicate how victims define a positive interaction with the prosecutor, although European countries offer some interesting possibilities. In Poland, victim–prosecutor interactions look like a partnership, because victims have the opportunity to serve as "subsidiary prosecutor" in the case (Erez and Bienkowska 1993). Using a national sample of victims, Erez and Bienkowska (1993) found that victims who served as a "subsidiary prosecutor" in their case reported higher levels of satisfaction with the criminal justice system and the defendant's sentence than victims who did not. In the U.S.A., victims cannot serve as a subsidiary prosecutor, and the current literature does not even indicate whether American crime victims would want this type of interaction.

Victims' rights legislation may have a limited effect on victims' experience because of criminal justice workers' reluctance to welcome the victim's participation in the criminal justice process. Using in-depth interview data with rape victims and prosecutors, Konradi (1996) found that prosecutors welcomed victims' offers of case evidence but rejected victims' suggestions about case strategy. "Providing strategy appears to tread on prosecuting attorneys' toes, as it challenges their right to determine whether and how to proceed" (Konradi 1996: 423). Many prosecutors view the victim's role as a symbolic one, not a substantive one (Erez and Laster 1999). Following in-depth interviews with legal professionals, Erez and Laster (1999: 545) reported, "Victim participation reforms were understood by practitioners as only a minor or symbolic gesture that was not intended to modify court procedures and sentencing practices. The true intent of [victim impact statements], they maintained, was political." Frohmann (1998) concludes that rape reform legislation proves limited in its ability to empower victims, because to pursue a legal case, victims have to redefine their personal problem as a legal problem, omitting aspects of the victimization experience unrecognized by the law. In the U.S.A., victims' rights legislation has been passed without asking victims themselves what they want from the criminal justice system (see Rock 1998). This study asks victims to describe in their own words what they expected of prosecutors following their loved one's murder with the idea that these words will give meaning to victims' experiences and inform victims' rights efforts.

Setting and Methods

Community and Legal Setting

Union County had a population of more than 700,000 people (U.S. Bureau of the Census 2001) and approximately 45 murders per year ([Omitted State Name] Department of Health 2000) at the time of this study. The Union police department, sheriff's department, and district attorney's office had victim services counselors on staff full-time and the police and sheriff's departments had an extensive network of volunteer victim services counselors. These counselors, victim-oriented programs, and a strong victims' advocacy group have given Union a national reputation for being an innovator in victim services, making it an ideal location for a study on victims' experiences. If victims are not having a good experience in this criminal justice system, they are unlikely to be having a good experience in others.

When a murder occurred in Union County, law enforcement detectives collected evidence and interviewed witnesses, and they turned the case over to the District Attorney's Office for a grand jury indictment. After the indictment, a victim-witness counselor with the District Attorney's Office contacted the murder victim's family members, on behalf of the prosecutor, to notify them of the status of the case, give them information about criminal justice procedures, and invite them to meet with the prosecutor to talk about the case. Prosecutors and victim-witness counselors knew that most bereaved victims wanted a trial in their loved one's murder case, as opposed to a negotiated plea, and this knowledge shaped the direction and tone of their first few meetings. "[I]n almost all the homicide cases I've dealt with [the family] wants to go to trial. They think that a trial is a public airing of what happened, [and they think it] is going to fix them, and it doesn't fix them" (Prosecutor and Director of Trial Division). To prevent conflict over a trial versus a negotiated plea later in the case, Union County prosecutors and counselors tried to build a rapport with bereaved victims in the very early stages of the process with the idea that the rapport would help them if they needed to deliver bad news about the strength of the case, their plans to dispose of it through a plea bargain, or their views on an appropriate sentence for the defendant. Union County prosecutors and counselors often honored bereaved victims' wishes for a trial but they reserved the right to reject their wishes if a trial seemed unlikely to bring a guilty verdict.

At the time of this study, the victims' rights laws in this state were very comprehensive and did not distinguish between various types of crime victims.[1] The prosecution-related victims' rights included the right to the return of the victim's property when it is no longer needed by the criminal justice system, the right to information on the defendant's bail and criminal procedures and deadlines, and the right to give a victim impact statement during the sentencing phase of the defendant's trial.

Data Collection

The study included in-depth interviews with 32 bereaved victims whose loved ones were murdered between 1994 and 1999 in Union County and nine Union County criminal court professionals working on murder cases (e.g., prosecutors, judges, and counselors). The data also include interviews with three crime victim advocates (i.e., people who worked or volunteered for a non-profit victims' rights organization) in Union County. All interviews were conducted by the author and were tape-recorded and transcribed. The study also include more than 144 hours of participant observation data, which the author collected while working as a volunteer victim services counselor for the Union Police Department and while observing Union County murder trials.

Bereaved Victim Interviews

Bereaved victims were recruited by contacting: (1) the next-of-kin listed on death certificate records for 1997 to 1999 Union County murder victims (n = 25), (2) the next-of-kin mentioned in newspaper accounts of all 1995 to 1996 Union County murder victims (n = 4), and (3) the family members of Union County murder victims referred by the Union County District Attorney's Office (n = 3). Each bereaved victim interview took approximately two and a half hours. The interviews contained questions about the criminal justice system, relationships with others, the meaning of the loss, demographic characteristics, and advice for others. The data presented here come from bereaved victims' responses to questions about their positive and negative encounters with prosecutors and the District Attorney's Office.[2]

Criminal Court Professional and Victim Advocate Interviews

The interviews were with nine criminal court professionals (e.g., four prosecutors, three judges, and two counselors) working on murder cases in Union County and three crime victim advocates based in Union County; the court professional and advocate interviews took approximately one hour each. Participants were selected using judgment sampling, and all participants had two or more years of experience working on murder cases in Union County. The interviews continued until saturation point (i.e., when additional respondents provided little new information). Criminal court professionals and advocates were asked open-ended questions about their work with bereaved victims and the positive and negative aspects of including bereaved people in the criminal justice process.

Bereaved Victim Sample Profile

Seventy-eight percent of the bereaved victims were female. Fifty-three percent were white, 31 percent Hispanic, and 16 percent black. The mean age of bereaved victims was 49. Six percent of bereaved victim respondents had not completed high school, 32 percent had completed high school, 39 percent had completed some college, 13 percent had completed college, and 10 percent had completed graduate school. The median household income was $40,000 to $59,999 (for additional information on the sample, see Goodrum 2007).

Although it is not ideal to use a population-to-sample comparison of murder victims to infer a population-to-sample comparison of bereaved victim respondents, the comparison sheds light on the possibility that the bereaved victims of some murder victims were more likely than the bereaved victims of other murder victims to participate in the study. The comparison indicates that the population and sample of murder victims look very similar in age and gender but less similar in race. The population of murder victims was 33 percent white, 24 percent black, and 43 percent Hispanic, while the sample of murder

Table 1 Sociodemographic Characteristics of Bereaved Victims in the Sample*

Mean Age	Gender	Race	Marital Status	Level of Education	Next-of-Kin's Relationship to Victim[3]
49	22% Male	53% White	44% Married	6% Less than High School	9% Child
	78% Female	16% Black	41% Divorced[1]	32% High School	6% Spouse
		31% Hispanic	9% Widowed	39% Some College	63% Parent
			6% Never Married	13% College	19% Sibling
				10% Grad School[2]	3% Other

Notes

*Source: This information was obtained from in-depth interviews with bereaved victims.

[1] Divorced and Separated are combined under the label "Divorced."

[2] Grad School refers to people who either attended or completed Graduate School.

[3] Relationship to victim refers to the bereaved victim's relationship to the murder victim as listed on the death certificate. For example, if the mother is listed as the next-of-kin contact on the murder victim's death certificate, her relationship would be listed in this table as "Parent."

victims was 50 percent white, 12 percent black, and 38 percent Hispanic. Nineteen percent of the murder cases remained unsolved at the time of the interview.

Criminal Court Professional and Crime Victim Advocate Sample Profile

Five of the 12 court and advocate respondents were female. Nine of the 12 were white, one was Hispanic, and two were biracial (white and American Indian). These criminal justice professionals and advocates had an average of 10.9 years of experience on murder cases; the average number of murder cases dealt with was 115.

Findings

Defining the Prosecutor Role

Herbert Blumer's (1969: 2) first premise of symbolic interactionism states that people act "toward things on the basis of the meaning that the things have for them." When people consciously think about a "thing" (e.g., object, person, or situation), they assign it meaning, and this meaning proves important in helping people decide how to behave in a given situation and around others. Knowing the meaning that victims assign to the prosecutor role provides insight into the ideas shaping their feelings about and responses to the criminal justice process. By examining the way bereaved victims describe their encounters with prosecutors, we begin to understand victims' expectations for the prosecutor in their loved one's murder case. The findings presented here reveal several small but important differences in how bereaved victims and others define the prosecutor role. In addition, the findings reveal several neglected areas of victims' needs in current victims' rights legislation in the United States. Bereaved victims' definitions of the prosecutor role included two main components: (1) key informant, and (2) sympathetic warrior. The central idea linking both components is ally; bereaved victims expected the prosecutor in their loved one's murder case to act as their intimate ally, a finding not discussed in previous research. While the data come from people who have lost a loved one to homicide, the findings could come from any group of victims—as the desire for information and compassion from prosecutors cuts across all types of victimization experiences.

Prosecutor as Key Informant

The first theme in bereaved victims' responses to questions about the prosecutor in their loved one's murder case indicates that they expected the prosecutor to give them detailed information about the prosecution process in general and their loved one's murder case in particular. Victims wanted specific information about: (1) the date and nature of upcoming court proceedings, (2) the status of the prosecutor's investigation, and (3) the most likely outcome of the case. Bereaved victims wanted as much information about every possible aspect of the prosecution as they could obtain, and their poignant responses suggest that having this information gave them emotional comfort. Riches and Dawson's (1998) in-depth study of six murder cases confirms that access to information is critical to bereaved victims' well-being, and Konradi (1997) found that knowledge specific to their case and general to the criminal justice system helped rape victims feel more control over the process. Social psychologists describe knowledge as critical to a sense of personal control, and a sense of person control is positively associated with psychological well-being (Mirowsky and Ross 1989). Mirowsky and Ross write (1989: 170): "Without knowledge, control is impossible." The findings presented below lend further support to the idea that information benefits psychological well-being, particularly following a criminal victimization.

The first type of information bereaved victims wanted from prosecutors related to the timing and purpose of the court proceedings in their loved one's murder case. Melissa Iker, the mother of a 24-year-old murder victim, lived out-of-state at the time of her son's murder and during the court proceedings that followed. She expressed tremendous appreciation for the time and effort the prosecutor and counselor spent in keeping her informed about the case. She said:

> They kept contact with us . . . and they . . . [let] me know about the indictment [of the defendant] and then when it was time . . . for him to go in front of the judge to plead guilty. . . . They briefed us on what was going to go on [during the hearings] and what was going to happen, and there was always somebody with us during the day [during the court proceedings].

Bereaved victims wanted information about the dates for all of the court proceedings in the case, including the indictment, arrest, arraignment, preliminary hearing, and negotiated plea or trial. The victims' bill of rights in the state of study and in other states in the U.S.A. guarantees victims the right to information on the dates for all of the court proceedings in the case (see also Wiebe 1996). In fact, the President's Task Force on Victims of Crime (1982: 114) recommended that "[T]he victim, in every criminal prosecution shall have the right to be present . . . at all critical stages of judicial proceedings."

In addition to information on the court dates, Melissa and other participants also wanted the prosecutor to give them information on what to expect from those court proceedings, such as the purpose of the proceeding (e.g., defendant's arraignment), the difficult aspects of the proceeding (e.g., crime scene photos, coroner's testimony), and the likely outcome of it (e.g., defendant will enter a "not guilty" plea). Wendy Lawrence, the daughter of a 77-year-old murder victim, said that each day before they entered the courtroom, the prosecutors briefed her and her family on what to expect.
She said:

> They would tell us . . . this is going to happen . . . [or during a court recess they would say] they're discussing whether we can do this or that. . . . They explained the whole process to us as it was happening.

The second type of information bereaved victims wanted from prosecutors concerned the status of the prosecutor's investigation, including the content of witness testimony, the appearance of the crime scene, and the strengths and weaknesses of the evidence. Nora Harden, the mother of a 25-year-old man who was shot and killed during a party, wanted the prosecutor in her son's murder case to walk her through the crime scene and tell her about all of the evidence in the case, a practice not typically granted to victims. She said:

> I asked [the prosecutor] if [she] would come out [to the scene of the murder] and show me exactly where everything was; so I could picture everything in detail, exactly where the witnesses were standing [when my son was shot] and what they were saying. . . . So, I feel [the prosecutor] really did wonders in the case. I mean, honestly, I think she just was wonderful.

Nora even expressed a desire to act as an investigator in the case. She explained:

> I don't know what you [would] call it, but I was kind of being my own investigator . . . [I wanted] to have a handle on [the evidence in the case].

While many victims counted on the prosecutor to handle these details, several victims—like Nora—wanted to participate in the actual investigation, and they described this participation as helpful to their mental health. Wendy Lawrence (quoted earlier) felt frustrated when the prosecutors handling her elderly father's murder case neglected several pieces of evidence, including her 911 call, a towel from the crime scene, and her granddaughter's recorded testimony. She said:

> A week before we [went] to trial, I finally convinced [the DA] to listen to the 911 tape [where I described the crime scene] . . . I thought that wasn't good [that I had to remind him of the tape and that] he didn't allow [the jury to hear] the 911 tape or my granddaughter's [taped interview].

A review of other participants' comments and previous research on victim–prosecutor interactions (see Konradi 1996, 1997) indicates that Wendy's interactions with the prosecutor are more typical than Nora's. Few victims get to walk the crime scene or learn about *all* of the evidence in the case from their prosecutor, and even fewer victims get to act as an assistant investigator in the case.

The third type of information bereaved victims wanted from prosecutors concerned the most likely outcome in the murder case—including the prosecutor's plan for resolving the case (e.g., negotiated plea or trial) and the anticipated length of the defendant's sentence. They wanted this type of information even when it brought bad news. Wanda Diaz, the mother of a 20-year-old murder victim, said:

> [I appreciated] the DA being up front and truthful [with me], even though the case was ruined [because of the inappropriately obtained confession]. I think [it helped me anticipate things] with them letting us know, "This is what might happen. If the [defendants] don't go for the plea bargain, then this is what will happen, and we'll have to let them go."

Wanda and other participants reported heartfelt appreciation for prosecutors who gave them the ugly truth about the problems with the evidence in the case, and while they disliked the idea of not getting their "day in court," they often eventually came to understand the need to settle the case with a negotiated plea. During prosecutors' filing interviews with rape victims, Frohmann (1998) found that prosecutors often described the likely outcome in a case to rape victims, but they did so in a way that ensured victims' compliance with their plan for the case—either to pursue a charge or drop the case. Thus, Frohmann (1998) found that prosecutors' primary motive for sharing information on the likely outcome of the case with rape victims was to ensure victims' cooperation, not to emotionally prepare them for the outcome.

It is important to note that several bereaved victims expressed a specific desire to deal directly with the prosecutor in the case, not the counselor. Nora Harden, the mother quoted earlier, explained:

> [The] Victims' Services [Counselors] were fine ... but I basically stuck straight with Christina [the prosecutor in my son's murder case]. Whenever I called [the DA's Office], I called for her specifically to ask how the case was going. It was just too personal to feel I could go through anybody else.

In the conclusion of her study on rape victims' encounters with prosecutors, Konradi (1997) warned that counselors may have trouble fully addressing victims' needs, because they do not always have access to the type of information victims want and they sometimes feel obligated to side with prosecutors and the criminal justice system instead of victims. As bereaved victims' responses suggest, almost all of the prosecutors, counselors, and advocates in Union County recognized bereaved victims' need for information. A prosecutor with more than seven years of experience described it as follows:

> [O]ften [I meet with the family] after the case has already been through the grand jury process and [the defendant has] been indicted ... I'll answer all their questions as best I can. Sometimes I can't tell them everything about the evidence ... [but] I think it's very important that they know what actually happened, what the history of the people involved is, [and] I try to get them to understand what's going to happen [in the prosecution process].

As Wanda suggested earlier, prosecutors and counselors sometimes had to share bad news with victims, including unflattering aspects of the murder victim's history (e.g., drug use, domestic violence) or bad choices on the day of the murder (e.g., aggressor in altercation leading to murder). Prosecutors did not want victims to hear this bad news during the trial or from the media, and they viewed this type of "information sharing" as an important part of their role. Previous research on loss to murder indicates that part of prosecutors' motivation for sharing bad news is to prevent an emotional outburst from bereaved victims during the trial (Goodrum and Stafford 2003). A prosecutor explained:

> I have a case right now where it's going to be a battered wife syndrome defense, and the [murder victim's] family never had any idea that their brother or son was a batterer. They never saw that. So, it's very hard for them to believe that he [abused his wife]. So, you're breaking some news to them that they had no idea about.

For the most part, bereaved victim, prosecutor, counselor, and advocate participants defined the informant aspect of the prosecutor role similarly. Symbolic interactionists would argue that criminal justice workers' experiential knowledge and role-taking ability allowed them to imagine and anticipate victims' intense desire for detailed information about the case (see Blumer 1969). Current victims' rights legislation in the United States typically addresses crime victims' right to information about the court schedule in their case. This legislation, however, does not address the types of information victims want most from prosecutors, namely information on the status of the investigation and the most likely outcome in their loved one's murder case. The underlying message in the "key informant" component of victims' definitions of the prosecutor role suggests that bereaved victims wanted an ally in the prosecutor, not just a prosecutor.

Prosecutor as Sympathetic Warrior

The second theme in bereaved victims' responses to questions about the prosecutor in their loved one's murder case related to their desire for a sympathetic and emotionally connected prosecutor. Victims wanted the prosecutor to understand their profound grief over the loss and their tremendous anger toward the defendant. The frequency with which respondents mentioned the prosecutor's expression (or non-expression) of sympathy in the case suggests that they viewed compassion as a key component of the prosecutor role. In addition, this finding indicates that prosecutors (and other criminal justice workers) can enhance bereaved victims' experiences with the criminal justice system by expressing genuine sympathy for them and their deceased loved one. Nora, Donna, and Delia explained:

> [The prosecutor in my son's murder case] was very warm, always very warm.
>
> (Mother of 25-year-old murder victim).

> I could tell that it wasn't just any case to [the prosecutors]. They cared a lot about this case. . . . They were very sensitive as to the way I would feel about things.
>
> (Sister of 20-year-old murder victim).

> [The prosecutor] did a very thorough job. [He] understood what was going on, [and he] was able to express some of our anger at the injustice of the murder. So, it wasn't like he was without passion once we got to trial.
>
> (Aunt of 24-year-old murder victim).

Nora described the prosecutor as "very warm," Donna described the prosecutors as "sensitive" to her feelings, and Delia said the prosecutor conveyed her family's "anger" to the jury during the trial. A careful examination of these (and other) responses reveals that bereaved victims valued having an emotional connection with the prosecutor in their case.

Norman Denzin (2007) describes emotional connections as the cornerstone to meaningful relationships. Shared emotions "lie at the core of what it means to understand and meaningfully enter into the emotional experience of another" (Denzin 2007: 137). As this finding suggests and as Denzin (2007) might note, bereaved victims viewed "shared emotionality" with prosecutors as essential to the prosecutor role. To truly understand the devastating nature of the loss and the injustice of the murder, bereaved victims expected their prosecutor to move beyond an intellectual understanding of the case to an emotional understanding of the loss. Prosecutors' expressions of sympathy toward victims and statements of anger to the jury represented the best ways for prosecutors to convey that they had entered into the family's emotional experience of the victim, that they "got it." Entering into (as opposed to just observing) the emotional experience of another can improve a person's ability to understand another's situation, as well as their ability to offer emotional support. The literature on both crime victims and bereavement finds that social and emotional support aid recovery from trauma and loss (see Burgess 1975; Kelly 1990; Rando 1993). Thoits (1984) identifies socio-emotional support as instrumental in countering the effect of difficult life events. For victims of crime, an emotional connection with the prosecutor handling the case may prove particularly important because they cannot wage their own legal battle against the defendant; they must rely on someone else—a stranger—to wage it for them.

Bereaved victims' desire to share emotions with the prosecutor in the case may relate to Clark's (1987) discussion of sympathy in social life. People expect sympathy in times of need; people who do not express sympathy to those in need are under-investors whose "sin" is being "aloof and removed" (Clark 1987: 313). An emotionally *uninvested* prosecutor signaled a lack of sincere interest in the case, and as the participant quoted at the opening of this chapter suggests when she exclaimed, "That ain't your husband!" to the prosecutor, an unsympathetic prosecutor frustrated bereaved victims. Interestingly, only one of the four prosecutors (but both of the counselors) participating in the study defined the prosecutor role to include the sharing of victims' emotions.

> I think it's real important [that the murder victim's family] have a bond [with the prosecutor], and they trust [you as the prosecutor]. If you do go to trial, they need to trust that you really know what you're doing, that you really care [about the case], and that you're there to help them. If you're just some anonymous prosecutor . . . they're just not going to feel comfortable with what's going to happen to them.

The above prosecutor valued having an emotional connection with bereaved victims, but she was the exception. No other prosecutor participating in the study expressed an interest in emotionally connecting with victims. Counselors—the criminal court system's emotion managers—on the other hand, repeatedly mentioned the importance of "shared emotions" in their meetings with bereaved victims (see also Goodrum and Stafford 2003). A counselor and former victim advised prosecutors and counselors:

> Do not be afraid to tell [the murder victim's family] that you are really sorry that this happened to them . . . cos that's really what they need to hear; [they] need [you] to confirm with them the horror of what's happened in their life.

Including shared emotionality in the criminal justice system's and victims' rights legislation's definition of the prosecutor role presents a challenge, for main two reasons. First, the culture of the criminal justice system does not typically encourage the sharing of emotions (Goodrum and Stafford 2003). Criminal justice professionals value unemotional objectivity (Erez and Rogers 1999; Stenross and Kleinman 1989). Second, prosecutors and other criminal justice workers may distance themselves from bereaved victims because they know there is little that will alleviate their grief and they dislike the emotional burden that comes with bereaved victim interactions (Goodrum and Stafford 2003). Requiring prosecutors to develop close personal relationships with crime victims on a daily basis may lead to emotional exhaustion and professional burnout (see Copp 1998).

Discussion and Conclusion

The bereaved victim quoted at the start of this chapter describes poignantly what she and many other bereaved victims expected from the prosecutor in their loved one's murder case: a close partnership. Bereaved victims wanted the prosecutor to openly and easily share both information and sympathy with them, and they viewed the exchange of information and emotion as critical components of the prosecutor role. Symbolic interactionist theory— which emphasizes the importance of meaning in social interaction (Blumer 1969)—helps explain some of the reasons why victims' interactions with prosecutors prove so critical to their overall satisfaction with the criminal justice system (see Carr et al. 2003). In short, bereaved victims viewed the prosecutor as more than the state's representative in their loved one's murder case; they viewed the prosecutor as their intimate ally in their search for justice.

A challenge arises in how to incorporate all of victims' expectations for prosecutors into victims' rights legislation in the United States. The first change to victims' rights legislation implied by these findings concerns bereaved victims' access to information, a recurring theme in the larger literature on victims and the criminal justice system. When we carefully review the content of current victims' rights legislation, we see that victims are typically granted the right to be informed about and present at "all critical stages of judicial proceedings" (President's Task Force 1982: 114). In the state of study, for example, victims have "the right to be informed of relevant court proceedings and to be informed if those court proceedings have been canceled or rescheduled prior to the event" (Goodrum 2007: 732). This legislation, unfortunately, does not guarantee victims the right to information about the *content* or *purpose* of those court proceedings, nor does it guarantee victims the right to information about the investigation or the most likely outcome in the case (the second and third types of information requested by bereaved victims). According to both bereaved victims' and criminal court workers' comments, however, many of the bereaved victims encountering Union County prosecutors received this type of information—without the stated right. Of course, some prosecutors withheld information on the evidence to help build a strong case, and the prosecutor's power to control the flow of information frustrated some bereaved victims and hindered their recovery from the crime. When prosecutors shared information on the investigation and bereaved victims understood that evidence, bereaved victims appreciated it when prosecutors and counselors related the evidence in their case to the evidence in other, similar cases. The context gave them an idea of what to expect when their loved one's murder case went to trial and an idea of the possible outcomes.

To help address bereaved victims' concern about open access to all of the information in the investigation, state legislators in the U.S.A. could consider offering victims the opportunity to serve as a subsidiary prosecutor, as in Germany or Poland (see Erez and Bienkowska 1993; Doak 2005). This position may give victims more information about criminal court procedure and a greater sense of closeness to the prosecutor. This type of change may facilitate an ideological and substantive change in the victim–prosecutor relationship (Frohmann 1998). The subsidiary prosecutor position for victims may usher in a new alliance with prosecutors, an alliance which the bereaved victims in this study sought.

The second change to victims' rights legislation implied by these findings concerns prosecutors' emotional displays. Bereaved victims expected the prosecutor in their case to care about them and sympathize with their loss, an expectation that may prove difficult to guarantee through legislation. A question arises about whether it is practical or realistic to mandate sympathy for victims. Perhaps not. However, to help address victims' desire for some type of emotional connection with the prosecutor, the criminal justice system could encourage prosecutors to—at a minimum—recognize victims' emotions (e.g., "It sounds like this has been very difficult for you. It sounds like you are in a great deal of pain over your son's death"). In the ideal encounter, prosecutors would express sympathy for the bereaved victim (e.g., "I'm very sorry for your loss"). Norman Denzin (2007) might suggest that a prosecutor's willingness to emotionally connect with bereaved victims—to engage in "shared emotionality"—over the death of their loved one and over their anger at the murderer may help promote healing. Participants' responses suggest that shared emotionality, or "the intentional feelings of two or more persons [being] drawn together . . . to produc[e] . . . bonding" (Denzin 2007, 152–153) represents the most intimate form of advocacy in the criminal justice system.

The criminal justice system could consider offering prosecutors training exercises that facilitate their taking the role of the victim to increase their compassion for and understanding of victims. Of course, a shift in the emotional culture of the criminal justice system—from stoic to compassionate—would need to accompany these types of exercises, because traditionally, the criminal justice system has promoted unemotional objectivity (Erez and Rogers 1999; Stenross and Kleinman 1989) and delegated emotion work to the system's victim service counselors (Goodrum and Stafford 2003). Bereaved victims' responses indicate that relegating all of the criminal justice system's emotion work to counselors compartmentalizes victims' intense feelings of sadness and anger to a therapeutic encounter, and they wanted the *prosecutor* (not the counselor) to convey all of those emotions to them as well as to the jury and the judge during the trial. As Konradi (1997) anticipated in her study of rape victims' encounters with prosecutors, bereaved victims wanted to share their feelings with and have them validated by the criminal justice professional championing their case: the prosecutor. For bereaved victims, the prosecutor embodied an intimate ally in their fight for justice.

Critical Thinking

Goodrum's findings suggest that the fulfillment of the roles by court personnel aids family members in continuing the grieving process and ultimately recovering from their loss. The findings also suggest that bereaved families and court personnel perceive the important roles of court workers in a similar manner. However, only one of four prosecutors interviewed described empathy with victims' grief as important. In light of this finding, do you think prosecutors should become emotionally involved in cases as the victims' families suggest? What would be the advantages and disadvantages of prosecutors becoming more emotionally involved in murder cases? In addition, consider how expectations toward police differ from prosecutors. What occupational features of police and prosecutors may explain these differences?

Notes

1. The name of the state has been withheld to protect the identity of the study participants. Some of the details of bereaved victim respondents' experiences, as well as District Attorney's Office respondents' job titles and years of service, could make them identifiable if the name of the state were revealed.
2. These questions were asked only of the 19 bereaved victims whose loved ones' murder cases went to the District Attorney's Office, because the unsolved and murder-suicide bereaved victims had no contact with this part of the system at the time of the interview.

References

Amick-McMullan, Angelynne, Dean G. Kilpatrick, and Heidi S. Resnick. 1991. Homicide as a Risk Factor for PTSD Among Surviving Family Members. *Behavior Modification* 15: 545–559.

Amick-McMullan, Angelynne, Dean Kilpatrick, Lois J. Veronen, and Susan Smith. 1989. Family Survivors of Homicide Victims: Theoretical Perspectives and an Exploratory Study. *Journal of Traumatic Stress* 2 (1): 21–35.

Blumer, Herbert. 1969. *Symbolic Interactionism: Perspective and Method.* Berkeley: University of California Press.

Burgess, Ann Wolbert. 1975. Family Reaction to Homicide. *American Journal of Orthopsychiatry* 45: 391–398.

Carr, Patrick J., Kim A. Logio, and Shana Maier. 2003. Keep Me Informed: What Matters for Victims as They Navigate the Juvenile Criminal Justice System in Philadelphia. *International Review of Victimology* 10: 117–136.

Clark, Candace. 1987. Sympathy Biography and Sympathy Margin. *American Journal of Sociology* 93: 290–321.

Copp, Martha. 1998. When Emotion Work is Doomed to Fail: Ideological and Structural Constraints on Emotion Management. *Symbolic Interaction* 21: 299–328.

Davis, Robert C. and Barbara E. Smith. 1994. Victim Impact Statements and Victim Satisfaction: An Unfulfilled Promise? *Journal of Criminal Justice* 22: 1–12.

Denzin, Norman K. 2007. *On Understanding Emotion.* New Brunswick, NJ: Transaction Publishers.

Doak, Jonathan. 2005. Victims' Rights in Criminal Trials: Prospects for Participation. *Journal of Law and Society* 32(2): 294–316.

Elias, Robert. 1984. Alienating the Victim: Compensation and Victim Attitudes. *Journal of Social Issues* 40: 103–116.

Erez, Edna. 1994. Victim Participation in Sentencing: And the Debate Goes On. *International Review of Victimology* 3: 17–32.

Erez, Edna. 2000. Integrating the Victim Perspective in Criminal Justice through Victim Impact Statements. In *Integrating a Victim Perspective within Criminal Justice: International Debates,* ed. Adam Crawford and Jo Goodey. Burlington, VT: Ashgate.

Erez, E., & Belknap, J. 1998. In Their Own Words: Battered Women's Assessment of the Criminal Processing System's Responses. *Violence and Victims,* 13(3): 251.

Erez, Edna and Ewa Bienkowska. 1993. Victim Participation in Proceedings and Satisfaction with Justice in the Continental Systems: The Case of Poland. *Journal of Criminal Justice* 21: 47–60.

Erez, Edna and Kathy Laster. 1999. Neutralizing Victim Reform: Legal Professionals' Perspectives on Victims and Impact Statements. *Crime & Delinquency* 45(4): 530–553.

Erez, Edna and Linda Rogers. 1999. Victim Impact Statements and Sentencing Outcomes and Processes. *British Journal of Criminology* 39 (2): 216–239.

Erez, Edna, Leigh Roeger, and Frank Morgan. 1997. Victim Harm, Impact Statements, and Victim Satisfaction with Justice: An Australian Experience. *International Review of Victimology* 5: 37–60.

Frazier, Patricia A. and Beth Haney. 1996. Sexual Assault Cases in the Legal System: Police, Prosecutor and Victim Perspectives. *Law and Human Behavior* 20: 607–628.

Frohmann, Lisa. 1998. Constituting Power in Sexual Assault Cases: Prosecutorial Strategies for Victim Management. *Social Problems* 45: 393–407.

Goodrum, Sarah. 2007. Victims' Rights, Victims' Expectations, and Law Enforcement Workers' Constraints in Cases of Murder. *Law and Social Inquiry: Journal of the American Bar Association* 32(2): 725–768.

Goodrum, Sarah and Mark C. Stafford. 2003. The Management of Emotions in the Criminal Justice System. *Sociological Focus* 36(3): 179–196.

Hare, Sara C. 2006. What Do Battered Women Want? Victims' Opinions on Prosecution. *Violence and Victims* 21(5): 611–628.

Kelly, Deborah. 1990. Victim Participation in the Criminal Justice System. In *Victims of Crime: Problems, Policies, and Programs*, ed. Arthur J. Lurigio, Wesley G. Skogan, and Robert C. Davis. Newbury Park, CA: Sage.

Kenney, J. Scott. 1995. Legal Institutions and Victims of Crime in Canada: An Historical and Contemporary Review. *Humanity and Society* 19(2): 53–67.

Kilpatrick, Dean G. and Randy K. Otto. 1987. Constitutionally Guaranteed Participation in Criminal Proceeding for Victims: Potential Effects on Psychological Functioning. *Wayne Law Review* 34: 17–28.

Konradi, Amanda. 1996. Preparing to Testify: Rape Survivors Negotiating the Criminal Justice Process. *Gender and Society* 10: 404–432.

Konradi, Amanda. 1997. Too Little, Too Late: Prosecutors' Precourt Preparation of Rape Survivors. *Law & Social Inquiry* 22: 1–54.

Mirowsky, John and Catherine E. Ross. 1989. *Social Causes of Psychological Distress*. Hawthorne, NY: Aldine de Gruyter.

[Omitted State Name] Department of Health. 2000. Homicide Data for [Omitted County Names], 1994–98 [MRDF]. [Omitted State Name] Department of Health, Bureau of Vital Statistics, Statistical Services Division [producer and distributor].

President's Task Force on Victims of Crime. 1982. *Final Report on President's Task Force on Victims of Crime*. Washington, DC.

Rando, Therese A. 1993. *Treatment of Complicated Mourning*. Champaign, IL: Research Press.

Riches, Gordon and Pam Dawson. 1998. Spoiled Memories: Problems of Grief Resolution in Families Bereaved through Murder. *Mortality* 3(2): 143–159.

Rock, Paul. 1998. *After Homicide: Practical and Political Responses to Bereavement*. Oxford: Clarendon Press.

Stenross, Barbara and Sherryl Kleinman. 1989. The Highs and Lows of Emotional Labor: Detectives' Encounters with Criminals and Victims. *Journal of Contemporary Ethnography* 17: 435–452.

Thoits, Peggy A. 1984. Explaining Distributions of Psychological Vulnerability: Lack of Social Support in the Face of Life Stress. *Social Forces* 53: 2453–2481.

U.S. Bureau of the Census. 2001. *County Population Estimates for July 1, 1999 and Population Change for July 1, 1998 to July 1, 1999 (Population Estimates Program, Population Division)*. Washington, DC: U.S. Census Bureau (http://www.census.gov/population/estimates/county/co-99-1/99C1_48.txt) (accessed October 2, 2001).

Wiebe, Richard P. 1996. The Mental Health Implications of Crime Victims' Rights. In *Law in a Therapeutic Key: Developments in Therapeutic Jurisprudence*, ed. David B. Wexler and Bruce J. Winick. Durham, NC: Carolina Academic Press.

18

Female Recidivists Speak About Their Experience in Drug Court While Engaging in Appreciative Inquiry

Michael Fischer, Brenda Geiger, and Mary Ellen Hughes

Abstract: *Fischer, Geiger, and Hughes address the way in which female drug court participants assess the strengths and weaknesses of the program. The majority of participants described the drug court program in a positive light, often comparing the program to previous experiences in other drug programs. The participants described the intensive structure, supervision, and rule enforcement as helpful in their recovery. However, the participants also emphasized the importance of supportive staff members and court personnel. The women's accounts indicated that although structure and supervision are deemed helpful, these aspects of the program alone are not sufficient to encourage compliance with rules and active participation in the program. Instead, the findings indicate that a compassionate and supportive atmosphere is necessary to motivate the women to succeed in the program and attempt to change their behavior.*

Arrests and convictions for drug abuse and drug-related crimes have become the most frequent conviction offense for female offenders (Anglin and Perrochet, 1998; Chesney-Lind and Pasko, 2004; Merlo, 1995). As indicated by the National Institute of Justice (1998), between 33 and 82 percent of female offenders tested positive for drugs at the time of their arrest. From 1995 until 2000, the number of women convicted of federal methamphetamines charges increased by 133 percent (Chesney-Lind and Pasko, 2004). In addition, about a quarter of all women in prison had some form of drug treatment prior to imprisonment (Chesney-Lind and Pasko, 2004). Of those using drugs, 41.8 percent participated in a treatment program the month prior to being arrested. These figures suggest that most of the current interventions were not sufficient to address women's underlying needs (National Institute of Justice, 1998). Female offenders often share the same background characteristics of poverty and traumatic childhood experiences (Geiger and Fischer, 2003, 2005). Most of these women are mothers, oftentimes of minor children for whom there is no arrangement other than adoption or foster care. More than 70 percent of the 869,000 women under criminal justice surveillance have children under the age of 18—1.3 million children (Chesney-Lind and Pasko, 2004, p. 154). Loss of custody often shatters meaning and purpose in life and provides an additional reason to lose oneself in drugs (Chesney-Lind and Pasko, 2004; Chesney-Lind and Shelden, 2004; Geiger and Fischer, 2003, 2005).

The nation's 1,400 drug courts seem to provide an answer to the ever-increasing number of female recidivist felons with a desperate need for resources and services. Based on the philosophy of Therapeutic Jurisprudence (Hora, Schma, and Rosenthal, 1999), drug court provides its clients with intensive judicial supervision and community-based treatment alternatives without the stigma and dehumanizing effects of incarceration (Nolan, 2002). Suspended sentences are used to encourage offenders to participate in drug court and mandated mental health and substance-abuse treatment. Graduated intensive supervision, monitoring for compliance with treatment, and graduated sanctions for noncompliance develop offenders' accountability and allow for gradual reintegration into the community (Berman and Feinblatt, 2005).

Drug courts are required, when receiving federal funding, to be evaluated every six months in their efforts to rehabilitate drug offenders (Goldkamp, 2000; Goldkamp, Weiland, and Moore, 2001; Gottfredson and Exum, 2002). These evaluations employ a variety of process and outcome measures, including program-retention rates, urinalysis results, healthy babies, employment, and recidivism. Assessments show that by comparison to incarceration or standard rehabilitation programs, drug court programs have lower recidivism rates and are more cost-effective (Goldkamp, 2000; Goldkamp et al., 2001; Gottfredson and Exum, 2002).

Despite regular formal quantitative evaluations, appreciation of the components and processes that give life to this unique program as perceived by the program participants themselves has not yet been explored, especially in reference to female participants. In agreement with Patton (2002), the researchers believe that in order to evaluate the effectiveness of a program one must listen to the voices and the stories of those about whom the statistics have been compounded. To compensate for this lack, this action research engaged Northern California drug court female participants in an appreciative collaborative inquiry (Bushe, 1995, 1997).

The main tenets of appreciative inquiry are: (1) the focus on positive and effective programs, and (2) amplification of what participants want more of, even if what they want more of exists only in a small quantity (Cooperrider, 1990; Cooperrider and Srivastva, 1987; Whitney and Cooperrider, 2000). Congruent with the tenets of appreciative inquiry, this study adopts a social and postmodernist perspective that views people as continuously reconstructing social reality (Gergen, 1990, 1994). Program participants have the ability to evaluate and create new and better programs simply by talking about their program and envisioning new realities (Barrett, Thomas, and Hocevar, 1995; Cooperrider and Srivastva, 1987).

Female drug court participants were invited to talk about the characteristics of the people and processes that were conducive to their recovery. Engaged as core searchers and change agents, these women were empowered to amplify those qualities and envision new potentials and possibilities for future drug court programs.

Northern California Drug Court Program Description

The Northern California drug court program under study enrolled 119 felony-convicted offenders, of whom 30 were women. Following individual assessment by the case manager, clients are provided with resources and referrals to various treatment facilities. Clients progress through three phases each lasting for six months, and after-care that lasts for approximately six months. Participants are urine- and Breathalyzer-tested twice a week, with the days of the test selected at random. Continuous graduated intensive supervision and monitoring for compliance with treatment are made possible by the joint collaboration of a judge, three probation officers, 12 treatment providers, two case managers, and two counselors. A mental health specialist court liaison plays the dual role of case manager and liaison, evaluating and reporting to the judge the client's progress. The client appears in court three times a week in phase one, twice a week in phase two, and once a week in phase three. Satisfactory progress is symbolized by advancement through the phases. Compliance with the program requirements leads to a decrease in the intensity of supervision and to greater autonomy and individual choice. Graduated sanctions for noncompliance range from explanation and planning, to being dropped to a previous stage or remaining longer in a phase, to being sent to jail.

Method

Participant Selection

Participant selection criteria for this research were (1) being female, (2) having repeat drug or drug-related offenses, (3) enrollment in drug court program for at least seven months, and (4) being in phases two or three of the program. In the opinions of the probation officers and case managers, these criteria would guarantee that only clients who had enough experience and knowledge of drug court would participate in this study. Eighteen of the 30 female Northern California drug court participants satisfied these criteria. Of this eligible pool, 11 women consented to be interviewed. The age range of these 11 women was between 23 and 47 years, with a mean age of 34.1, and a median age of 32 years.

These women were felons convicted for drug-related offenses such as drug dealing and use, possession of drug paraphernalia, embezzlement, child endangerment, Driving Under the Influence, theft, possession of firearms, hit and run, forgery, possession of stolen property, and stolen credit cards. The reported average number of years of drug addiction was 13.4 years, with 64 percent of the women starting between ages 12 to 16. The drug of choice for 10 of these women was methamphetamine (meth). Five of these women had survived incest, rape, and/or had a family history of drug and alcohol abuse. The remaining six women did not report any family history of drug abuse or incest. In the words of Kim, "A lot of us are from the middle class, without a drug history."

All research participants were mothers of between one and five children, with a mean of 2.5. They had all experienced separation from their children, of whom they had either temporarily or permanently lost custody.

Procedure

A semi-structured in-depth interview that included an interview guide was the main research tool of our appreciative collaborative inquiry. Aside from background information and a history of drug and sexual abuse, questions inquired about participants' experience in the criminal justice system, their experience in the present drug court program, and the components that were conducive to their progress and recovery. Additional questions directed these women to envision innovative aspects of future drug court programs. In order not to interfere with the flow of the narrative, the order of questions in the interview guide was not always adhered to (Brunner, 2004; Denzin, 1989; Patton, 2002; Plummer, 1995).

Before obtaining participants' consent, the two researchers conducting the interviews introduced themselves as a designated drug court evaluator and coordinator from another state. The researchers wanted to hear the participants relate in their own words the components, activities, and people in the program that had assisted them to succeed and change. It was also specified that participation was voluntary. The lack of a therapeutic role of the interviewers and the informal nondirective style of the interview increased ease and facilitated rapport (Baron and Hartnagel, 1997; Hagan and McCarthy, 1992).

Results

Research participants were in awe of what drug court had offered them in their community. In the words of Paula, "Our drug court here is absolutely incredible. I never want them to retire. We are losing one gal due to budget cutbacks, and that will hurt us all."

In trying to comprehend what makes drug court so unique, these women often compared negative past experiences with positive present experiences. To them it was the staff that composed drug court that made this program so special and so different from previous experiences in the criminal justice system and, in a few cases, with other drug courts. Whether in drug court, in the treatment program, or in aftercare, these women felt supported by people who cared about them. The judge emerged in the foreground as one of the most if not the most important figure. He was described as fair, helpful, encouraging, and concerned about the client's progress. In the words of Arlene, "He is really nice, encouraging, doing something positive. He makes it much known to everybody. Actually, it makes you feel good."

Despite a rich past in the cogwheels of the criminal justice system, it seems that for the first time these women were treated with dignity. The judge was talking to them, not past them, or about them to someone else. He genuinely listened to what they had to say about their progress. In the words of Candy, "I think the judge is very fair and honest. He always treats me with respect. He does not talk to me as if I am some worthless addict. I think it is helpful to go in front of the judge." Similarly, Theresa explained while comparing past and present drug court judges,

> There is a big difference. This time he actually wants you to talk to him. You get up in front of him and report how you are doing weekly, or how your program is going, and if you have a relapse, and if there

is any trouble. You can tell him what the problem was and how you solved it. Before they called your name and you stood up and they have this piece of paper and the probation officer and drug court counselor would read it to the judge and say you are doing OK. Bye! It was the drug court staff talking.

The judge's uniqueness was related to a combination of empathy, professionalism, and knowledge about recovery. "He is very compassionate, very understanding, and very knowledgeable about recovery. He has our best interests and our welfare at heart" (Sharon). The drug court probation officer and counselor were also appreciated for their concern and respect. To them, they were no longer a number, but people.

> You see them [probation officer and case manager] once a week. And they ask how are you doing, they want to know what's going on, and a regular probation officer isn't necessarily like that. They want to know everything, which is kind of nice because you know that they really care. You are not just a number.
>
> (Arlene)

> I go in and test on Tuesdays and Fridays. But it's just like, whenever I need to talk, I will go in and talk, and they will sit down and talk to me. They are always helpful.
>
> (Candy)

Sharon remembers how indifferent her other probation officers were: "The probation officer, before, she did not have any compassion. These guys even though they had to send me to jail, they are still smiling." Positive comments were also made in reference to the treatment providers and counselors. Attentive to these women's needs, they gave the women the feeling that they were there for them 24 hours a day.

> I couldn't say enough good things about this treatment staff. They are very conscientious about recovery. When I lost my last sister two months ago, they told me to go home, but I needed to be with people. They just gave me my space, whatever I needed, all I had to [do] was ask.
>
> (Paula)

Similarly, in aftercare and Narcotics Anonymous their sponsors were also always available.

> A counselor may not be available all the time, but somebody is always available from 12 Steps. The people in the meetings have been very supportive. I did not realize how much support there is around here.
>
> (Kim)

> On weekends you have sponsors you may call. Mine lives right up the street. I have had a sponsor for the last 10 months.
>
> (Paula)

Clear Rules and Consequences for Rule Transgression

For these women, intensive supervision, structure, and consequences for rule transgressions and delinquent behavior in the drug court and treatment program were judged helpful as long as they were not humiliating and the participants were treated with respect. In the words of these women,

> And the structure, having to be tested twice a week, forces you to be off of drugs. There are consequences. That helped me clean up long enough to get my bearings.
>
> (Kim)

> New Beginnings is one of the most structured programs. But it's a neat program. They treat me very well.
>
> (Theresa)

Testing positive—relapsing—could require remaining longer at a stage or being moved back to a prior stage, and, in serious cases, being sent to jail. In drug court, participants knew they had to play by the rules. In the words of these women,

> They don't take any crap off of you. If you are going to be defiant and are not going to follow the rules, you'll have a bracelet slapped on you in a heartbeat.
>
> (Paula)

> When you try to take advantage of the court you will get caught. They do not like it. You can only play games for so long. They will put you right in jail. Once you stop using, and stop playing games with them, you realize how good it is.
>
> (Kathe)

Accurate Drug Testing

Participants' confidence in the drug court system was increased because of accurate drug-testing procedures. Reliable laboratory results protected them from false positives. In the words of Theresa, "They sent it to the lab to break it down. They sent it to determine if it was drugs or a false positive. And they figured out that it was a false positive." Similarly, Thelma explains, while comparing past and present testing procedures,

> Back in 1997 tests were not accurate. They accused me of using pot, and told me I was really in denial. "You had a dirty test, and you are going to jail." Today tests are very accurate. If you get a false positive they send it to the criminal lab and they test it, they break it down. It costs the client 45 dollars to send it to them, whereas it costs 6 dollars to do the regular test.

For these women, punishment and accurate testing were, however, still insufficient to prevent rule transgression and promote active participation in recovery. Piaget (1966) often mentioned in the context of moral development that it is the respect, firmness, and warmth of those who communicate the rules that motivate people to adopt and follow them. The women in this research expressed the same sentiment. In their own words,

> You know not to mess up. You can feel the support. People in the front row, you can tell if they have screwed up or not.
>
> (Kim)

He will pull a lot of people's collars and put them in jail. They are not serious about recovery. But for those of us who are, he has a lot of respect for us.

(Paula)

Realizing that drug court had their best interests at heart motivated these women to be honest. Being honest often meant communicating one's failure. It meant reporting drug use and alcohol consumption even when they were sure such use would not be detected by the test. Candy and Kathe recounted,

Around Mother's day, I used marijuana, I got sick to my stomach, I got dizzy, and I had to sit down. What do I do? Do I tell, or not? I drank a 32-ounce bottle of cranberry juice to clean my system out. I had to tell, it's not truthful and honest. I walked in there and told them. I just talked to them about it, and they made me write a little piece of paper about who I was with, and where I was. They tested me, and my test came back clean. It just set me back two months.

(Candy)

Alcohol gets out of your system really fast. I could drink on weekends and get away with it. Alcohol is the one thing you can get away [with] in drug court. All the other drugs will show in your system even after three days.

(Kathe)

In drug court these women learned to assume responsibility and become active participants in their progress. In case of relapse, the judge would ask for the client's input and plans to prevent future drug and alcohol use. In the words of Thelma,

The judge asks you, "So what are you going to do next time? How can you stop it from happening again?" I answer, "I am going to do this and going to do that. I am not going to hang around with those people."

Assuming responsibility was also to accept the consequences of relapse, which at times meant returning to jail.

I did use; I did get a dirty test a couple of times. I told them I slipped up and used meth. I was sent to jail a couple of times. Now I am doing real good.

(Thelma)

I spent 68 days in jail, and I have done 90 days in jail, a week in jail, a couple of months. I know when I will have a dirty test, I have messed up. I will tell them about it, and they will arrest me right then and there.

(Sabina)

These women evoked the need to differentiate between drug and house rule violations. Although the consequences for drug violation were accepted as fair, they requested more flexibility concerning treatment program rule transgressions that were unrelated to drugs and supervision. To be sent to jail for technical violations such as smoking or drinking coffee was for them too extreme and unfair. In their own words,

Well, when I was in jail pregnant with my son I was not arrested for using; I was arrested for being kicked out of a program for smoking cigarettes and drinking coffee; and it was a nonsmoking program. So I had a really hard time with it, that was a violation, I hadn't used, but I had violated. Actually I did go to jail for four months. And they were going to send me to prison for three years. But the judge decided to give me another chance.

(Arlene)

I call it [treatment facility] boot camp: no coffee, no soda, or cigarettes, or chocolate. You get one cup of sugar. Nobody can know where you live, your phone number.

(Candy)

Personal Attitude and Motivation to Mature Out of Crime

As they progressed in the interview, these women emphasized that a client's personal attitude and motivation were conditions *sine qua non* for successful recovery. The client must be ready to change and mature out of drugs. Kathe explained,

And if you are not ready to change it, then you are not going to last long. And the turnover is like crazy. There have been over 100 people in this treatment facility in the six months I have been coming, and I have seen maybe six people graduate since I have been there.

Thelma explained, "Drug court and New Beginnings. Everyone can say I have to quit all they want, but you have to do it."

These women understood that, no matter how much support they received from relatives, friends, or professionals, the desire to change had to come from within. If one is not ready to change, no change will occur. Kristine, who had been surrounded by many caring relatives, knew it best:

If you want drugs, you will take drugs. I had everybody around me telling me to change; I had people trying to help me, my mother, my ex-husband, and everybody else. I did not want to hear it. I still went out to drink.

Being ready means "wanting off those chemicals" (Paula), whatever the reason one had for starting or continuing. The women in this study stated that to change one had to "hit bottom." In the words of Paula,

When I entered New Beginnings we had 11 people in the outpatient program. Now we have four. That's how many have left to use drugs. They were not serious. I think you have to hit rock bottom. . . . Each person's bottom is different.

For these women the phrase "hitting bottom" meant being tired of the vicious circle of drugs, prostitution, crime, and jail.

The same vicious circle, the lies, the stealing, not knowing where I am going to sleep. I have slept on people's cars, bushes, porches. I have prostituted to get my drugs. I am not ashamed of what I did, just some of what I have gone though, you know, is crap. I am 24 years old and I have not accomplished anything but being a drug addict.

(Candy)

"Hitting bottom" also meant coming close to losing it all, including oneself: "It devastated my life. I went from having everything in the world to having nothing. . . . Looking backward my relationship with my family, my sobriety are more important than any drug in the world" (Paula).

Only at the bottom could one reach a deeper level of understanding. Such an understanding was not related to their knowledge about the devastating effects of drugs. Rather, it came from the depth of one's being. In the words of Candy,

> Drug court is a big motivator and a big help, but you have to be ready, from in here [showing her chest]. Not just from your head, but from your heart too. You must really want to change from the inside. You must be ready to grow up.

To be successful one must want to mature; that is, to take personal responsibility for one's fate. Candy explained concerning her parents,

> Mom was also a heroine user, my father would dabble in alcohol, methamphetamine, heroine, marijuana, and I used meth and marijuana with my dad. I feel that they had something to do with how I started off my life; but the problems that I created for myself with the law were my own doing.

Research participants also searched for the components of community-based residential and aftercare treatment programs that were conducive to their progress and recovery.

Individualized Treatment Plan

All these women reported that only an individualized treatment plan could provide the services and supervision they needed. The intake interview with a case manager was, therefore, an essential step in this process. In the words of these women,

> He assesses, determines which program you should enter, whether you need to live in a residential facility. If there is a problem, he will ask you what's going on, etc. If you are doing well, you only have to test once a week, otherwise three times a week. Then both drug court and probation will test you if you need that much supervision.
>
> (Thelma)

Remembering past negative experiences, Kim spoke of a rigid counselor who was deaf to her wishes and excluded her from the decision-making process:

> My counselors in Prop 36 wanted me to go into a battered women's shelter with my 17-year-old-son, but he could not move in because he was too old. When I would have gotten out of there, I would have been homeless. It made absolutely no sense to me, so I did not sign their paper, and so I got a probation violation. I got kicked out of the program because I was being insubordinate. It frustrated me so much that I screwed up and used again.
>
> (Kim)

Learning from past experiences, these women emphasized that decisions about treatment plans had to involve the client and to take into consideration the client's concerns and preferences. Furthermore, assessments must be given periodically because the client changes, and so do her needs for services and supervision.

> When you are originally assessed you may need more intensive treatment. However, going through the process of recovery, whether you are waiting to go to jail or waiting to get into that treatment facility, you have changed. You may no longer need an intensive treatment facility. Without being reassessed you may be sent to a place that does not fit you any longer.
>
> (Kim)

Treatment Facilities That Accept Children

Separation from their children and concern for their welfare remain major preoccupations. To these women, especially for those who did have close relatives to assume custody, there was an eminent need for facilities that accepted children. Kathe was one of the lucky few with a helpful mother and treatment facility that accepted children. She recounts,

> My mom moved into my apartment to take care of the kids when I was in jail. Then they came with me to the residential center. I was extremely lucky, as this is one of the few programs that accept children over the age of 4. So my son and daughter came to live with me.

By contrast, Theresa did not have such a choice. Her children were put up for adoption as a result of a lack of close relatives to take care of them and/or residential facilities to accept them. The loss embittered her. Theresa recounted,

> They put me in a program where I could not have my kids, knowing that I was running out of time. Knowing that if they put me in a program where I could not have my kids, I would lose my kids. I have a real problem with that. If they would have put me in a treatment facility with my children back then, maybe it would have made a big difference. But I wasn't in drug court yet, and it took me a few years to get to drug court. And even then they put me in a place where I could not have my children. That kind of screwed me and my children up.

Choice of Therapy

The women interviewed in this research generally found the intensive therapy and counseling instrumental to their recovery. It was helping them understand the source of their problems. In the words of Kim,

> It does make a difference to find the root. They may say it's because your parents drank or drug used, but a lot of it isn't. A lot of us are from the middle class, without a drug history. Now I understand myself more, and feel more confident with myself, not to let people push me around.

These women also mentioned the need to match therapy (group or/and individual) with the client's need. A mismatch often led to regression. Candy, who wanted individual therapy, complained about a treatment facility:

It's always in a group. No one-on-one. They really don't work with you on an individual basis. They work with you in a group, and then they judge you individually.

Issues Addressed in Therapy

Group therapy had often helped these women confront past sexual abuse and unresolved anger. In the words of these women,

> We worked through a lot of underlying issues, a lot of anger that we had. That I did not know I had. If you learn to hide it at a younger age, drugs just mask it at an older age. With me it was incest.
>
> (Thelma)

> I had a lot of abuse in my past, and I get very anxious and angry, and so I have been in there and talked to people. I didn't really know where the anger was coming from, but they kind of helped me get down to the bottom of it, after I steamed off, like where is this anger coming from, which is really from abuse years ago. And that was really helpful. Because I had no idea as to why I was so angry, I was just mad at everything. And they helped me figure it out.
>
> (Arlene)

Another Issue Confronted: Self-blame and Guilt Consequent to the Separation From Children

Therapy was also needed to deal with separation and loss of the children. In the words of Thelma, who had lost custody of her children,

> Separation from the children creates more issues of guilt and shame, issues that a woman cannot face, and it's going to hurt, and she just wants to use more. To heal the family would be to heal the person.

Candy, similarly, wondered whether there was some kind of therapy that could help her deal with the feeling of loss over her children.

> I regret the loss of my children. I lost them for drugs. [Silence for 10 seconds.] I feel very messed up in the head over it. That I have lost them all. I lost them for drugs. It makes me sad, makes me think. Drug court does not really help with the feeling part.

Treatment Staff: Preference for Counselors Who Are Ex-addicts

All the women interviewed mentioned the advantage of facilities that hired counselors who were ex-addicts. The reason for such preference was that only people who had gone through the same experience could understand and be compassionate. In Arlene's words,

It's hard to make a person understand what you are going through if they have not been there. If you have not been there, you have no idea what it's really like. You may be able to understand what they think and why, but unless you have been there, you really don't know.

For these ex-addicts, counselors' judgment and insight as to what was best for them could be trusted. In their own words,

And that's a really big thing, to trust someone, especially in the system. And I have been in the system since I was 12 years old. If they do not think it's right for you, they will give you another option. If they do not think it's right, they will tell you "This is what we're really thinking." And I really trust their judgment now.

(Theresa)

I do believe that they do have insight, and a lot of them have been through the process themselves, so they understand the problems we face as we go through the stages. I have been here for just over a year and I know that they know what they are doing. I trust them.

(Arienne)

Gender of the Counselor

Most of the participants mentioned that the gender of the counselor is important. In their opinion, female counselors were better able to help them deal with underlying "female" issues of separation of children, physical abuse, and sexual abuse. "It is nice to have a female counselor. It seems like everybody in the program had an abuse issue, sex, and incest" (Kim).

Paula formulated the golden rules for counselors: "(1) don't be judgmental with people; you don't know what they are going though, (2) have an open mind, (3) give that person the benefit of the doubt until they prove otherwise, (4) don't condemn an addict, because you are going to send that person right back out, (5) try being as positive as possible, and (6) maintain confidentiality."

Treatment Facilities' Comprehensive Set of Services

The treatment facilities that were considered superior were those that offered a comprehensive set of services. Project Innovation, which unfortunately closed due to lack of funding, was often cited as the prototype for such a facility. In the words of these women,

Project Innovation was from 8 until 4, with an hour for lunch, Monday through Friday. We had an hour of Alcohol and Other Drugs (AOD) program in group, and then a break, and then relapse recovery for an hour. . . . A speaker came in. It was a job thing and we learned how to do resumés. It was a really good program.

(Arlene)

It offered family recovery, women's issues, individual, group, parenting, anger management, art therapy, and relapse prevention. If you needed legal assistance, there was a counselor who would give it. If you needed medical assistance, they would provide it. If you needed a ride, they had a car. They would get you there and make sure you could get back.

(Thelma)

Resources and Referrals

These women also appreciated resources and referrals at every phase, which enabled them to become independent. In Theresa's words,

> They are hooked up with the EDD [Employment Development Department] place, and they should also be hooked up with Voc Rehab, which is different from the job place. It actually gets you started in something you want to do, hooks you up in school or finds you a job, or pays for tools if you do not have them, if you cannot get on your feet.

Sensitivity to the client's financial problems was also mentioned as an asset. If need be, drug court paid for drug rehabilitation, testing, counseling, transportation, and so on.

> When you are in a residential program drug court helps you with your finances, when you can't pay for bus tickets, they will pay.

(Kathe)

> They pay for my drug rehabilitation, my books [for drug rehabilitation] and stuff; they pay for my aftercare, 10 dollars every time I go. They pay for the one-on-one counseling, if that's what you need; people here in the office will help you get it.

(Arlene)

Skill Acquisition and Vocational Training

For these women, skill acquisition and vocational training were also crucial. The only way to leave welfare as a way of life is to acquire a job. In their own words,

> There are women here who need help and training to get skills and stuff like that. To get them off of welfare, to feel better, stronger. But me, I am happy with what they have done for me.

(Paula)

> People should be made to do something, where they get a skill, such as a welder. Then they could go to work when they get out rather than going back on the streets and drugs. Most of the people who end up incarcerated it's because they don't have a job, or a good job, a good paying job.

(Thelma)

To these women, receiving wages during vocational training was an additional incentive to enroll. Kathe who had enrolled in a vocational training project, explains, "They will pay your wages for up to three months; they will pay you for school if you need it."

Children as Anchor to Remain Clean and Sober

The prospect of being with or seeing their children renewed their hope and faith in life. When asked what would help them remain clean, Jasmine answered, "My daughter!" Similarly, Kathe explained, "For 17 years I was either doing meth, alcohol, or just getting high. And now I am sober, for me, and for them." Candy, who was about to receive four-hour visitation rights, was very excited by the prospect: "I really only have contact with one of my children. I am excited. I am so happy. It starts on his birthday."

Several of these women wished to become productive and work. Kim enjoyed her work:

> I am a waitress. I am getting ready to go back to work. I like work. It keeps me busy. I was stagnant then, it was a lot of wasted time, and I was not using my potential. I have been like this for too long.

Candy was very excited to have, for the first time, a paying job even if it is only on weekends and may result in her losing all governmental aid. "I really want to work; it's my first job ever. I have never had a job. And I just started two weeks ago and I really like it."

Another sign of complete recovery was to give back by helping other drug addicts. For Paula, this was a way to express gratitude to all those who had helped her recover.

> I had wonderful people support me in my recovery, and it's important to give it back, to close the circle. I take them out shopping, or help them with reading, or take them to a movie. It's really important to get that support. These young people don't have the opportunity to get out. I have my freedom, my own space.

Discussion

This qualitative study engaged in an appreciative inquiry with female repeat felons participating in a drug court program in Northern California. Eleven out of 18 females enrolled in phases two and three of the program consented to be interviewed. They were given a voice to talk about the strengths of the program and of the key persons who had helped them change. Empowered as change agents, these women looked at their past and present experiences in drug court and the criminal justice system, and looked forward to envision future drug court innovations. From these women's perspectives, the strongest component of the drug court they were enrolled in was being surrounded by many caring people who listened to them and who were genuinely concerned about their progress. These women did not mind the intensive supervision and graduated and immediate sanctions as long as they were imposed fairly by people who sought to educate rather than punish or humiliate them. Wraparound services, resources, and referral; treatment facilities that accepted children; and individualized treatment plans were essential components of a successful program. Group and individual therapy and counselors who were ex-addicts and preferably women helped these women get to the root of their drug problem and address women's issues of incest, anger, and guilt over the separation from their children.

In drug court they were empowered to put the past behind them and start a new life "without the rush of drugs." It is to be noted that not all of these women were from disadvantaged social-economic strata, and not all of them had abusive parents. Remaining clean and sober as they moved through the three phases and aftercare, acquiring skills, finding a job, and visiting or regaining custody of their children increased confidence in their ability to lead drug-free, meaningful lives.

Drug court assumes that reform can be achieved through coerced court and community intervention without requiring clients to obtain the highest levels of motivation (Prochaska, DiClemente, and Norcross, 1992). It furthermore assumes that motivation can be cultivated through suspended sentences and by having participants remain for longer periods of time than is customary in drug rehabilitation programs (Satel, 1998, 2000). Our findings indicated that clients' participation in drug court increased motivation as they were supported and rewarded for progress through phases. The public announcement of such progress enhanced self-efficacy perception (Bandura, 1977) and motivation to complete recovery. Nevertheless, participants stressed that a condition *sine qua non* for drug court program success was the participants' readiness to mature out of drugs, to stop being deceitful, and to be honest with themselves.

It is possible that the presently examined drug court program was successful with the 11 women precisely because they were already in the process of maturing out on their own. Greater insight concerning the level of motivation and readiness of female drug court participants could be obtained by conducting further research that would compare the subjective experience of female drug court participants who did not go beyond phase one (that is, had failed the program) with those of female drug court participants who progressed beyond phase one.

The women interviewed in this research repeatedly mentioned the human element of care, concern, and fairness of drug court and treatment staff. What these persons gave them could not be compared with any other experience they had had in the criminal justice system, including in a few cases other drug courts. Given the unique personal characteristics of this drug court's personnel, it is recommended to replicate this appreciative inquiry with several drug courts located in the various counties of Northern California. Such a replication would allow us to find out whether the uniqueness of the drug court team was related to the adoption of therapeutic jurisprudence philosophy or a single phenomenon related to the special mix of personal characteristics of drug court staff and clients.

In conclusion, despite the small and selected sample of women who engaged in this appreciative inquiry in one drug court in Northern California, this research expands our knowledge in the field by showing the benefits of a drug court program from female participants' perspective. The components of quality care of drug court and of the process of recovery go beyond traditional criteria of success—lack of recidivism and sobriety statistics so far compiled on drug courts. Terms such as caring drug court staff concerned with the client's recovery, respect, honesty, bottoming out, wanting out of chemicals, relapsing and trying again, putting the past behind them, having hope for the future, wanting therapy to deal with the roots of their drug problems and with the feeling of guilt consequent to separation with children, developing a sense of efficacy that increases motivation to take care of the children, work, and giving in return to other drug addicts are some of the many criteria of successful recovery that could only be comprehended through qualitative research. This study, therefore, shows the invaluable data obtained by conducting qualitative evaluations of drug court programs.

Critical Thinking

Although the women evaluated the drug court program positively, they did provide some suggestions for improvement. The women expressed interest in gaining access to programs with vocational training and continuing education classes, residential programs that allow children, and counseling programs that included therapy for women separated from their children. The women also preferred programs where they could choose between secular or Christian-based treatment and programs that primarily employed female counselors who were ex-addicts. Considering these women's suggestions, do you think these additions are feasible or important? In short, should evaluations of programs to deter or rehabilitate offenders take the perceptions of offenders into account?

References

Anglin, M.D., and Perrochet, B. (1998). Drug use and crime: An historical review of research conducted by the UCLA Drug Abuse Research Center. *Substance Use Misuse 33*, 1871–1914.

Bandura, A. (1977). *Social learning theory*. Englewood Cliffs, NJ: Prentice Hall.

Baron, S. and Hartnagel, T. (1997). Attributions, affect, and crime: Street youths' reactions to unemployment. *Criminology, 35*, 409–434.

Barrett, F.J., Thomas, G.F., and Hocevar, S.P. (1995). The central role of discourse in large-scale change: A social construction perspective. *The Journal of Applied Behavioral Science, 31*, 352–372.

Berman, G. and Feinblatt, J. (2005). *Good courts*. New York: The New Press.

Brunner, J. (2004). Life as narrative. *Social Research, 71*, 691–711.

Bushe, G.R. (1995). Advances in appreciative inquiry as an organization development intervention. *Organization Development Journal, 13*(3), 14–22.

Bushe, G.R. (1997). *Attending to others: Interviewing appreciatively*. Vancouver. BC: Discovery & Design Inc.

Chesney-Lind, M. and Pasko, L. (2004). *The female offender. Girls, women, and crime* (2nd edn). Thousand Oaks, CA: Sage.

Chesney-Lind, M. and Shelden, M. (2004). *Girls, delinquency, and juvenile justice* (3rd edn). Belmont, CA: Wadsworth.

Cooperrider, D.L. (1990). Positive image, positive action: The affirmative basis of organizing. In S. Srivastva and D.L. Cooperrider (eds), *Appreciative management and leadership* (pp. 91–125). San Francisco, CA: Jossey-Bass.

Cooperrider, D.L. and Srivastva, S. (1987). Appreciative inquiry in organizational life. In R. Woodman and W. Pasmore (eds), *Research in organizational change and development* (Vol. 1, pp. 129–169). Greenwich, CT: JAI.

Denzin, N.K. (1989). *Interpretive interactionism*. Newbury Park, CA: Sage.

Geiger, B. and Fischer, M. (2003). Female repeat offenders negotiating identity. *International Journal of Offender Therapy and Comparative Criminology, 47*(5), 496–515.

Geiger, B. and Fischer, M. (2005). Naming oneself criminal: Gender differences in offenders' identity negotiation. *International Journal of Offender Therapy and Comparative Criminology, 49*(2), 194–209. (Reproduced in *In her own* words: Women offenders' views on crime and victimization (pp. 45–54), by L.F. Alarid and P. Cromwell (eds), 2006, Los Angeles, CA: Roxbury.)

Gergen, K. (1990). Affect and organization in postmodern society. In S. Srivastva and D.L. Cooperrider (eds), *Appreciative management and leadership* (pp. 153–174). San Francisco, CA: Jossey-Bass.

Gergen, K. (1994). *Toward transformation in social knowledge* (2nd edn). Thousand Oaks, CA: Sage.

Goldkamp, J.S. (2000, October). *What we know about the impact of drug courts: Moving research from "Do they work?" "When and how do they work?" Testimony before the Senate Judiciary Subcommittee on Youth Violence.* U.S. Department of Justice, Bureau of Justice Assistance.

Goldkamp, J.S., Weiland, D., and Moore, J. (2001). *The Philadelphia treatment court, its development and impact: The second phase (1998–2000).* Philadelphia, PA: Crime and Justice Research Institute.

Gottfredson, D. and Exum, M.L. (2002). The Baltimore city drug treatment court: One year results from a randomized study. *Journal of Research in Crime & Delinquency, 39,* 227–356.

Hagan, J. and McCarthy, B. (1992). Streetlife and delinquency. *British Journal of Sociology, 43,* 533–561.

Hora, P.E, Schma, W.G., and Rosenthal, J.T.A. (1999). Therapeutic jurisprudence and the drug court movement: Revolutionizing the criminal justice system's response to drug abuse and crime in America. *Notre Dame Law Review, 74,* 439–538.

Merlo, A. (1995). Female criminality in the 1990s. In A. Merlo and J.M. Pollock (eds), *Women, law and social control* (pp. 119–134). Boston, MA: Allyn & Bacon.

National Institute of Justice. (1998). *Women offenders programming needs and promising approaches.* Washington, DC: Office of Justice Programs.

Nolan, J., Jr. (2002). *Drug courts in theory and in practice.* New York: Walter de Gruyter.

Patton, M.Q. (2002). *Qualitative research and evaluation methods* (3rd edn). Thousand Oaks, CA: Sage.

Piaget, J. (1966). *The moral judgment of the child,* trans. M. Gabois. New York: Free Press.

Plummer, K. (1995). Life story research. In J.N. Smith, R. Harre, and L.V. Langenhove (eds), *Rethinking methods in psychology* (pp. 50–63). London: Sage.

Prochaska, J.O., DiClemente, C.C., and Norcross, J. (1992). In search of how people change: Applications to addictive behavior. *American Psychologist, 47,* 1102–1114.

Satel, S.L. (1998). Observational study of courtroom dynamics in selected drug courts. *National Drug Court Institute Review, 1*(1), 56–87.

Satel, S.L. (2000). Drug treatment: The case for coercion. *National Drug Court Institute Review, 3*(1), 1–57.

Whitney, D. and Cooperrider, D.L. (2000). The appreciative inquiry summit: An emerging methodology for whole system positive change. *Journal of the Organization Development Network, 32,* 13–26.

19

Jurors' Views of Civil Lawyers: Implications for Courtroom Communication

Valerie P. Hans and Krista Sweigart

Abstract: *Valerie Hans and Krista Sweigart find that communication skills are necessary for lawyers to convey the merits of a case to jurors. Despite the significance of these exchanges, there have been surprisingly few studies on how jurors perceive attorneys. According to the authors, many attorneys overestimate the importance of their opening and closing statements. Although the opening and closing statements prove important as a means of structuring a logical argument, the majority of jurors remain neutral after the opening statement and claim that the closing statement did not overly affect their decision. The authors claim that the popular conception that attorneys do not have to be likeable to present an effective case is a myth. Instead, the authors find that demeanor and likeability was a key factor in the jurors' evaluations of the credibility and sincerity of the lawyer. Hans and Sweigart also determine that excessive use of emotional appeal and dramatics can hinder the credibility and sincerity of an attorney's case. Attorneys that employ overly aggressive interrogation tactics are also deemed less credible.*

Introduction

Conceptions and Misconceptions of Attorneys

In a recent address to a conference on communication in the courtroom sponsored by The Annenberg Washington Program, Robert Sayler, Chair-Elect of the Section of Litigation for the American Bar Association, asserted that many trial lawyers miscommunicate because they hold fundamental misconceptions about juries. The first misconception is that many attorneys believe that they should not be concerned about whether or not the jury likes them. Sayler (1988) claims that it does matter how jurors feel about attorneys because people accept a message more readily when they like the messenger. The second misconception is that jurors want to see a warrior or "Rambo" attorney. Sayler argues that warrior tactics reduce the attorney's credibility when it counts. An attorney who is constantly on the attack loses the opportunity to signal to the jury when he or she feels the witness really is lying. The idea that juries expect to be entertained is the third misconception that Sayler attributes to attorneys. He maintains that it is not bad to entertain, but cautions that entertaining can come to overshadow the evidence. The use of drama may cause juries to think that dramatics are necessary because the case is weak. Drama can also hurt the attorney's case if jurors do not like the theatrical presentation. Then, too, constant entertainment can become old and boring. The fourth misconception is that juries decide cases by the end of the opening statements. Sayler flatly rejects this premise, stating that although there used to be evidence supporting this view, more current work shows that jurors decide cases based on the evidence presented during trials. The idea that preparation can hurt an attorney's case because it produces nonspontaneous responses is the fifth misconception identified by Sayler. On the contrary, preparation is necessary and produces relaxed witnesses who are more credible. Finally, Sayler refutes the ideas that jurors respond to emotional rather than rational arguments, and that the trial judge does not matter. Sayler concludes that attorneys may miscommunicate with juries because attorneys simply do not know what factors jurors believe are important when making a decision. By relying on false assumptions, attorneys may not be defending their clients as effectively as they otherwise might.

Sayler appears to have based his assessment of attorney misconceptions about jurors on his own extensive experience and knowledge about the jury, but many of the observations he makes are supported by standard trial tactics handbooks and by social science data.

Several studies buttress Sayler's general point that attorneys have significant misconceptions about jurors' views of them. Opinion surveys conducted by Mindes and Adcock (1982) discovered divergence among (1) the public's view of lawyers, (2) lawyers' views of themselves, and (3) lawyers' views of how the public perceives them. These researchers polled 321 lay respondents and 305 lawyers to determine what images each group held about the occupation of the lawyer. Lawyers were also asked to estimate how the public viewed their occupation. There was a great deal of overlap across lay and lawyer samples in the characteristics ascribed to lawyers. However, lawyers believed that the public view of them was worse than it really was. Attorneys thought the public saw them as more likely to be greedy, tricky, evasive, manipulative, and overbearing than the public really did. They also thought the public saw them as less helpful, cooperative, understanding, and likable than the public actually did. Overall, the attorneys attributed to the public a view of lawyers that was high on "trickster" or "shyster" qualities and low on "helper" qualities. Attorneys apparently believe that their profession is viewed in a poor light, which may cause attorneys to act in the courtroom in a way more congruent with the way they think the public sees them rather than the way the public actually does.

When attorneys step into the courtroom, they may overestimate their own abilities as attorneys. In one inventive study conducted by Linz, Penrod, and McDonald (1986), trained in-court observers watched the opening statements of 50 criminal trials and rated attorneys on factors such as friendliness, enthusiasm, and nervousness. The researchers compared the observers' ratings and jurors' evaluations of the attorneys with the attorneys' own self-perceptions. Although prosecutors showed no such difference, defense attorneys' ratings of their opening statements differed significantly from the evaluations of the courtroom observers along several dimensions. For both types of attorneys—prosecutors and defenders—there was no correlation between the number of trials in which they had participated or their years in practice and the observers' judgments of their rapport, enthusiasm, or articulateness. The researchers discovered that jurors' judgments and lawyers' self-evaluations correlated significantly for only some characteristics. The researchers also found that the greater the number of years an attorney was in practice, the greater the likelihood that the attorney would underestimate his or her level of nervousness, and overestimate his or her level of friendliness. Thus, although attorneys did not necessarily become more effective communicators as their careers progressed, they became more confident in their skills. It is not surprising to learn that lawyers hold misconceptions about effective trial tactics or even about their own abilities and performances. One of the key factors in promoting accurate self-perception is feedback. Frequent, specific feedback increases our chances of learning what others think of us. Yet the trial situation is one that precludes attorneys from learning what the key decision-makers, namely the jurors, think about them and their actions. True, the jurors reach a verdict in each case, but that verdict reflects the multiple influences of the merits of the evidence, the strengths of the witnesses, the idiosyncrasies of the individual jurors, and the lawyers' impact. Litigators are often stymied in learning from experience because it is difficult to disentangle the different factors producing a favorable or unfavorable outcome in a case.

It would be valuable, then, to know what is in the minds of jurors as they observe attorneys' courtroom communications. A few studies have looked at the impact of lawyer characteristics on juror outcomes by examining actual jury trials and verdicts. In Kalven and Zeisel's (1966) landmark study of judge–jury agreement, the researchers asked trial judges presiding over criminal jury trials to indicate whether the attorneys were evenly balanced or whether the defense or the prosecution was superior. In 76 percent of the trials, the judges viewed the attorneys as evenly matched, and approximately the same percentage of defense and prosecuting attorneys were seen as superior (11% versus 13%, respectively). Additional analyses led Kalven and Zeisel to conclude that in only a little over 1 percent of all trials did the presence of superior defense counsel cause the jury to reach a verdict that was different from one that the judge would have reached had the judge been trying the same case without a jury.

While Kalven and Zeisel had to rely on global judicial evaluations of attorney behavior, another study conducted by Norbert Kerr (1982) correlated student observers' in-court ratings with the case outcomes in 113 criminal jury trials in San Diego. Kerr found that specific ratings of the defense and the prosecuting attorneys were in some instances significantly related to which side won the case. The greater the defense attorney's working knowledge of the evidence, the more convincing the arguments the defense advanced, and the more supportive the defense was toward the prosecutor, then the more likely the defense was to prevail. In a counterintuitive set of findings, the more supportive the prosecutor was toward the defense attorney and the more interested and respectful the prosecutor appeared to be, the *less* likely the prosecutor was to prevail.

Because many different factors varied, along with attorneys, in both the Kalven and Zeisel study and the Kerr study, it is difficult to make causal inferences about how the specific tactics or characteristics of an attorney influence case outcomes. Several mock-juror research studies, most using college students as subjects, have looked at aspects of attorney behavior or characteristics that appear to influence mock jurors. These studies have an advantage in that only one or a few characteristics are varied in a single study, making causal inferences possible. But, they are limited in that the evaluations are based on hypothetical cases, and most use college students as subjects, representing a skewed group of respondents.

Although trial tactics manuals evidence great interest in juror perceptions, this brief summary of the available research shows that few studies, aside from the one conducted by Linz and his colleagues (1986), have taken a systematic look at actual jurors' perceptions of attorneys and their communication strategies, indicating the value of the present project.

Summary

In light of the limited research in the area and the misconceptions that attorneys appear to hold about jurors, it is important to look more methodically at what qualities and actions impress jurors during actual cases. We attempt to identify some of these factors in our analyses of interviews with civil trial jurors.

Research Method

Cases and Participants

This study of jurors' views of civil lawyers, based on a total of 99 tape-recorded interviews, is part of a larger interview study examining the reactions of 269 jurors to cases with business and corporate parties. During a one-year period in a state court of general jurisdiction, every civil jury trial that involved a business or corporate party was identified and included.

With the trial judges' permission, the names, addresses, and telephone numbers of jurors were obtained from the court files. Letters were sent to jurors on University of Delaware stationery requesting them to participate in an interview study about their experiences as jurors. Following the initial letter, a research assistant telephoned each juror. In an effort to contact the jurors, up to ten telephone calls and two additional letters were sent to the jurors. Only a small percentage of jurors could not be contacted by these methods.

The overall response rate of the jurors was 64 percent, with an average of seven out of 12 jurors on each case agreeing to participate. In total, there were 269 participants from 36 cases involving businesses and corporations. There were 28 tort and eight contract cases. The subjects of the cases consisted of disputes over contracts, job-related injuries, consumer injuries, product liability, automobile accidents, and medical malpractice.

All quotes and data used in this article are from the tape-recorded interviews with 99 jurors in these particular cases. In the 14 cases being used, one or more plaintiffs sued business, corporate, or professional defendants. Nine of the cases dealt with personal or consumer injuries, four with contract disputes, and one with medical malpractice. The plaintiffs were successful in 12 of the 14 cases, a success rate similar to that in the total sample of cases. The juror response rate for the cases used was comparable to the overall response rate for the entire project.

Forty-one attorneys were listed in court records as participating in the 14 cases. Twenty-two represented defendants, and 19 represented plaintiffs. One attorney represented a defendant in two cases. Using the *Martindale-Hubble* directory of lawyers, state bar directories, and telephone contacts, the law schools attended by 36 of these attorneys were identified. The remaining five attorneys could not be traced using any of these methods.

Procedure

Jurors were interviewed individually using a semi-structured interview format. In the interviews, jurors were asked to give their reaction to the parties, attorneys, and evidence in their case. The interviews were audio-taped and open-ended responses were allowed. A lengthy set of questions were used to determine the factors that jurors considered significant in reaching the verdict in their case.

Results

Influence of Opening Statements

In the interviews, the jurors were asked if they were drawn to either the plaintiff's or the defendant's side after the opening statements, or if they had remained neutral. While trial consultant Donald Vinson (1986) and others claim that most jurors' minds are made up after the opening statements, 63 percent of the jurors we interviewed maintained that they had remained neutral after the opening statements. In ten of the 14 cases in our sample, the majority of jurors in those cases indicated that they were not drawn to either side after the opening statements. In two other cases, the majority of jurors interviewed reported being drawn to the plaintiff, while in the final two cases there was no clear majority position.

Why Jurors Said They Tried to Stay Neutral

In responding to the question about whether they had been drawn to one side or the other by the opening statements, jurors indicated a number of factors that led them to try to remain neutral. In their accounts, jurors cited the following factors: the judge's instruc-

tions, the lack of evidence at that point in the trial, the fact that they were genuinely undecided, or a desire to resist the impulse to be swayed by their emotions.

The main reason jurors said they were undecided after the opening statements was that
they were following the judge's instructions to remain neutral. One juror who wanted to
be careful to heed the judge's instructions stated: "[T]he whole idea that really stuck with
my mind was that the opening [statements] were to be something you heard, but really
didn't hear; you didn't base your decision on what was said in an opening [statement], but
more what was going to come later." When maintaining that they were undecided after the
opening statements, jurors often referred specifically to the instructions the judge had
given them. A male juror explained, "The judge instructed us at the beginning not to take
sides . . . but to just . . . soak up the information. Take your notes and think about it." Jurors
who mentioned the judge's instructions regarding opening statements support the contention that most jurors strive to be responsible, to be "good jurors," and to follow the instructions they are given as closely as possible.

Other jurors who did not choose sides following the opening statements expressed a
desire to be as neutral as possible. A 47-year-old male juror showed a keen understanding
of the nature of the adversarial process when he stated: "I was keeping an open mind
throughout, because I know there's always two sides to a story, and sometimes you can be
drawn [to one], and then later on see more evidence and sway to the other." A female juror
with some college education wanted to wait to make a decision until she had heard from
the plaintiff and the witnesses. She did not want to base her decision solely on the lawyers'
opening statements: "I got an impression of both the lawyers themselves, but I kept on
trying to repeat to myself that it's not those particular people that we were judging, and so
I would have to say that that [was not] a deciding factor."

Lack of evidence was the second reason jurors commonly gave for remaining undecided
after the opening statements. Without any proof to back up what the lawyers were saying,
the jurors were unwilling to make even a tentative decision. One juror from an asbestos
case said, "I had no feeling because I didn't have enough detailed information to really
draw a conclusion one way or the other." The unwillingness of the jurors to take the lawyers'
words at face value may be due to a distrust of lawyers. In the same asbestos case, another
juror expressed some suspicion when he stated that he was not favoring one side over the
other because "I wanted to hear the actual evidence . . . to see what was actually presented
and whether they could back up their statements . . . [to see] if they were true or not."

Another rationale jurors gave for not being swayed by the opening statements was that the
jurors understood that the lawyer's job was to sway them, and they intended to resist being
influenced so early in the case. When one male juror was asked if he had been "drawn to one
side or the other," he responded, "That's what they wanted us to [do]. They were drawing us
out, they were choosing sides, that's what the lawyers were trying to do." A 60-year-old male
juror with a high school diploma said that he did not want to make a premature decision:

> At that stage of the game, no. Not until I actually had in my hot little hands the documents that the
> lawyers were presenting, back and forth. Because they're great at picking up a piece of paper and
> reading off what they want you to read, and then . . . when it's time for rebuttal, they read what [the

other lawyer] read, and then they read the rest of it. So, actually between lawyers, as far as I'm concerned, it's all a big act.

The juror saw that the attorneys were trying to sway him, and he wanted to wait for the actual evidence to make a decision.

Some jurors genuinely felt that they were not drawn to either side during the opening statements because both sides sounded so convincing. These jurors frequently mentioned that they felt both lawyers had brought out good points in their openings.

> [H]e made such a convincing introduction that before the other man got up, you would think, "Well, boy, I know I'm going to be on this guy's side." Or, "I know that this really sounds right." But, then when the other guy got up, he made such convincing statements, which were just the opposite, that you said, "Oh, well, I didn't think of that before."

With persuasive information from both the plaintiffs' and the defendants' attorneys, the jurors chose to remain undecided because, for them, there was no clear choice of who should win. A female juror explained, "I was half and half. There was a time I was gone for the plaintiff, and then there was a time I was gone for the defendant."

One element that some jurors felt was inappropriate in the opening statements was an exceptional amount of emotional appeal. This foreshadowed the jurors' negative reaction to excessive emotional appeals in later stages of the trial. Although most conceded that emotional appeal was an inevitable part of a case involving an injured plaintiff, they refused to make it their sole basis for being swayed by the opening statements in most cases. When one juror was asked if she favored one side or the other, she responded:

> No. I felt that the opening [statements] were a lot of sob stories, and they weren't that, especially on the plaintiff's part, they wanted you to really feel sorry for these guys . . . [to] draw you into their personal lives, and I was determined I wasn't going to get drawn in, so no, I personally was not swayed by the opening [statements].

A young female juror discussed how her neighbor had suffered problems from asbestos similar to the ones the plaintiff had experienced in the case in which she was a juror. She felt an emotional urge to side immediately with the plaintiff, but she was firm when she stated, "I can't let my emotional feelings interfere with what . . . I'm supposed to be doing."

One can observe from these statements that jurors struggled to resist efforts to appeal to them emotionally. This resistance is reminiscent of some of the psychological research on how people react to one-sided persuasive communications in a two-sided communication context.

Why Jurors Said They Were Drawn to One Side After the Opening Statements

In a minority of instances, jurors reported being swayed by one side or the other by the opening statements. Overall, 20 percent of the individual jurors interviewed sided with the plaintiff following opening statements, and 8 percent sided with the defendant.

In one case in which the majority of the jurors reported being drawn to the plaintiff's side after the opening statements, the defense attorney was trying his first case and was painfully nervous. Jurors cited this factor as the reason they were drawn to the other side. In another case where the jurors were drawn to the plaintiff's side, the defense attorney was viewed by many of the jurors as especially slovenly and obnoxious. The jurors were offended by his demeanor and chose early on to side with the plaintiff.

Other jurors reported that after the opening statements it seemed clear that the side they had chosen was right. One juror favoring the plaintiff said that she had decided, right from the beginning: "I don't know why. I thought that it seemed reasonable, how the accident happened, and I didn't have any trouble with it. I sort of leaned right to his side from the very beginning." Thus the minority of jurors who admitted being drawn to one side or the other after the opening reported that either attorney demeanor or the merits of the case had influenced them. What is most striking, however, is how few jurors acknowledged that they were drawn to one side or the other by the opening statements.

Influence of Closing Arguments

Near the end of many of the interviews, jurors were asked if the closing arguments had an impact in convincing or changing their minds. In 44 percent of the interviews, the question was either not asked or not answered. This was usually because, in the course of the interviews, many jurors stated their preference before the interviewer reached that question, so the question was omitted. However, 80 percent of those jurors who were asked the question said that the closing arguments had not caused them to be drawn to one side or the other. In many cases, the jurors had already decided what side they were going to favor before the closing arguments.

Of the jurors asked about closing arguments, those who reported being drawn to the plaintiff's side and those who reported being drawn to the defendant's side by the closing arguments were nearly even. Eleven percent of the jurors said they were drawn to the plaintiff's side, while 9 percent reported being drawn to the defendant's side. In none of the 14 cases did a majority of the jurors report being drawn to either one side or the other by the closing arguments.

Some jurors reported not being swayed by the closing arguments because they saw them more as a summary of the case than an actual argument. They realized that the attorneys were trying to remind them of all that had transpired during the case. Some jurors expressed disappointment that the closing arguments were not as exciting as those they had seen on television or in the movies. One juror explained: "They weren't as strong as I thought they would be. Basically, it was just a brief summation from what went on. . . . [I]t was nothing glorifying, like you see on Perry Mason." Some jurors did feel that the attorneys were trying to sway them: "They were, at that point, both trying to leave their impression upon us, to convince us one way or the other. If the evidence didn't do it, possibly their last remarks would." These jurors often mentioned the fact that the plaintiff's attorney not only gave a closing argument but could also rebut the defense attorney's closing argument. They felt it was unfair that the plaintiff had "two shots" at the jury:

> The [plaintiff] had the last word if I remember right, and I think he did. I think the last words said [are] what sticks in the jurors' minds the most; he's got the opportunity to contradict everything that [the defense attorney] said in his closing argument and I think that stuck with most people. I think he had a distinct advantage there.

Overall, the jurors expressed some disappointment in the closing arguments. They were frustrated that they were once again hearing what they had already heard in the opening statements and in the actual case. Some had envisioned climactic endings to their trials and were let down in realizing that the closing arguments were basically a summation of the facts. A retired female juror said, "Well, they were very much the same . . . rehashed over the same things. It was such a repetition." By the end of the trial some jurors also seemed disheartened by the adversarial nature of the cases. A juror complained that the closing arguments were "too long, too drawn out, too predictable. You knew what [the plaintiff] was going to say, you knew what [the defendant] was going to say, the complete opposite."

Creating a Framework

Although most jurors reported that their preference for one side or the other was not influenced exclusively by the opening statements and closing arguments, it would be a mistake to infer that the opening and closing had no impact. Further analysis of jurors' comments revealed that the opening and closing were critically important in providing a framework. Many jurors mentioned that the opening statements and closing arguments created a framework within which they viewed the case, and gave the case a clear structure that it might have otherwise lacked. By outlining in the opening statements the ideas they were going to advance and later summing up the facts in the closing arguments, the attorneys gave the jurors a coherent idea of what to expect in the trial and of what they had delivered. This use of attorney communication is, of course, quite consistent with the story model of jury decision-making described earlier.

The jurors used the opening statements to help them determine what they should be looking for in the case. After hearing the statements, the jurors felt they had a good idea of what was going to happen throughout the case. As a male college graduate explained:

> The plaintiff went first. He told the general overview of the case, and how he was going to try to prove his point. And the defense did the same thing. He gave a general overview of the case: and how he was going to prove his point, who he was going to call, [and] that we were going to have some taped testimony on videotape.

Similarly, a 20-year-old juror felt that the opening statements were an attempt to "set the stage" of the case.

Many of the jurors thought the closing arguments were useful in clarifying issues that had become confused during the trial. A female juror said the closing argument "was just summing things up to me and refreshing my memory. Kind of like making me go back to the beginning, to make me remember what was important down the road until this point for me."

Lawyers also had the opportunity in closing arguments to show the jurors the consistency of their arguments throughout the trial. A juror in a personal injury case said, "I believe the [plaintiff's attorney] put a lot of things back together as far as what he tried to do right from the start and how it paralleled his introduction." Without the closing arguments, jurors may not have been able to sift through the information the attorneys presented. Especially in long trials, jurors apparently began to confuse the arguments presented by the plaintiff and the defendant. One juror expressed the importance that the closing arguments held for her:

> I think it sort of just tied up some loose ends; it reiterated some stuff that was said in the beginning that I might have lost track of along the way. And it also led me to realize that they were boxing heads, solidified in my mind that they had actually two sides. Because when you get to hear all these plaintiffs and witnesses, and folks are up cross-examining each other, you begin to think, "Well, just who was for who, what was for what?" And you're taking down all the facts, but you have to go back and look over your notes to just really decide what you're going—you know, what your idea is, or what your thoughts are. However, in the closing arguments, it sort of brought it all back into perspective . . . [and made] you . . . remember that there are two sides.

Even if jurors reported that they stayed neutral during the opening statements and closing arguments, an attorney who clearly expressed the structure of the case appeared to have an advantage in encouraging jurors to focus on and recall the material that supported his or her client.

Jurors' General Views of Attorney Qualities

In addition to asking specific questions about opening statements and closing arguments, we also asked jurors to provide a general evaluation and ranking of the attorneys in their cases. Slightly more jurors reported favoring the plaintiff's attorney (37%) than the defendant's attorney (31%). The remainder expressed no opinion or thought that the attorneys were evenly matched. Similarly, in five of the 14 cases in the sample, a majority of jurors chose the plaintiffs representative as superior, compared to three cases in which jurors chose the defendant's attorney as the superior one. The small number of cases precluded us from conducting a statistical test to determine whether the perceived superiority of the attorney translated into a favorable case outcome.

What Made One Attorney Better

Issues that appeared to influence the way jurors evaluated attorneys were the credibility and demeanor of the attorneys, the emotionality of their arguments, and their organization of the case. Attorneys who were not credible, had poor demeanor, used excessive appeals to the jurors' sympathy, or were poorly organized tended to alienate the jurors.

It is interesting to note that jurors expressed ambivalence about emotionality in the arguments. They liked a small amount, but resented extreme appeals to their sympathy. In addition, the level of emotionality in argument was evaluated against the severity of injuries claimed in the case.

These points are best illustrated by specific examples from cases in which one attorney was considered to be better than the other. In one case involving a sports injury that left the plaintiff paralyzed, the majority of the jurors who favored the plaintiff's attorney referred to the level of the attorney's organization in explaining why they preferred him. Since he appeared to be better organized, the jurors concluded that he was a better attorney. Moreover, the defendant's lawyers did not seem to be as involved in the proceedings. A female juror explained:

> [The defense attorney] used the plaintiff's material so often, I felt that he was not as prepared as the other lawyer. He was forever leafing through, like he was confused, he wanted to find this, he wanted to find that. . . . And I felt that the lawyer from the company, as the time went on, he was not there 100 percent of the time. But when he was there, he just didn't . . . seem to be interested.

The plaintiff's attorney came across as more likable. He used an amount of emotional appeal that the jurors felt was appropriate in this particular case. Although he tried to evoke the jurors' sympathy, his approach was not viewed as excessive given his severely injured client. None of the jurors felt he was exaggerating the injuries in order to play upon their emotions. A male juror said, "His was more of an emotional plea, whereas the other man was more of a legal correctness, who made a mistake and who didn't." This approach, focusing on the legal aspects of the case, tended to make the defense attorney appear unsympathetic to the plight of the severely injured victim. Throughout the interviews, the jurors described the defense attorney as "cold," "calculating," and "callous."

Even though no juror favored the defendant's lawyer over the plaintiff's, jurors did not believe that he was a bad attorney. The jurors simply tended to favor the approach of the plaintiff's attorney. A male juror explained the differences between the two lawyers:

> They were both good lawyers, and the thing of it was that they both have opposite personalities. One man was . . . a more story-type, personable, warm-type guy, and the other man was very legal and precision-minded, very dry, cut and dry, unemotional. . . . [The plaintiff's attorney], he was more positive and more flowery and descriptive and colorful and story-type. The other man was negative. He was . . . looking for everything that was wrong all the time, picking out all the dark, negative things, and enlarging on them deliberately. He seemed to be like one of these birds in the air that fly over, he never sees any beautiful scene, he just sees a dead cat on the ground or something like that. You know, always seeing the bad, the negative. So . . . those . . . were . . . their two different approaches.

In the case mentioned previously in which the defendant's attorney was trying his first case and was apparently very nervous, his nervous appearance put him at a disadvantage in the jurors' minds. The majority of jurors evaluated the plaintiff's attorney more positively. A male juror with graduate school experience explained:

> I thought that [the plaintiff's lawyer] had a better composure; I don't know that he displayed more skill or more insight or more intelligence about the case or the way to handle a case. Nor do I think

that he displayed less. I thought in those respects they were equal, except [the defendant's lawyer] was a lot more nervous.

Throughout the interviews with jurors from this case, the main topic in the discussions of the quality of the attorneys was the defense lawyer's extreme nervousness. His nervousness was so intense that it made some jurors uncomfortable. A female juror said, "I felt embarrassed at the defendant's lawyer because he was new and he was making all these mistakes." The plaintiff's attorney may have looked better in relation to the defendant's attorney simply because he was more composed, but there are suggestions in some juror interviews that the nervousness also detrimentally influenced the organization of the case presentation. A 35-year-old female compared the attorneys:

> There was a great difference. I mean, [the plaintiff's attorney] knew what he was doing or appeared to know what he was doing, and he was very cool and very collected and had all his facts together. I mean, he went through every witness and you could tell that his questions were preplanned. And when he crossed he had everything written down and went right down in order. . . . [The defendant's attorney], on the other hand, had a very confusing way of addressing everything. He would put a chart up as to certain dates when the accident occurred, when she was released from the hospital, the first time she went to the doctor, and he would just put them up there in sort of a jumbled fashion. And he would bounce around, and it was very distracting at first, until you got used to him. And he was very, very disorganized all through the whole thing.

The defense attorney did help his situation somewhat by informing the jury that it was his first trial. A male juror reported:

> I thought it was wise of him at a point in the trial to indicate to the jury that, "this is my first trial." But not come out and say, "I'm nervous because this is my first." [While examining a witness,] he very wisely pointed out that, "You're very nervous. Are you normally like this?" And she said, "No, I've never been on trial before." And he said, "Well, I've never been on trial either, this is my first trial so we're both nervous." And they kind of kept going. But I thought it was excellent of him to point out to us, "I'm nervous because this is my first trial, not because of the case."

The lawyer's comments about his first trial let the jurors know that he was nervous for a reason other than the quality of his case. Otherwise, the jurors could have misread his nervousness to be an indication that he was not confident about the information he was presenting.

The preparedness of the lawyers was an important issue to the jurors in many of the cases. Not surprisingly, a well-prepared case tended to appear stronger. In a contract dispute case in which 75 percent of the jurors favored the plaintiff's attorney, the plaintiff presented a significantly greater amount of evidence than the defendant. Jurors saw this as an indication that the defense attorney was either too confident or had no case at all. A female juror said:

> The plaintiff's attorney was definitely well prepared. There's no doubt about it, he definitely had enough [evidence]. As a matter of fact he had too much information as it kept getting him into trouble. If he wouldn't drop it, he'd be looking for it, constantly fumbling through all pages looking for what he was looking for. He reminded you of the absent-minded professor, but he presented his

case very well, needless to say. The defense attorney, I think they thought the case was out and dry, that they didn't have to present anything to us.

Although the plaintiff's attorney may have been a little disorganized, his huge volume of material impressed the jurors enough to make up for it. The defense attorney's lack of material to present made him appear cocky or arrogant.

A female juror with some college experience also felt that the defense attorney was doing the minimum necessary to present the case:

> All along I felt that the defense attorney just—really, I don't know, . . . he really was defending. I mean he was doing what he was supposed to do but, it was not like a proactive kind of an argument. It was just, "Well you said this, but, . . ." He wasn't as strong as [the plaintiff's attorney].

In another personal injury case, many of the jurors did not perceive the defendant's attorney as professional or credible. Four of the six jurors who chose the plaintiff as the superior lawyer mentioned that the appearance or demeanor of the defendant's attorney was inappropriate. A male juror stated: "The key issue had to be appearance, demeanor, credibility. [The defendant] or his attorney did not come across as professional, trustworthy, honest. We all said this in that courtroom. It was not very difficult to reach a decision." The difference between the two attorneys was clear to that juror:

> You had the clean-cut, professional-looking attorney, and you had this guy, [the defense attorney,] who certainly didn't appear—he did not have the credibility he should have [had, because of] his appearance. . . . I think his appearance took away from a lot of what he had to say. . . . His shirttails were hanging out, his shirt was wrinkled. He really did not have a professional [attitude].

The plaintiff's attorney, on the other hand, was well respected by the jurors. A female juror said, "I thought he did an excellent job. He kept to the facts and didn't exaggerate anything and didn't make it emotional or anything."

An unusual aspect of this case was the fact that the defendant himself was an attorney. The defendant tended to get involved in the defense of his case, and two of the six jurors who sided with the plaintiff's attorney mentioned that his involvement had disturbed them. A male juror explained:

> I think [the defense attorney] was a puppet and he was doing what he was told to by [the defendant]. Because [the defendant] was at his side, and anything that the plaintiff would present, [the defendant] would go ahead and tell [the defense attorney] what it was, he would whisper in his ear a bunch of things. [The defendant] would write something down and would hand it to him and he would get up there and talk. It seems he was doing what he was told to by [the defendant].

These jurors felt that the defendant's attorney should have controlled the case, not the defendant. The defense attorney's lack of control in the case made him look weak in the jurors' eyes.

The final case in which the plaintiff's attorneys were viewed as better by a majority of jurors was an asbestos case. No single issue arose that marked the plaintiff's attorneys as superior; rather, the jurors generally felt they were better lawyers. Unlike another asbestos case in our study, the plaintiff's attorneys did not suffer in this instance because they specialized in a particular type of claim. In the other asbestos case, jurors were hostile to the idea that a lawyer would bring numerous asbestos claims. They saw this practice as attorneys "manufacturing" cases in order to make more money and described the plaintiffs' attorney as an "ambulance chaser." In contrast, in this case, jurors actually saw it as an advantage to specialize: "I know that there [are] lawyers that specialize in different fields—[prosecuting] murder[ers], suing, corporations, paperwork, and that kind of thing. I know there must be at least a half dozen categories or whatever it is. And when you specialize in that one field you become good at it." In this case, jurors did not seem at all disturbed by the idea that the lawyers were repeatedly bringing one type of claim. They rejected the notion put forth by the defense that this practice was unfair. A female juror said: "There was a little conjecture, and the defense tried to point out that there was a conspiracy of some sort. But as the trial progressed, we all came to the conclusion that there was damage that had been done to these people, and it really wasn't their fault." The defendants' attorney suffered because he did not appear as knowledgeable about cases involving asbestos injuries. A male high school graduate explained:

> This other fellow, [the defendant's attorney], he didn't know it that well. It just seemed like he took a crash course in it and got as much information pertaining to it and had to study it the night before to come in prepared. But the other guy, he knew his stuff.

There were three cases in which the defendant's attorney was considered the better attorney. In all three cases, calm defense attorneys opposed very emotional plaintiffs' attorneys. The defense attorneys seemed to have benefitted from the comparison.

The plaintiff in one case was injured as the result of a car accident. Her attorney used many arguments that jurors felt were designed to appeal to their emotions. Although jurors recognized that the woman had been hurt, they felt the plaintiff's attorney was exaggerating her injuries. It is useful to contrast jurors' negative reactions to emotionality in this case with their more neutral reactions to emotionality in the case involving the paralyzed plaintiff in the sports injury case. It appears to be important that attorneys carefully calibrate the amount of emotion they express in a case to the seriousness of the injury. Jurors did not automatically resent emotion, but instead resisted emotion that seemed out of proportion with the injury. Since the attorney in the car accident case made the plaintiff's injuries seem more serious than they appeared to be, he lost credibility. A male juror who works as a security officer explained:

> He was overly dramatic. You know what I'm talking about? Since it was about the case, he kept saying how perfect her body was before the accident . . . he made her almost seem like a cripple, but we could all look at her and see that there was no neck brace, no wheelchair, nothin', you know? And we're all just like . . . she looks fine to me.

It appears that jurors were annoyed by the constant emotional appeals in a case that they did not consider to be very serious. Also apparent is some suspicion on the part of the jurors about the plaintiff's claim of severe injury. Later in the interview the same juror said:

> [The plaintiff's lawyer] kept repeating: "This is our one shot. This lady has been calling for me for the last two years on the phone about this case, about her injuries, and her pain. And her pain will not go away, and this is our only shot, you people here. If we don't win, we can't come back. This is it." And we were all like, "So?"

The jurors were also confused in this case by the fact that the plaintiff's young son sat with her throughout the trial but did not testify. Six out of the eight jurors commented on this. They wanted to know why he was not in school. Many jurors saw this as a tactic to induce sympathy for the plaintiff and felt it was inappropriate. A female juror explained the reaction of the others involved in the case:

> We had one woman on the jury, she said, "as soon as I walked in there and saw that boy sitting at the table I wondered why he wasn't at school." And they had said that he was having a civics lesson, the lawyer had said that he was there because this was a good civics lesson. [The jurors] didn't buy that, they weren't a bit sympathetic that the boy was there.

The son sitting with his mother seemed out of place to the jurors, and it became a major source of discussion during their deliberations. Most jurors assumed that it was a tactic or trick on the part of the plaintiff's attorney.

Throughout this personal injury case, few jurors referred to the defendant's attorney as a good attorney. It seemed that the jurors were rejecting the plaintiff's lawyer rather than commending the defendant's. The jurors seemed better able to respond to the calm, unemotional arguments that the defendant's attorney put forth, but this fact did not mean that they thought he was a superb attorney. A female juror described him: "He asked questions, he was very to the point, said what he had to say, that type." Another juror described him as "the lesser of two evils."

In another case pitting a calm defense attorney against a lawyer who was more emotional, one juror compared the attorneys:

> I guess [the defense attorney], you'd have to say, was a slicker. If you knew what a slick attorney was, that was a good definition of him. [The plaintiff's attorney] got a little more emotional sometimes. He'd get a little loud, scream and yell. [The defense attorney] would make his subtle theatrics: raise his eyebrows up in the air, look around the room. He'd sort of say "ha" without really saying it. He didn't really say it, but the jury could see him.

Jurors were more comfortable with the defense attorney's approach. He was thorough, but not excessive. The following juror explained, "[h]e was the best lawyer, because he was fighting for the case, but he wasn't going to an extreme." In contrast, the jurors distrusted the excessive emotional appeals of this plaintiff's lawyer, and felt he was exaggerating the case in his statements. As a result, the defense attorney and his client benefitted.

The final case where a defendant's attorney was favored by a majority of the jurors was another in which the plaintiff's lawyer was very emotional (several of the jurors described him as a "showboat"), while the defendant's lawyer was calm and quiet. A male juror in his forties described the differences between the two attorneys:

> [The plaintiff's attorney] basically played on the emotional factor. Here's poor [plaintiff]: he's been damaged, he can't work, he can't bend, he can't walk, he can't stoop, he can't sit in a chair for more [than] ten minutes. Yet the guy sat in the chair for seven solid days and never moved. And he got to be quite flamboyant. And I had a little trouble with that. . . . [The defendant's] case was basically the facts. Here's what happened, here [are] the photographs, here's the testimony. Base your decision on what really happened in the case.

Jurors also felt that the plaintiff's attorney was exaggerating the plaintiff's injuries:

> I think his attorney was a little overzealous in trying to say [the plaintiff's] life had just come to an end and that if he didn't receive this settlement his life was going to be destroyed and he would never be able to take care of himself or his family and that . . . the thing that we as good citizens just had to do was award [the plaintiff] his $600,000. So I started to develop kind of a negative attitude about him probably around the third day of the case. The case went for seven days.

The emotionality of the plaintiff's attorney made him appear less believable to the jurors. They began to see him as a lawyer they could not trust. The defendant's attorney presented a straightforward argument; although the jurors did not feel she was exciting or especially talented, they did feel she was worthy of their trust. A male juror said, "I think I probably like [the defendant's attorney] a little better because she seemed to be playing it more legitimate than the [plaintiff's attorney] was."

Badgering the Witness

Jurors, especially female jurors, did not respond favorably to attorneys who attacked or badgered witnesses. It made the jurors feel uncomfortable and sometimes more sympathetic to the witness than they otherwise would have felt. In a knee injury case, the defense attorney badgered a female witness to the extent that a female juror began to identify with the witness and feel sorry for her:

> Another thing the plaintiff's attorney did at that point was to ask her if she had walked to the courtroom. She said, "Yes, I parked two blocks away." He said, "Do you have high heels on?," and she said, "No." And he, he frankly took her shoe off, and I would have been mortified if this were me, and showed it to the jury. And there was a small heel on there, but most working women do not wear flats. Even if you're in mortal pain, you're at least going to get a little bit of a heel out of it. And he really tried to rake, rake her over the coals over that. . . . So I really felt sorry for her there.

Being aggressive with a witness made the jurors dislike an attorney. A female juror described an especially forceful attorney:

> He was really cocky, and sometimes he'd be really mean and ugly to those people. [One witness] had a stutter, and as soon as he got up on the stand, it really came out. You couldn't understand him, and

> I thought [the attorney] was a little rude to him. I mean, I wanted to yell out, "Would you leave him alone!" But [I] didn't. I almost felt like you're in school. You didn't yell out, you didn't do any of that. You just kind of sat there, and it was like, "Urghh, leave, this guy alone!" . . . I wouldn't . . . like him at all if he came on to me that way.

Another juror acknowledged that she thought it was the role of the attorneys to try to upset and confuse witnesses, but she also understood that people cannot remember things perfectly—so witnesses are occasionally going to be inconsistent:

> I guess maybe . . . [the defendant's attorney] did a real good job of confusing him with dates and things like that which was annoying. He was kind of picking on him, but that's [his] job. And [the witness] was getting confused about some of the dates and the way that it had happened a long time ago. Anyone would be fuzzy about certain dates, when he had a doctor appointment and all that stuff.

In a case in which the defense attorney was reported by the jurors to have badgered a medical witness, the witness performed well under the circumstances and increased his credibility in the minds of many jurors. A male juror said:

> The lawyer kept baiting him, and baiting him, and baiting him. . . . He was getting pretty mad at the end. I think we all sympathized with the guy, so after a while the lawyer hurt himself more than anything because the doctor came with fixed straightforward answers, but he kept trying to bait the guy.

By constantly pressing the plaintiff's witness, the defendant's attorney made the jurors feel uncomfortable and sympathetic to the witness. Because the witness was consistently able to answer the attorney's questions during the cross-examination, the attorney actually increased the witness's credibility instead of decreasing it.

Thus, in these cases the attorneys seemed to gain nothing from badgering a witness. The jurors were more likely to sympathize with roughly treated witnesses, and less likely to believe, when witnesses were badgered, that inconsistencies in their testimony were a result of weaknesses in the case.

Actors and Tricksters

Many of the jurors did not believe that the attorneys' actions were worthy of their trust. The word "actor" came up repeatedly throughout the interviews. Some jurors did not believe that the behaviors or the arguments of the attorneys were genuine; rather, they suspected the attorneys of playing a role in each case. Emotional displays by the attorneys were especially suspect. A male juror with some college experience said:

> When [the plaintiff] was on the witness stand, [the lawyer] started to break down in tears himself. Which I don't know if that . . . came natural, or whether that was part of the act. I don't know . . . when she started breaking down, he did too.

The juror had trouble believing that the lawyer might feel sympathy for the plight of his client. In the case with the nervous defense attorney, a female questioned his nervousness:

"I just wondered, 'Is this a ploy to get our sympathy?,' because he was so nervous or 'Is he really like that?,' and that's the one thing that really stuck out in my mind, more than anything else." Instead of believing the attorney was nervous, the juror suspected the attorney of lying. Lawyers who showed excessive emotion—even nervousness—during the trial were considered by some jurors to be acting to elicit the jurors' sympathy.

Attorneys were also considered to be acting when they deviated from a straightforward approach while trying the case. Raised voices or abrupt actions were supposedly part of an act. A female juror said: "They were both very good at their theatrics, as far as hopping around, making faces. It was kind of funny. [The attorney] for the plaintiff—little guy— he'd get all fired up and hoot and holler. [The attorney] for the defense was very quiet." A male juror with college experience also saw these types of actions as part of an act:

> I enjoyed watching the lawyers go back and forth and some of the tactics that they would use. And, you know, the way they would roll their eyes. . . . I was really quite interested in the way the different attorneys played to the jury and played against each other. It was, it was very good. They must have been in drama class at one time.

Jurors seemed to neglect the possibility that the attorneys might actually get excited or frustrated during the progress of their case. Extreme displays of emotion appeared frequently to lower the attorney's credibility in the jurors' eyes.

Sometimes jurors suspected the attorneys of outright lying. They saw the lawyers as tricksters who would lie or try to manipulate the jury in order to sway them to their side. A female homemaker said: "I think sometimes lawyers try to play games with your mind to try and make you, well, think their way. And I think it gets to the point where the jury has to decide who's lying." A juror from another case explained:

> [A]nd he was a lawyer, which was in the back of my mind too . . . because I kind of think . . . lawyers try to take you over. Maybe that was in the back of my mind too. [Lawyers] know the ins and outs to the whole thing, you know. While [the plaintiff] was just, a first time thing for him, he had an entirely different background.

Jurors also thought that attorneys might persuade plaintiffs to lie or to exaggerate their injuries. A juror who was a high school graduate thought the attorney had done this. "I think that [the plaintiff's] lawyer told her how to act and react. . . . She was very emotional and upset about it. I mean, she acted like it was yesterday when his hand got cut." The presentation of evidence by adversary attorneys thus appeared to alert jurors to be on their guard for ways in which the evidence itself might be influenced by the attorneys.

Discussion

Opening Statements and Closing Arguments

One of the most interesting sets of findings pertains to the jurors' estimates of how they were influenced by opening statements and closing arguments. Most jurors rejected the idea that they were strongly swayed by such arguments alone. They offered a variety of explanations for why they were not drawn to one side or the other after the opening statements. The most significant, of course, were judicial instructions to remain neutral. Closing arguments were similarly judged by jurors as not being particularly influential.

It is always difficult to evaluate the accuracy of people's responses to questions when strong cues indicate the socially desirable answer. The judge instructed the jurors that they must not allow themselves to be swayed by the opening statements, and thus it was clear what the court wanted them to do in order to fulfill their role as good jurors. Some jurors may well have been strongly influenced by the opening statements and closing arguments, but still attempted to maintain that they were not influenced—or reported to us that they were not—because of the judicial admonition. Yet the jurors' comments about trying to remain neutral have a compelling and realistic quality. Many jurors revealed some mistrust of the opening statements and expressed a desire to see whether or not the evidence would support these statements. This reported resistance to persuasion has also been found among subjects in studies of one-sided and two-sided communications.

Jurors remarked that the prime value of opening statements and closing arguments was that they provided a framework within which jurors could evaluate the cases. In this relatively subtle way, attorneys were able to affect jury decision-making. By outlining the arguments they were going to advance, attorneys gave the jurors a way to order information in the case. The jurors' descriptions of the impact of opening statements in this study converge nicely with the findings of Pyszczynski (1981) that opening statements create cognitive schemata that structure the jurors' processing and interpretation of evidence. In addition, the jurors' descriptions about the impact of opening statements correlate well with the theoretical arguments of other scholars about the importance of a story or script for ordering trial evidenced. Many jurors mentioned that the opening statements and closing arguments helped them to understand and recall information—but they did not consider this to constitute "influence." Attorneys, of course, might well disagree!

The comments by jurors showed that the summary statements were quite helpful to them in organizing the evidence. In this light, it is worthwhile to note that jury experts have recommended that, to enhance jury comprehension, attorneys should be permitted to make mini-summary statements throughout the trial in addition to their standard opening statements and closing arguments. The results of our study suggest that such statements would have maximum impact if they help generate a strong framework within which jurors may organize the ongoing evidence.

Although jurors are affected by opening statements in that they use them to create stories or frameworks to organize the evidence, the jurors' comments that they were not swayed by the opening statements strongly support Sayler's contention that jurors do not make up their minds right after the opening statements. In contrast to the claims of some trial consultants and attorneys, our study suggests that instructed jurors are aware of the adversary pressure during the openings and try to resist early persuasion attempts. The judge's forewarning about the opening statements appeared to alert jurors to attorneys' efforts to persuade them. This is an interesting finding in that many studies on the impact of judicial instructions upon jurors have shown them to have little effect on jury decision-making. To test whether jurors who are admonished are actually more apt to resist persuasion attempts during the opening statements, or whether they are simply responding in a socially desirable way by reporting that they were not swayed by the openings, one could conduct a mock-juror experiment that includes or excludes a judicial instruction concerning opening statements and then observe whether jury decision-making is thereby affected.

Qualities of Good Attorney Communication

Returning to Sayler's comments about how jurors respond to attorney communications, many of his points about jurors are confirmed by the juror interview results. The jurors in this project reported that the primary factors that influenced their opinions of an attorney were the attorney's credibility, organization, demeanor, emotionality, and treatment of witnesses. Jurors evaluated positively those attorneys who were credible, well organized, and moderate in their use of emotion. Poorly prepared or extremely emotional attorneys, and attorneys who badgered witnesses, were all viewed negatively by jurors. This fits well with Sayler's recommendation to steer clear of "Rambo" lawyering, and to avoid relying exclusively on emotional—rather than rational, evidence-based—appeals.

In a related vein, our study reinforces one public opinion poll's findings that some people perceive attorneys as "tricksters." Jurors thought that many of the attorneys were behaving unnaturally, acting out a role specific to the case rather than behaving truthfully and naturally. Jurors were cognizant of the adversary nature of the trial and the opposing roles of the attorneys, and considered these roles in responding to lawyers' communications. The jurors' comments and reactions show the hazards of employing excessive or overly dramatic trial tactics, and the value of developing a highly credible courtroom style.

One interesting pattern in this study is that attorneys who expressed emotion were not universally disliked. The most important consideration in the jurors' evaluations of attorneys' emotional expression seemed to be the amount of emotionality that the attorneys used in proportion to the plaintiffs' injuries. It was necessary for an attorney to calibrate the emotionality of the argument to the level of injury or harm the plaintiff sustained. Thus, jurors viewed emotionality as appropriate when the plaintiff was severely or chronically injured, but not when the plaintiff had suffered a minor injury that could be corrected.

The peril of a defense attorney appearing cold and unsympathetic in a catastrophic injury case has been noted by the trial advocates who are members of the Federation of Insurance and Corporate Counsel. Recently, the Federation produced a videotape on handling sympathy in jury trials. In the video, they maintain that defense attorneys in severe personal injury cases should acknowledge to the jury the natural sympathy anyone feels for a badly injured person and should treat the injured plaintiff with dignity and respect. However, attorneys should caution the jury not to decide the case on the basis of sympathy alone.

On the other hand, it is clear that in cases where the plaintiff suffers relatively minor injuries, the plaintiff's attorney faces many suspicious jurors who are predisposed to believe that plaintiffs and their attorneys may, and are likely to, attempt to bring frivolous lawsuits and to exaggerate the plaintiff's injuries. These predispositions were revealed in an analysis of tort juror responses to a post-interview questionnaire from our larger study of jurors in business and corporate cases. A majority of the jurors in the study expressed disbelief and even hostility toward personal injury plaintiffs. Eight out of ten jurors believed that there are far too many frivolous lawsuits today; only about one-third of the tort jurors in the entire sample agreed that "most people who sue others in court have legitimate grievances." The "litigation explosion" appears to exist in the minds of jurors, if not in reality, and is currently a factor that attorneys must consider in shaping their persuasive communications in the courtroom.

Critical Thinking

According to Hans and Sweigart, many popular opinions about attorneys and litigation are actually myths. For instance, the idea that many court cases are tried based on emotional appeal is debunked by these jurors. However, Hans and Sweigart's sample includes only corporate or business-related cases. If the same study were applied to criminal cases and violent crimes, do you think the authors would have obtained similar results? Would emotional appeal become more important in a criminal case? Would aggressive interrogation tactics be deemed as ruthless when applied to suspected violent criminals?

References

Kalven, H. and Zeisel, H. (1966). *The American Jury*. Boston, MA: Little, Brown, & Co.

Kerr, N. (1982). Trial participants' behaviors and jury verdicts: An exploratory field study. In V.J. Konecni and E.B. Ebbeson (eds), *The Criminal Justice System: A social-psychological analysis*. (pp. 261–268) San Francisco, CA: W.H. Freeman.

Linz, D., Penrod, S., and McDonald, E. (1986). Attorney communication and impression making in the courtroom: Views for the bench. *Law and Human Behavior*, 10, 281–302.

Mindes, M.W. and Adcock, A.C. (1982). Trickster, hero, helper: A report on the lawyer image. *American Bar Foundation Research Journal*, 7, 177–233.

Pyszczynski, T.A. (1981). Opening statements in a jury trial: The effect of promising more than the evidence can show. *Journal of Applied Social Psychology*, 11, 434–444.

Sayler, R. (1988). Rambo litigation: Why hardball tactics don't work. *ABA Journal*, March, 79–81.

Vinson, D. (1986). *Jury Trials: The psychology of winning strategy*. Charlottesville, VA: Lexis Law Publishers.

20

Engaging With Criminal Prosecution: The Victim's Perspective

Melissa E. Dichter, Catherine Cerulli, Catherine L. Kothari, Frances K. Barg, Karin V. Rhodes

Abstract: *Despite more than a decade of policies that encourage prosecutors to proceed without the victim's input or actions in cases of intimate partner violence (IPV), prosecutors still often rely on the victim's participation to move a case forward. The purpose of this study was to identify the barriers and motivators influencing female IPV victims' engagement with the criminal justice system and their preferences regarding prosecution. Findings from focus groups with women who had experienced police response to IPV related that women wanted the violence to end but faced numerous barriers to engaging with the criminal prosecution process. The dominant voice favored police and prosecutors taking action toward prosecution without depending solely or heavily on the victim's active participation.*

Introduction

Background

In the United States in the 1970s, the battered women's movement worked to bring the social problem of violence against intimate partners into public discourse. Advocates successfully campaigned for a criminal legal system response to "wife abuse," previously considered a "private family matter" (Ferraro 1989). Less than 65 percent of intimate partner violence (IPV) cases, however, are reported to the police (Durose et al. 2005); of those, a smaller portion proceeds to prosecution. Whether an IPV case reaches and moves through the criminal legal system often depends on the extent of the victim's participation in the process.

In most cases, it is the victim who solicits intervention from police. In other cases, a third party—a child, neighbor, doctor, or bystander—calls for police help. If the police make an arrest, the case goes to the prosecutor's office for approval for prosecution and further adjudication. The victim then becomes a witness for the prosecution's case. Prosecutors have traditionally relied on victim participation in the prosecution process. Victim participation may include showing up at the prosecutor's office, coming to court appearances, providing written or oral statements or testimony, and affirmatively expressing a desire that the abuser be prosecuted.

Participating in the prosecution process, however, may be unsafe or at least undesirable for some victims, who may experience further violence, perhaps in retaliation, as a result of their participation. One solution to the problem of victim nonparticipation has been the adoption of evidence-based or "no-drop" prosecution policies that allow the prosecutor to proceed with the case based on evidence alone without the victim's testimony or authorization (Hanna 1996). These policies were accepted in the context of research findings that indicated a decline in abuse for those who secured protection orders (Carlson, Harris, and Holden 1999). However, even with well-intended pro-prosecution policies, if there is insufficient evidence and the victim does not participate, the prosecutor may be unable to proceed with the case. For this reason, IPV prosecution has continued to rely heavily on victim participation.

IPV victims underutilize the criminal justice system, and lack of victim participation in the prosecution process continues to be a problem for prosecutors. Victims may be faulted or dismissed when they do not call the police—for example, they may be told that their reports of previous violence are not valid because they did not previously report the violence, or they may be criticized for continuing to live with their abuser. Victims are also criticized and labeled as "uncooperative" for not participating in the prosecution process (Fleury-Steiner et al. 2006; Rebovich 1996).

Study Purpose

The purpose of this study was to understand motivations for seeking criminal system intervention in response to IPV, factors that prevent victims from pursuing intervention and participating in prosecution, and recommendations for IPV prosecution from the perspective of female victims who have experienced police response to IPV. The goal of this study was to develop knowledge, from the victim's perspective, to inform further refinements of the criminal legal system response to IPV. Specifically, these refinements could improve victim engagement with the system to facilitate offender accountability and victim safety. We define *victim engagement* as action taken to support and advance prosecution; this could include calling 911, attending court dates, and/or providing statements. We recognize that a lack of engagement does not necessarily mean that a victim does not want her offender arrested or prosecuted; therefore, it is important to understand both how she feels about being an active participant in prosecution and how she feels about prosecution itself, as these may not correspond.

Literature Review

Previous research on IPV victims' preferences for prosecution has documented a range of responses. Buzawa and Austin (1993) interviewed IPV victims following police intervention and found that 34 percent of the victims said that they wanted the offender arrested and prosecuted. In contrast, Weisz (2002) reported that 62.5 percent of victims interviewed said that prosecution was "a good idea," and 70.2 percent of the victims Hare (2006) interviewed said they wanted charges filed against their offenders. Bui (2001) found that in 40 percent of police reports from IPV incidents there was a record of the victim wanting prosecution. Kingsnorth and MacIntosh (2004) found documentation in prosecutor records that 74.8 percent of victims (whose offenders were arrested and approved for prosecution) wanted the offender arrested but that only 28.6 percent of victims were supportive of prosecution later in the process.

Previous studies have identified factors that are associated with victims wanting—and pursuing—criminal prosecution of their abusers. Victims may pursue prosecution because they want to prevent further violence as well as to hold the abuser accountable for violence already committed (Erez and Belknap 1998; Ford 1991). Goodman, Bennett, and Dutton (1999) found that severity of violence was correlated with participation in the prosecution process. Quantitative and qualitative studies conducted in the 1980s and 1990s identified other motivations for participating in prosecution, including concern for children and encouragement or support from others (e.g., family, friends, co-workers, legal or health professionals; Erez and Belknap 1998; Ford 1991; Goodman et al. 1999).

Regardless of whether they favor or oppose prosecution, there is evidence that victims face barriers to seeking help from and engaging with the criminal legal system. Interviews and surveys conducted with female IPV victims in the 1990s identified fear of retaliatory violence as a primary barrier to seeking help or participating in prosecution (Bennett, Goodman, and Dutton 1999; Erez and Belknap 1998; Fugate et al. 2005). Abusive partners or ex-partners may threaten further harm if the woman engages with the police, and women have reported further assaults even following arrests and incarceration (Fleury-Steiner et al. 2006; Moe 2007; Wolf et al. 2003).

Victims may also avoid engaging the system because they are emotionally and/or financially dependent on their partners and fear that arrest or prosecution will cause them to lose this support and the relationship (Bennett et al. 1999; Erez and Belknap 1998; Fleury-Steiner et al. 2006; Fugate et al. 2005; Hare 2006). They may also be hesitant because they believe that the relationship will improve, that they deserved the assault, and/or that the violence was not "bad enough" to justify intervention or that they lack sufficient evidence for the system to act (Hare 2006; Fugate et al. 2005; Wolf et al. 2003). Concerns regarding other family members may also play a role as women worry about the impact of prosecution on their children or lack support from other family members (Bennett et al. 1999; Erez and Belknap 1998).

Some women may lack sufficient understanding of the criminal legal system or may hold negative views of the system based on their assumptions or prior experiences (Apsler, Cummins, and Carl 2003; Barata 2007; Erez and Belknap 1998; Moe 2007; Wolf et al. 2003). In some cases, women choose not to pursue system involvement for fear that they themselves will be arrested for illegal activity (including drug use or undocumented immigrant status). It is not uncommon for batterers to threaten their victims with allegations of illegal activity, including perpetration of IPV, if the latter call the police (Miller 2001;

Moe 2007). In addition, women may lack trust and confidence in the system or be confused by and frustrated with the process, especially with the complexity, length of time, demands on her time and emotional energy, and difficulty involved in obtaining information or support (Bennett et al. 1999; Erez and Belknap 1998). In Fugate and colleagues' (2005) study, "hassle" emerged as a primary reason for not seeking police help.

Studies conducted in the 1980s and 1990s have provided a foundation to inform researchers' understanding of barriers that women face in calling the police or pursuing prosecution of their abusive partners. We expand on this earlier work by reporting on factors that motivate women to seek help from the criminal legal system, as well as those that inhibit participation in prosecution, within a community that employs recommended best practices for IPV prosecution. We also include women's recommendations for ways in which the system should act to prevent them from further violence. Use of a qualitative methodology allowed us to use an inductive approach, to let the themes emerge from the participants, and to include women's own voices in describing their experiences.

Methods

To solicit women's perspectives, we used a focus group methodology. Qualitative research allows the themes and constructs to emerge from the participants rather than limiting the findings by imposing preformed options through quantitative methodology. Focus groups hold an advantage over individual interviews in that the group process can stimulate and elicit themes through discussion and the sharing of experiences. We held focus groups with women who had shared the experience of having police respond to an incident of IPV but who varied in their experiences of participation in soliciting police intervention and proceeding with prosecution.

Setting

The study took place in a mid-western county that contains two mid-sized cities and several rural communities and has a total population of nearly 250,000. The county has a coordinated community response team for IPV cases that includes representatives from law enforcement, prosecution, victim services, health care, district court, circuit court, probation, and batterers' intervention and that follows best practices as identified at both the state and national levels for handling IPV cases in the criminal system.

All calls coming into the police departments in the county are screened for IPV, and when IPV is identified or suspected, the case is flagged and an officer is immediately dispatched. As in many states across the country, if there is evidence of IPV, the officer can execute a warrantless arrest and place the accused offender in the county jail, or if the defendant has fled the scene the officer will file a charging request with the prosecutor's office. As soon as the prosecutor's office receives a charging request, a victim advocate attempts to contact the victim and works with her throughout adjudication, functioning as the primary source of information for the victim and extensively documenting victim input and wishes. The IPV prosecution protocol provides for vertical prosecution and requires that police, advocates, and attorneys all engage in evidence collection to support cases in which the victim may be reluctant to testify. An example would be the photographic documentation of injuries, such as bruises, over time.

Recruitment

Participants were recruited for the focus groups through flyers posted throughout the community as well as ads placed in the local community newspaper of a mid-sized midwestern city. Eligibility criteria included being female, being age 18 or older, speaking English, having had a police call for IPV, and not having an open criminal case. A total of 22 women called in response to the ads and were eligible to participate in the study. After hearing about the details of the study, 18 women agreed to participate. Of these women, 15 participated in one of four focus groups (the remaining three women did not show up for a focus group).

Procedures

Focus groups were conducted at community-based agencies. Upon the participant's arrival, a member of the research team reviewed the informed consent document with her. The participant then completed a brief survey to collect individual demographic and case data before the start of the group. The focus groups were co-facilitated by an anthropologist (Frances K. Barg) and a former domestic violence prosecutor with a PhD in criminal justice (Catherine Cerulli). The facilitators used a list of open-ended questions and themes, developed by the research team members in advance, to guide the discussion. With participant permission, the focus groups were recorded by digital voice recorder and transcribed. The group sessions lasted for up to two hours.

Data Analysis

The quantitative questionnaire (demographic and incident) data were reviewed and analyzed using SPSS statistical software, Version 14.0 for Windows (SPSS, Inc., Chicago, IL). Transcriptions of the focus groups were coded and analyzed using QSR NVivo qualitative data analysis software (QSR International, Victoria, Australia). We used a modified grounded theory and inductive analysis methodology (Glaser and Strauss 1967) when approaching the qualitative data analysis. Most of the research team members (Karin V.

Rhodes, Catherine Cerulli, Catherine L. Kothari, Melissa E. Dichter) had extensive experience collecting qualitative data and providing services to victims of IPV; they were advised by an anthropologist with expertise in qualitative data analysis (Frances K. Barg). All team members read each of the transcripts and developed coding schemes independently. We then collaboratively developed a list of preliminary coding themes, allowing for additional codes that emerged during the analytic process. Each transcript was then coded by two team members (Karin V. Rhodes and Melissa E. Dichter). Discrepancies in coding were resolved by consensus. Once coding was completed, we identified relationships among the codes and drew interpretations of the data.

Limitations

The focus group methodology has inherent benefits as well as limitations. Using qualitative methods allows researchers to hear women's own voices; however, the focus group modality can inhibit some participants from expressing feelings, beliefs, attitudes, or experiences that may conflict with those of the dominant voices in the group. As the study was conducted in a single community with a self-selected sample of women, the findings cannot be generalized to other communities. The women who volunteered to respond to ads and participate in the focus groups may have been different from those who would not have volunteered to participate. The women who participated in the focus groups had all experienced police intervention because of violence victimization perpetrated by a male partner. IPV cases that reach the police tend to be those on the higher end of the severity spectrum (Bonomi et al. 2006), and the violence described by the women in our focus groups was likely more severe than that occurring in the larger population. Finally, the women's accounts were retrospective; the intervening time period between their decision-making and the focus groups may have impacted their responses.

Results

Sample Description

Participants were women who had experienced a police call for IPV; at the time of the focus groups, none of the women had an open criminal case (an eligibility criterion). Some of the participants had been with the partner involved in the IPV incident for many years; others had shorter relationships. In general, with a few exceptions, the participants were no longer in the relationship with that partner at the time of the focus group. The participants spanned a nearly 40-year age range and included black, white, and Latina women, with two-thirds identifying as white. Most (80 percent) had children, and a little more than half were employed.

Incident Factors

At the time of the police call, a little more than a quarter (26.7%) of the participants were married to their abusers; the other participants had non-marital intimate relationships. In two-thirds of cases, the women themselves called the police. An arrest was made (or a warrant for arrest issued) in more than half (53.3%) of the cases; in two (13.3%) cases, the women were arrested along with their partners. Four (50%) of the cases in which there was an arrest resulted in the conviction of the male partner.

Motivators for Engaging the Criminal Legal System

Focus group participants described factors that motivated them to seek or to move forward with the prosecution process. Women typically associated prosecution with ending or leaving the relationship and escaping the abuse. Women spoke about the point at which they decided to take action; they were ready to move away from the relationship and turned to the criminal legal system to help them do so.

"Enough is Enough"

In describing when and why they made their decisions to move forward with prosecution, some women referred to a "breaking point," or a point at which the violence had built up to the point that they decided that they were no longer going to tolerate it. They were exhausted by the violence. Women used phrases like "I just had my fill." For example, "I started getting tired and started thinking, 'You know, this is not life and I'm not gonna take this,' and I start kind of breaking out of that, that shell and that cycle . . . I thought, 'Enough is enough.'" And, "Once you go through it so many times, you just have enough. I just got to the point where I had enough."

Concern for Children

Women may reach the point of readiness to take action toward prosecution when they feel that the abuse is potentially damaging to their children. Mothers were concerned that their children would learn and repeat the behaviors they saw at home; they wanted their children to know that such behavior is not okay: "One of the very last straws for me was the last time my kids were there and I thought I'm raising boys; they have to know this is not okay, so I called the police." Mothers also worried about their children directly experiencing the abuse: "He went after my 7-year-old son and that was when I said, 'It's not gonna get better.'"

Social Support: Friends, Family, Co-Workers, Advocates

Friends, family members, advocates, or others may present women with the "extra push" to move forward with engaging or participating with the criminal legal system. This theme illustrates the ways in which other people involved in the women's lives influenced their decision to move forward with prosecution.

> So I had to go to [my supervisors at work] and I had to tell them what was happening . . . and they said, "Take as much time as you need, go file a police report, go get the personal protection order."
>   I was talking to my mom about it and she said, "Well he should have been arrested" and so I called the police.

Barriers to Victim Engagement in Prosecution

Reaching a tipping point with violence that motivates one to action does not mean that prior to the tipping point abuse or violence is acceptable, tolerable, or desirable. Women did not enjoy or want to experience violence. They recognized, however, that engaging in prosecution was a challenging endeavor and that it did not guarantee freedom from violence. The focus group transcripts revealed numerous instances of women explaining and providing examples of barriers they faced to participating in prosecution, including soliciting police assistance and following through with filing charges. Lack of participation did not necessarily indicate that a woman was opposed to prosecution; she may have wanted her partner prosecuted but faced barriers to actively participating with the criminal legal system.

Fear of Retaliation

Fear of retaliation was a major barrier to women calling the police and in particular following through with pressing charges against their partners. In some cases a third party, such as medical personnel, a neighbor, or a bystander, called the police, but women were then pressed to decide whether they wanted to participate in the prosecution process. Respondents shared that it sometimes felt safer not to press charges to avoid retaliation. As one respondent explained,

> I was scared to press charges, 'cos the last time I pressed charges on somebody he broke in my house and cut my throat, you know, before that. I was scared to press charges. [Name]'s a mean man. I found that out the hard way, you know? I was just plain scared.

Such responses indicate that the victims did not believe that criminal prosecution would necessarily prevent further violence and also noted that it might exacerbate the violence.

Love and Dependence

Prosecuting a partner can signify the loss of the relationship, as described by focus group participants, and the women were not always comfortable with that loss. Women spoke about their feelings of loving and caring for their partners and feeling fearful about losing the relationship. In speaking about why women might drop charges against a partner, participants explained, "You know all anybody ever wants is somebody to love them and care about them and if we don't have that and the only place that we're feeling any love is from this man, we'll take him back."

Fear of the loss of tangible—typically financial—support if their partners were arrested and charged emerged as a barrier to prosecuting and losing the relationship.

> I had four kids, two were in diapers, one was a newborn. He had me convinced that there's no way I could make it out there by myself and I believed him and that's why I stayed. . . . It's hard to pick up four kids and run.

Concern for Children

Concern for children, for not wanting to take them away from their fathers, and for keeping the family together left some women hesitant to seek help or intervention. "I didn't want to put [my children] through that and 'Momma, where's daddy?' . . . all they know is that their momma crying and their daddy's being taken away." A few women were caring for their partners' children but had no legal relationship to the children, which complicated the situation. For example, one woman talked about staying with her abusive partner to protect his son:

> I have a step that I raised since he was 6 weeks old. I wasn't allowed to take my son anywhere. I had to stay there for eight years just to protect my son 'cos my ex-husband wanted to—well, I had a stepson and he wanted to kill him and I had no say so over it. But if I did take my son, I'll go to jail for kidnapping.

Women with biological or legal ties to their children feared that if they involved the criminal system, they would risk child welfare system involvement that would separate them from their children. Local policy requires police to notify child protective services when a child is present in a domestic violence case. One respondent explained, "That's a big deterrent in calling." Another woman revealed that she took her children to a neighbor's house before calling the police to avoid child welfare system involvement: "The truth is, I sent my kids away before the police got there because I had a girlfriend who had her kids taken away. And that probably prevents women from calling a lot."

Privacy and Stigma

Concern regarding the violation of privacy, especially if it led to family or community members becoming aware of the abuse, can hold a woman back from pursuing prosecution presumably because of a perception of a stigma attached to IPV victimization. Two young women said they did not want to report the abuse because they did not want their parents to know about it. Other women indicated that their parents discouraged prosecution because the parents did not want others to know, particularly when they held visible professions in the community. For example, one woman's father was a member of the religious clergy, and another woman's parents were also concerned about public awareness and social stigma:

> A lot of people know [my parents] and know their name and they wanted to keep it out of the news-paper and so they were more for picking me up and moving me someplace . . . they were not inter-ested in me pursuing [prosecution] at all even though they totally hated him and would have liked to see him in jail.

Lack of Information

All of the women in this study had had encounters with police intervention in an IPV case. But some of these women had not previously been aware that they had the option to seek police help; some felt that the abuse was not "bad enough" for the police to respond. When women did not think of their partner's behavior as traditionally abusive, they did not think the partner could be held criminally liable: "I didn't know that he could be arrested for just pushing me." And, "I didn't know I could call the police just for him leaving a knife on my pillow so I never did." Others expressed a lack of awareness of options and an inability to understand ways in which to access the system.

> I didn't even know what I was supposed to be asking for or asking about or who I should ask for like, my parents weren't helping and I didn't know anything about the whole court system or what he could get in trouble for or anything like—I just think that was like my biggest problem. But I don't know, like if I would have got in contact with somebody if I would have ever went ahead with anything or not, but I didn't even know what the choices were to go ahead with.

Lack of System Follow-through

When women did take the initiative in pursuing prosecution, they often encountered system personnel who failed to follow through with or communicate about cases, leaving women confused and frustrated:

> And so I had [the police officer's] card, and I didn't hear anything, you know, so I kept calling and they're like, you know, it's a long process and there's nothing really to tell you and it went on longer, like months went by and like nothing happened and I kept calling and like nothing, nothing ever happened.

When the system did not respond to the women and seemed to lack interest or concern, the women often let the case go:

They told me I had three days within to change my mind to press charges. The third morning, I called the prosecutor's office and talked to the attorney and she told me that she would have an advocate call me back when they came in at 9:30 and nobody ever called and I didn't push it.

Logistical Barriers

Some women intended to call the police or, further along in the process, the prosecutor's office, but they were unable to do so because of logistical barriers such as not having access to a telephone at work or having a partner who prevented them from accessing a telephone or leaving the house. Logistical barriers, therefore, can interfere with the ability to participate in the process, even if the victim otherwise supports prosecution.

> But everybody else is asking me, "Well, why didn't you just go to the police station?" Because . . . he was right there with me, in the car, the whole time that he was hitting on me, so it's like "How am I going to get to the police station if he's sitting next to me? He can grab the wheel at any minute."
>
> I couldn't do anything because he sat, my bed is right here and there was a bookcase, he sat on my bookcase staring at me for hours, you know, said he wasn't gonna go to bed but he sat there and stared at me. . . . And then when I finally got him to lay down, he was actually sleeping so much lighter than he always does that any little movement I made, he was awake, so I couldn't [call the police] at any point.

Victim Recommendations for Prosecution Practices

Study participants tended to favor prosecution initiated and driven by the criminal legal system, even in cases of victim ambivalence at the time of the incident. A victim might be hesitant to proceed with prosecution at the time of the event and the legal proceedings but in retrospect might have wanted her partner to be prosecuted fully. A theme emerged of participants recommending that the system take over. For example, one participant reflected,

> There were times when I wished they would just drop the charges, you know? But after having been through what I've been through now, I wish, you know, that they would have pressed harder every time . . . even if that woman doesn't feel like that's the best thing for her, until she's out of that situation she won't see it.

Women indicated that they felt that their participation came through initially contacting the police. They wanted the system to take over prosecution without requiring their participation in that process. As one participant pointed out, "If somebody steals something and they're arrested. . . . Do they say 'Your store was robbed but if you don't want to press charges now, you don't have to'?" Even though some women felt that the victim should assert control over the situation, others felt that the prosecutor should override reluctant victims in some cases. For example,

If it's a bad enough case then the prosecutor should just pick it up, you know, because like the victim could be scared or you know, the family might get mad at the victim for pressing charges, you know, anything. So like if this is really bad, I think the prosecutor—like if he break her legs and she in the hospital and stuff like that—I think that the prosecutor should really pick it up.

Discussion

Many of the barriers to participating in prosecution identified in our study parallel the factors associated with staying with an abusive partner or avoiding calling the police found in other studies (e.g., Anderson et al. 2003; Apsler et al. 2003; Bennett et al. 1999; Fleury-Steiner et al. 2006; Fugate et al. 2005; Hare 2006; Wolf et al. 2003). The women in our focus groups recognized the barriers they faced, and because the dominant voice of each of the groups was in retrospect in favor of prosecution, they recommended having a system whereby others (e.g., police and prosecutors) take more action toward achieving the ultimate outcome (prosecution) rather than depending solely or heavily on the victim herself. Our findings are consistent with previous studies which have found that female victims of IPV endorse using the criminal legal system to protect their safety and to ensure that their abuser gets rehabilitation and/or justice despite recognizing the problems with and limitations of the system (Barata 2007; Hare 2006).

Implications

This study documents the compelling personal barriers women face to engaging with the criminal prosecution of an abusive partner. Because victim involvement in the process is so critical to the prosecution's ability to move forward with the case, prosecutors would be well served to assess barriers, develop ways to overcome or minimize them, and improve outreach to the victim. Our study and others suggest support for system-driven prosecution outside of victim input. Such policies, however, remove the victim's agency in decision-making and can be disempowering and potentially harmful to victims (Bennett et al. 1999; Davis et al. 2008). It is imperative, therefore, to assess individual safety concerns rather than following blanket policies to pursue prosecution with or without victim input.

The barriers to engaging with prosecution that emerged from the focus groups each hold implications for system and society response. Given victims' expressed concerns that moving forward with prosecution may lead to—or fail to prevent—further violence, additional safeguards are needed to protect victims both during and after prosecution. Victims also need support, both emotional and practical, to assist them in managing the potential losses associated with leaving an intimate relationship. Services to provide for the safety and well-being of children and to help them cope with the loss or trauma associated with criminal legal system intervention could help reduce the barriers related to concerns for children. These services should not additionally put the mother at risk for adversarial child protective services involvement.

The criminal legal system could also facilitate participation by providing more public education about the options available to victims and the processes involved so that victims know when and whom to call. The system may also need to improve follow-up with victims to avoid the problem of victim dropout due to lack of follow-through and discouragement. There may be innovative ways to facilitate participation, for example, by extending hours so that victims could call before or after work. The system may not be able to remove abuser-imposed barriers, such as preventing the victim from leaving the house or using the telephone, but understanding that victims do face such barriers would be helpful in reducing victim blaming. Given that some victims avoid seeking or pursuing help from the criminal system because of shame or embarrassment about having been victimized, efforts to "break the silence" about the problem of IPV, and educate the public about the realities of victims' experiences are important for reducing the stigma against victims.

Acknowledgments

Support for this project was provided by Grant 2006-WG-BX-0007 from the National Institute of Justice (Rhodes/Cerulli), "Victim Participation in Intimate Partner Violence Prosecution: Implications for Safety." Additional support was provided by National Institute of Mental Health (NIMH) K23 MH64572 (Rhodes) and NIMH K01 MH75965-01 (Cerulli).

The contents of this article do not necessarily represent the views of the U.S. Department of Veterans Affairs or the U.S. government.

We acknowledge the help of the staff of the domestic violence program in the community in which this study took place, the many research assistants who contributed to this project, and, most of all, the women who shared their experiences with us.

Critical Thinking

There were multiple barriers that inhibited participants from seeking help from law enforcement officials. Discuss these barriers and, from a law enforcement perspective, what kinds of changes need to be implemented to remedy these issues.

References

Anderson, Michael A., Paulette M. Gillig, Marilyn Sitaker, Kathy McCloskey, Kathleen Malloy, and Nancy Grigsby. 2003. " 'Why Doesn't She Just Leave?' A Descriptive Study of Victim Reported Impediments to Her Safety." *Journal of Family Violence* 18: 151–155.

Apsler, Robert, Michele R. Cummins, and Steven Carl. 2003. "Perceptions of the Police by Female Victims of Domestic Partner Violence." *Violence Against Women* 9: 1318–1335.

Barata, Paula C. 2007. "Abused Women's Perspectives on the Criminal Justice System's Response to Domestic Violence." *Psychology of Women Quarterly* 31: 202–215.

Bennett, Lauren, Lisa Goodman, and Mary Ann Dutton. 1999. "Systemic Obstacles to the Criminal Prosecution of a Battering Partner: A Victim Perspective." *Journal of Interpersonal Violence* 14: 761–772.

Bonomi, Amy E., Victoria L. Holt, Diane P. Martin, and Robert S. Thompson. 2006. "Severity of Intimate Partner Violence and Occurrence and Frequency of Police Calls." *Journal of Interpersonal Violence* 21: 1354–1364.

Bui, Hoan N. 2001. "Domestic Violence Victims' Behavior in Favor of Prosecution: Effects of Gender Relations." *Women & Criminal Justice* 12: 51–76.

Buzawa, Eve S. and Thomas Austin. 1993. "Determining Police Response to Domestic Violence Victims." *American Behavioral Scientist* 36: 610–623.

Carlson, Matthew J., Susan D. Harris, and George W. Holden. 1999. "Protective Orders and Domestic Violence: Risk Factors for Re-abuse." *Journal of Family Violence* 14: 205–226.

Davis, Robert C., Chris S. O'Sullivan, Donald J. Farole, and Michael Rempel. 2008. "A Comparison of Two Prosecution Policies in Cases of Intimate Partner Violence: Mandatory Case Filing Versus Following the Victim's Lead." *Criminology & Public Policy* 7: 633–662.

Durose, Matthew R., Caroline W. Harlow, Patrick A. Langan, Mark Motivans, Ramona R. Rantala, and Erica L. Smith. 2005. *Family Violence Statistics: Including Statistics on Strangers and Acquaintances.* Washington, DC: U.S. Department of Justice, Office of Justice Programs.

Erez, Edna and Joanne Belknap. 1998. "In Their Own Words: Battered Women's Assessment of the Criminal Processing System's Responses." *Violence & Victims* 13: 251–268.

Ferraro, Kathleen J. 1989. "Policing Woman Battering." *Social Problems* 36: 61–74.

Fleury-Steiner, Ruth E., Deborah Bybee, Cris M. Sullivan, Joanne Belknap, and Heather C. Melton. 2006. "Contextual Factors Impacting Battered Women's Intentions to Reuse the Criminal Legal System." *Journal of Community Psychology* 34: 327–342.

Ford, David A. 1991. "Prosecution as a Victim Power Resource: A Note on Empowering Women in Violent Conjugal Relationships." *Law & Society Review* 25: 313–334.

Fugate, Michelle, Leslie Landis, Kim Riordan, Sara Naureckas, and Barbara Engel. 2005. "Barriers to Domestic Violence Help Seeking: Implications for Intervention." *Violence Against Women* 11: 290–310.

Glaser, Barney G. and Anselm L. Strauss. 1967. *The Discovery of Grounded Theory: Strategies for Qualitative Research.* Chicago, IL: Aldine.

Goodman, Lisa, Lauren Bennett, and Mary Ann Dutton. 1999. "Obstacles to Victims' Cooperation with the Criminal Prosecution of Their Abusers: The Role of Social Support." *Violence and Victims* 14: 427–444.

Hanna, Cheryl. 1996. "No Right to Choose: Mandated Victim Participation in Domestic Violence Prosecutions." *Harvard Law Review* 109: 1849–1910.

Hare, Sara C. 2006. "What Do Battered Women Want? Victims' Opinions on Prosecution." *Violence and Victims* 21: 611–628.

Kingsnorth, Rodney F. and Randall C. MacIntosh. 2004. "Domestic Violence: Predictors of Victim Support for Official Action." *Justice Quarterly* 21: 301–328.

Miller, Susan L. 2001. "The Paradox of Women Arrested for Domestic Violence: Criminal Justice Professionals and Service Providers Respond." *Violence Against Women* 7: 1339–1376.

Moe, Angela M. 2007. "Silenced Voices and Structured Survival: Battered Women's Help Seeking." *Violence Against Women* 13: 676–699.

Rebovich, Donald J. 1996. "Prosecution Response to Domestic Violence: Results of a Survey of Large Jurisdictions" (pp. 176–191), in *Do Arrests and Restraining Orders Work?* edited by E.S. Buzawa and C.G. Buzawa. Thousand Oaks, CA: Sage.

Weisz, Arlene N. 2002. "Prosecution of Batterers: Views of African American Battered Women." *Violence and Victims* 17: 19–34.

Wolf, Marsha E., Uyen Ly, Margaret A. Hobart, and Mary A. Kernic. 2003. "Barriers to Seeking Police Help for Intimate Partner Violence." *Journal of Family Violence* 18: 121–129.

III Corrections

It is in the last stages of the criminal justice process that we find the lowest public visibility for organizational practices. Prisons, unlike police and judicial organizations, operate with very little scrutiny until something occurs that comes to the attention of the public. This is why field research is so important in these institutional settings. Although there have historically been numerous studies about the various aspects of prison life, the enormous growth of prison construction and heterogeneous inmate populations has changed the way in which these facilities operate. In addition, the past several decades have seen a dramatic change in the population of those who now occupy the positions of correctional officers. These two fundamental changes in the prison environment necessitate the need for a better understanding of the prison as a work world.

The five naturalistic oriented studies selected for the section on correctional practitioners explore some areas of our prison system that have not received a great deal of attention in recent years. The articles address such issues as how correctional officers negotiate formal rules and regulations, how officers stereotype inmates and treat them accordingly, how gender influences the way in which correctional workers treat one another and those they supervise, and the impact of changing treatment models upon those who work in probation and parole.

The experiences of those confined to prison and their families are often overlooked. Ignoring inmates' perspectives is likely due to their status. However, such a view does a great disservice to those interested in finding ways to deter and rehabilitate offenders. The five articles included in this section were chosen because they represent a broad overview of some of the salient issues inmates face both in prison and upon release to the community. These readings address such topics as how prisoners make sense of parole board decisions, sex offender registries, financial obligations and employment, women's problems with attaining employment while on work release, and parental contact with children while incarcerated. Inmates are not the only ones affected by their confinement. Thus, we have included an article that addresses the difficulties families face due to their loved ones' incarceration and the difficulties faced by being on parole.

The articles in both sections should cause readers to consider how current corrections policies and practices directly affect the organizational operations of institutional corrections. Certainly there are numerous other issues that are of great importance to inmates and their families. If nothing else, we trust that these field studies will enlighten readers to the realities and effects that the correctional environment has on both employees and prisoners.

A Practitioners

21

Accounts of Prison Work: Correction Officers' Portrayals of Their Work Worlds

Stan Stojkovic

Abstract: *Stan Stojkovic examines correctional staff interactions with inmates in a maximum security prison to shed light on the gap between formal policies and the practices that officers actually carried out. His findings suggest that correctional officers portray their work worlds as filled with problems that stem from both correctional administrators and inmates. According to officers, administration implements unrealistic rules that hinder their ability to do their jobs effectively. Correctional officers believe that they must overlook some of these formal rule violations; otherwise their jobs would be too difficult and too dangerous.*

Sykes (1958) offers a sociological explanation for correctional officers' tendency to develop unapproved work routines, relationships, and orientations stating that the prison social system involves contradictions and pressures that undermine and, ultimately, "corrupt" correctional officers' authority. Although it is concerned with a variety of human service and social control organizations, Lipsky's (1980) analysis of street-level bureaucracies also emphasizes how low-level staff in prisons and similar organizations adapt to organizational problems and pressures over which they have little or no control. Lipsky focuses on the ways in which human service and social control professionals cope with such problems by approaching their work in officially disapproved but functional ways in order to fulfill their professional obligations. He concludes that street-level bureaucrats' coping strategies are realistic and necessary because organizational goals are seldom achievable in officially prescribed ways. Unauthorized procedures are often functional for organizational systems and the larger society.

This analysis offers a new way of understanding correctional officers and their work worlds. I consider many of the issues raised in the corrections literature but my focus is on how correctional officers explain and justify their development of officially disapproved work routines, relationships, and orientations. Thus, I am not concerned with why correctional officers "really" modify organizational rules and expectations or the function of their actions for the prison system. Rather, I attempt to explicate correctional officers' *accounts* of the actions and relationships. As Scott and Lyman (1968, p. 46) state,

An account is a linguistic device employed whenever an action is subjected to valuative inquiry. Such devices are a crucial element in the social world since they prevent conflicts from arising by verbally bridging the gap between action and expectation. Moreover, accounts are "situated" according to the statuses of the interactants and are standardized within cultures so that certain accounts are terminologically stabilized and routinely expected when activity falls outside the domain of expectations.

By taking accounts as its topic, this article focuses on the ways that correction officers verbally bridge the gap between their work activities and relationships and official organizational expectations. Accounts are rhetorical; that is, they are all expressed as rationales intended to anticipate and counter others' criticisms of persons' actions (Miller and Holstein 1989). Officers use these accounts to make sense of the actions that constitute their everyday work routines. Correctional officers' accounts of their work circumstances and relationships are thus both descriptions of their work world and features of it. The descriptions and rationales are available to, and used by, correctional officers to manage troublesome persons who may criticize them for acting in improper ways.

Setting and Organization of the Study

The study was conducted over a 12-month period in 1982/1983 and involved the observation of correctional staff interactions with prisoners in a maximum security prison. The prison was built to house prisoners classified as especially dangerous to the public. During the research period, over 75 percent of the inmates were serving sentences of 20 years or more. Further, most of the inmates had records of violent and disruptive behavior in other prisons in the state. The correctional officer staff consisted of 150 persons, most of whom were new to correctional work. The inexperience of the correctional officer staff was intentional. The warden stated that he wished to put together a correctional officer staff that would bring new ideas, work habits, and attitudes to their work. He stated that hiring correctional officers with little or no experience was important because they would be unfamiliar with the "old ways of doing things," including the corrupt practices that flourish in many prisons.

I observed interactions in all areas of the prison, including its most restrictive segregation unit. In addition, 20 correctional officers were interviewed about their work. The interviews were conducted at the officers' homes and/or in a local tavern. The questions asked of correctional officers were open-ended and intended to elicit portrayals of the purposes of the prison, the officers' work in it, and officers' relations with others, particularly inmates, administrators, and other correctional officers. The portrayals may be analyzed as accounts because they were responses to questions which asked the officers to evaluate aspects of their work world and explain disjunctures between officers' depictions of organizational ideals and their behavior. Put differently, the officers' responses are treated as culturally standardized explanations for bridging the gap between organizational expectations and practices.

Most correctional officers portrayed the primary purpose of the prison as maintaining institutional security and control over the prisoners. They expressed little concern for prisoners' rehabilitation. They stated that rehabilitation was not why the prison was built; rather, it was intended to make prisoners more manageable. As one officer stated, "We get all the fuck-ups from the other prisons that nobody else wants." Although correctional officers stated that the security and control of prisoners was the prison's central purpose, they also stated that the accomplishment of this goal was made problematic by the prison's administrative structure and the conflicting demands placed on them by supervisors.

Thus, correctional officers' explanations and justifications of how they maintained a secure prison in an often hostile, uncertain, and contradictory environment is the primary topic of this article. Officers stated that they maintained order by developing accommodative relationships with prisoners which violated officially prescribed rules and procedures, but which the officers portrayed as realistic and necessary adjustments to their work circumstances. In this way the officers described themselves as acting much as the street-level bureaucrats Lipsky (1980) analyzed. Central to both descriptions is the depiction of low-level organization members as competent and responsible persons trying to cope with difficult work circumstances.

The Prison as a Problematic Work World

For correctional officers, the prison world was organized in terms of routine activities and relationships. In the abstract, at least, the routines were interrelated ways in which correctional officers achieve the prison's organizational purposes. The officers stated, however, that the meaning of their everyday work activities and relationships was not so simple or clear-cut. They portrayed their work activities and relationships as adaptations to problematic circumstances. Specifically, the correctional officers stated that their work involved three major sources of uncertainty and problems: (1) prison system and correctional officers' place in it, (2) prison administrators' actions and interests, and (3) inmates. According to the officers, each of these aspects of the prison involved different practical problems which they sought to manage. The rest of this section is concerned with the way in which the correctional officers portrayed and oriented to aspects of the prison world as problems.

The Prison System as a Problem

The officers often portrayed themselves as forgotten people in a hostile social system made up of politicians, the public, prison administrators, and inmates. They stated that their problems and low social standing reflected politicians' and the public's negative attitudes toward prisons and correctional officers. The officers stated that members of each of these groups treated them as insignificant, largely incompetent, and expendable parts of the prison organization. Of most immediate importance to the officers, however, were prison administrators' orientations to them. They stated that prison administrators treated correctional officers as scapegoats; that is, administrators protected themselves by passing the blame for system problems from administrators to correctional officers. The officers portrayed prison administrators' and others' attitudes toward correctional officers as counterproductive and self-fulfilling prophecies because correctional officers partly adapt to the prison system by taking on the traits attributed to them by others.

Consider, for example, the following descriptions of the prison world. They are explanations of why correctional officers "have no togetherness" and eventually confirm others' negative evaluations of them. The portrayals center in treating correctional officers' work problems as system problems.

> We are Indians in the correctional system. Everyone shits on us. We have no togetherness in this place.... We are the screws no one really cares about.... We are shipwrecked in the society and are always labeled as the bad guys ... they [administration] treat us like assholes and we will eventually become nothing but assholes.

> Who gives a fuck about corrections officers? We have to deal with all the assholes in the system and they expect us to like it.... It's this kind of attitude we have to live with ... then they wonder why we are all alcoholics.

The correctional officers further explained that their problems and low standing in the prison were relatively recent developments. According to the officers, the problems were a result of changing prison policies which expanded prisoners' rights and reduced correctional officers' discretion, particularly their right to discipline prisoners as they saw fit. The officers explained that the changes were counterproductive restrictions on their abilities to effectively respond to troublesome prisoners. They stated that the ultimate effect of the changes was a reduction in correctional officers' authority and inmates' respect for officers. Consider, for example, the following discussions of how correctional officers' work circumstances had been adversely affected by changes in prison policies.

> It is not like in the old days when you could beat the shit out of an asshole. I wish they did still have this for some of these guys in this place. Some guys need a good ass kicking, then we wouldn't have that many problems at all in trying to keep them in line.

> There is no real punishment in this place. What would have happened in the old days is that the guy would have gotten his ass beat for about two weeks straight and the other inmates would have known it right away ... the sad thing is that the inmates know that there is no real punishment and they flaunt it in our faces.

According to the correctional officers, a related problem with the prison system involved officers' inconsistent enforcement of prison rules. They stated that, while every correctional officer was supposed to strictly follow prison rules, they frequently deviated from them. Although the officers' comments might be taken as a call for the strict enforcement of prison rules, they were intended as critiques of the rules which the officers portrayed as unrealistic expectations and standards. Indeed, many officers stated that flexible rule enforcement was needed in the prison because officers could not effectively run their units under a policy of literal enforcement. In this way, the officers cast the enforcement of prison rules and their responsibility to effectively manage prisoners as contradictory aspects of the prison system. As one officer explained,

> If you [inmate] are doing time and you are decent, you will be alright in this place. Rules are meant to be bent in a place like this; you have to be flexible in how you deal with the inmates. If you are not flexible, then you will be in trouble.

However, while the officers portrayed flexible rule enforcement as a necessity, they also stated that it was a major source of work problems because too many officers were too flexible. Officers framed the issue as a practical dilemma. They stated that, on the one hand, the official prison rules to which they were accountable were unrealistic and inadequate because the rules did not take account of the practical contingencies faced by officers in managing inmates. Consequently, correctional officers engaged in selective enforcement to fulfill their larger obligation to maintain order in the prison. On the other hand, the officers stated that, although most of them agreed that they had to be flexible in enforcing prison rules, they did not agree on when and how to do so. According to the officers, the result was inconsistency and uncertainty among officers and inmates about appropriate inmate behavior.

Officers stated that this circumstance had practical consequences because inmates could get by with rule breaking by playing one officer off against another much as children negotiate with, and get permission from, their parents by telling one parent that the other approves of their requests. Specifically, inmates responded to correctional officers who tried to strictly enforce prison rules by stating that other officers did not enforce them. The officers stated that such problems were most serious when supervisory officers were more lenient than the officers they supervised. In this circumstance, officers could actually be punished for enforcing prison rules. Consider, for example, the following correctional officer's complaint about the inmates' practice of taking food from the prison kitchen. He portrays the practice as a practical dilemma and problem which focuses on how officers were sometimes punished for "doing their jobs."

> I am sick and tired of guys bringing all this shit from the kitchen into the housing units. It is something that just has to stop. But the problem is that so many officers allow it to happen and you can't get consistency . . . in rule enforcement . . . remember one time when two officers stopped a guy with a whole coat full of stuff from the kitchen. The inmate responded that [another] officer allowed it to come to the unit. When they checked it out with the officer, who was their superior, he reprimanded them for enforcing the rules. All they were doing was their jobs. That type of shit is what really pisses me off about this job.

In sum, the correctional officers portrayed the prison system as fraught with problems, contradictions, and dilemmas that made it difficult—if not impossible—for them to fulfill their organizational obligations. They further stated that in attempting to cope with the problems of the prison system, correctional officers sometimes generated new problems and injustices, making their work circumstances even more complex and difficult. The officers stated that these problems were exacerbated by problems in the correctional officer–prison administrator relationship. We turn to these problems next.

Prison Administrators as a Problem

The correctional officers portrayed the officer–administrator relationship as filled with tensions and distrust resulting from the prison administrators' lack of respect for correctional officers, over-concern for protecting themselves from criticism and negative publicity, and willingness to use correctional officers as scapegoats. In other words, the officers described themselves as *victims* of the policies and practices of prison administrators in order to exonerate themselves from blame for their, and the prison's, failures (Holstein and Miller 1990). Specifically, the officers explained that the tensions and distrust underlying the officer–administrator relationship were based on three factors.

First, correctional officers expressed concern that prison administrators were changing the rules and regulations of the prison so rapidly that officers and inmates did not know what was expected of them. According to the officers, the changes created uncertainty among prisoners about organizational rules and expectations. As one officer stated,

> By fucking with the inmates' minds is where the problems begin. The inmates need to have rules and regulations consistently enforced. But the problem is that the administration always changes the rules of the game for both inmates and staff. Inconsistency pisses off a lot of inmates. Convicts want and need consistent rules. How can we expect them to follow the rules when the rules are always changing?

The officers explained that the problem was a result of the prison administrators' unrealistic emphasis on controlling both inmate groups and the correctional officer's union. They stated that maintaining control over such groups was the administrators' highest priority. They further explained that frequent changes in prison policies created uncertainties and divisions between officers and inmates that served the administrators' interests. "All these different rules put inmates against officers and officers against themselves," stated one officer. According to the officers, the major results of the administrators' actions were that correctional officers learned to distrust prison administrators and to rely on their own judgment and methods in controlling inmates. As one correctional officer explained,

> You do what you think is right and you disregard anything the administration says. You are the one who is doing the job, and you do anything that you think will make your job more effective and easy in the long run.

A second issue raised by the officers in explaining their distrust of prison administrators was safety. Specifically, they stated that the administrators were unconcerned about the officers' safety. The officers further stated that the administrators' lack of concern increased the risks associated with their jobs. The officers cited a number of incidents in explaining and justifying their concerns about their personal safety and prison administrators' attitude toward it. One such incident involved an especially violent and disruptive inmate assault on a correctional officer in the cafeteria. The assault occurred in the presence of over 30 correctional officers and 100 prisoners. Immediately following the incident the inmate shouted, "What can these assholes do to me anyway? I am serving double-life." The inmate was given segregation and punishment time, yet the officers stated that the assault warranted greater punishment and that the administration should have attempted to transfer the prisoner to another less "luxurious" prison in the state system.

The officers used such incidents to cast the prison as an unsafe place and prison administrators as unconcerned with officers' welfare. They also used the incidents to explain and justify a work orientation that involved avoiding actions that threatened their safety, including allowing inmates to flagrantly violate some prison rules. According to the officers, they had to take care of themselves first because prison administrators were unwilling to protect them. As one officer stated,

> Them administration types don't care about us or our jobs. So, why should I stick my neck out for them? I'll do anything to keep myself safe. . . . If that means letting them [inmates] burn down the place, that's fine with me.

Finally, correctional officers stated that prison administrators were too concerned with inmate lawsuits. According to the officers, the prison administrators' concern resulted in an improper emphasis on pleasing inmates. The effect of the emphasis was to reduce correctional officers' authority and discretion in dealing with inmates. The officers further stated that prison administrators responded to inmate lawsuits by allowing the officers to be blamed for the problems of the prison system. Consider, for example, the following officer's portrayal of the effect of prison administrators' concern for inmate lawsuits. Through his portrayal, the officer casts correctional officers as victims of prison administrators' overemphasis on inmate lawsuits. He also explains and justifies his interest in returning to law enforcement.

> The only reason I became a guard is because I was laid off from my job as a sheriff. . . . As soon as that picks up, I am getting the fuck out of this place. . . . A lot of these administrators just care for the inmates. That's because inmates file lawsuits and the public thinks we are all assholes. . . . We can't even do our jobs without being thought of as bad by the public.

In sum, the officers stated that many of their problems with inmates were caused by prison administrators' policies. Specifically, prison administrators' policies and actions made it impossible for correctional officers to act as they preferred and/or as required by prison policies. We next consider the officers' descriptions of other sources of tension in the correctional officer–inmate relationship.

Prisoners as a Problem

Although we might expect inmates to resent and resist all rule enforcement by correctional officers, the officers stated that most inmates recognized the importance of prison rules. They stated that, although inmates expected the rules to be enforced in realistic and flexible ways, most inmates recognized that the rules were important to the maintenance of prison order. Officers added that flexibility in rule enforcement was especially important when it involved events which were the most relevant to the prisoners' ability to cope and adapt to the demands and constraints imposed by the prison environment. For example, the officers stated that telephone calls were very important to prisoners because they were the only way in which inmates could regularly interact with friends and relatives on the outside. Thus, for the officers, flexibility in enforcing rules about inmates' use of the telephone was an important way of maintaining stable relations with prisoners. As one officer stated,

> Phone calls are really important for guys in this place . . . you cut off their calls and they get pissed. So what I do is give them a little extra and they are good to me.

While flexibility in rule enforcement was important in interactions between correctional officers and prisoners, the officers stated that they selectively enforced the rules to achieve organizational goals. Put in the officers' language, they enforced the rules to "squeeze" inmates who were severely disruptive to the housing units or posed threats to other inmates. The officers stated that, in doing so, they solved problems for both themselves and the inmates, both of whom had an interest in maintaining an orderly prison world. Consider, for example, the following correctional officers' explanations of the usefulness of selectively enforcing prison rules.

> I'll be easy on the rules if the guy is not causing trouble. . . . If he is into all those bullshit games, then I want his ass out of my unit. The problem is that nobody wants him . . . but if you are smart you can get the real troublemakers out of the place.

> For the inmate who doesn't force himself on anyone you got to give him a break. . . . I do that by giving him more dayroom [recreation] time and he respects that. . . . You know, you're not always on the guy and inmates admire that in an officer.

A related aspect of the correctional officer–inmate relationship centered on the officers' classification of inmates into those who "knew how to do time" and those who did not. The officers stated that it was the latter group of inmates who were most troublesome because they had no commitment to prison policies and procedures. Specifically, the officers stated that the younger inmates serving longer sentences had no understanding of what it meant to do time and that their adjustment to prison was, therefore, more difficult. Further, the officers stated that the presence of younger inmates in the prison made their jobs more difficult and problematic. They stated, for example, that although they warned younger inmates about the possible consequences of rule infractions, the warnings had no effect on their behavior.

> It's the bugs [young inmates] that cause all the problems. . . . They are the ones involved in spud juice [alcohol], dope, and sex . . . they don't give a shit about nothing and most have been state raised so they know nothing but prison.

The officers added that their concern for managing troublesome young inmates was shared with the older inmates who had been in prison for a number of years and viewed the prison as their home. According to the officers, the older inmates also saw the younger inmates as troublemakers who were upsetting the established order developed and perpetuated by themselves and correctional staff.

> It seems to me that the older inmates understand the officer's job and buy into the system of rules and regulations. On the other hand, the younger inmates cause more problems because they don't buy the rules of the enforcers.

> Them older guys know what prison life is all about. They know that you're just doing your job and don't want any hassle. . . . You never have any problems with them.

Thus, although the correctional staff were officially obligated to enforce all prison rules all the time, they did not always do so. Rather, they selectively enforced prison rules to control troublesome prisoners and reward cooperative ones, always seeking to manage the practical contingencies associated with their jobs. The officers also used selective enforcement of prison rules to build alliances with inmates who could help them control troublesome inmates. Specifically, the officers depended on and used older inmates to control younger, more troublesome inmates. The older inmates aided the correctional officers by encouraging the younger inmates to cooperate with the officers. They did so by instructing the younger inmates on the practical advantages of cooperation. Thus, although it was not recognized in official prison policies and rules, the correctional officers stated that one way in which they fulfilled their professional responsibilities was by selectively enforcing rules in order to secure cooperation from older inmates.

The officers stated that it was one of several ways in which they adapted their relationship with inmates to the practical constraints and circumstances of their work. The adaptations were the basis for the accommodative relationships which prevailed in the housing units. We further consider how correctional officers portrayed and justified their relationships with inmates in the next section.

The Social Organization of Officer–Inmate Relations

Although not all the correctional officers agreed that capitulation to inmates' desires and needs was appropriate, most of the officers who regularly interacted with inmates were accommodative, particularly those assigned to the housing units. The officers explained that accommodation was necessary because strictly enforcing prison rules did not produce inmate compliance; rather, it destabilized the prison environment and officer–inmate relationships. The officers gave two major reasons for this circumstance. Both reasons involved portraying accommodation with inmates' desires as a practical response to the constraints of correctional officers' work.

First, they stated that the strict enforcement was counterproductive because there was no real punishment attached to many of the violations. They stated that prison punishments were too soft and prison administrators did not support correctional officers in their disputes with inmates. For example, the correctional officers stated that officers who relied on ticket writing as their only way of controlling prisoners were doomed to failure. Ticket writing was the officially approved method of documenting inmates' misbehaviors and, according to the prison administrators, was the first step in taking formal action against troublesome inmates. The officers stated, however, that tickets were not taken seriously in the prison. As one officer stated,

> Your only formal authority is the tickets you write, but tickets are not written by a lot of officers because they do not really do anything in this place. A lot of tickets are thrown away by superiors anyway.

The officers also stated that writing tickets for many inmate rule violations did not make sense because many of the behaviors were "bullshit"; that is, they were minor offenses that did not warrant official responses. The officers stated that ticketing inmates was only appropriate when nothing else could be done with troublemakers. For example, I observed two prisoners pushing and shoving each other in one of the housing units. An officer broke up the disturbance and sent the inmates on their way. Later, I asked him why he had not given them tickets for fighting. He replied,

> What for? It only produces trouble between those two guys and myself. If someone got stabbed or seriously hurt, then I would have to write a ticket, but no one did.

Second, the officers stated that, although they could use physical force to gain short-term inmate cooperation, coercion was a last-resort response to troublesome inmates because it involved unacceptable long-term costs. They stated that inmates resented such treatment and would respond by withholding future cooperation. Equally importantly, the officers stated that if they used physical force to manage inmates it could lead to violent inmate responses, a circumstance they wished to avoid. Thus, although the correctional officers had official access to resources which presumably allowed them to compel acquiescence from inmates, they did not emphasize them. Rather, they sought to build "noncoercive" relationships with inmates. According to officers, such relationships were realistic and necessary ways of dealing with inmates.

In so explaining and justifying their relationships with inmates, then, correctional officers cast accommodation to inmates' desires and behaviors as a rational response to the practical circumstances of prison life. They further stated that accommodation was good for both officers and inmates. The officers explained that accommodative relationships served the officers' interest in maintaining orderly and stable housing units and inmates' interest in reducing the insecurities of prison life. Although it was less emphasized by the officers, a related reason why accommodative officer–inmate relations prevailed in the housing units was because officers who sought to strictly enforce prison rules seldom remained in the housing units for long. Officers portrayed this approach as unrealistic because it was overly strict. Indeed, inmates referred to "strict" correctional officers as the "police," thereby highlighting their emphasis on rule enforcement.

The officers stated that many strict officers left the housing units and sometimes correctional work because they became frustrated by the selective rule enforcement of other correctional officers. According to the officers, strict officers were caught between their desire to enforce all prison rules and inmates' claims that they should ignore rule violations because other officers did so. In addition to strict officers' requests to leave, their time in the housing units was reduced by the intervention of prison administrators who frequently transferred them to jobs that did not involve regular contact with inmates. The administrators usually did so in response to inmates and/or correctional officers' complaints portraying the strict officers as unreasonable and sources of problems in the housing units. In so responding to officer and inmate complaints, the prison administrators helped maintain and perpetuate accommodative officer–inmate relationships which centered in selected rule enforcement.

According to the officers, then, there were several practical reasons for the prevalence of accommodative officer–inmate relationships in the housing units. The officers further stated that, although the relationships involved violations of formal prison policies and rules, they were realistic, necessary, and served the interests of inmates, prison staff, and the public. The remainder of this section considers correctional officers' accounts of their accommodative orientation to inmates' desires and behaviors and treatment of some inmate rule violations as deviance. They were explanations and justifications of the correctional officers' routine violation of official prison rules and policies. I discuss the issues in turn.

The Accommodative Orientation

Accommodative relationships between correctional officers and prisoners were rooted in three practices that may be stated as officers' claims:

1.   Because correctional officers could not have total control over the inmates, negotiations were central to prisoner control.
2.   Once an officer defined or negotiated a set of informal rules with a prisoner or group of prisoners, the rules were to be respected by all parties.
3.   Some rule-violating behaviors in the prison setting were "normal" and, consequently, did not merit officer attention or sanctioning.

More specifically, the officers stated that proper accommodation to inmates' desires and interests involved "giving respect" to inmates and restricting officers' interactions with inmates. In doing so, correctional officers stated that they sought to effectively control and manage inmates while avoiding troublesome encounters with them.

> The officers stated that giving respect to inmates was a central aspect of building effective relationships with inmates. It involved enforcing only those prison rules that most inmates and correctional officers deemed important and realistic. For the officers, such selective rule enforcement allowed them to maintain an acceptable degree of control in the housing units while enabling inmates to "save face" by providing them with a sense of respect, dignity, and self-control. As one officer stated, the importance of giving a man his respect is key to this place. I have found if you give respect you get respect in here. The inmates know it, and for the most part the good guards know it too.

The officers stated that a related and important aspect of giving respect to inmates was that in selectively enforcing prison rules they clearly defined the rules that mattered. That is, both correctional officers and veteran inmates knew and agreed on the types of behavior that called for official action by the officers. The officers stated that their selective enforcement of prison rules resulted in officer–inmate consensus about acceptable inmate behavior and, based on the consensus, a greater sense of predictability and order existed in officer–inmate interactions. The officers further stated that new correctional officers and inmates were partly a problem because they were unfamiliar with the working assumptions and rules of the prison. In learning the practical meaning of giving and getting respect, new officers learned how to properly do their jobs and new inmates learned to do their time.

The second aspect of the correctional officers' accommodative orientation to the officer–inmate relationship involved restricted interaction with inmates. Specifically, correctional officers tried to limit their interactions to those inmates who could help them control other inmates in the housing units. Thus, many inmates had limited and perfunctory dealings with correctional officers, such as fleeting contacts during count times or when inmates were leaving the housing units for jobs, school, or other institutional assignments. The officers explained that they did not interact with most inmates because it was not a necessary part of their jobs. One officer explained his orientation to interactions with inmates in the following way.

> Why should I get involved in something with a prisoner when I don't want to know him? I am not here to love him, only to watch him and make sure the housing unit is secured.

Nonetheless, the correctional officers did regularly interact with some inmates. They did so with inmates who were willing to help the officers fulfill their organizational responsibilities, the most important and cumbersome being the counting of inmates. The counts were conducted at 6:00 a.m. (right before many prisoners went to work), 11:00 a.m. (right before the staggered lunch-times for prisoners), 4:00 p.m. (right after the shift changes of officers), and 10:00 p.m. (right before lights out in the prison). Counting inmates was a cumbersome task for the correctional officers because it required that prisoners be locked in their cells. To ensure this, correctional officers used "trusted" inmates to do their counts for them and help them move prisoners into their assigned cells. In return, the inmates were given privileges that other prisoners did not enjoy, such as extra phone time or dayroom time. They also had greater contact with the correctional officers, although their interactions were focused on the practical problems of counting inmates.

In sum, the correctional officers described their accommodative orientation to prison rules and inmate relationships as a pragmatic adaptation to their work circumstances. They gave respect to inmates because it was an effective way of gaining inmate cooperation and they restricted their interactions with inmates to those who could help them better manage their work problems. Put differently, the officers' portrayals of the accommodative orientation centered in avoiding trouble with inmates. A related way in which they managed inmates and avoided trouble was by treating some inmates' behaviors as normal deviance. The officers described normal deviance as rule violations that were not serious enough to warrant removing prisoners from their housing units or the normal daily activities of the prison. I next consider how the officers explained and justified their treatment of some inmate behaviors as normal deviance.

Avoiding Normal Deviance

According to the correctional officers, the two most important kinds of normal deviance engaged in by inmates were sexual relations and drug use. They were significant to the officers because the behaviors affected the correctional officers' orientation to their work and social control. Specifically, the correctional officers stated that although the behaviors were violations of prison rules, they were ongoing inmate activities which, at best, could only be partly controlled by the strict enforcement of prison rules. For the officers, then, a more realistic and productive orientation to the activities was to treat them as matters of negotiation and accommodation. Officers explained that in treating inmate sexual activities and drug use as negotiable, they were able to maintain a degree of control over them while not engendering the hostility associated with the strict enforcement of prison rules.

The officers stated that sexual relations between inmates was the most problematic kind of normal deviance. It was problematic because, although the correctional officers assumed that it was happening, they did not know when and where to be in the prison in order to avoid discovering it. The officers stated that avoiding the discovery of inmate sexual activities was important because the discovery of inmates having sexual relations was a threat to their safety. The officers explained that an inmate who is confronted by an officer with the fact that he is not a man but a "sissy," "punk," or "fag" would resort to violence to ensure his respect among other inmates. They stated that no inmate wants to be viewed as being sexually weak, nor does he want other inmates to view him as a "woman" who can be exploited by other prisoners for sexual favors.

Thus, to avoid such confrontations the correctional officers watched for signs of inmate sexual activities and removed themselves from settings where signs of sexual activity were present. The officers explained and justified their actions as a realistic and necessary accommodation to the practical circumstances of prison life. As one officer stated,

> If I see three or four guys crowding around a guy's cell, I know something is going down, either they are getting high or someone is sucking or fucking. If I get in the middle of that shit, I would be crazy because I will either get seriously hurt or killed. I am not going to go down there and write tickets. It would be plain stupid.

This is not to suggest that the correctional officers tolerated all forms of inmate sexual activities. Specifically, they did not tolerate the public display of sexual behavior, inmates "squeezing off" other inmates into the "hole" (a segregation cell for those inmates who were afraid of being sexually assaulted), or coercing sexual relations from weaker inmates. The officers stated that both they and inmates viewed these forms of sexual relations as intolerable and that they worked to control sexual exploitation. Finally, correctional officers justified their treatment of inmate sexual activities as normal by portraying the amount of such activity in the prison as less than that found in other prisons in the state. In doing so, they cast inmates' sexual activity as less of a problem than in other settings and, therefore, a tolerable form of rule breaking.

The correctional officers also portrayed their orientation to inmates' drug use as accommodative. They stated that, as in other prisons, narcotics were readily available to inmates in their prison and that they took account of it in their dealings with inmates. The officers further stated that so long as inmates were not causing trouble or exhibiting violent behavior, inmate drug use was a tolerable activity. Indeed, they stated that inmate drug use was a normal and expected part of the inmates' social world. As with inmate sexual activity, the correctional officers avoided confronting inmates about their drug use. The officers tried to anticipate occasions when inmates would be using drugs and avoid situations in which enforcement of prison rules forbidding drug use might be required. They explained that their orientation was realistic because the problems resulting from their enforcement of drug-related rules were more serious than those associated with inmates' drug use. As one correctional officer stated,

> One thing that you don't want to get involved in is the illegal bullshit between inmates. . . . If I know inmates are going to be smoking [marijuana], I'll let it slide if it isn't going to cause any problems. . . . Once you try to step in, then you got problems.

The correctional officers further justified their accommodative orientation to inmate drug use by stating that while drug use was common in the prison, it was not as problematic in this prison as in others in the state. They stated that the most serious danger stemming from inmates' drug use involved new dealers' efforts to move in on the markets of established dealers. According to the correctional officers, however, this problem could be controlled through proper negotiations with dealers, not the strict enforcement of prison rules.

Discussion and Conclusion

Looked at one way, the correctional officers' accounts discussed here are excuses intended to explain away the officers' selective enforcement of prison rules. Viewed this way, they are techniques of neutralization which the officers used to deny responsibility for failing to carry out their officially prescribed responsibilities (Sykes and Matza 1957). The officers did so partly by blaming others (particularly prison administrators) for their actions. In doing so, they cast themselves as victims both of others' actions and, more generally, of the prison system which the officers portrayed as organized to undermine their authority and efforts to fulfill their responsibilities in organizationally approved ways. The officers further described their selective enforcement of prison rules as realistic and necessary adaptations to the prison system.

Implicit in the analysis of the officers' accounts as excuses, however, is an assessment of their accuracy; that is, the accounts are treated as adequate or inadequate explanations of the officers' circumstances, actions, and motives. Further, such an analysis involves taking a side in the officers' disputes with others. By treating the accounts as accurate portrayals of their circumstances, actions, and motives, persons align themselves with the officers in their disputes with inmates, prison administrators, and others in their social world. On the other hand, emphasizing the inadequacy of the officers' accounts implicitly undermines their claims and the legitimacy of their positions in disputes with others.

There is, however, an alternative orientation to the officers' accounts that treats it as rhetoric; that is, as claims about reality intended to persuade others. Rhetoric is partisan discourse through which persons anticipate and/or counter others' criticisms of their actions and positions on practical issues (Perelman 1979). It is also an interactional procedure for assigning preferred identities to one's self and others. By formulating accounts of their activities that emphasize the practical constraints and injustices making up the prison system, correctional officers anticipated and countered others' criticisms of them as corrupt and uncaring functionaries. They also assigned preferred identities to themselves by portraying their actions as professionally responsible efforts to cope with difficult work circumstances. If we treat officers' accounts as *partisan* and *purposeful*—but not necessarily flawed—versions of reality, we can begin to analyze both how officers experience their work worlds and how they managed and made sense of those worlds through their accounting procedures. A rhetorical analysis can provide insight into how officers *produce* the social organization of their work lives. I conclude by discussing some of the implications of treating the officers' accounts as rhetoric.

First, rhetorical analysis does not involve assessing the truthfulness or accuracy of persons' accounts. Rather, it focuses on the practicalities of account-making; it considers how persons produce accounts to solve practical problems. Such problems include explaining why actions which might be seen as improper are "really" proper, as well as efforts to preserve a preferred image of self while acknowledging that one's actions might be taken as evidence of dispreferred motives. Equally importantly, rhetorical analysis of the officers' accounts highlights the multiperspectival nature of social relations in the prison. The officers' accounts are expressions and justifications of their orientations to aspects of the prison social world. We should expect that they will differ from prison administrators' and inmates' accounts of prison life.

The difference is not a matter of the truthfulness or accuracy of the officers' and others' accounts; rather it is a matter of orientation. We should expect diverse orientations to everyday prison life and partisan positions on correctional officers' work practices from officers, administrators, and inmates. Members of these groups bring different concerns and interests to their prison experiences, including their experiences with one another. Thus, the accounts of none of the groups are "better" than the accounts of the others, although they involve different reality claims and are used to pursue different practical interests.

A second and related implication of treating the officers' accounts as rhetoric involves the larger social and political context of prison life and relationships. To the extent that they are organized as conflicts of orientation and interest, we would anticipate that correctional officers', inmates', and prison administrators' accounts will involve differing, even opposed, reality claims. Indeed, the data reported here show that correctional officers also differ in their orientations to everyday life in the prison and their professional responsibilities. Although I have emphasized the ways in which the officers justified their accommodative orientation to inmate relationships, all of the correctional officers were not so oriented.

Some officers portrayed their jobs as involving the strict enforcement of prison rules. They justified the orientation by portraying selective rule enforcement as having long-term detrimental consequences for officer–inmate relations and the officers' authority. According to the strict officers, the most serious and detrimental consequence of the accommodative officer–inmate relationship was the encouragement of snitching among inmates. They stated that, although snitches served the short-term interest of correctional officers in maintaining control over the housing units, they created an atmosphere of distrust and increased inmates' sense of uncertainty in their dealings with officers and other inmates. Other officers countered this claim and justified their encouragement of snitching among inmates by stating that it was a necessary part of maintaining control over inmates and had no serious, detrimental consequences for prison life.

Thus, a third implication of analyzing the correctional officers' accounts as rhetoric is that it points to the variety of ways in which members of the same occupational and organizational group may orient to aspects of their work. But rhetoric and account-making are more than simple reflections of persons' orientations to practical issues; they are also interactional procedures for formulating orientations and perspectives. For example, the officers' responses to my interview questions were more than reports on their thoughts and feelings about their work. The questions were occasions for the officers to produce and justify a perspective on their work which they portrayed as based on enduring thoughts and feelings. Further, because the practical circumstances of correctional officers' account-making differ across situations, we should expect that their rhetoric will also vary situationally. For example, their positions on practical issues and justifications of them may differ when dealing with inmates, administrators, and correctional officers assessed as friendly and supportive versus those assessed as antagonistic.

Critical Thinking

In their role as social control agents, correctional officers are asked to maintain order among inmates while simultaneously carrying out administrative policies that pose a working dilemma for them. This conflict, between administrative demands for fair treatment of inmates and the actual realities of maintaining order, results in officers accommodating prisoner deviance on a daily basis. Do you think such discretion should exist? If, like those Stojkovic interviewed, you think that it should, do you think such discretion contributes to the inconsistencies in how inmates are treated by staff? Taking the role of an inmate, consider how you might interpret the distribution of this discretion.

References

Holstein, J.A. and G. Miller. 1990. "Rethinking Victimization: An Interactional Approach to Victimology." *Symbolic Interaction* 13(1): 101–120.

Lipsky, M. 1980. *Street-level Bureaucracy*. New York: Russell Sage.

Miller, G. and Holstein, J.A. 1989. "On the Sociology of Social Problems" (pp. 1–16), in *Perspectives of Social Problems*, Vol. 1, edited by J.A. Holstein and G. Miller. Greenwich, CT: JAI Press.

Perelman, C. 1979. *The New Rhetoric and the Humanities*. Dordrectht, Holland: D. Reidel.

Scott, M.B. and S.M. Lyman. 1968. "Accounts." *American Sociological Review* 33: 46–62.

Sykes, G.M. 1958. *The Society of Captives*. Princeton, NJ: Princeton University Press.

Sykes, G.M. and D. Matza. 1957. "Techniques of Neutralization." *American Sociological Review* 22: 664–670.

22

Sense-making in Prison: Inmate Identity as a Working Understanding

John Riley

Abstract: *John Riley examines the ways in which correctional officers who work in a maximum security prison formulate, communicate, and justify a shared understanding of how they construct identities for inmates. These shared inmate identities are then used by officers to stereotype the prisoners who come under their supervision. In short, sense-making causes correctional staff to stereotype prisoners in order for them to gain a working understanding of who the prisoners are. Riley suggests that this process of identifying inmates (what he calls "sense-making") by officers allows for them to categorize (stereotype) inmates for the purpose of maintaining social control functions within the prison.*

Cultural studies of the justice system often direct our attention to activities through which actors construct the categories that structure collective action and promote cooperation in professional life (Bridges and Steen 1998). Sudnow (1965), for example, shows how courtroom workgroups use the category of "normal crimes" to promote collaboration and organize the efficient processing of cases. In the field of policing, Van Maanen (1978) describes "the asshole," a category used by street cops to distinguish between those who share an insider's view of the criminal justice process and citizens who bring naïve, unrealistic expectations to their encounters with police officers. Hunt's (1989) discussion of "normal force" focuses on related processes through which rookie police officers come to revise standards generated by academy training as they gain experience as street cops.

Although correctional officers do not share the long period of professional socialization common to members of courtroom workgroups, or the strong subcultural ties observed in policing, informal understandings about the nature of correctional work remain important (Farkas and Manning 1997; Klofas 1984; Klofas and Toch 1982; Philliber 1987). Crouch and Marquart (1980) increase the appreciation of these understandings by describing categories used by correctional officers when they encounter inmates. They suggest that these categories are similar to those described by Van Maanen in his work on policing, and include "good inmate" and "inmate troublemaker" types. Marquart (1986) describes "tune-ups," "attitude adjustments," and "ass whippings," unofficial categories of physical coercion observed in a Texas prison. And Guenther and Guenther (1980) discuss the "stick man," a term used to describe traditional correctional officers, and the "stick man ideology," a view of institutional life characterized by suspicion of inmates and resistance to change.

In this article I examine some of the ways in which correctional officers in a maximum security prison construct, communicate, and defend a shared account of inmate identity. This process allows them to make sense of their work by making sense of the people they supervise. These efforts produce a generic categorization of inmates that is demeaning, derogatory, and often contradicted by firsthand experience (Goffman 1961; Jacobs and Retsky 1975). Even so, it is central to the continuing reproduction of authority in the prison.

Members of most groups come to share operational understandings that define the typical people, places, and situations which demand their professional attention (McNulty 1994). These understandings are the building blocks of larger, socially constructed inter-subjectivities that promote a sense of common identity and facilitate collective action. The identification and description of cultural categories that give structure and meaning to collective action in the justice system constitute an established tradition in the social sciences. Somewhat less, however, is known about the processes by which members maintain these understandings through time and in the face of criticism and experiential contradiction. In focusing on some of the ways in which correctional officers sustain a particular understanding of "the inmate," I examine strategies employed to preserve the functional integrity of a cultural category through which members construct accounts that make sense of their experience and coordinate collective action in the workplace.

Understanding Sense-making

Much of what we know about the construction and maintenance of practical, working accounts of experience is captured by the literature on sense-making. According to Weick (1995), sense-making may be described as a continuous social process, which is retrospective, grounded in efforts at identity construction, and "en-active of sensible environments" (Weick 1995: 30; see also Turner 1987). Sense-making links belief with action, as participants generate meaning in uncertain or ambiguous situations by searching for cues that allow them to connect past experiences with the challenges of the present. The accounts produced, and the processes that produce them, have important implications for the coordination of collective action, for the identity of the individual actors who contribute to their production, and even for the accomplishment of social change (Giddens 1984; Weick 1995). Sense-making gives meaning to the activities of groups and their members. It turns events into accomplishments, converts problems into opportunities, and transforms individuals into leaders, team members, friends, and even enemies of the organization.

While sense-making activities are grounded in "retrospective interpretation of past events" (Weick 1995: 24), they also have important implications for future behavior. Sense-making practices are a means by which participants may work to understand and actually influence change within the organization and in the larger society (Crank 1996; Weick 1995). Research on sense-making suggests that relatively subtle interpretive practices, such as those embodied in tropes, play an important role in the social creation of meaning, in processes of occupational socialization, and particularly in shaping the course of change in complex organizations (Crank 1996; Shearing and Ericson 1991).

Tropes, which include metaphor, synecdoche, metonymy, and irony, are important to the study of occupational socialization and organizational change because they provide shorthand terms for the communication of professional sensibilities and so shape orientations toward collective action (Crank 1996). Like sense-making in general, tropes may be used to create strategic links between past and present events. Metaphor, for example, may reduce uncertainty by demonstrating the essentially familiar nature of an apparently novel experience. In suggesting that a colleague will "meet his Waterloo" or that a candidate for a job might be "Borked," we communicate economically and precisely an evaluation of what may be fairly complex events.

The correctional officers studied here participate in a systematic and categorical devaluation of their prisoners that is grounded in a shared account of inmate identity. Their efforts generate a working understanding of the prisoner and help sustain a sensibility that guides interaction in the prison. Like workers in other occupations, the correctional officers whose work is discussed in this article engage in predictable conversational routines. Such sense-making routines may be understood as ritual efforts to promote cooperation and solidarity. They may also be understood as efforts to preserve and defend the cultural categories the officers use to understand their work and to structure collective action.

Research Design

The data discussed here were obtained between July 10, 1992 and February 17, 1993 at High Mountain Correctional Center (a pseudonym), a facility located in a small community in a western state. At that time High Mountain, a maximum security prison for men, housed approximately 426 inmates who were supervised by 150 correctional officers. During the data-collection period I was granted virtually unrestricted access to all areas of the prison, at any time during the day or night, with the exception of the institution's two armed posts: a watch tower and a roving perimeter vehicle. The data represent approximately 125 hours of on-site observation and an equal number of hours spent outside the institution, talking and socializing with members of the institutional staff.

I gathered the data through observation and unstructured interviews with correctional officers, administrators, and other staff members. Inevitably, researchers seeking to understand correctional officers' sense-making practices face a number of difficult decisions about the collection and analysis of data. Understanding sense-making activities depends heavily on analysis and interpretation of conversational activities in natural settings. These conversations must be either electronically recorded or reconstructed from fieldnotes taken during or shortly after the events observed. When used ethically, electronic recording devices have the potential to alter the events we want to study in significant and unpredictable ways.

Three Occasions for Sense-making

In any group, sense-making activities become most apparent, and thus most amenable to study, when circumstances call into question dominant assumptions about identity, behavior, and the nature of the environment in which members find themselves. Sense-making activity is perhaps most obvious where routine patterns of activity are repeatedly called into question by events not easily reconciled with the understandings accepted and shared by members of a group. In most organizations, opportunities for sense-making often present themselves in the form of new members or inquisitive visitors, who require additional socialization if they are to share the workgroup's understanding of behavioral norms and occupational realities.

At High Mountain Correctional Center, one of the chief products of sense-making is a working understanding of the inmate as an untrustworthy, manipulative, and dangerous individual. The inmate is understood by the staff to be unrestrained by a normal conscience and unwilling to take responsibility for his own behavior. Such failings are assumed to reflect serious faults that are essential, unchanging features of individual personality or character. Supported by the doctrine of "less eligibility" and consistent with the ideology of the "new penology," this view involves a conscious and collective effort to see the prisoner in disparaging and stereotypical terms (Feeley and Simon 1992). Correctional officers' common understanding of inmates may be described as a form of categorical devaluation. It is akin to a legal fiction, or one of the counterfactual safety maxims that we learn to accept for its utility even while maintaining reservations about its factual content. Correctional officers learn to regard all inmates as untrustworthy, manipulative, and dangerous for the same reason that firearms enthusiasts are taught to treat all guns as loaded, and dentists are taught to see all patients as potential carriers of infection. Therefore, this understanding of inmates' character expressed by correctional officers serves as a universal precaution. Like universal precautions in medicine and dentistry, it also serves as a touchstone of competent professional practice.

At High Mountain, three kinds of events routinely call into question the working sense of inmate identity that guides custodial staff members. This stereotypical view is challenged by favorable evaluations of individual inmates often voiced by newcomers to the institution, by instances in which the informal exercise of discretion in rule enforcement seems to favor the inmate, and by the formal requirements of due process associated with the institution's internal disciplinary procedures. Such events create dissonance by challenging the working assumptions about inmates and by raising important questions about the correctional officers' loyalty and character. In responding to the uncertainty reflected in each of these situations, correctional officers employ various sense-making strategies to reconcile apparent inconsistencies and to communicate what they take to be an appropriate professional sensibility.

Reading the Record

Newcomers to the institution frequently question the custodial staff's blanket assessments of inmates' character and identity. In a well-managed institution, newcomers interact with inmates in a variety of settings. Finding that these interactions conform in predictable ways to the expectations that govern life outside the institution, visitors often conclude that inmates are essentially normal. Remarking favorably on a particular inmate's behavior, and so calling into question the working understanding of experienced correctional staff members, frequently gives rise to a form of sense-making activity that may be called "reading the record."

Throughout the institution, officers have access to a thick computer printout called the Confidential Register, which provides selective biographical information on each inmate. Other than documenting institutional work assignments, these records contain no material that could be used to portray the inmate in a favorable way. They provide a succinct portrait of the inmate as an offender, describing his criminal history and his sentence, release date, security classification, and housing assignment. When treatment workers, visitors, or new staff members question an experienced correctional officer's categorical devaluation of inmates by referring to a particular inmate's success in program participation, his cooperative demeanor, or his strong work ethic, a reading of the record virtually guarantees that the working understanding of the custodial staff will be supported.

Reading the Confidential Register is a form of status degradation ceremony in absentia. Because High Mountain is a maximum security prison, inmates' criminal histories generally involve extremely serious, often violent offenses. Institutional records show that in 1992, when data collection for this study began, 32 percent of the inmates were serving time for crimes involving homicide. Another 17 percent were serving sentences for sexual assault. But these "facts" have a compelling official quality. They portray a one-dimensional man, a man whose identity has been reconstructed to serve the needs of those who hold him captive. With this style of presentation, officers can confirm to skeptical outsiders, with apparent objectivity, the dominant view of an inmate's character and identity. Reading the record allows the custodial staff to participate in the social construction of inmate identity without committing themselves to a position that inexperienced outsiders might construe as unprofessional or inappropriately prejudicial. Claims about an inmate's identity thus become documented facts rather than subjective assertions. This form of sense-making is compelling and influential in the prison. Like all such activities, reading the record links the past with the present so as to reinforce a particular set of dispositions.

Exercising Discretion

For those correctional officers who work most directly with inmates, the routine of a shift is typically punctuated by events requiring the exercise of individual discretion in enforcing institutional rules. These events, usually quite minor, challenge officers to find creative solutions to the many human relations problems associated with managing inmates. Like their law enforcement counterparts on the outside, correctional officers cannot respond to every instance of rule breaking with formal sanctions. To do so would be time-consuming, inefficient, and counterproductive.

A formal response to rule violation is a complicated process requiring the participation of perhaps four or five other officers, generating substantial paperwork, and often making demands on the institution's superintendent. An officer who places too much emphasis on formal sanctions imposes upon others, creates doubt about his or her ability to manage inmates, and is viewed by inmates and staff as weak and ineffectual. For these reasons, officers at High Mountain often rely on informal strategies as they exercise their authority, overseeing the production of order through continuous negotiation with the individuals they encounter.

Because pressures to handle rule violation informally are strong, officers must frequently ignore, at least temporarily, obvious violations of relatively minor institutional rules. Sometimes they disregard such violations until an inmate can be isolated from potential sources of support and reprimanded in private, or until an inmate who is obviously very angry has a chance to "cool off." Although it is illegal to smoke in any building in the High Mountain compound, a prudent officer might ignore an inmate caught smoking in a doorway on a cold day if he or she is aware that the inmate has just received news of a family member's death or the loss of an important appeal.

Such exercise of discretion may reflect the officer's perception that tolerance is an investment in cooperation. This perception is reflected in remarks recorded in the project fieldnotes, though these remarks sometimes indicate ambivalence and uncertainty:

> Treat the inmates like human beings and they will treat you OK.
>
> (housing unit officer)

> [Officer Ryan] said he can never let himself see inmates as human beings. Then [he] said he could [treat an inmate like a human being] if he had to tell an inmate his father died. "I'm not going to go to him and say your dad just shit the bed."

Although tolerance sometimes makes good sense, and no officer would fault another for reluctance to turn a minor problem into a possible confrontation, the exercise of tolerance and understanding may be interpreted as inconsistent with the experienced correctional officers' understanding of inmates' character. Where it appears to involve tolerance, the exercise of discretion may seem to some to suggest, inappropriately, that an inmate deserves the special consideration we usually reserve for friends, neighbors, co-workers, and others who live law-abiding lives. Particularly when witnessed by a newcomer, a correctional officer's decision to tolerate an inmate's misconduct constitutes an important occasion for sense-making.

When officers find themselves in situations where discretion may be interpreted contrary to their commonsense notions of inmate identity, they may choose from among a variety of sensemaking options. Typically, discretion that might imply undeserved tolerance toward inmates is justified pragmatically with apparent acts of kindness reframed as maneuvers in the struggle to maintain control. Such pragmatic justification links the current minor infraction with previous experience demonstrating the wisdom of toler-ance or delay. Storytelling about examples of institutional disturbances frequently focuses on the minor nature of confrontations that eventually escalate into major events. According to one account, the 1971 Attica uprising was sparked when a guard tackled an inmate who refused to leave his cell for a disciplinary hearing. Simple requests for inmates' compliance take on new meaning when linked with historical accounts of prison violence.

The language of pragmatic justification may be used to recount stories of violence in abbreviated ways, using the shorthand of metaphor. As the following expressions suggest, the language of guarding offers a number of convenient ways to communicate danger and uncertainty:

> Inmates sometimes go off when you don't expect it, so you have to be careful about how you handle things.

> He's hot now because we just wrote him up this morning. We'll let him blow off a little steam now, but I'll talk to him later about this.

> Sometimes it pays to give them a little air. Screw the lid down too tight and you can make things worse. A tough attitude can come back to bite you.

Metaphors that bring to mind unvented boilers, explosions, and volcanic eruptions all succinctly communicate the need for caution; they may be used to justify correctional practices that seem inconsistent with a militant, oppositional approach to inmates.

Pragmatic justification is a strategy that allows custodial staff members to exercise discretion and show some tolerance toward inmates without undermining the under-standing of inmates' character that informs their professional decision-making. By linking minor infractions with serious trouble in the past, officers can demonstrate their commit-ment to control even while it might appear to some observers that they are failing to exercise complete control in the present.

Ritual Insubordination and Institutional Due Process

Institutional due process frequently provides occasions for sense-making because it combines opportunities to exercise discretion with a process that forces officers to confront the inadequacy of their assumptions about inmates. Institutional due process highlights the contradictory role expectations that characterize correctional work. In the work of the institutional disciplinary committee, individual officers struggle to reconcile belief in fair-ness and the rule of law with commitment to a working conception of inmate identity that is ultimately demeaning and stereotypical. Disciplinary hearings may be understood as status degradation ceremonies, in which group activity focuses on the moral failings of deviant members in an effort that ultimately affirms moral boundaries and the social solidarity of members in good standing (Garfinkel 1956).

Although institutional due process at High Mountain involves important elements of status degradation, it would be a mistake to understand such events solely in these terms.

These events have a double character: They are motivated as much by a rejection of efforts to impose an "official" view of the world upon the correctional officer as by a rejection of the inmate's moral worth. In institutional due process, and perhaps in offensive speech more generally, we see both status degradation ceremony and ritual insubordination. At times it may be impossible to separate one from the other.

During the course of this study, institutional due process frequently elicited derogatory remarks that called into question the inmates' moral worth and the legal requirements associated with disciplinary proceedings. Although the unflattering language of the degradation ceremony sustains the inmate's unenviable position in the moral order of the institution, it also appears to have another, equally important, quality. Because the remarks made at these hearings both disparage inmates and show a lack of respect for institutional due process, they also distance the officers who make them from an official, administratively approved version of prison life that challenges the officers' understanding of inmate identity. In short, they constitute an instance of ritual insubordination.

The term *ritual insubordination* encompasses complaining, swearing, griping, or bitching, particularly when those forms of expression form a collective response to occupational stress. In contrast to more utilitarian versions of protest, the meaning of the term is partly captured in the commonsense notion of "blowing off steam." It applies when insubordinate behavior "is not realistically expected to bring about change" (Goffman 1961: 315). Goffman chose to treat ritual insubordination as a largely expressive act, lacking in practical utility but important in the identity work of individuals experiencing conflict between institutional role expectations and conceptions of personal identity.

The "D-board"

I routinely observed ritual insubordination during meetings of the institution's disciplinary committee, a group of correctional officers organized to hear charges of internal infractions brought against inmates. Known in the institution as the "D-Board," this committee provides inmates with the first elements of due process required by law when individuals are charged with consequential violations of institutional rules. Disciplinary hearings observed at High Mountain are conducted before a senior officer, who serves as chairperson, and three other officers. Service on the D-Board depends on availability, on shift assignments, and ultimately on the discretion of the officer in charge. The committee hears testimony from the accused inmate, from the officer making the charge, and from other officers, inmates, or staff members who might provide relevant testimony.

Although these hearings are roughly analogous to a courtroom trial, those who expect elaborate due process may be surprised by their organization. Because of the need to maintain institutional security, and particularly to protect witnesses from retaliation, prison inmates do not enjoy the right to confront witnesses or even to be present when testimony is offered against them. Disciplinary committees may elect to withhold information where security concerns are an issue. Both testimony and committee deliberations may take place in a room where only correctional officers are present. The routine of these hearings is such that the disciplinary committee is frequently alone: waiting for witnesses, deliberating the facts of the case, or considering punishment options in private. Although a tape-recorder is used to produce an official record of each case, tape-recording is routinely suspended when inmates are requested to leave the hearing room to facilitate private discussion.

When the D-Board is in session, a substantial amount of time is spent waiting for cases to begin or for witnesses to arrive. Committee members typically view these "in-between" periods as opportunities for gossip, storytelling, jokes, and other forms of social activity. These relatively private moments are frequently characterized by the sort of griping or bitching that Goffman called ritual insubordination. Disciplinary committee members frequently comment on the character of both particular prisoners with whom they are called to interact and the "typical" prisoner incarcerated at High Mountain.

In the 36 cases I observed during the study, I heard many derogatory remarks and stories about inmates, and numerous cynical remarks about the disciplinary process. Members commonly referred to the individual about to be heard by the board as "the next victim." Officers sometimes engaged in tongue-in-cheek discussion of punishment options before the facts of the case were heard. In one typical instance, an officer inquiring about the charge at issue in a pending case asked "What's this one guilty of?" One inmate who refused to attend his hearing was said to have "PMS today," a particularly provocative remark in an environment where few things are considered more offensive than remarks that call into question another man's masculinity. Inmates were described as "stupid," were denigrated for their sexual preferences, and were compared to animals. Officers also complained about "ACLU lawyers," "liberal judges," and "out-of-touch" administrators.

These remarks are as much a rejection of the legitimacy of institutional due process and those who support it as they are a derogatory characterization of inmates. Equally importantly, they were always made off the record and out of the prisoners' hearing. Although these efforts may be regarded as status degradation in absentia, they lack the full force of ceremonies in which all parties meet face-to-face. They go beyond symbolic attack on the inmate. Officers explicitly criticize the due-process demands supported by "out-of-touch" administrators who spend too much time in their offices and by "liberal" judges who "think more of inmates than they do of guards." Those people do not seem to share the correctional officer's working understanding of the inmate. Hearings that involve inmates' testimony, after all, cannot make sense to those who share the operational assumption that inmates are dishonest and manipulative. And hearings in which an inmate can call into question an officer's account of a disciplinary write-up make even less sense in the partisan world of the prison.

In relation to the disciplinary hearing, ritual insubordination represents an effort to distance oneself not only from inmates but also from an official version of the situation which suggests that an inmate's version of events has value. This implied assumption of credibility cannot be reconciled with the officers' understanding of inmates' character. In the officers' view, those who impose demands for due process challenge that understanding and force the prison staff to support their effort. Ritual insubordination gives assembled officers an opportunity to verbally express allegiance to workgroup norms in circumstances in which the actions they are legally required to take may cast doubt on that loyalty.

Those seeking justification for moral outrage would find it easily if the informal conversation that accompanies disciplinary hearings were presented out of its larger context. Ultimately these exchanges are grounded in a generally derogatory conception of inmate identity. In the understanding that emerges and is reinforced in these conversations, inmates are characterized as immature, untrustworthy, unpredictable, weak, perverse, and a potential source of trouble for the staff.

Disciplinary boards are required to choose between the version of events offered by the officer who made the initial charge and the version offered by an inmate. In situations where the board finds that punishment of an inmate is unjustified, board members, in a sense, are breaking ranks. This is particularly clear to the officer in charge of the hearings. When interviewed, he described his role as leader of the disciplinary committee by saying "I'm here to make sure the officer doesn't get stepped on out there."

Correctional officers who show too great a concern for an inmate's rights are not only placed in a position in which they may seem, to some, to side with an inmate. They are also acting so as to call into question the working understanding of inmate identity, an important expression of group loyalty. Such action may be justified pragmatically, like any expression of discretion, but it creates high levels of cognitive dissonance for those involved. This is exactly the sort of situation in which one would expect conscientious correctional officers to suffer a great deal of stress, with a need to reaffirm their commitment to colleagues and to the central tenets of their occupational culture. In disciplinary hearings, offensive speech may sometimes serve as a way to affirm one's loyalty and professional identity under difficult and confusing circumstances.

Discussion

In reading the record, correctional officers respond to challenges to their working understanding of inmate identity by making an apparently objective biographical presentation from an official source. In the informal exercise of discretion, episodes that may be understood as suggesting sympathy for apparently deserving inmates are recast as strategic maneuvers in the struggle for control of the prison. In instances of ritual insubordination associated with due process, officers reaffirm commitment to the dominant assumptions of the group through symbolic protest, and work to elaborate a vision of occupational life that reconciles group loyalty with a commitment to the rule of law.

Working understandings, and the sense-making activity that produces and maintains them, are inevitable features of collective action, and correctional officers' sense-making activity may inevitably be somewhat oppositional. In view of their professional responsibilities, this is probably appropriate. A working definition of the inmate that discourages trust and encourages vigilance is necessary for correctional work in maximum security facilities. Without such operational assumptions, it is hard to understand how the job could be done.

If conversational routines that disparage inmates are to be expected in corrections, problems will arise when the categorical devaluation of inmates is unchecked by competing elements of organizational culture, or when newcomers are exposed to these routines without first learning to appreciate their significance. New employees or prison visitors are unlikely to appreciate the difference between language that enthusiastically affirms unflattering working assumptions and language expressing a genuine contempt for prisoners' human rights. Demeaning and derogatory remarks may promote pluralistic ignorance, a condition that exists in institutions where many guards support legitimate institutional goals but feel that most others do not (Kauffman 1981; Philliber 1987). Even more importantly, they may create the impression that inmates are fair game for more serious forms of abuse.

Offensive speech associated with the categorical devaluation of inmates may create problems for some employees; certainly it does so for the inmates in their care. Regardless of the speaker's intention, language that denigrates others may encourage abusive and even violent behavior. Language gives license, whether we intend it or not. Therefore, it is as important to discourage offensive speech as to understand it. Because casual conversation may set the stage for violent behavior in the nature, and because we know that such behavior occurs regularly in American prisons, correctional supervisors must take casual conversation seriously.

In focusing on collective efforts to affirm and protect a working understanding of inmate identity, it is easy to forget the diversity that characterizes the workforce of correctional institutions (Klofas 1984). Officers may acknowledge the value of a shared definition of the inmate in connection with collective action, but no officer is required to fully embrace this one-dimensional view, and many clearly do not. Officers approach the routines that express these understandings with varying levels of approval, enthusiasm, and commitment. Existing research suggests that many correctional officers hold attitudes favorable to inmates, and to the provision of services facilitating rehabilitation (Kauffman 1981; Klofas and Toch 1982; Logan 1996; Lombardo 1982). In addition, many observers of prison life indicate that correctional officers have more in common with the inmates they supervise than they might care to admit (Hassine 1999; Lombardo 1989; Owen 1988).

Conclusion

The sense-making accomplishments of the correctional staff at High Mountain are frequently called into question by the people and events that constitute the routine of prison life. By focusing on ways in which officers respond to such challenges, I explore the processes through which members repair and maintain the categorical understandings produced through sense-making activities. By participating in these processes, officers in one prison reproduce established patterns of social control.

Like police officers, correctional officers make sense of their world through conversational routines that often appear to take place when the real work of their profession does not require their full attention (McNulty 1994). In fact, informal conversational routines are the medium through which participants engage in work that is a fundamental precondition of effective collective action. As Gronn (1983: 1) observes, "[T]alk is the work," and these efforts to fill the time are essential moments in the reproduction of occupational culture and social control in the justice system.

Social scientists have worked to identify and describe the activities through which actors construct and maintain the categories that structure collective action and promote cooperation in professional life. Such efforts are an important undertaking in the social sciences. Studies of the ways in which such categories contribute to the reproduction of social control in the prison offer opportunities to learn more about inmates and correctional workers, and to understand more clearly the strategies of social control that now shape the lives of millions of incarcerated Americans. Further research on sense-making in correctional facilities, and particularly on the categories used by correctional officers to understand their work, would contribute to a more satisfactory account of workplace culture in the justice system, and to a fuller understanding of the dynamics of social control.

Critical Thinking

This article, as did the previous one by Stojkovic, discusses the realities of prison work and the necessity for social control methods beyond formal policy. Yet, officers seem to justify their negative perceptions of inmates, often without cause, and consequently treat inmates as if they are all disciplinary problems. Further, officers consistently violate prison rules and policies by claiming such actions are necessary to maintain social control. Viewed with a critical eye, do you think that the informal social structure of the prison allows correctional officers to act in this way?

References

Bridges, G.S. and S. Steen. 1998. "Racial Disparities in Official Assessments of Juvenile Offenders: Attributional Stereotypes as Mediating Mechanisms." *American Sociological Review* 63: 554–570.

Crank, J.P. 1996. "The Construction of Meaning During Training for Probation and Parole." *Justice Quarterly* 13: 265–290.

Crouch, B.M. and J.W. Marquart. 1980. "On Becoming a Guard" (pp. 63–106), in *The Keepers: Prison Guards and Contemporary Corrections*, edited by B.M. Crouch. Springfield, IL: Thomas.

Farkas, M.A. and P.K. Manning. 1997. "The Occupational Culture of Corrections and Police Officers." *Journal of Crime and Justice* 20: 51–68.

Feeley M.M. and J. Simon. 1992. "The New Penology: Notes on the Emerging Strategy of Corrections and Its Implications." *Criminology* 30: 449–474.

Garfinkel, H. 1956. "Conditions of Successful Degradation Ceremonies." *American Journal of Sociology* 61: 420–424.

Giddens, A. 1984. *The Constitution of Society: An Introduction to the Theory of Structuration*. Berkeley: University of California Press.

Goffman, I. 1961. *Asylums: Essays on the Social Situations of Mental Patients and Other Inmates*. New York: Anchor Books.

Gronn, P.C. 1983. "Talk as the Work: The Accomplishment of School Administration." *Administrative Science Quarterly* 28: 1–21.

Guenther, A.L. and M.Q. Guenther. 1980. "Screws vs. Thugs" (pp. 162–182), in *The Keepers: Prison Guards and Contemporary Corrections*, edited by B.M. Crouch. Springfield, IL: Thomas.

Hassine, V. 1999. *Life Without Parole: Living in Prison Today* (2nd edn). Los Angeles, CA: Roxbury Publishing.

Hunt, J. 1989. "Police Accounts of Normal Force" (pp. 345–363), in *Deviant Behavior*, edited by D. Kelly. New York: St. Martin's Press.

Jacobs, J.B. and G.R. Retsky. 1975. "Prison Guard." *Urban Life* 4: 5–29.

Kauffman, K. 1981. "Prison Officers' Attitudes and Perceptions of Attitudes: A Case of Pluralistic Ignorance." *Journal of Research in Crime and Delinquency* 18: 272–294.

Klofas, J. 1984. "Reconsidering Prison Personnel, New Views of the Correctional Officer Subculture." *International Journal of Offender Therapy and Comparative Criminology* 28: 169–275.

Klofas, J. and H. Toch. 1982. "The Guard Subculture." *Journal of Research in Crime and Delinquency* 19: 238–254.

Logan, C.H. 1996. "Public vs. Private Prison Management: A Case Comparison." *Criminal Justice Review* 21: 62–85.

Lombardo, L.X. 1982. "Alleviating Inmate Stress: Contributions from Correctional Officers" (pp. 285–298), in *The Pains of Imprisonment*, edited by R. Johnson and H. Toch. Beverly Hills, CA: Sage.

Lombardo, L.X. 1989. *Guards Imprisoned: Correctional Officers at Work* (2nd edn). Cincinnati, OH: Anderson Publishing.

Marquart, J.W. 1986. "Prison Guards and the Use of Physical Coercion as a Mechanism of Social Control." *Criminology* 24: 347–366.

McNulty, E.W. 1994. "Generating Common Sense Knowledge Among Police Officers." *Symbolic Interaction* 17: 281–294.

Owen, B. 1988. *The Reproduction of Social Control: A Study of Prison Workers at San Quentin*. New York: Praeger.

Philliber, S. 1987. "Thy Brother's Keeper: A Review of the Literature on Correctional Officers." *Justice Quarterly* 4: 9–37.

Shearing, C.D. and R.V. Ericson. 1991. "Culture as Figurative Action." *British Journal of Sociology* 42: 481–506.

Sudnow, D. 1965. "Normal Crimes: Sociological Features of the Penal Code in a Public Defender Office." *Social Problems* 12: 255–276.

Turner, J.H. 1987. "Toward a Sociological Theory of Motivation." *American Sociological Review* 52: 15–27.

Van Maanen, J. 1978. "The Asshole" (pp. 221–238), in *Policing: A View from the Street*, edited by P. Manning and J. Van Maanen. Santa Monica, CA: Goodyear.

Weick, K.E. 1995. *Sensemaking in Organizations*. Thousand Oaks, CA: Sage.

23

Gender and Occupational Culture Conflict: A Study of Women Jail Officers

Eric D. Poole and Mark R. Pogrebin

Abstract: *Offering a female perspective of custodial corrections work in county jails, Poole and Pogrebin consider the adjustment problems and work strategies of women deputy sheriffs. The authors discuss the issues of employment integration, sex role stereotyping, gender-based work strategies, and differential treatment within the organization. The authors find that in their role as jail officers, female deputies experience work integration difficulties predominantly imposed upon them by their male co-workers. These difficulties increase gender stereotyping, role conflict, and differential performance expectations. Poole and Pogrebin also depict numerous obstacles that prevent women correctional deputies from being promoted to supervisory positions. They conclude with a discussion of the personal and occupational consequences of a system rife with institutionalized sexism, and they offer some possible means for addressing these occupational barriers that presently exist in the jail organizational culture.*

Since the early 1980s, the number of women working in state and federal jails has grown dramatically. According to the Bureau of Justice Statistics of the U.S. Department of Justice, the number of females employed as correctional officers rose from 16,545 in 1988 to 42,500 in 1999—an increase of 157 percent (Perkins, Stephan, and Beck, 1995; Stephan, 2001). Females now comprise 28 percent of the custodial/security staff in jails nationwide. The primary stimulus for the increased employment and utilization of female officers has been the need to comply with federal guidelines on hiring (Equal Opportunity Act of 1972 amending Title VII of the Civil Rights Act of 1964), as well as with various court orders to implement hiring quotas to increase female representation or to rewrite entrance exams and requirements to encourage the employment of women (see Camp, Steiger, Wright, Saylor, and Gilman, 1997). While the initial stimulus for increased hiring of women was prompted by legislative and judicial mandates, several administrative factors have also driven the need for more women employees. First, jails must house both male and female inmates, and women are needed to supervise the female residents. Second, female officers are needed to conduct searches of female visitors. Third, a rapid expansion of the jail workforce has increased demand and opened up job opportunities for qualified female applicants.

Despite women's increased presence in corrections work, the position of female jail officer is a unique form of non-traditional work for women; it is qualitatively different from other work in that violence is prevalent in the work environment and the job is perceived to be a highly sex-typed male one requiring qualities of dominance, aggressiveness, and authoritativeness (Hemmens, Stohr, Schoeler, and Miller, 2002). Female qualities of nurturing, sensitivity, and understanding are thought by many male jail officers to be not merely unnecessary, but potentially detrimental to job performance. Because female officers are expected to conform to masculine sex-typed work norms, it is likely that the integration problems faced by women entering this occupation are severe; however, little research attention has been focused on female officers working in local jails.

Based on studies of women working as guards in male correctional facilities, sexism and sexual harassment have emerged as persistent obstacles to workforce integration (Farnworth, 1992; Pogrebin and Poole, 1997). Women correctional officers experience a hostile work environment where they endure resentment, harassment, and discrimination. The research suggests that male officers seek to maintain male dominance and subordination of female co-workers by sexualizing the prison work environment (Pogrebin and Poole, 1997). What is lacking almost entirely from the research literature is a focus on the impact of the sexualized work environment on women jail officers. This article seeks to lay an initial qualitative research foundation upon which this area of concern may be addressed.

We will frame our study by focusing on gender as a normative system, a pervasive network of interrelated norms and sanctions through which female and male behavior is evaluated and controlled (West and Zimmerman, 1987). This conception of gender as a scheme of interpersonal evaluations is, of course, implicit in most critiques of the concepts of "femininity" and "masculinity." Guided by how workplace perceptions and practices bear a close relation to these sociocultural constructions of reality, we will stress what Padavic (1991) has described as the "re-creation of gender in the male workplace" (p. 279) and what Stockard and Johnson (1980) have termed "the reproduction of male dominance in everyday interactions" (p. 10).

Diverse studies of the gender system have irrefutably shown how the subordination of women is sustained through their being socialized for, and restricted to, limited aspirations, options, roles, and rewards. The weighty significance of such factors, along with the basic learning processes and major societal institutions that produce and perpetrate them, is unquestionable. Equally important is the role of interpersonal evaluation in ordinary life situations. In particular, informal social control must be recognized as a key mechanism that backs up and enforces many of the restrictions and limitations placed on women. There are various ways, then, in which gender—as a sociocultural complex of meanings, behaviors, and assessments—is instilled and maintained. Hochschild (1973) identifies four main perspectives adopted in studies of women and the gender system. One focuses on the nature of biological and psychological "sex differences"; a second emphasizes "sex roles and the norms which govern them"; a third treats "women as a minority group"; and the fourth—a "politics of caste" outlook—stresses power differentials and exploitation as a tool of control. As Hochschild notes, these alternative approaches reflect different disciplinary traditions, tend to favor different "conceptual vocabularies," and may carry different implications with respect to social change and public policy. In the present work, the first orientation ("sex differences") receives little attention. Each of the other three approaches, however, provides concepts and emphases that are useful for the analysis of women's work experiences. Our central concept of "gender norms" has close ties to the study of "sex roles," even if the focus here on reinforcement in daily interaction departs somewhat from the more usual stress on socialization. In exploring the basic perceptions and responses through which women are devalued, the analogy to deviance labeling and stigmatization will prove valuable. Finally, power and control differentials are going to be critical sensitizing concepts in examining the sexualization of the work setting, in general, and sexual harassment, in particular. In developing an overview of women working in jail it is unnecessary, therefore, and may even prove counterproductive, to attempt to adopt one of these orientations. The sociological penchant for identifying supposedly competing "schools" should not lead us to neglect points on which otherwise different approaches may converge or complement each other. Because the topic of women working in traditional male occupations is highly complex, to study it we may well need a varied arsenal of sociological concepts and outlooks.

Occupational Norms and Workplace Organization

Both early studies and the contemporary literature reveal that women who have entered a variety of traditionally male occupations have faced discriminatory hiring and assignment practices, resistance and opposition from male co-workers, and inadequate on-the-job training. The experiences of women entering the corrections field are illustrative of these organizational obstacles and challenges to changing occupational norms in a work setting undergoing integration (Britton, 2003; Carlson, Anson, and Thomas, 2003). To understand the persistence of an organizational climate of resentment, skepticism, and hostility toward women working in corrections, we must first examine the nature of the occupational norms that are at stake.

Occupational norms have traditionally been linked to work segregation by sex (Jacobs, 1989). For the most part, the sex typing of specific jobs is arbitrary and follows one basic rule: men and women are different and should be doing different things. Such stereotypical thinking has long sustained the stigmatization of those who violate such norms of occupational segregation, thus reinforcing sex-role typing in the workplace. Sex-role stereotypes function to keep women in ancillary and supportive roles rather than in positions of independence, authority, and leadership (Safilios-Rothschild, 1979). A consequence for women who challenge these sex-role stereotypes is the negative evaluation of their skills, capabilities, and competence. While women in corrections work may perform the job as well as men, they tend not to be seen as being men's equals (Belknap, 1996).

Negative reactions to or sanctioning of occupational "deviants" constitutes a powerful social control mechanism in maintaining a polarized male and female workforce (Schur, 1984). Particularly when women enter what have traditionally been viewed as ultra-masculine occupations (such as coal-mining, steel manufacturing, firefighting, corrections, etc.), intense reactions are expected to occur. Several common responses are likely to be found in such situations of female occupational deviance (Schur, 1979). Consciousness of the deviant's femaleness will be heightened. Consciousness of the female's deviance will also be high, and she will be devalued, restricted, and otherwise punished for it. Finally, male workers may convince themselves that a woman who commits such occupational deviance deserves whatever she gets. Women come to be viewed as "fair game" for whatever abuses— verbal, emotional, or physical—male co-workers decide to dispense. In such a work situation, then, a specific imputation of deviant identity to the woman is used to rationalize diverse forms of inappropriate male behavior directed toward her (Schur, 1984). This rationalization suggests that harassment may sometimes implicitly constitute punishment for women's perceived violation of specific gender norms.

Some observers contend that a generalized perception of threat to male power and control on the part of male workers lies behind most harassment in the workplace (Erez and Tontodonato, 1992). It is important, however, to keep in mind that something besides occupational power and control is involved in the harassment phenomenon. As MacKinnon (1979, p. 162) notes,

> The sense that emerges from incidents of sexual harassment is . . . [that men] want to know that they can go this far this way any time they wish and get away with it. . . . The practice seems an extension of their desire and belief that the woman is there for them, however they may choose to define that.

Harassment functions to sustain both male workplace power and male power to treat women as sexual objects (Zimmer, 1988). Workplace harassment, then, is not merely a result of women's violating occupational norms or their being vulnerable as tokens (i.e., being in the numerical minority). On the contrary, it also reflects the socialized and reinforced tendency of male co-workers to view women primarily as visual sexual objects (MacKinnon, 1979). From this standpoint, harassment of women workers has as much to do with the daily harassment they experience in many other contexts as it has to do with the specific features of women's work situations.

The sexualized work environment embodies the treatment of women as objects and a denial of personal autonomy (Farley, 1978). According to MacKinnon (1982), "Sexual objectification is the primary process of the subjection of women" (p. 541). This process is thus central to perceptions of female violations of occupational norms and gender roles, as individual women are submitted to standardized and stereotype-laden categorizations and responses. In this respect the sexualized work environment is the linchpin of occupational inequality (Martin, 1989). The research presented here seeks to explore the dimensions of the sexualized jail setting that women corrections officers face and to understand the significance of gender in their work experiences.

Method

Four county jails and three adult detention centers located in four counties in the Denver metropolitan area were selected for the present study. These facilities were managed and staffed by personnel from four sheriffs' departments. Utilizing personnel rosters of deputy sheriffs provided by the respective facilities, we drew a 50 percent systematic random sample (n = 135) of all female officers from each institution. We contacted sampled officers individually in order to inform them of the purpose of the study, request their participation, and obtain informed consent. A total of 119 women agreed to participate, and interview times were then scheduled. Because of conflicts related to vacation, sick leave, work assignment, transfer, etc., interviews with 11 women could not be conducted. Thus, the present study was based on interview data from 108 women deputies. Their ages ranged from 24 to 51 (median = 37), and their length of experience at their present facility ranged from one to 15 years (median = 5).

Interviews were conducted at the respective facilities in private conference rooms, library carrels, or visitation rooms during off hours. Each interview lasted for approximately 90 minutes and was tape-recorded with the subject's consent. A semi-structured interview format was used, which relied on sequential probes to pursue leads provided by subjects. This allowed the deputies to identify and elaborate upon important domains they perceived to characterize their experiences in jail work, rather than the researchers eliciting responses to structured questions.

Findings

Second-class Status

According to Belknap (1991), the conflict between gender-role norms and occupational-role norms in jail work poses unique obstacles for female officers. The traditional male attitude about the inherent masculine nature of the job of jail guard makes the prospect of a female co-worker particularly offensive to some men officers. For example, corrections officers associate masculinity with physical ability and view the use of force as a defining feature of the job (Belknap, 1991). Jurik (1985) reports that male officers believe that women are incapable of exercising sufficient physical force to perform the social tasks required to control incorrigible inmates; moreover, women are often seen as less reliable in back-up or cover roles when handling violent encounters with inmates. Implicit trust and reliance that an officer will come to another's aid and use any means necessary to protect a peer's life are vital components of the work expectations among corrections officers. Male staff are fearful that the presumed physical limitations of women will place officers at greater risk and make the environment potentially more threatening and dangerous because of the inmates' perception of diminished staff ability to maintain control. Women in line positions are thus regarded as second-class officers, unable to meet reliably job performance criteria of male officers.

Zimmer (1986) reports that female officers are afforded few opportunities to build skills or gain confidence in controlling prisoners in threatening situations. Since women are perceived as weak, indecisive, emotional, and timid, male officers tend to take charge in physical encounters between women deputies and inmates. This action, although necessary in aiding a fellow officer as back-up, reinforces male feelings of physical superiority over women and diminishes the status of female officers. One woman officer describes her experience:

> I've been on many codes [officer back-up] when there is a physical altercation going on and male officers have run in with me and I'm shoved aside so the guys can get in on the fight. . . . I don't know if it's ego. Some of it is patronizing, some protective, "We've got to take care of the little women."

The attitude that female officers need protection from aggressive inmates is also shared by supervisory staff. Instead of developing policy which is inclusive of women in these dangerous encounters, supervisory personnel tend to reinforce the stereotype of women's heightened vulnerability. A deputy illustrated this problem:

> We had a fight in the girls' pod day room, and there was all this concern all of a sudden that we can't have two female officers in the pod. . . . It's just not safe. The male supervisors think we can't handle it.

If women corrections officers are not afforded the opportunity to resolve inmate physical altercations, they are restricted in their repertoire of social control techniques. To the extent that supervisory personnel reinforce this subordinate position, women officers will have limited opportunities to demonstrate their physical abilities and gain experience and confidence in the skilled use of force. Such paternalistic treatment thus serves to undermine the authority of women officers and calls into question their ability to perform their job:

> A male deputy, in front of some inmates, put his arm around me and said, "Dear, I'm going to go to lunch. Can you handle this?"

The paternalistic treatment of women is in itself a denial of their basic role identity as agents of security and control. The notion that women officers can't take care of themselves subjugates them in their work relations with men, as well as imputing diminished capacities in their routine job performance. In her participant observer role as a coal handler in a power plant, Padavic (1991) reports that paternalistic treatment made her "unsure of [her] abilities, afraid of undertaking something new, doing it wrong, and thereby confirming a stereotype" (p. 286). Millett (1971) further notes that while paternalism is held as "a palliative to the injustice of women's social position, chivalry is also a technique for disguising it" (p. 37).

The irony of the self-fulfilling prophecy that operates in the jail setting is twofold. First, women officers who are subjected to paternalistic protection and control are not given the opportunity to develop or prove their physical skills, which in turn tautologically confirms the male co-workers' stereotypes. Second, when women officers are treated as second-class employees who are perceived in need of protection they may experience heightened anxiety, exhibit less self-confidence, and even react in inappropriate or unsatisfactory ways. Thus the circle is complete: paternalistic actions serve to foster the stereotypical behavior that in turn confirms the original expectations.

Occupational Subculture

Pollock (1986) notes that the guard subculture is an important component of work social-ization. Yet male officers tend to adhere to a cult of masculinity that serves to isolate women co-workers as outsiders (Belknap, 1991). By excluding women staff from the informal organizational network of male deputies, the former are often forced to learn much of the job on their own. As a result of this purposive exclusion, women are denied occupational socialization opportunities and a sense of belonging associated with colle-gial relations. Because much of the job training is done on an informal basis as situations arise, the isolation of female officers undermines their ability to learn the particulars and peculiarities of the job from experienced male colleagues.

Zimmer (1986) reports that female officers are viewed by many of their male peers as being inferior and are therefore denied entree to the officer subculture. One deputy describes her experience of exclusion from informal work networks:

> The male officers go out for drinks after work. Nobody ever bothers to tell me until later on and I find out just in conversation. . . . I once asked a male deputy to let me know when the shift goes out and he said that he knows that some of the men bother me, so he didn't ask me along.

The social exclusion of women deputies makes them easy targets for jocular aggression and derogatory nicknames; moreover, male workgroup solidarity may be enhanced by directing humor at female officers. This "laughter of inclusion" (Dupreel, 1928) affirms the gender distinctions and relative male superiority. Innuendo, insinuation, and character assassina-tion are effective strategies in maintaining social distance and social boundaries between the male in-group and the female out-group. As one deputy notes, "You're always mindful of your position here. You're at work doing your job, but you always feel somehow you don't really belong here." In short, women officers are often ostracized and belittled by their male co-workers. The male officers view women with a mixture of hostility and resentment, treating them with disdain or simply ignoring them.

According to Millett (1971), men have a vested interest in sustaining conventional sexual distinctions in role relationships, which reflect a recognition and acceptance of gender-based status and power differentials. In this point we can see a link between gender identity and work role dynamics. Gender norms and work relationships are concerned with maintaining boundaries: moral, social, and psychological. Imputed male work superiority and dominance require female devaluation and subordination. Thus Dworkin (1974) asserts: "The truth of it is that he is powerful . . . when contrasted with her" (p. 44).

Sustaining male workplace superiority dictates that women be isolated so that they cannot compete with males. In this way the strength of women's efforts to compete deter-mines the force required by men to limit or restrict these attempts. Change on one side of the equation invariably affects the other side as well. It is the perception of a threat, regard-less of whether that perception is well founded, that constitutes a central basis for resis-tance to change and triggers the systematic devaluation of women workers (Kanter, 1977).

When male workers' conceptions of their masculinity are closely linked to the nature and conditions of their work (particularly in what have traditionally been viewed as ultra-masculine occupations), they are especially likely to feel threatened by female job entrants and resort to more overt subjugation (see Lutze and Murphy, 1999). Of course, if women are cowed into lowering their aspirations or limiting their efforts, it may not matter whether this happens because their workplace threats to men are real or imagined. Either way, the overall subjugation of females would again be taking its toll in lost work contributions and occupational achievements.

Emotion Work

Fox and Hesse-Biber (1984) suggest that certain forms of workplace harassment and abuse are so commonly tolerated that many women have come to regard such activity as inevitable and as virtually a condition of employment. These researchers report that women are reluctant to try to do anything about harassment out of fear of reprisals that may include being fired, demoted, passed over for promotion or a raise, transferred to an undesirable job, or given a poor performance evaluation. In hopes of protecting their job security, female officers often accept and endure the harassment as part of the work environment. Such stressful work conditions often produce feelings of anger, irritability, fear, anxiety, powerlessness, and depression. A female deputy described the types of emotional problems they have had to face:

> I became something of a zombie. I was emotionally numb. I didn't care about anything or anyone and as a result I was very lonely and isolated. Even at parties or at other social occasions I just didn't feel comfortable.... People like to talk about work, tell stories, you know. But I couldn't bring myself to talk about what I did at work.

Research in law enforcement agencies and correctional settings has shown that women and minority officers are especially vulnerable to the psychological and physiological disorders associated with sustained exposure to job-related stress. For example, Wexler and Logan's (1983) study of the sources of stress among women officers in a large metropolitan police department indicated that their greatest obstacle was in demonstrating that they could be effective officers without compromising their femininity:

> the most significant stressors seem to be ones in which others were denying them as officers, as women, or both. It is psychologically a very threatening and uncomfortable situation when one's self-perception is substantially different from the perception of others. This is particularly the case when such fundamental identities are at stake as one's gender and profession.
>
> (p. 53)

Individuals who feel or know they are deemed marginal employees experience anxiety and are more sensitive about their job performance, often assuming a defensive posture, attempting to overcompensate to prove others wrong in their attitudes, or otherwise reacting in ways that may be perceived as inappropriate or undesirable (Wright and Saylor, 1991). Two deputies relate their reactions:

> I found that I would lose my temper over the littlest of things. . . . Stupid little things would happen and I would start crying.

> I just stayed mad. I became defensive. I had a big chip on my shoulder. I hated the constant abuse and kept thinking that one day I would just kill someone.

The job stress experienced by women working in jails is further exacerbated by their lack of access to the peer-group support structure of fellow male deputies. The informal work subculture often functions to reduce stress, providing individual officers with a forum within which they can vent safely. Women deputies' lack of acceptance in this traditional male fraternity thus denies them a critical organizational coping mechanism to mitigate the impact of work-related stress.

Female officers sometimes attempt to deal with their male co-workers by adopting a "give-and-take" approach, a sort of verbal jousting. This tactic, however, is risky, as shown by a woman deputy:

> Bantering back and forth with the men takes a lot of stress out of the situation and kind of neutralizes the harassment we experience. But once it goes beyond or crosses the line, there seems to be no course of action for female officers.

Such inability on the part of female deputies to engage in verbal horseplay on an equal footing with male co-workers reflects their lack of acceptance in the work subculture. Pogrebin and Poole (1988) observe that "Joking relations among peers generate feelings of implicit understanding and camaraderie, thus strengthening group norms and bonds" (p. 184). The rub is that women deputies are not accepted as "peers" in the jail work setting; thus, women may find that their attempts to act like "one of the boys" via joking relations are met with "punitive" responses from male co-workers (Seckman and Couch, 1989).

Unequal Opportunity

Women in corrections routinely experience derision, hostility, and exclusion from male supervisors and co-workers. Their attitudes toward job commitment and aspirations to advance in the profession are adversely affected by such treatment (Belknap, 1991). Chapman and her colleagues (1983) report that female corrections officers perceive unequal opportunities and unequal treatment in promotion. Poole and Pogrebin (1988) uncover a similar perception among women police officers; specifically, after only three years on the job, policewomen view their chances of ever being promoted to be greatly diminished. A veteran officer who had spent many years working in the patrol side of the sheriff's department tells of her disappointment in not having an opportunity for advancement:

> I came off the street as a road deputy after 12 years on the front lines. I really did think I had the skills to come here and make some rank and do well, but that will never happen.

Jurik (1985) claims that supervisors who are biased against females working as corrections officers use performance evaluations to discourage them and keep them in subordinate positions. Since performance history is a critical criterion in advancement to supervisory ranks, women officers are viewed as less promotable. One deputy notes the nature of the inequality:

> There is one woman who really is an exceptional deputy and I like her a lot. She is really strong and stern and she knows her job very well. If she were a man, they would think she is the best deputy in the world, but because she is female they think she is a bitch. But if a male deputy would act like her, they would promote him real fast.

In those rare instances when a female officer receives a choice assignment or a promotion, she is perceived by male staff as not having earned it. For example, females are often teased about trading sexual favors for advancement:

> There are men on this job that think anytime a woman gets ahead the first thing out of their mouth is: "Oh, I wonder who she's sleeping with?" . . . That's their way of dealing with women who're better than them.

Such sexist attributions of female career advancement serve to impede the acceptance of women into the work subculture, which robs them of important training, peer support, sponsorship, and access to inside information for job assignments and promotional opportunities (Zimmer, 1986). If sexist attitudes and actions are allowed to prevail, women officers are unlikely to be seen as capable of becoming supervisors and joining the ranks of management.

Among those women in our sample who had attained supervisory positions (n = 6), there was a consensus that they now experience more hostility and resistance than they had encountered when they were line officers. These women perceive greater resentment on the part of not only the male line staff but their fellow male supervisors as well:

> I finally realized after years on the job that I've been playing gin rummy and the men have been playing poker. . . . We are socialized to be a team player and sacrifice for the good of the group. . . . Men are like sharks. Play on a team with sharks, they'll eat you alive.

Supervisory work in many respects is associated with male role characteristics like independence, initiative, forcefulness, competitiveness, and tough-minded objectivity. Ironically, although the image of the supervisor is one that emphasizes masculine traits, the tasks that the supervisor actually performs are not exclusively those associated with maleness. Compassion, understanding, and interpersonal warmth, traits associated with the female role, have been shown to be just as important to supervisory success as male qualities (Kim, DeValve, DeValve, and Johnson, 2003). Moreover, women in supervisory positions in jail are a new phenomenon, representing a complete reversal of the historically all-male management staff and directly challenging the traditional conceptions of the relationship between sex and power.

Given the greater exclusiveness of supervisory positions, especially the inner circles of upper management, the entry of women into positions of increased status and power may be seen as disruptive and detrimental to the intimacy, solidarity, and informality of the nearly all-male colleague group. Exclusion from this more powerful male management subculture again results in a lack of access to information, contacts, and informal participation, representing yet another barrier to career advancement.

Another source of resistance to women supervisors is the organizational perception that women simply do not make good managers. They are often viewed as overbearing and domineering, as well as inflexible and overly concerned with bureaucratic routines and details (Rosen and Jerdee, 1973; Schein, 1973). The women supervisors in our study do report sex differences in how they do their jobs, and these differences seem to originate in their performance as line officers. For example, Worden (1993) reports that women police officers emphasize rules and regulations more and exercise discretion less frequently than do their male counterparts. This is because the standard operating procedures define roles and evaluation criteria, establishing a level playing field with the men. Women jail officers similarly perceive "going by the book" as a safer method of operation, thus avoiding risky discretionary decision-making which may lead to criticism.

> I've learned it's best to know the rules and stick to them in everything you do in here. Someone's always waiting for you to mess up . . . so it's better to have rules you can rely on to do your job. . . . Because if a female officer messes up because she wasn't following the rules, then it's made ten times worse.

Most women in our sample also believe that adhering to rules and regulations is a function of their gender socialization:

> Women pay more attention to detail, more strict abidance to the rules. I mean, the rules are the rules; that's the way we've been socialized. We follow the rules or we lose our turn. And we follow the rules well. Even if some rules don't make sense, if it's a rule, we still follow it.

It is likely that women officers who have successfully survived and advanced in the jail organization still embrace these work strategies, tending to rely on what has worked for them in the past. The consequences of employing such a work strategy in the role of a manager, however, are deleterious, if not predictable, as three women supervisors observe:

> On my last [performance evaluation] I received several negative comments about how I handle officers. . . . I was criticized for how I write them up. They think I'm too picky and that I demand too much.

Kanter (1977) argues that negative perceptions of women in supervisory positions reflect sex differences in power and influence within organizations. In particular, performance ratings by supervisors are affected by the supervisor's power and influence; and more powerful supervisors generate higher morale, tend to be less rigid and authoritarian, and are generally better liked. Powerless supervisors, on the other hand, are more likely to be controlling in their relationships with subordinates, show favoritism, and generate lower morale. Since men are more likely to be in formal positions of power and authority and to be part of the informal networks of organizational influence, differences in the perception and behavior of female supervisors are more a function of the unequal distribution of organizational power than a reflection of sex differences in managerial or personal style.

Discussion

Women jail deputies find themselves in an occupational dilemma. Many male jail officers harbor negative attitudes toward competent women co-workers because they perceive women who can perform their job-related tasks satisfactorily as threatening. On the other hand, they view female officers who fail to perform the job adequately as confirming the stereotypical "unfitness" of female workers. Thus, the better officers women become, the greater their threat to the male establishment.

Several observers have noted that gender remains the defining or controlling (i.e., master) status in traditionally male occupations, with women treated first on the basis of their sex role and second on the basis of their work role (Williams, 1989). Hunt (1990) argues that gender-based norms support discriminatory practices and sexual harassment in the work setting, which in turn reinforce and maintain power differentials. The sexualized work environment is intended to keep a woman subservient by making her feel unwelcome, insecure, and fearful. The strategy is to exert control through intimidation and humiliation.

The consequences of institutional sexism may be such as to discourage aspirations and restrict opportunities, or to instill fear of being maligned or punished for even trying. In short, sexism may reduce the efforts of females to demonstrate their full potential. Systematic devaluation of women's work roles easily becomes self-fulfilling and self-perpetrating. It can create and maintain conditions that minimize the need for males to confront evidence contradicting their stereotypes, or to experience dissonance when they demean female co-workers (Schur, 1984).

Sexual harassment represents a violation of Title VII of the U.S. Civil Rights Act, which bans sex-based discrimination (Deitch, 1993). Any conduct which has the purpose or effect of substantially interfering with an individual's work performance or creating an intimidating, hostile, or offensive working environment is prohibited; moreover, employers have an affirmative duty to take "all steps necessary" to prevent such conduct and to take remedial actions when it does occur. Yet, we find a great deal of misunderstanding as to what constitutes sex-based discriminatory practices. For example, Gutek and Morasch (1982) note that "men are more likely than women to project sexuality into ambiguous behavior between sexes at work, and to feel that such sexuality is appropriate in the work environment" (p. 59); consequently, what female workers perceive as unwelcome sexual advances may be viewed by male employees as innocent flattery. Konrad and Gutek (1986) further report that men employed in male-dominated jobs are less inclined than men working in gender-integrated jobs to define their gender-based behavior toward women co-workers as sexual harassment. It appears that gender-integrated work settings foster a greater congruence of definitions of acceptable behavior between the sexes, which may serve to reduce the nature and extent of gender-based behavioral misunderstandings.

A complicating factor in effecting change in the jail setting is the social pathology of a male-dominated work culture. The occupational culture of jail work is based on the values and eccentricities of a cult of masculinity, largely exemplified in behaviors such as aggression, taunting, horseplay, and sexually related conversation and innuendo (Belknap, 1991). Despite significant increases in the number of women in local corrections, the generally higher caliber (and more educated) people entering the field, better professional training, and implementation of policies to control sexual harassment and related misconduct, vestiges of the long-established characteristics of the occupational culture still persist. Since survival in the informal organization requires adherence to the subcultural norms, women must develop appropriate adjustment or coping strategies not only in doing their jobs but also in managing their work relations with male officers. Men tend to misinterpret culturally related behaviors of women jail deputies—largely holding them to a double standard—and cannot understand why they are accused of harassment or conduct unbecoming to an officer.

The sexualized work environment of the jail is thus grounded in and supported by a combination of structural factors (e.g., occupational segregation, tokenism, hierarchical power arrangements) and cultural themes and processes (e.g., occupational norms, gender-based stereotypes, status inequality) that become manifest in social interaction. Sex discrimination and job segregation regularly place working women under male supervision and control, heavily dependent on males for their economic security. Because of their subordinate economic and occupational situations, most women have neither autonomy nor authority in workplace relations (Kanter, 1977). These consequences of the sexualized work environment thus have implications that go beyond the job itself.

The prevailing opinion of female officers in all seven facilities was that the elimination of harassment in local corrections organizations was dependent on top administrators enforcing policies against sexual harassment. As long as sexist stereotypes are allowed to pervade the work setting, women officers will be viewed and treated as second-class workers. Lovrich and Stohr (1993) further argue that managers and supervisors in corrections need to transform the work environment into one where women officers are recognized and appreciated as valuable resources and are fully integrated into both formal and informal organizational cultures, both of which are intolerant of sexual and gender harassment. In addition, there must be a strong advocacy role adopted by jail administrators in order for female deputies to gain equal opportunities for career advancement (Zimmer, 1989).

In order to minimize harassing behavior in the jail setting, administrators need to invest in the career development of all employees, advance the ideals of professionalism, and establish closer linkages to line staff (Belknap, 1996; Zimmer, 1989). Such a work climate would help lower the level of animosity and offensive behavior directed at women officers by male co-workers. The "affirmative duty" of jail management lies not simply in fostering a general atmosphere which will combat harassing behavior but also in implementing proactive mechanisms to monitor and prevent the conditions that give rise to such actions.

The organization of corrections work itself plays a role in producing and reinforcing workplace attitudes and behavior, and thus the extent to which sexism and sexual harassment may be institutionally tolerated. These discriminatory practices and subsequent difficulties faced by women officers can be affected significantly if the organization implements adequate administrative strategies to promote gender integration and institutionalize measures to provide equality of opportunity.

Conclusion

The presence of women in what has long been an exclusively male occupation creates a multitude of individual and organizational conflicts. The workplace functions as a complex occupational and organizational entity that shapes workers' perceptions of self and others. The relationship between gender and organizational status reveals that those work roles assigned to women are seen as appropriate extensions of their more diffuse social role of nurturance. These arrangements can act to reflect, magnify, or distort gender differences, which then confirm prevailing stereotypes and organizational norms. This situation has culminated in male co-workers' and supervisors' limited and often inaccurate appraisal of women officers' true potential and capabilities in the field.

To persist in this state of affairs is untenable because evaluating female officers on the basis of male sex-typed norms detracts from the organization's efforts to implement competency-based standards and reduces its ability to analyze work problems and formulate solutions. The jail must demonstrate a philosophical commitment to the thorough integration of women within the formal and informal organizational structure. The more barriers women face in accessing informal channels of information and conflict resolution, the more they are compelled to respond formally with its associated implications of lesser control and power. Jail officers, whether male or female, are less likely to perform effectively if they are not perceived as exercising legitimate authority under conditions of equality.

The nature and scope of jail work continue to increase in complexity, presenting new job expectations and challenges for male and female officers alike. Given the need to adjust and respond to changing organizational demands, it becomes increasingly critical that officers have the opportunity to hone their unique talents and utilize their special skills with greater latitude. Developing alternative or multiple work strategies would thus permit officers to maximize their effectiveness and accomplish tasks otherwise beyond their capacity. An important initiative in realizing such change in organizational culture is to flatten the hierarchical control mechanisms and eliminate the administrative pressures for worker uniformity that have served to reinforce and maintain traditional job stereotypes in the jail setting. Finally, Wexler and Quinn (1985) report that the number of women present in an organization is a critical mass variable in facilitating gender-integrated workgroups. This finding would seem to encourage more aggressive recruitment and retention of women officers who by their sheer numbers may promote the development of an androgynous work culture where an individual officer's success is predicated on ability, rather than on sexual physiology.

Critical Thinking

Institutionalized sexism is found in numerous professions and limits women's opportunities for employment and occupational advancement. This is especially true in the criminal justice fields of law enforcement and institutional corrections, where males dominate in large numbers. Based on the readings on women police officers, can you think of ways in which women correctional officers adapt to the masculine norms of jails?

References

Belknap, J. (1991). Women in conflict: An analysis of women correctional officers. *Women & Criminal Justice, 2*, 89–115.

Belknap, J. (1996). *The invisible woman: Gender, crime, and justice.* Belmont, CA: Wadsworth.

Britton, D.M. (2003). *At work in the iron cage: The prison as gendered organization.* New York: New York University Press.

Camp, S.D., Steiger, T.L., Wright, K.N., Saylor, W.G., and Gilman, E. (1997). Affirmative action and the "level playing field": Comparing perceptions of own and minority job advancement opportunities. *Prison Journal, 77*, 313–334.

Carlson, J.R., Anson, R.H., and Thomas, G. (2003). Correctional officer burnout and stress: Does gender matter? *Prison Journal, 83*, 277–288.

Chapman, J.R., Minor, E.K., Rieker, P.P., Mills, T.R., and Bottum, M. (1983). *Women employed in corrections.* Washington, DC: U.S. Department of Justice, National Institute of Justice.

Deitch, C. (1993). Gender, race, and class politics and the inclusion of women in Title VII of the 1964 Civil Rights Act. *Gender and Society, 7*, 183–203.

Dupreel, E. (1928). Le probleme sociologique du rise. *Revue Philosophique, 106*, 213–260.

Dworkin, A. (1974). *Woman hating.* New York: E.P. Dutton.

Erez, E. and Tontodonato, P. (1992). Sexual harassment in the criminal justice system. In I.L. Moyer (ed.), *The changing roles of women in the criminal justice system: Offenders, victims, and professionals* (pp. 227–252). Prospect Heights, IL: Waveland Press.

Farley, L. (1978). *Sexual shakedown.* New York: McGraw Hill.

Farnworth, L. (1992). Women doing a man's job: Female prison officers working in a male prison. *Australian and New Zealand Journal of Criminology, 25*, 278–296.

Fox, M.F. and Hesse-Biber, S. (1984). *Women at work.* Palo Alto, CA: Mayfield.

Gutek, B.A. and Morasch, B. (1982). Sex-ratios, sex-role spillover, and sexual harassment of women at work. *Journal of Social Issues, 38*, 55–74.

Hemmens, C., Stohr, M.K., Schoeler, M., and Miller, B. (2002). One step up, two steps back: The progression of perceptions of women's work in prisons and jails. *Journal of Criminal Justice, 30*, 473–489.

Hochschild, A.R. (1973). A review of sex role research. In J. Huber (ed.), *Changing women in a changing society* (pp. 249–267). Chicago, IL: University of Chicago Press.

Hunt, J. (1990). The logic of sexism among police. *Women and Criminal Justice, 1*, 3–30.

Jacobs, J.A. (1989). *Revolving doors: Sex segregation and women's careers.* Stanford, CA: Stanford University Press.

Jurik, N.C. (1985). An officer and a lady: Organizational barriers to women working as correctional officers in men's prisons. *Social Problems, 32*, 375–388.

Kanter, R.M. (1977). *Men and women of the corporation.* New York: Basic Books.

Kim, A.S., DeValve, M., DeValve, E.Q., and Johnson, W.W. (2003). Female wardens: Results from a national survey of state correctional executives. *Prison Journal, 83*, 406–425.

Konrad, A.M. and Gutek, B.A. (1986). Impact of work experiences on attitudes toward sexual harassment. *Administrative Science Quarterly, 31*, 422–438.

Lovrich, N.P. and Stohr, M.K. (1993). Gender and jail work: Correctional policy implications of perceptual diversity in the work force. *Policy Studies Review, 12*, 66–84.

Lutze, F.E. and Murphy, D.W. (1999). Ultramasculine prison environments and inmates' adjustment: It's time to move beyond the "boys will be boys" paradigm. *Justice Quarterly, 16*, 709–734.

MacKinnon, C.A. (1979). *Sexual harassment of working women*. New Haven, CT: Yale University Press.

MacKinnon, C.A. (1982). Feminism, Marxism, method, and the state: An agenda for theory. Signs, *7*, 515–544.

Martin, S.E. (1989). Sexual harassment: The link joining gender stratification, sexuality, and women's economic status. In J. Freeman (ed.), *Women: A feminist perspective* (pp. 57–75). Mountain View, CA: Mayfield.

Millett, K. (1971). *Sexual politics*. New York: Avon Books.

Padavic, I. (1991). The re-creation of gender in a male workplace. *Symbolic Interaction, 14*, 279–294.

Perkins, C.A., Stephan, J.J., and Beck, A.J. (1995). *Jails and jail inmates 1993–94*. Washington, DC: U.S. Department of Justice, Bureau of Justice Statistics.

Pogrebin, M.R. and Poole, E.D. (1988). Humor in the briefing room: A study of the strategic uses of humor among police. *Journal of Contemporary Ethnography, 17*, 183–210.

Pogrebin, M.R. and Poole, E.D. (1997). The sexualized work environment: A look of women jail officers. *Prison Journal, 77*, 41–57.

Pollock, J.M. (1986). *Sex and supervision: Guarding male and female inmates*. New York: Greenwood.

Poole, E.D. and Pogrebin, M.R. (1988). Factors affecting the decision to remain in policing: A study of women officers. *Journal of Police Science and Administration, 16*, 49–55.

Rosen, B. and Jerdee, T.H. (1973). The influence of sex-role stereotypes on evaluation of male and female supervisory behavior. *Journal of Applied Psychology, 57*, 44–48.

Safilios-Rothschild, C. (1979). *Sex Role Socialization and Sex Discrimination: A Synthesis and Critique of the Literature*. Washington, DC: National Institute of Education.

Schein, V.E. (1973). The relationship between sex stereotypes and requisite management characteristics. *Journal of Applied Psychology, 57*, 95–100.

Schur, E.M. (1979). *Interpreting deviance*. New York: Harper & Row.

Schur, E.M. (1984). *Labeling women deviant: Gender, stigma, and social control*. Philadelphia, PA: Temple University Press.

Seckman, M.A. and Couch, C.J. (1989). Jocularity, sarcasm, and relationships. *Journal of Contemporary Ethnography, 18*, 327–344.

Stephan, J.J. (2001). *Census of jails, 1999*. Washington, DC: U.S. Department of Justice, Bureau of Justice Statistics.

Stockard, J. and Johnson, M.M. (1980). *Sex roles*. Englewood Cliffs, NJ: Prentice-Hall.

West, C. and Zimmerman, D.H. (1987). Doing gender. *Gender and Society, 1*, 125–151.

Wexler, J.G. and Logan, D.D. (1983). Sources of stress among women police officers. *Journal of Police Science and Administration, 11*, 46–53.

Wexler, J.G. and Quinn, V. (1985). Considerations in the training and development of women sergeants. *Journal of Police Science and Administration, 13*, 98–105.

Williams, C.L. (1989). *Gender differences at work: Women and men in nontraditional occupations*. Berkeley: University of California Press.

Worden, A.P. (1993). The attitudes of women and men in policing: Testing conventional and contemporary wisdom. *Criminology, 31*, 203–237.

Wright, K.N. and Saylor, W.G. (1991). Male and female employees' perceptions of prison work: Is there a difference? *Justice Quarterly, 8*, 505–524.

Zimmer, L.E. (1986). *Women guarding men*. Chicago, IL: University of Chicago Press.

Zimmer, L.E. (1988). Tokenism and women in the workplace: The limits of gender-neutral theory. *Social Problems, 35*, 64–73.

Zimmer, L.E. (1989). Solving women's employment problems in corrections: Shifting the burden to administrators. *Women & Criminal Justice, 1*, 55–80.

24

Criers, Liars, and Manipulators: Probation Officers' Views of Girls

Emily Gaarder, Nancy Rodriguez, and Marjorie S. Zatz

Abstract: *Drawing upon theories and research that focused on gender, race, ethnicity, and social class, Gaarder, Rodriguez, and Zatz study how democratic factors influence family court personnel's perceptions of juvenile girls as manipulative and more difficult to work with than boys. The authors focus on the repercussions of this image and address the issue of probation officers understanding the need for gender and culturally specific programs for girls under their supervision. They find that as a result of scarce resources, gender and racial/ ethnic stereotypes on the part of probation staff leave girls with few treatment options and services provided by the family court. In short, there is a lack of program options for girls under probation supervision. This frustrates some staff members who see the need to offer gender, ethnic, and culturally based treatment for juvenile girls who come under the court's jurisdiction.*

Feminist scholars and practitioners who work with girls in the juvenile justice system have long been searching for ways to raise awareness about girls' experiences and how their needs and issues may differ from boys' (Alexander, 1995; Belknap and Holsinger, 1998; Chesney-Lind, 1997; Chesney-Lind and Shelden, 2004; Kunzel, 1993; Odem, 1995; MacDonald and Chesney-Lind, 2001). A number of contemporary works by academics and practitioners alike call for an emphasis on gender, race, and class to fully understand girls' social and economic realities, and to provide programming appropriate to that context (Acoca, 1998b; Bloom, Owen, Deschenes, and Rosenbaum, 2002a; MacDonald and Chesney-Lind, 2001). Accordingly, we reviewed juvenile probation case files and interviewed juvenile probation officers in one metropolitan county in Arizona to better understand how girls are perceived, how their unique histories of abuse and related problems are interpreted, and how juvenile courts respond to these perceptions and interpretations in prescribing treatments for girls.

Drawing from theories and research on the social construction of gender, race, culture, and class, we observe how such constructions influence perceptions juvenile court personnel hold and how such perceptions sustain the "disconnect" between girls' images and their realities. How are ideas about "acceptable" behaviors and lifestyles embedded in notions of gender, culture, and class? To the extent that girls are seen as manipulative or "harder to work with," we ask: What are the repercussions of this image? Finally, we address whether and how probation officers understand gender and culturally specific needs and programming, and the availability of such programming. One of the conundrums faced in this court, as elsewhere, is that these constructions are nested within an environment characterized by scarce resources. We end by discussing how attitudes of probation officers interact with the structure and priorities of juvenile probation, including especially treatment options (given scarce resources), and implications for girls in the system.

Review of the Literature

We still lack adequate knowledge of how probation officers and other court officials view girls' pathways to crime, personal attributes, and future possibilities (Miller, 1996). Such descriptions can tell us a great deal about how girls are perceived and socially constructed according to race, gender, and class. They also allow us to compare these perceptions with the reality of girls' lives, helping us discover whether common stereotypes permeate probation officers' analyses of girls and influence treatment or confinement decisions.

The Disconnect Between Girls' Lives and Treatment Programs

We draw upon the literature on the social construction of gender, race, and class to develop a more informed approach to effective programming for delinquent girls (e.g., Bloom et al., 2002b; Hoyt and Scherer, 1998; Miller, 1998; Messerschmidt, 1997; Chesney-Lind, 1999). Unfortunately, institutions and programs that house girls have often reinforced stereotypical gender norms such as femininity and passivity. These programs and institutions usually lack a more holistic approach to treatment, such as family involvement, drug/alcohol treatment, sexual/physical abuse counseling, and community involvement (Chesney-Lind, 1997).

What Does Gender and Culturally Responsive Programming Mean?

Given the importance that feminist scholars and practitioners place on the intersection of gender, class, race, and culture, the second part of our study explores how knowledgeable probation officers are with regard to gender and culturally specific needs and programming. Defining gender and culturally appropriate programming is extremely important given the relatively few programs that address such needs. A national report by Girls Incorporated (1996, p. v) recommends that any program for juvenile female offenders "be gender specific, designed to meet the needs of young women as individuals, to take female development into account, and to avoid perpetuating limiting stereotypes based on gender, race, class, language, sexual orientation, disability, and other personal and cultural factors."

While there are few templates that demonstrate these characteristics, some programs do exist that can help us identify and measure what kinds of programming work for girls. Nationally based organizations such as Girls Incorporated, and local programs such as P.A.C.E. Center for Girls, can serve as examples of successful programming (Girls Incorporated, 1996). Such programs provide comprehensive evaluations of girls based on gender-specific education and therapeutic services in educational-based settings. In Canada, Toronto's Earlscourt Child and Family Centre has developed promising early interventions. Their Girls' Connection program is the first-known attempt in Canada to offer girls and their families a gender-specific, holistic intervention that provides long-term services and follow-up care (see Chesney-Lind, Artz, and Nicholson, 2001; Levene, 1997).

Data and Methods

To address whether and how gender, race/ethnicity, and class influence perceptions of girls held by juvenile court personnel and how such perceptions may contribute to the already limited treatment options for girls, we use two primary data sources. The first are official case file narratives from court records for a random sample of 174 girls referred to juvenile probation in Maricopa County, Arizona during 1999. These files include juvenile court petition information, disposition reports, progress reports, and psychological evaluations normally maintained by the juvenile court, both from the 1999 case and from any earlier referrals of these girls to juvenile probation.

Our intent with the girls' case files was threefold. First, we retrieved narrative statements about the girls and about juvenile court officials' presentations of their cases (i.e., perceptions of girls' behavior and situations). The majority of our data are these narratives written by probation officers, but we also include psychological reports. Although the latter are not written by probation officers, they contribute to the overall "image" of a girl that is created in a probation file. These psychological reports are used by probation and other court officers to assess a girl's background, behavior, and delinquency issues, and can influence the type of treatment or programming she receives. Second, in an effort to better assess girls' lives, we collected narrative information on the girls' parents/guardians, siblings, and extended family members. Third, given the well-documented need for gender-appropriate treatment, we examined the treatment recommendations made by juvenile court staff and relate them to the experiences of girls (i.e., substance abuse, sexual abuse, pregnancy).

We supplemented the case file narratives with 14 semi-structured interviews conducted with juvenile probation officers. The women we interviewed included five whites, two African Americans, one Asian American, one Hispanic, and one Middle Eastern. Of the four male probation officers, two were African American, one white, and one Hispanic. The probation officers averaged 11.2 years of experience, with a range from 1 to 24 years. Probation officers represented various units, including standard probation, intensive probation, detention, a school safety program, treatment services, community services, a sex offender program, drug court, transfers, and program services. The semi-structured interviews lasted for 45 to 90 minutes. All interviews were taped and transcribed by the interviewer.

The 174 girls in the sample were racially and ethnically diverse: 58 percent were white, 24 percent Hispanic, 13 percent black, 4 percent American Indian, and fewer than 1 percent Asian Pacific Islander. All were between 12 and 17 years old and had been referred to juvenile court for person, property, drug, and status offenses and for probation violations. To capture information on the structural dimensions of the girls in our sample, we linked their residential zip codes with 2000 census data (United States Census Bureau, 2000). While these data are aggregate, they provide insights into the demographic characteristics of the geographic areas where the girls lived. The median family income for census respondents within the girls' zip codes was $42,258 a year. Twenty-two percent reported having less than a high school education, 6 percent reported being unemployed, and 10 percent lived below the poverty level. The majority of the communities were occupied by whites (61%) and Hispanics (28%). Twenty-two percent identified Spanish as their primary language.

Findings

Three dominant themes emerge from the case file narratives and interviews with probation officers. The first of these is the gap between probation officers' and other court officials' perceptions of the girls as whiny and manipulative and the realities of the girls' lives, including sexual abuse and teen motherhood. The second is the disconnect between official perceptions of the girls' families as "trashy" and irresponsible and the realities of the girls' family circumstances, including such structural dimensions as poverty as well as individual histories of abuse. The third is the lack of knowledge and understanding on the part of probation officers regarding culturally and gender-appropriate treatments, as well as the reality of limited programming services for girls.

It is important to note that prevalence speaks not to how often girls in the sample were abused or how many mothers fit negative stereotypes, for example. Rather, prevalence refers to how often a juvenile court official noted a particular issue in the girls' files. Thus, the percentages that we present are underestimates if the court officials, for whatever reason, did not explore and/or comment on a particular theme (e.g., abuse that was part of the girls' family history and circumstances).

While the realities of girls' lives were consistently emphasized in case file narratives and interviews, we found that stereotypical images of girls outweighed any realities. We also found that girls were often referred to treatment services that did not appear to match their needs. Moreover, the juvenile court lacked the insight and capacity to meet their needs. That is, we found that probation officers, like other criminal justice officials, seem to inadvertently "blunder" when attempting to be sensitive to race, gender, and class (Zatz, 2000, p. 519). They also had little training and few resources at their disposal to match the gender and culturally specific needs of girls on their caseloads.

Perceptions of Girls: Criers, Liars, and Manipulators

Consistent with the findings of Baines and Alder (1996), Belknap, Holsinger, and Dunn (1997), and Bond-Maupin, Maupin, and Leisenring (2002), common images in girls' probation files included fabricating reports of abuse, acting promiscuously, whining too much, and attempting to manipulate the court system. In our sample, about 20 percent of the girls were depicted by probation officers and other court officials as sexually promiscuous and 16.5 percent as liars and manipulators. For example, girls were described in case files as: very manipulative, whining, pouting (#126—African American girl); not inhibited in any way . . . possesses loose morals (#39—Hispanic girl); and manipulative, unpredictable personality (#12—Hispanic girl).

Interviews with probation officers revealed similar images. Several probation officers used words like promiscuous, manipulative, liars, and criers in their descriptions. Girls were "harder to work with," "had too many issues," and were "too needy." The following responses convey these messages.

> They play the system real well. Girls play the system better than the boys do. They're manipulative. They, you know: "Pity poor me. I'm the innocent bystander and nobody's listening to me." They play the role as if they're so helpless . . . and the majority of the judges are male and they fall into that trap every single time.

> They're more like criers. Girls will do that. They'll break down and you'll be in the sympathy thing for a while you know, but then you realize what they're doing.

Another officer who worked in the detention unit offered a different perspective.

> Oh yes, that's their survival sometimes . . . getting what they need by going around the back door, not giving the truth, or just flat out lying.

She recalled a recent incident where a girl had reported being raped at her residential treatment center. The girl wanted to speak to a counselor about it. The probation officer later discovered that the incident did happen, but more than two years ago. The girl had reported it as though it had just happened.

> What she wanted was some one-on-one attention with an adult staff. Girls get their needs met through attention, through their relationships with people.

When attempting to explain the cause of girls' delinquent behavior, Baines and Alder (1996) found that youth workers often relied on the abuse histories of girls to contextualize their path into delinquency. Consistent with their findings, 11 of the 14 probation officers we interviewed felt that most of the girls on their caseload had histories of sexual and/or physical abuse, emotional abuse, and neglect. Most made connections between the offending behaviors and past victimization. One remarked, "I hardly ever get a girl who hasn't been raped, sexually abused, or physically abused," noting an apparent direct correlation. Another indicated that girls have usually been victims and that "involvement in sexual activity, criminal activity, is increased after that."

Although most officers were sympathetic to the girls' histories, a few believed that the abuse stories girls told were untrue or exaggerated, or that girls were partially responsible for being abused.

> They feel like they're the victim. They try from "Mom kicked me out" to "Mom's boyfriend molested me" to "My brother was sexually assaulting me." They'll find all kinds of excuses to justify their actions. Because they feel if I say I was victimized at home that justifies me being out on the streets. . . . Or while they were out there they got raped. Or, they were mistreated. Personally, I think 98 percent is false . . . 98 percent of the girls say the exact same story, so it's as if they just get together on the units and think up these things.

> [The interviewer asked about victimization/offending connections.] I think there is a connection but it starts before that. It started with their behavior, being out there on the streets, being out there with those people. You know, they end up in these situations. One of them—she was already incorrigible before this—took off with her boyfriend. She was raped and she refused to give his name because he was in a gang and she was afraid. She came home and did detention for a little while because she had run away, so yeah, because I don't think she's dealt with these issues, she runs away from them. So they do have a correlation, but I don't know which one comes first. The behavior came first because she, you know, got in that situation.

As these probation officers and court psychologists indicate, girls are seen as being very difficult to work with. Whether the officers blame or sympathize, they perceive the girls as being troubled and troublesome. We turn next to the realities of the girls' lives, paying particular attention to their histories of sexual abuse, substance abuse, and teen motherhood.

Reality of Girls' Lives: Sexual Abuse and Teen Motherhood

The direct and indirect relationships between girls' emotional, sexual, and physical abuse and delinquency have been substantially documented in prior work (Alexander, 1995; Belknap and Holsinger, 1998; Chesney-Lind and Shelden, 2004; McCormack, Janus, and Burgess, 1986; Rhodes and Fischer, 1993). Given the prevalence of sexual abuse histories reported in previous studies (e.g., Acoca, 1998a; Belknap and Holsinger, 1998), we were surprised to find that a relatively low percentage of girls in this study (18.8%) were identified as victims of sexual abuse. However, as previously noted, these data represent instances where a court official was informed of such abuse and actually reported it in the girl's file.

The depiction of girls' sexuality as "dirty" or inappropriate has led to an assumption that girls need to be protected from the dangers associated with their sexuality. Interestingly, we found minimal effort to protect or assist these girls. Girls' sexual activity, while documented in case files, was not dealt with in conjunction with other risk factors such as sexual abuse or mental health problems. In fact, even when these two girls had suffered extensive sexual abuse, they were still perceived as manipulators.

> [Girl's name] also claims a history of rape on two occasions, but according to her mother, she did not report it to anyone and did not mention it to anyone for over a year after it supposedly happened. She also was pregnant in [date omitted] and attempted suicide. The letter in the record is suggestive of a long and somewhat chronic history of mental health issues and it would appear that she has

been somewhat manipulative in her behavior. There are indications to suggest that she has superficial lacerations on her forearms, suggestive of cutting herself subsequent to an argument with the parents. In the past, [Girl's name] was raped four different times. The first occurred when she was 7 years old; twice at age 13 (once by three boys) and another time at a party. She would not talk about the most recent incident, the fourth rape.

(#82—white girl)

She reports being sexually active and also reports having an abortion two months ago. She states that the father of her child is actually a 35-year-old man who has his own business. She reports being sexually active, as she prostituted herself on and off since she was 13. [Girl's name] reports for her evaluation in a very candid manner, yet she does appear to be somewhat manipulative. She likely, in fact, sexualizes many of her relationships when communicating with males. She states that she tried to commit suicide recently while in detention, reporting trying to tie a sheet around her neck.

(#165—white girl)

We found these depictions of girls as manipulative thought provoking. On the one hand, it is not surprising that girls with a history of abuse might be seen as manipulative. For example, the mental health literature tells us that victims of incest may try to control or manipulate individuals (e.g., an abusive father) or situations to reduce the likelihood of further abuse. Manipulating others thus becomes a survival tactic.

Yet our reading of the case files and our reflections on the interviews with probation officers suggest that rather than simply describing a behavior as manipulative, the probation officers take the further step of ascribing a personality trait. There is a difference, we argue, between a recognition that girls may be manipulative in specific situations to achieve a desired end (e.g., not being abused) and the construction of the girl herself, and of all girls by extension, as manipulative by nature and therefore difficult to work with.

The key, we suggest, is whether the probation officers reflect on the girls' contexts and the underlying problems to which manipulative behaviors may be a reasonable response. If they do, we should expect to see them searching for appropriate programs that can adequately respond to the girls' problems and needs. Unfortunately, we do not find that to be the typical response. Rather, some probation officers simply assume that the girls are making up stories. Too many others recognize that girls have problems due to their histories of victimization but do not respond in sympathetic ways, instead writing the girls off through gendered stereotypes and treating the victimization and manipulative behaviors as independent realities.

Perceptions of Girls' Families: Trashy, Manipulative, and Sexually Irresponsible

Perceptions of girls' families were also examined. The majority of the probation officers interviewed felt that the family was crucial to the juvenile's success. In particular, they commented on how important it is that parents take responsibility for their children, seek help for their parenting problems, and be willing to work with probation officers.

Yet some of the same probation officers spoke of the girls' mothers in terms similar to those used to describe the girls themselves—"promiscuous" and "sluts." Indeed, in 6.1

percent of the case files, the probation officers made such notes. Again, we emphasize the particular language used to describe girls' mothers, and not using such statements as an indicator of mothers' behavior.

> [From an interview] Her background is the classic. Her sister uses drugs. The other sister has a baby, has had two or three kids. Mom—she's a slut. Mom—she's on her third marriage.

> [From an interview] The daughters and sons are going through life with no supervision, no rules. All of the sudden the girl is 14, comes home with hickeys and dressed like a slut and Mom wants to give her rules. And Mom comes home at 3 a.m. with five different guys.

Interestingly, not a single probation officer commented on the fathers' marital status, physical attire, or sexual activities in the case files. We also found that 7.9 percent of mothers described in case files were presented as liars, or as manipulating the juvenile court system.

Class was an important factor in assessments of the girls' families, though this seemed to operate in several, perhaps contradictory, ways. The most extreme examples of economic disadvantage were cases where families were homeless. Three case files noted that girls living in homeless families were being punished for not attending treatment sessions regularly or missing appointments with their probation officers, both of which are considered probation violations. Probation officers sometimes noted that girls were being labeled delinquent simply because they were homeless. Some probation officers expressed sympathy for girls and families with economic challenges. One derogatory comment, however, targets the economic situation of a low-income, single-parent household.

> This officer has tried to work with this family in order for [Girl's name] to be successful on probation, since much of her problems appear to be related to the lifestyle which they choose to live. This officer was not raised in an environment where people chose to live around discarded items, even having disabled vehicles permanently placed in the driveway, but it is still this officer's opinion that it is a choice of lifestyle that [Girl's mother] chooses for herself and her family.
>
> (#6—white girl)

During interviews, some officers said that lower-income parents were easier to work with because they were uneducated, intimidated by the court, and not knowledgeable of court services. Another probation officer, however, identified these as barriers that poorer families face in seeking help for their children.

> Basic communication skills and having the confidence to interact with government and community agencies. A lot of lower-class/working-class parents are afraid to get the phone book out or go to the police station or their community center and start asking what they think are maybe awkward or silly questions.... Middle- and upper-class parents are more confident through their jobs and education and everything. They're more confident to interact with the bigger system.

This officer also noted that very poor and middle-class families receive more services than working poor families, because they either qualify for free services (in the case of poor families) or can afford to pay for treatment (in the case of middle-class families).

> The lower middle-class or working poor make $20,000 and don't qualify for welfare or have medical benefits. They can't pay $50 per hour for a counselor.

As a result, these girls are left with few options. If their families are working but do not qualify for federal assistance they do not receive services.

An African American probation officer noted that because his caseload was predominantly Hispanic and African American, it limited the types of services he was able to provide. He saw a relationship between race/ethnicity and class. Some services were located in geographic areas at a considerable distance from neighborhoods where economically disadvantaged minority families tended to live. Girls were frequently unable to travel to the locations where they could receive treatment. In essence, services were simply not an option for all.

Realities of Girls' Families: Abuse, Poverty, and Racism

Culture and class are central to the social construction of gender, including both what girls see as their available options and what others see as appropriate behaviors for girls. Portillos (1999) has shown how Chicanas and Mexicanas, in search of independence from the expectations of the family, may turn to gangs to alleviate experiences as marginalized women. Others have identified the traditional household duties of Hispanic girls (see Burgos-Ocasio, 2000) and the development of values such as strength and independence among African American girls to deal with the challenges of labor markets (Rice, 1990). We found that 12.3 percent of Hispanic women in our sample dealt with language barriers, poverty, discrimination, and familial and economic expectations associated with living close to the Mexican border.

> It is believed that this family is somewhat economically disadvantaged, which may influence the family, on occasions, to change their address. [Girl's name] parents are Spanish speaking only, but the juvenile seems to have a fairly good grasp of the English language.
>
> (#75—Hispanic girl)

Interestingly, and consistent with Bridge and Steen's (1998) findings regarding court officials' perceptions of intrinsic causes of African American delinquency and extrinsic causes of white delinquency, when Hispanics and/or their families contradict some of these cultural dimensions, their involvement in delinquent acts are viewed as mishaps. For example, a Hispanic girl's family are described as cooperative and functional because they speak English and are in the country legally.

Substance abuse plays a significant role in these girls' lives. Case file narrative data showed that 43 percent of the girls were current drug users or had a history of drug use. For some, language barriers made treatment or assessment difficult given the probation officer's inability to communicate effectively with parents.

> There was no response from the family regarding my initial letter to them and the request to contact me. I was able to finally get a hold of the father at his work number. [Father's name] speaks mostly

Spanish and therefore conversation with him was limited. He speaks some English but may not have fully understood some of my questions. Parents are divorced but are still living together. They both work long hours and [are] rarely home in the day. Both parents admitted that lack of supervision is contributing to the behaviors of their daughter. It was very clear that the parents know their children are using drugs but that there is little that they feel they can do to stop the behavior. This officer found their complacency about the activities in their home disturbing.

(#59—Hispanic girl)

In 18.8 percent of cases, we found that extended family members served as guardians when biological parents were unable to raise their children.

There are eight other children also living with grandparents. The grandparents are in their seventies and both are still working; they seem to be very responsible caring people. Both natural parents have histories of problems with the law. Mom has problems with alcohol and "rock" and dad also has alcohol problems.

(#105—Hispanic girl)

Research has found that girls are much more influenced by family expectations and family conflict than boys (Hoyt and Scherer, 1998). These experiences vary by race/ethnicity. For example, Taylor, Biafora, Warheit, and Gail (1997) found that Hispanics are significantly influenced by family substance abuse, and African American youths by the levels of family communication. For some girls, substance abuse in combination with other family problems, including financial stability, domestic violence, and sexual abuse, compound their situations. Two narratives illustrate this clearly.

[Girl's name] is currently a ward of the state and is living in a group home. She was brought to the interview by her CPS caseworker B. [Girl's name's] mother is living somewhere on the streets in [city omitted] and reportedly is dying of AIDS while her father is incarcerated in Mexico for murder. The caseworker reported that [Girl's name] has had a lot of problems with anger but seems to be making some progress recently. She was kicked out of her grandmother's house for assaulting her and then kicked out of her foster mother's house for assaulting her also. She has run away, attempted suicide, been assaulted and abused, been involved with gangs, drugs, and marijuana and has been on probation previously. However, as I stated, it appears that there has been progress and [Girl's name] seems to have mellowed out some. According to her grandmother, [Girl's name] was sexually abused at 6 years of age.

(#48—Hispanic girl)

[Girl's name] is a 17-year-old American Indian youth who, at the present time, is doing quite well with her counseling and doing well at [school name]. She has had a very sad and rocky childhood, she had to watch her mother die in front of her eyes from drug and alcohol abuse and has been from foster home to youth home and in hospitals and numerous counseling sessions to deal with her depression, her anger, and some of the violent and abusive situations that she has been exposed to.

(#58—American Indian girl)

Bond-Maupin et al. (2002) found that probation officers were often sympathetic to the conflicts Hispanic girls faced (i.e., having "traditional" parents and living as an "Americanized" girl). During our interviews with probation officers, we found they also identified with the struggles faced by Hispanics and commented on the valuable support system that extended families provide:

> Personally I think some of the girls, especially Hispanic girls, are brought up to believe that their purpose in life is to stay home and have kids and do nothing. But they're growing up in the 90s. . . . I think a lot of them feel really torn—well, am I supposed to go out and have kids or am I supposed to have a career?

Regarding family conflict, many probation officers expressed concern about domestic violence and noted that children were often punished for fights started by parents.

> The whole thing just burns a hole in me. . . . Say the police respond to a case of domestic violence. You have a 3-year-old girl, a 16-year-old girl, and the mother fighting. Say the mother grabbed that girl and started pounding her face into cement. They're not going to take Mom to jail when there is a 3-year-old daughter there. But they need to separate the two of them. So a lot of times it really is the parent's fault but the kid gets hauled away to jail for protection and they're not going to take Mom who has to support the 3-year-old and go to work the next morning.

Although some probation officers identified the conflicts at home, economic instability, and substance abuse as the root of the problems the girls faced, they were unable to provide the needed services. The lack of appropriate treatment options and services for girls is our third theme.

Gender-specific Needs

Many scholars and practitioners recognize the need for more appropriate treatment for girls but the small number of girls relative to boys makes it difficult for court officials to justify specialized, often expensive, treatments that are culturally and gender appropriate (Alder, 1998; Bloom et al., 2002a; Freitas and Chesney-Lind, 2001; McDonald and Chesney-Lind, 2001).

In our interviews, we asked probation officers whether they believed girls had different problems or needs than boys. We also asked if they worked differently with the girls on their caseloads. The majority of probation officers noted immediately that girls were more likely to be referred for incorrigibility or domestic violence offenses. Other likely offenses included probation violations (usually running away), truancy, drugs, and prostitution. Half of the probation officers reported that girls were more likely to be arrested for status offenses. These officers said that parents tend to "keep a closer eye" on girls, or try to "over-control" them. They also noted that boys were more likely to be rewarded for sexual behavior and girls punished. As one probation officer noted, "Girls get picked up for stuff that males don't." Another said, "Girls are involved with the court process more for their best interests, not necessarily because she is a danger to the community, but for her own safety." Yet not all officers saw this as positive. One commented, "Domestic violence and incorrigibility needs to be directed away from the courtroom and into specialized programs. We're turning a lot of these girls into criminals."

However, four of the 14 probation officers asserted that juveniles all had similar needs and should not be treated or approached any differently based on gender. They rejected the need for gender-specific programming, preferring to decide on treatment options based on individual characteristics or circumstances. When asked about the kinds of programs in which girls were successful, another officer replied,

> I don't feel like you can just say that this program works for girls or whatever—they're children. Some of them are ready and some of them aren't. Whether they be boys or girls.

Some of these officers believed that treating girls "differently" would be assuming that all girls had the same issues and problems. They alluded to the fact that some girls were not in fact acting normally.

> These days you can't do that. I have some young ladies on my caseload that are kind of like—they have a macho side, I guess.

> They're not your typical girls . . . you know, the fingernails, the make-up, the Ms. Prissy. They're just like the boys. They're worse than some of the boys. They go out and they prove themselves like they're not feminine. You know they don't want anybody to think . . . well, I'm helpless. I can take care of myself, so they play the role as portraying to be something that they're not.

When girls did not adhere to "feminine" behaviors or attitudes there was often an assumption that they were "becoming more like boys," and should be treated as boys would be. Probation officers also relied on gender stereotypes to define specific issues facing girls. Several of the probation officers believed that the girls were promiscuous and needed sexual education programming. Early sexual activity, pregnancy, and sexually transmitted diseases were seen as feminine issues. As one officer commented,

> It would be good to have gender specific—all girls—for feminine problems or feminine-related issues—we have a lot of STDs transmitted.

Another suggested that sex education was needed, "definitely for the females because they . . . they produce the seed." Interestingly, one probation officer who had earlier called promiscuity a "girl problem" began to question herself after prompting from the interviewer.

> *Probation officer*: You know what? [long pause] I think there is . . . umm . . . you know I think there is, but maybe with the girls it's more noticeable. They're always getting STDs—but they must be getting them from the guys, so . . . [trails off].

In addition to labeling girls' sexuality as specifically problematic (as opposed to boys), probation officers also made reference to the "hormonal" issues underlying girls' tendency to be "difficult."

> Girls are much more difficult to case manage. Their affect is different—they will push you away when really they want to come closer. They will make your life miserable—whereas boys will just sort of go along with the program. . . . A lot of it, I think, in my opinion, is hormones. In fact, when I had a lot of girls on a caseload, you could almost watch the ebb and tide. When their hormones are on the move and they're ovulating, you couldn't stand to be around them.

Despite gender stereotyping, or conversely, the denial that any differences existed, nearly all the officers admitted that they "talked to girls more." Girls were more open than boys to sharing details about their lives and relationships. This was in spite of the fact that many of the probation officers felt uncomfortable "acting like counselors."

Research suggests that one of the most important factors in working with girls is establishing relationships (see Alder, 1998; Chesney-Lind and Shelden, 2004; Taylor et al., 1997; Lindgren, 1996). For example, Belknap et al.'s (1997) data from focus groups with incarcerated girls outlined the importance of respectful and caring relationships between girls and adult staff. In general, girls did not feel respected by the staff in their agencies and institutions. They wanted to be listened to by caring adults, and desired one-on-one relationships in which they could discuss their feelings. In step with this, when asked what kinds of problems the girls on her caseload faced, one officer had this to say:

> Girls face relationships. Their number one problem in my opinion is self-esteem issues, and how to relate to the world around them. . . . Girls are more interested in whether the relationship—you know, if they like you as a P.O. or whatever. You have to get through that barrier first.

Despite a few exceptions, which we have noted, most of the probation officers understood gender-specific needs and programming for girls as sex education (especially STD and pregnancy prevention), good parenting skills, and building self-esteem. Their interpretations are not surprising, given the attention to issues such as sexual activity, pregnancy, and victimization in case file narratives. When it came to dealing with these issues, however, the only resources that the probation officers offered the girls were Planned Parenthood and Parents Anonymous.

Gender-specific Programming

Both the interviews and our review of case files revealed a severe lack of programming for girls. The majority of probation officers in our study could not name a single program designed specifically for girls. A persistent theme regarding treatment services for girls was the disconnect between the realities of the girls' lives and appropriate treatment options. As mentioned before, a girl whose family was homeless and living on the streets had probation violations for not attending her drug treatment and for not staying in contact with her probation officer. Sadly, the only option the probation officer could suggest was counseling. In another case, a pregnant teen received sex education as part of her terms of probation.

> [Girl's name] is currently pregnant. She reports that she has used marijuana since being pregnant. She denies any other usage. [Girl's name] and her grandmother are hopeful that they can find an adoptive family for the baby. At her doctor's appointment on [date omitted], [Girl's name] admitted to having an abortion in [date omitted]. She is in need of life skills training and sex education.
>
> (#5—white girl)

Case file narrative data reveal that nearly 16 percent of the girls were referred to detention or a state institution for treatment. Unfortunately, a lack of available and appropriate treatment programs made confinement the only option for some.

In some cases where girls were sexually active and suffered from histories of abuse, probation officers openly admitted to being "confused as to what is best for the child." For others, institutionalization was the only alternative given the "difficult" nature of girls' cases—often meaning that girls frequently ran away or did not succeed in existing programs. Many probation officers expressed frustration with the lack of funding for programming in general and for girls specifically. This attitude is consistent with Kempf-Leonard and Sample's (1991) survey of juvenile and family court judges and officers. The majority of those surveyed noted that females did not have adequate access to treatment, especially for mental health problems, status offending, chemical dependency, and sexual victimization.

Half of the officers believed that gender-specific programming was a good idea. "Maybe it would be good to have a gender-specific program for girls—just to see how they'd react," one officer said, adding, "I don't know if any are available." Different reasons were given, however, for why gender-specific programming might be needed. Some reasoned that girls and boys become distracted by each other when they are together. Others recognized that girls may be reluctant to talk about their situations when boys are present.

Attempts to address girls' needs result all too often in ill-fitting programs and frustration regarding the limited options available. Most all-girl programs were in locked institutions. There were even fewer options for early intervention programming or chemical dependency issues. Once a psychological evaluation was conducted and mental health issues were identified, girls were usually placed on medication and sent for counseling.

Culturally Specific Needs

The cultural differences identified in prior works have stressed the importance of addressing the cultural dimensions of girls' lives (e.g., Fishman, 1998; Miller, 1998; Chesney-Lind, 1999). Recognizing the relationship between gender, culture, and class is a first step toward providing girls with the services they need. Some officers spoke at length about cultural differences and needs of the girls on their caseloads. One response was particularly representative.

> Girls of color have a double whammy pretty much. They are minorities from ethnic standing. They are female from gender standing. There are different psychodynamics when you talk about different ethnic females. If you have Hispanic females—the male's the machismo. If you have African American—African American females tend to be the backbone of the black culture. It's just different. It's different all the way down the line.

Other officers tried to incorporate culturally sensitive methods into their work, but lacked training and resources. Racial stereotypes and misunderstandings regarding cultural differences can persist if probation officers are not adequately trained. False assumptions about cultures can lead to inappropriate assessments of girls' needs. For example, a probation officer told the story of a Hispanic boy molesting a cousin, and of their therapist not being aware that cousins do marry in some Hispanic cultures. The officer suggested that therapists should better understand the cultures of those with whom they work.

Culturally Specific Programming

When asked about culturally sensitive programs, we found that, again, probation officers could not name even one program that was culturally aware. Many officers reported that they referred kids to programs based on the gender and race of the counselor, not on what the program itself offered. The growing and varying racial/ethnic make-up of juveniles on probation seems to only compound the problems associated with providing proper programs for juveniles. Probation officers mentioned that there were no culturally appropriate resources available to deal with the growing Asian American population.

> We don't have anything within the probation department that focuses on Asian American issues. Right now, I'm seeing more kids of Asian parents . . . the parents may be first or second generation in the U.S. They don't know the language. They're more easily manipulated by their kids. And the kids are more quickly sucked into the drugs and alcohol and partying and rebellious stuff . . . that's happening a lot with Asian American families. I got a bunch of Filipino families. . . . They do not know how to be a parent in the U.S. with all these problems. They're just desperate. They're begging for help. [But] they're not real receptive once we start making suggestions, because it is totally foreign to them.

When asked if there were differences in terms of race/ethnicity that needed to be considered in programs or counseling, one probation officer remarked:

> The only time I'll typically look for ethnicity is when I have a Spanish-only speaking kid and I need a counselor who speaks Spanish. . . . I don't like making big issues about that. I have major issues with people saying a lot of rights are broken because of the color they are, when a lot of rights for white people are as well. My perspective is, if they're a good counselor, they can work with any of them. It's only an issue if it's a language barrier or an ethnic issue in it. Like Indians—they do their sweat lodges and they do all that. I can't do one of those. So in essence, they need to have an Indian do that.

On the other hand, another probation officer saw her race/ethnicity (Asian American) as a helpful attribute in working with girls of color:

> I went with another probation officer to see the girls on our caseload. She had an American Indian girl on her caseload and the girl would not talk to her. She made some kind of comment about "just another white agency person coming to see me." But she would talk to me.

Discussion of the Findings

The social construction of gender, race/ethnicity, and class has a profound impact on girls in the juvenile justice system. In this study, we found that juvenile court staff often act based more on the perceptions they have of girls and their families than on the realities the girls face, including both individual and societal factors. Our findings suggest that gender and racial/ethnic stereotypes leave girls few options for treatment and services in juvenile courts.

There is still much discussion and debate around the meaning of "gender-specific" needs and programming. Not surprisingly, the lack of clarity regarding the concept of gender or cultural needs/programming (along with the relative "newness" of the terminology) leads to confusion among practitioners about how to implement such ideas. In step with our findings, Belknap et al. (1997) found that practitioner awareness of gender differences and appropriate services varied widely. One of their recommendations includes the coordination of "regional gender-specific sensitivity training and information sharing sessions for juvenile justice and youth serving professionals" (1997, p. 33). They also note that "few individuals have developed the ability to identify appropriate and effective programs for delinquent girls" (1997, p. 33). They urge the development of assessment tools to measure the effectiveness of girls' programs, as well as periodic program evaluations. While we recognize that additional resources are needed to better serve all juvenile offenders in the juvenile court system, risk/needs tools that focus on mental health (e.g., depression, which is more often internalized by girls than by boys) and victimization would more appropriately address female delinquency than current efforts. Programming that highlights relationship building and incorporates an understanding of how culture directly influences girls' delinquent and nondelinquent behavior is also needed. Finally, family-based treatment can provide girls with an important support system, one that is often lacking in girls' lives.

Conclusion

The juvenile justice system has long been criticized for inadequate attention to the situations and needs of girls. We suggest that framing the problem theoretically as the social construction of gender, race, and class in juvenile probation helps us better understand the disjunctures between court actors' perceptions of girls and what they see as culturally appropriate gendered behaviors. Probation officers expect one set of behaviors and attitudes from the girls and their families, but due to economic and social forces (e.g., homelessness, immigration restrictions, histories of sexual abuse) as well as individual factors (e.g., mental health problems), the girls do not manifest these hegemonic expectations. This results in disappointment on both parts—girls are not treated according to the reality of their lives, and probation officers continue to express frustration and even hostility toward girls who are not responding favorably to the programming being offered.

As Chesney-Lind and Shelden (2004, p. 6) remind us, "An appreciation of a young woman's experience of girlhood, particularly one that attends to the special problems of girls at the margins, is long overdue." We urge the continued development and implementation of gender and culturally responsive approaches and programming that can help confront the social and economic realities of girls. More detailed information and rigorous evaluation of programming for girls is needed. Without these analyses, probation officers and other court officials will continue to rely on stereotypical images of "proper girl behavior" and psychological assessments of their conduct, while discounting the power that oppressive structures and institutions hold over people. As contemporary feminist research begins to solidify its definition and understanding of "what works for girls," we face the equally enormous task of communicating this information to practitioners, administrators, and other decision makers. It is apparent from this study that the message has not yet been heard.

Critical Thinking

Similar to the gender issues discussed previously by Poole and Pogrebin, it appears that juvenile females on probation are perceived by some probation staff as more difficult to work with than juvenile males, and they receive less program treatment resources for gender specific and cultural needs. One critical issue raised by this article is: should court and probation staff incorporate gender, class, and cultural perspectives into their treatment of juvenile girls in their supervision practices?

References

Acoca, L. (1998a). Outside/inside: The violation of American girls at home, on the street, and in the juvenile justice system. *Crime & Delinquency, 44*, 561–589.

Acoca, L. (1998b). Defusing the time bomb: Understanding and meeting the growing health care need of incarcerated women in America. *Crime & Delinquency, 44*, 49–69.

Alexander, R. (1995). *The "girl problem": Female sexual delinquency in New York, 1900–1930.* London: Cornell University Press.

Alder, C.M. (1998). "Passionate and willful" girls: Confronting practices. *Women and Criminal Justice, 9*, 81–101.

Baines, M. and Alder, C. (1996). Are girls more difficult to work with?: Youth workers' perspectives in juvenile justice related areas. *Crime & Delinquency, 42*, 467–485.

Belknap, J. and Holsinger, K. (1998). An overview of delinquent girls: How theory and practice have failed and the need for innovative changes. In R. Zaplin (ed.), *Female crime and delinquency: Critical perspectives and effective interventions* (pp. 13–64). Gaithersburg, MD: Aspen.

Belknap, J., Holsinger K., and Dunn, M. (1997). Understanding incarcerated girls: The results of a focus group study. *The Prison Journal, 77*, 381–404.

Bloom, B., Owen, B., Deschenes, E., and Rosenbaum, J. (2002a). Moving toward justice for female juvenile offenders in the new millennium: Modeling gender specific policies and programs. *Journal of Contemporary Criminal Justice, 18*, 37–56.

Bloom, B., Owen, B., Deschenes, E., and Rosenbaum, J. (2002b). Improving juvenile justice for females: A statewide assessment in California. *Crime & Delinquency, 48*, 526–552.

Bond-Maupin, L., Maupin, J., and Leisenring, A. (2002). Girls' delinquency and the justice implications of intake workers' perspectives. *Women and Criminal Justice, 13*, 51–77.

Bridge, G.S. and Steen, S. (1998). Racial disparities in official assessments of juvenile offenders: Attributional stereotypes as mediating mechanisms. *American Sociological Review, 63*, 554–570.

Burgos-Ocasio, H. (2000). Hispanic women. In M. Julia (ed.), *Constructing gender: Multicultural perspectives in working with women* (pp. 109–137). Belmont, CA: Brooks/Cole.

Chesney-Lind, M. (1997). *The female offender: Girls, women, and crime.* Thousand Oaks, CA: Sage Publications.

Chesney-Lind, M. (1999). Girls, gangs, and violence: Reinventing the liberated female crook. In M. Chesney-Lind and J.M. Hagedorn (eds), *Female gangs in America: Essays on girls, gangs and gender* (pp. 295–310). Chicago, IL: Lake View Press.

Chesney-Lind, M. and Shelden, R.G. (2004). *Girls, delinquency, and juvenile justice.* Los Angeles, CA: West/Wadsworth.

Chesney-Lind, M., Artz, S., and Nicholson, D. (2001). *Making the case for gender-responsive programming.* Paper presented at the Annual Meeting of the American Society of Criminology, Atlanta.

Fishman, L. (1998). Images of crime and punishment: The black bogeyman and white self-righteousness. In C.R. Mann and M.S. Zatz (eds), *Images of color, images of crime* (pp. 109–125). Los Angeles, CA: Roxbury.

Freitas, K. and Chesney-Lind, M. (2001). Difference doesn't mean difficult: Practitioners talk about working with girls. *Women, Girls and Criminal Justice, 2,* 65–79.

Girls Incorporated. (1996). *Prevention and parity: Girls in juvenile justice.* Washington, DC: Office of Juvenile Justice and Delinquency Prevention.

Hoyt, S. and Scherer, D. (1998). Female juvenile delinquency: Misunderstood by juvenile justice system, neglected by social science. *Law and Human Behavior, 22,* 81–107.

Kempf-Leonard, K. and Sample, L. (1991). Gender bias in the disposition of juvenile court referrals: The effect of time and location. *Criminology, 29,* 677–699.

Kunzel, R. (1993). *Fallen woman, problem girls: Unmarried mothers and the professionalization of social work.* London: Yale University Press.

Levene, K. (1997). The Earlcourt girls connection: A model intervention. *Canada's Children, 4,* 14–17.

Lindgren, S.J. (1996). Gender specific programming for female adolescents. Unpublished Master's thesis. Minneapolis, MN: Augsburg College.

MacDonald, J. and Chesney-Lind, M. (2001). Gender bias and juvenile justice revisited: A multiyear analysis. *Crime & Delinquency, 47,* 173–195.

McCormack, A., Janus, M., and Burgess, A.W. (1986). Runaway youth and sexual victimization: Gender differences in an adolescent runaway population. *Child Abuse and Neglect, 10,* 387–395.

Messerschmidt, J.W. (1997). *Crime as structured action: Gender, race, class, and crime in the making.* Thousand Oaks, CA: Sage Publications.

Miller, J. (1996). An examination of disposition decision making for delinquent girls. In M.D. Schwartz and D. Milovanovic (eds), *Race, gender, and class in criminology: The intersection* (pp. 219–245). New York: Garland Publishing.

Miller, J. (1998). Up it up: Gender and the accomplishment of street robbery. *Criminology, 36,* 37–65.

Odem, M.E. (1995). *Delinquent daughters: Protecting and policing adolescent female sexuality in United States.* Chapel Hill: University of North Carolina Press.

Portillos, E.L. (1999). Women, men and gangs: The social construction of gender in the barrio. In M. Chesney-Lind and J.M. Hagedorn (eds), *Female gangs in America: Essays on girls, gangs, and gender* (pp. 232–244). Chicago, IL: Lake View Press.

Rhodes, J.E. and Fischer, K. (1993). Spanning the gender gap: Gender differences in delinquency among inner city adolescents. *Adolescence, 28,* 879–889.

Rice, M. (1990). Challenging orthodoxies in feminist theory: A black feminist critique. In L. Gelsthorpe and A. Morris (eds), *Feminist Perspectives in Criminology* (pp. 57–69). Bristol, PA: Open University Press.

Taylor, D.L., Biafora, F.A., Warheit, G., and Gail, E. (1997). Family factors, theft, vandalism, and major deviance among a multiracial multiethnic sample of adolescent girls. *Journal of Social Distress and the Homeless, 6,* 71–87.

United States Census Bureau. (2000). Summary File 3. Available at: http://www2.census.gov/census_2000/datasets/Summary_File_3/Arizona/.

Zatz, M.S. (2000). Convergence of race, ethnicity, gender, and class on court decision making: Looking toward the 21st century. In J. Homey (ed.), *Policies processes, and decisions of the criminal justice system* (pp. 503–552). Washington, DC: U.S. Department of Justice, Office of Justice Programs, National Institute of Justice.

25

The Construction of Meaning During Training for Probation and Parole

John P. Crank

Abstract: *John Crank assesses the ideological changes in the training environment of proba-*
tion and parole officers. He illustrates how the organizational culture of a Peace Officer
Training Division reflects a changing correctional philosophy that has moved from a treat-
ment model to a more punitive one. Crank shows how the shift toward a crime control and
surveillance model changed the method of teaching probation and parole personnel new
values, practices, and beliefs that fit in with the mandated, public safety oriented policies that
currently exist. This punitive change in probation and parole functions was instituted on a
national level and is best characterized as favoring a public safety emphasis for probation
and parole staff at the expense of an offender rehabilitative model.

According to conventional wisdom on organizational reform in criminal justice, local agency culture will blunt efforts to institute meaningful change. Efforts for change have had only a limited impact on the day-to-day activities of criminal justice practitioners, as has been cited widely (Fogelson 1977; Guyot 1986; Kerner Commission 1967). Among courtroom actors, the resistance of courtroom work groups to change has been described in terms of the influence of local legal culture (Church 1982). Among the police, occupational resistance to change has been characterized in terms of organizational culture and described in terms of police insularity, the blue curtain, and the code of secrecy (Manning 1970; Pollock-Byrne 1988; Stoddard 1968; Westley 1956). In the field of corrections, the guard subculture, some-times with the support of charismatic administrators, has been associated with widespread resistance to the expansion of prisoner rehabilitation programs (Jacobs 1977) and with the use of violence to maintain social control (Marquart and Crouch 1984, 1990).

This literature has frequently described resistance to organizational change in terms of individual or group self-interest—the idea that the agent of resistance to change lies in purposeful individual or group behavior. From this perspective, advocates seeking reform through organizational change have failed because changes are perceived to be inconsis-tent with the self-interest of members of the particular organizational culture or subcul-ture. For example, a factor in the failure of team policing reforms in the 1970s has been described as the resistance of mid-management personnel who feared losing their jobs in the wake of command decentralization (Skolnick and Bayley 1986; Walker 1992). Similarly, resistance to change from local legal cultures has been attributed to courtroom actors' vested interest in maintaining established relations (Walker 1985).

While acknowledging the powerful influence of self-interest as a source of resistance to change (DiMaggio and Powell 1991), I argue here that change efforts may encounter local customs regarding how action should be organized in particular organizational cultures (Jepperson 1991). Organization members' response to change may not be resistance for reasons of self-interest, but assimilation of that which is new into customary ways of doing and thinking about things (Meyer and Rowan 1977). In other words, how an organizational culture responds to change will depend on the meanings and values carried by its members. This point suggests that the study of the impact of change on organizational culture requires three steps: first, the identification of the changes bearing on the organization; second, an assessment of the values and meanings embedded in a particular organizational culture; and third, an analysis of how those changes are perceived in terms of prevailing patterns of cultural meaning. In this article I perform these three steps in order to understand how a particular parole and probation organization is affected by contemporary changes in parole and probation.

POST Training and the Diffusion of Institutional Knowledge

Three broad areas of change affect the field of parole and probation today: the shift toward crime control and surveillance, accountability to the rule of law, and the rationalization of the work environment (Feeley and Simon 1992; Fogel 1984; Simon 1993).

Over the past 60 years, Peace Officer State Training (POST) training has evolved as a carrier of formal training across the institutional environment of criminal justice. As an institutional form, POST legitimates individuals as "sworn" officers: it prepares recruits who will occupy positions in corrections, parole and probation, and policing for duties associated with the status of professional peace officer with the license to carry a weapon. POST training emerged relatively recently as an institutional form for the transmission of training and education. In the 1920s and 1930s, August Vollmer and two of his proteges, William Wiltberger and O.W. Wilson, emerged as advocates of educational reform in California and in Wichita; all three made use of facilities available at institutions of higher education for providing peace officer training (Morn 1984). In 1959 California founded a commission on POST training to establish minimum standards for hiring and training peace officers. By 1969 there were 45 police academies in California; 17 of these were housed in colleges, and 14 others were affiliated with colleges.

Areas of Institutional Change

POST, a means for transmitting knowledge across the institutional environment of parole and probation, also transmits changes that occur within that environment. That is, changes in values, practices, and beliefs will be reflected in the selection and content of topics and classes provided by the POST curriculum (Meyer and Rowan 1977). In the current era, these changes can be organized into three categories, discussed below: those which emphasize the role of surveillance and crime fighting, those which involve officers' accountability to the rule of law, and those which emphasize the rationalization of administrative process.

The first area of institutional change is the reconstruction of the work of parole and probation officers around ideas of law enforcement and surveillance. With the decline of the rehabilitative ideal in the 1980s, probation has shifted its emphasis from traditional ideas of offender counseling to a public safety enterprise oriented around ideas of surveillance and enforcement (Fogel 1984; Rothman 1980). This shift occurred simultaneously with the federal government's divestment of funding for community-based rehabilitation for offenders during the Reagan era (Duffee 1990). At the same time, a deinstitutionalization process has increased the population of probationers and parolees. Legislators have responded by trying to make parole and probation look "tough" (Gordon 1991). The continuing intensification of peace officers' law enforcement role has been noted in current research on community corrections (Feeley and Simon 1992; Petersilia 1989).

Many elements of the curriculum and topics of POST training reveal the emphasis of parole and probation on enforcement and surveillance. Peace officer skills, an area that includes topics such as range safety, firearms handling, and handcuffing, is the single largest block, accounting for 66 of the 240 hours of instruction. Topics such as survival skills, aimed at preparing recruits mentally for work in a hazardous environment, promote a perception of parole and probation as dangerous work dealing with lawbreakers. To illustrate the extent to which parole and probation focus on crime control, the instructors of defensive tactics, two parole and probation officers, also teach defensive tactics to the city-county police department.

The second area of institutional change is peace officers' accountability to the rule of law. Although parole and probation historically have been perceived as correctional functions, accountability concerns are increasingly comparable to those confronted by police rather than those addressed by correctional agents, whose authority is limited by the confines of a correctional institution. The traditional tasks of reintegrating offenders are being delegated to community organizations, while officers focus on control (Harris, Clear, and Baird 1989). Consequently, issues of accountability increasingly parallel those of municipal police officers.

Accountability is a topic of sustained interest in POST training, as indicated by the large numbers of classes on aspects of that subject. In this context, accountability aims to upgrade individual officers. Many of the POST courses, which focus on procedures regarding arrest and detention, paperwork preparation and timeliness, and community relations, instruct recruits in the nature and limits of their authority. Other courses related to accountability include Professional Ethics, Legal Liability, Undercover Activity, and Search and Seizure. The class titled Strategies of Case Supervision, for example, includes the topic of legal and illegal officer behavior in a practicum. The Bill of Rights is disseminated to students and discussed. In short, accountability to the rule of law is a topic of continual discussion in POST classes.

The third area of change is the rationalization of the administrative process in parole and probation work (Feeley and Simon 1992). This rationalization has also been noted in criminal justice institutions, including police (Crank and Langworthy 1992) and the courts (Heyderbrand and Seron 1990). Feeley and Simon (1992), discussing the "new penology," distinguish this process from the rightward shift in penal thinking that characterized the 1980s. The new penology, they suggest, is marked by the development of bureaucratic strategies that focus on the management of risk groups and dangerous populations (Cohen 1985). Community-based sanctions become risk-management strategies whose purpose is to maintain control and surveillance over offenders (Feeley and Simon 1992: 461, 450). System goals have shifted from the reintegration of offenders to the efficient control of internal system processes—for example, the use of urine testing to determine whether offenders are using drugs.

Occupational Culture, Common Sense, and Tropic Knowledge

Information transmitted by POST across the institutional environment of parole and probation is not accepted unconditionally, but is subjected to evaluation by local organizational cultures. In this process of evaluation, institutional information is weighed against standards of "common sense."

Common sense is the lifeblood of occupational culture. Occupational cultures embody "accepted practices, rules, and principles of conduct that are situationally applied" (Manning 1989: 360). These practices and rules are recipes for behavior, and are codified loosely into organizing themes that participants perceive as common sense. The use of commonsense judgments in assessing justice has been noted at all stages of the criminal justice process (Walker 1985).

The presence of commonsense knowledge is indicated by the use of linguistic devices called tropes (Shearing and Ericson 1991). A trope is essentially something described in terms of something else. In occupational cultures this something else is often a story, an irony, a metaphor, or some combination of these, constituted from everyday experience. The accumulation of tropes makes each organizational culture unique, depending on its work circumstances and its members' collective experiences.

Tropes are processes of "analogous reasoning" or "cultural repertoires" that "allow action to be both orderly and improvisational" (Shearing and Ericson 1991: 482). They provide culturally acceptable ways for organizing knowledge under commonsense ideas. The craft of policing, for example, may be characterized as an extensive repertoire of tropes that enable officers to move easily from one ambiguous situation to the next, practicing their craft according to commonly held ideas, embodied in a story-based vocabulary, of what policing is (McNulty 1994).

Four types of tropes are frequently cited (Eco 1984). Metaphor, defined as a "way of seeing something as if it were something else" (Manning 1979: 661), has been called the master trope in that other types of tropes are special types of metaphors. Stories are metaphors in that they explain something in terms of personal, concrete experience, although the stories themselves may be constructed from strings of tropes. The other tropes are special cases of metaphors. Synecdoche refers to seeing a part for the whole. Burke (1969) defined synecdoche as representation—that is, the presentation of one thing to represent another. Metonymy takes a whole and reduces it to its constituent parts (Turner 1974). Ironies convey meaning through their opposites.

Tropes are often carried by stories about what peace officers do. Storytelling among peace officers to depict their work is recognized widely (Harris 1973; VanMaanen 1979). That these stories may be the object of research, however, has been noted only recently (McNulty 1994; Shearing and Ericson 1991). Stories are not merely glosses that arise from peace officers' inability to articulate why they do what they do; rather, they represent a "narration that is the quintessential form of customary knowledge" (Shearing and Ericson 1991: 488–489). Put another way, stories provide a vocabulary of precedents that construct an appropriate cultural, or intersubjective, way of seeing the world (Mills 1940). A member of an organizational culture learns not how to act, but "rather the sensibility out of which she or he ought to act" (Shearing and Ericson 1991: 493). McNulty (1994) describes an interactive training scenario in which police recruits are taught the "problematic quality of the truth" (Ericson 1982: 62).

Because stories use the intersubjective world of occupational activity as their referent, culture is transmitted as knowledge about the natural order of things (McNulty 1994). Thus recruits, when taught the lore of police work, simultaneously receive a vocabulary of police culture whenever tropes are used to convey information. When training occurs in a classroom provided for POST academies, the use of stories imparts a lexicon of organizational culture masquerading as commonsense knowledge.

POST instructors, by virtue of their occupational position, span the boundaries between the institutional environment and the local organizational culture. As members of the organizational culture, they participate in its commonsense language. Their natural language for organizing action is metaphoric and story-based (McNulty 1994). These individuals are also responsible for providing rational instruction as it is embodied in the content of the curriculum and the topics selected for POST training. Thus they are ideological boundary spanners: as instructors they are expected to provide the rational discourse of institutional change, while as members of the local organization they participate in a culturally created commonsense worldview communicated by tropes.

Boundaries between areas of institutional change and local organizational culture emerge when instructors are asked a question or when they feel compelled to explain something during a class. Explanations based on the instructors' lore will be drawn from their commonsense worldview, and consequently will be expressed as a trope. These explanations thus convey organizational or cultural perspective presented as commonsense knowledge (Shearing and Ericson 1991). In this way, instructors convey cultural tools that enable trainees to organize the knowledge presented in POST training (Kappeler, Sluder, and Alpert 1994). Because these tools are conveyed in regard to particular topics, trainees learn to use Shearing and Ericson's (1991) phrase, "the sensibility out of which" to think about whatever material is being taught. When topics involve changes in the institutional environment of parole and probation, recruits are taught how to think about those changes.

This toolkit—the stories and tropes used by instructors to convey local culture—is the object of the present analysis. Because tropes emerge frequently in discussions involving institutional change, an assessment of tropes helps us consider how local organizational culture responds to those changes.

Research Design

In the summer of 1992 I conducted research as a nonparticipant observer of a POST training session offered by the Nevada Department of Probation and Parole. The session lasted for six weeks, from June 15 to July 27. The academy employed 35 POST-certified instructors during this period; all but three were members of the Department of Probation and Parole. All instructors were sworn peace officers and were employed by the Department of Probation and Parole.

The integration of training into organizational structure, process, and culture was indicated by the organization of the regional Department of Probation and Parole. This department consisted of five units. Three units supervised offenders; one provided court services. The fifth, the POST training unit, was housed in the same building complex as the three supervisory units. The unit manager and both supervisors of operations carried offender caseloads, as did the district trainer, the rangemaster, and the program coordinator. These individuals were also instructors in the POST academy. The other instructors also typically carried caseloads. Consequently, the instructors' values and beliefs complemented the occupational perspectives of the members of the organization, among both administrators and line officers.

During the session, I gathered data primarily from classroom observation and conducted follow-up interviews with training staff members and students. POST instructors were informed of my presence before class. I took the role of a nonparticipant observer to minimize the impact of my presence on the conduct of the class. With the passage of time, however, I was increasingly accepted as a member of the group, and was occasionally invited to participate in class activities. In this way my nonparticipant status was breached on several occasions. This breaching probably aided in the collection of valid data: at the outset, I suspected that information was filtered in that students and instructors, distrustful of academic outsiders, were guarding their conversations and discussions. With the relaxing of the nonparticipant barrier, however, I sensed that instructors, particularly those who appeared before the class on multiple occasions, were more "open"—that is, likely to lecture, speak, or reveal their sentiments as they would if I were not present.

Findings

Findings are presented here by domain. Tropes in each domain are presented in what follows as vignettes and are organized into themes of cultural meaning.

Crime Fighting

The first domain, crime fighting, was marked by tropes that emphasized the role of the parole and probation agent as a crime fighter. Instructors' crime-fighting stories dominated the tropic landscape. The tropes were organized into two themes.

The first theme cast probationers or parolees as lawbreakers or, in the metaphorical parlance of probation and parole officers, "the bad guys," and emphasized the need to control their behavior and surveil their activities. Tropes with this theme underscored the importance of labeling probationers or parolees as offenders and as persons probably engaged in continuous wrongdoing. The following synecdoche, in which the appropriate term *parolee* or *probationer* was replaced by the figurative term *offender*, was stated several times in academy classes:

> Keep in mind: we do not service clients. We supervise offenders.

This dictum carried the weight of administrative authority:

> The district administrator is very adamant about that. They are offenders, not clients.

The following trope, from a class on home visits, emphasized the idea that offenders were engaged in continuous wrongdoing:

> A fella just got out of jail, and I gave him one of my cards. The next day Metro called, and asked me about my cards, they had found a card at the scene of a burglary. I asked them to read it to me, and they did, and it was this guy. We went to his place, and the police checked for the stolen items. When he came home we arrested him. He was out only one day.

The labeling process was reinforced with interrogative interviewing strategies. The following example and associated trope refer to "wedging the alibi with a minor admission" to uncover wrongdoing during interviews.

> Most offenders will not admit all at one time, they will admit by hints and pieces at a time. Any time you can get the offender to admit a little bit of it, you've opened the door.

An instructor told a long story of an individual who would not admit to a crime. The agent, however, by gaining admission to small units, one at a time, was able to obtain evidence that this individual had committed the crime. In the same class, this was another principle of interviewing:

> They forget to cover up their closest associations. You can get a lot of information from loved ones.

This statement was followed by a story about an offender who had thoroughly alibied his offense but had failed to provide the alibi to his sister. These tropes characterized an ordinary component of probation and parole activity—interviewing the probationer or parolee—in terms of strategies which, when followed correctly, would uncover law-breaking. The tropes revealed the extent to which interviewing has shifted from rehabilitative counseling to interrogation aimed at uncovering wrongdoing (Cohen 1985).

The second theme concerns tropes that describe the potential danger of routine activities. These were the most common of the crime-fighting tropes. In a class on lethal force, the following advice emphasized the potential for danger in a home visit:

> If someone says "I can kill you six ways before you hit the ground," well, maybe they can. Get an extra one or three people before you go in. Most of the time they are bluffing, but don't take any chances.

This theme was echoed in a class on operations. Students were provided with a vocabulary list of terms used by the agency. Two of these terms were tropes which, according to the instructor, provided direction for home visits. The first was "JDLR," defined as "Just don't look right. Refer to GTHO, p. 5." The definition of GTHO was "Get the hell out." These two tropes were ironies by which a keen observer transformed apparently safe circumstances into perilous ones.

The following story, from a class on the return of violators, emphasized the dangerousness of offenders and the need to search carefully, however repugnant the process might be. The instructor was discussing body searches and was referring to the area around the groin:

> This is the place where people hide all kinds of stuff. There was a case in California where a guy was up for parole. He went before the board, and they turned him down. He bent over and pulled a stabbing tool out of his anal cavity. He jumped over the desk and stabbed a parole board member that he didn't like in the shoulder a couple of times.

Tropes can be chillingly persuasive. The following tropes were taken from a class on officer survival. The class opened with a two-minute film in which an officer was talking against the backdrop of a city street (a visual metaphor of the street as a place where the work takes place). This example illustrates the metaphorical richness of tropes that can imbue even a brief statement with meaning. In this instance, tropes (in bold type in the following quote) emphasized the crime-control aspect of the work.

> I'm not going to let any **son-of-a-bitch** [depraved animal: metaphor for violator] get me **out there** [the street: metaphor for work]. No **animal** [animal: metaphor for client] **out there** [the street: metaphor for work] is going to **beat me** [physical confrontation: metaphor for doing one's job]. You'll have to **cut my head off** [cutting one's head off: metaphor for keeping from doing one's job] to **stop me** [stop me: metaphor for physical resistance obstructing someone's work].

The instructor presented this statement as an example of a healthy attitude that would enable a recruit to survive in a hostile environment. It was followed by a heuristic trope, a film story of unpredictability and danger during a routine activity. The film was taken by a videocam mounted on an officer's car. The officer was engaged in a routine traffic stop of a car when he was suddenly and violently assaulted by the occupants. The footage showed the officer being beaten and murdered at the side of a dark road. In the last few minutes of the film, the officer was shown lying dead on the pavement behind the patrol car, enveloped in the somber Texas night. This story served as a powerful irony; it transformed a traffic stop into an activity with peril, in which the greatest peril was to take things as they appeared to be.

The theme of unpredictability as a basis for storytelling has been noted by other scholars (Harris 1973; VanMaanen 1979). The following story, from a class on probable cause, uses the irony of difficulty in gaining entry to convey unpredictability.

> A door can *hurt* you. I've got a big foot [points at his foot]. We were over at a fellow's place, and we could see him on the bed. I kicked the door, and that door it kicked back. I kicked that door nine times. When it finally broke open, there was a great big piece of the door around the deadlock still stuck to the wall. When I pulled it out, there was a deadbolt that long [gestures about nine inches] in concrete reinforced wall. It was specially reinforced.

The Morality of Personal Responsibility

Many tropes identified a precept of personal responsibility for both offenders and officers: responsibility for one's own actions morally imbued probation and parole work at all levels. Whether such responsibility involved the behavior of a probation and parole officer in the courtroom or when making house calls, or whether it involved an offender's ability to maintain personal cleanliness or conform to terms of probation or parole, these tropes emphasized the morality of responsibility for one's own behavior.

Among officers, personal responsibility involved personal demeanor, emotions, and case preparation. In a class on courtroom procedure, accountability for probation and parole officers was linked to their demeanor and case preparation, as indicated by the following tropes:

> Don't read a paper. I was in reviewing a case, leafing through the pages, and the judge stopped, pointed at me, pointed to the bailiff, and the bailiff made a big circle around the courtroom, a big show, and came up to me and said "Please don't rustle your paper."

> If a judge asks you a question, and you don't know the answer, he'll ask "Who knows?" He'll call for a new date for the hearing, and instruct you to bring in everyone who has that information.

In these examples, responsibility was an immediate, concrete issue of demeanor and preparation. Responsibility, however, also involved the control of emotions. The following story, stated in a class on lethal force, provided local cultural perspective on personal emotions:

> A PR24 [baton] is a deadly weapon. A few years ago an LASD officer saw a fellow he knew standing on a corner, a guy he knew was a burglar. He told him to leave. He drove around the block, and when he came back the guy was still there. He executed a power takeout with a PR24 and hit the guy across the skull, and literally knocked his brains out the side of his head. So be careful. You may be tempted to strike someone, but you'll end up in the trick bag.

The message here was to avoid being overcome by anger; this was viewed as a loss of emotional integrity.

The extent to which moral responsibility was perceived as an issue of personal integrity was underscored in a class titled "Hazardous Attitudes." Such attitudes were detrimental to the use of common sense. The five hazardous attitudes—anti-authority, impulsiveness, macho, apathy, and invulnerability—were presented ironically as exemplars of the absence of common sense.

After the instructor's opening presentation the class divided into five groups, each charged with acting out one of the hazardous attitudes. These skits were heuristic dramas on the ironies. Thus recruits were taught to think tropically by constructing and enacting tragic dramas that demonstrated how a hazardous attitude could conflict with the application of common sense to daily work. Inevitably each drama ended in mock tragedy, affirming the trainees' understandings of local cultural values. The instructor's concluding trope, "Don't drive faster than your guardian angel can fly," conveyed the sentiment that agents should not let their emotions get the better of them.

Among offenders, personal responsibility was presented thematically in terms of "taking responsibility for [the offender's] life." The director of the training unit emphasized this theme in cited discussions with offenders. She stated the following trope many times:

> I had an offender accuse me of building a case against him. "Are you building the case?" No sir. I told him he was building his own case. Am I writing it down? You betcha!

This theme was echoed in the following statement that made use of a correctional metaphor: doing time for someone else.

> You've got to avoid doing time for them. They'll have a million excuses. They have to be responsible for themselves.

The morality of offenders' responsibility justified retribution. An instructor in a class on probable cause defined the probable cause standard for probation and parole: a crime has been committed, or is about to be committed, or a condition of probation or parole has been violated. The instructor then stated:

> Suppose you have a guy that is usually clean, starts dressing dirtier, makes payments late, but doesn't show drugs in his urine. Is this basis for a search? Yes. Behavioral change. This is probable cause.

In this hypothetical story, behavioral changes indicating untidiness in demeanor, even in the absence of legal or technical violations, become grounds for reinvoking the intervention of the criminal justice system.

Bureaucracy

Many classes dealt with issues salient to participants in bureaucracies, and tropes were frequently bureaucratic in reference. These tropes were organized into two themes. First, they provided guidance for organizing action in terms of local values on topics made complex by a proliferation of legal or organizational structure. Second, they allowed recruits to consider ways to offset some of the more dehumanizing aspects of the crescive rationality of the organizational and legal bureaucracy.

I obtained the following metaphorical trope in a class on case supervision that presents the offender as a construction of the record-keeping system:

> Until Central receives the Initial Risk and Needs Assessment form, the person does not *live*. They do not *die* until Central gets the Termination Data form. The computer says this person lives and dies, and no logic prevails.

In regard to the first theme, several tropes acted as cultural guideposts for action to simplify bureaucratic complexity in order to act more directly and sometimes more retributively against offenders. Drug use is one such topic for which these tropes come into play. This offense classification is highly rationalized by the state legal code. Drugs are categorized by type in five schedules; each contains several different drugs. For example, Schedule 2 includes amphetamines, methaqualone, morphine, thebaine, and hydrocordane. Moreover, three quantities differentiate the charges of trafficking; each charge carries different recommended sentences and fines. Each offense in turn is compounded by previous offenses. From this mass of legal complexity emerged cultural bases for organizing retributive action for drug violators:

> I had a woman, I work over at Gersham Park, that just wouldn't quit (using drugs). I just couldn't get her to quit. So we went in, took her kid away. Stopped her welfare, told her she couldn't get her kid back until she cleaned up her act. She was in a program in three days.

Another way to organize retribution was provided in a class on filing new charges. This example also reveals how local organizational culture was presented as commonsense knowledge. Here a trainee was told to use common sense, and then was provided with a cultural recipe to organize commonsense action:

> Basically, the rule of thumb is that if you have a lot of stuff on them, go ahead. Just use common sense. We had a bad guy that was causing a lot of trouble. He was picked up, searched, and a small piece of a roach was found. They found him guilty of a gross misdemeanor, and he pled it way down to introducing a controlled substance into interstate commerce. That's the lowest of the low. They'll use that when they really want to get someone.

The following story reveals how organizational culture was masked as organizational process by adding new charges for drug violators:

> INSTRUCTOR: *We rarely do these [file new charges]. I did three over the past year, and that's a lot. For example, you might have a pregnant mother using drugs.*
> TRAINEE: *Is that a case where we don't do this?*
> INSTRUCTOR: *No, that's the kind of case where we usually make an arrest.*

These tropes revealed how violators, particularly individuals who use drugs, were legally chastised. In these stories, tropic language simplified organizational complexity with rule-of-thumb guides for delivering sanctions to drug-using offenders.

This simplification of procedure occurred around important local values—for example, assisting one's partner. I witnessed this in a class on radio communications. Communications have become highly rationalized, and agents are expected to learn a complex array of procedures to communicate by radio. Recruits were introduced to the five types of radios used in the district, details of radio panels, basic radio functions, and the 400 code; officers were advised to memorize this code. Heuristic dramas introduced officers to the complexities of the communications system and emphasized Code 444—assisting another officer.

Dramas were scripted from known events involving officers in the department. The first drama was about a traffic accident that changed to a Code 444 when an officer received gunfire and an armed suspect was chased on foot. The second concerned an aborted holdup that changed into a siege situation when the offender escaped to the roof of a building and shot a medical officer. Both of these skits were about officers in trouble. Through the administrative and technical complexity of police communications emerged one fundamental cultural precept: always respond to officers' calls for assistance.

The second theme was that of balancing bureaucratic excess against offenders' particular needs. The first trope reveals a sympathy for individuals whose circumstances make it difficult to deal with conditions of probation or parole.

> We have a bad situation in our country. A lot of times it is impossible to find work for an unemployed mother. There's no way minimum wage can provide the support [she can get] from unemployment and ADC. However, a condition of parole is employment. You may have to talk to your supervisor. A low-skill offender with three children, her children will literally starve if she has to take a minimum-wage job. They can't afford child care. You can write it up so that they have to work, but you can write it up so that they can take care of their children at home.

The theme of balancing bureaucracy against offenders' needs was revealed particularly by the "success story" tropes, which described how offenders had overcome particular problems in dealing with the bureaucratic apparatus of the criminal justice system. The following story was told in a class on offender services:

> There is essentially no public transportation in the city. When classes are over, people may be dumped at the terminal and be stuck. There is no bus service when classes are over at 9:15. Also, transportation is a significant problem for many of them. One woman started catching buses at 3 to be at class at 7. One kid took a skateboard every morning to get from Henderson to the Bonanza office. He always managed to get there on time.

Another story was told in a class on case supervision:

> The judge ordered a high school completion (a needs form) for a woman with an IQ of 70. What I did was put my woman into Rancho High School classes. She wrote a book report she was exceptionally proud of. I sent a report to the judge telling him what she had accomplished. The judge liked it.

These tropes suggest that probationers or parolees who have displayed the ability to overcome personal hardships become "success stories," a valued commodity in the storytelling language of the organizational culture.

Discussion

Domains are a cognitive map of the organization of common sense in the local culture. Because common sense is produced in POST training, these domains become a cultural interface with the institutional environment and, by implication, with areas of institutional change. Here I discuss domains in the light of contemporary changes in the institutional environment of parole and probations.

The first domain, crime fighting, revealed local accommodation to surveillance and crime-control trends in contemporary probation and parole (Duffee 1990; Gordon 1991; Simon 1993). Themes of tropes in the crime-fighting domain— labeling the probationer or parolee as an offender, and the danger and unpredictability of routine activities— suggested that the role of crime fighter was integrated fully into the organizational culture. The commonsense worldview, with its emphasis on crime fighting, danger, and unpredictability, is similar to the worldview of occupational activity frequently attributed to police officers (Manning 1970; McNulty 1994).

Tropes favorable to crime control appear to be matched by a corresponding devaluation of rehabilitative concerns. Probationers and parolees were labeled offenders rather than clients, a label from which there was no escape as long as an offender remained under the department's administrative authority, yet, if formal terms of probation or parole and informal norms of personal responsibility were honored, offenders were not subjected to further status degradation. The awkward accommodation between the supportive nature of rehabilitation and the adversarial nature of surveillance was revealed in an incident related by the director of the training unit. A prisoner said "You don't trust us, do you?" She responded "You're right, I don't trust you, but I care."

The second domain, the morality of personal responsibility, is particularly relevant to officers' accountability to the rule of law. Accountability issues are more complex for probation and parole officers than for other sworn officers in criminal justice. Probation and parole officers have broader search-and-arrest authority than do police officers. Although probation and parole officers are subject to the same due process constraints as police officers regarding revocation of probation or parole, the due process standard for the former is more lenient. Evidence seized in violation of the Fourth Amendment, for example, cannot be entered into evidence for any new crime, but it can be used as a basis for revocation of probation or parole. Searches of a probationer's residence do not require probable cause. In addition, violation of contractual terms of probation or parole is a basis for the rearrest of offenders for existing charges, but it has no legal bearing on new charges. These examples reveal that issues of accountability vary according to the legal situation encountered by the officer.

Throughout the six-week period, not a single trope disdained due process concerns. Tropes suggested that these issues were interpreted in terms of pre-existing cultural meanings—specifically the morality of individual responsibility. These criteria were behavioral: how an individual dresses, courtroom demeanor, and the following of technical procedures for arrest. Thus, contrary to the often-cited resistance of policing cultures to accountability, probation and parole instructors provided tropes favoring such accountability. The officer's personal integrity and, by application, the integrity of the organization were of utmost importance.

The third domain, bureaucracy, revealed how the local organizational culture accommodated the contemporary process of rationalizing the administrative environment of parole and probation (Feeley and Simon 1992). Rationalization was revealed in the elaboration of record-keeping systems. The increasing emphasis on surveillance facilitates the rationalization and centralization of the record-keeping and information-collecting systems used by criminal justice agencies; officers were taught detailed procedures when dealing with interstate compacts, for returning violators, and in court services. As one student noted, "P and P stands for paperwork and more paperwork."

Tropes emerged to facilitate problem-solving in bureaucratically complex areas. I noted simplifying strategies in the sanctioning of offenders in areas that were organizationally or legally complex, and also in limited efforts to counter the bureaucratic rigor of particularly stringent probation contracts or parole conditions. In institutional terms, tropes instructed how officers could "loosely couple" their behavior to areas of administrative or legal complexity by using local cultural recipes for action.

Conclusions

"One must pick one's root metaphors carefully" (Turner 1974: 25).

A POST training class, viewed through the lens of culture, is a practical theory of action grounded in the experiential world, steeped in rational knowledge, and based on powerful metaphorical imagery. Its metaphors are consequential. The above quote by Turner (1974), with its suggestion that foundational metaphors may have far-reaching implications, is accepted here as an invitation to illuminate some of those implications.

First, the "crime fighting" metaphor has sweeping implications for the organization and activity of parole and probation. That crime fighting is accomplished by individual officers with superior skills was made evident in tropes that labeled probationers or parolees as offenders, and in the use of investigative skills to uncover possible wrongdoing this metaphorical imagery is similar to Hobbs's (1991) description of the master detective as the organizing principle for much of police work, in which the ability to ferret out and control offenders' crime stems from the skill of the individual peace officer. Tropes also scripted surveillance and enforcement with stories of the danger and unpredictability of enforcement activity. In a national climate of intense crime-control activity and in the face of cultural expectations of controlling crime among offenders, temptations to circumvent due process may become strong, particularly in view of the already relaxed due process protections for probation and parole officers. Organizational pressures to make arrests have strongly influenced the corruption of undercover police officers (Manning and Redlinger 1978). Probation and parole officers, facing increased pressures to convert to a crime-control mode, may find it difficult to avoid similar problems with due process, particularly in view of their expanded enforcement authority.

Second, personal responsibility infuses cultural morality; this finding supports Simon's (1993) important work on the history of parole. Simon (1993: 105) conceptualizes parole officers' perceptions of their work in terms of controlling "poor discipline." Parole provides an ideological corrective; it seeks to ensure that offenders are returned to a condition of social normality (see also Garland 1985). I observed this ideological corrective in the current research in the use of streamlined disciplinary tactics to sanction drug offenders. The diverse accounts of organizational short cuts for penalizing drug violators suggest that normalization of offenders is pursued with a moral vengeance. On the other hand, offenders who displayed moral responsibility in the face of administrative adversity become "success stories." These stories may consequently serve as a moral counterweight to the legal degradation of offenders who violate precepts of morality, and thus, in an ironic logic, may justify retribution for offenders who violate the local culture's moral sensibility.

Third, bureaucratic tropes provide organizational short cuts for dealing with areas swathed in technicality to facilitate control of offenders. Put another way, the bureaucratization of probation and parole appears to be accompanied by the development of informal processes to facilitate the organization of officers' day-to-day routines. This was particularly evident in the development of short cuts for dealing with problem cases in areas dense with legal complexity. If, as Feeley and Simon (1992) suggest, the process of system rationalization continues to accelerate for probation and parole, one might anticipate the increasing decoupling of probation and parole officers' work from the administrative processes of the organization, and the increasing isolation of line-level probation and parole officers from the administrative process.

In the aggregate, findings suggest that rather than resisting change, as suggested by common wisdom, the local organizational culture absorbed changes in terms of existing areas of meaning, such as offenders' and agents' morality. In doing so, however, the culture itself changed: it adapted to increased legal complexity, for example, by developing rules of thumb for dealing with particular types of offenders. The organizational culture apparently responded to the content of POST training by incorporating areas of change into a continual redefinition of itself. Organizational culture is thus passed on to each new cohort in ever-changing form, providing the flexibility to adapt and survive regardless of changes imposed externally on the organization.

Fourth is the finding that stories are integral to the language of motive. Stories are not simply illustrative fillers that ground a technical lecture empirically; they imbue an account with cultural meaning and value. By the tropes an instructor uses, he or she adds organizational "spin," or cultural interpretation and value, to an area of instruction. This point has a powerful policy implication: a class is a transmitter of organizational culture. POST leaders at the agency level should not only monitor the technical quality of classes, as they do currently through an assessment of testing materials, instructor evaluations, and evaluations of performance, they should also be sensitive to the tropic devices used by instructors to convey information. The transmission of information through tropes will affect recruits' loyalties and the meanings they acquire about their work as powerfully as the technical knowledge will affect their skills and abilities. POST leaders who fail to recognize the power of tropes for instilling cultural knowledge may find that all of their efforts to instill change or knowledge in a particular area are circumvented by offsetting cultural precepts and values.

Both cultural and institutional perspectives rely heavily on case study methods of observing and presenting information. The usual call to develop quantifiable measures for future research will not be issued here. I believe that additional and more elaborate case study research can contribute most to these perspectives. We need to assess the wellsprings of organizational meaning and to learn how meanings are modulated through cultural and institutional contexts.

I have examined here only one source of organizational change. Actors have sought to change the administration and behavior of criminal justice organizations in many ways: through the efforts of the chief executive, college education, civilian review boards, media supervision, and policy-oriented research. The central thesis of this article, however—that organizational culture will influence how particular changes are perceived, and ultimately will determine the success or failure of those changes—should apply to those sources of change as well.

Critical Thinking

The 1990s were the era of the incapacitation model for corrections. Longer sentences for offenders, fewer treatment programs, and a tremendous increase in the correctional population occurred on a national level. Only recently have state legislators begun to question the expense and failure of our correctional institutions to transform prisoners into law-abiding citizens. They emphasized concern for public safety at the expense of treatment programs, which also directly affected the operations of probation and parole departments throughout the country. Why do you think these changes in penal philosophy (i.e., massive incarceration) occurred during the 1990s? Do you think the rise in incarceration rates is responsible for the drop in crime rates across the United States? What do you think are some of the unintended consequences of this trend toward incarceration?

References

Burke, K. 1969. *A Grammar of Motives*. Berkeley: University of California Press.

Church, T. 1982. *Examining Local Legal Culture: Practitioner Attitudes in Four Criminal Courts*. Washington, DC: National Institute of Justice.

Cohen, S. 1985. *Visions of Social Control: Crime, Punishment and Classification*. Oxford: Polity Press.

Crank, J.P. and R. Langworthy. 1992. "An Institutional Perspective of Policing." *Journal of Criminal Law and Criminology* 83: 338–363.

Crouch, B.M. and J.W Marquart. 1990. Resolving the Paradox of Reform: Litigation, Prisoner Violence, and Perceptions of Risk. *Justice Quarterly*, 7(1): 103–123.

DiMaggio, P.J. and W.W. Powell. 1983. "Institutional Isomorphism and Collective Rationality: The Iron Cage Revisited." *American Journal of Sociology* 48: 147–160.

DiMaggio, P.J. and W.W. Powell 1991. "Introduction" (pp. 1–40), in *The New Institutionalism in Organizational Analysis*, edited by W. Powell and P. DiMaggio. Chicago, IL: University of Chicago Press.

Duffee, D. 1990. *Explaining Criminal Justice: Community Theory and Criminal Justice Reform*. Prospect Heights, IL: Waveland Press.

Eco, U. 1984. *Semiotics and the Philosophy of Language*. Bloomington: Indiana University Press.

Ericson, R. 1982. *Reproducing Order: A Study of Police Patrol Work*. Toronto: University of Toronto Press.

Feeley, M.M. and J. Simon. 1992. "The New Penology: Notes on the Emerging Strategy of Corrections and Its Implications." *Criminology* 30: 449–474.

Fogel, D. 1984. "The Emergence of Probation as a Profession in the Service of Public Safety: The Next Ten Years" (pp. 65–99), in *Probation and Justice: Reconsideration of Mission*, edited by P. McAnany, D. Thompson, and D. Fogel. Cambridge, MA: Oelgeschlager, Gunn and Hain.

Fogelson, D. 1977. *Big-city Police*, Cambridge, MA: Harvard University Press.

Garland, D. 1985. *Punishment and Welfare*. Brookfield, VT: Gower.

Gordon, D.K. 1991. *The Justice Juggernaut: Fighting Street Crime, Controlling Citizens*. London: Rutgers University Press.

Guyot, D. 1986. "Bending Granite: Attempts to Change the Rank Structure of American Police Departments" (pp. 43–68), in *Police Administrative Issues*, edited by M. Pogrebin and R. Regoli. Millwood, NY: Associated University Press.

Harris, P., T. Clear, and S.C. Baird. 1989. "Have Community Supervision Officers Changed Their Attitudes toward Their Work?" *Justice Quarterly* 6: 233–246.

Harris, R.N. 1973. *The Police Academy: An Inside View*. New York: Wiley.

Heyderbrand, W. and C. Seron. 1990. *Rationalizing Justice: The Political Economy of Federal District Courts*. New York: State University of New York Press.

Hobbs, D. 1991. A Piece of Business: the Moral Economy of Detective Work in the East-End of London. *The British Journal of Sociology*, 42(4): 597–608.

Jacobs, J. 1977. *Stateville: The Prison in Mass Society*. Chicago, IL: University of Chicago Press.

Jepperson, R.L. 1991. "Institutions, Institutional Effects, and Institutionalism" (pp. 143–64), in *The New Institutionalism in Organizational Analysis*, edited by W. Powell and P. DiMaggio. Chicago, IL: University of Chicago Press.

Kappeler, V.E., R.D. Sluder, and G.P. Alpert. 1994. *Forces of Deviance: Understanding the Dark Side of Policing*. Prospect Heights, IL: Waveland Press.

Kerner, O. and the National Advisory Commission on Civil Disorders. 1967. *Report of the National Advisory Commission on Civil Disorder*. Washington, DC: U.S. Government Printing Office.

Manning, P. 1970. *Police Work*. Cambridge, MA: MIT Press.

Manning, P. 1979. "Metaphors of the Field: Varieties of Organizational Discourse." *Administrative Science Quarterly* 24: 660–671.

Manning, P. 1989. "Occupational Culture" (pp. 360–364), in *The Encyclopedia of Police Science*, edited by W. Bayley. New York: Garfield.

Manning, P. and L.J. Redlinger. 1978. "The Invitational Edges of Corruption: Some Consequences of Narcotic Law Enforcement" (pp. 147–166), in *Policing: A View from the Street*, edited by P.K. Manning and J. VanMaanen. Santa Monica, CA: Goodyear.

Marquart, J. and B. Crouch. 1984. "Coopting the Kept: Using Inmates for Social Control in a Southern Prison." *Justice Quarterly* 1: 491–509.

McNulty, E.W. 1994. "Common-Sense Making among Police Officers: The Social Construction of Working Knowledge." *Symbolic Interaction* 17: 281–294.

Meyer, J. and B. Rowan. 1977. "Institutionalized Organizations: Formal Structure as Myth and Ceremony." *American Journal of Sociology* 83: 430–463.

Mills, C.W. 1940. "Situated Actions and Vocabularies of Motive." *American Sociological Review* 5: 904–913.

Morn, F. 1984. "The Academy of Criminal Justice Sciences and the Criminal Justice Education Movement: Some History." Unpublished manuscript.

Petersilia, J. 1989. "The Influence of Research on Policing" (pp. 230–248), in *Critical Issues in Policing*, edited by R. Dunham and G. Alpert. Prospect Heights, IL: Waveland Press.

Pollock-Byrne, J. 1988. "Ethics and Criminal Justice." *Justice Quarterly* 5: 475–485.

Rothman, D. 1980. *Conscience and Convenience*. Boston, MA: Little, Brown.

Shearing, C.D. and R.V. Ericson. 1991. "Culture as Figurative Action." *British Journal of Sociology* 42: 481–506.

Simon, J. 1993. *Poor Discipline: Parole and the Social Control of the Underclass, 1890–1990*. Chicago, IL: University of Chicago Press.

Skolnick, J. and D. Bayley. 1986. *The New Blue Line: Police Innovation in Six American Cities*. New York: Free Press.

Spradley, J.P. 1979. *The Ethnographic Interview*. New York: Holt, Rinehart and Winston.

Spradley, J.P. 1980. *Participant Observation*. New York: Holt, Rinehart and Winston.

Stoddard, E.R. 1968. "The Informal Code of Police Deviancy: A Group Approach to Blue-collar Crime." *Journal of Criminal Law, Criminology, and Police Science* 59: 201–213.

Turner, V. 1974. *Dramas, Fields, and Metaphors: Symbolic Action in Human Society*. Ithaca, NY: Cornell University Press.

VanMaanen, J. 1979. "Observations on the Making of Policemen" (pp. 292–308), in *Policing: A View from the Street*, edited by P. Manning and J. VanMaanen. Santa Monica, CA: Goodyear.

Walker, S. 1985. *Sense and Nonsense about Crime*. Belmont, CA: Wadsworth.

Walker, S. 1992. *The Police in America*, 2nd edn. New York: McGraw-Hill.

Westley, W.A. 1956. "Secrecy and the Police." *Social Forces* 34: 254–257.

B Outsiders

26

Denial of Parole: An Inmate Perspective

Mary West-Smith, Mark R. Pogrebin, and Eric D. Poole

Abstract: *West-Smith, Pogrebin, and Poole examine inmates' perceptions of being denied parole. Inmates find it difficult to understand the rationale of the board and believe that board members were searching for any reason to deny their parole. Many of these complaints are based on various other aspects of their hearing, such as composition of the board, behavior and attitude of members, setbacks due to previous parole violations, denial despite family needs, unhelpful case managers, retroactive application of laws, general denial of all inmates on that particular day, and unfair hearings due to lack of individual consideration.*

Like many other discretionary decisions made about inmates (e.g., classification, housing, treatment, discipline, etc.), those involving parole are rather complex. Parole board members typically review an extensive array of information sources in arriving at their decisions, and empirical research has shown a wide variation in the decision-making process. The bulk of research on parole decision-making dates from the mid-1960s to the mid-1980s (e.g., Gottfredson and Ballard, 1966; Rogers and Hayner, 1968; Hoffman, 1972; Wilkins and Gottfredson, 1973; Scott, 1974; Carroll and Mondrick, 1976; Heinz et al., 1976; Talarico, 1976; Garber and Maslach, 1977; Sacks, 1977; Carroll et al., 1982; Conley and Zimmerman, 1982; Lombardi, 1984). Virtually all of this research focuses on the discretion exercised by parole board members and the factors that affect their decisions to grant or deny parole. Surprisingly, only one study, conducted over 20 years ago, has examined the inmate's perspective on the parole decision-making process (Cole and Logan, 1977). The present study seeks to advance the work on parole decision-making from the point of view of those inmates who have had their release on parole denied.

Inmates denied parole have often been dissatisfied with what they consider arbitrary and inequitable features of the parole hearing process. While those denied parole are naturally likely to disagree with that decision, much of the lack of acceptance for parole decisions may well relate to lack of understanding. Even inmates who have an opportunity to present their case through a personal interview are sent out of the room while discussions of the case take place (being recalled only to hear the ultimate decision and a summary of the reasons for it). This common practice protects the confidentiality of individual board members' actions; however, it precludes the inmate from hearing the discussions of the case, evaluations of strengths and weaknesses, or prognosis for success or failure. More importantly, this practice fails to provide guidance in terms of how to improve subsequent chances for successful parole consideration. A common criticism of parole hearings has been that they produce little information relevant to an inmate's parole readiness (Morris, 1974; Fogel, 1975; Cole and Logan, 1977); thus, it is unlikely that those denied parole understand the basis for the decision or attach a sense of justice to it.

Parole Boards

The 1973 Supreme Court decision in *Scarpa v. United States Board of Parole* established the foundation for parole as an "act of grace." Parole is legally considered a privilege rather than a right; therefore, the decision to grant or deny it is "almost unreviewable" (Hier, 1973, p. 435). In fact, when federal courts have been petitioned to intervene and challenge parole board actions, the decisions of parole boards have prevailed (see *Menechino v. Oswald*, 1970; *Tarlton v. Clark*, 1971). While subsequent Court rulings have established minimal due process rights in prison disciplinary proceedings (*Wolff v. McDonnell*, 1974) and in parole revocation hearings (*Morrissey v. Brewer*, 1972), the parole hearing itself is still exempt from due process rights. Yet in *Greenholtz v. Nebraska* (1979) and *Board of Pardons v. Allen* (1987), the Supreme Court held that, although there is no constitutional right to parole, state statutes may create a protected liberty interest where a state's parole system entitles inmates to parole if they meet certain conditions. Under such circumstances, the state has created a presumption that inmates who meet specific requirements will be granted parole. Although the existence of a parole system does not by itself give rise to an expectation of parole, states may create that expectation or presumption by the wording of their statutes. For example, in both *Greenholtz* and *Allen*, the Supreme Court emphasized that the statutory language—the use of the word "shall" rather than "may"—creates the presumption that parole will be granted if certain conditions are met. However, if the statute is general, giving broad discretion to the parole board, no liberty interest is created and due process is not required. In Colorado, as in most other states with parole systems, the decision to grant parole before the inmate's mandatory release date is vested entirely within the discretion of the parole board. The legislatively set broad guidelines for parole decision-making allow maximum exercise of discretion with minimal oversight.

Normalization and Routinization

Sudnow's (1965) classic study of the processes of normalization and routinization in the public defender's office offers insights into the decision-making processes in parole board hearings. Like Sudnow's public defender, who works as an employee of the court system with the judge and prosecutor and whose interests include the smooth functioning of the court system, the parole board member in Colorado works with the prison administration, caseworkers, and other prison personnel. Public defenders must represent all defendants assigned to them and attempt to give the defendants the impression they are receiving individualized representation. However, public defenders often determine the plea bargain acceptable to the prosecutor and judge, based on the defendant's prior and current criminal activities, prior to the first meeting with the defendant (Sudnow, 1965).

The parole board theoretically offers individual consideration of the inmate's rehabilitation and the likelihood of future offending when deciding whether or not to release an inmate. However, the parole board, like the public defender, places a great deal of emphasis on the inmate's prior and current criminal record. The tremendous volume of cases handled by the public defender necessitates the establishment of "normal crime" categories, defined by type and location of crime and characteristics of the defendant and victim, which permit the public defender to quickly and easily determine an appropriate and acceptable sentence. Such normalization and routinization facilitate the rapid flow of cases and the smooth functioning of the court system. Similarly, a two-year study of 5,000 parole decisions in Colorado in the early 1980s demonstrated that the parole board heard far too many cases to allow for individualized judgments (Pogrebin et al., 1986, p. 149).

Observations of parole hearings illustrate the rapid flow of cases and collaboration with other prison personnel. Typically, the case manager, in a brief meeting with the parole board member, discusses the inmate, his prior criminal history, current offense, institutional behavior, compliance with treatment programs, progress, and current attitude, and makes a release or deferral recommendation to the parole board member prior to the inmate interview. The inmate and family members, if present, are then brought into the hearing room. The parole board member asks the inmate to describe his prior and current crimes, his motivation for those crimes, and the circumstances that led to the current offense. Typical inmate responses are that he was "stupid," "drunk," or "not thinking right." Inquiries by the parole board about the programs the inmate has completed are not the norm; however, the inmate is often asked how he thinks the victim would view his release. The inmate typically tries to bring up the progress he has made by explaining how much he has learned while institutionalized and talks about the programs he completed and what he learned from them. A final statement by the inmate allows him to express remorse for the pain he has caused others and to vow he will not get into another situation where he will be tempted to commit crimes. Family members are then given time to make a statement, after which the inmate and family leave the hearing room. A brief discussion between the parole board member and the case manager is followed by the recommendation to grant or defer parole. A common reason given for a deferral is "not enough time served." If parole is granted, the parole board member sets the conditions for parole.

"Normal" cases are disposed of very quickly. The time from the case manager's initial presentation of the case to the start of the next case is typically 10 to 15 minutes. Atypical cases require a longer discussion with the case manager before and after the inmate interview. Atypical cases can also involve input from other prison personnel (e.g., a therapist), rather than just the case manager. Those inmates who do not fit the norm, either through their background or the nature of their crime, are given special attention. The parole board member does not need to question the inmate to discover if the case is atypical, since the case manager will inform him if there is anything unusual about the inmate or his situation.

During the hearing, the board member asks first about the prior and current crimes and what the inmate thinks were the causal factors that led to the commission of the crimes. Based on his observations of public defenders, Sudnow (1965) concludes, "It is not the particular offenses for which he is charged that are crucial, but the constellation of prior offenses and the sequential pattern they take" (p. 264). Like the public defender who attempts to classify the case into a familiar type of crime by looking at the circumstances of prior and current offenses, the parole board member also considers the criminal offense history and concentrates on causal factors that led the inmate to commit the crimes. It is also important for the board member that the inmate recognize the patterns of his behavior, state the reasons why he committed his prior and current crimes, and accept responsibility for them. The inmate, in contrast, generally wants to describe what he has learned while incarcerated and to talk about the classes and programs he has completed. The interview exchange thus reveals two divergent perceptions of what factors should be emphasized in the decision-making process. In Sudnow's (1965) description of a jury trial involving a public defender, "the onlooker comes away with the sense of having witnessed not a trial at all, but a set of motions, a perfunctorily carried off event" (p. 274). In a similar manner, the observer at a parole board hearing has the impression of having witnessed a scripted, staged performance.

As a result of their journey through the criminal justice system, individual inmates in a prison have been typed and classified by a series of criminal justice professionals. The compilation of prior decisions forms the parole board member's framework for his or her perception of the inmate. The parole board member, with the help of previous decision-makers and through normalization and routinization, "knows" what type of person the inmate is. As Heinz et al. (1976) point out, "a system premised on the individualization of justice unavoidably conflicts with a caseload that demands simple decision rules. . . . To process their caseloads, parole boards find it necessary to develop a routine, to look for one or two or a few factors that will decide their cases for them" (p. 18). With or without the aid of parole prediction tools to help in their decision, parole board members feel confident that they understand the inmate and his situation; therefore, their decisions are more often based on personal intuition than on structured guidelines.

Theoretical Framework

Based on a combination of both formal and informal sources of information they acquire while in prison, inmates believe that satisfactory institutional behavior and completion of required treatment and educational programs, when combined with adequate time served, will result in their release on parole. They also believe that passing their parole eligibility date denotes sufficient institutional time. Denial of parole, when the stated prerequisites for parole have been met, leads to inmate anger and frustration. As stories of parole denials spread throughout the DOC population, inmates are convinced that the parole board is abusing its discretion to continue confinement when it is no longer mandated.

Control of Institutional Behavior

The majority of inmates appearing before the parole board have a fairly good record of institutional behavior (Dawson, 1978). Inmates are led to believe that reduction in sentence length is possible through good behavior (Emshoff and Davidson, 1987). Adjustment to prison rules and regulations is not sufficient reason for release on parole; however, it comprises a minimum requirement for parole and poor adjustment is a reason to deny parole (Dawson, 1978). Preparation for a parole hearing would be a waste of both the prisoner's and the case manager's time and effort if the inmate's behavior were not adequate to justify release.

Research suggests that good behavior while incarcerated does not necessarily mean that an inmate will successfully adapt to the community and be law-abiding following a favorable early-release decision (Haesler, 1992; Metchik, 1992). In addition, Emshoff and Davidson (1987) note that good time credit is not an effective deterrent for disruptive behavior. Inmates who are most immature may be those who are most successful at adjusting to the abnormal environment of prison; inmates who resist conformity to rules may be those who are best suited for survival on the outside (Talarico, 1976). However, institutional control of inmate behavior is a crucial factor for the maintenance of order and security among large and diverse prison populations, and the use of good time credit has tradition-ally been viewed as an effective behavioral control mechanism (Dawson, 1978). Inmates are led to believe that good institutional behavior is an important criterion for release, but it is secondary to the background characteristics of the inmate. Rather than good behavior being a major consideration for release, as inmates are told, only misbehavior is taken into account and serves as a reason to deny parole.

Inmates are also told by their case manager and other prison personnel that they must complete certain programs to be paroled. Colorado's statutory parole guidelines list an inmate's progress in self-improvement and treatment programs as a component to be assessed in the release decision (Colorado Department of Public Safety, 1994). However, the completion of educational or treatment programs by the inmate is more often consid-ered a factor in judging the inmate's institutional adjustment (i.e., his ability to conform to program rules and regimen). Requiring inmates to participate in prison programs may be more important for institutional control than for the rehabilitation of the inmate. Observations of federal parole hearings suggest that the inmate's institutional behavior and program participation are given little importance in release decisions (Heinz et al., 1976). Noncompliance with required treatment programs or poor institutional behavior may be reasons to deny parole, but completion of treatment programs and good institu-tional behavior are not sufficient reasons to grant parole.

Release Decision Variables

Parole board members and inmates use contrasting sets of variables which each group considers fundamental to the release decision. Inmates believe that completion of treatment requirements and good institutional behavior are primary criteria which the parole board considers when making a release decision. Inmates also feel strongly that an adequate parole plan and demonstration that their families need their financial and emotional support should contribute to a decision to release on parole.

In contrast, the parole board first considers the inmate's current and prior offenses and incarcerations. Parole board members also determine if the inmate's time served is commensurate with what they perceive as adequate punishment. If it is not, the inmate's institutional behavior, progress in treatment, family circumstances, and parole plan will not outweigh the perceived need for punishment. Inmates, believing they understand how the system works, become angry and frustrated when parole is denied after they have met all the stated conditions for release.

Unwritten norms and individualized discretion govern parole board decision-making; thus, the resulting decisions become predictable only in retrospect as patterns in granting or denying parole emerge over time. For example, one of the difficulties Pogrebin et al. (1986) encountered in their study of parole board hearings in Colorado was developing a written policy based on previous case decisions:

> This method requires that a parole board be convinced that there exists a hidden policy in its individual decisions. . . . [M]ost parole board members initially will deny that they use any parole policy as such . . . [and] will claim that each case is treated on its own merits. . . . [However,] parole decisions begin to fit a pattern in which decisions are based on what has been decided previously in similar situations.
>
> (p. 149)

Method

In October 1997, Colorado-CURE (Citizens United for Rehabilitation of Errants), a Colorado non-profit prisoner advocacy group, solicited information through its quarterly newsletter from inmates (who were members of the organization) regarding parole board hearings that resulted in a "set-back" (i.e., parole deferral). Inmates were asked to send copies of their appeals and the response they received from the parole board to Colorado-CURE. One hundred and eighty inmates responded to the request for information with letters ranging in length from very brief one- or two-paragraph descriptions of parole board hearings to multiple-page diatribes listing not only parole board issues, but also complaints about prison conditions, prison staff, and the criminal justice system in general. Fifty-two letters were eliminated from the study because they did not directly address the individual inmate's own parole hearing. One hundred and twenty-eight inmate letters were analyzed; 125 from male and three from female inmates. Some letters contained one specific complaint about the parole board, but most inmates listed at least two complaints. Several appeals also contained letters written to the parole board by family members on the inmate's behalf. Two hundred and eighty-five complaints were identified and classified into 13 categories utilizing content analysis, which "translates frequency of occurrence of certain symbols into summary judgments and comparisons of content of the discourse" (Starosta, 1984, p. 185). Content analytical techniques provide the means to document, classify, and interpret the communication of meaning, allowing for inferential judgments from objective identification of the characteristics of messages (Holsti, 1969). In addition, parole board hearings, including the preliminary presentation by the case manager and the discussion after the inmate interview, were observed over a three-month period in 1998. These observations were made to provide a context for understanding the nature of the hearing process from the inmate's perspective and to document the substantive matter of parole deliberations.

The purpose of the present study is not to explore the method the parole board uses to reach its release decisions; rather, our interest is to examine the content of the written complaints of inmates in response to their being denied parole.

Findings

Those complaints relating to parole hearings following a return to prison for a parole violation and those complaints regarding sex offender laws will not be addressed in the following discussion. Parole revocation hearings are governed by different administrative rules and are subject to more rigorous due process requirements, and are thus beyond the scope of the current study. In addition, sex offender sentencing laws in Colorado have evolved through dramatic changes in legislation over the past several years and a great deal of confusion exists regarding which inmates are eligible for parole, when they are eligible, and what conditions may be imposed when inmates are paroled. We now turn to an examination of the remaining categories of inmate complaints concerning parole denial.

Inadequate Time Served

Forty-eight percent of the inmates reported "inadequate time served" as a reason given for parole deferment. Their attempt to understand the "time served" component in the board's decision is exemplified by the following accounts:

> if you don't meet their [the parole board's] time criteria you are "not" eligible. Their time criteria is way more severe than statute. . . . [The risk assessment] also says, if you meet their time amounts and score 14 or less on the assessment you "shall" receive parole. This does not happen. The board is an entity with entirely too much power.

> If the court wanted me to have more time, it could have aggravated my case with as much as eight years. Now the parole board is making itself a court!

[Enclosed] is a copy of my recent deferral for parole, citing the infamous "Not enough time served" excuse. This is the third time they've used this reason to set me back, lacking a viable one.

These responses of the inmates to the "inadequate time served" reason for parole deferral demonstrate that they believe the parole board uses a different set of criteria than the official ones for release decisions. Inmates do not understand that the "time served" justification for parole deferment relates directly to the perception by the parole board member of what is an acceptable punishment for their crime. They believe the parole board is looking for a reason to deny parole and uses "time served" when no other legitimate reason can be found.

Completed Required Programs

Thirty-five percent of the inmates complained that their parole was deferred despite completing all required treatment and educational programs. Related complaints, expressed by 9 percent of the inmates, were the lack of mandatory classes and the long waiting lists for required classes. The following excerpts from inmate letters reflect this complaint:

> When I first met with them [the parole board] I received a 10-month setback to complete the classes I was taking (at my own request). But was told once I completed it and again met the board I was assured of a release. [,] Upon finishing these classes I met the board again [a year later]. . . . I noticed that none of my seven certificates to date were in the file and only a partial section of the court file was in view. I tried to speak up that I was only the fifth or sixth person to complete the 64-week class and tell about the fact that I carry a 4.0 in work plus have never had a COPD conviction or a write-up. He silenced me and said that meant nothing. . . . I later was told I had been given another one-year setback!!!

> They gave me a six-month setback because they want me to take another A.R.P. class. . . . [I]t was my first time down [first parole hearing], and I have taken A.R.P. already twice. . . . I have also taken . . . Independent Living Skills, Job Search, Alternatives to Violence, workshops and training in nonviolence, Advanced Training for Alternatives to Violence Project, mental health classes conducted by addiction recovery programs. I also chair the camp's A.A. meetings every week and just received my two-year coin. I have also completed cognitive behavioral core curriculum.

Inmates view completion of required programs as proof that they have made an effort to rehabilitate themselves and express frustration when the parole board does not recognize their efforts. The completion of classes was usually listed with other criteria the inmates viewed as important for their release on parole.

Parole Denied Despite Parole Plan

Deferral of parole even though a parole plan had been submitted was a complaint listed by 27 percent of inmates. It is interesting to note that this complaint never appeared as a solo concern, but was always linked to other issues. These inmates seem to believe that a strong parole plan alone will not be sufficient to gain release and that the parole plan must be combined with good institutional behavior and the completion of required classes. Even when all required criteria are met, parole was often deferred. The frustration of accomplishing all of the requirements yet still being deferred is expressed in the following excerpts:

> I was denied for the third time by the D.O.C. parole board even though I have completed all recommended classes (Alcohol Ed. I and II, Relapse Prevention, Cognitive Skills and Basic Mental Health). I have a place to parole to [mother's house], a good job and a very strong support group consisting of family and friends. . . . To the present date I have served 75 percent of my three-year sentence.

> [After having problems with a previous address for the parole plan] . . . my parents and family . . . were assured . . . that all I needed to do is put together an alternative address. I managed to qualify for and arrange to lease a new low-income apartment at a new complex. . . . My family was helping with this. I also saw to it that I was preapproved at [a shelter in Denver], a parole office approved address, so that I could go there for a night or two if needed while I rented and had my own apartment approved by the parole office. My family expected me home, and I had hoped to be home and assisting them, too. I arranged employment from here, and looked forward to again being a supportive father and son. . . . I received a one-year setback! I was devastated, and my family is too. We are still trying to understand all of this. . . . I am . . . angry at seeing so many sources of support, employment, and other opportunities that I worked so hard at putting together now be lost.

Preparing an adequate parole plan requires effort on the part of both the inmate and the case manager. When a parole plan is coupled with completion of all required treatment and educational programs and good institutional behavior, the inmate is at a loss to understand how the parole board can deny parole. Inmates often expressed frustration that the plans they made for parole might not be available the next time they are eligible for parole. "Inadequate time served" is often the stated reason for parole deferment in these cases and does not indicate to the inmate the changes he needs to make in order to be paroled in the future.

Parole Board Composition and Behavior

Twenty-one percent of the inmates complained about the composition of the parole board or about the attitude parole board members displayed toward the inmate and his or her family. Several inmates expressed concern that at the majority of hearings only one parole board member is present and the outcome of an inmate's case may depend on the background of the parole board member hearing the case:

> The man [parole board member] usually comes alone, and he talks to the women worse than any verbal abuser I have ever heard. He says horrible things to them about how bad they are and usually reduces them to tears. Then he says they are "too emotionally unstable to be paroled!" If they stand up for themselves, they have "an attitude that he can't parole." If they refuse to react to his cruel proddings, they are "too cold and unfeeling." No way to win!! Why in the *world* do we have ex-policemen on the parole board?? Cops always want to throw away the key on all criminals, no matter what. Surely that could be argued . . . as conflict of interest!

My hearing was more of an inquisition than a hearing for parole. All of the questions asked of me were asked with the intent to set me back and not the intent of finding reasons to parole me. It was my belief that when a person became parole eligible the purpose was to put them out, if possible. My hearing officer did nothing but look for reasons to set me back.

Inmates often expressed the view that the parole board members conducting their hearings did not want to listen to their stories. However, if parole board members have generally reached a decision prior to interviewing the inmate, as indicated by the routinization of the hearing process, it is logical that the board member would attempt to limit the inmate's presentation. In addition, if board members have already determined that parole will be deferred, one would expect the questions to focus on reasons to deny parole. One inmate stated, "I believe that the parole board member that held my hearing abused his discretion. I had the distinct feeling that he had already decided to set me back before I even stepped into the room."

Family's Need for Inmate's Support

Many inmates criticized the parole board for failing to take into account their families' financial, physical, and emotional needs. Seventeen percent of the inmates expressed this concern, and several included copies of letters written by family members asking the board to grant parole. The primary concerns were support for elderly parents and dependent young children:

My mom has Lou Gehrig's disease. . . . [S]he can't walk and it has spread to her arms and shoulders. . . . [No] one will be there during the day to care for her. The disease is fast moving. . . . My mom is trying to get me home to care for her. . . . I am a non-violent first-time offender. I have served eight years on a 15. I have been before the parole board five times and denied each time. . . . (I got six-, six-, nine-, six-, 12-month setbacks in that order). Why I'm being denied I'm unsure. I've asked the board and wasn't told much. I've completed all my programs, college, have a job out there, therapy all set up, and a good parole plan.

[My 85-year-old mother] has no one. Her doctor also wrote [to the chair of the parole board] as well as other family members, including my son. All begging for my release. She *needs* me!! I wish you could [see] . . . how hard I have worked since I have been in prison. . . . Being good and trying hard does not count for much in here. . . . This is my fifth year on an eight-year sentence.

The parole board does not consider a dependent family as a primary reason to release an inmate on parole; however, inmates regard their families' needs as very important and are upset that such highly personal and emotionally charged circumstances are given short shrift during their parole hearing. And if they believe they have met the conditions established for release, inmates do not understand why the parole board would not allow them to return home to help support a family.

Case Manager Not Helpful

Thirteen percent of the inmates expressed frustration with their case manager, with a few accusing the case manager of actually hurting their chances to make parole. Although the inmate was not present during the case manager's presentation to the board member, many inmates declared satisfaction with their case manager and felt that the board did not listen to the case manager's recommendation. Since the present study focuses on inmate complaints, the following excerpts document the nature of the dissatisfaction inmates expressed concerning their case managers:

> [The case manager] has a habit of ordering inmates to waive their parole hearings. Many inmates are angry and do not know where to turn because they feel it is their right to attend their parole hearings. . . . [He] forces most all of his caseload to waive their parole hearing. That is not right! . . . How and why is this man allowed to do this? I would not like my name mentioned because I fear the consequences I will pay. . . . [T]his man is my case manager and I have not seen the parole board yet.

> I have not had any write-ups whatsoever and I have been taking some drug and alcohol classes since I have been back [parole revoked for a dirty U.A.]. I had a real strong parole plan that I thought that my case manager submitted but he never bothered to. I was planning on going to live with my father who I never asked for anything in my life and he was willing to help me with a good job and a good place to live. My father had also wrote to [the chair of the parole board] and asked if I could be paroled to him so he can help me change my life around.

> [Some] case managers are not trained properly and do not know what they are doing. Paperwork is seldom done properly or on time. Others are downright mean and work *against* the very people they are to help. Our liberty depends on these people, and we have no one else to turn to when they turn against us.

Inmates realize they must at least have a favorable recommendation by the case manager if they are to have any chance for parole. Yet they generally view the case manager as a "marginal advocate," often going through the motions of representing their interests but not really supporting or believing in them. Case managers after all are employees of the Department of Corrections, and their primary loyalties are seen by inmates to attach to their employer and to "the system."

Few Inmates Paroled the Same Day

Five percent of the inmates related in their letters that very few inmates were paroled on a given hearing day, leading them to suspect that the parole board typically denies release to the vast majority of inmates who come up for a hearing.

> I just received a letter . . . and she told me that two out of 24 made parole from [a Colorado women's facility]. . . . [Also] out of 27 guys on the ISP non-res program from [a community corrections facility] only four made parole!! . . . What is going on here?!! These guys [on ISP] are already on parole for all intents and purposes.

> Went [before parole board] in June '97; 89 went. Two made it (mandatory).

> I realize they're not letting very many people go on parole or to community. It's not politically correct to parole anyone. Now that Walsenburg is opening, I'm sure they will parole even less people. I have talked to 14 people that seen the Board this week. Two setbacks.

Inmates circulate such stories and cite them as evidence that the parole board is only interested in keeping prisoners locked up. Many inmates express their belief that the parole board is trying to guarantee that all the prisons are filled to capacity.

Appeals Not Considered on an Individual Basis

Although Colorado-CURE asked inmates to send copies of their appeal and the response to the appeal, the majority of inmates mailed copies of their appeal before they received the response. Thus, it is not surprising that only 4 percent of the inmates discussed the apparent uniformity of appeal decisions. The standard form letter from the chair of the parole board, included by those who stated this complaint, reads as follows:

> I have reviewed your letter ... along with your file, and find the board acted within its statutory discretion. Consequently, the decision of the board stands.

Word of the appeals circulates among the general prison population and between prisons via letters to other inmates. Inmates suggest that the form letters are evidence that the parole board is not willing to review cases and reconsider decisions made by individual board members.

> I finally got their response. They are basically sending everyone the same form letter. I was told by someone else that it [is] what they were doing and sure enough that is what they are doing.

> After receiving the denial of my appeal, I spoke with a fellow convict about his dilemma, which prompted him to show me a copy of his girlfriend's denial of her appeal. . . . It seems that [she] was given an unethical three-year setback, even though she has now completed three-quarters of her sentence. And she too received a carbon copy response from the [chair of the parole board's] office. It should be crystal clear that these files are *not* being reviewed as is stated in [the] responses, because if they had been, these decisions would surely seem questionable at best.

Conclusion

The nature of the written complaints reflects the belief among many inmates that the parole board in Colorado is using criteria for release decisions that are hidden from inmates and their families. A parole board decision, made without public scrutiny by members who have no personal knowledge of the inmate, depends on the evaluation of the likelihood of recidivism by others in the criminal justice system. While guidelines and assessment tools have been developed to help with the decision-making process in

Colorado, it is unclear the extent to which they are used. Release decisions by the parole board appear to be largely subjective and to follow latent norms that emerge over time. The emphasis on past and current crimes indicates that inmates—regardless of their institutional adjustment or progress in treatment, vocational, or educational programs—will continue to be denied parole until they have been sufficiently punished for their crimes. As one inmate lamented in his letter of complaint,

> When the inmate has an approved parole plan, a job waiting, and high expectations for the future and then is set back a year ... he begins to die a slow death. They *very often* use the reason: *Not enough time served* to set people back. If I don't have enough time served, why am I seeing the parole board? Or they will say: *Needs Continued Correctional Treatment*. If I have maintained a perfect disciplinary record and conformed to the rules, what more correctional treatment do I need. . . . I had a parole plan and a job in May when I seen the board. I was set back one year. I will see them in March. . . . I will have no job and nowhere to live. . . . The Colorado Dept. of Corrections does not rehabilitate inmates. That is solely up to the inmate. What they do is cause hate and bitterness and discontent.

Findings of this study indicate that the factors which inmates believe affect release decisions are different from the factors the parole board considers, and thus suggest why inmates fail to understand why their parole is deferred despite compliance with the prerequisites imposed upon them. As evidenced by the above examples, inmates are not only confused and angry when they believe parole should be granted, they begin to question whether or not it is worth the effort if they are only going to "kill their numbers" (i.e., serve the full sentence). The prison grapevine and the flow of information among the entire Department of Corrections inmate population allow such stories and theories to spread. Prison officials should be concerned that if inmates feel that compliance with prison rules and regulations is pointless, they will be less likely to conform to the administration's requirements for institutional control. Currently, inmates who are turned down for parole see themselves as victims, unfairly denied what they perceive they have earned and deserve. Each parole-eligible case that is deferred or set back becomes another story, duly embellished, that makes its rounds throughout the prison population, fueling suspicion, resentment, and fear of an unbridled discretionary system of power, control, and punishment.

Inmates denied parole are entitled to a subsequent hearing usually within one calendar year. But the uncertainty of never knowing precisely when one will be released can create considerable tension and frustration in prison. While discretionary release leaves them in limbo, it is the unpredictability of release decisions that is demoralizing. As we have found, this process has resulted in bitter complaints from inmates. Perhaps the late Justice Hugo Black of the U.S. Supreme Court best summarized the view of many inmates toward the parole board:

> In the course of my reading—by no means confined to law—I have reviewed many of the world's religions. The tenets of many faiths hold the deity to be a trinity. Seemingly, the parole boards by whatever names designated in the various states have in too many instances sought to enlarge this to include themselves as members.

(quoted in Mitford, 1973, p. 216)

Critical Thinking

It is common for members of parole boards to want inmates to accept full responsibility for their crimes. When inmates present excuses or justifications for their acts, parole board members interpret this as evidence that they will likely go back to crime. In short, parole board members expect inmates to accept "criminal" as an identity status. Think about some of the improper things you have done. Were there "legitimate" excuses for why you did them? Should your identity be tied solely to these acts? Think about some excuses that you would accept from inmates if you were on a parole board and ones you would not.

References

Board of Pardons v. Allen, 482 U.S. 369 (1987).

Carroll, J.S., Wiener, R.L., Coates, D., Galegher, J., and Alirio, J.J. (1982). Evaluation, diagnosis, and prediction in parole decision making. *Law and Society Review*, 17, 199–228.

Carroll, L. and Mondrick, M.E. (1976). Racial bias in the decision to grant parole. *Law and Society Review*, 11, 93–107.

Cole, G.F. and Logan, C.H. (1977). Parole: The consumer's perspective. *Criminal Justice Review*, 2, 71–80.

Colorado Department of Public Safety (1994). *Parole guidelines handbook*. Denver, CO: Division of Criminal Justice.

Conley, J.A. and Zimmerman, S.E. (1982). Decision making by a part-time parole board: An observational and empirical study. *Criminal Justice and Behavior*, 9, 396–431.

Dawson, R. (1978). The decision to grant or deny parole. In B. Atkins and M. Pogrebin (eds), *The invisible justice system: Discretion and the law* (pp. 360–389). Cincinnati: Anderson.

Emshoff, J.G. and Davidson, W.S. (1987). The effect of "good time" credit on inmate behavior: A quasi-experiment. *Criminal Justice and Behavior*, 14, 335–351.

Fogel, D. (1975). . . . *We are the living proof: The justice model for corrections*. Cincinnati: Anderson.

Garber, R.M. and Maslach, C. (1977). The parole hearing: Decision or justification? *Law and Human Behavior*, 1, 261–281.

Gottfredson, D.M. and Ballard, K.B. (1966). Differences in parole decisions associated with decision-makers. *Journal of Research in Crime and Delinquency*, 3, 112–119.

Greenholtz v. Nebraska Penal Inmates, 442 U.S. 1 (1979).

Haesler, W.T. (1992). The released prisoner and his difficulties to be accepted again as a "normal" citizen. *Euro-Criminology*, 4, 61–68.

Heinz, A.M., Heinz, J.P., Senderowitz, S.J., and Vance, M.A. (1976). Sentencing by parole board: An evaluation. *Journal of Criminal Law and Criminology*, 67, 1–31.

Hier, A.P. (1973). Curbing abuse in the decision to grant or deny parole. *Harvard Civil Rights—Civil Rights Law Review*, 8, 419–468.

Hoffman, P.B. (1972). Parole policy. *Journal of Research in Crime and Delinquency*, 9, 112–133.

Holsti, O.R. (1969). *Content analysis for the social sciences and humanities*. Reading, MA: Addison-Wesley.

Lombardi, J.H. (1984). The impact of correctional education on length of incarceration: Non-support for new paroling policy motivation. *Journal of Correctional Education*, 35, 54–57.

Menechino v. Oswald, 430 F.2d 402 (2nd Cir. 1970).

Metchik, E. (1992). Judicial views of parole decision processes: A social science perspective. *Journal of Offender Rehabilitation*, 18, 135–157.

Mitford, J. (1973). *Kind and unusual punishment: The prison business*. New York: Knopf.

Morris, N. (1974). *The future of imprisonment*. Chicago, IL: University of Chicago Press.

Morrissey v. Brewer, 408 U.S. 471 (1972).

Pogrebin, M.R., Poole, E.D., and Regoli, R.M. (1986). Parole decision making in Colorado. *Journal of Criminal Justice, 14,* 147–155.

Rogers, J. and Hayner, N.S. (1968). Optimism and accuracy in perceptions of selected parole prediction items. *Social Forces, 46,* 388–400.

Sacks, H.R. (1977). Promises, performance, and principles: An empirical study of parole decision making in Connecticut. *Connecticut Law Review,* 9, 347–423.

Scarpa v. U.S. Board of Parole, 414 U.S. 934 (1973).

Scott, J.E. (1974). The use of discretion in determining the severity of punishment for incarcerated offenders. *Journal of Criminal Law and Criminology,* 65, 214–224.

Starosta, W.J. (1984). Qualitative content analysis: A Burkean perspective. In W. Gudykunst and Y.Y. Kim (eds), *Methods for intercultural communication research* (pp. 185–194). Beverly Hills, CA: Sage.

Sudnow, D. (1965). Normal crimes: Sociological features of the penal code in a public defender's office. *Social Problems, 12,* 255–276.

Talarico, S.M. (1976). The dilemma of parole decision making. In G.F. Cole (ed.), *Criminal justice: Law and politics,* 2nd edn (pp. 447–456). North Scituate, MA: Duxbury.

Tarlton v. Clark, 441 F.2d 384 (5th Cir. 1971), *cert, denied,* 403 U.S. 934 (1971).

Wilkins, L.T. and Gottfredson, D.M. (1973). *Information selection and use in parole decision-making: Supplemental report V.* Davis, CA: National Council on Crime and Delinquency.

Wolff v. McDonnell, 418 U.S. 539 (1974).

27

How Registered Sex Offenders View Registries

Richard Tewksbury

Abstract: *Richard Tewksbury assesses the perceptions of registrants about the value of sex offender registries as a tool to enhance community awareness and promote public safety. In addition, he examines offenders' perceptions of the strengths and weaknesses of the registry format and structure. Results show that registrants see significant potential for registries but seriously question the efficacy and efficiency of how registries are currently constructed and used.*

Sex offenders are considered by many in society as the "worst of the worst" among criminal offenders. Sex offenders are subjected to increasingly stringent sentences and post-sentence restrictions on where they may live, work, and with whom they may spend their time. These are not entirely new issues, however. Historically, sex offenders have been subject to severe sentencing laws and harsh treatment (Quinn, Forsyth, and Mullen-Quinn, 2004). The recent enhancements of sentences and restrictions, including sex offender registries and community notification, are premised on the idea of deterrence. The idea is that known sex offenders can be more closely monitored and potential sex offenders will recognize that sanctions are extreme; thus offending will not be in his or her best interests. Sex offender registries and community notification are also designed to "shame" the offender and further deter future unlawful behavior. However, little research has been devoted to examining the way in which sex offenders perceive their sanctions (do they experience shame?), and if and how sex offender registration may be related to such perceptions.

The goal of the present study is to assess how registered sex offenders perceive registration, and the ways in which perceptions structure their responses. Obtaining such insights from sex offenders may therefore allow both policy-makers and criminal justice practitioners to better understand how the sanction of sex offender registration may or may not have an effect on offenders.

Research on Sex Offender Registries

Research regarding sex offender registries and community notification comes in four general types: statistical profiles of registrants (Adams, 2002; Szymokowiak and Fraser, 2002), assessments of recidivism (Adkins, Huff, and Stageberg, 2000; Pawson, 2002), evaluations of the accuracy of registry information (Levenson and Cotter, 2005; Tewksbury, 2002), and assessments of collateral consequences of registration (Tewksbury, 2004, 2005; Zevitz and Farkas, 2000a, 2000b, 2000c). The most important of these foci for the present study is the last focus: assessment of if and how sex offender registration provides additional punishments and consequences for offenders.

Collateral Consequences

Research on sex offender registries and community notification has clearly shown that there are numerous collateral consequences that accompany sex offender registration. Researchers have identified numerous legal consequences that accompany criminal convictions of any variety. These collateral consequences include disenfranchisement, loss of the ability to own or possess a firearm, and numerous employment restrictions. Social consequences such as stigmatization, relationship difficulties, employment problems, and feelings of shame and diminished self-worth have also been found to accompany felony convictions (Dodge and Pogrebin, 2001; Pogrebin, Dodge, and Katsampes, 2001). Such consequences can create a very difficult reintegration into society for the offender (Harding, 2003).

Collateral consequences specific to sex offender registration include all of the above, as well as additional consequences arising from registration and community notification. Interestingly, research has also suggested that the nature and extent of these consequences may be much greater for sex offenders than for other felons. For instance, beginning in 2005, numerous communities across the nation began to pass ordinances establishing residential buffer zones around locations known to be frequented by children, including schools, day care centers, churches, libraries, public parks, and bus stops. Evaluations of the effects of these restrictions suggest both that many offenders live in violation of such buffer zones (Tewksbury and Mustaine, 2006) and that these have little, if any, effect on rates of sex offender recidivism (Duwe, Donnay, and Tewksbury, 2008). In addition, numerous studies (Levenson and Cotter, 2005; Mustaine and Tewksbury, 2008; Tewksbury, 2004, 2005; Zevitz and Farkas, 2000a) have documented stigmatization, damaged relationships, and harassment, as well as housing and employment difficulties for registered sex offenders in Kentucky and Indiana.

Collateral consequences of sex offender registration also affect people other than the convicted offender. Included among those who suffer from restrictions imposed upon sex offenders are their family members and criminal justice officials. Tewksbury and Levenson

(2009; see also Levenson and Tewksbury, 2009) have shown that spouses, children, and parents of registered sex offenders suffer socially, financially, and emotionally from legal restrictions placed upon their loved ones. In regard to criminal justice officials, probation and parole officers in Wisconsin reported a loss of personnel, time, and budgetary resources as a result of a recent community notification program (Zevitz and Farkas, 2000b). Negative consequences have even been experienced by the very people that sex offender registration was designed to help. Zevitz and Farkas (2000c) report increased levels of anxiety for citizens attending community notification meetings in Wisconsin. Zevitz and Farkas (2000a) also explain that citizens who are notified of sex offenders' presence in the community may be held at least partly responsible for preventing successful reintegration of the offender into society.

Offenders' Perceptions of Sanctions

Research findings consistently identify a strong relationship between offenders' perceptions of the legitimacy of the criminal sanctions imposed upon them and recidivism (see Makkai and Braithwaite, 1994). As Sherman (1993, p. 452) explains, "People obey the law more when they believe it is administered fairly than when they don't." Studies have linked positive offender perception of sanctions to increased compliance with the law (Williams and Hawkins, 1992). Conversely, offenders who do not believe sanctions are fair, effective, or appropriately administered have been reported to commit crime as a result of such beliefs (Sherman and Berk, 1984; Sherman, 1993; Petersilia and Deschenes, 1994).

Research has not only looked at perceived legitimacy of received sanctions, but also at offenders' perceptions of the severity of sanctions. If a penalty is seen by an offender as too severe, it may be viewed as too hard to overcome, which may in turn lead to the offender repeating their crime(s). Strong evidence of this comes from Sherman and Berk's (1984) classic study of the effects of mandatory arrest for domestic violence cases in Minnesota. They concluded that only for certain types of individuals did the arrest effectively deter future crime. The authors noted that men with "high interdependencies," such as married and employed offenders, were likely to be deterred by mandatory arrest policies. However, the authors also reported that a majority of individuals (who were unemployed and unmarried) showed a counter-deterrent effect and rather than seeing mandatory arrest as reducing their likelihood of reoffending it led to additional, sometimes more extreme, violent behavior.

Taking this idea a step further, Williams and Hawkins (1992) have suggested that collateral consequences of sanctions may be seen as especially punishing and consequently serve an important role in deterring reoffending. In short, offenders who perceived their punishment as severe yet fair and appropriate were less likely to anticipate reoffending, and those who do not perceive their sanctions as such may be likely to act out against those they feel are just as responsible for their situations.

As a result of this line of research, Sherman (1993) argued that the ways offenders view the sanctions they receive are important for understanding the likelihood of recidivism. When an offender believes that a punishment holds a fair and reasonable level of severity, deterrence is likely to occur. Punishments that are most likely to be viewed as fair are those that are perceived to be proportional to the offenses committed (Petersilia and Deschenes, 1994). This perception of fairness is consequently seen in whether offenders' future behavior is criminal or not.

The Present Study

The goal of the present study is to identify perceptions registered sex offenders have about the sex offender registry as a tool for public safety. The existing literature on offenders' perceptions of sanctions has shown that perceptions of sanctions may influence behavior. However, this line of inquiry has yet to be extended to a sex offender registration. The views sex offenders hold of their received sanctions, as well as their suggestions for where sanctions can be improved or enhanced, may enable lawmakers, correctional administrators, and the public to re-evaluate the current structure and practice of sanction imposition.

Methods

Data for this study are all qualitative and were collected by way of one-on-one, personal interviews conducted with a sample of offenders listed on the Kentucky Sex Offender Registry (http://kspsor.state.ky.us) at the time of data collection. The Human Studies Protection Program office at the author's university reviewed all materials. Data collection was conducted in February and March 2005.

Sample

A total of 22 sex offenders participated in the study. These individuals were randomly selected from Kentucky's sex offender registry, and all lived in the city of Louisville. The sample of interviewees is almost exclusively male (95%), primarily white (86%), and has a mean age of 48. In terms of their registration characteristics the sample is evenly distributed between lifetime and ten-year registrants. In addition, the sample has a mean length of time on the registry of just over three years. In regard to their conviction offenses, 27 percent have been convicted of rape, 59 percent have a sexual abuse conviction, 45 percent have a conviction for sodomy, and 5 percent have a conviction for some other sexual offense.

Procedure

All data are from one-on-one, in-person semi-structured interviews. Interview length ranged from 30 to 90 minutes. Interviews covered a range of topics, including registrant's knowledge of the sex offender registry, perceptions of reactions from family members, friends, acquaintances, and co-workers, perceptions of strengths and weaknesses of the registry as a tool for public safety, general social/work/educational experiences as a known, convicted, registered sex offender, and whether or not (and to whom) the registrant had disclosed their registration status and demographics. No questions were asked about the offenses or criminal justice processing of the registrant's case, although a large majority of interviewees did discuss their offenses, victims, and case processing.

Findings

Analysis of the interviews shows that registered sex offenders do perceive the sex offender registry as a good and valuable entity, believe the existence of the registry can and does make positive contributions to society, but also believe there are a number of problems and difficulties in the structure, form, and uses of the registry. Although registered sex offenders (RSOs) have a generally positive view about the existence and use of sex offender registries, registrants question whether or not the registry in its current form can be and is effective in enhancing community awareness of sex offenders and public safety. There is also widespread belief among registrants that while use of a sex offender registry for some types of offenders may be valuable and important, there needs to be more differentiation, classification, and/or distinction between which offenders are subject to registration and what information is provided on the registration about registrants.

Registrants' Perceptions of the Value of Sex Offender Registration

When viewing sex offender registration as a concept, and while attempting to remove themselves from the picture, registrants universally recognize the value and potential contributions to community awareness and public safety that registries offer. The value of having a listing of known sex offenders, along with their residences and descriptions, is seen as something that makes sense and is perceived to be a possible contributor to public safety. Almost without exception, RSOs expressed an understanding of why society would want to have a sex offender registry. However, there is also widespread dissatisfaction with having oneself listed.

As a concept and tool for both the public and law enforcement, sex offender registries are perceived in mixed ways. Two questions are central to RSOs' perceptions about the practical value of sex offender registries. First, there are mixed views expressed by registrants about whether registries can raise community members' awareness of the dangers and potential predators in their neighborhoods. Second, RSOs are also of varying mind-sets regarding whether being listed on the registry is likely to influence the likelihood of offenders recidivating.

Among those registrants who believe the registry may be an important tool for enhancing community awareness, this belief appears to be largely based on their assumptions that registries are regularly consulted by community members. As other research has shown, RSOs generally believe that sex offender registries are checked by many (if not most) community members. Because of this assumption, RSOs also commonly believe that these community members who consult the registry will be vigilant about both watching registrants in their neighborhoods, and informing other neighborhood residents about RSOs. This sentiment is expressed clearly by Preston, a child molester and lifetime registrant:

> I think it's a good thing. If my being there and the other people being there will help cut down on the child sex abuse and all that, then it's a damn good thing.

Or, in a more concise statement, Andy, who has been on the registry for nine months for conviction for more than a dozen counts of sodomy with a 14-year-old boy, says, "I think people should be knowledgeable."

However, not all RSOs share this view. Many also question whether a registry, especially in its present form, can realistically be expected to promote widespread community awareness. These registrants recognize that the registry is quite large and that locating specific individuals, especially by chance, is not a very likely event. In addition, those who question the efficacy of the registry for promoting community awareness point out that for it to be effective, community members need to regularly go to the Internet site and search for registrants. Many registrants recognize that this is also not very likely to occur. Arthur, a 53-year-old, three-times divorced registrant who has had no contact with his siblings or adult children for nearly a decade, explained:

> I don't see that it would prevent a lot of sexual abuse occurring. One, I don't see where a large enough segment of the public is aware of the registry to take advantage of it. I don't see where it—it's too broad for all the people it has on it. . . . I just don't see where it has a major impact on the public or on the prevention of sexual abuse.

Or, in the words of Jon, a lifetime registrant who has been on the registry for only a year and a half:

> By literally taking 95 percent of the people who come out and putting us all on the list for life—and they put how many more thousand people on there every year. At some point there will be so damn many people on that list that, to some extent, you're just another face in the crowd. I think that lessens the impact of it to the public. When they look at it and there is 400 people on there—you say, "Hell, it's everywhere, what can you do?"

Just as the population of RSOs is split in their beliefs about whether sex offender registries may or may not be effective for raising community awareness of the presence of sex offenders in a neighborhood, so too are they split in their beliefs about registries' abilities to reduce recidivism. A minority of registrants do believe that RSOs are less likely to reoffend, primarily because they believe registrants are under careful and constant watch by community members. In addition, this assumption is complemented by the view that registrants' knowledge of their existing label will deter them from reoffending, since they are likely to be suspects and investigated in any future reported instances of sexual offenses.

More common, however, is the view that having a sex offender registry is a highly inefficient and ineffective means for deterring offenders and reducing recidivism. As Jon very bluntly puts it, "If I'm going to reoffend, that registry is not going to keep me from it." Explaining this common view a bit more, Mike, a 10-year-registrant convicted of molesting his stepson, suggested that:

> There has to be a deterrent so if people know about the registry before they offend, maybe they won't offend again. It might act as a good deterrent, but I doubt it. The electric chair doesn't keep people from killing people.

Questions about the abilities of sex offender registries to achieve their stated purposes—raising community awareness and reducing recidivism—lead RSOs to point out that a number of changes to the structure, format, and process of registries and the registration process are needed. Changes, whether in who is registered, what information is listed about registrants, or how determinations about who is listed and for how long, are perceived by registrants as critical to the success of the registry, and vitally important for both community safety and "fairness" for offenders.

Remembering that RSOs universally believe in the concept and idea of sex offender registries, their near-universal call for (varying) changes to the registry reinforces their expressions of support for the concept. No registrant interviewed for this project called for the end of the registry or registration process, but nearly all advocated for at least some types of modifications so that the registry would be more likely to achieve its stated goal(s).

As discussed below, a number of specific changes are suggested by RSOs, typically focusing on providing some degree of categorization or differentiation between types of registrants. It is important to be able to differentiate between "true sex offenders, those that are actually a danger" and those not seen as dangerous (i.e., themselves). Without such distinctions, users of the registry may not be able to effectively distinguish RSOs that they should and should not fear. As one registrant summed up what he sees as the problem with the lack of differentiation in registrants' listings, "It's one size fits all. . . . So, in its present form, it's a waste of time."

The failure to distinguish between RSOs based on degrees of dangerousness, whether registrants have or have not completed a treatment program, and those that target children sits at the core of registrants' frustrations with the registration experience. More than any other issue, registrants decry being equated with predators, "real pedophiles," and offenders they themselves define as "dangerous," "heinous," and " a real threat to others." Commenting on his frustrations at being registered in the same way and virtually indistinguishable from more serious sex offenders, Tyler, a 29-year-old lifetime registrant, reflected that:

> I don't think it's really appropriate for me. I'm sure there are some people who it is appropriate for. I think it should go more into repeat offenses with different victims, different dates—more into people who are deemed more predatory. . . . I think there's a place for it, but I don't think they took a lot of time to think about the effective way to use it. I think they've done it like running cattle through fields, it's just massively done.

For many registrants, their frustration and dissatisfaction with the registry and their experiences with it could be significantly diminished if only they believed that the information provided to the public about them and their offense(s) allowed others to "see that I'm not like those others."

"I Don't Associate with Those Kinds of People"

A near-universal theme expressed by RSOs is the belief that they are different from "those kinds of people" who are—and are generally believed should be—on the sex offender registry. RSOs express a strong desire to distinguish themselves from those whom they see as the "real criminals" and sex offenders that they believe are "dangerous," "vicious," or "sexual predators."

Almost without exception, the RSOs interviewed for this project explained, sometimes in lengthy detail, that they did not believe themselves to be dangerous or "as extreme" as other RSOs. Scott, a lifetime registrant with convictions on 11 counts of molesting 12- and 13-year-old boys, explained his frustration at being listed alongside and not distinguished from other sex offenders, saying:

> To read some of the things on there, you can't make a distinction between the monsters and the people that are in there for lesser evils. The wording on there is so brief and simple. My own charge—if I read that and I was John Q. Citizen, I would say, "Lord, that's a dangerous guy right there!"

The belief that one is different from other sex offenders is not only pervasive, but is also seen as a major contributor to both strong social stigmas experienced by RSOs and negative interactions experienced with others who know of one's status as a RSO. Registrants generally believe that they are widely perceived and defined simply by their status as a "sex offender" and not as individuals. Arthur lamented what he perceived as his being inaccurately perceived by others, saying:

> Just being on the registry and being called a sex offender. People have visions of the most extreme cases. They don't think, "Oh, I wonder if Arthur put his hand on an underage female's breast through her clothing while he thought she was asleep?" They think, "I wonder if Arthur dragged some 6-year-old out into the woods and repeatedly raped her and then left her to die on the side of the road?" That's what people think of when they hear "sex offender."

One of the most bothersome parts of being seen "just like all those others" for RSOs is the belief that when the public think of a registered sex offender they assume all such persons are child molesters or pedophiles. Frustrations at being perceived as such are present across the sample and expressed in often very strong and sometimes harsh language. When comparing themselves with other RSOs it is common for interviewees to explain that although their victims may have been legally too young to consent to sexual activity of any form, they did not victimize "children." Charlie, convicted for sexually abusing his preadolescent stepdaughter, complained that:

> They don't differentiate between the guy that goes out and goes to a party and runs across a 16-year-old girl and has oral sex with her, or the guy that drags a 5-year-old off the playground and rapes and kills her. It's still a sex offender.

Andrei, a 64-year-old convicted child molester who was not sure if he was a ten-year or lifetime registrant, argued that he was not a pedophile and strongly disliked having others (presumably) assume he was. Explaining his view, he stated:

> If a guy goes out here and stalks a kid at a school yard or a young Kid—I think he ought to be (on the registry). . . . But this girl . . . she was 13 years old and, in my opinion, old enough to have said "no." I basically didn't have sex with her—it was oral sex. . . . I never was exposed to her, I had my clothes on, fully dressed—it was here in this house. And I kissed her vagina and put my finger in it.

In his mind Andrei did not have sex with a child, since he believed she was "old enough to have said 'no.'" Therefore, he reported being extremely frustrated that his sex offender registry listing might lead others to assume he was a pedophile.

Across the sample of interviewed RSOs there was an expressed sentiment that to be considered one and the same as "those kinds of people" (i.e., pedophiles, sexual predators, and "real" sex offenders) was both insulting and perhaps the worst aspect of registration. Jordan, a 51-year-old convicted of molesting his daughter, explained this experience:

> I hate to be categorized and monitored with all these people who are serial, reoffender or vicious child predators. I don't put myself in that category with them. I hate to be looked upon as that kind of person because I don't feel I am that kind of person. . . . It's degrading and dehumanizing to know that people can pull my picture up and compare me to the guy under me or the guy they saw before me.

Related to the frustration regarding being seen "just like all of those other guys" is RSOs questioning why only sex offenders are subject to placement on a publicly accessible registry. For many RSOs there is a belief that the existence of the sex offender registry serves only to reinforce stereotypes and stigmas of sex offenders as the "worst kind of criminal." However, in the minds of RSOs there are a number of other varieties of offender that are "much worse, and much more of a danger than we are." One of the most common sentiments expressed by RSOs was that having a registry for only sex offenders was unfair, illogical, and an inefficient use of resources.

Having a sex offender registry, but not a registry for all (other) violent offenders, or, as suggested by a few RSOs, any criminal offenders, serves only to exacerbate stereotypes and stigmas, and fails to provide much additional safety for society. Frequent mention was made in interviews of the efficacy of sex offender treatment programs; many RSOs recited statistics about the low recidivism rates of sex offenders (especially those who complete treatment programs), followed by questioning about why such "low-risk" types of offenders are subject to registration, but the "truly violent" and "more dangerous types" of criminal offenders are not.

Many RSOs offered suggestions along with their questioning and criticism of how a more valuable registry might be structured and operated. Primary suggestions centered on requiring registration for offenders convicted of all forms of violent offenses, registering offenders who victimize children (but not adults), and registering only repeat offenders.

Questions persisted across the sample of RSOs. Questions regarding why only sex offenders were subject to registration, questions about whether the registry could be effective, and questions about what registering only sex offenders says about society and common values in society emerged from all of the interviews. Preston, a 63-year-old convicted of multiple counts for fondling and performing oral sex on a 12-year-old girl, expressed his belief that the sex offender registry shows that society may have misplaced values. In his words:

> I wish we could do the same thing for burglars and drunk drivers and some of the others. My problem is that it seems like I committed the crime du jour. I mean had I got drunk and run over the same 12-year-old girl and killed her I probably would have got three years (in prison) and it all would have been over with. But, to use a vulgar term, her ass was worth more than her life.

Sex offenders see registration in its current form as particularly frustrating and the source of many problems in their lives. Registrants call into question the consistency and proportionality of registries when compared to other criminal justice policies and practices. Changes in the process and form of registration would seem to placate offenders and increase their perceptions of registries as a fair and just tool for society.

Registrants' Suggestions for Improving the Sex Offender Registry

As indicated above, nearly all registrants identified and advocated changes to the structure and form of the registry or the registration process. Although numerous suggestions for change were offered, three main modifications were commonly expressed. First and most frequently and strongly articulated, RSOs desired to see the registry distinguish between types of sex offenders. Second, the process by which individuals are assigned to registration for either ten years or lifetime was questioned, and, based on their assumptions about how this determination is made, suggestions for alterations were offered. Third, restrictions on who would be provided access, and under what conditions or circumstances, were voiced by a number of RSOs.

The strong, collective call for better differentiation between types of offenders listed on the registry is a direct outgrowth of registrants' frustrations at being equated with and listed alongside offenders they define as more serious and more disdained than they perceive themselves. Nearly all RSOs offered explanations of how and why they believed they were different from other RSOs. And, again reinforcing their general support for the concept of a sex offender registry, almost all registrants acknowledged the value of having "those other kinds of sex offenders" on a registry. However, they also desperately wanted to be able to point to something on their own registry listing to show they were "not nearly as bad as some of those others on there."

Matt, a 28-year-old convicted of multiple counts of sodomy with his 15-year-old step-daughter, expressed his desire to see distinctions between listed registrants, saying:

> I just wish that they would categorize it. There's guys that are.... There—a guy rapes a 15-year-old girl, cuts her clothes off, then cuts her throat—yeah, put them on there. They need to be on there. Like myself, it was non-violent, consensual—it was wrong—but put me on there in a different category. Like the guy who was 18 and his girlfriend (was underage)—they was going together. He got charged with rape just because they broke up. That's wrong—he didn't hit her or beat her or nothing and he's in that category too—and there's no getting off of it.

Or, as Jordan suggested, "I can understand these repeat offenders and killers. We've got to do something with them."

In a related issue, a majority of RSOs also call for having an objective assessment or evaluation of registrants completed and used to determine dangerousness and registration status. It is at this point in the registration process that RSOs believe clinicians need to be included. Those who suggest that registries should have clinicians—generally mentioning psychiatrists, psychologists, or those who run sex offender treatment programs—involved in the decision also expressed a belief that presently the decisions about who is listed and whether registration is for a period of ten years or lifetime seemed random or based on little objective evidence. Whether an individual is included on the registry is not really a decision, but is based on one's conviction offenses. Determinations about length of registration are based on a risk evaluation, although many registrants believed that "the people who made this decision . . . weren't more qualified than I am to do so." Or, as another RSO stated, "the psychiatrists know who's likely to reoffend."

Having some type of evaluation completed is believed by registrants to be the first step toward limiting which convicted sex offenders are included on the registry. It is the belief of these individuals that if objective, clinically based evaluations were completed on sex offenders, those deemed to be low (or "no") risk would be unlikely to be listed. As Chris, a 67-year-old convicted eight years earlier for molestation of his granddaughter, explained:

> I don't think they should have it for people who are not a threat, not violent folks. I don't think they should have it for exhibitionists. I think some of those people are not harmful but just got screwed up somewhere along the way and need some counseling. I think the therapists who have them could sign off and say they should be or shouldn't be (on the registry). I don't think that the courts should be, I think that the therapists and doctors should be the ones to sign off. In other words, if they make that positive move to sign off that they wouldn't have to be on it.

Registrants not only call for having objective, clinical assessments completed as a tool for determining whether particular individuals should be listed on the sex offender registry, but so too is there a belief that completing a risk evaluation during the time that a registrant is on the registry would be productive. The idea here is to identify registrants that could be removed from the registry, or having their listing reflect a diminished threat level. Again, the belief is that this needs to be done by qualified, specially trained clinicians. The idea of reviewing registrants with an eye toward identifying those who need to remain on the registry and those who could be removed was thoughtfully presented by Tyler.

> I think there needs to be a way that after X amount of time people can be reviewed or interviewed again, tested, psychology-wise, to see if it's really efficient leaving these people on there for lifetime. I think after a while it's kind of not necessary.... It needs to be more about how we deal with these guys after they've been on there for a period of time. Instead of just saying they're on there and to hell with them. There needs to be like a committee to review the people on it after a certain amount of time to see if it's really serving a purpose by still listing these people on here after X amount of years.

For some registrants, having a risk evaluation completed while on the registry is perceived as providing an incentive and motivation for RSOs to pursue treatment, to avoid problematic situations, and to simply provide yet another reason for maintaining a crime-free lifestyle. However, this is not a possibility at the present time (although several registrants thought it was the case). Jordan also put forth the idea of an evaluation of registrants at some point following their listing. As he suggested,

> I've paid the price and I feel that enough should be enough. There should be some way that I could be able to cut the leash from this program, and I am not being given this opportunity and I don't think it's fair.... If I'm ever given the opportunity where I could have my name taken off the sex offender registry, I would like to see, in the future, about maybe some way a person could earn a way to get off it. Even a life sentence in prison is 20 years. A life sentence on this is until death.

Some RSOs had their biggest problem with the registry center on the fact that anyone, anywhere, at any time can access the registry and find their name, description, home address, and photograph. For these registrants they desired to see strict limits placed on who could access the registry. In essence, although claiming to support the idea of a sex offender registry in concept, these registrants believed the registry should be used primarily/exclusively by law enforcement and other "officials," not by the general public. Paul, a 52-year-old lifetime registrant who transferred his registration from another state following a rape conviction, summed up this argument and well represents the views of this set of registrants.

> I would probably change the fact that it's too easy for people to have access to a sex offender registry and then form their own opinion about the person on the registry just by the information they are looking at. If I could change anything about the registry, I wouldn't even allow people to know that person is on there unless it directly affects them personally.

An additional suggestion, although offered by only a few of the RSOs, is to remove registrants' pictures from their listings. The issue of including registrants' photographs is perceived by those calling for their removal as "an invasion of my privacy" and "just going too far, having your name and address on there should be enough." Others, however, while not necessarily liking the fact that their picture is included, recognize the reasons why they are included. The suggestions for modifications to the sex offender registry offered by RSOs directly arise from their experiences, and frustrations, with how registration has affected RSOs on a personal level. Stemming from their beliefs that "not all sex offenders are the same," these registrants believe that there should be a more detailed and careful review and classification of offenders, and these distinctions should be reflected in individual listings. Suggestions are also related to registrants' desires to be able to more carefully manage who knows about their status, and what information others are able to access about them and their offenses. This is not to imply that the suggestions which RSOs offer are without merit. Implementation of some of the approaches and structural changes that are presented in fact could be beneficial, for both registrants and the wider community.

Conclusion

The purpose of this study was to identify and understand the perceptions of registered sex offenders regarding sex offender registration as a tool for public safety. Overall, this study suggests that sex offenders generally believe that the concept of a sex offender registry is a valuable and worthwhile tool. Although they may believe that registries are generally a "good thing," most still dislike being included on the registry. In addition, while seeing registration as good in concept, there is disagreement among registrants regarding the practicality of sex offender registries. Some offenders believe that goals of community awareness and increased safety are unlikely to be achieved since the registry contains a large number of offenders and requires community members to actively seek out information. Individuals holding this view simply doubt the effectiveness of registries, since they feel it is unlikely that very many citizens actually check the registry and would be able to locate a specific individual out of thousands of listed names. Conversely, many offenders are under the assumption that citizens look at the registry often and are keenly aware of who is on the registry. For those who hold this belief, there is significant impact upon the offender's lifestyle and interactions with others. This also means that for these sex offenders, the experience of collateral consequences is greater.

Sex offenders interviewed in this study also expressed mixed views in the way that being listed as a sex offender may affect recidivism. A small portion of offenders believe that registries are able to prevent reoffending. Among those believing this, most offenders believe that registered sex offenders are more carefully watched and monitored by society and would be likely suspects when sexual offenses do occur. However, the majority of sex offenders hold the cynical view that registries are highly inefficient and ineffective for reducing recidivism.

Commonly, sex offenders expressed a belief that registries could deter future sex crimes if changes were made in the format, structure, and process of sex offender registration.

Overwhelmingly, the main flaw that offenders saw in the current system was the failure to distinguish between different types of sex offenders and the "one size fits all" mentality displayed in the current form of the registry. This sentiment was typically coupled with the belief that individually they were not the same as the "other" registrants, perceiving themselves as neither dangerous nor predatory.

A second frustration held by many offenders was the process by which registrants were assigned to lifetime or ten-year registration. Most offenders did not feel that this process was well thought out and failed to show uniformity. They also expressed discontent at the fact that they were "trapped" with being listed on the registry for a predetermined period of time. Here it is important to recall that other studies have shown that offenders viewing punishment as too severe or inescapable may be more likely to reoffend (Sherman and Berk, 1984; Petersilia and Deschenes, 1994). In the eyes of many registrants, the use of lifetime registration may be an overly strict and restrictive sanction. This may be especially damaging for registrants convicted as teenagers or during their early twenties.

A final suggestion for improvement mentioned by a number of sex offenders was the accessibility of the registry. Some offenders were frustrated with the fact that any person can access the registry for any reason, at any time. Most registrants did not question whether law enforcement officials should have access, but they did not understand the rationale for allowing registries to be accessible to others. In the minds of many offenders this simply invites harassment, stigmatization, and increased collateral consequences.

In the end, this study both identifies how sex offenders subject to registration and community notification perceive their sanctions and identifies suggested possible improvements to the format, process, and structure of sex offender registries. While the perspective of offenders is often of minimal concern to those who oversee and implement sex offender registry programs, the insights provided by offenders may offer opportunities for modifications which could lead to a more efficient and effective system. In order for the goals of decreased recidivism and community awareness to be achieved, changes may need to be made to meet the needs of both offenders and society.

Critical Thinking

Tewksbury finds varied opinions as to whether the registry serves as an effective deterrent. The minority of participants who claim that community members regularly consulted the registry think that the policy was an effective deterrent. However, most participants claim that the registry does not serve as a deterrent or reduce recidivism and is not consulted regularly by community members. Although the participants describe many issues with the current implementation of the policy and provide several suggestions for improvement, no participants suggest complete eradication of the policy. How effective do you think the sex offender registry is in reducing recidivism? If you were given the task of improving the effectiveness of sex offender registries, how would you change them based on the findings of this study?

References

Adams, D.B. (2002). *Summary of state sex offender registries, 2001*. Washington, DC: U.S. Department of Justice.

Adkins, G., Huff, D., and Stageberg, P. (2000). *The Iowa sex offender registry and recidivism*. Des Moines: Iowa Department of Human Rights.

Dodge, M. and Pogrebin, M.R. (2001). Collateral costs of imprisonment for women: Complications of reintegration. *Prison Journal, 81*(1), 42–54.

Duwe, G., Donnay, W., and Tewksbury, R. (2008). Does residential proximity matter? A geographic analysis of sex offense recidivism. *Criminal Justice and Behavior, 35*, 484–504.

Harding, D. (2003). Jean Valjean's dilemma: The management of ex-convict identity in the search for employment. *Deviant Behavior, 24*(6), 571–596.

Levenson, J.S. and Cotter, L.P. (2005). The effects of Megan's Law on sex offender reintegration. *Journal of Contemporary Criminal Justice, 21*(1), 49–66.

Levenson, J.S. and Tewksbury, R. (2009). Collateral damage: Family members of registered sex offenders. *American Journal of Criminal Justice, 34*, 54–68.

Makkai, T. and Braithwaite, J. (1994). Reintegrative shaming and compliance with regulatory standards. *Criminology, 32*(3), 361–386.

Mustaine, E.E. and Tewksbury, R. (2008). Registered sex offenders, residence, and the influence of race. *Journal of Ethnicity in Criminal Justice, 6*, 65–82.

Pawson, R. (2002). *Does Megan's Law work? A theory-driven systematic review*. ESRC UK Centre for Evidence Based Policy and Practice: Working Paper 8. London: University of London. (Available at: http://www.evidencenetwork.org/cgi-win/enet.exe/biblioview?780.)

Petersilia, J. and Deschenes, E.P. (1994). What punishes? Inmates rank the severity of prison vs. intermediate sanctions. *Federal Probation, 58*(1), 3–8.

Pogrebin, M., Dodge, M. and Katsampes, P. (2001). The collateral costs of short-term jail incarceration: The long-term social and economic disruptions. *Corrections Management Quarterly, 5*(4), 64–69.

Quinn, J., Forsyth, C., and Mullen-Quinn, C. (2004). Societal reaction to sex offenders: A review of the origins and results of the myths surrounding their crimes and treatment amenability. *Deviant Behavior, 25*(3), 215–233.

Sherman, L.W. (1993). Defiance, deterrence, and irrelevance: A theory of the criminal sanction. *Journal of Research in Crime and Delinquency, 30*(4), 445–473.

Sherman, L.W. and Berk, R.A. (1984). The specific deterrent effects of arrest for domestic assault. *American Sociological Review, 49*(1), 261–272.

Szymkowiak, K. and Fraser, T. (2002). *Registered sex offenders in Hawaii*. Honolulu, HI: Department of the Attorney General.

Tewksbury, R. (2002). Validity and utility of the Kentucky sex offender registry. *Federal Probation, 66*(1), 21–26.

Tewksbury, R. (2004). Experiences and attitudes of registered female sex offenders. *Federal Probation, 68*(3), 30–33.

Tewksbury, R. (2005). Collateral consequences of sex offender registration. *Journal of Contemporary Criminal Justice, 21*(1), 67–81.

Tewksbury, R. and Levenson, J.S. (2009). Stress experiences of family members of registered sex offenders. *Behavioral Sciences and the Law, 27*, 611–626.

Tewksbury, R. and Mustaine, E.E. (2006). Where to find sex offenders: An examination of residential locations and neighborhood conditions. *Criminal Justice Studies, 19*, 61–75.

Williams, K. R. and Hawkins, R. (1992). Wife assault, costs of arrest, and the deterrence process. *The Journal of Research in Crime and Delinquency, 29*(3), 292–310.

Zevitz, R.G. and Farkas, M. (2000a). Sex offender community notification: Managing high risk criminals or exacting further vengeance? *Behavioral Sciences and the Law, 18*(2–3), 375–391.

Zevitz, R.G. and Farkas, M. (2000b). *Sex offender community notification: Assessing the impact in Wisconsin*. Washington, DC: National Institute of Justice.

Zevitz, R.G. and Farkas, M. (2000c). Sex offender community notification: Examining the importance of neighborhood meetings. *Behavioral Sciences and the Law, 18*(2–3), 393–408.

28

Keeping Families Together: The Importance of Maintaining Mother–Child Contact for Incarcerated Women

Zoann K. Snyder

Abstract: *Snyder examines the effectiveness of special visitation programs designed to keep imprisoned mothers and children connected. Using semi-structured interviews with incarcerated mothers, she discusses their perspectives about how their children are coping with the separation, their concerns for their children, their views of their roles as mothers, and their post-release needs. Snyder suggests that keeping mothers and children connected may produce positive behavioral and emotional outcomes for both the mothers and their children that could possibly reduce correctional costs and increase community safety.*

Contemporary U.S. crime control policy stresses individual responsibility for crime, with an emphasis on such retributive penalties as mandatory minimum sentences, determinate sentencing structures, habitual offender statutes, and truth-in-sentencing policies. Such policies do not take into account the social, political, and economic factors that may contribute to an individual's criminality. This focus also fails to take into account the social connections damaged or severed by state intervention. Failure to consider the personal situation of the offender when punishing can have devastating consequences for the family of the offender. This devastation can be particularly severe for women offenders and their children.

Women prisoners carry the burden of a criminal conviction and the violation of societal norms about what good women and mothers are supposed to be. Although state penal codes do not explicitly state that women with criminal convictions are bad mothers and should be denied contact with their children, contemporary correctional practices often result in the loss of family contact and control for incarcerated mothers. More recent studies (cf. Hagan and Coleman, 2001; Radosh, 2002) have proposed that punishing incarcerated mothers with separation from and loss of contact with children may be more deliberate than has been previously acknowledged.

Although many readers may presume that children are better off separated from their criminal mothers, I discuss why that assumption is not necessarily true and may be a greater threat to the well-being of affected children and mothers, and to the safety of the larger community. The popular argument "Why should I pay for criminals to have family privileges?" prompts a critical and overlooked question: "What will be the harm if incarcerated mothers and their children are not kept together?"

Greene, Haney, and Hurtado (2000) called for the need to listen to the voice of incarcerated women to better understand the issues for mothers and their children. They suggested that one can learn from the women themselves their needs and, hopefully, provide better, more relevant services to women and children at risk. Toward that end, the current research addresses how incarcerated women and their children are affected by the forcible separation of incarceration. Through the use of interviews, incarcerated mothers were encouraged to share their perceptions of how incarceration has impacted their children, their relationships with their children, their perceptions of themselves as mothers, and the needs they see for themselves and their children post-release. A demographic overview places the women interviewed within the larger frame of offenders and prisoners in the United States.

Demographics

The separation of children from their families due to a parent's incarceration is a large and growing problem. The U.S. Bureau of Justice Statistics (BJS, 2000) estimated that nearly 1.5 million children had at least one parent in prison in 1999. This number represents an increase of more than 33 percent since 1991. In state institutions, 65 percent of incarcerated women and 55 percent of imprisoned men had at least one minor child (younger than age 18). Of these minor children, 22 percent were younger than age 5 (BJS, 2000). Nearly two-thirds of women housed in state prisons reported living with their minor children prior to their incarceration as compared to 44 percent of men (BJS, 2000). Proportionately more mothers (46%) than fathers (15%) were the sole care provider for their children prior to arrest. The majority of incarcerated fathers' children (90%) were reportedly living with the child's mother, whereas only 28 percent of the children of imprisoned mothers were with the child's father (BJS, 2000).

Between 1990 and 2000, the women's prison population increased by 108 percent while the men's population grew by 77 percent (BJS, 2001). Although men remain the numerical majority of the incarcerated population, the incarceration of women has the potential for greater impact on minor children. When a father goes to prison a child is more likely to live with his or her mother, whereas the children of incarcerated mothers are more likely to be passed along to other family members (BJS, 2000).

The growing number of incarcerated women increases the proportion of minor children who will be impacted by family separation. The disruption caused by the mother's incarceration is impacting more children and for potentially longer periods as mandatory minimum sentences and truth-in-sentencing guidelines increase the length of confinement. The majority of these young children will not be living with their fathers. Consequently, these children may be at risk of placement in foster care and/or permanent loss of their mothers as their primary guardians.

Punishment Versus Rehabilitation

The majority of incarcerated women are serving sentences for nonviolent crimes and drug offenses (Belknap, 2001; Pollock, 1999). Radosh (2002, p. 310) argued that the current get-tough-on-crime approach "does not fit either the crime or the offender" when it comes to women:

> Women's crime commonly reflects prior life experiences with men who clearly perpetrated serious criminal acts, such as childhood sexual molestation, rape, incest, and domestic violence. The fact that such offenders frequently were not prosecuted or punished cannot frame the defense of women in their current offense. Yet the underlying injustice inherent in societal tolerance of suffering on one level, while overreacting to less crime on another level, frames a basic violation of human rights.

Although all criminal offenders are subject to state penalties, the impact of women's punishment extends beyond the individual offender. Two-thirds of incarcerated women are mothers to minor children and were living with these children immediately prior to their incarceration (BJS, 2000). Crime control efforts do not recognize the harm being extended to children when state officials punish mothers with forcible removal from their children (Radosh, 2002). The physical separation of incarcerated mothers from their children may rightfully be addressed as a crisis for the family members involved. This particular occurrence needs to be viewed within the context of families that may already be at risk due to physical, emotional, and sexual abuse; addiction to drugs and alcohol; mental illness; unemployment; or poverty (Adalist-Estrin, 1986; Gabel, 1992; Greene et al., 2000; Myers, Smarsh, Amlund-Hagen, and Kennon, 1999; Sharp and Marcus-Mendoza, 2001). Many young children will face changes in caregivers and possibly their home environments (Koban, 1983; Myers et al., 1999; Phillips and Harm, 1997; Schafer and Dellinger, 1999; Sharp and Marcus-Mendoza, 2001). Most children will be placed with family members which may include the same individuals who reportedly abused the incarcerated mothers (Greene et al., 2000; Sharp and Marcus-Mendoza, 2001).

These life changes often extract a sizable toll on the emotional and behavioral well-being of the children. Researchers have noted that children are harmed when separated from their mothers (Bloom and Steinhart, 1993; Clark, 1995; Gabel, 1992; Greene et al., 2000; Hairston, 1991; Johnston, 1995; Kampfner, 1995; LaPoint, Pickett, and Harris, 1985; Martin, 1997; Myers et al., 1999; Schafer and Dellinger, 1999; Schoenbauer, 1986; Sharp and Marcus-Mendoza, 2001; Young and Smith, 2000). Children experience a gamut of emotions: anger, fear, depression, anxiety, and frustration. Behavioral problems may also occur, such as truancy, poor school performance, expulsion from school, running away, fighting and aggression toward others, and conflict with caregivers (Gaudin, 1984; Henriques, 1982; Johnston, 1995; Kampfner, 1995; McGowan and Blumenthal, 1976; Myers et al., 1999; Sach, Siedler, and Thomas, 1976; Sharp and Marcus-Mendoza, 2001; Stanton, 1980).

Children who witness their mother's arrest may suffer from posttraumatic stress disorder and fear of state agents such as the police and court officials (Hannon, Martin, and Martin, 1984; Kampfner, 1995; LaPoint et al., 1985; Myers et al., 1999). Although none of these authors suggests that state officials actively intend to punish or harm the children of adult offenders, the failure to provide for the needs of children to be with their mothers penalizes the children for their parent's behavior.

The extant literature has also noted the connection between a child having an incarcerated parent and ending up in the criminal justice system (Bloom, 1993, 1995; Gabel, 1992; Greene et al., 2000; Henriques, 1982; Johnston, 1995; Light, 1993; Moore and Clement, 1998; Muse, 1994; Thompson and Harm, 1995). The estimates of how many children with a family history of incarceration end up in the justice system are varied. About half of all incarcerated women have at least one family member who has been incarcerated (BJS, 1994). Muse estimated that about one-third of incarcerated juveniles have had at least one parent who has been incarcerated. Regardless of the actual numbers, there is evidence to suggest that an intergenerational link exists between parental incarceration and children entering the criminal justice system as defendants. More attention is needed to examine the connection between parents' imprisonment and children engaging in juvenile and/or adult criminal behavior.

The temporary separation caused by prison may become permanent for some incarcerated women and their children. Hagan and Coleman's (2001) critical analysis of the 1997 Adoption and Safe Families Act (ASFA; Public Law 105–89) indicated that efforts to shorten children's stays in foster care may impede or prevent family reunification post-release. Under the ASFA, the state may initiate termination of parental rights when children have been in foster care for 15 of the preceding 22 months. With an average sentence length of 18 months, incarcerated women may lose custody of their children if there are no other caregivers and the children are placed in foster care. Although intended to prevent children from being housed long term in the foster care system, ASFA may be used as a "second sanction" for mothers in prison who are viewed as not fulfilling their parenting roles as required by the state (Hagan and Coleman, 2001, p. 359).

Hagan and Coleman (2001) noted that the ASFA presumes that foster care is not safe-keeping for children. Its supervision should be limited and children placed with permanent caregivers as soon as possible. But state action creates the need for foster care. State officials claim that children should not spend too long in foster care. The language of the law creates a presumption of parental failure when mothers are incarcerated and unable to provide for the daily living needs of their children. The policy fails to take into account the state's responsibility for the forcible separation rather than child neglect or abandonment by the mothers.

Incarcerated mothers who seek to parent from prison encounter numerous obstacles. Institutional policies in place to control the conduct of prisoners may hinder efforts at communication and contact between incarcerated mothers and their children. Incarcerated mothers face such communication barriers as limits on number and length of phone calls, restrictions on days and times of visitation, and geographical distance between the institution and the location of families (Bloom, 1995; Clement, 1993; Hairston, 1991; Snyder, Carlo, and Mullins, 2001; Young and Smith, 2000). Institutions with restrictive visitation policies or limited parenting services may further erode mothers' efforts to maintain their roles as parents (Beckerman, 1991; Coll, Miller, Fields, and Mathews, 1997; Young and Smith, 2000).

Incarcerated mothers no longer have their children in their custodial care. They have concerns for the emotional and physical safety and well-being of their children (Browne, 1989; Hairston, 1991; Koban, 1983; LaPoint et al., 1985; Moore and Clement, 1998; Sharp and Marcus-Mendoza, 2001; Snyder et al., 2001; Thompson and Harm, 1995; Weilerstein, 1995; Young and Smith, 2000). The mothers also experience guilt about failing their children, anxiety about their parenting abilities, and remorse for being removed from their children (Baunach, 1985; Browne, 1989; Clark, 1995; Moore and Clement, 1998; Young and Smith, 2000).

Release back into the community will not be the end of mothers' concerns and needs. The transition to life in the community and with their children has many pressures for women. There will be multiple demands on their time as they attempt to satisfy the requirements of parole, such as establishing a permanent residence, seeking and securing employment, caring for children, and possibly attending substance abuse treatment and counseling. Harm and Phillips (2001) noted a complex relationship between substance abuse, familial relationships, and employment for women post-release. Anxiety about meeting the needs of their children while attempting to fulfill requirements of supervision may overwhelm some women. Although children may be seen as positive motivators for women, they can also be stressors that trigger substance use/abuse to cope. It will be difficult for women to meet all of the technical requirements of parole and still fulfill societal expectations of mothers (Richie, 2001; Young and Smith, 2000).

Research Setting

Given the issues of concern for incarcerated mothers and their children, the current research examines if and/or how women and children remain connected during incarceration and the impact that such contact has on their relationships. The Nebraska Correctional Center for Women (NCCW) in York, Nebraska was the research site. The research participants were women with one or more minor children who were incarcerated at NCCW in 2000. The targeted participants included women who were participating in the Mother Offspring Life Development (MOLD) program. MOLD provides classes in parenting, child development, and personal development, and onsite overnight and day visits for women prisoners and their children. The MOLD program has been in place since 1974 and is the first and oldest continuously operating mother–child visitation program offered in any U.S. prison. MOLD requires that women who want to take part in the program enroll in and complete a portion of the parenting classes prior to having special visitations with their children. These women must also maintain a good institutional conduct record to begin and retain the specialized visits. These visits take place at the prison but in an atmosphere very different from that of the standard visitors' room. Through MOLD, mothers are permitted to meet with their children in a more neutral environment where guards are not present. During these visits, the women and children are permitted to have close contact and play games, build crafts, read, and so on.

Methods

The current research was designed with the intent of enabling and empowering incarcerated women to identify and discuss the issues of concern central to them and their families. Through personal interviews, the incarcerated mothers were invited to engage in a dialogue about their roles as mothers and their interaction with their children. The interview questions and format were developed using feminist standpoint epistemology (cf. Harding, 1991; Stanley and Wise, 1993), and emphasized the importance of understanding incarcerated mothers' concerns from their position and not according to socially defined perspectives of mothering.

Efforts were made to reduce the hierarchical structure often found in traditional interviews (cf. Finch, 1981; Oakley, 1981). Interviews were completed with only myself and one woman present at a time. Questions were offered as prompts for conversation, and the women were encouraged to expand upon issues as they chose. Topical areas of interest were grouped together, but the numbering of questions was not rigidly adhered to in order to facilitate a more normal conversation.

The sample was limited to the first 50 participants who met the research criteria. A total of 25 mothers active in the MOLD program and a comparison group of 25 mothers not in MOLD participated. The women in the comparison group were not receiving visits through the MOLD program but were not prohibited from doing so by the NCCW, the Nebraska Department of Correctional Services, or any other legal restrictions. Women could not receive visits if they had not completed the required parenting classes. Lack of space availability, children living out of state or too far from the institution to make regular visits, or caregivers for the children who could not or would not bring the children to the prison may have prevented participation.

The women were asked a series of open-ended questions focusing on their experiences as mothers and their separation from their children. Central to the inquiry were their observations about their relationship with their children, how incarceration has impacted them and their children, and their plans following release. Text from the interviews is used throughout this article to give voice to the women's observations. It is important to note that the names of the mothers and their children have been changed to protect their privacy.

Findings

Maintaining Contact with Children

The women at the NCCW have a variety of media for maintaining contact with their children, including cards and letters, telephone calls, audio- and videotapes, messages communicated through friends and family members, and regular visitation in the standard visitors' room. MOLD program participants also have the opportunity for on-grounds visits and overnight stays for younger children. Most mothers have nearly the same opportunities for contact with their children with few institutional restrictions. Whether women are able to access these opportunities, however, is affected by social and financial considerations. Some women reported that family members have placed phone blocks or refuse incoming collect calls. Lynelle (not in the MOLD program) addressed this issue:

> My ex has no kind of long distance, so collect calls are out of the question. My fiancé told me that he'd call my ex and offer to bring my daughter to my house where I could call and talk to her, but as of yet I don't know whether that's gonna happen.

Geographical distance, time constraints, or lack of money necessary for onsite visits may preclude regular family contact for some women. Other mothers noted that their children are in juvenile facilities, jail, or treatment programs and are unable to visit. Caregivers for children may refuse visits in the best interests of the child. Laura (non-MOLD) addressed why she does not have visits with her preschool-age son: "Yeah, they [her family] thought that if he came up here, it would damage him in some way and so they chose not to have him come up."

With regard to the frequency of written or phone contact, a greater proportion of MOLD mothers (88%) reported writing several times per month in comparison to non-MOLD mothers (75%). MOLD and non-MOLD mothers are equally likely (48%) to receive several letters per month from their children. MOLD mothers (84%) are more likely to have several phone conversations per month with children in comparison to non-MOLD mothers (64%). A greater proportion of non-MOLD mothers (36%) than MOLD mothers (24%) communicate with their children through family members.

Family members can provide a vital link that may otherwise be missing between mothers and children. Laura was able to have some contact with her son through her mother and brother:

> My brother will tell him that "your mom called and she loves you" and "she called and she was asking about you." I get lots of pictures and he sees pictures of me and they talk about me every day. My mother said on the phone that she missed me and wanted a picture of me and so I sent a picture and he pointed to me and said "mommy," so he knows. I haven't seen him for 342 days.

Bonnie, a MOLD participant, reflected on the importance of letters in her relationship with her children:

> Being in communication through correspondence has opened up a different facet of our relationship because we've really never been apart and the written word is something I think that you can hold onto and look back on and read over and over again. It's not something like a phone call or even a conversation that is just gone. It's there in black and white, so I think in that way it's been helpful.

There is a significant difference between the MOLD and non-MOLD mothers with regard to regular visits and the frequency of such contact. The majority of MOLD program participants (92%) reported visits from their children in the standard visitors' room, whereas less than half of the non-MOLD women (48%) have face-to-face contact with their children. For the mothers receiving visits with children, 65 percent of the MOLD mothers have at least monthly contact as compared to 33 percent of the women not participating in MOLD.

Although the frequency of contact other than visitation is comparable for the two groups of mothers, there is a significant distinction when physical contact is addressed. MOLD mothers and their children have more regular contact in comparison to mothers not in the MOLD program. Mothers in MOLD suggested that their contact visits form the basis for phone calls and letters. The women and their children discuss their recent time together or plan future visits. It is very likely that phone calls, cards, and letters are the links that strengthen the connection between mothers and children. Regular communication may help mothers and children feel less awkward when they come together for visits. Extra-visitation exchanges may provide greater continuity in relationships than can be achieved through traditional visitation alone. Regular contact may also account for why MOLD mothers do not have significantly greater extra-visitation communication in comparison to non-MOLD mothers. Frequent visits may take the place of additional phone calls, cards, and letters.

Mothers' Observations About Their Children

Another essential component of inquiry was the mother–child relationship. The women were asked questions regarding how they view their relationships with their children and their perceptions of how their incarceration has affected their children.

The variable for a mother's assessment of her relationship with her child/children was coded into dichotomous categories of "fair to good" and "poor to none." More MOLD mothers (92%) than non-MOLD mothers (80%) reported that their relationships with their children are positive, but these assessments are tempered by the reality of families divided by incarceration.

One MOLD mother, Celine, spoke with candor of her relationship with her children:

> It's a good relationship, but there's a lot of room for improvement. They're mad that I came here. Well, I was incarcerated from 1995 to 1998 and I got out on parole, and then in 1999 I came back, so that really angered them that I didn't do good and had to come back.

Monica (MOLD) addressed the difficulties she is experiencing with her children:

> My relationship with my children is not where I want it to be at this point in their lives. There's a lot of damage. My youngest daughter, they're getting ready to terminate my rights as a parent, and I'm trying to just soak her in as much as I can. I'll probably lose her before I get out of here. My oldest daughter I'm struggling with because I know she's going through a lot and I know that there are some problems at her dad's house. I feel frustrated. I have no control, and I think that's got to be one of the worst things about being incarcerated is that you don't have any control and you know that your children are hurting and there's nothing you can do about it. It's almost like just holding my breath and pray that they can hold on.

Janine (non-MOLD) provided insight about what is needed to improve her relation-ship with her children:

> I think it's as good as it can be for the moment. I think on the phone they're reassuring that they love me and I reassure them. We talk about different things and we try to give them a lot of positive reinforcement. I think that their trust was broken by my parole violation.

When asked how their incarceration has impacted their children, MOLD mothers were more likely than non-MOLD mothers to suggest that their children are having difficulty dealing with the incarceration. A greater proportion of non-MOLD mothers (23%) than MOLD mothers (4%) felt that their children are coping with their incarceration.

The concern that children are having difficulties dealing with their separation from their mothers was expressed by Tamica, a MOLD program participant:

> My kids get counsel. They counsel once a week and that's good because they have a lady that comes and talks to them. They also work with the counselors at their school. I don't know. When I see my children, I almost feel like it's weird because I get this sense that they are desensitized somehow. Just like with my son, some children at that age it would've happened to them, they would've been crying. My son didn't even do that. He didn't share a tear. I'm not trying to read too much into that, but it almost makes me wonder if they are not used to [the separation] already, that, okay, this is what might happen sometimes. I might be taken from mom. Mom might be taken from me. Dad might be taken. So we're just going to numb ourselves to not show any emotion. I'm just so scared that that's happening with them.

Tamica reported having twice-monthly contact in the traditional visitors' room with her son, who is too old for on-grounds visits. Her younger children see her weekly, either in the regular visits or in the MOLD area.

Rose, another MOLD mother, discussed her preschool-age daughter:

> Well, when I first got here, she was—I could tell that she had anger towards me from the way she acted out, and as I'm getting closer to going home, her attitude changes when she comes to visit. It's easier for her to leave. She doesn't cry anymore. When we talk on the phone, you know, it's just simple conversation. So she's understanding now that I'm where I'm at. My mom felt that there was probably a little bit of abandonment, thinking she was abandoned by me. That's basically why my parents keep bringing her up every week, and I'm allowed to call home every day to keep us close to reassure her that I did not abandon her. She's like me where when we're hurt, we express it more in anger.

Maria (non-MOLD) has contact visits with her children about twice a year, though she indicated weekly phone conversations. She feels that her children have benefited from her incarceration:

> I think [her incarceration has] affected them in a positive way. In the beginning they were very angry. It was tough at first because they were very angry at me, but I think as I explained to them how I've changed and how things are gonna change when I get home, I think they've let go of that anger. They're starting to regain that trust.

There are several things to consider from these responses. Regular visits provide mothers with the opportunity to see their children and to talk about what is happening in their lives. The reality of incarceration is clear and perhaps less frightening when children can visually confirm that their mothers are okay. Deeper communication into thoughts and feelings may be more difficult to express or address in letters and relatively brief phone calls. Younger children do not have the language skills to express their feelings, and body language cannot be intuited from phone calls or letters. MOLD mothers' participation in parenting classes may also provide them with more skills with which to observe and communicate with their children. Mothers with more contact time with their children may have a more balanced and realistic view of their children and their children's emotions.

It is important to note that although children's health and well-being may be intact, this does not preclude the possibility that children are negatively impacted by separation from the mother. The positive aspects of visitation and contact do not completely offset the trauma and pain of living apart. Rather, the mothers with more stable connections to their family may have a broader and more informed perspective on their children and their children's lives.

Mothers' Views of Their Roles as Parents

The mothers were also asked to discuss their roles as parents. The women reflected on how incarceration affects them as mothers. The question was divided into categories of "coping" and "difficult and painful." MOLD mothers were slightly more likely to indicate that they are coping with their incarceration than were non-MOLD mothers. In all, 72 percent of the MOLD mothers and 76 percent of the mothers not in the program were candid about the pain and anxiety associated with being separated from their children. Although MOLD participants may have more opportunities to explore their roles as mothers through parenting classes and other related activities, they are still apart from their children. Contact visits and communication cannot completely offset the loss and pain incurred through incarceration.

Women not in the MOLD program shared their experiences:

> It's hard. It hurts a lot. I had to put my trust in God because I can't do much until I get out. I don't really feel like a mother anymore in here.
>
> (Jaycee)

> I think for me the hardest thing was my fear. The first time I didn't fear it. I don't know why. The first time here was good. It really was. It was not fun but it was not hard either. This time it's been miserable from the day I got here and I don't want to come back. I don't want my children to have this. It's hard knowing that they may not want me to be a part of their life. They may not want me around.
>
> (Janine, reflecting on her second incarceration)

Mothers who participate in MOLD noted similar feelings about how incarceration has affected them as mothers:

> It's tore me down. I've spent the past seven years ... I've spent all this time being a mother and nothing else. That was my main thing in life. That was my career. I guess you could say it's damaged me, the fact that I'm gonna have to try to get over the fact that I wasn't there for my kids for two years.
>
> (Josie)

> At times I feel guilty. I feel like I should be there with them and helping to take care of them. I feel like I abandoned them. A mother should be there. My mother was there to raise me and I should be there with them.
>
> (Meg)

> It's been a huge kick in the ass, a lot of guilt, a lot of shame.
>
> (Monica)

The anxiety, guilt, shame, and fear for their children during their separation add to the pain of incarceration experienced by many of the women in the NCCW. These issues are compounded for the mothers who do not have regular contact with their children. The enforced estrangement from their children causes anguish during the mothers' incarceration and flavors how they think about their lives post-release. With an awareness of how incarceration has affected their roles as mothers, the women were asked to discuss their future needs.

Needs and Plans for the Future

The final question put to the women was what types of services could be offered to help the mothers and children following release. The four categories of the question were "shelter and subsistence needs," "counseling and therapy," "more parenting classes and support groups," and "nothing more is needed." Significant differences were expressed by the two groups of mothers regarding their post-release needs. The primary concern expressed by the majority of mothers is the need for ongoing counseling and therapy for themselves and for their children. In all, 68 percent of the non-MOLD and 48 percent of the MOLD mothers identified counseling and therapy as an important need. In addition, 12 percent of the non-MOLD women said subsistence concerns, such as shelter, food, and employment, are their primary needs. Additional parenting classes and support groups were viewed as necessary by 20 percent of the women in MOLD and 12 percent of the women not in the program. Nearly one-third of the MOLD mothers indicated that no further services are necessary following release, as it is up to them to make their own way in the community.

The women's concerns for after their release were summed up by two of the mothers:

> I think that they should have some kind of housing for women that stay in Nebraska with their children because a lot of times when they get out and they don't have anywhere to go to so they leave their

children with their mother, and then they get stressed out and go to drugs or drinking or whatever problem that come the first time. If they had a halfway house or some kind of organization out there that would benefit the mother and the child, it would give the mother some responsibility because they don't give them any responsibility when they're in prison. The only thing they do is give them $100 and 99 percent of these women don't have nowhere to go, so they go back to what they know best.

(Rowena, non-MOLD)

I'm gonna need more parenting classes. I know that for a fact. When I had my oldest, when I got pregnant, my case workers let me in . . . a program for teenage mothers . . . I really feel like I'm gonna need a visiting nurse just to get me back into things with my kids, or a family support worker. I had one of those when I was in foster care. Something like that to get you back into the swing of being with my children and the things they like to do and did want to do. . . . It's just that I'm gonna need somebody to support me through—my bond with my kids is really strong—but through reuniting after being gone for so long. I'm gonna need a support person.

(Randi, MOLD)

There are differences in the women's views of post-release needs. Mothers participating in the MOLD program identified with the need for both counseling/therapy and a parenting support group following their release. Women not in the MOLD program expressed the most concern for counseling and therapy services. The mothers' recognition of needs and the resources to provide these services are very much at odds with one another. Community-based programs for drug and alcohol abuse counseling are limited primarily to Narcotics Anonymous and Alcoholics Anonymous or programs for a fee. Community mental health programs do exist but are often stretched for financial support and/or human resources to meet the demands for services. Most of the women expressed concerns about their financial status post-release and will likely not have the resources necessary for private counseling services. The findings leave the paradox of those most in need of services being least likely to receive them.

Criticisms of MOLD and the NCCW

Although many of the women spoke favorably of the MOLD program and its staff, parenting classes, and institutional staff, there were criticisms aimed at institutional personnel and programs. A total of 28 percent of the women interviewed noted that they do not the have the opportunity to speak about their concerns as parents. The lack of opportunity was attributed to several different sources.

Some women reported that the prison administrator in place at that time did not support the MOLD program or parenting initiatives. Carrie, a MOLD participant, expressed her feelings about MOLD and its place in the prison:

The program is great because that's what keeps us in touch with our kids and that's what makes— the warden, she's trying to cut it out. She just don't want it here and the institution, they're not fighting for us to keep it. You have inmates that aren't fighting for us to keep it because they don't have any children, so they don't care if we have the program or not. It's the institution that will eventually make the program fall.

Kaylee (MOLD) voiced a similar concern:

> Now since Warden Wayne is gone, it's like nobody cares. There's talk that they should get rid of the MOLD program. If people do, like the TV people come, the staff people come and talk to them, but the real people that has real concerns, they're afraid to let it all come out. They just hush it up like it's really wrong.

Staff indifference was cited as a barrier to talking about family concerns: "I don't think the staff really care about your kids, but other women will listen to you, yeah. The staff, you're just a number to them. They're just doing their job," said Brenna (non-MOLD). "These people don't give a darn. They have parenting classes but they're a joke, so you're pretty much kind of on your own," said Carrie (MOLD).

Janine, not in the MOLD program, did not talk about her parenting concerns due to lack of confidentiality: "I don't really share much with the other women. I have people I talk to, but I stay to myself. The minute you tell somebody something or share something, it's everywhere. I don't like that."

For other women, institutional programming is tailored more toward women in crisis or for mothers with marginal parenting skills:

> We take classes and stuff, but it's really more surface. There's too many for us to be a one-on-one kind of thing. . . . To be quite honest, I don't think it has [affected her relationship with her children] because this is stuff that I already know because even if you're the worst parent, these are things that maybe strengthen you or things that I already knew and did.
>
> (Celine, MOLD)

> If you're not a drug addict or an alcoholic or not an habitual offender or something like that, you really don't get much.
>
> (Naomi, non-MOLD)

As with most programs, MOLD is not able to meet all of the needs of all of the women incarcerated in the NCCW. Although it is unlikely that any one project could provide complete user satisfaction, the women offered insights into their needs and expectations that could be integrated into institutional or community-based parenting services.

Summary

Mothers in the MOLD program have more regular visitation with their children and a higher frequency of visits than do mothers not in the program. These visits can form the foundation for understanding and caring for their children. The parenting classes combined with visitation may enable the women to identify their needs during and after incarceration. Empowering and privileging the voices of mothers in prison can provide the knowledge necessary to better serve women and families impacted by incarceration. Their needs must be central to and addressed by community-based and institutional programs.

Institutional programs designed to help incarcerated mothers meet post-release demands are crucial for mothers' successful transition back into society. Incarcerated women do not stop being mothers despite their geographical separation from their children. Martin (1997) found that imprisonment did not break the family ties for all women. She noted the existence of *connected mothers*, defined as women who had "not only legal custody, they also had an emotional connection with their children and a mature grasp of their needs" (p. 3). Although she noted that not all women can become connected mothers, institutional programs and services can provide a valuable support structure for mother–child relationships.

Contact visits can comfort both mothers and children. Speaking face-to-face and visually confirming one another's well-being can reduce anxiety and fear for both mothers and children. Although onsite visitation cannot reproduce the normalcy of daily living for families, it can provide a means for mothers and children to build or retain relationships. Such bonds may help facilitate post-release reunification.

Critical Thinking

In light of Snyder's findings, how do you think the pain and loss the women describe hampers their recovery? How do you think the pain and loss of their children affects their current and future behavior? Why do you think the non-program mothers believe their children are coping better, even though they enjoy less contact with their children than the other mothers?

References

Adalist-Estrin, A. (1986). *Parenting from behind bars* (Family Resource Coalition Report No. 1). Jenkintown, PA: Parent Resource Association.

Baunach, P.J. (1985). *Mothers in prison*. New Brunswick, NJ: Transaction Books.

Beckerman, A. (1991). Women in prison: The conflict between confinement and parental rights. *Social Justice, 18*(3), 171–183.

Belknap, J. (2001). *The invisible woman* (2nd edn). Belmont, CA: Wadsworth/Thomson Learning.

Bloom, B. (1993). Incarcerated mothers and their children: Maintaining family ties. In *Female offenders: Meeting the needs of a neglected population* (pp. 60–68). Laurel, MD: American Correctional Association.

Bloom, B. (1995). Imprisoned mothers. In K. Gabel and D. Johnston (eds), *Children of incarcerated parents* (pp. 21–30). New York: Lexington Books.

Bloom, B. and Steinhart, D. (1993). *Why punish the children? A reappraisal of the children of incarcerated mothers in America*. San Francisco, CA: National Council on Crime and Delinquency.

Browne, D.C.H. (1989). Incarcerated mothers and parenting. *Journal of Family Violence, 4*(2), 211–221.

Chesney-Lind, M. and Immarigeon, R. (1995). Alternatives to women's incarceration. In K. Gabel and D. Johnston (eds), *Children of incarcerated parents* (pp. 229–309). New York: Lexington Books.

Clark, J. (1995). The impact of the prison environment on mothers. *Prison Journal, 75*(3), 306–329.

Clement, M.J. (1993). Parenting in prison: A national survey of programs for incarcerated women. *Journal of Offender Rehabilitation, 19*(1/2), 89–100.

Coll, C.G., Miller, J.B., Fields, J.P., and Mathews, B. (1997). The experiences of women in prison: Implications for services and prevention. *Women & Therapy, 20*(4), 11–28.

Finch, J. (1981). "It's great to have someone to talk to": The ethics and politics of interviewing women. In H. Roberts (ed.), *Doing feminist research* (pp. 70–87). London: Routledge & Kegan Paul.

Gabel, S. (1992). Behavioral problems in sons of incarcerated or otherwise absent fathers: The issue of separation. *Family Process, 31*, 303–314.

Gaudin, J.M., Jr. (1984). Social work roles and tasks with incarcerated mothers. *Social Casework, 65*, 279–286.

Greene. S., Haney, C., and Hurtado, A. (2000). Cycles of pain: Risk factors in the lives of incarcerated mothers and their children. *Prison Journal, 80*(1), 3–23.

Hagan, J. and Coleman, J.P. (2001). Returning captives of the American war on drugs: Issues of community and family reentry. *Crime & Delinquency, 47*, 352–367.

Hairston, C.F. (1991). Mothers in jail: Parent–child separation and jail visitation. *Affilia, 6*(2), 9–27.

Hannon, G., Martin, D., and Martin, M. (1984). Incarceration in the family: Adjustment to change. *Family Therapy, 11*(3), 253–260.

Harding, S. (1991). *Whose science? Whose knowledge?* Ithaca, NY: Cornell University Press.

Harm, N.J. and Phillips, S.D. (2001). You can't go home again: Women and criminal recidivism. *Journal of Offender Rehabilitation, 32*(3), 3–21.

Henriques, Z.W. (1982). *Imprisoned mothers and their children*. Washington, DC: University Press of America.

Johnston, D. (1995). Effects of parental incarceration. In K. Gabel and D. Johnston (eds), *Children of incarcerated parents* (pp. 59–88). New York: Lexington Books.

Kampfner, C.J. (1995). Posttraumatic stress reactions in children of imprisoned mothers. In K. Gabel and D. Johnston (eds), *Children of incarcerated parents* (pp. 89–100). New York: Lexington Books.

Koban, L.A. (1983). Parents in prison: A comparative analysis of the effects of incarceration on the families of men and women. *Research in Law, Deviance and Social Control, 5*, 171–183.

LaPoint, V., Pickett, M.O., and Harris, B.F. (1985). Enforced family separation: A descriptive analysis of some experiences of children of Black imprisoned mothers. In M.B. Spencer, G.K. Brookins, and W.R. Allen (eds), *Beginnings: The social and affective development of Black children* (pp. 239–255). Hillsdale, NJ: Erlbaum.

Light, R. (1993). Why support prisoners' family-tie groups? *Howard Journal, 32*(4), 322–329.

Martin, M. (1997). Connected mothers: A follow-up study of incarcerated women and their children. *Women & Criminal Justice, 8*(4), 1–23.

McGowan, B.G., and Blumenthal, K.L. (1976). Children of women prisoners: A forgotten minority. In L. Crites (ed.), *The female offender* (pp. 121–135). Lexington, MA: Lexington Books.

Moore, A.R. and Clement, M.J. (1998). Effects of parenting training for incarcerated mothers. *Journal of Offender Rehabilitation, 27*(1–2), 57–72.

Muse, D. (1994). Parenting from prison. *Mothering, 72*(fall), 98–105.

Myers, J.M., Smarsh, T.M., Amlund-Hagen, K., and Kennon, S. (1999). Children of incarcerated mothers. *Journal of Child and Family Studies, 8*, 11–25.

Oakley, A. (1981). Interviewing women: A contradiction in terms. In H. Roberts (ed.), *Doing feminist research* (pp. 30–61). London: Routledge & Kegan Paul.

Phillips, S.D. and Harm, N.J. (1997). Women prisoners: A contextual framework. *Women & Therapy, 20*(4), 1–9.

Pollock, J.M. (1999). *Criminal women*. Cincinnati, OH: Anderson.

Radosh, P.F. (2002). Reflections on women's crime and mothers in prison: A peacemaking approach. *Crime & Delinquency, 48*, 300–315.

Richie, B.E. (2001). Challenges incarcerated women face as they return to their communities: Findings from life history interviews. *Crime & Delinquency, 47*, 368–389.

Sach, W.H., Siedler, J., and Thomas, S. (1976). The children of imprisoned parents: A psychological exploration. *American Journal of Orthopsychiatry, 46*, 618–628.

Schafer, N.E. and Dellinger, A.B. (1999). Jailed parents: An assessment. *Women & Criminal Justice, 10*(4), 73–91.

Schoenbauer, L.J. (1986). Incarcerated parents and their children—Forgotten families. *Law & Inequality, 4*, 579–601.

Sharp, S.F. and Marcus-Mendoza, S.T. (2001). It's a family affair: Incarcerated women and their families. *Women & Criminal Justice, 12*(4), 21–49.

Snyder, Z.K., Carlo, T.A., and Mullins, M.M.C. (2001). Parenting from prison: An examination of a children's visitation program at a women's correctional facility. *Marriage & Family Review, 32*(3–4), 33–62.

Stanley, L. and Wise, S. (1993). *Breaking out again*. London: Routledge.

Stanton, A.M. (1980). *When mothers go to jail*. Lexington, MA: Lexington Books.

Thompson, P.J. and Harm, N.J. (1995). Parent education for mothers in prison. *Pediatric Nursing, 21*, 552–555.

U.S. Bureau of Justice Statistics. (1994). *Women in prison*. Washington, DC: Author.

U.S. Bureau of Justice Statistics. (2000). *Incarcerated parents and their children*. Washington, DC: Author.

U.S. Bureau of Justice Statistics. (2001). *Prisoners in 2000*. Washington, DC: Author.

Weilerstein, R. (1995). The prison M.A.T.C.H. program. In K. Gabel and D. Johnston (eds), *Children of incarcerated parents* (pp. 255–264). New York: Lexington Books.

Young, D.S. and Smith, C.J. (2000). When mothers are incarcerated: The needs of children, mothers, and caregivers. *Families in Society, 81*, 130–141.

29

Employment Isn't Enough: Financial Obstacles Experienced by Ex-prisoners During the Reentry Process

Mark R. Pogrebin, Mary West-Smith, Alexandra Walker, and N. Prabha Unnithan

Abstract: *One of the greatest needs for persons leaving prison and returning to their communities is immediate employment. Although this has been researched and written about by many in the field of criminology and criminal justice, this study, based on interview data obtained from 70 men and women on parole in Colorado, expands on the recognized need for employment by identifying and analyzing the additional collateral financial obligations that are rarely addressed by researchers and correctional practitioners. In addition to describing barriers to obtaining employment, we explore financial obligations that may significantly prevent ex-offenders from gaining an economic foothold even when employed, including mandatory parole expenses and other debts incurred prior to and following incarceration. Without the ability to meet these financial obligations, many returning former prisoners came to believe they will never achieve economic success. A lack of financial stability and little hope for a better future may significantly affect the ability of many persons leaving prison to successfully reenter society.*

In the past three decades, the prison population in the United States has more than quadrupled, expanding from approximately 369,000 to more than 1.5 million inmates (U.S. Department of Justice, 1982, 2012a). The tremendous growth in the inmate population has resulted in a subsequent increase in offenders returning to their communities, with as many as 730,000 offenders being released from federal and state correctional facilities per year (U.S. Department of Justice, 2011). By 2011, 853,900 persons were being supervised in the community as parolees, while 80 percent of persons who left prison that year did so under some form of parole supervision (U.S. Department of Justice, 2012b, 2012c).

The parole population is in a state of constant flux. Within one year, the membership of the parolee population changes dramatically, with almost two-thirds of the individuals on parole exiting parole through various ways, including completion of the terms of parole, return to incarceration, abscondence, deportation, and death (U.S. Department of Justice, 2012c). However, only about one-third of persons who exited parole in 2011 did so through successful reentry to their communities (U.S. Department of Justice, 2012c). More than a decade ago, two-thirds of released persons were rearrested within three years of release (U.S. Department of Justice, 2002). While there has been a great deal of variability in the return-to-prison rates in individual states over the last decade, the frequency of parole failure remains stubbornly high (Pew Center on the States, 2011).

It has been long recognized that there are several circumstances linked to successful reentry, including employment that pays wages that cover basic living expenses (Travis and Petersilia, 2001). However, the use of criminal justice fees associated with parole conditions, such as payments for drug testing, treatment, and monitoring, are increasingly being assessed and may reduce available funds to pay for basic expenses (Bannon, Nagrecha, and Diller, 2010). Restitution, child support, and additional mandated expenses may also be contributing to financial barriers to successful reentry that available employment cannot overcome.

Literature Review

Individuals returning to their communities do not experience equally the multiple dilemmas of reentry, but the vast majority encounter difficulties in various areas of adjustment. Employment opportunities, access to governmental benefits, stable housing, treatment programs, family support, access to health care, and a positive parole experience are needed for successful reentry (Naser and La Vigne, 2006; Travis and Petersilia, 2001). Becker (1968) recognized decades ago that loss of human capital creates additional challenges for reentering prisoners. The depreciation of human capital resulting from incarceration diminishes prospects for success in many areas, but it is especially problematic when ex-offenders are trying to find employment. If employment is found, it is commonly unskilled work that pays low wages (Becker, 1968; Kling, 2006). Western, Kling, and Weiman (2001) note that the experience of discrimination in employment and lowered chances for economic success for reentering prisoners has been well established.

Ex-inmates have lower earning capacities and rates of employment when measured against comparable groups (Freeman, 1992; Grogger, 1995; Lyons and Pettit, 2011; Western et al., 2001). Compared to 18 percent of the general population that does not have high school diplomas, 68 percent of inmates reported having not completed high school, while approximately quarter received their GED certificates, which serve as high school equivalency assessments, while serving time in an institution (U.S. Department of Justice, 2003). People who lack the education and training employers value have difficulty finding employment, but, as Pager (2003, p. 956) notes, "criminal records close doors in employment situations." Pager also found that employers stated they were twice as likely to hire nonoffenders as they were to give jobs to equally qualified offenders. According to Holzer, Raphael, and Stoll's (2007) study involving employer surveys, two-thirds of the respondents reported that they would not hire people with criminal backgrounds. Additionally, only 6 percent of those surveyed reported that they would be willing to employ people who not only have criminal backgrounds but who also have spent time in prison, leaving 94 percent of these surveyed employers as apparently viewing persons with prison stays ineligible for employment in their organizations.

Job applicants may try to hide their past criminal records by not informing prospective employers of their prior incarceration (Harding, 2003). In a study of formerly incarcerated persons' perception of stigma, more than one-third of the study participants reported that they had avoided disclosure of their criminal histories on job applications in an attempt to avoid rejection based on their ex-inmate status (LeBel, 2012). This risky strategy is effective primarily in situations where the job is short term or where background checks are not required (Harding, 2003). More desirable jobs, especially those that have mandatory background checks, are likely out of their reach, since ex-inmates are unable to conceal their former inmate status.

Having a family support system has also been shown to be important for successful reentry (Kushel, Hahn, Evans, Bangsberg, and Moss, 2005; La Vigne, Visher, and Castro, 2004). Providing a home when a person leaves prison greatly relieves many financial pressures, but family members can also improve job opportunities for returning ex-prisoners through their network of friends, employers, and religious institutions (Visher, Debus-Sherrill, and Yahner, 2008). Parolees who find employment shortly after release often do so by making use of connections through friends and family members with whom they maintained contact during their incarceration (Cobbina, 2009; Mallik-Kane and Visher, 2008; Nelson, Dees, and Allen, 1999; Visher and Kachnowski, 2007). Without the help of family and friends, returning ex-inmates are likely to face much longer periods of time before finding employment, if they find it at all (Nelson et al., 1999).

Parolees who were employed prior to incarceration may be able to reestablish contact with former employers prior to release, which improves their chances of quickly finding employment (Visher et al., 2008). However, since many former inmates do not have decent legitimate employment records, few likely can take advantage of such former relationships. Although one of the best ways for ex-prisoners to find work is through family, community, and former employment contacts, many persons leaving prison lack connections that can lead to employment since many of their contacts in the community may be criminally active and are not in the position to offer leads for legitimate employment (Hagan, 1993). Their stigmatized backgrounds, their deficiencies in education and appropriate skills, and their lack of prosocial contacts can affect many ex-inmates' ability to find work, which can inhibit both their current and future economic status (Pager, 2003; Western, 2006; Western et al., 2001).

The stakes for quickly finding employment are high for persons returning from prison. Parolees generally must have jobs to meet their parole conditions, and the inability to find and keep work can result not only in a marginalized existence, it may also result in a return to prison for violation of parole requirements. However, employment alone may not be sufficient for many persons leaving prison, since employment that may barely cover basic living expenses likely will not pay enough to meet the additional financial obligations that many parolees confront as they leave prison. Debts incurred prior to incarceration may continue to mount while a person is in prison. Griswold and Pearson (2005), in a study of child support obligations of incarcerated parents, found that parents often enter prison with thousands of dollars in unpaid child support and by the time they leave prison, the arrears they owe include not only the original debt but interest and child support accumulated while in prison. In addition to child support obligations, ex-inmates are often released from prison with significant financial liabilities, such as court costs and fees, tax deficiencies, and other domestic bills (Richards and Jones, 2004).

In the 15 states with the largest prison populations, expenses frequently assessed through the criminal justice system include restitution and fees associated with parole supervision, alcohol and drug testing, and mandatory treatment (Bannon et al., 2010). Additional noncriminal justice obligations, such as child support and "poverty penalties," including late fees, interest fees, payment plan fees, and collection fees associated with the inability to pay debts, may further reduce funds available to cover basic living expenses and may contribute to a return to prison (Bannon et al., 2010, p. 19). Such fees may discourage ex-inmates from seeking legitimate employment if wages are garnished and income tax refunds are intercepted to pay debts incurred through criminal justice and other legal obligations.

Finding and maintaining employment, having a residence at which a parolee can be contacted, submitting to and paying for medical and drug testing, and paying fees and restitution are now common standard conditions of parole (Travis and Stacey, 2010). An increasing dependence on surveillance and ongoing treatment and testing in the community has shifted the costs from the supervising authorities to persons leaving prison. In the past, employment that ex-inmates may have had access to and that may have provided wages sufficient to pay for minimal living expenses might not be sufficient to cover the now-mandated additional expenses associated with parole.

While some states allow prisoners to voluntarily "max out" their sentences, thereby forgoing parole supervision (Ostermann, 2011, p. 596), Colorado is not one of these states. In 1993, the Colorado Legislature passed H.B. 93–1302, which requires felony offenders to serve mandatory parole periods of one to five years after their first release from prison. From 1995 to 2011, the average daily parole population in Colorado increased from 1,185 to 8,422 (Colorado Department of Corrections, 1999, 2013), a much larger increase than would be expected, based only on the increase in the prison population. With the dramatic increase in the parole population, the number of individuals returned to prison for parole violations also increased. From 1997 to 2013, the percentage of Colorado parolees who exited parole by returning to prison for technical violations of parole rose from 16.5 percent to 40 percent (Colorado Department of Corrections, 1999, 2013), despite many intermediate sanctions steps taken by Colorado to minimize the number of parole violators returned to prison. In stark contrast, the national percentage of exits from state parole by return to prison for technical violations dropped from 25 percent to 21 percent between 2008 and 2011, and in 2012, this number dramatically decreased to 14 percent, largely driven by California's efforts to curtail the use of prison as a response to technical parole violations (U.S. Department of Justice, 2013). Nonetheless, Colorado's percentage of parolees who exit parole by returning to prison for technical violations is significantly higher than the national average.

Maintaining employment, if one is not physically or mentally disabled, is a typical parole condition requirement. Without the ability to find and maintain employment, parolees may have little chance of avoiding reincarceration. However, merely finding employment may not be sufficient to overcome other financial barriers that may prevent parolees from gaining any type of financial stability and, thus, a foothold in conventional society.

The purposes of the current study are multiple. First, we explore the employment and financial challenges that parolees confront as they leave prison in Colorado. Second, we seek to improve our understanding of how additional financial burdens may prevent parolees from achieving financial security. Finally, we focus on how such burdens and financial insecurity may create conditions where parolees believe they cannot successfully reenter society.

Method

The current study was approved by both the Colorado State University Institutional Review Board and the Colorado Department of Corrections, the parent agency of the Division of Adult Parole. Data were collected from 70 parolees: 48 males and 22 females. The ethnic/racial composition of our study population was 45.6 percent Anglo, 31.5 percent Hispanic, and 18.4 percent African American, which closely mirrors the ethnic and racial composition of the inmate population in Colorado. We recruited study participants from four district parole offices, two in urban locations and two in suburban areas, all within the greater Denver metropolitan area. The age range of respondents was from 23 to 57 (median = 29 years old) and the incarceration lengths ranged from one to 20 years (median = 5.8 years). Median time on parole at the time of the interview was 18 months.

We used a purposive sampling technique to contact potential research participants. We had approval to contact parolees at the time they had appointments to see their parole officers, to describe our research, and to ask if they were interested in participating in the research. Each person was told the purpose of the study and if they agreed to participate, they signed a consent form approved by the Colorado State University Institutional Review Board (IRB). With the exception of one male parolee who declined to participate, all of the parolees we contacted agreed to be study participants. Study participants were told that their responses would be confidential and that they could choose not to tape the interview or stop the interview at any time. All of our 70 paroled ex-prisoners were cooperative, agreed to be recorded, and seemed willing to discuss the problems they were facing on parole. The men and women who were interviewed appeared to be open and frank in relating their personal experiences, although at times relating difficult experiences was an emotionally painful process. While there is always concern regarding potential harm to research participants, as Linn (1997) noted, relating their stories may allow respondents to better comprehend their feelings about what they have experienced.

Findings

Reentering offenders are in desperate need of employment to financially survive and to successfully complete the mandates of parole, but they may be in the position of facing a vast majority of employers unwilling to consider hiring them. This leaves very few employers and jobs available for the hundreds of parolees leaving Colorado prisons each month, most of whom appear to be competing with each other for the same low-wage positions. The accounts of our study participants revealed the difficulty and frustrations involved in trying to find work, which rarely resulted in employment shortly after leaving prison.

Seeking Employment

Felony convictions and incarceration hampering a search for employment were common themes among our research participants, as related by one male parolee.

> I request an application, I'll go in there and fill it out and I'll return it, give it back to them. About a week or two later I'll give them a call back just to check on the status of my application, and they just say "They don't hire felons." That's the way it is. Or they tell me, "We will call you back," or something like that. But I never hear back.

This particular parolee's rejection in his job search was typical of the vast majority of our study participants.

At times, temporal circumstances prevented some of our study participants from obtaining employment; they claimed that they were not yet out of prison when a job they could have had opened up. One married 37-year-old male parolee expressed his frustration in trying to get a public transportation position.

> They were like "Sorry, we could have hired you back then" [when I was still in prison]. I could have had a job with RTD (Regional Transportation District) Access. Those small buses where they pick up elderly and mentally challenged people. I now have to wait four and a half months. I applied seven or eight months ago, me and my wife ... she went ahead and filled out the application with me for the hell of it and she ended up getting a job.

In this parolee's account, his wife was laid off from a credit union where she had worked for nine years. She had no criminal history and had excellent job references and was selected to be a Regional Transportation District (RTD) driver, the job her husband was seeking. The paroled applicant continued to try to get a job with RTD and was quite persistent in his attempts to gain employment with the public bus line.

> I've been keeping contact with the district manager there. He knew me after I got my ankle bracelet off. I called him and he says, "There's another issue. They (RTD) want to make sure that you have been driving for a year. If you're still unemployed after a year, I'll hire you."

Returning ex-offenders often find themselves in "Catch-22" positions due to restrictions and requirements of parole that can inhibit a successful job search. Many people on parole are prevented from attaining certain types of employment due to state laws or parole rules. For example, they often cannot have a driver's license until a certain period of time has elapsed without a violation of parole. Such restrictions place many positions that pay decent wages out of reach. While this study participant had been led to believe that he could have had the job if only he had been out of prison, the requirement that he have held a valid license for one year prior to being hired would have prevented him from obtaining this desirable job shortly after leaving prison.

Job applicants may try to hide past criminal records from prospective employers, a risky strategy since not reporting one's past criminal history may be considered a technical violation of the conditions of parole and can result in a return to prison. However, parole officers may use their discretion to overlook this type of violation if the parolee is employed and complying with the other conditions of parole. For most jobs, employers conduct criminal background checks, but these checks are often not completed before the applicant is hired. Lying about a criminal history that is later discovered through a background check is grounds for termination. One participant described how he was willing to take this risk and was able to obtain and keep a job, despite failing to disclose his criminal history.

> I kind of told a white lie at my interview. It was the only way I could get my foot in the door. They (Subway) were interviewing hundreds of people. The lady that I was interviewing with, I told her that I was married and that my wife got in a car accident and passed away that's what I told her, to get in the door . . . I'm 49 years old and I've been welding for some years. So, working in a sandwich shop, well, I had to do something to start paying the rent at the halfway house. I needed money coming in. I had to have a job to keep on parole, so I kind of told a white lie to get that job. Once I got in the door and showed them how hard I could work and everything, I 'fessed up and told them the truth.

This parolee, the only person out of all who were interviewed for this study who admitted to being deceitful on his job application, was very fortunate to not be fired when his criminal history came to light. His employer did not terminate him and he had been working for seven months at the time he was interviewed for this study. Many employers are likely to not be so willing to retain an employee who not only lied on a job application but who also had a criminal record that included time spent in prison.

Family Networks and Employment

About 40 percent of our study participants resided with their families upon release from prison. These respondents found employment more readily than those who did not parole to their families' homes. Numerous examples clearly demonstrated the role that family support and family members' knowledge of available jobs or contacts played in helping parolees find work. In the following examples, employers knew the respondents had been in prison and these parolees were able to find work without having to conceal their former inmate status or to face background checks. One male parolee described finding work through his mother's contacts.

> Luckily, my Mom knows the owner and is good friends with her. They go to the same church. She talked to her before I came home. So that's how I got the job. But, I put in many, many applications, several a day for weeks, and to this day, since I got out (eight months ago), I haven't got a call back once.

Another parolee offered an explanation of how he found work through friends of his father.

> My dad's got a lot of friends that have small farms, so I've been helping them all summer, tossing hay bales and doing all kinds of different stuff. My dad and uncle always do side work, like we built a cow shed. Stuff like that's been basically keeping me afloat. For a couple of months I had a job. That was nice.

While one study participant described that he was fortunate his mother owned a construction company that hired him immediately upon release, ex-inmates typically come from families with low socioeconomic backgrounds and do not have family members who own profitable and legitimate businesses that can provide the type of employment required to meet parole conditions. Some of our study participants had family members and relatives who played major roles in utilizing community networks to help them find employment, but many returning parolees do not have family members who are willing or able to help them with their job searches. These parolees often depend on friends or acquaintances they knew prior to their imprisonment to help them find work.

Friend Networks and Employment

One female study participant described being fortunate to be rehired as a waitress where she had worked prior to incarceration. At the time of the interview, she had been promoted to night manager. However, her experience was uncommon among our research participants. Many men and women in our study had poor employment histories prior to incarceration and could not contact former employers and realistically hope to be rehired as they left prison.

A more common theme was that of using connections parolees had in their communities prior to their imprisonment, as described by one male participant.

> I have a friend that has got his own remodeling business. I have known him for 10 years, from the streets. He used to be my neighbor. I told him "Hey, I'm back out. I need work." [He said] "Okay, come on over." I remodel houses, drywall, and install floors.

Another ex-offender described making use of friendship connections.

> The best way to find jobs is through a friend or somebody you know. You ask around. You go there first. 'Cos that's how 90 percent of people get jobs, through somebody they know. Then, from there, you crack down on other jobs, try to make them better. If it's crappy, you deal with it and then try to make it better. You try to get a better job.

At the time of the interview this respondent held two jobs, both found by using his network of friends and acquaintances.

One important condition of parole is to not have contact with persons who have criminal records or those who are involved in criminal behavior. These restrictions are designed to prevent parolees from reconnecting with criminally oriented friends and falling back into criminal lifestyles. While they may reduce the chances of connecting with former criminal associates, they can also significantly narrow many offenders' networks of friends and acquaintances who could potentially offer job information tips.

Finding employment in recent years has been made even more difficult for persons leaving prison. Employment for citizens who have no criminal history has been difficult in our nation's depressed labor market and many unemployed law-abiding persons compete for similar low-wage positions that, in the past, ex-offenders were often able to obtain. Thus, the burden of finding any employment for those with a criminal record has been made even more challenging.

Employment Isn't Enough: Additional Financial Obligations

Parolees are expected to find work that pays wages adequate for self-sufficiency. Paying for room and board, if one is not living with family members, is just the beginning of many parolees' financial obligations. Some obligations are internal to parole, such as payment for drug testing, mandatory treatment, court costs and fines, and restitution. Other legal obligations outside of the conditions imposed by parole may include child support, tax liabilities, and family debt incurred prior to or during incarceration.

Financial Obligations Related to Parole

Ex-prisoners who are not able to live with family members after release and who reside in halfway houses as per their parole plans face additional pressures to find work. Halfway houses in Colorado are operated by private for-profit or nonprofit vendors and have rules regarding rent payment. One halfway house resident spoke of the challenges he encountered in finding work.

> We went out Monday through Friday about 7:30 a.m. in the morning until 4 p.m. in the afternoon looking for jobs. There were quite a few guys there in the halfway house, and I think about 60 to 80 of us were looking for work every day. There were some guys that had been there for months and hadn't found work.

Halfway house rents average approximately US$400 per month, which parolees are obligated to pay (Colorado Department of Corrections Parole Officer, personal communication, February 20, 2014). Many of our study participants who resided in halfway houses did not find employment for months, which meant that when they did find jobs, they owed several months' back rent. The majority of jobs parolees secure pay minimum or close to minimum wages and are often not full time. If they do finally find work, much of their income goes to the halfway house to pay the back rent and they may find themselves no better off than they were when unemployed. As one parolee related, his stay in the halfway house did not ease his return to the community.

> I think I was there (the halfway house) about a month and a half before I found work. My checks were going straight to the halfway house. I didn't even get money for the bus or any funds for anything from my payments. The halfway house took my whole check and didn't give me any of it. I'm still paying them off, actually.

Offenders are often paroled to a halfway house as part of their initial parole plan developed prior to their release from prison. Approximately 25 percent of our sample were parolees who were required to live in halfway houses upon release. These individuals may suffer the greatest financial burden when compared to other ex-prisoners who reside with their families or those who end up staying in homeless shelters. An important point to note is that if halfway house residents do not pay all of the rent monies owed, they have violated the conditions of their parole and can be returned to prison on a technical violation for nonpayment. Many of our study participants who had paroled to halfway houses spoke of a fear of returning to prison because they had accumulated large debts which they were having difficulty paying.

In many instances, the courts include restitution payments as part of the felony sentence. Restitution technically is not "punishment," but, rather, a requirement that offenders reimburse their victims for the victims' financial losses. The restitution obligation follows individuals during their time in prison and payment of restitution is attached as a condition for parole. The determination of the monthly amount of money paid to the victim by the offender is usually set by the parole officer. Payments can vary depending on the parolee's employment status and amount of income earned, and may increase over time if the ex-offender earns a higher salary in the future.

Payments for restitution, charges for mandatory drug and alcohol testing, supervision fees, and mandatory treatment expenses may all be conditions of parole. The total number of required payments was succinctly summed up by one participant.

> It's not that I don't like my job. It's an alright job. I mean, it's not something I want to spend the rest of my life at, that's for sure. Nobody wants to work at Wendy's forever. I get, like 18 to 25 hours a week. I have bills to pay. I've got restitution payments, supervision fees, child support, [and] I've got to live. I've got UAs (urine tests for drug use), BAs. I get like $300 a paycheck, and that's for two weeks. A person can't live off that.

Another study participant described the difficulty of meeting the financial obligations for parole.

> I have restitution, which is $152 every month. And then I have three UAs a month, so that's $45 a month and a $10 parole supervision fee, so that's about $207 a month.

This parolee was fortunate to not have to make payments to a halfway house, since, unlike the majority of our respondents, he lived with his parents and did not have to pay rent. Despite this advantage, he was struggling to meet his financial obligations in order to remain compliant with his parole conditions, since the only work he could find was part-time minimum-wage work. In addition, like many in our study, he was not eligible to receive benefits, such as health insurance, sick pay, or retirement, due to his part-time employee status.

Many of our research participants were unclear about the restitution they were required to pay. Unlike other states that do not rely as heavily on restitution, Colorado makes extensive use of restitution and many persons leaving prison do so with significant debts owed to their victims. The majority of offenders do not have the assets to repay their victims prior to leaving prison and few of them obtain employment that provides sufficient income to repay their victims in a timely manner. None of the interviewed parolees knew if they were obligated to pay the entire amount of their restitution. However, they had been told that being discharged from parole was not contingent on a full repayment of their restitution. Even parole agents we spoke with informally were unclear as to what happens to restitution requirements once the other conditions of parole had been fulfilled. When a parolee is discharged from parole, there is no mechanism for ensuring that restitution payments continue. The remaining restitution balance may be sent to collection, which further damages the credit of an individual attempting to make a clean start.

Financial Obligations External to Parole

Besides parole-required payments, additional financial obligations such as child support and other prior debt may create problems for persons leaving prison. In some cases, prior liabilities may affect family members on the outside. One participant described how his child support debt affected his wife after he went to prison.

> Schooling is very important to me, but right now I need money. We are homeowners and we have bills. I had an issue; they took my wife's income because of my past obligations when I was in prison. I owed back child support; they took all of her income tax refund, $6,800, to pay for it.

He and his wife were not able to start over debt-free, which, according to this respondent, would have allowed him to change his life by pursuing an education when he left prison.

Parole Success

A few participants related more positive economic situations. One woman planned for her release from prison by not using the savings she had prior to being sentenced. Another female respondent described her careful use of money while in prison.

> I had just saved it. I basically used it very minimally. I only used what I needed. I wasn't greedy. When I got out I had enough money to get my own place. It's not the best. It's a little two bedroom.

She was also employed and, unlike many of the research participants, she stated that between her job and her prior savings, she had no trouble paying for her parole-mandated programs.

One respondent described how an unexpected income tax return helped him become less reliant on his parents.

> I was living with my parents and I would borrow money from them. On my birthday I got an income tax return for the last year I was out, and that helped a lot. That really kind of covered my expenses that I had to pay for, UAs and everything. Really, I was just lucky.

Inmates who were able to plan for their release and who had the ability to leave prison with some financial resources identified themselves as lucky to be able to meet the mandated expenses required of parole. These individuals appeared to be much less likely to run into problems with technical violations of parole related to nonpayment of mandated parole expenses than their "unlucky" counterparts who left prison with little money, who paroled to halfway houses, who had extreme difficulty in finding employment, and who had multiple financial obligations they had little hope of being able to pay.

Parole Failure

Between interviews with parolees, we spoke casually with parole officers and supervisors about the financial mandates for parole. From these conversations, we learned that it was not uncommon for parolees to abscond or return to criminal activity because they felt overwhelmed by the payments they were unable to make. This was especially true for halfway house residents who were in debt for large sums of money and had no legitimate way to make payments. Study participants who paroled to halfway houses spoke of the dilemma they faced: fearing a return to prison for failing to pay a debt they felt was impossible to overcome or making a decision to abscond because they felt that a return to prison was inevitable.

In addition to the difficulty in paying off halfway house debt, the inability to pay for mandated parole programs, such as required treatment and urine analysis (UA), can result in a technical violation and a potential return to prison. Respondents explained that if one shows up for a UA and is unable to pay, the company giving the test for drug use counts the parolee as a no-show. Two or more missed UAs are grounds for a technical parole violation. One unemployed parolee described his decision to abscond because he was not able to pay for his required UAs and group counseling sessions and was in danger of being returned to prison for a technical violation.

> The first time I absconded for nine months so they caught me. The second time I missed four UAs and four group sessions because I didn't have a job. The place that I took the UAs at told me I couldn't take them anymore.

This offender's explanation for absconding was not unique. In short, parolees' inability to pay for parole mandates that require access to money they do not have may push them to abscond and into parole failure.

Ex-offenders on parole who have difficulty finding employment also suffer frustrations from their inability to find work and, as the following account demonstrates, these frustrations can lead to negative consequences.

> It's most stressful. Either you go out and get a job right away, or you're looking and looking. And because you have so much time on your hands, you go back to your old life, relapse, or go back and hang out with the homies.

Not only can unemployment and associating with felons be violations of parole, reconnecting with criminal associates and living the "old life" can result in a return to prison for committing new crimes.

Discussion

Our focus for this study was on financial problems encountered by people leaving prison. As such, this article does not address additional collateral problems, such as mental illness, poor health, drug use, lack of housing and transportation, and other reentry challenges, that many offenders face upon their release from prison and return to their communities (Petersilia, 2003; Pogrebin, Dodge, and Katsampes, 2001). We also did not address racial/ ethnic, gender, or age differences because we did not find significant differences between these groups in our sample. However, the median length of time on parole in our sample was 18 months and we likely did not have a good representation of individuals who failed quickly on parole, where racial/ethnic, gender, and age differences may be more apparent. Rather, the stark contrast in our sample appeared to be between those who had access to housing and/or employment help as they left prison and those who were trying to "make it" on their own. Despite the length of time many of our research participants had been out of prison and on parole, the problems they emphasized more than any others related to the financial challenges awaiting them upon release and that subsequently continued and often increased throughout their time on parole.

Parolees must often turn to family members for help, which can be humiliating. One participant described his primary focus as "Getting a job . . . paying for my parole, my UAs, and all that stuff. [So] I won't have to ask people to help me with money." It must be understood that our study consisted of adults and not juveniles. Not having enough money to pay the mandated parole requirements and having to depend on others can place adult ex-inmates in childlike and dependent situations where they may be perceived by others as the same irresponsible individuals they were before they were convicted and imprisoned.

Those who are not able to achieve long-term and legitimate successes are often viewed by the wider society as possessing individual deficits that result in their economic failure. Without the necessary social capital via economic capital that is so highly regarded in American society, ex-prisoners confront nearly insurmountable odds against becoming productive and accepted citizens in this nation, even if they have a desire to do so. This is a greater challenge for offenders of color, who represent a disproportionate number of imprisoned persons. Not only do they suffer from the pains of societal and institutional discrimination (Western, 2006) they are also competing with many other ex-offenders who are very much like them: individuals who are poorly educated, have minimal legitimate employment histories, and are returning to impoverished communities that offer few chances for legal employment that pay wages sufficient for the basic necessities of life, let alone the additional payments required for successful parole completion.

A large percentage of formerly incarcerated men and women may be free from their inmate status but may later find themselves trapped by insurmountable challenges of a different nature: the longevity of stigma and discrimination in a capitalist social structure which places great emphasis on economic success. It is little wonder that reentry so often fails, since for the vast majority of returning felons the odds of attaining legitimate economic stability is almost nil, given the extremely limited financial opportunities available to them. Failure is a realistic consequence of the inability to progress economically in the short term. However, equally concerning is the foreshadowing of a future characterized by persistent failure to succeed. When one cannot succeed economically immediately upon release from prison, when debts incurred related to incarceration and to mandated parole expenses cannot be paid off, and when the future appears bleak for being able to economically succeed, it is understandable why a large percentage of parolees reoffend, abscond, or violate parole rules and return to prison.

In a five-year follow-up study of inmates released in 30 states in 2005, the Bureau of Justice Statistics reported that 67.8 percent of ex-prisoners were rearrested within three years of their release and 76.6 percent were rearrested within five years (U.S. Department of Justice, 2014). While many look at these discouraging numbers and attribute reentry failure to personal failings for individuals leaving prison, it may be appropriate to explore whether the low rate of parole success may be partially attributable to various financial challenges placed upon reentering offenders as they return to their communities. The parole system, originally designed to not only provide supervision of individuals leaving prison but to also provide support during the difficult transition from prison to life on the outside, may be playing a significant role in parole failure through the often unrealistic financial expectations that persons recently released from prison have little hope of meeting.

Our study participants' accounts were filled with frustration and hopelessness. As Wanberg, Glomb, Song, and Sorenson (2005) noted, the inability to achieve even a small piece of the American dream has detrimental effects that can lead to poor self-concepts and bleak futures. The heavy toll of repeated rejection can create a stigma that results in discrimination (Branscombe, Schmitt, and Harvey, 1999) and a negative self-concept (Goffman, 1963), added burdens on ex-offenders as they attempt to return to society. If, as LeBel, Burnett, Maruna, and Bushway (2008) argue, feeling stigmatized is a predictor for reimprisonment, and if hope and self-efficacy are necessary but not sufficient to desist from crime, current parole practices do little to reduce the well-known barriers to successful reentry and may create nearly impossible financial burdens, which give Colorado parolees little reason to hope that they will succeed.

Conclusion

The tremendous increase in the prison population since the 1980s required that the majority of state correctional budgets be spent on the construction of new prisons to house the growing number of inmates. This building boom, combined with the downturn of the economy, has left few financial resources for states to spend on reentry and other correctional programs designed to assist offenders in making successful transitions from prison to the community. High reentry failure rates and a continued lack of resources to adequately address prisoner reentry problems suggest that many parolees will be unable to overcome imposing reentry barriers and will continue to present society with numerous economic and social challenges.

Too many ex-prisoners on parole, as we have attempted to illustrate, are unable to acquire any type of sustainable employment and seem to be on their own as their debts mount. The system itself appears to bear some responsibility for the large amount of debt many parolees incur within a few months after they are released. If parolees encounter nearly insurmountable barriers to obtaining employment that pays enough to meet their financial obligations, if inmates are unable to accumulate "nest eggs" during the imprisonment that could help to offset some of the initial required parole expenses, and if they view parole failure and returning to prison as the likely result of parole, we should not be surprised that so many parolees are unable to successfully reenter society. The privatization of halfway houses and the use of vendors who provide fee-based UA testing, anger management groups, sex offender therapy, and other mandated fee-for-service programs appear to have added to the punitive nature of the parole system while creating barriers that many offenders simply cannot overcome. All play an important role in the "pay or fail" parole-mandated programs, where obligations related to parole place the unemployed, underemployed, and those who suffer from overwhelming financial burdens at a distinct disadvantage. Their path back to a society that cares little and understands less about the challenges these individuals face is not easy. What others see as an uphill climb may be, for many, an insurmountable mountain.

It is little wonder that our research participants all spoke of the financial challenges they were facing and most described feelings of frustration and desperation that they would not be able to "make it" on the outside. Although future research is certainly needed not only in Colorado but in other states to try to understand the full effect of financial limitations on parole success, there is little doubt that returning ex-offenders confront tremendous challenges in finding legitimate employment that allows for self-sufficiency. However, if there are additional structural barriers, such as those in Colorado, that create even more financial difficulties for individuals leaving prison, future research to examine alternative approaches for parole mandates could help to identify whether or not parole outcomes may be related to the economic requirements placed upon persons leaving prison.

Improving reentry outcomes over the last decade has been a major focus for both correctional researchers and practitioners. Practices such as the use of transitional housing and ongoing treatment to help with the change from prison existence to life in a community have been encouraged. However, if the costs of such practices are assigned to individuals who have little ability to pay for these requirements and if a threat of a return to prison for nonpayment of these debts hangs over parolees' heads, attempts to improve reentry outcomes may be making reentry for many persons leaving prison even more difficult. Finding ways to ease the mandated obligations related to parole may help many persons leaving prison to overcome some of the economic challenges they face, which, in turn, may also allow them to believe that a path to economic stability through the legitimate workforce may be more than an impossible dream.

Critical Thinking

As the authors mention, a stipulation of parole is that offenders refrain from any contact with individuals who have a criminal record of their own. What is the rationale behind this from a crime control perspective? What unintended consequences could result? How do you think this policy affects rates of recidivism?

References

Bannon, A., Nagrecha, M., and Diller, R. (2010). *Criminal justice debt: A barrier to reentry*. New York: Brennen Center for Justice, New York University School of Law. Retrieved from http://www.brennancenter. org/sites/default/files/legacy/Fees%20and%20Fines%20FINAL.pdf.

Becker, G. (1968). Crime and punishment: An economic approach. *Journal of Political Economy, 76*, 169–217. doi:10.1086/259394.

Branscombe, N., Schmitt, M., and Harvey, R. (1999). Perceiving pervasive discrimination among African-Americans: Implications for group identification and wellbeing. *Journal of Personality and Social Psychology, 77*, 135–149. doi:10.1037/0022-3514.77.1.135.

Cobbina, J. (2009). *From prison to home: Women's pathways in and out of crime*. Retrieved from http://www. ncjrs.gov/pdffiles1/nij/grants/226812.pdf.

Colorado Department of Corrections. (1999). *Statistical report: Fiscal year 1998*. Colorado Springs, CO.

Colorado Department of Corrections. (2013). *Statistical report for fiscal year 2013*. Colorado Springs, CO.

Freeman, R. (1992). Crime and unemployment of disadvantaged youths. In G. Peterson and W. Vroman (eds), *Urban labor markets and job opportunity*. Washington, DC: Urban Institute Press.

Goffman, E. (1963). *Stigma: Notes on the management of spoiled identity*. Englewood Cliffs, NJ: Prentice Hall.

Griswold, E.A. and Pearson, J. (2005). Turning offenders into responsible parents and child support payers. *Family Court Review, 43*, 358–371. doi:10.1111/j.1744-1617.2005.00039.x.

Grogger, J. (1995). The effects of arrests on the employment and earnings of young men. *Quarterly Journal of Economics, 110*, 51–71. doi:10.2307/2118510.

Hagan, J. (1993). The social embeddedness of crime and unemployment. *Criminology, 31*, 465–491. doi:10. 111/j.1745-9125.1993.tb01138.x.

Harding, D. (2003). Jean Valjean's dilemma: The management of ex-convict identity in the search for employment. *Deviant Behavior, 24*, 571–595. doi:10.1080/713840275.

Holzer, H., Raphael, S., and Stoll, M. (2007). The effects of an applicant's criminal history on employer hiring decisions and screening practices: Evidence from Los Angeles. In S. Bushway, M. Stoll, and D. Weiman (eds), *Barriers to reentry: The labor market for released prisoners in post-industrial America* (pp. 117–150). New York: Russell Sage.

Kling, J. (2006). Incarceration length, employment, and earnings. *American Economic Review, 96*, 863–876. doi:10.1257/aer.96.3.863.

Kushel, M., Hahn, J., Evans, D., Bangsberg, D., and Moss, A. (2005). Revolving doors: Imprisonment amongst the homeless and marginally housed population. *American Journal of Public Health, 95*, 1747–1752. doi:10. 2105/AJPH.2005.065094.

La Vigne, N., Visher, C., and Castro, J. (2004). *Chicago prisoners' experiences returning home*. Washington, DC: The Urban Institute.

LeBel, T. (2012). Invisible stripes? Formerly incarcerated persons' perceptions of stigma. *Deviant Behavior, 33*, 89–107. doi: 10.1080/01639625.2010.538365.

LeBel, T., Burnett, R., Maruna, S., and Bushway, S. (2008). The "chicken and egg" of subjective and social factors in desistence from crime. *European Journal of Criminology, 5,* 131–159. doi:10.1177/1477370807087640.

Linn, R. (1997). Soldier's narratives of selective moral resistance. In A. Lieblich and A. Josselson (eds), *The narrative study of lives* (pp. 95–112). Thousand Oaks, CA: Sage.

Lyons, C. and Pettit, B. (2011). Compounded disadvantage: Race, incarceration and wage growth. *Social Problems, 58,* 257–280. doi:10.1525/sp.2011.58.2.257.

Mallik-Kane, K. and Visher, C. (2008). *Health and prisoner reentry: How physical, mental and substance abuse conditions shade the process of reintegration.* Washington, DC: The Urban Institute.

Naser, R. and La Vigne, N. (2006). Family support in the prisoner reentry process: Expectations and realities. *Journal of Offender Rehabilitation, 43,* 93–106. doi:10.1300/J076v43n01_05.

Nelson, M., Dees, P., and Allen, C. (1999). The first month out: Post incarceration experiences in New York City. *Federal Sentencing Reporter, 24,* 70–71. doi:10.1525/fsr.2011.24.1.72.

Ostermann, M. (2011). Recidivism and the propensity to forgo parole release. *Justice Quarterly, 29,* 596–618. doi:10.1080/07418825.2011.570362.

Pager, D. (2003). The mark of a criminal record. *American Journal of Sociology, 108,* 937–975. doi:10.1086/374403.

Petersilia, J. (2003). *When prisoners come home: Parole and prisoner reentry.* New York: Oxford University Press.

Pew Center on the States. (2011). *State of recidivism: The revolving door of America's prisons.* Washington, DC: The Pew Charitable Trusts.

Pogrebin, M., Dodge, M., and Katsampes, P. (2001). Collateral costs of short-term jail incarceration. *Corrections Management Quarterly, 5,* 64–69.

Richards, S. and Jones, R. (2004). Beating the perpetual incarceration machine: Overcoming structural impediments to re-entry. In S. Maruna and R. Immarigeon (eds), *After crime and punishment: Pathways to offender reintegration* (pp. 201–232). Collompton, England: Willan Publishing.

Travis, J. and Petersilia, J. (2001). Reentry reconsidered: A new look at an old question. *Crime and Delinquency, 47,* 291–313. doi:10.1177/0011128701047003001.

Travis, L. and Stacey, J. (2010). A half century of parole rules: Conditions of parole in the United States, 2008. *Journal of Criminal Justice, 38,* 604–608.

U.S. Department of Justice, Bureau of Justice Statistics. (1982). *Prisoners in 1981* (NCJ 82262). Retrieved from http://www.bjs.gov/index.cfm?ty=pbdetail&iid=3366.

U.S. Department of Justice, Bureau of Justice Statistics. (2002). *Recidivism of prisoners released in 1994* (NCJ 193427). Retrieved from http://www.bjs.gov/index.cfm?ty=pbdetail&iid=1134.

U.S. Department of Justice, Bureau of Justice Statistics. (2003). *Education and correctional populations* (NCJ 195670). Retrieved from http://www.bjs.gov/index.cfm?ty=pbdetail&iid=814.

U.S. Department of Justice, Bureau of Justice Statistics. (2011). *Prisoners in 2009* (NCJ 231675). Retrieved from http://www.bjs.gov/index.cfm?ty=pbdetail&iid=2232.

U.S. Department of Justice, Bureau of Justice Statistics. (2012a). *Correctional populations in the United States, 2011* (NCJ 239972). Retrieved from http://www.bjs.gov/index.cfm?ty=pbdetail&iid=4537.

U.S. Department of Justice, Bureau of Justice Statistics. (2012b). *Prisoners in 2011* (NCJ 239808). Retrieved from http://www.bjs.gov/index.cfm?ty=pbdetail&iid=4538.

U.S. Department of Justice, Bureau of Justice Statistics. (2012c). *Probation and parole in the United States, 2011* (NCJ 239686). Retrieved from http://www.bjs.gov/index.cfm?ty=pbdetail&iid=4538.

U.S. Department of Justice, Bureau of Justice Statistics. (2013). *Probation and parole in the United States, 2012* (NCJ 243826). Retrieved from http://www.bjs.gov/content/pub/pdf/ppus12.pdf.

U.S. Department of Justice, Bureau of Justice Statistics. (2014). *Recidivism of prisoners released in 30 states in 2005: Patterns from 2005 to 2010* (NCJ 244205). Retrieved from http://www.bjs.gov/content/pub/pdf/rprts05p0510.pdf.

Visher, C., Debus-Sherrill, S., and Yahner, J. (2008). Employment after prison: A longitudinal study of former prisoners. *Justice Quarterly, 28,* 698–718. doi: 10.1080/07418825.2010.535553.

Visher, C. and Kachnowski, V. (2007). Finding work on the outside: Results from returning home project in Chicago. In S. Bushway, M. Stoll, and D. Weiman (eds), *Barriers to reentry: The labor market for released prisoners in post-industrial America* (pp. 80–113). New York: Russell Sage.

Wanberg, C., Glomb, T., Song, A., and Sorenson, S. (2005). Job-search persistence during unemployment: A 10-wave longitudinal study. *Journal of Applied Psychology, 9,* 411–430. doi:10.1037/0021-9010.90.3.411.

Western, B. (2006). *Punishment and inequality in America.* New York: Russell Sage Foundation.

Western, B., Kling, J., and Weiman, D. (2001). The labor consequences of incarceration. *Crime and Delinquency, 47,* 410–427. doi:10.1177/0011128701047003007.

30

Navigating the Job Search After Incarceration: The Experiences of Work-release Participants

Andrea Cantora

Abstract: *When prisoners return to the community they often strive to obtain immediate employment; however, finding work after being released from prison is one of the major challenges which returning prisoners face. With few employment prospects due to legal restrictions, discrimination from prospective employers, and multiple individual and community barriers offenders often end up accepting low-skilled work with little opportunity for growth. This qualitative study examines the job-searching process for women residing in a community correction work-release facility. The researcher identified several barriers to securing employment, as well as many factors that facilitated the process. Sources of help, types of jobs secured, and experiences with stigma and discrimination are discussed. Implications for improving the job-searching process for this population are discussed.*

Introduction

Each year approximately 600,000 prisoners return to the community (Carson and Golinelli, 2013). Upon release from prison, concerns about housing, employment, family reunification, and treatment needs are core issues that require immediate action. When prisoners return to the community they often strive to obtain immediate employment. Work serves as an informal social control mechanism to prevent criminal behavior (Sampson and Laub, 1993; Visher, Debus-Sherrill, and Yahner, 2011). However, finding work after being released from prison is one of the major barriers to successful re-entry (Travis, 2005; Visher et al., 2011). There is a wealth of literature on the multiple barriers returning prisoners experience when searching for employment. These include state laws preventing employers from hiring (Legal Action Center, 2004), the availability of low-skilled jobs, the correctional systems' low capacity to enhance prisoner vocational skills (Lynch and Sabol, 2001), and individual factors such as low educational attainment, unemployment history, and lack of work experience (Western, 2007). Other challenges associated with securing employment include health issues, mental health problems, and having a history of substance abuse (Visher, Debus-Sherrill, and Yahner, 2008). Most of the barriers identified are experienced by prisoners released straight to the community after incarceration, or on parole supervision. There is little research examining employment barriers from prisoners released to a work-release halfway house. This study examines women's experiences obtaining employment while residing at a work-release community correction facility.

Employment Barriers

There are many challenges related to finding work after incarceration. To start with, educational attainment levels contribute to the complexities associated with securing and maintaining employment. For example, 37 percent of state and federal inmates do not have a high school diploma or GED; and 78 percent lack postsecondary education (Greenberg, Dunleavy, and Kutner, 2007). These statistics are troubling considering that educational attainment is linked with employability and earnings. According to the U.S. Census Bureau, individuals with an associate or bachelor's degree earn more than those with a high school diploma or less (Bureau of Labor Statistics, 2003). Research finds that higher educational levels and higher earnings are correlated with lower levels of recidivism (Chappell, 2004; Visher et al., 2008). Higher education, however, is not the only indicator of employment success. Research conducted on a sample of Texas women offenders found that women with a high school diploma or GED, prior work experience, and engagement in prison job training are more likely to obtain and maintain employment within the first year of release from prison compared to women without these characteristics (La Vigne, Brooks, and Shollenberger, 2009).

In addition to limited education, many returning prisoners have poor employment histories and lack the skills necessary for securing work. Visher et al. (2011) studied former prisoners' employment experiences by examining individual factors that impact their ability to find work. They found that individuals with little to no-employment history had poorer work outcomes than individuals with a history of recent and consistent employment. There is a long-standing theory that legitimate employment enhances social ties to conventional norms, therefore decreasing crime (Sampson and Laub, 1993). Empirical research finds support for this theory—having stable employment decreases recidivism (Visher and Travis, 2003). Specifically, research finds that returning prisoners who work more hours and earn higher incomes have lower levels of recidivism (Visher et al., 2008). Furthermore, the quality of work also plays a role in future crime and social control, whereas higher quality jobs decrease criminal motivation and increase social control (Uggen, 1999).

Health factors also serve as a barrier to employment. For example, Visher et al. (2011) found that drug relapse immediately after release, and the presence of chronic physical and mental health conditions, impacted length of employment prior release. Women, specifically, struggle due to the lack of treatment options for substance abuse, physical and mental health problems, and unresolved trauma issues (Richie, 2001). Other life factors play a role as well. Obligations to pay debt also played a role in maintaining work, as did being married and having close relationships with children (Visher et al., 2011). Furthermore, women face additional work challenges because they are often the primary caregiver for young children, and access to affordable childcare is not always available (Berman, 2005; Flower, 2010; Richie, 2001). For women, re-establishing relationships with family and children is critical to successful re-entry (O'Brien, 2001; Richie, 2001).

With few employment prospects and little money to support themselves, returning prisoners rely heavily on social networks. Family and friends often end up financially supporting returning family members (Mallik-Kane and Visher, 2008). Although some research indicates that learning about job opportunities through social networks is often weakened as a result of incarceration (Western, Kling, and Weiman, 2001), many returning prisoners often secure job opportunities through friends, family, and former employers (Nelson, Perry, and Allen, 1999; Solomon, Roman, and Waul, 2001). Visher et al. (2011) found that one of the most successful job-searching strategies for participants was returning to a previous job. Participants in Visher et al.'s study also believed that employers were reluctant to hire them due to their criminal record. Maintaining a job after securing one was another challenge for participants. Sixty-five percent of Visher et al.'s sample found a job after release, but under half maintained their job. Relying on family and friends for financial support was a common occurrence for almost half of the sample eight months after release.

Economic conditions within communities also impact the employment prospects for returning prisoners. Considering most returning prisoners are released to urban areas, access to jobs may be a barrier. Both the loss of labor markets in urban areas, and the competition with other low-skilled residents, impacts employment options (Lynch and Sabol, 2001). While most research on labor markets and the ex-offender population has focused mostly on men, Lalonde and Cho's (2008) research on women offenders indicated that spending time in prison may actually enhance employment prospects for women rather than harm them. Their research indicates that prison time is associated with increased employment rates. Specifically, they suggest that their findings indicate women are more likely to enter the workforce after leaving prison. Although they don't elaborate on why this may be the case, it is possible that parole work requirements force women to enter the labor market.

Another major barrier to securing employment is the public perception of criminal records and the discrimination that results. When searching for work, returning prisoners must also deal with the stigma associated with having a criminal record (Sampson and Laub, 1993; Solomon et al., 2001; Western et al., 2001). Employers may view people with criminal records as untrustworthy, a threat to their business, and a potential legal liability (Holzer, Raphael, and Stoll, 2004). This stigma is known to decrease employers' willingness to hire returning prisoners, resulting in difficulties finding jobs (Pager, 2002; Petersilia, 2001). For example, Holzer et al.'s (2004) study examining employers' reluctance on hiring a person with a criminal record indicated that a majority were unwilling to hire. For women in particular, the social and economic marginalization they have historically faced adds to the barriers of finding equal work and pay after spending time in prison (Scroggins and Malley, 2010). In addition, women returning from prison face even greater stigma than their male counterparts due to their higher rates of substance abuse, mental health issues, and health-related problems (LeBel, 2012). Furthermore, LeBel found that women perceive more reasons for discrimination than men, including criminal record, gender, sexual orientation, and mental health disorders.

To alleviate some of the barriers returning prisoners experience, many states utilize community corrections programs to address employment needs. Halfway house facilities are one type of community intervention that offers returning prisoners an opportunity to secure employment, save money, and have a place to "get back on their feet" (Latessa, 2004, p. 138). Halfway houses, also called community correction facilities, were originally developed due to the ineffectiveness of traditional prison programs to reduce overcrowding, and as a cost-effective strategy to keep prisoners in the community (Donnelly and Forschner, 1987; Latessa and Allen, 1982). As described by Latessa and Travis (1991, p. 54):

> Halfway houses provide the security of a structured controlled residence, similar to incarceration, combined with the freedom of residents to seek and engage in employment and other activities in the free community.

Researchers who have evaluated halfway house programs reported that women who transitioned through these programs have lower recidivism rates than those who did not (Mackey and Fretz, 2007; O'Brien, 2002). Other re-entry programs that share common characteristics with the services provided by halfway house facilities have also been successful in reducing recidivism. For example, transitional job programs that place returning prisoners into temporary employment while also providing support services have been successful at reducing recidivism (Redcross, Bloom, Azurdia, Zweig, and Pindus, 2009). In addition, holistic case management programs that provide comprehensive services for up to two years post-release improve offenders' employment outcomes and reduce recidivism (see Rossman and Roman, 2003). Although the larger body of research on employment programs and recidivism is not encouraging (see Bushway and Apel, 2012) the studies mentioned above illustrate that some programs—especially those that include comprehensive services—are promising.

Few studies have examined the role work-release halfway houses play in helping women secure employment after release from prison. To add to the research, this qualitative study aims to answer the following questions: How do women prepare for the job market, what are the challenges of securing work, and what factors facilitate the process? In-depth qualitative interviews with 33 women were conducted and analyzed to understand the job search process. It is important to understand some of the nuanced challenges and facilitators of the employment process for women returning from prison. While evaluation research tells us whether programs are effective, qualitative studies on the process are necessary for practitioners interested in implementing, or improving, correctional employment programs.

The following section provides an overview of the work-release halfway house program. Next, a detailed description of the methods used to carry out the study is discussed. The results are then presented to illustrate the job search process. Finally, the article ends with a discussion of the findings, study limitations, and program implications for improving the employment process for women.

The Program

The Halfway House[1] follows a gradual three-phase system that provides residents with privileges as they achieve certain goals and maintain good standing in the program. Once residents arrive at the Halfway House they are required to participate in a two-week program orientation and are unable to leave the facility unescorted. During the first 24 hours of admission, residents are assigned a bed,[2] provided with linen, and meet with staff for an in-depth program orientation that covers program expectations and regulations. During the first week residents are administered the level of service inventory—revised (LSI—R) and complete an employment and educational assessment. After this, they complete a job readiness training which includes an orientation to the job-searching phase of the program, developing a resumé, how to fill out applications, and interviewing strategies. During the second week of Phase I, residents meet with their case manager to develop a 30-day service plan that includes individualized treatment goals. Residents are required to sign and follow the treatment plan and are evaluated weekly by their case manager.

After residents complete the two-week orientation, they move into the second phase of the program where they are allowed to begin job searching and receive more visitation and community privileges. All residents are required to obtain full-time employment or enroll in a full-time educational/vocational program. Residents are permitted to work part-time if they are enrolled in a part-time educational program. Residents with financial obligations (e.g., restitution or childcare) are required to work at least part-time. Residents are allowed to search for jobs from Monday to Thursday between the hours of 8:00 a.m. and 3:00 p.m., and must secure employment (or an education/vocational program) within 30 days of beginning their job search. When on the job search, residents are required to make "accountability calls" to the Halfway House once they arrive at a potential job site and before they leave. If they are at a job site for several hours, residents are required to call every two hours. In addition to making routine calls, residents are required to obtain the signature of the prospective employer to confirm their job-searching activities.

The employment counselor works with residents to identify potential employers and even provides petty cash for travel to residents with limited funds. After a resident receives a job offer, the employment counselor will visit the site and either grant or deny the resident permission to work at the selected employment site. Residents unable to obtain employment within 30 days are placed on an employment contract. The employment contract further restricts their privileges in the community and inside the house. Residents on an employment contract must continue their job search. If employment is not secured within ten days of being placed on the contract, residents face disciplinary action which could result in their return to prison. In addition to obtaining employment and/or enrolling in education programs, residents must meet weekly with their employment counselor and case manager. These meetings are arranged to assist residents with the job search and their other individual needs. During the job-searching phase, residents are eligible to receive one two-hour visit per week. Visitation and other community privileges increase once residents begin to work.

Once residents secure employment they must maintain a 35-hour work week. Residents are not permitted to leave the work site at any time during their schedule, nor are they allowed to take days off without prior approval from Halfway House staff. The employment specialist maintains contact with all employers. To ensure residents are working a full-time schedule, they are required to submit their pay stubs to program staff. After residents receive their first paycheck, they are mandated to pay 30 percent of their wages toward house maintenance fees. Residents are also required to open a savings account, maintain a budget, and are only permitted to have $50 in spending money per week.

Methods

The findings discussed in this article were extracted from interview transcripts of women residing at the Work-Release Halfway House in New Jersey. The larger study from which these findings came was designed to capture women's perceptions and experiences with prison and halfway house programming, their support systems, childhood experiences, and release plans. This article, however, focuses on women's experiences of job searching and working while at the Halfway House. The study aimed to answer the following questions: How do women prepare for the job market?, What are the challenges of securing work?, and What factors facilitate the process?

Data Collection

All women residing at a New Jersey Halfway House between June 2007 and November 2007 were eligible to participate in this study. All participants were previously incarcerated in New Jersey's Edna Mahan Correctional Facility (NJDOC). Forty-three women were residing in the Halfway House on the day of the first interview. Thirty-five women were conveniently selected (based on availability) to be interviewed and 33 agreed to participate.[3] Before each interview the researcher informed participants about the voluntary nature of the interview and that confidentiality and anonymity would be protected. After each woman agreed to participate, the researcher asked for further permission to record the interview. Twenty-nine participants agreed to have the interview recorded. Each interview ranged from 30 minutes to two hours. Drawing on existing literature, the interview protocol was structured around a series of broad questions on women's pathway to prison, their experience during incarceration, the transition to the Halfway House, daily life at the house, searching for employment, addressing other re-entry needs (e.g., housing, family reunification, and treatment), and expectations for re-entry to the community. All recorded interviews were transcribed by the researcher afterward. The researcher took detailed notes during the four interviews where participants refused to be recorded. In addition, demographic and criminal history data were collected from participant case files. Data from case files included Pre-Sentence Investigation Reports, a Correctional Facility Assessment, and the LSI—R conducted by Halfway House staff.

Analysis

Analytical memos were written throughout the interviewing process to identify early themes. This step was useful in probing participants on emerging themes, and was also used to develop an initial code list. Since the interviews covered a wide range of topics, the researcher identified subsections of the transcripts where respondents spoke specifically about searching for employment, challenges with finding work, help in securing a job, and types of employment secured. A process of initial coding then took place as a method of studying fragments of transcripts (Charmaz, 2006). As segments of transcripts were labeled using the initial code list, the researcher analyzed the meaning of the participants' words by writing additional analytical memos (Strauss and Corbin, 1998). After this step, a second analytical phase of focused coding was applied. During this phase the qualitative software program, *Atlas.ti*, was used to aid in making connections between interviews and to search for additional themes related to women's job search experience. This phase allowed the researcher to further identify aspects of the data that may have been overlooked during initial coding and also allowed for greater comparison among participants (Charmaz, 2006). This comparison method was useful in further developing themes related to the employment search process. Lastly, to develop a sample profile, the researcher reviewed case files and analyzed the data using descriptive statistics related to demographic and criminal history. Case files were especially useful in reviewing the employment history of women in the sample. Comparing participants' employment history with their job search experience was a useful triangulation method that provided greater context for their experiences.

Study Sample

The average age of interviewees was 39. Women were primarily African American (52%), followed by 27 percent white, and 21% Hispanic. The average length of time participants remained in the program was 202 days (with a range of 51–475 days). The length of time in the program varied and often depended on how much time remained on their sentence until parole eligible. More than half of the sample was unmarried (61%), and the majority had at least one child under the age of 18 (64%). Sixty percent of participants had a high school diploma or GED. Sixty-seven percent were frequently unemployed prior incarceration. Fifty-four percent had little to no work history, and 45 percent had extensive work experience. The majority of the sample had an extensive criminal history, with 58 percent having three or more criminal convictions. Sixty-four percent of the sample had a history of substance use; however, only 49 percent had a current substance abuse problem. An indication of a mental health problem was less frequently identified. Twenty-four percent of the sample reported receiving previous mental health treatment. In addition, 46 percent experienced domestic violence and 30 percent were sexually abused in their childhood.

Results

The majority of participants (76%) were able to secure employment while residing at the Halfway House. Those not working were either enrolled in a full-time education, substance abuse, or mental health program. Three participants did not find work due to health issues. Participants found work in various fields, including the medical, restaurant, fast food, and customer service. Most participants were able to secure employment within 30 days of beginning the job search, although a few took longer. The majority (64%) landed work in low-skilled jobs. Employed participants, and those actively job searching were asked various questions about the job-searching process and establishing employment. Below are several themes that emerged from the interviews. Themes are categorized into two broad categories: job-search barriers and sources of help.

Job-search Barriers

Participants shared many stories about the discouragement and anxiety of the job-searching process. Participants expressed frustration and anxiety over explaining their halfway house status, not landing a job, the inability of finding a pay phone to make accountability calls, fear of returning late to the Halfway House due to public transportation delays, legal and program job restrictions, and, for non-local participants, the stress of being unfamiliar with the area.

Double Stigma

An additional stressor, frequently cited in the literature, was the stigma associated with having a criminal record (Sampson and Laub, 1993; Solomon et al., 2001; Western et al., 2001). Experiencing stigma and employment rejection is a common experience for prisoners returning home. In this study, participants had to deal with a double stigma—having a criminal record and living in a halfway house.

During the job search, residents were required to disclose their halfway house status to potential employers. This policy was developed to hold residents accountable for all community movements, and to verify job-search activity. When out on the job search, residents were required to obtain the signature of all potential employers. Many participants perceived this policy as off-putting and several stated that they felt humiliated over disclosing their status. Similar to what other researchers found (Hattery and Smith, 2010), some participants felt that the disclosure hurt their chances of obtaining employment. According to Debbie,

> It was embarrassing. I lost a couple of jobs because of that, to tell you the truth, you know—they knew I was from a halfway house or a program and they didn't want to hire me.

Another participant, Susan, would not have disclosed her criminal status if she was living elsewhere.

> The only fear I had was, I mean I am so used to job searching. The only fear was telling them where I was coming from. If I had been on my own I would have never said it or mentioned it.

Although the majority of participants felt stigmatized and embarrassed about disclosing their halfway house status, a few participants did not appear bothered by this disclosure. They saw it as part of the process of being in a halfway house. The researcher asked a participant, Nancy, how employers react when presented with the job search verification form.

> They have to stamp it [job search form] with the company name. Basically that will show that you have been there. Me—I take care of my business. Everything else I just sit back. It is not hard for me cos I am not ashamed of as far as my criminal behavior and drug addiction. I am not ashamed. They [employers] are very understanding. If you ask them to please sign this because I am in a halfway house. You have to present yourself that you are in a halfway house so that is what I did. You need that paper stamped stating that I was there. Or if they don't have a stamp they give me their business card so I come back with that.

Although the experience was stressful, for many women going through the job search process, the rejection related to their criminal records was also perceived as beneficial. Women spoke about how the employment rejection prepared them for the reality of dealing with stigma after release from the program. They learned to manage the stress and disappointment, and how to respond to questions about their criminal history (see Cantora, 2013).

Program Regulations

Making accountability calls when out on the search was another challenge participants spoke about. Participants were fearful of missing these calls because they did not want to violate program rules and risk returning to prison. Participants described struggling to find working phones and running out of money to make calls.

You have to call every hour or every two hours when you're at a place, and that's kind of like confusing because if you had a job interview how are you going to get out the next couple of hours, you know what I'm saying? You know, when—it's kind of hard when you don't have money. They give you the money to pay the bus fare, they do give you that.

(Anna)

The expense of making accountability calls and transportation also placed additional stress on residents. Several participants were able to save money from their prison job and others received assistance from their families. Residents with no financial support were provided with petty cash with the condition that they would reimburse the House once employed. To avoid paying for accountability calls, participants sometimes asked potential employers to use their telephone. Two participants described situations where they were denied access to the employer's telephone. They both attributed the refusal to their halfway house status.

Oh my God, I went to [names business]; I don't know if you heard of that place. That lady looked at me, she had her purse on the floor like this and I said I am from the House, may I use the phone please, I need to make my contact call and I came here for an interview. She looked at me and looked at her purse, grabbed it and put it on her lap and would not let me use the phone. So I am running around looking for a phone, because if you don't make that contact call you get in trouble. It's very hard thing to do, to find people like that, they not going to understand. All they know is that you're a criminal and you're in front of her, she not going to see I am a changed person. I felt like crying. She thought I was going to steal her purse and run. I felt humiliated.

(Jenny)

The requirement to find work within 30 days of starting the job search added an additional layer of anxiety for many residents. This requirement pushed residents to search for work in places that would more likely result in quick employment. For example, most women sought out work in fast food restaurants. These women were able to obtain work within the 30-day mandate. Women who had higher qualifications (i.e., had a college education or certified in a specific field) were discouraged from working in the fast food industry. These participants often had extensive employment histories and were encouraged by staff to find a skilled job. Although these participants were anxious about not having a job within the 30-day requirement, staff informed them that so long as they were making an effort to find work they would extend their search time. When participants wanted to give up and settle for a low-skilled job, staff encouraged them to continue searching.

After a month of unsuccessful job hunting, Beth was ready to apply to McDonald's. Program staff encouraged her to take more time to search for employment that would fit her skill set. She eventually found a job she was satisfied with and one that also paid well.

I wasn't just trying to get any kind of job. After like two months of not getting a job I was like look can I just go to McDonald's? And Ms. A was like "No, you're too qualified to go to McDonald's." I am like but I can't find anything else and McDonald's would hire me. This is a work-release program you have to work. When I first got here they said I would give you 30 days to find a job and if you don't find a job you go back to Clinton [prison]. I was like oh my God, yeah it was 16 and I was still looking. The reason they didn't put me on an employment contract, because they see me trying every day. I was spending a fortune. I was going out every day. I was persistent; I was not giving up until I found a job. I was like someone is going to get me a job. Like one lady I went to dental care, she said "you know you are overqualified for the job but I can't hire you because of your background." So yeah a lot of jobs didn't give me . . . but I was determined I was going to get a job and it was going to be the kind of job I wanted. I finally found something making $13 an hour. And I get bonuses!

Several residents discussed turning down a job because it interfered with the mandated in-house treatment group. During the time period this study was conducted, two mandatory treatment groups were offered inside the Halfway House. Based on their individual needs, women were enrolled in either the three-month substance abuse or gender-responsive program. Treatment groups occurred twice a week from 6 p.m. to 8 p.m. Gail, a college-educated resident, described being told by program staff that she could not apply to McDonald's because she had a college education and the qualifications to obtain a more skillful job. After being rejected numerous times,[4] the employment counselor allowed Gail to apply to McDonald's and she was immediately hired.

It took me a while to find a job, I was told that I could not work in fast food so I went to [names retail store][5] and I got the job but then they rejected me because of my [violent] charge. My second offer I had to reject because of the [treatment] groups I had to take at night. I tried [names retail store]— didn't get it. It annoyed me, but it's a reality and I am glad to be going through it here and not at home. I finally got a job at McDonald's, I don't love it, but I am happy to get a pay check and to have a routine. I work with my friend [another resident].

Other participants spoke about changing their work schedules around to attend groups. Even though most employers were understandable and allowed participants to change their work schedules, participants expressed frustration over leaving work early but were willing to do so because attending groups was a program requirement.

Legal and Program Restrictions

An additional barrier was the restrictions on working in certain professions. The New Jersey state laws prohibiting offenders from certain work were part of the challenge for some women (some examples include: establishments serving liquor; businesses that handle personal records; security work; places that work closely with children, the elderly, and the physically/mentally ill). Additional regulations developed by the Halfway House further restricted residents from certain jobs. For example, residents were prohibited from working certain hours (i.e., overnight) and from working in a location without a telephone. Residents were also unable to work in a business where another resident acted as a manager.

Some residents wanted to find "easy" jobs, even though they were overqualified for the job. Aspiring to work at McDonald's was a common response because residents were aware of their non-discriminatory policy of hiring people with criminal records. As illustrated below, Pauline discussed plans to obtain employment at McDonald's not only because they hired individuals with criminal records, but also because she knew she could later transfer to a store closer to her home. At the time this interview was conducted, Pauline was getting ready to begin the job search and was worried staff would not allow her to pursue this job choice.

> The reason I want to go there is (A) they hire ex-convicts and (B) they're all over, you know, so I can just transfer—if I go home transfer to one right up there and I'll have a job, you know. I won't have to go through searching for a job again. So I'm hoping that she allows me to do that. My understanding is that she—They don't want you to go into the fast food service, like oh, God, you're a typical inmate. You know what I mean? Well, you know, I mean, it's—it's not a bad job. In the management end of it, it's not a bad job.

Location

Another difficult aspect of the job search was the unfamiliarity of the area for non-residents. Many non-area participants expressed frustrations about not knowing the area and not having connections. According to Jamie,

> I haven't found a job yet. I mean, I don't know nothing about this place, I don't know where to go or I don't know where to look. Even Ms. A. tells me she'll have something for me Monday, whatever. I mean, I need a job, I want a job, I want to work. I want to get out of this building.

Several also spoke about wanting to return to old employers but were unable to do so due to the distance. These participants discussed returning to old employers, working with family, or finding and securing a specific job in their home community once released from the Halfway House.

The multiple barriers associated with finding work, coupled with the pressure to find employment within 30 days, left many participants discouraged with the job search experience. As participants waited for employers to call them, they expressed anxiety of never obtaining a job. For many participants, living at the Halfway House did not make the job-search experience any less challenging; it did, however, provide residents with a realistic perspective of the challenges associated with finding work after release from prison. Regardless of the multiple barriers experienced during the job search, participants received help through various sources that eventually led to obtaining employment.

Sources of Help

The second category related to the employment search phase is the various sources of help women received when trying to obtain work. Participants received help through various sources: Halfway House staff, the local *One Stop*, other residents, understanding employers, and social networks.

Program Staff Help

Participants had mixed responses about the role the Halfway House plays in facilitating the job search. Several spoke about receiving some assistance from the employment counselor, which often included basic preparation on how to answer interview questions and a few discussed receiving job leads.

> Yes, she gives us a lot of leads and she has given us instructions on how to go out there and be presentable and how to be on interviews. She does a lot for us and she deals with a lot of people. I am not saying she is under a lot of stress it's just that she has to deal with a lot of residents in here. But she always gives us job leads every day. She always got something for us. I don't mean one thing, it will be a couple things that we can put our pass in to go out.
>
> (Nancy)

Several residents went to other halfway houses either before entering the Halfway House or when they were previously incarcerated. This experience shaped their expectations and perceptions of the program. They compared the employment assistance between halfway houses, and felt that the Halfway House should do more to help residents find work. Stacy felt that the employment counselor should find her a job, since that had been her experience in the past. Most participants recognized that the employment counselor was overburdened and felt that staff should provide more assistance with finding work, including hiring additional staff to help.

> If you are supposed to be a work counselor then you are supposed to be getting us a job and you should be doing that. It shouldn't be about me getting on the phone to get the job. Like at [names other halfway house] Ms. D. is the employment counselor and she has two assistants. When I got there and I went on work release she said, "look I got a contract already in the work and I am going to send you there." I got off work release on Monday, Tuesday I went for interview. I came home and was working on Wednesday. She already was out in the community and set up jobs for us to go to. Where this employment counselor—they don't have that here. She is only one person. They don't have other people—employment staff—only one person can't do that. There are so many women in there.

When asking participants how the Halfway House can improve their programs and services, several recommended hiring additional staff to help with employment. Participants shared the perception that the employment counselor was overburdened with "too many residents" and could not provide full support to all residents. In addition to hiring more staff, women recommended setting up a resource board with job openings, receiving information about specific places that hired formerly incarcerated people, and opportunities to leave the facility early in the morning to job search.

One-stop Career Center Help

Halfway House staff also refer residents to the One-stop Career Center for additional employment assistance. The One-stop provides employment assistance to all individuals seeking employment, including services such as resumé preparation, interview skills, job readiness, life skills, referrals to education and vocational programs, and job placement services. Participants discussed receiving some of these services, but none receive job placement. The most common services that participants received were job leads, applications, and employment-related workshops. The researcher asked Rachel how job searching was going. She described some benefits and drawbacks of the One-stop.

> I went to One-stop yesterday from 11.30 to 4. What happened was I was on the computer. I was looking up stuff. I didn't find anything, then I went to the desk and asked for a counselor. She gave me a website called Career Builders. The thing with that is they have jobs for you but they don't have the addresses and the phone numbers and stuff like that, because that's what we need to give Ms. A. so we can go out. And so I was just on the computer. Then we went to this boring orientation. The lady didn't know what she was talking about, whatever, so it just basically got me out of the building, just to say I went out. But I'm going to go back Monday because they give out applications for the [names business] place. And there was like seven of us from—from here at One-stop yesterday.

Another participant discussed receiving job leads from both the One-stop and the Halfway House employment counselor. Although one of the job leads resulted in employment, the job was not stable and she ended up unemployed. After this interview, Monique started the job search all over again and eventually found another job a few weeks before her release.

> I went to One-stop. The women there, she is excellent, she is always given me leads to go. Ms. A. I guess got a call from [names business], so she sent me and several other females out to [names business]. I just wish I went to another job, I would still be working right now. They laid us off, like last Monday and only called us back because people are on vacation. I mean truthfully speaking. I wish I would have went another route and got a stable job where I wouldn't have had that problem. But it is what it is.

Social Networks

Returning to the same neighborhood strengthened employment opportunities for local women. These women described finding jobs through social contacts, previous employers, and by just knowing where to search. Jenny described finding a job through an old acquaintance. Not only did she land a job, but she was also able to help other residents find employment through this contact.

> Took me two weeks. I went to One-stop and there was this guy I knew and he gave me his card and said they were hiring there. See it's good to be from [area], again. So, I took the card and gave it to the Employment Specialist to let her check into it. So I kept calling the guy and calling him until he was sick of hearing my voice and he called me. I am not the only one that works there. Two other girls work with me. And then Ms. A. just sent I think it was four or five other girls.

Another participant discussed being restricted to returning to her previous job due to the Halfway House policies. However, because she had worked in the local area for many years prior to her incarceration, she was able to reach out to an old employer. Knowing employers and having an extensive record of employment allowed Ella to return to an employer who recognized her work ethic.

> Actually, I knew I could go back to the job I had but due to the procedures here I wasn't allowed to go back to the jobs I had. Some you can't do with personal records and some you couldn't work because of the time frame. So, I knew [names restaurant] because I had worked there part-time and I knew the manager and I asked him . . . he knew the predicament I was going through. He said you worked so hard. I explained to him what happened. Like I said, I didn't think I was going to be incarcerated for so long. I thought I would just get a bracelet and go home.

Anna, a participant familiar with the area, did not believe knowing the area would help her find a job. Anna had little job experience and was unemployed for most of her life. Even though she was unable to depend on social networks, she was able to receive assistance from both the Halfway House employment counselor and the local Onestop. The employment counselor helped her with her resumé and contacted several places to inquire about hiring. The One-stop provided her with information on which employment establishments hire people with criminal records.

> No, I don't feel like that because I know the area, but it's still hard for ex-offenders to get jobs, and you have to know exactly which place that does hire ex-offenders. And when we went to the meeting—we went to One-stop yesterday and we had to actually take the orientation thing yesterday, and they gave us a list of places that hire ex-offenders. So, you know, that kind of helped me a little bit, so I can look for the places that they gave me and call them and ask them if they're hiring, so that's a good thing. A lot of McDonald's stores hire ex-offenders. I got real good leads going for all next week.

Resourceful Residents

Most participants with limited employment histories were able to secure low-skilled jobs within the 30-day job-search period. Several participants spoke about receiving job leads from other residents at the Halfway House. Employed residents shared information about job openings at their workplace. Learning about job opportunities from other residents appeared to help many participants land jobs. Participants often discussed working with friends they made at the Halfway House. Kate spoke about taking over the job of a resident who was about to be released.

> I got lucky. Someone who was leaving—I took her job—and now they're like you're not leaving when you leave are you? It's a diner. I like it. I'm tired, but I like it. They were waiting for me and then off blackout [orientation phase], I got off Friday and I started Saturday. There are people still job searching and they been here a few months.

Understanding Employers

Although many participants described experiences of employers turning them away because of their status, others described encountering employers who understood their situation. Even participants with serious violent crimes were able to find employers who gave them a chance. Carol discussed using the tools she had learned at a previous halfway house, and at the current house, to help answer tough interview questions about her criminal past.

> They never asked me. At the [restaurant] did. The guy Frank did. He definitely did. We sat down and had lunch over it. I did not want to talk about it. But he asked. I told him I was young and it was a mistake and I rectified my mistake. And that I'm asking to be given a chance. He said I am going to give you a chance. He said it is a small world it's like you're not by yourself. I don't know what he's talking about that. But I guess it happens to a lot of people and I am not the only one. That is how I took it. That was it. I did not get into details though. I went around and in and over and back.

After serving 11 years in prison, Carol had her first employment experience at a different halfway house program. When job searching at her prior halfway house, she discussed being afraid to leave the building alone and was accompanied by staff until she felt comfortable on her own. She worked for two months before violating parole and returning to prison. She stated that her job-searching experience at this halfway house was less stressful because of her prior experience at the first halfway house. For Carol, finding a job was not the cause of her anxiety; rather it was the fear of going out into the community and interacting with other citizens—"Like you just have to break the fear, once you're out there, you're out there."

As illustrated above, the Halfway House provides some assistance preparing residents for the workforce. Frequent forms of help were preparing residents for interviews, providing job leads (i.e., places to inquire about employment), and referrals to the local One-stop. Even though participants received some assistance from staff, most were left to find work on their own and did so with the help of other residents or understanding employers. Residents from the local area were at a greater advantage to find work through social networks, old employers, and by just being familiar with the area. Regardless of the help residents received with employment, having a criminal record and living in a halfway house aggravated the challenges typically associated with finding work at the skill level of the applicant.

Discussion

The purpose of this study was to understand the job-searching process for women residing at a work-release halfway house. Many of the nuanced challenges and facilitators of the employment process have been highlighted. Some of the challenges with the job-searching process included the double stigmatization of having a criminal record and living in a halfway house. As a result, participants became discouraged, experienced rejection, and felt humiliated disclosing their status. Regardless of release location, dealing with the stigma of a criminal record has been well documented in the literature (Sampson and Laub,1993; Solomon et al., 2001; Western et al., 2001). The additional stigma of halfway house status further contributed to the stress and anxiety of searching for work. Due to these stigmas, participants, even those with extensive employment histories, struggled to find jobs within their fields and often settled with fast food restaurant jobs because these jobs were the easiest to secure. Participants also complained about the employment counselor not having enough time or resources to help residents find jobs. Although there were multiple barriers experienced during the search process, 76 percent of participants secured employment through various sources.

The Halfway House provided some assistance in preparing residents for the workforce. Frequent forms of help were preparing residents for interviews, providing job leads (i.e., places to inquire about employment), and referrals to the local One-stop. Even though participants received some assistance from staff, most were left to find work on their own. Residents from the local area were at a greater advantage to find work through social networks, old employers, and by just being familiar with the area. Regardless of the help residents received with employment, having a criminal record and living in a halfway house aggravated the challenges typically associated with finding work at the skill level of the applicant. Consistent with the literature (see Nelson et al., 1999; Solomon et al., 2001; Visher et al., 2011), the importance of social networks was a common theme throughout the interviews. There was also a qualitative distinction between participants from the local area vs. those from other areas of New Jersey. Local residents were at an employment advantage due to their familiarity with the area and their access to acquaintances and old employers, whereas participants from other parts of the state were unfamiliar with the community and did not have access to local social networks. Unlike local residents, non-residents sought temporary employment and had to quit their job once released. Many discussed plans to return to old employers or had ideas about where they would seek employment once back in their former community.

For those with an extensive employment background, the jobs secured were obtained just to fulfill the requirements of remaining in the program. These women had bigger plans than just working low-skilled jobs. This was evident in their persistence to enroll in educational and vocational courses to advance their job prospects. Most women, regardless of their employment background, had no plans to maintain the same job when released. For many, their release location was too far from the Halfway House job, making it impossible to maintain their position. Several women, working in the fast food industry, did speak about transferring to another store in their home community.

Three women with health-related problems were unable to work. Consistent with the literature (Richie, 2001; Visher et al., 2011) health conditions impact maintaining a job. Although a very small percentage of the sample in this study were unable to work, it is important to recognize that women with serious health conditions need a different host of services than what is typically provided in work-release programs. It should also be mentioned that women in this study were provided with temporary housing and did not have any household or family obligations. A valid assessment of their employment experience is lacking because of their current housing situation. As indicated in the literature, women experience a range of additional barriers related to family care and re-establishing relationships (Berman, 2005; Flower, 2010; O'Brien, 2001; Richie, 2001). Future research on women's employment process should address these issues.

Study Limitations

It is important to note the limitations of this study. Due to the small sample size and nature of data collection this method does not allow for generalizing findings to other female community correction programs within the state or other states. While some of the findings from this study are comparable to other research on the topic, women residing in other, similar programs may have different experiences. A further limitation is the lack of follow-up. The researcher was unable to conduct follow-up interviews to determine whether participants maintained their jobs once released, found new ones, struggled to find work in the same way they did at the Halfway House, and whether new barriers arose. Was the experience easier because of the head start received at the Halfway House? Future research should compare the job-search experience process while residing in a community correction setting, to the experience of living in a non-restrictive setting.

Due to time constraints, another limitation was the lack of member checking. Member checking is an important strategy often conducted in qualitative studies to avoid researcher bias and data misinterpretation. The stress of living at a halfway house and feeling pressure to secure employment within a brief time period may have impacted women's perceptions of the program and their responses to the interview. It should be noted that several participants made comments about how the interview was actually helpful for them. For example, one resident was forced to end the interview early because of a scheduled meeting with the employment specialist. She asked if she could continue the interview later in the day and stated that the interview was helping her think about her plans for the future. There were many other anecdotes that led me to believe that the women were genuinely forthcoming and truthful. The fact that I was of the same gender as participants and had previously worked as a re-entry service provider with a similar population may have helped develop quick rapport. Perhaps my presence over a six-month period made participants feel comfortable talking about their experiences. Of course, there were exceptions—the few women who provided very short responses and finished the interview in less than an hour.

Program and Policy Recommendations

Several program and policy recommendations should be considered for future research and program development. First, it should be noted that residing in a community corrections facility enhances the surveillance over the job-search process and forces residents to secure low-skilled jobs. As evident by the findings from this study, the requirement to find work within 30 days restricted residents' ability to find jobs that met their employment/education skills. Securing work that is compatible with skills should be a priority of work-release programs. Even if securing immediate work is a mandate of the program, residents—especially those who plan to live in the surrounding community—should be encouraged (if not required) to continue their job search until they find compatible employment. As highlighted in the literature, higher quality jobs increase social control and decrease recidivism (Uggen, 1999), especially when jobs focus on skill-building (Latessa, 2012). According to Latessa (2012), low-quality jobs that don't enhance skill development may not lead to behavioral change. To be successful, Latessa argues that employment programs must also target attitudes and values about work. Securing work just to satisfy a program requirement may not lead to positive attitudes toward that job, and will likely result in low-skilled work. Focusing on skill-building and attitudes toward employment are two components that will potentially lead to sustainable and meaningful work.

Since many women secure temporary jobs due to the 30-day work requirement and the distance between the Halfway House and their intended release location, a second program recommendation is warranted. Developing a state-wide transitional job program may be beneficial to individuals released to halfway houses. Considered a promising employment model (Redcross et al., 2009), individuals are placed into temporary jobs, offered a range of support services, and provided with assistance finding permanent work. Since most women at the Halfway House engage in significant efforts to secure temporary work it may be useful to develop a program that places them in a transitional job while simultaneously working with them to find permanent jobs in the community to which they plan to return. This continuity-of-care approach would ensure that there is no employment gap between the time released from the halfway house and the time they return to their home community.

Critical Thinking

Many of the participants struggled to find work. What kind of "job search barriers" impeded their employment opportunities? Are these impediments fair? Do the current rules and regulations governing ex-offenders increase the likelihood for recidivism?

Notes

1. To protect the identity of staff and participants, the halfway house program is referred to as the "halfway house," and participant and staff names have been changed to a pseudonym.

2. Room sizes at the Halfway House vary. Some rooms are very small and accommodate two to four residents, while others are large and accommodate up to 11 residents. Residents share common bathrooms.

3. Eight women were not included in the study because they were released from the Halfway House before the researcher had a chance to approach them for an interview. The characteristics of these eight women are unknown.

4. This resident was incarcerated for a manslaughter charge and attributes this charge to not finding a skillful job.

5. The names of certain businesses are excluded to protect the identity of the participants. McDonald's is the only business named in this manuscript because many participants in this study applied and/or obtained work at this restaurant.

References

Berman, J. (2005). *Women offender transition and reentry: Gender responsive approaches to transitioning women offenders from prison to the community*. Washington, DC: US Department of Justice, National Institution of Corrections.

Bureau of Labor Statistics. (2003). *Earnings by educational attainment and sex, 1979 and 2002*. Washington, DC: US Department of Justice, The Bureau of Labor Statistics.

Bushway, S.D. and Apel, R. (2012). A signaling perspective on employment-based reentry programming: Training completion as a desistance signal. *Criminology & Public Policy, 11*, 21–50.

Cantora, A. (2013). Building grounds for release: Women's perceptions of a community corrections program. *Journal of Qualitative Criminal Justice and Criminology, 1*, 197–220.

Carson, A. and Golinelli, D. (2013). *Prisoners in 2012. Trends in admissions and releases, 1991–2012*. Washington, DC: US Department of Justice, The Bureau of Justice Statistics.

Chappell, C.A. (2004). Post-secondary correctional education and recidivism: A meta-analysis of research conducted 1990–1999. *Journal of Correctional Education, 55*, 148–169.

Charmaz, K. (2006). *Constructing grounded theory: A practical guide through qualitative analysis*. Thousand Oaks, CA: Sage.

Donnelly, P.G. and Forschner, B.E. (1987). Predictors of success in a co-correctional halfway house: A discriminant analysis. *Journal of Crime and Justice, 10*, 1–22.10.1080/0735648X.1987.9721346.

Flower, S.M. (2010). *Employment and female offenders: An update of the empirical research. Gender responsive strategies for women offenders*. Washington, DC: US Department of Justice, National Institution of Corrections.

Greenberg, E., Dunleavy, E. and Kutner, M. (2007). *Literacy behind bars: Results from the 2003 national assessment of adult literacy prison survey*. Washington, DC: US Department of Education, National Center for Education Statistics.

Hattery, A. and Smith, E. (2010). *Prisoner reentry and social capital: The long road to reintegration*. Latham, MD: Lexington Books.

Holzer, H.J., Raphael, S., and Stoll, M. (2004). Will employers hire ex-offenders? Employer preferences, background checks, and their determinants. In M. Patillo, D.F. Weiman, and B. Western (eds), *Imprisoning America: The social effects of mass incarceration* (pp. 205–246). New York: Russell Sage Foundation.

La Vigne, N.G., Brooks, L.E., and Shollenberger, T.L. (2009). *Women on the outside: Understanding the experiences of female prisoners returning to Houston Texas*. Washington, DC: The Urban Institute.

Lalonde, R.J. and Cho, R.M. (2008). The impact of incarceration in state prison and the employment prospects of women. *Journal of Quantitative Criminology, 24*, 243–265.10.1007/s10940-008-9050-x.

Latessa, E.J. (2004). Homelessness and reincarceration. Editorial introduction. *Criminology & Public Policy, 3*, 137–138.

Latessa, E. (2012). Why work is important, and how to improve the effectiveness of correctional reentry programs that target employment. *Criminology & Public Policy, 11*, 87–91.

Latessa, E.J. and Allen, H.E. (1982). Halfway houses and parole: A national assessment. *Journal of Criminal Justice, 10*, 153–163.10.1016/0047-2352(82)90006-X.

Latessa, E.J. and Travis, L.F. (1991). Halfway house or probation: A comparison of alternative dispositions. *Journal of Crime & Justice, 14*, 53–75.

LeBel, T.P. (2012). "If one doesn't get you another one will": Formerly incarcerated persons' perceptions of discrimination. *The Prison Journal, 92*, 63–87.10.1177/0032885511429243.

Legal Action Center. (2004). *After prison: Roadblocks to reentry. A report on state legal barriers facing people with criminal records*. New York: Author.

Lynch, J. and Sabol, W. (2001). *Prisoner reentry in perspective*. Washington, DC: The Urban Institute, Justice Policy Center.

Mackey, R. and Fretz, R. (2007). *Female offender outcome research study (Community Education Centers)*. Philadelphia, PA: Drexel University Press.

Mallik-Kane, K. and Visher, C. (2008). *Health and prisoner reentry: How physical, mental, and substance abuse conditions shape the process of reintegration.* Washington, DC: The Urban Institute.

Nelson, M., Perry, D., and Allen, C. (1999). *The first month out: Post-incarceration experiences in New York City.* New York: The Vera Institute of Justice.

O'Brien, P. (2001). *Making it in the free world: Women in transition from prison.* Albany: State University of New York Press.

O'Brien, P. (2002). *Reducing barriers to employment for women ex-offenders: Mapping the road to reintegration.* Chicago, IL: Safer Foundation.

Pager, D. (2002). The mark of a criminal record. *American Journal of Sociology, 108,* 937–975.

Petersilia, J. (2001). When prisoners return to the community: Political, economic and social consequences. *Corrections Management Quarterly, 5,* 1–10.

Redcross, C., Bloom, D., Azurdia, G., Zweig, J., and Pindus, N. (2009). *Transitional jobs for ex-prisoners: Implementation, two-year impacts, and costs of the Center for Employment Opportunities (CEO) prisoner reentry program (A report from MDRC-Building Knowledge to Improve Social Policy).* New York: MDRC.

Richie, B.E. (2001). Challenges incarcerated women face as they return to their communities. *Crime and Delinquency, 47,* 231–245.

Rossman, S.B. and Roman, C.G. (2003). Case managed reentry and employment: Lessons from the opportunity to succeed program. *Justice Research and Policy, 5,* 75–100.10.3818/JRP.5.2.2003.75.

Sampson, R.J. and Laub, J.H. (1993). *Crime in the making: Pathways and turning points through life.* Cambridge, MA: Harvard University Press.

Scroggins, J.R. and Malley, S. (2010). Reentry and the (unmet) needs of women. *Journal of Offender Rehabilitation, 49,* 146–163.10.1080/10509670903546864.

Solomon, A., Roman, C.G., and Waul, M. (2001). *Summary of focus group with ex-prisoners in the district: Ingredients for successful reintegration.* Washington, DC: The Urban Institute.

Strauss, A. and Corbin, J. (1998). *Basics of qualitative research: Techniques and procedures for developing grounded theory.* Thousand Oaks, CA: Sage.

Travis, J. (2005). *But they all come back: Facing the challenges of prisoner reentry.* Washington, DC: Urban Institute Press.

Uggen, C. (1999). Ex-offenders and the conformist alternative: A job quality model of work and crime. *Social Problems, 46,* 127–151.10.2307/3097165.

Visher, C. and Travis, J. (2003). Transitions from prison to community: Understanding individual pathways. *Annual Review of Sociology, 29,* 89–113.10.1146/annurev.soc.29.010202.095931.

Visher, C.A., Debus-Sherrill, S.A., and Yahner, J. (2008). *Employment after prison: A longitudinal study.* Washington, DC: The Urban Institute.

Visher, C.A., Debus-Sherrill, S.A., and Yahner, J. (2011). Employment after prison: A longitudinal study of former prisoners. *Justice Quarterly, 28,* 698–718.10.1080/07418825.2010.535553.

Western, B. (2007). The penal system and the labor market. In S. Bushway, M.A. Stoll, and D.F. Weinman (eds), *Barriers to reentry? The labor market for released prisoners in postindustrial America* (pp. 335–360). New York: Russell Sage Foundation.

Western, B., Kling, J.R., and Weiman, D. (2001). The labor market consequences of incarceration. *Crime and Delinquency, 47,* 410–427.10.1177/0011128701047003007.

Credit Lines

Kurtz, Don. L., Travis Linnemann, and L. Susan Williams
Kurtz, Don. L., Travis Linnemann, and L. Susan Williams. 2012. "Reinventing the Matron: The Continued Importance of Gendered Images and Division of Labor in Modern Policing." *Women and Criminal Justice* 22: 239–263.

Dabney, Dean A., Heith Copes, Richard Tewksbury, and Shila R. Hawk-Tourtelot
Dabney, Dean A., Heith Copes, Richard Tewksbury, and Shila R. Hawk-Tourtelot. 2013. "A Qualitative Assessment of Stress Perceptions among Members of Homicide Unit." *Justice Quarterly* 30: 811–836.

Vera Sanchez, Claudio G. and Dennis Rosenbaum
Vera Sanchez, Claudio G. and Dennis Rosenbaum. 2011. "Racialized Policing: Officers' Voices on Policing Latino and African American Neighborhoods." *Journal of Ethnicity in Criminal Justice* 9: 152–178.

Pogrebin, Mark R. and Eric D. Poole
Pogrebin, Mark R. and Eric D. Poole. 1988. "Vice Isn't Nice: A Look at the Effects of Working Undercover." *Journal of Criminal Justice* 21: 383–394.

Pogrebin, Mark, Mary Dodge, and Harold Chatman
Pogrebin, Mark, Mary Dodge, and Harold Chatman. 2000. "Reflections of African American Women on their Careers in Urban Policing: Their Experiences of Racial and Sexual Discrimination." *International Journal of the Sociology of Law* 28: 311–326.

Gau, Jacinta M. and Rod K. Brunson
Gau, Jacinta M. and Rod K. Brunson. 2010. "Procedural Justice and Order Maintenance Policing." *Justice Quarterly* 27: 255–279.

Durán, Robert
Durán, Robert. 2010. "Urban Youth Encounters with Legitimately Oppressive Gang Enforcement." Original contribution to the book.

Stretesky, Paul, Tara O'Connor Shelley, Michael J. Hogan, and N. Prabha Unnithan
Stretesky, Paul, Tara O'Connor Shelley, Michael J. Hogan, and N. Prabha Unnithan. 2010. "Sense-making and Secondary Victimization." Original contribution to the book.

Stephens, Joyce and Peter G. Sinden
Stephens, Joyce and Peter G. Sinden. 2000. "Victims' Voices: Domestic Assault Victims' Perceptions of Police Demeanor." *Journal of Interpersonal Violence* 15: 534–547.

Brunson, Rod K., Anthony Braga, David Hureau, and Kashea Pegram
Brunson, Rod K., Anthony Braga, David Hureau, and Kashea Pegram. 2015. "We Trust You, But Not That Much: Examining Police–Black Clergy Partnerships to Reduce Youth Violence." *Justice Quarterly* 32: 1006–1036.

Goodrum, Sarah, Mark R. Pogrebin, and Matthew W. Greife
Goodrum, Sarah, Mark R. Pogrebin, and Matthew W. Greife. 2015. "Representing the Underdog: The Righteous Development of Death Penalty Defense Attorneys." *Criminal Law Bulletin* 51: 329–356.

Butler, Paul
Butler, Paul. 2013. "How Can You Prosecute These People?" (pp. 15–28). In A. Smith and M.H. Freedman (eds), *How Can You Represent These People?* New York: Palgrave-Macmillan.

Bowen, Deirdre M.
Bowen, Deirdre M. 2009. "Calling Your Bluff: How Prosecutors and Defense Attorneys Adapt Plea Bargaining Strategies to Increased Formalization." *Justice Quarterly* 26: 2–29.

DioGuardi, Sherri
DioGuardi, Sherri. 2014. "Examining the Death Penalty Insider Perspective: Capital Bench and Bar Interviews." *Journal of Qualitative Criminal Justice and Criminology* 2: 148–173.

Rosecrance, John
Rosecrance, John. 1988. "Maintaining the Myth of Individualized Justice: Probation Presentence Reports." *Justice Quarterly* 5: 235–256.

Konradi, Amanda
Konradi, Amanda. 1996. "Preparing to Testify: Rape Survivors Negotiating the Criminal Justice Process." *Gender and Society* 10: 404–432.

Goodrum, Sarah
Goodrum, Sarah. 2010. "Expecting an Ally and Getting a Prosecutor." Original contribution to the book.

Fischer, Michael, Brenda Geiger, and Mary Ellen Hughes
Fischer, Michael, Brenda Geiger, and Mary Ellen Hughes. 2007. "Female Recidivists Speak about their Experience in Drug Court while Engaging in Appreciative

Inquiry." *International Journal of Offender Therapy and Comparative Criminology* 51: 703–722.

Hans, Valerie P. and Krista Sweigart
Hans, Valerie P. and Krista Sweigart. 1993. "Jurors' Views of Civil Lawyers: Implications for Courtroom Communication." *Indiana Law Journal* 68: 1297–1332.

Dichter, Melissa E., Catherine Cerulli, Catherine L. Kothari, Francis K. Barg, and Karin V. Rhodes
Dichter, Melissa E., Catherine Cerulli, Catherine L. Kothari, Francis K. Barg, and Karin V. Rhodes. 2011. "Engaging with Criminal Prosecution: The Victim's Perspective." *Women and Criminal Justice* 21: 21–37.

Stojkovic, Stan
Stojkovic, Stan. 1990. "Accounts of Prison Work: Correction Officers' Portrayals of Their Work World." *Perspectives on Social Problems*, Vol. 2, pp. 211–230.

Riley, John
Riley, John. 2000. "Sense-making in Prison: Inmate Identity as a Working Understanding." *Justice Quarterly* 17: 359–376.

Poole, Eric D. and Mark R. Pogrebin
Poole, Eric D. and Mark R. Pogrebin. 2009. "Gender and Occupational Culture Conflict: A Study of Women Jail Officers" (pp. 423–443). In R. Tewksbury and D. Dabney (eds), *Prisons and Jails: A Reader*. New York: McGraw Hill.

Gaarder, Emily, Nancy Rodriguez, and Marjorie S. Zatz
Gaarder, Emily, Nancy Rodriguez, and Marjorie S. Zatz. 2004. "Criers, Liars, and Manipulators: Probation Officers' Views of Girls." *Justice Quarterly* 21: 547–578.

Crank, John P.
Crank, John P. 1996. "The Construction of Meaning During Training for Probation and Parole." *Justice Quarterly* 13: 265–290.

West-Smith, Mary, Mark R. Pogrebin, and Eric D. Poole
West-Smith, Mary, Mark R. Pogrebin, and Eric D. Poole. 2000. "Denial of Parole: An Inmate Perspective." *Federal Probation* 64: 3–10.

Tewksbury, Richard
Tewksbury, Richard. 2010. "How Registered Sex Offenders View Registries." Original contribution to the book.

Snyder, Zoann K.
Snyder, Zoann K. 2009. "Keeping Families Together: The Importance of Maintaining Mother–Child Contact for Incarcerated Women." *Women and Criminal Justice* 19: 37–59.

Pogrebin, Mark R., Mary West-Smith, Alexandra Walker, and N. Prabha Unnithan

Pogrebin, Mark R., Mary West-Smith, Alexandra Walker, and N. Prabha Unnithan. 2014. "Employment Isn't Enough: Financial Obstacles Experienced by Ex-prisoners During the Reentry Process." *Criminal Justice Review* 39: 394–410.

Cantora, Andrea

Cantora, Andrea. 2015. "Navigating the Job Search after Incarceration: The Experiences of Work-release Participants." *Criminal Justice Studies* 28: 141–160.

Index